COUNSELING

Women

EVIDENCE-BASED TREATMENT
WITH FAITH INTEGRATION

Kendall Hunt
publishing company

PATTI HINKLEY | APRIL CRABLE | JAMA DAVIS | ANITA KUHNLEY

www.kendallhunt.com
Send all inquiries to:
4050 Westmark Drive
Dubuque, IA 52004-1840

CONTENTS

ABOUT THE EDITORS

April R. Crable specializes in teletherapy, crisis and trauma and counseling, substance abuse, ethics, and sex offender treatment. She has been a distance educator for ten years. Dr. Crable is currently a professor at co-owner of Fruition Counseling and Consulting Services, LLC. The practice specializes in providing teletherapy services. Dr. Crable has worked in the mental health field for over a decade providing services to various populations. She is a Licensed Professional Counselor in the states of Arizona, Florida, Virginia, Texas, and New York. Additionally, she is both a Certified Substance Abuse Counselor and Sex Offender Treatment Provider in the state of Virginia. Her research and teaching interests include field experience, ethics, crisis and trauma, and distance counseling and supervision.

© April Crable

Jama Davis, PhD, LMHC (IN), LPC (NC), NCC is an Associate Professor in the CACREP accredited Clinical Mental Health Counseling program at Liberty University. Her work in the counseling profession as a counselor, supervisor and professor spans over 30 years, leading her to counsel and teach internationally. She regularly presents at conferences and has published for professional associations.

© Randall Davis

Patti Hinkley, Ed.D. is a professor for the CACREP accredited Clinical Mental Health Counseling program at Liberty University. In addition, for the past 40 years, she has been actively involved in various administrative roles for Liberty including Executive Director of LU's Distance Program, Associate Dean, and Department Chair. Dr. Hinkley is also a Licensed Professional Counselor, a Licensed Marriage and Family Therapist, and a Nationally Certified Counselor. She practiced as a professional counselor for 19 years with Light Counseling Associates in Lynchburg, Virginia.

© Tom Hinkley

Anita Knight Kuhnley, Ph.D. is a licensed professional counselor (LPC) in the state of Virginia and an Associate Professor of Counseling in Regent University's School of Psychology and Counseling. Kuhnley earned her doctorate in Counselor Education and Supervision from Regent University. Kuhnley is certified as a highly reliable coder of the Adult Attachment Interview (AAI) through Mary Main and Eric Hesse's UC Berkeley AAI coder certification program and is the coauthor of several books including *Redeeming Attachment* and *Research Based Counseling Skills*. Her most recent book is *The Mister Rogers Effect*, which unpacks the psychological secrets Mister Rogers used to reach his television neighbors. You can find out more about her via her website: https://dranitakuhnley.com/books/

ABOUT THE AUTHORS

Dr. Andrea Barbian is a LCMHC in the state of NC and a professor at Liberty University. She has received specialized training in and has over 6 years of experience in treating eating disorders. She is passionate about eating disorder research and promoting best practice in eating disorder treatment.

© Andrea Barbian

Dr. Jennifer Beres is an Assistant Professor and Instructional Mentor for Liberty University. She is also an individual and family counselor who has been in clinical practice since 1999. She has written literature and presented on a host of topics related to the counseling profession. Her current area of specialization is trauma and complex PTSD.

© Jennifer Beres

Dr. Deborah Braboy is an Assistant Professor at Liberty University. She is an LPC-Supervisor in Arkansas and Oklahoma. Her clinical expertise includes a thriving private practice, Anchored Hope Counseling, working with individuals with grief and loss issues, depression, anxiety, and co-parenting. Because of her journey as a young widow, she has used her experiences to help others on the often uncertain path of grief and loss. She enjoys mentoring and training individuals as they enter the counseling field.

© Kendee Hughes

© Tate Tullier

Dr. Capri Brooks is a professor of Counselor Education at Liberty University. Prior to becoming a counselor educator in 2014, Brooks spent time working in both clinical counseling and school counseling where she specialized in children and adolescents. Dr. Brooks serves as volunteer counselor at a local school.

© Dustin Clark

David R. Brown, PhD is a professor at Liberty University. Professionally active in the counseling profession, he presents regularly at state, regional, and national conferences. His research interests include assessing spirituality and religiosity, technology in counseling, and pedagogy related to studying abroad and global mental health.

© Emmy Barron

Jonna Byars has taught counseling courses at the college and graduate level for over twenty years. In her own practice she specializes in addiction and women's issues. Her current research interests include the effects of social media and technology, and complex trauma.

© Rhonda Smiga

Janice Caudill is a psychologist who specializes in treating sex addiction and related betrayal trauma, helping partners and couples heal in the wake of intimate deception. She is the author of *Full Disclosure: Seeking Truth After Sexual Betrayal* and co-author of *Full Disclosure: How to Share Truth after Sexual Betrayal*.

Dr. Timothy Crable, Ph.D., M.B.A., is CEO and co-owner of Fruition Counseling and Consulting Services, LLC; a teletherapy private practice spanning five states. Additionally, Dr. Crable is a college professor, business consultant, motivational speaker, and USN Chief (Retired).

© Timothy Crable

Dr. Cynthia Doney is an Assistant Professor at Liberty University. Her expertise is in Counselor Education and Supervision (PhD), and Clinical Mental Health Counseling (Master's). Her passion is teaching graduate students, specifically as a mentoring professor. Clinically, she specializes in marriage and family therapy, military resilience, and adoption adjustment/attachment issues.

© Cynthia Doney

Nivischi Edwards, PhD, LMHC, LPC, NCC, BC-TMH received her Doctorate in Counselor Education from the University of Central Florida. She believes true accomplishment is love; unconditional love for God, self, and others. She operates a virtual practice, teaches counseling at Liberty University, and is passionate about healthy relationship. Learn more here: https://drnivischi.com

© Adam Dean

Dr. Marlene Estenson is an Associate Professor at Liberty University, in the School of Behavioral Sciences, Counselor Education and Family Studies Department. Educationally, she has a doctorate in Educational Leadership, a master's in Counseling, and a bachelors in Human Development. She and her husband, Dan reside in Tennessee.

© Katie Estenson

© Jake Ford

Dr. Kristy Ford is a Licensed Mental Health Counselor specializing in clinical supervision and counseling research. Her clinical experience includes private practice, pastoral counseling, managed care, and community based care. Her research has focused on the use of spiritual interventions in counseling and multicultural issues related to religious accommodation of mindfulness practice in treatment, and she has presented research findings at national conferences. Her continued research and teaching interests include the integration of spirituality and effective counseling practice, mindfulness practice, attachment-based treatments, and neuroscience.

© Amber Ruffin

Angel Golson, PhD, LPC-S is an Assistant Professor at Liberty University and is involved in teaching, advising, researching, and student development. Her clinical experience includes working with children, college students, and their families. Her research interests include wellness, addiction, and faculty advising and supervision for online programs.

© Maranda Griffin

Maranda Griffin, PhD, is a higher education administrator at Walden University. She received her doctorate in counselor education from Auburn University. She is the founder of MG Consultation, a small private practice, coaching, and consulting organization that helps transform the lives of people and the way agencies do business.

© Jim Jerniga

Holly Johnson, PhD, LPCS, NCC is an assistant professor at Liberty University. She is the founder of a non-profit agency that provides hunger relief, advocacy, and counseling to impoverished individuals. Dr. Johnson has clinical experience in working with adults, adolescents, and children in both agency and private practice settings.

Sarah Kitchens, Ph.D., is an associate professor at Liberty University in the School of Behavioral Sciences. She also works part-time as a counselor at a private practice. Prior to joining the faculty in 2014, Dr. Kitchens worked as a school counselor and a coach/counselor for a non-profit.

© Jamie Kitchens

Summer Perhay Kuba, Ph.D., Ed.S., MSW is an assistant professor at Liberty University in the School of Behavioral Sciences. Prior to joining the faculty in 2018, she worked in a clinical setting and more recently as a school counselor. Dr Kuba actively presents at state and national conferences and continues to seek out opportunities to advocate for students, school counselors and the profession as a whole.

© Sabrina Walsh

Edward John Kuhnley, M.D. is a board-certified child, adolescent, and adult psychiatrist. He is an Adjunct Clinical Assistant Professor of Psychiatry at Liberty University College of Osteopathic Medicine. and an adjunct faculty member in the School of Behavioral Sciences, Department of Counselor Education and Family Studies at Liberty University.

© Brett Hartley

Stacey C. Lilley, Ph.D., LPC-S, received her doctorate in Counselor Education from Virginia Tech in 2007. She has experience as a licensed school counselor, wellness director, college counselor, private practice, clinical supervisor, and assistant professor. When she's not working, she enjoys reading, musicals, and traveling to golf and scuba dive.

© Lori Hedrick

Dr. Marrah is an Assistant Professor at Liberty University. She has presented research on racial trauma and on mentorship for Black women in doctoral programs. Dr. Marrah has written book chapters on cultural humility and sexual trauma. Her teaching interests include race-based trauma and women issues in counseling.

Robyn Trippany Simmons, Ed.D., LPC-S (AL), NCC, RPT-S is Professor of Counseling in the CACREP accredited Clinical Mental Health Counseling program at Liberty University. Dr. Simmons received her Ed.D. in Counselor Education from the University of Alabama in 2001 and has been a practicing counselor since 1996. Her research and clinical interests include sexual trauma, vicarious trauma, play therapy, and professional identity issues. Dr. Simmons publishes and presents locally, regionally, nationally, and internationally on play therapy, creative approaches to therapy and clinical supervision, counselor education, and trauma counseling.

Dr. Dallas E. Speight is an ordained Southern Baptist minister, a board-certified chaplain, CPE Supervisor, Approved Clinical Supervisor (ACS), a licensed professional counselor in Florida and Tennessee. He retired from the U.S. Army as a Chaplain (Colonel) after serving for 30 years. His education includes a Bachelor of Arts, Master of Divinity, Master of Science in Counseling degree and Human Development, Doctor of Ministry in Pastoral Care and Counseling, and a Doctor of Education in Counseling Psychology.

Dr. Sheila Speight is a licensed professional counselor in Florida and Tennessee, and a nationally certified counselor, and holds certifications in several areas. She has years of experience working in the field of education, private practice counseling, conference speaking, and leader for Army conferences and Christian organizations as well as volunteer work in various venues. Her education includes an Associate of Divinity, Bachelor of Arts, Master of Science in Counseling and Human Development, and a PhD. in Counseling.

Barbara Steffens, PhD, LPCC, specializes in helping women recover from sexual betrayal and trains others on how to help this special population of women. She served as the founding President of a The *Association for Partners of Sex Addicts Trauma Specialists* (APSATS) from 2012 until she retired in February of 2019. She is Core Faculty for Liberty University Online CHMC program.

© Dan Ledbetter

Dr. Rebecca Taylor is a professor at Liberty University serving in the Department of Counselor Education and Family Studies. In addition to her academic career, Dr. Taylor has a background in community mental health. In her counseling career, she has worked extensively with survivors of childhood sexual abuse.

Copyright © Image Group Photography, LLC. Reprinted by permission.

Dr. Tyre, LPC-S, NCC, has been working as a counselor, counselor educator, author and higher education professional for the past 15 years. Her research interest includes counselor wellness and self-care, compassion fatigue and issues surrounding college counseling. She is owner of Reignite, LLC, Counseling and Consultation Services.

© Felix Tyre

Christina Villarreal-Davis, Ph.D., LPC-S, NCC, RPT-S is an Assistant Professor at Liberty University and the clinical director/owner of Wellspring of Life Counseling & Play Therapy Center. She has published and presented on topics related to trauma and grief, helping women overcome perinatal loss, neuroscience-informed approaches, and play and expressive therapies.

© Toni Arauza

Dr. Waldenstrom holds a Ph.D in Clinical Psychology. Her post-graduate work includes forensic assessments and counseling within community mental health agencies. Her specialization is in sexuality issues, mostly with adolescent girls. Dr. Waldenstrom teaches with Liberty University, while also serving as an Instructional Mentor, and Subject Matter Expert for human development classes.

Dr. White is a Professor at Liberty University. She has 20 years of experience in the fields of mental health counseling, social work, and peacebuilding. Her work focuses on individuals who have experienced personal, communal, current and transgenerational trauma, understanding cultural barriers and resources for resilience.

Charity D. Williams earned a PhD in psychology and counseling from New Orleans Baptist Theological Seminary. She currently is an assistant professor for Liberty in the Department of Community Care and Counseling and coaches and counsels church leaders alongside her husband, Mike. She also has discipleship conversations with church members.

CHAPTER 1

Cultural Issues Facing Women in Today's Society

Yulanda Tyre, Ph.D., Deborah Braboy, Ph.D., & Kristy Ford, Ph.D.

> "The fastest way to change society is to mobilize all the women of the world."
> ~Charles Malik (2000)

> "I praise you, for I am fearfully and wonderfully made. Wonderful are your works; my soul knows it very well." (Psalms 139:14, ESV)

Wisdom from Above: Standing in His Grace

© somrak jendee/Shutterstock.com

Start a new diet, try a different style, change your routine, eat this - not that. The media messages that surround women daily can leave us spinning. Which fragrance, food, novelty item, dress style or diet is best for me? How can I look and feel like the woman in the advertisement? Should I even look like that? …am I too old, too round, too tall?

Even friends and family from home, work, and church can place demands and expectations on our lives that at times leave us searching for how to achieve the best version of ourselves. This self-appraisal can intersect with moments of doubt and prompt feelings of inadequacy and insecurity. It seems we have all been there, asking if we are enough and if we will be able to do all that is asked of us. Thankfully, God offers us a shield from competing expectations and provides truths and promises that can be used to withstand the tumultuous moments. God encourages us to stand our ground, putting on the belt of truth, the body armor of God's righteousness and the shoes of peace that comes from the good news (Ephesians 6:14-15) "Stand firm then, with the belt of truth buckled around your

CHAPTER LEARNING OBJECTIVES

Upon completing this chapter, you should be able to:

- Identify current sociocultural norms influencing the roles and expectations of women
- Evaluate clinical considerations for working with women in the current context of social messaging
- Evaluate opportunities for advocacy and social justice for women
- Analyze Biblical constructs that inform and empower women

waist, with the breastplate of righteousness in place, and with your feet fitted with the readiness that comes from the gospel of peace" (*New International Bible*, 1973/2011). He holds us as worthy, even when we may not find worthiness in ourselves, He esteems us as His children and has a promising future planned for us (Jeremiah 29:11) "For I know the plans I have for you, declares the Lord, plans for welfare and not for evil, to give you a future and a hope" (*English Standard Bible*, 2001). In His love, we can stand firmly while drowning out the negative voices in our head and resisting the social pressures around us.

CHAPTER OVERVIEW

This chapter focuses on the conflicting messages related to roles and expectations that women receive in social contexts and their compounding impact on mental health throughout the lifespan. Specifically, this chapter will review social media messaging, messaging in the workplace and the home, and the role of advocacy in counseling to support the specific clinical needs of women related to socio-cultural issues. Additionally, this chapter will review the role of women in society as presented from a Biblical context, highlighting the unique value that God places on adolescent and adult

© Rawpixel.com/Shutterstock.com

COUNSELING WOMEN

females. While other chapters in the book will specifically address considerations of race, ethnicity, and class in relation to women and mental health, it is important to note that these compounding factors may dramatically impact women as they determine the messaging and social norms they are exposed to. This section of the textbook will explore how consistent, oppressive, negative, and restrictive views can cause undue hardship to women, impacting their overall wellbeing. These considerations highlight the importance of counseling and advocacy aimed at women's issues related to the influence of sociocultural norms and social messaging.

WOMEN AND SOCIOCULTURAL NORMS

Cultural norms and practices have shaped views on the identity and value of women since the beginning of time, often negatively. For example, in Biblical times, women were often viewed as sinful in nature and second in value to men (Bellville, 2005). Scripture notes stories such as the woman at the well who had several previous husbands and was currently living unmarried with a man (John 4:4-26), the woman who was almost stoned for committing adultery (John 7:53-8:11), and even Eve who is infamous for convincing Adam to take a bite of the forbidden apple (Genesis 2:4-3:24). For centuries, women were not allowed to own land, any significant property, and they were not allowed a voice outside of their husbands and sons —consider the trials of Naomi and Ruth (Ruth 1-4). Women were also not able to take positions of leadership outside of the home make decisions regarding the communities they lived in. Women during this time might only have been valued for their childbearing ability to produce a male offspring.

© Rawpixel.com/Shutterstock.com

In modern times, women continue to face challenges based on social norms. In the 19th century, women were forced to petition for their right to vote in hopes of establishing equality comparable to their male counterparts (Ware, 2015). In the 1950's women emerged on the college scene after demanding opportunities for education; however, they were primarily seen as homemakers and community service volunteers as they rarely moved into career settings, often marrying and starting a family. In the 1960's, the increase in women's education opportunities evolved into a fight for rights in the workplace (Ware, 2015). The 60's and 70's led to concepts of compounding multigenerational, multicultural factors, feminism, and the continuation of the Suffrage Movement. Each wave of challenge worked toward change in the concepts of women's roles in society.

These components of change made way for a Second Demographic Transition (SDT) (Shultz et al., 2018). During this transition, fertility declined, divorce, recoupling, and premarital cohabitation increased. SDT enhanced the flow of women in the workplace, including women with young children. The emergence of women and mothers in the workplace, highlighted unfair practices and promoted an outcry for fair and comparable wages along with opportunities for egalitarian roles. Women desired and still desire to be valued for their ideas, contributions, and unique characteristics that they bring to the work setting. Furthermore, this fight for value and voice can be seen in areas of leadership, entrepreneurship, medical care, politics, sports, education, advertising, and even in counseling. Social norms related to the value of women permeates culture through our families and churches, further impacting the development of policy and community standards and expectations. These norms are often perpetuated through social messages in social media, in the workplace, and in the home.

SOCIAL MESSAGES TO WOMEN IN THE MEDIA

It is impossible to explore social messaging and its impact on women without first examining the role of messaging through various forms of media in society. Media such as television, magazines, and social networking platforms, can be a significant source of negative messaging, and it is important to keep a watchful eye on the issue at hand: How do negative messages in media impact women and what are the consequences for mental health?

Social networking sites like Twitter, SnapChat, Facebook, and Instagram have mesmerized society with the next selfie, live video feed, hashtag, celebrity post, or charity challenge. Not only has social media captured our

curiosity, it has changed how we define, make and maintain friendships, find jobs, keep up with the latest news, remain in the loop with our political party or community events, or make choices about our next purchase, church to attend, or babysitter to choose for our children. More notably, it has changed the way we communicate with others, how we see ourselves, how we compare ourselves to others, and how we define our self-worth and the worth of others. These shifts in self-identification have had the biggest impact among women; changing how they see themselves and interact with the world around them (Baruth, 2014).

The Negative Impact of Media Messages

The impact of media on women is commonly noted during adolescence (ages 13-17); however, advertising in other forms such as cartoons, television commercials, video games, and teen focused magazines lay the groundwork for negative social media impact at earlier stages (Baruth, 2014; Guinta, 2018). During adolescence, young girls begin to look outside of themselves for identity formation. This can be a critical time period for development and growth. Observable behaviors that mark the influence of social media can be seen in increased cell phone and social media usage that may intrude on family time, social engagement, personal decision making, educational engagement, and activities once enjoyed that did not include technology. This age group is at a greater risk for experiencing the negative influences of social media due to developing maturity levels, low self-regulation, and vulnerability to peer pressure (DePaolis & Williford, 2019; Guinta, 2018). These considerations, along with limited parental guidance or authoritative oversight, make this group susceptible to internet addiction, social impairment, and legal ramifications related to issues such as sexting and sharing inappropriate information (Rosenthal et al., 2016).

© Tero Vesalainen/Shutterstock.com

Body Image and Sexuality

The influences of social media can compound and expand through late adolescence (ages 18-24) as social media engagement and access is less restricted. Girls and young women who more frequently engage with mainstream media content are exposed to a heavily emphasized, narrow, and unrealistic standard of beauty. Moreover, they are exposed to stereotypes that depict women as sexual objects (e.g., dressed in revealing clothing; bodily postures or facial expressions that imply sexual readiness; focused on body parts rather than the whole person). Professional models skew the perspective on healthy femininity, presented for young girls and women to study and emulate and leading them to model the unrealistic messages. This has the potential to lead to a negative body image which may result in issues, such as unhealthy eating habits (dieting, fasting, and purging), in an effort to obtain the portrayed ideal body weight or shape (Rosenthal et al., 2016). In fact, the hyper-sexualization of women is linked to three of the most common mental health problems of girls and women: eating disorders, low self-esteem, and depression or depressed mood (American Psychological Association, 2007). Each of these will be discussed in greater detail in other chapters in this textbook.

In 2007, The APA Task Force on the Sexualization of Girls was developed and tasked with examining the psychological theory, research, and clinical experience addressing the sexualization of girls via media and other cultural messages. It included the prevalence of these messages and their impact on girls and the role and impact of race/ethnicity and socioeconomic status. The task force noted that there are several components to sexualization, setting it apart from healthy sexuality. Sexualization occurs when:

1. a person's value comes only from his or her sexual appeal or behavior, to the exclusion of other characteristics;
2. a person is held to a standard that equates physical attractiveness (narrowly defined) with being sexy;
3. a person is sexually objectified—that is, made into a thing for others' sexual use, rather than seen as a person with the capacity for independent action and decision making; and/or
4. sexuality is inappropriately imposed upon a person.
   (American Psychological Association, 2007, p. 1)

Societal messages that contribute to the sexualization of girls come not only from media and merchandise but also through girls' interpersonal relationships such as parents, teachers, and peers (Brown & Gilligan, 1992). Parents can contribute to the sexualization of girls by reinforcing the importance of an attractive physical appearance and social norms in "women's roles" related to sexuality (wearing heels, make-up, skills for finding a husband, etc.). An example of this can be seen in parents who purchase clothes designed to enhance the sexual appeal of girls; this can include agreement if asked to make the purchase by the girl. Female peers can also play a role in sexualization of other girls by reinforcing standards of thinness and sexiness, through encouragement to be thin, or negative comments about weight. Peers also provide allowances for boys to sexually objectify or harass girls as part of normal and/or genetic behavior that cannot be avoided. Girls can also objectify themselves, in their choice of dress (provocative and oversexualized dress) and when they think of themselves in objectified terms, commonly noted as self-objectification whereby girls *learn* to think of and treat their own bodies as objects of others' desires.

Cyberbullying

Cyberbullying (bullying that takes place over digital devices like cell phones, computers, and tablets) can occur through SMS, Text, and apps, or online in social media, forums, or gaming where people can view, participate in, or share content. Cyberbullying includes sending, posting, or sharing negative, harmful, false, or mean content about someone else. It can include sharing personal or private information about someone else causing embarrassment or humiliation. Some cyberbullying crosses the line into unlawful or criminal behavior (U.S. Department of Health and Human Services, 2019).

Social media can also be a breeding ground for psychological harm that has the potential to evolve into physical threats and harm. Predators and perpetrators can use social media platforms to send insensitive, harmful, and demeaning messages and/or pictures to victims. Social media sites along with advances in the use of smartphones, blogs, private messaging, private chat rooms, private email accounts, and the use of anonymous accounts or public accounts with anonymous names have increased, making it an optimal platform for those wanting to do harm (Baruth, 2014). These types of users can cause great harm to victims by invoking fear and the dissolution of feelings of safety and trust. Cyberbullying can occur in a number of ways as noted by DePaolis & Williford (2019); on-line fighting; where two or more parties engage in hostile exchange to include messaging and/or pictures. Online gossiping, which includes an intentional effort to slander one's reputation; harassment, which includes threatening and hostile messaging used to promote fear or coercion; exclusion, blocking someone from joining or gaining access to an on-line group; and outing, which is a current and commonly noted form of cyberbullying where the assailant shares private and personal information about someone via messaging, pictures, or video. This form of cyberbullying is commonly used as a coercion technique toward the victim. The availability and 24-hour access to digital tools along with the long-lasting digital imprint, and anonymity that social media provides makes cyberbullying a unique impacting form of bullying. These factors can make it hard for victims to receive relief, support or protection (U.S. Department of Health and Human Services, 2019).

SOCIAL MESSAGES TO WOMEN AT HOME AND IN THE WORKPLACE

Mothering and Mom-Guilt

A couple was wanting to capture a "moment" with their young children on their way to an event with everyone looking happy and smiling. Instead, what they got was the reality of life with two small children. Both children were having major meltdowns, but the couple went ahead and posted it on social media. It was raw, real, and risky! More often though, instead of posting the "real life" photos, we only post the ones that will be "good enough" – the photos that make up the "highlight reel" of our lives. This sets up the atmosphere for comparison and shaming.

Parents have numerous decisions to make when it comes to their children: what form of discipline is used (do you count to 3, use time outs, spank, etc.), breastfeeding versus formula, stay-at-home mom versus working mom, and homeschool versus public or private school all set up moms/parents who are "trying to get it right". But what often happens is comparison, judging, and shaming. Instead, it is important to support and build one other up regardless of whether there is agreement on every decision. Current research supports the importance of this kind and supportive attitude toward one another and the self. For example, research on self-compassion indicates that if we can move from the self-comparison culture toward a culture that emphasizes self-compassion and a kind attitude toward the self that normalizes mistakes this is more adaptive for our mental health (Hinkley et al., 2020; Kuhnley, 2020).

Women may receive social messages that indicate it is unacceptable to have negative feelings about parenting and create pressure to deny those thoughts or feelings. In 2017, a study was conducted by Schoppe-Sullivan and colleagues to identify notable differences between new young mothers in their use and experience of Facebook. They found "higher levels of maternal identity confirmation and societal-oriented parenting perfectionism were associated with greater Facebook activity" (p. 285). Their findings were also consistent with previous research which showed that Facebook use may undermine the mental health of new moms. The reality is women often have realistic and conflicting feelings about parenthood, and the pressure to be perceived as the perfect mom has the potential to lead to disappointment and self-condemnation. Mom-guilt is real. A "psychological consequence of modern motherhood that scholars have argued is actually an inherent part of motherhood – guilt" (Henderson et al., 2016, p. 515). Evolutionary psychologists Rotkirch and Janhunen (2009) addressed this topic in an article titled "Maternal Guilt" writing that "guilt focuses on wrongful behavior and is connected to a concern for oth-

© Nicoleta Ionescu/Shutterstock.com

ers and how they are affected by one's behavior" (p. 92). Therefore, when it comes to mothering, in a desire to attain perfection, **mom guilt** (feelings of guilt that result from internal and external pressure to be perfect alongside perpetual feelings of inadequacy) can emerge frequently as a result of the pressure to be perfect and the perpetual feelings of inadequacy.

Counselors working with moms can help them gain a healthy perspective.

- Happy moms learn how to let go. Realize that you did your best and understand that there are a lot of factors out of your control.
- Happy moms do not need to be attached to outcomes. Realize that you can't make your children perfect or happy.
- Happy moms set boundaries over which children (or others who may guilt you) cannot cross. Expect to be treated with respect (from your children and others as well).
- Happy moms allow others to help out and do not have to do it all. Realize that others love your children and are willing to step in when you are too tired or need a break.
- Happy moms pursue some personal interests and maintain a balanced life.
- Happy moms have a tribe with whom they can feel authentic, validated, and affirmed.

Working Women and Family Systems

© Dashu/Shutterstock.com

A long-standing way of thinking in American culture is the belief that women should be the primary caregivers in the family while men should be the primary breadwinners (Cuddy et al., 2004). Many studies have investigated the perceptions of and behaviors toward women who occupy both roles: a mother and a professional. The results show unique disadvantages suffered by female professionals (as compared to male professionals) who happen to be parents (Cuddy et al., 2004). Gender discrimination in the workplace continues to be a reality in our society.

Despite changes in values, examples of bias and prejudice are evident – women and men are not equally represented in management positions, particularly at higher levels of organizations (Wynn, 2017). The increase of women occupying a more significant proportion of the full-time labor force in the 1980s led to more families identifying as dual-earner couples. The traditional gender stereotypes of women as "caregivers" and men as "breadwinners" had impacted the way partners defined their roles within the family. Masterson and Hoobler (2015) introduced five dual-earner couple types that stem from distinct combinations of the partner's family identities: (1) the "traditional dual-earner couple" wherein the female family identity prioritizes caregiving over career while the male family identity prioritizes career over caregiving, (2) the "non-traditional dual-earner couple" wherein men assume the role of caregiver as a stay-at-home dad, (3) the "family first dual-earner couple" wherein both male and female partners define their primary roles in terms of caregiving, significantly more so than career, (4) the "outsourced dual-earner couple" wherein both male and female partners construe their role in the family in terms of career, significantly more than care, and (5) the "egalitarian dual-earner couple" wherein both partners strongly incorporate both family-based roles and career-based roles into their family identity.

The egalitarian dual-earner couple type incorporates men's societal shift toward increased involvement in day-to-day care of the family as well as women's shift toward greater involvement in the financial security of the home (Haas & O'Brien, 2010; Masterson & Hoobler, 2015). This family dynamic encourages an equal division of the household responsibilities (Zuo, 2004) and values employment while accommodating the desire to spend time with family (Hammer et al., 2009). In summary, each of these family dynamics have both positive and negative implications for counseling women. What may work for one family, may not necessarily work for another. While there are no "right" or "wrong" family systems, just as there are no "cookie cutter" families, it is important to explore the current family dynamic of clients during intake and assessment to consider implications for the presenting problems.

Pregnancy and Maternity Leave

The United States is one of the few countries that does not offer guaranteed paid leave for women after childbirth. The Department of Labor estimates that paid family leave (through the employer) is only available to a small percentage (12%) of private sector workers (2015).

The Department of Labor (2015) estimates that only 12% of private sector workers have access to paid family leave through their employer.

Maternity leave not only helps a woman recover from childbirth but also helps her bond with her newborn during crucial early days and weeks of the infant's life. This bonding has a positive impact on the mother's physical health, on her mental and emotional wellbeing, and on the development of secure attachment between her and her child (Clinton & Sibcy, 2002; Sibcy & Knight, 2017). However, maternity leave often has negative consequences for family finances, job security, and opportunities for promotion. Without pay during maternity or paternity leave, the likelihood that parents can afford to stop working is lowered. With the introduction of the Family and Medical Leave Act, the potential for businesses to discriminate against women who are or who are likely to become pregnant is increased. Smaller businesses face the potential of being temporarily short-staffed and saddled with higher medical costs, and possibly taking on higher wage costs, when women take maternity leave (Zagorsky, 2017).

In 1993, the Family and Medical Leave Act (FMLA) was introduced, providing maternity leave (eligible workers receiving up to 12 weeks of unpaid time off during the first 12 months after birth to care for a newborn) for eligible workers, including up to 12 weeks of *unpaid time off* during the first 12 months after birth to care for a newborn (Zagorsky, 2017). However, because of the criteria for companies to meet (length of employment >1 year, hours worked >1250 hours in the past 12 months, and employer size >50 employees), not all workers are covered. It is important to note that FMLA is *unpaid time off* and this can, and often does, put a financial hardship on the new mother. Low-wage employees are even less likely to have access to paid family leave through their employers, which includes maternity leave.

According to the 7th edition of *Guidelines for Perinatal Care*, published by the American Congress of Obstetricians and Gynecologists (ACOG) and the American Academy of Pediatrics (AAP), most women need **4 to 6 weeks** to physically recover from giving birth before returning to work. And, recovery from a cesarean delivery typically takes **1 to 2 weeks longer**, according to ACOG (2015).

Because many women can't afford to have unpaid maternity leave, they and their babies face potential harm. The lack of paid maternity leave has been linked to lower rates of breastfeeding and childhood immunizations, and higher rates of infant and child mortality and depression in mothers (Rubin, 2016). According to the 7th edition of Guidelines for Perinatal Care, published by the American Congress of Obstetricians and Gynecologists (ACOG) and the American Academy of Pediatrics (AAP), most women need 4 to 6 weeks to physically recover from giving birth before returning to work.

Additionally, recovery from a cesarean delivery typically takes 1 to 2 weeks longer, according to ACOG.

The then-Surgeon General Regina Benjamin, MD, issued "The Surgeon General's Call to Action to Support Breastfeeding" in 2011 and one of the 20 actions she recommended was for all employed mothers to have access to paid maternity leave. Dr. Benjamin noted that breastmilk has immunological and anti-inflammatory properties that protect mother and child from a host of illnesses. Although mothers may be well-intentioned, returning to work can get in the way of their breastfeeding plans. Counselors need to be aware of all of these changes in addition to the potential for postpartum depression in women who have recently given birth.

Working Women and Mothering

Working moms are often viewed as more motherly than professional, and as more nurturing than task-oriented, which upholds the social structure that maintains the female caregiver/male breadwinner ideology. But caregiving is not often viewed as a promotable quality in many professions. Because men and childless women are viewed as available to work longer hours (and often as having fewer responsibilities at home), they can anticipate and expect higher promotion chances (Wynn, 2017). Less than a quarter of full professors are women, even though more than 50 percent of college graduates are now women. Women comprise approximately one third of Masters of Business Administration classes (MBA) and 47 percent

© Monkey Business Images/Shutterstock.com

of the labor force but only 4 percent of *Fortune 500* CEOs and 8 percent of top-earning leadership positions (Wynn, 2017). Wynn (2017) goes on to say that entry-level positions are somewhat comparable between men and women; however, women still face substantial obstacles for attaining upper level positions.

Working Women and the Gender Pay Gap

The **gender pay gap** (women in the United States earning less than their male counterparts in spite of having equivalent experience, education, and job skills) is still in existence today, as it was more than 50 years ago when it was first addressed by the Equal Pay Act and Title VII (Stanberry, 2018). The Civil Rights Act of 1964 was enacted more than half a century ago, yet there is little improvement in delineating between *women's work* and *men's work*. The Civil Rights Act denied employers from overtly advertising jobs based on gender but "invisible and taken-for-granted non-cognitive job demands are influential in differentiating 'women's' jobs from 'men's' jobs" (Guy, 2017, p. 49). Women in the United States earn less than their male counterparts even when they have equivalent experience, education, and job skills. A plethora of studies have produced empirical data to substantiate the existence of the gender pay gap, so much so that the topic has become somewhat stale.

FIGURE 1.1

Wage and Expectation Gaps for Women by Years of Experience

Graph © Kendall Hunt Publishing Company. Data source: Hired.com The State of Wage Inequality in the Workplace 2019 Report

The gender pay gap increases with age, but so does the expectation gap – the more experienced women are, the lower is their salary expectations with women with 9-10 years of experience having the biggest gap. Thus, women are not only experiencing gender discrimination, but also age discrimination. This graph by Forbes (Grobman, 2019) illustrates the wage and expectation gaps for women by years of experience.

Although progress has been made (and is projected to get better), it is not appropriate or ethically acceptable to tell any victim of discrimination that even though things have gotten better over the last 50 years that they should wait another 10 or 20 for a level playing field. Women have a right to expect equal pay now.

A Voice from the Field
One Woman's Step in Providing
a Platform for Other Women
Sasha Shilcutt, MD, CEO, Brave Enough

© Kylee Pack

Sasha K. Shillcutt, MD, MS, FASE is a Tenured Professor and the Vice Chair of Strategy and Innovation in the Department of Anesthesiology at the University of Nebraska Medical Center (UNMC). Sasha CEO & Founder of Brave Enough, a well-published researcher in cardiac anesthesiology and gender equity, cardiac anesthesiologist, author, and international speaker. She leads conferences and retreats for professional women through her organization, Brave Enough. Her first book, *Between Grit and Grace: How to be Feminine and Formidable*, released in February 2020. In response to a question about the development of her passion for advocating for women through the Brave Enough platform, Sasha said (personal communication, December 4, 2019):

I was in a very low place about 5 years ago when I had a lot of academic success but inside; I was completely empty. I asked myself, "Is this what I envisioned my life to be?" I realized I was incredibly lonely. I was under a lot of pressure to be successful at work and at home. I heard many social messages to "do more", "be more", etc. I invited a few friends to a text group which turned into a social media group in 2015. As of today, that group is made up of 11,000 women! I realized that women need com-

munity and we heal through community. I created a virtual "women's lounge" where you can get advice and not be ashamed about it (from what lipstick do I choose to how do I negotiate something in my job). All the things that were perceived as non-academic, but were crucial to a woman's mental wellbeing, are allowed. This is why I do what I do – to be able to help women live authentically.

As women, we have so many similar struggles. I was encouraged when I decided to host my first Brave Enough conference and it sold out in one hour after opening registration in the group. So many wonderful and real relationships have developed from women since the establishment of the Brave Enough community: women have gathered to go on trips together, engage in community activities, and strategically supported one another in career advancement. I have learned that building connection is so important. The number one thing that women face is the incredible pressure to be more. This constant feeling of not being enough creates isolation. Living authentically as women, when we live our authentic self, it allows others to live their authentic selves too. Sometimes, as women, we are afraid to step into our authentic self – because we fear what others might say or think about us.

I realize every year as I look back and reflect, I think, "I cared so much about what other people thought of me and the truth is I probably wasn't even on their radar." The narrative that society creates is that women are "catty", and not supportive of one another. We, as women, need to choose to NOT play into that narrative. All of us have had the "mean girl" experience, or may, at one point or another, have been the mean girl, for whatever reason. We don't know what the other person is going through, and so let's err on the side of assuming positive intent. The natural result of our society is that women are labeled as not being able to get along. As women, let's change that narrative. My life goal is to gather, unite, and inspire women.

You can follow Sasha at www.becomebraveenough.com

CLINICAL CONSIDERATIONS FOR WOMEN FACING CULTURAL ISSUES

The foundational practices of the counseling profession have been developed and shaped primarily by a male worldview, initially leaving minimal if any consideration to the differences between males and females or the perspectives of women and how they view the evolution of illness, wellness, research, and pedagogical development surrounding women's issues. While some research and theory have evolved over the years, considerations for women's development, counseling concerns, barriers to treatment, and best clinical practices are limited although women are the primary partakers in counseling services (Gelaye et al., 2016; National Institute of Mental Health (NIMH), 2017). Overlooking or minimizing this gap in understanding and research to women's specific needs can lend itself to stifled competency among counselors providing therapeutic services to women, limit quality care to women, and possibly elicit ethical violations.

Considering Sex, Gender, and Ethical Issues

To competently provide mental health treatment to women, they should be seen in their entirety. Women must be viewed in the context of their race, culture, educational level, disability, sexual orientation, socio-economic class, religious preference, and societal gender role expectations as each of these considerations intertwine in ways that impact women across the lifespan. To truly understand the complexity of a woman we will have to look beyond her

© GBALLGIGGSPHOTO/Shutterstock.com

sex and the assumed differences that exist between a woman and her male counterparts. To do this, we have to have an understanding of the term "sex" and how it differs from the term "gender". "Sex" generally denotes biologically determined characteristics, while "gender", on the other hand, identifies culturally and socially-shaped roles, like differences in how to think or act, among men and women (Durbin et al., 2017; Hamovitch et al., 1997; Lovejoy et al., 2013).

In exploring and developing an understanding of these terms, it is important to note that the absence of discrimination on the basis of a person's sex in opportunities, and the allocation of resources or benefits, or access to services, is gender equality. Whereas gender equality refers to fairness and justice in the distribution of benefits and responsibilities between women and men

(Durbin et al., 2017). An awareness of these terms and factors support clinical considerations that can enhance the ethical treatment of women in therapy.

The American Counseling Association through its *Code of Ethics* (2014) provides a standard of practice for counselors and counselors in training for avoiding harm, imposing personal values, standards of advocacy and (A.4.a, b; 7.b.) in working with diverse groups, in this case women. Section C, Professional Responsibilities of the ACA *Code of Ethics* encourages counselors to engage in educational training, develop skills, and engage in experiences that enhance their ability to meet the needs of diverse populations (including women). This section goes on to prompt counselors to practice in a nondiscriminatory manner in working with specialty groups, to advocate to promote changes at the individual, group, institutional, and societal levels that improve the quality of life for individuals and groups, to remove potential barriers to the provision or access of appropriate services being offered, and to engage in counseling practices that are based on rigorous research methodologies.

Considering Gender Differences in Mental Health

© BlurryMe/Shutterstock.com

Women and men, while created equally, differ greatly. Exploring gender differences in mental health services provides a platform to assess the interplay between biological and social factors that impact the inequality of mental health treatment outcomes across the gender line. In 2002, the World Health Organization (WHO) passed its first Gender Policy. This policy acknowledged gender as an important issue for consideration in world health. During this same time, WHO additionally established the UN's Millennium Development Goals which expanded focus beyond general Health for All framework's on equity and shifted focus to gender equality and the empowerment of women (2017).

Women are diagnosed with mental health disorders at a higher rate than males. Research indicates that women encounter higher rates of childhood abuse, including physical, psychological and sexual abuse, compared to abuse reported by males. These traumas and adverse childhood experiences can be linked to behavioral issues as well as psychological disorders such as depression, post-traumatic stress, panic disorder, and eating disorders among women throughout their lives (Gelaye et al., 2016; Hamovitch et al., 1997).

Mental health disorder diagnoses also vary across age groups with differences in prevalence between genders. Conduct disorder, the most prevalent psychiatric disorder in childhood, is diagnosed among boys at a rate of three times that for girls. However, during adolescence, girls have a higher prevalence of depression and eating disorders; they are also noted to engage more in suicidal ideation and suicide attempts than boys, who are more prone to engage in high risk behaviors and commit suicide more frequently. In adulthood, women have a higher prevalence of most affective disorders and non-affective psychosis and men have higher rates of substance use disorders and Antisocial Personality Disorder. Men in adulthood are also noted to develop alternative disorders in response to stress, such as antisocial behavior and alcohol abuse (Alegria et al., 2008; Gelaye et al., 2016; NIMH, 2017).

> Men are more likely to have been socialized to express anger or other forms of acting out, while women may be more likely to be socialized to express dysphoria in response to stress. Awareness of these factors can play a vital role for counselors in working with women, however they may often go unrecognized in assessing the evolution of a woman's distressed physical and mental health.

In later life, the prevalence of disorders differed significantly by gender, ethnicity, education, household income, and marital status. Specifically, women are noted to have significantly higher rates of mood and anxiety disorders, whereas men have significantly higher rates of substance use. Mental health disorders become less prevalent and appear to level off for both women and men in late age; 85 and older. Older adults adopt a limited perception of time and a present-focused state of awareness, seek the fulfillment of emotionally meaningful goals, and select the company of familiar social partners which decreases the likelihood that stressful social situations will occur, and increases the likelihood of experiencing positive emotions (NIMH, 2017; Reynolds et al., 2015).

Considering the Impact on Wellness Functioning

Mental health distress or impairment can have a pervasive impact on various areas of wellness functioning. Individuals, specifically women suffering with mental illness, are less likely to maintain long-term, stable, and up-wardly mobile employment. This can be a significant consideration as most US families are now dual wage income homes or are led by a single mother. A woman's inability to maintain solid footing in employment can negative-ly impact the financial stability of the family, which can lead to issues in maintaining housing, transportation, food stability, access to quality medi-cal care, among other things (Lerner & Henke, 2008; Wynn, 2017). Mental health disorders are also linked to health problems such as cardiovascular disease, diabetes, stroke, certain types of cancers, substance use disorders, and even suicide (World Health Organization, 2017). Within families where women are generally the primary caregiver for children, issues of mental health can impact the quality of parenting; limited or negative engagement can increase the risk of child maltreatment (Lovejoy et al., 2013). These are sobering factors considering the aforementioned high rates of abuse and maltreatment that already exist among girls and women.

Mitigating the Negative Impact of Social Media

Negative social media influences can have a detrimental impact on several domains of functioning: cognitive health, physical health, mental health, sexuality, and attitudes and beliefs. These compounding factors make it important for counselors to be aware of steps that can be taken to mitigate impact. The following are a few considerations:

- Counselors working in a school setting have a captive audience of adolescent girls and boys. Because media is a prominent source of sexualizing images, the development and implementation of school-based media literacy training programs can be a key in combating the influence of sexualization by promoting critical thinking skills in stu-dents viewing and consuming media that highlight the sexualization of women and girls.
- Counselors working in schools and colleges can advocate for increased access to athletic and other extracurricular programs for girls and wom-en. As counselors, we can encourage and support engagement in activi-ties that allow our female clients to focus on, develop, or refine physical attributes that do not include their looks and enhance opportunities for achievement that can build confidence and self-esteem.
- Counselors can develop a comprehensive sexuality education pro-gram that can be implemented in community settings such as girl

scouts, community centers, summer programs and church settings where young girls and women frequent. As counselors, we can encourage involvement in these settings to enhance understanding and meaning of healthy sexuality.

- Counselors can garner engagement from parents and families to help in confronting sources of sexualized images of girls. Educate parents and other caregivers about the impact of sexualization of girls and encourage co-viewing of media with their children in order to influence the way that media messages are interpreted, offering girls practical and psychological alternatives to the values conveyed by popular culture.

- Counselors should also be aware that while social media has its pitfalls, it also provides opportunities for connection, increasing the perceptions of relationship closeness, and connectedness among users (Ellison et al., 2007, Jacobsen & Forte, 2011). Healthy social media use can provide opportunities for collaboration, communication, self-esteem enhancement, health promotion, and access to vital health information (Guinta, 2018).

- Counselors can use group modalities, cognitive behavior models, and wellness approaches that emphasize skills for developing healthy connections with others, for speaking authentically about thoughts and feelings, and for coping with life's demands more effectively (e.g., Beck, 1995; Myers & Sweeney, 2005; Tolman & Brown, 2001). Counselors should engage in ongoing research and training that bolsters our understanding and supports competent therapeutic engagement.

Mitigating Barriers to Treatment

The negative and pervasive nature of mental health concerns for women support a need for mitigating the impact of mental health issues. As we have looked at the specific differences that occur between women and men in prevalence and impact, it is important to explore barriers to access, engagement, and positive therapeutic outcomes from treatment (Alegria et al., 2008). The identification of mental health issues among women seeking ser-

© BCFC/Shutterstock.com

vices are often met by agency level waitlists for services, cost of services, fears about losing custody of their children, and mistrust of the mental health system. Women can also be impeded by negative personal opinions about the perceived relevance, helpfulness, and acceptability of treatment. The perceived lack of therapeutic bonding or the perception of fit and connection in the therapeutic relationship can lead to premature drop-out of services (Hamovitch et al., 1997).

Women often become aware of mental health needs or issues while seeking health care. However, health services for women tend to focus on their reproductive functions, neglecting the needs of women outside of reproductive ages and omitting assessment and treatment for things like postpartum depression, in which 1 in 9 women suffer (American College of Gynecologists and Obstetricians, 2015; Gelaye et al., 2016; NIMH, 2017). A lack of female medical personnel is sometimes a barrier for women who do utilize healthcare services. Women can also find themselves without access to healthcare more often than men from the same social group, even in rich countries like the United States. In many developing countries, women complain about lack of privacy, confidentiality, and information about options and services available. Additionally, women face the bias of medical doctors who attribute different meanings to identical symptoms for women and male patients, or attribute women's illnesses to psychiatric disorders and prescribe inappropriate medication (American College of Gynecologists and Obstetricians, 2015). Women disproportionately face a higher mental and physical morbidity than men. This has been hypothesized to be caused by their gender sensitivity to physical cues and to the social acceptability of "sick roles" for women. Women facing certain issues such as substance abuse are less likely to seek treatment than men. Barriers to treatment also stem from high rates of coexisting mental health issues, such as posttraumatic stress disorders and depression which lead to self-medication of substances to include alcohol, medication, and/or over-indulgences in other self-harming behaviors (Alegria et al., 2008; NIMH, 2017).

BIBLICAL PORTRAYALS OF WOMEN

Genesis explains that God created men and women to fulfill different roles within the home, church, and workplace. However, some may interpret Scriptures to limit, distort, or dismiss a woman's role in each of these settings. God created men and women in His image, and He created them to be male and female (Genesis 1:27). Genesis indicates that God concluded man was not complete without woman, and many would argue that it takes both man and woman together in order to fully reflect the divine image of God — they complement each other and are equal in that respect (Rea, 2016). Although culture shapes our definitions of differences between men and women, the Bible portrays women as faithful, as strong, and as inspiring leaders.

Old Testament Women

While the Bible is often considered more patriarchal in nature, the text supports equal standing of men and women in all facets of God's intent when He created Adam and Eve (Hughes, 2006). Even in the Old Testament, there are many examples of strong women who were active in their communities and whom God used for His purposes.

Miriam, Esther, and Deborah are just three of many women whose lives and stories are recorded in the Old Testament. Miriam was a model of wisdom, intelligence, and confidence in the protection of her baby brother, Moses. She watched over his life as he was hidden in a papyrus basket among the reeds along the bank of the Nile and therefore played a role in

© Katie Braboy

the deliverance of Israel from Egypt (Exodus 2). Esther risked her life to save her people. She exemplified faith, grace, principles, and conviction while she was brave and courageous in approaching the King to state her case for her people (Esther 5). Deborah was a prophetess and judge to Israel (Judges 4-5). She led with wisdom, courage, and a compassionate zeal for justice. She exhibited both spiritual and civil leadership (Eldredge & Eldredge, 2010). These women are all examples of strong leaders!

The Proverbs 31 Woman

Proverbs 31 gives an example of a Godly, wise woman – one who takes care of her family and household while also being active in the market or business. She is an industrious housewife, a shrewd businesswoman, an enterprising trader, a generous benefactor, and a wise teacher. Consider the verse, "She is clothed with strength and dignity; she can laugh at the days to come; She speaks with wisdom and faithful instruction is on her tongue" (*New International Bible*, 1973/2011, Proverbs 31:25-26).

Peter Rios, in his article *Wife as Entrepreneur: A Business View of Proverbs 31:10-31,* identifies the values of the wife spoken of in Proverbs 31 (2015). The narrative that Rios (2015) presents of the Proverbs 31 woman is one of a modern-day entrepreneur; she has all the characteristics of a successful business owner. She is a respected woman who is valued and cherished by her husband (vs. 10-12). She gets up early to attend to her business and keeps her home in order (vs. 13-15). She serves the community, and she confidently conducts herself in the marketplace (vs. 16) which reflects that she is an excellent manager and has empathy for disadvantaged persons (vs. 20). A Proverbs 31 woman is admired and imitated and while she empowers others, she has a stellar reputation, she teaches others (vs. 26), and her husband is a leader in the community (vs. 23). She has a strong work ethic (vs. 27) and is valued by her family and throughout the community (vs. 28-31) (Rios, 2015).

New Testament Women

In the New Testament, Matthew's genealogy includes women when providing the lineage of Jesus Christ. It was uncommon at that time to provide women in genealogies; however, if they were included, one would expect them to be without flaws, which could not be further from the truth for some of the women listed who had pretty scandalous histories (Moore, 1996). It is important to note that men listed throughout the Bible were not without flaws either — except for Jesus, the Son of God. The genealogy list includes Mary, the mother of Jesus. She was strong and showed immense courage for such a young woman. Can you just imagine, she was in a relationship with an older man and announced she was pregnant … and impregnated by God? She was virtuous, but others surely speculated about her story and her relationship with Joseph. She allowed herself to be used by God in a mighty way and is an example of true faith.

© WarArt/Shutterstock.com

Along with Mary, Jesus' genealogy includes four other women, four broken women — women who felt like outsiders. Women who didn't quite fit in. There was Tamar who some say was guilty of prostitution and incest (Genesis 38:6-30). Bathsheba committed adultery with King David (2 Samuel 12:24) and possibly because of her marriage to a Hittite, she was also considered a foreigner. Rahab has often been referred to as "the harlot" but she hid two spies that Joshua sent out to investigate the military strength of Jericho, and by doing so, committed treason; thus the harlot of Jericho saved her family and was included in the lineage of Christ (Joshua 2:1, 3; 6:17, 23, 25; Hebrews 11:31). And then there was Ruth. Ruth was a Gentile, a foreigner who was widowed and saw that she needed to inspire Boaz to marry her. She took a risk by making herself vulnerable to Boaz (Ruth 4:13) (Eldredge & Eldredge, 2010). Jesus claimed these four women!

The stories of these women in the New Testament who faced great challenges give hope to women of all generations. Most women have decisions in their life that they would like to have back; most women have faced rejection and grief and some women have been victimized in deeply painful ways. Sometimes life circumstances lead to guilt and shame. These Biblical examples show that EVERYONE can be redeemed, that recovery is possible, and that even scarred lives can be redeemed to find purpose and meaning.

Jesus' Perspective on Women

The New Testament also includes many examples of Jesus loving and treating women with great respect and dignity. For example, in Matthew 15:24, he heals the demon-possessed daughter of a Gentile woman. She represented everything a good Jewish man would want to avoid. Jesus was not only teaching her; He was also teaching his disciples who were observing his interactions. He wanted this woman, as well as his followers, to understand that she has a place in the kingdom of heaven. Also, John's gospel (John 7:52-8:5) gives an account of a woman caught in adultery and brought by the Pharisees to Jesus, wanting Him to weigh in on the circumstances. There are several interesting questions about this such as: Where is the man she was caught with? Why are they not punishing the man as well? And, how did they know this was even taking place? But one thing is clear: Jesus cared for this woman – His actions unquestionably displayed his compassion for her and His love for broken people. His character was on full display as He identified, criticized, and dismantled the whole group of men there to condemn this woman. Furthermore, in Mark 12:41-44 and Luke 21:1, Jesus used the example of an unassuming widow to teach the disciples that it is not the size of the currency but the size of the sacrifice that matters to God. He told the disciples that this woman had given far more than all the rich because she gave all she had. And, after Jesus' resurrection, He first appeared to a woman – Mary Magdalene. She was alone and He instructed her to go and tell the disciples that she had seen Jesus (Mark 16:10-11).

The triune God is a God who values and has offered counsel to women. God the Father created women in His image and used their gifts. Jesus' validation and affirmation of women is documented throughout the Gospels Matthew, Mark, Luke, and John. Unfortunately, the value of women that is evident throughout the Bible is lacking in religious and social cultures today as much as it was during Biblical times.

God never discriminated against women. He valued them and respected them. He advocated for them and stood by them. He met them where they were. He heard them. He treated them with dignity, compassion, and love. Jesus learned from the way God valued and continues to love and affirm women. As counselors-in-training (CITs), a great deal can be learned by Jesus' examples in the way he treated women. Christian counseling can be a pivotal experience for women of today, facing difficulties and trials not unlike those experienced by the women portrayed in the Bible.

Women have always had their hands on the wheels of change. Women have led reform in voting rights, temperance, religious movements, moral, and political reform. While women have accomplished a great deal through history, there are still many more areas for continued work in shaping the practices, policies, laws, and conversations that can positively impact the lives of women. Unfortunately, today's woman is faced with many of the same issues as her sisters from the past: opportunities for work, leadership, and wage equality in the workplace, confining socio-cultural role expectations, access to and quality healthcare, protection from sexual assault, physical abuse, trafficking, and welfare of young girls who are abused, neglected, and unwanted in our society. In recognizing this, we must ask ourselves two questions: What is the mental health impact on women living in a marginalized society followed by the next question, what does it take to promote long lasting or permanent change? In addressing this consideration then we must ask ourselves what is our part? As a part of the community, in consideration of our moral, professional, and ethical responsibility, we must examine ourselves and continue to move with focus, passion, knowledge, and skill toward the true work of being the light of the world.

CHAPTER SUMMARY

This chapter provided an overview of several areas of sociocultural messaging facing woman today along with implications for mental health considerations and treatment. Advances in media platforms and technology have enhanced the scope of access to women about women, bolstering persistent, consistent and negative concepts. As counselors it is important to understand the implications of negative, sexualized and marginalizing images, music, print media, and social media and their impact on the self-image and self-esteem of young girls throughout their lifespan. Counselors are challenged to gain awareness and insight and act on behalf of women, with specific consideration for gender issues, barriers to treatment, and a Biblical worldview.

KEY TERMS

Cyberbullying - bullying that takes place over digital devices like cell phones, computers, and tablets

Gender Pay Gap - women in the United States earning less than their male counterparts in spite of having equivalent experience, education, and job skills

Maternity Leave - eligible workers receiving up to 12 weeks of unpaid time off during the first 12 months after birth to care for a newborn

Mom Guilt - feelings of guilt that result from internal and external pressure to be perfect alongside perpetual feelings of inadequacy

SUGGESTED RESOURCES

Books

Captivating: Unveiling the Mystery of a Woman's Soul by John and Stacey Eldridge

Two Views on Women in Ministry by James Beck, Stanley Gundry, and Linda Belleville

Organization

U.S. Department of Health and Human Services. (2019). *What is cyberbullying.* https://www.stopbullying.gov/cyberbullying/what-is-it

REFERENCES

Alegria, M., Polo, A., Gao, S., Santana, L., Rothstein, D., Jimenez, A., Hunter, M. L., Mendieta, F., Oddo, V., & Normand, S. L. (2008). Evaluation of a patient activation and empowerment intervention in mental health care. *Medical Care, 46,* 247–256.

American College of Gynecologists and Obstetricians. (2015). *ACOG committee opinion. Number 757.* https://www.acog.org/Clinical-Guidance-and-Publications/Committee-Opinions/Committee-on-Obstetric-Practice/Screeningfor-Perinatal-Depression.

American Counseling Association. (2014). *2014 ACA code of ethics.* https://www.counseling.org/knowledge-center

American Psychological Association. (2007). *Report on the APA task force on the sexualization of girls.* https://www.apa.org/pi/women/programs/girls/report-full.pdf

Baruth, K. (2014). Psychological aspects of social media and mental well-being. *Journal of Human Services, 34*(1), 84-88.

Beck, A. (1995). *Cognitive therapy: Basics and beyond.* Guilford Press.

Bellville, L. (2005). Women in ministry: An egalitarian perspective. In S. N. Gundry, & J. R. Beck (Eds.), *Two views on women in ministry* (pp. 21-51). Zondervan.

Brown, L. M., & Gilligan, C. (1992). *Meeting at the crossroads: The landmark book about the turning points in girls' and women's lives.* Ballantine.

Clinton, T. & Sibcy, G. (2002). *Attachments: Why you love, feel and act the way you do.* Integrity Publishers.

Cuddy, A. J. C., Fisk, S. T., & Glick, P. (2004). When professionals become mothers, warmth doesn't cut the ice. *Journal of Social Issues, 60*(4), 701-718.

DePaolis, K. J., & Williford, A. (2019). Pathways from cyberbullying victimization to negative health outcomes among elementary school students. *Journal of Child & Family Studies, 28*(9), 2390-2403.

Durbin, S., Page, M., & Walby, S. (2017). Gender equality and 'austerity': Vulnerabilities, resistance and change. *Gender, Work & Organization, 24*(1), 1-6.

Eldredge, J., & Eldredge, S. (2010). *Captivating: Unveiling the mystery of a woman's soul.* Thomas Nelson Publishing.

Ellison, N., Steinfield, C., & Lampe, C. (2007). The benefits of Facebook "friends:" Social capital and college students' use of online social network sites. *Journal of Computer-Mediated Communication, 12*(4), 1143–1168. https://doi.org/10.1111/j.1083-6101.2007.00367.x

English Standard Bible. (2001). English Standard Bible Online. https://www.esv.org/

Gelaye, B., Rondon, M. B., Araya, R., & Williams, M. A. (2016). Epidemiology of maternal depression, risk factors, and child outcomes in low-income and middle-income countries. *The Lancet Psychiatry, 3*(10), 973–982.

Grobman, M. (2019, April 1). *Making sense of the gender pay gap in five graphs.* Forbes. https://www.forbes.com/sites/miriamgrobman/2019/04/01/making-sense-of-the-gender-pay-gap-in-five-graphs/#2d4e6f671a3e

Guinta, M. R. (2018). Social media and adolescent health. *Pediatric Nursing, 44*(4), 196-201.

Guy, M. (2017). Mom work versus dad work in local government. *Administration & Society, 49*(1), 48-64.

Haas, L., & O'Brien, M. (2010). New observations on how fathers work and care: An Introduction to the special issue – Men, work and parenting – Part 1. *Fathering, 8*(3), 271-275.

Hammer, L. B., Kossek, E. E., Yragui, N. L., Bodner, T. E., & Hanson, G. C. (2009). Development and validation of a multidimensional measure of family supportive supervisor behaviors (FSSB). *Journal of Management, 35*, 837-856.

Hamovitch, E., Acri, M., & Gooplan, G. (1997). Relationships between the working alliance, engagement in services, and barriers to treatment for female caregivers with depression. *Child Welfare, 97*(3), 23-40.

Henderson, A., Harmon, S., & Newman, H. (2016). The price mothers pay, even when they are not buying it: Mental health consequences of idealized motherhood. *Sex Roles, 74*(11-12), 512-526.

Hinkley, P., Kuhnley, A. K. Nguyen, T., & Lim, J. (2020, March12). *Aligning your heart for clients: Self compassion and its relationship to empathy for better clinical success.* Christian Association for Psychological Studies (CAPS). Atlanta, GA.

Hughes, R. S. (2006). A Biblical worldview in support of the worth of women's work. *Forum on Public Policy: A Journal of the Oxford Round Table.* https://forumonpublicpolicy.com/archive06/hughes.pdf

Jacobsen, W. C., & Forste, R. (2011). The wired generation: Academic and social outcomes of electronic media use among university students. *Cyberpsychology, Behavior, and Social Networking, 14,* 275-280.

Kilpatrick, S. J., Papile, L.-A., Macones, G. A., & Watterberg, K. L. (2017). *Guidelines for perinatal care* (8th ed.). American Academy of Pediatrics.

Kuhnley, A. K. (2020). *The Mister Rogers effect.* Baker Books.

Lerner, D., & Henke, R. M. (2008). What does research tell us about depression, job performance, and work productivity? *Journal of Occupational and Environmental Medicine, 50*(4), 401–410.

Malik, H. C. (2000). *The challenge of human rights: Charles Malik and the universal declaration.* I B Taurus Academic.

Masterson, C. R., & Hoobler, J. M. (2015). Care and career: A family identity-based typology of dual-earner couples. *Journal of Organizational Behavior, 36,* 75-93.

Moore, M. E., (1996). *The chronological life of Christ: Volume I from glory to Galilee.* College Press Publishing Company.

Myers, J. E., & Sweeney, T. J. (2005). *Counseling for wellness: Theory, research and practice.* American Counseling Association.

National Institute of Mental Health. (2017). *Major depression.* https://www.nimh.nih.gov/health/statistics/major-depression.shtml

New International Bible. (2011). New International Bible Online. https://www.thenivbible.com/ (Original work published 1973)

Rea, M. (2016). Gender as a divine attribute. *Religious Studies, 52*(1), 97-115.

Reiner, S. M., Dobmeier, R. A., & Hernandez, T. J. (2013). Perceived impact of professional counselor identity: An exploratory study. *Journal of Counseling and Development, 91,* 174-183.

Reynolds, K., Pietrzak, R. H., EL-Gabalawy, E., Mackenzie, C. S., & Sareen, J. (2015). Prevalence of psychiatric disorders in U.S. older adults: Findings from a nationally representative survey. *World Psychiatry, 14,* 74–81.

Rios, P. (2015). Wife as entrepreneur: A business view of Proverbs 31:10-31. *Journal of Ethics & Entrepreneurship, 5*(2), 71-76.

Rosenthal, S., Buka, S., Marshall, B., Carey, K., & Clark, M. (2016). Negative experiences on facebook and depressive symptoms among young adults. *Journal of Adolescent Health, 59*(5), 510-516.

Rotkirch, A., & Janhunen, K. (2009). Maternal guilt. *Evolutionary Psychology, 8*(1), 90-106.

Rubin, R. (2016). Despite potential health benefits of maternity leave, U.S. lags behind other industrialized countries. *Journal of American Medical Association, 315*(7), 643-645.

Schoppe-Sullivan, S. J., Yavorsky, J. E., Bartholomew, M. K., Sullivan, J. M., Lee, M. A., Kamp Dush, C. M., & Glassman, M. (2017). Doing gender online: New Mother's Psychological Characteristics, Facebook use, and depressive symptoms. *Sex Roles, 76,* 276-289.

Schultz, K., L., Tuffs, P., & Alwin, D. (2018). The cultural divide and changing beliefs about gender in the United States, 1974–2010. *Sex Roles, 79,* 393-408. https://doi.org/10.1007/s11199-017-0874-4

Sibcy, G. A., Knight, A. M. (2017). Emotional Intelligence and the Attachment Behavioral System. In R. Summers (Ed.) *Social Psychology: How other people influence our thoughts and actions.* Greenwood.

Stanberry, K. (2018). Closing the gender pay gap: New approaches to an old problem. *Compensation & Benefits Review, 504*(4), 189-195.

Tolman, D. L., & Brown, L. M. (2001). Adolescent girls' voices: Resonating resistance in body and soul. In R. K. Unger (Ed.), *Handbook of the psychology of women and gender* (pp. 133–155). Wiley.

U.S. Department of Health and Human Services. (2019). *What is cyberbullying.* https://www.stopbullying.gov/cyberbullying/what-is-it

U.S. Department of Labor. (2015). *DOL fact sheet: Paid family and medical leave.* http://www.dol.gov/wb/PaidLeave/PaidLeave.htm

Ware, S. (2015). *American women's history: A very short introduction.* Oxford University Press.

World Health Organization. (2017). *Depression and other common mental disorders: Global health estimates.* WHO Document Production Services. https://www.who.int/mental_health/management/depression/prevalence_global_health_estimates/en/

Wynn, A. T. (2017). Gender, parenthood, and perceived chances of promotion. *Sociological Perspectives, 60*(4), 645-664.

Zagorsky, J. L. (2017). Divergent trends in U.S. maternity and paternity leave, 1994-2015. *American Journal of Public Health, 107*(3), 460-465.

Zuo, J. (2004). Shifting the breadwinning boundary: The role of men's breadwinner status and their gender ideologies. *Journal of Family Issues, 25,* 811–832. https://doi.org/10.1177/0192513X03259144

CHAPTER 2

Multicultural Considerations When Counseling Women

Christina Villarreal-Davis, Ph.D., Nivischi Edwards, Ph.D., & Arleezah Marrah, Ph.D.

"As women, we must stand up for ourselves. We must stand up for each other. We must stand up for justice for all." ~Michelle Obama

"I looked again. I saw a huge crowd, too huge to count. Everyone was there-all nations and tribes, all races and languages. And they were standing, dressed in white robes and waving palm branches, standing before the Throne and the Lamb and heartily singing: Salvation to our God on his Throne! Salvation to the Lamb!" (Revelation 7:9-10, MSG)

Wisdom from Above: Standing in His Grace

Women are the foundation of the Earth. Without women, it is impossible to "be fruitful and multiply, and repopulate the earth" (*New Living Bible*, 1996, Genesis 9:2). As such, women often carry a heavy load while attempting to balance and support herself as she navigates life. Juggling the roles of daughter, wife, mother, sister, friend, and career women are sometimes exhausting, especially when women are viewed as less than, not only because of their gender, but also because of their skin color. Despite these realities, you see many women from various walks of life, surviving, striving, and thriving.

© Rawpixel.com/Shutterstock.com

CHAPTER LEARNING OBJECTIVES

Upon completing this chapter, you should be able to:

- Identify statistical facts, population growth, and reported psychological distress of Latinas, Black women, and Asian American women
- Describe challenges faced for Latina, Black women, and Asian American women
- Recite counseling considerations for Latina, Black women, and Asian American women
- Employ effective strategies and counseling recommendations for Latinas, Black women, and Asian American women
- Demonstrate Biblical integration and insights when counseling Latinas, Black women, and Asian American women
- Discuss key cultural concepts and counseling recommendations when counseling Native American women

CHAPTER OVERVIEW

Being a woman, especially a woman of color in America today, is much different than it was a century ago, when women's overall well-being was largely disregarded. In fact, pioneers in the field, whose approaches were largely uninfluenced by a woman's perspective but instead by a gender-biased, White male perspective, developed the foundational theories in counseling (Sue & Sue, 2003). Even the research on counseling theories and techniques lacked the voices of women and women of color (Sharf, 1996). However, with the perseverance and tenacity of many women in the field, significant changes in research and practice now highlight women's issues. We know a lot more today than we did twenty, thirty, and even forty years ago. The research on women's issues has provided greater insight and understanding on specific concerns of women, including the complexities of culture and how that impacts women of color in counseling today.

In this chapter, we will provide a brief overview of three major culture groups: Latinas, Black women, and Asian American women. This chapter highlights important issues counselors need to know, challenges faced in counseling, counseling considerations, and counseling recommendations for each culture group. Additionally, the chapter provides insights on

© pixelheadphoto digitalskillet/Shutterstock.com

Biblical and Christian integration. A case study concludes each major section to promote further understanding and integration. Lastly, this chapter spotlights a Native American woman's cultural journey and a Black woman's story on the superwoman persona.

COUNSELING LATINAS

What Counselors Need to Know

The Latina/o culture is very diverse and includes people from various Spanish-speaking and Latin countries. The terms *Hispanic* and *Latina/o* are frequently used interchangeably, but these terms tend to have different meanings within the culture. *Hispanic* generally refers to those individuals who can trace their heritage back to Spain or Spanish-speaking countries, whereas *Latina/o* generally refers to individuals from Latin American countries (American Psychiatric Association [APA], 2017). Moreover, *Latina* refers to the feminine version of Latino and describes females of Latin descent.

© Cabeca de Marmore/Shutterstock.com

The Latina/o population has experienced rapid growth over the years. According to the U.S. Census Bureau (2019), as of July 1, 2018, the Hispanic/Latina/o population constituted 18.3% (59.9 million) of the nation's total population, considered the nation's largest ethnic minority group. According to the Pew Research Center, the five largest U.S. groups by Hispanic origin included Mexican, Puerto Rican, Salvadoran, Cuban, and Dominican (Noe-Bustamante, 2019). Additionally, the 2017 American Community Survey indicated that 40.2 million Latinas/os are aged 18 and over, with 49.8% of those being Latinas (U.S. Census Bureau, 2018). Taking a closer look at mental health, it is important to note that Latinas are more likely to report serious psychological distress than non-Hispanic Whites, and the percentage increases for those who live in poverty (Centers for Disease Control and Prevention [CDC], 2019b).

© pixelheadphoto digitalskillet/Shutterstock.com

Challenges Faced in Counseling

Latinas encounter many challenges when accessing mental health services. The National Alliance on Mental Illness ([NAMI] 2019) identified two major disparities that Latinas/os face, including access to treatment and the quality of treatment. Because of these disparities, Latinas/os are at a greater risk for increased severity of mental health symptomatology. Moreover, Latinas/os are often misdiagnosed when a clinician performs an evaluation in the client's non-dominant language, and the continued insufficient number of bilingual professionals further complicates this issue (Arredondo et al., 2014). For example, one study revealed that the counselor's proficiency in Spanish was significantly related to caretaking outcomes (Guerrero et al., 2013). Other barriers in accessing mental health care include: (1) a lack of health insurance or insufficient insurance; (2) a lack of understanding about mental health concerns and treatment availability; (3) cultural shame connected to mental health problems; (4) privacy concerns (Latinas/os talk to family members, not outsiders); (5) the legal status of immigrants; (6) a tendency toward traditional healers and home remedies; (7) a lack of **culturally responsive services** (culturally responsive services refers to the counselor's knowledge of their client's cultural background, beliefs, values, and traditions. It involves making cultural adaptations in their theoretical and therapeutic approaches) and providers; (8) the struggle to recognize the initial signs of mental health concerns; and (9) an inability to connect the chief somatic complaint to a mental health concern (APA, 2017; NAMI, 2019).

Additionally, a growing body of research suggests that counselors need to study the unique cultural variables to provide effective counseling to Latinas (Serrata et al., 2019). In other words, do counselors really understand the unique cultural aspects of Latina such as immigration status, aspects of cultural identity, aspects of religious beliefs, country of origin, social class, family, and social support? Numerous researchers and experts in the field have also noted the lack of culturally responsive counseling practices, including "culturally-specific practices" (Serrata et al., 2019, p. 3), "culturally responsive care" (Guerrero et al., 2013, p. 2896), and "Latino-centered counseling" (Arredondo et al., 2014, p. 173), all of which are unique to the Latin culture.

Counseling Considerations

Having a better understanding of Latinas/os worldviews and cultural values will lay the foundation for best practices and considerations when counseling Latinas/os individuals and families. Did you know that strong family-centered values continue with third- and fourth-generation Latino families, who would rather provide care for aging parents than put them in a nursing care facility (Arrendondo et al., 2014)? This relates to the primary cultural worldview shared by many Latinos from differing geographical origins, *familismo* (a central relational value that represents the importance of familial relationships [including extended family members] and is family-centered, interdependent, and shows concern for others' health and happiness [Arrendondo et al., 2014]) (Ceballos & Bratton, 2010). This worldview has been shaped and influenced by *dichos* (proverbs

© Monkey Business Images/Shutterstock.com

or sayings) that reveal the beliefs, traditions, and attitudes of the Latina/o culture (Arrendondo et al., 2014).

Another paramount and influential value is *la familia*, which sheds light on family beliefs and expectations of family members. For example, Latina mothers are highly regarded for their dedication to their family and putting their children first. Latina mothers also display significant devotion to the oldest child and an only or favorite son (Falicov, 1998). Other cultural values include *respecto* (respect) in Latina/o relationships, well-mannered and respectful children, *marianismo* (sex role behaviors), religion (predominately Catholic), and *curanderos*, or folk healers (Arrendondo et al., 2014).

> **Curanderismo** integrates present and deceased significant loved ones (i.e., it is a systemic intervention that includes grief processes and family supportive involvement), uses symbols for intuitive connections, and provides experiences of change through the manipulation of symbols (i.e., multisensorial and cognitive-symbolic interpretations that lead to the release of personal pain to an object) (Arredondo et al., 2014, p. 189).

The Young Latina - Motherhood or Cultural Trailblazer?

High esteem and respect for Latina mothers and motherhood continues to be a cornerstone of the Latino culture. It is not uncommon for mothers to work outside the home to provide additional household income; however, *la familia* perpetuates their values and the family always comes first. For example, many Latina mothers hold true to the cultural value of *marianismo* and sacrifice their own needs (in the same manner as the

Virgin Mary) to put the needs of their *hijos* (sons) and *hijas* (daughters) first (Arrendondo et al., 2014). Even career-oriented Latinas are prompted by their parents about the significance of motherhood, which can create a quandary for women who prefer not to have children or prefer waiting longer such as after college to have children (Arrendondo et al., 2014).

So, what occurs when a Latina decides she would rather attend college than start a family? In their study of first-generation Latina college students, Storlie et al. (2016) found that Latina women felt alone and isolated in their family, social, and academic settings. Moreover, these women were in an uncharted territory in the academia world and unsure how to navigate these waters. Despite their fears, these first-generation Latinas broke the traditional family and cultural expectations by attending college to gain an education toward their chosen career. The Latinas in this study identified themselves as "cultural trailblazers" (Storlie et al., 2016, p. 313) and had a sense of pride in defining other non-stereotypical roles of Latina women. Furthermore, the career paths chosen by these Latina women involved giving back to their family and community, which is truly reflective of the Latina/o cultural value of *familisimo* (family values).

Counseling Recommendations

During your first meeting with a Latina, cultural responsiveness starts with a culture-centered assessment and evaluation. It is important to con-

© antoniodiaz/Shutterstock.com

vey the strong Latina/o values of *Personalismo* (the importance of personal relationships) and *respecto* (respect) during the initial assessment. The skilled counselor also utilizes their fine-tuned relational building micro-skills to provide an atmosphere of safety and cultural affirmation so that Latinas feel safe to disclose their concerns (Arrendondo et al., 2014). Considerations must be given to the Latina's acculturation level and preferred language for therapy (Arrendondo et al., 2014).

> "Relationship building is essential to culturally effective counseling with Latinos." (Arrendondo et al., 2014, p. 145).

Cultural adaptations and a multidimensional perspective must also be considered when working with Latinas. The Latina-sensitive counselor would need to make adaptations on two levels: the surface level (the interventions/materials provided that target Latinas, such as language and ethnic metaphors) and the deeper level (contextual factors, such as Latina/o family values and experiences, socioeconomic status, and political influences that manifest in behaviors; Resnicow et al., 1999). For example, a study on Latina survivors of intimate partner violence and sexual assault found that "cultural-specific practice contributes uniquely to the well-being of Latinas beyond that of trauma-informed practice..." (Serrata et al., 2019, p. 10).

With a push towards evidence-based practices, it is important to highlight other studies on cultural adaptations with Latinas. Various parenting programs (Ceballos & Bratton, 2010; D'Angelo et al., 2009; Garza et al., 2009; Matos et al., 2006; Parra Cardona et al., 2009, 2012; Villarreal, 2008), cognitive behavioral therapy (Piedra & Byoun, 2012; Shae et al., 2012), behavior therapy (Santiago-Rivera et al., 2008), guided imagery (La Roche et al., 2006), and strategic family therapy (Muir et al., 2004) have revealed empirical support. Other recommendations include applying strength-based models ("Strength-based therapy [SBT] is a client-directed approach that invites people to participate in every aspect of care and to apply their *indigenous* [emphasis added] strengths and resources toward personally meaningful goals...SBT draws from a variety of sources, ideas, and methods" [Murphy & Sparks, 2018, p. 3]), supporting spirituality and healing practices (*curanderismo*), working from a social justice therapeutic orientation, and engaging in advocacy to support any painful experiences of discrimination and marginalization (Arrendondo et al., 2014).

> "Sabías que/ Did you know that engagement in spiritual healing activities can lead to positive physical and mental health outcomes?" (Arredondo et al., 2014, p. 173)

LOOKING THROUGH THE LENS OF CHRISTIANITY: BIBLICAL INTEGRATION WITH LATINAS

With the majority of the current Latino population in the U.S. identifying with some form of faith, it is imperative to understand the importance of integrating religious and spiritual beliefs. According to the Pew Research Center (2019), 47% of Hispanics describe themselves as Catholic, 24% as Protestant, and 23% as religiously unaffiliated. Only 3% describe themselves as having a non-Christian faith.

© Stephen Coburn/Shutterstock.com

Many Christian beliefs and values are present in the everyday lives of Latinas. This is seen in the cultural value of *espiritualidad* (spirituality) and embedded in the cultural language and *dichos*, or sayings (see a list of "Spiritual Dichos" below). For example, one study found that Latinas/os declared God as an active force in their lives, practicing faith through daily prayers, monthly church attendance, and decorating their homes with religious symbols (Pew Hispanic Center, 2007). Christians and Latinas also share their journey of hope (*esperanza*) and inner strength (*fortaleza interna*) through personal testimonies (*testimonios*) of God's healing in their lives. For Latinas, *testimonios* (giving witness) has been used to help empower self-disclosure and overcome adversity through the message of faith and victory (Arrendondo et al., 2014).

> Catholics are no longer the majority among U.S. Hispanics. According to the Pew Research Center (2019), surveys conducted in 2018 and 2019 reveal a 10% decline, from 57% to 47% of Hispanics describing themselves as Catholic, and an 8% incline, from 15% to 23% of Hispanics describing themselves as religiously unaffiliated.

Lastly, the integration of Christianity and spirituality with Latinas/os have been encouraged through religious-based counseling practices (Moreno & Cardemil, 2013). This integration makes perfect sense knowing that Latinas/os use spirituality as a common source of cultural resilience. In one study, researchers found that higher religious affiliations in Mexican Americans were correlated with a lower risk of depression (Cokley et al., 2012).

Spiritual Dichos (Sayings)
- *Qué Dios te bendiga* - May God bless you
- *Qué Dios te ampare* - May God protect you
- *Estoy bien, gracias a Dios* - I'm fine, thanks be to God
- *Vaya con Dios* - Go with God
- *Qué sea lo que Dios quiera* - Let it be God's will
- *Dios dice ayudaté, que yo te ayudaré* - God says help yourself and I will help you
- *Tengo que poner de mi parte* - I have to cooperate or I have to help myself
- *Tienes que poner de tu parte* - You have to do your part to start helping yourself

(Arrendondo et al., 2014, p. 190-191).

CASE STUDY

© Dubowa/Shutterstock.com

Consuela (Connie; pseudonym) is a 67-year-old Latina who identifies herself as a Mexican American woman. She recalls her early childhood living in Mexico and migrating to the United States around the age of five. Although Spanish was her first language, she attributes her English proficiency to beginning public school education at the age of 6. She reports that she dropped out of high school at 15-years-old to help financially support the family. She obtained her first job at a local fast-food restaurant. When she was twenty, Connie met her first "real" boyfriend and married him a year later. They had two children together, but after twenty-one years of marriage, they divorced because he was "unfaithful" over the years and physically abusive. Two years later, Connie married again, but this only lasted three years, as he was also physically abusive. Since then, Connie has never remarried and has not been interested in an intimate relationship. However, the effects of the abuse and a strained relationship with her daughter have brought her into counseling. She reports feelings of sadness, uncontrollable crying spells, and loneliness related to the broken relationship with her daughter who stopped talking to her five years ago because of the domestic violence she was subjected to as a child. She also reports anxiety, panic attacks, excessive worries, sleep disturbance, and somatic symptoms related to past traumas. She stated that her relationship with her sister and her Christian faith have been the only things that help get her through each day.

Multicultural Considerations for Connie

First, Connie needs to feel understood and heard to feel safe opening up about the concerns that brought her into counseling. Therefore, during the intake, the counselor should determine her preferred language and if it is Spanish, the counselor should provide an appropriate referral if he/she is not bilingual. Next, the counselor should acknowledge her bravery in seeking help (this is very difficult, as going outside the family for help is not encouraged traditionally) and thank her for choosing the counselor to start her journey. The counselor should also take on a person-centered approach where the therapeutic conditions (congruent/genuineness, perceived acceptance and unconditional positive regard, and empathy) for growth are present. For example, as Connie starts to open up and share about her traumatic experiences, acknowledge her feelings by saying (with a deep empathy in her tone of voice), "Wow! That must have been extremely scary and hard for you. You must have been so frightened." It is also very critical that the counselor assess all family relationships and see how they can be included in the therapeutic process. For example, the therapist can invite her sister to join her for sessions, which can also highlight her social support systems and familial strengths (i.e., strengths-based approach). In addition, when Connie is ready, the counselor can suggest family sessions with Connie and her daughter. Lastly, the counselor should discuss the importance of Connie's faith and find spiritual strengths to overcome adversity. For example, the counselor might ask, "Tell me more about your Christian faith?", "How important is it to you?", and "How does faith help you now or how has it helped you in the past to overcome difficult times?" Overall, providing the therapeutic conditions for change and incorporating approaches (strengths-based, family-based, and spiritually based) that align with her culture and beliefs will help her reach her goals in counseling and experience optimal well-being. Also, accept small gifts and gestures that convey the building of a therapeutic relationship, such as an authentic homemade dish or dessert.

A Native American Woman
Frances Callow

© Frances Callow

Frances Callow is a member of the White Mountain Apache Tribe on the **Ft. Apache Indian Reservation in Whiteriver, AZ** and a graduate student studying Clinical Mental Health Counseling. Here's the greeting you'll receive when you visit the White Mountain Apache website: " *'Dagot' ee'*- Hello and welcome to the website of the White Mountain Apache Tribe...We believe that we come from the Earth, and that we belong to the Earth. Our beautiful home was given to us by our Creator and is rich in tradition, resources, wildlife, and outdoor recreation" (White Mountain Apache Tribe, n.d., para. 1). She vividly recalls many rich Native American traditions growing up on the reservation. One cultural norm relates to the famous phrase, "It takes a village to raise a child," which accurately describes the Apache family lifestyle. Additionally, breastfeeding is strongly encouraged, and the women support and help each other when a mother cannot breastfeed. In fact, Frances' sister helped breastfeed her children on occasions when she was not able to breastfeed herself. Women are also expected to stay home with their children for the first 3-5 years. She commented, "You're a mother before anything else" (F. Callow, personal communication, November 22, 2019).

Another cultural Apache tradition is the **Sunrise Dance** (this is a 4-day ceremony that starts with a blessing from the girl's father followed by traditional Apache songs and dances; setting up wikiups (traditional home); receiving instructions from the Godmother on how to grow spiritually, mentally, and physically; and learning homemaking skills). Recordings of Sunrise Dance ceremonies are now viewable on YouTube, which was historically not allowed until recent years (F. Callow, personal communication, November 22, 2019), a celebration for girls transitioning to womanhood on their 15th birthday. Unfortunately, Frances did not have a Sunrise Dance because her grandfather had recently passed away. In her culture, the ceremony cannot be performed if the girl has a family member that has passed away within the last year. Although Frances understood, she feels she missed learning more about her culture and traditions. The running joke of the family is that Frances does not know how to make bread like her older sister.

An interesting fact about the Apache tribe is that they are known for being the most ruthless tribe and stealing from other tribes. Historically, hatred exists between Apache and Navajo Indians. Frances recalls her own experiences of micro-aggression, such as being jokingly told, "I better check her at the door for any knives because she is Apache," and a Navajo Indian asking, "Can we have our horses and cattle back?" However, today they are highly respected and honored for their strong firefighting skills and often called upon to fight fires in Texas and California. They also had the first female firefighting crew called the "hot shot female crew" (F. Callow, personal communication, November 22, 2019).

Additionally, Frances comes from the Susan family who are well-known cattle ranchers within their tribe. An interesting fact about cattle ranching is that veterinarians are not allowed. If a cow or horse becomes ill, they attend to the animal's needs and let nature take its course, believing that whatever happens is God's will. Related to cattle ranching, the rodeo is a popular cultural tradition that serves as entertainment. In fact, Frances' uncle, Daniel Susan, is a championship bull rider inducted into the INFR Hall of Fame in 2019.

However, Frances' life on the reservation was not always filled with tribal dances and rodeos. She discussed her own experiences of not fitting in with her own tribal family, such as not looking Apache because of her lighter skin tone. She resembles her father who was half Navajo Indian and half Hispanic. She still remembers some of the words said to her such as, "You were the milk man's baby," and being called "apple" because she was red on the outside but white on the inside. Even her Apache name Dizahan ("little White girl") reflects this belief (F. Callow, personal communication, November 22, 2019). When Frances was 15 years old, she made a risky but brave decision to leave the reservation that did not fully accept her and escape her mother and stepfather's alcoholism and domestic violence. With two hundred and fifty dollars in her pocket, she found her way to her father's family in California, whom she felt accepted her. After high school graduation, she pursued her education at the University of Arizona, which is very rare in her culture. Moreover, after college graduation, she continued to experience micro-aggressions within her culture because of her degree, such as being told, "You're too good for us now. You speak better English than us."

Due to her multiple traumas, Frances has sought counseling three different times but has never really felt that these counselors understood her or her cultural values. As such, Frances makes the following recommendations for counselors: 1) realize that not all Native Americans are drunk savages who live in the casinos, and recognize they are moving forward economically, 2) Native Americans like to give homemade gifts to show appreciation, and not accepting it is a sign of disrespect, 3) use a person-centered approach to build the relationship and Gestalt methods as they align with Native American healing and embodied approaches, 4) understand the culture's spiritual beliefs, which also integrates Catholicism and Christianity, 5) consult with one of the elders of the tribe to learn more, and 6) understand and grasp the effects of the generational trauma that lives in all Native Americans today. Concerning the last recommendation, Frances commented,

"Our generation is still going through a huge loss of culture and tradition because of the boarding school era" (F. Callow, personal communication, November 22, 2019). During the **boarding school era** (the most traumatic era for Native Americans as many children never saw their families again, and a lot of them died from the diseases they caught due to the lack of medical treatment), children were removed from their homes and assimilated with European children in boarding schools. Frances' great-grandmother was one of those children; she was lured by a lollipop into a black vehicle and taken away from her family, never seeing them again.

Today Frances is married, has four children, and lives in Texas. She continues to practice her cultural traditions, but struggles living in a city without the support of her siblings and her mother, who has been sober now for ten years. She also struggles with maintaining her cultural values and instilling them in her children. However, she often listens to traditional Apache songs and dances to calm herself. She remarked, "It's the beating of the drums that calms me and my kids down; it helps us regulate and helps me cope better with my anxieties" (F. Callow, personal communication, November 22, 2019).

© Lamar Molina

COUNSELING BLACK WOMEN

What Counselors Need to Know

In this section, we will explore the multicultural perspective of Black women. However, consider this question first: Did you know that in 2018, among persons 18 years of age and older, the percentages of Non-Hispanic Black women who reported sadness, hopelessness, and worthlessness were sig-

© Monkey Business Images/Shutterstock.com

nificantly greater than those reported by Non-Hispanic White women (CDC, 2019a)? This is an astounding fact! Furthermore, it is important to note that some women who identify as Black come from a variety of races and cultures. In America, it is often the case that Black women are lumped together into one group and labeled African Americans. When using the terminology *Black*, some counselors overlook the importance of identifying their Black female clients by their individual ethnic or cultural background. In a study on racial labels, Hall et al. (2015) researched stereotypes and identified the consequences of identifying racial group members using African American versus Black. Additionally, Clark et al. (1999) and Meyer (1995) explored the fact that because the dominant culture sustains norms and marginalizes individuals in minority cultures, the oppression experienced by these individuals is a very taxing stressor termed as *minority stress* (a significant amount of stress faced by individuals of a disparaging minority groups). For some Black women, minority stress is a reality on a daily basis. Dealing with these stressors in society and facing these realities in the counseling setting can significantly affect the therapeutic process.

© And-One/Shutterstock.com

> **Gendered racism** has been defined as the simultaneous experience of both racism and sexism (Essed, 1991), and Black women everywhere in America experience this reality in their everyday lives.

Being culturally aware and exhibiting **cultural humility** ("Cultural humility incorporates a lifelong commitment to self-evaluation and self-critique, to redressing the power imbalances in the patient-physician dynamic, and to develop mutually beneficial and non-paternalistic clinical and advocacy partnership with communities on behalf of individuals and defined populations" [Tervalon & Murray-Garcia, 1998, p. 117]). will be beneficial to the counseling relationship.

Meyer (2007) suggested in the minority stress model that, in addition to general stressors experienced by all people, stigmatized minority groups experience additional stressors due to their group membership. For example, simply being Black and female are stressors. These identity-based stressors include rejection, prejudice, and discrimination. They may also cause additional distress because they challenge an individual's sense of self, requiring that they make decisions regarding the concealment or expression of their identities (Meyer, 2007).

Furthermore, being Black and female are often overlooked; however, the mere titles carry with them what many would entitle a "double-negative," an intersection of racism and sexism. For example, Black women experience racism because of the color of their skin and sexism because of their gender. As such, the **intersectionality** ("an analysis claiming that systems of race, economic class, gender, sexuality, ethnicity, nationality, and age form mutually constructing features of social organization" [Collins, 1998, p. 278]) of being Black and a woman results in unique experiences due to both social identities (Davis, 2015; Davis et al., 2018; Ghavami & Peplau, 2012; Hall, 2018; Shavers & Moore, 2014; Warner et al., 2018).

Challenges Faced in Counseling

There are a number of challenges to be mindful of when counseling Black women. As a result of intersectional oppression (being Black and female), many "Black women have mastered the art of portraying strength while concealing trauma—a balancing act often held in high esteem among Black women" (Abrams et al., 2019, p. 517). Although this facade has become

© Hogan Imaging/Shutterstock.com

a norm for Black women, it is a serious threat to the mental health and well-being of all Black females, to the point where they enter the counseling relationship with various masks that may take time for them and you as a counselor to decipher and unravel.

Another often overlooked challenge that Black women experience is the very subtle reality of **micro-aggressions** (indirect, subtle, or unintentional discrimination). Although a number of studies have explored racial micro-aggressions experienced by persons of color, including Black women, Lewis et al. (2016) extended Sue's (2010) theory and research on micro-aggressions to include an intersectionality framework that simultaneously explored the experience of racial and gender micro-aggressions. This body of research explored the struggles that Black women face on an ongoing basis. Some of these include a decrease in help-seeking behaviors, a higher rate of many diseases including depressive episodes, and a constant feeling of being overwhelmed and overworked (Longmire-Avital & Robinson, 2017; Shillingford et al., 2013; Versey & Curin, 2016).

Counseling Considerations

Heightened Awareness of the Challenges Black Women Face

Having this knowledge about the plight of Black women, counselors may enter the therapeutic relationship with a Black female having an awareness that, outside of the counseling room, the woman across from them faces a myriad of oppressive experiences and needs a safe place to share. This space must take into consideration the multiple hats that Black women wear outside of the session. Therefore, it is vital to counsel the Black woman with sensitivity to the challenges she faces, roles she plays, and masks she needs to wear, in conjunction with the presenting need(s) she brings to the counseling relationship.

Asking for Help Is Often Difficult and Sometimes Foreign

It is also important to note that "although U.S. Black women have historically and relentlessly felt pressure to be strong for their families and communities, many struggle with depending on others for support. Despite the experience of psychological distress, many Black women find it foreign and difficult to emote openly" (Abrams et al., 2019, p. 524). In other words, asking for help is often difficult and sometimes foreign for Black women. Since they have had to navigate the many areas of their lives on their own while shouldering the burdens of others (often being the primary or only support - financially, emotionally, or socially - for their immediate and extended family systems), Black women generally give the appearance that they can be independent and do it all. Furthermore, for a woman who focuses on family and community as a priority, it is easy for her to neglect herself and her needs. As a result, her counselor will do well to emphasize the strength the Black woman possesses while giving her permission to become unguarded and serve herself while in the counseling session.

Counseling Recommendations

Coker (2004) purported that Black women often view the use of formal counseling as a sign of deficiency, opting instead to gain support from family, friends, and religious/spiritual mentors. "African American women counsel each other in church communities; beauty shops; laundromats; and sitting side-by-side in cars, buses, or trains en route to work. Wherever African American women gather, there is an exchange of emotions, experiences, and coping strategies" (p. 133).

When counseling Black women, the counselor may consider beginning the therapeutic relationship by asking the client about the roles she plays in her life (see call out box below). Provide active listening and reflection

© Krakenimages.com/Shutterstock.com

continuously throughout the session. Black women need to feel heard, especially since for a large portion of their existence, they have been dismissed. A person-centered counseling approach, which includes congruence, empathy, unconditional positive regard, and perceived acceptance, may effectively provide a space where these women experience a sense of safety and support.

Three questions that may help facilitate rapport with Black women:
- Would you prefer that I address your race/culture as Black or African American or something else?
- Please help me understand all of your roles and responsibilities outside of this office by walking me through the things and people you support.
- During our time together, you are the priority, so how may I best support you in my role as your counselor? (Coker, 2002, 2003)

With these things in mind, there is much room in the counseling field to make theoretical approaches and techniques more relevant to Black Women. When offering support, consider their long cultural legacy of juggling multiple responsibilities, wearing a number of hats, and navigating multiple life stressors. Living life as a superwoman trying to accomplish many tasks without adequate physical or mental relief can have harmful effects on one's life. One way to support these women is to integrate cultural issues into the counseling session or link it to the presenting problem and treatment goals.

LOOKING THROUGH THE LENS OF CHRISTIANITY: BIBLICAL INTEGRATION WITH BLACK WOMEN

This section discusses considerations for counseling Black women from a spiritual and multicultural perspective. You have learned that the Black woman juggles varied responsibilities as she balances the intersectionality of her "double negative," being Black and a woman. Proverbs 31 introduces another woman who also juggles many areas of her life and wears a variety of hats. The chapter affectionately calls the Proverbs 31 woman, *a virtuous woman*. It posits virtues of a woman to include faith, marriage,

© Shift Drive/Shutterstock.com

mothering, health, service, stewardship, homemaking, time, and beauty. As the counselor of a Black woman it would be wonderful to support her during the therapeutic relationship, highlighting the varied roles she plays despite her many hats of virtue and the problem(s) she presents in session. Research supports that Black women (Black people in general) utilize religion and the church as a source of support when experiencing difficulties (Avent & Cashwell, 2015; Woodward, 2011). Instead of seeking help from a professional counselor, you may often find that Black women will seek religious or spiritual guidance by choosing a pastor or spiritual leader to support their mental health needs. A level of trust is usually primarily established here. With this knowledge, to become an effective counselor for a Black woman, it is important to enhance your awareness of her religious/spiritual lenses and incorporate her religious or spiritual background into the counseling experience (Cashwell & Young, 2011).

CASE STUDY

© PT Images/Shutterstock.com

Tara was in her mid-fifties, had obtained two graduate degrees, was in a managerial position at her place of employment, drove a high-end vehicle, lived in her own home in an upper-middle-class neighborhood, made a six-figure income, had a solid relationship with her family, and a consistent church-life where she held a number of leadership positions. The one area of Tara's life where she felt unfulfilled was in her intimate relationship. She had a number of past relationships with potential partners; however, each relationship ended in disappointment. When Tara came to you to begin counseling, she shared her longing to be in a loving relationship and her anxiety that it would never happen. She shared the number of times she was a bridesmaid in her friends' weddings and while she celebrated their joy, she often went home at the end of

COUNSELING WOMEN

the ceremony and cried herself to sleep. She also shared about her concern for her aging parents and the reverse role she finds herself in, as she had become their primary emotional and logistical (taking them to doctor's appointments, driving them around, etc.) support. At the end of your initial session, Tara shared, "I wonder if I will ever meet the right man. Is it me?"

Multicultural Considerations for Tara

As her counselor, where do you begin with Tara? What do you address first? How do you best support and provide a safe environment for her to share? After gathering this information about Tara, as stated in the "Call Out Box" above, you may ask in progressive counseling sessions: 1) Would you prefer that I address your race/culture as Black or African American or something else? 2) Please help me understand all of your roles and responsibilities outside of this office by walking me through all the things and people you support. 3) During our time together, you are the priority, so how may I best support you in my role as your counselor? Ask Tara where she wants to begin, and then listen attentively as she chronicles these details to you. Prize her as she talks about the challenges she experiences, the pressure she feels, and the internal challenges she has. Support her with verbal and nonverbal encouragers. You may encourage Tara to utilize her support (including the church) and find someone with whom she may choose to risk becoming vulnerable. Say, "We can use the counseling session as an opportunity to 'practice/rehearse' what you can do outside of session to change your circumstances." As she becomes more comfortable, have Tara tell you about her past intimate relationships and emphatically help her see the recurring themes that may present themselves.

Black Women and the Superwoman Persona
My Experience as a Strong Black Woman (SBW)
Dr. Raquel Guidry

© Raquel Guidry

I am strong. I am Black. I am a woman. However, those characteristics alone do not make me a Strong Black Woman. My identification as a Strong Black Woman is based upon lived experiences, encompassing societally, culturally, and self-imposed standards and demands that are not attributed to Caucasian women. I have been labeled superwoman, demanding, over-achieving, resilient, fierce, lioness, super independent, abrasive, withdrawn, distant, and guarded with a tough shell to crack, to name a few. While some of those attributes have a negative connotation, they are typically uttered with respect and admiration. I am known for stating, "Me and Jesus, we got this!" While other Black women applaud and say "Get it, sis!! I'm proud of you!! I wish I had your strength." and "Wow, when I grow up…" Black males and Caucasian friends (male and female) have responded with "Chill out, take a breather, why are you so driven? Does it really take all that? Don't you want some help? Everything doesn't have to be perfect, it's okay to fail sometimes…" Ultimately, they do not comprehend the internal driving force.

On the contrary, I don't recall ever being labeled as needy, sensitive, inadequate, gentle, vulnerable, or weak, and I would likely take offense to these characterizations. However, the truth is that I am actually all of these things at times, including the latter, but the SBW in me would never allow others to see those characteristics. In retrospect, it has been this way since I was probably five years old. I was taught very early on that I had to be strong, self-reliant, respectable, and an overachiever in a White male-dominated society. Less than was never an option and I seldom recall crying, other than tears of joy. This sense of responsibility and fortitude to my family, my culture, and myself was communicated directly as my parents shared their expectations. I internalized them and this narrative became my personal reality.

All of this has resulted in a feeling of always having to be "on" (i.e., at my best, ready for anything at all times, up to any challenge and able to overcome any obstacle, while simultaneously meeting the needs of my spouse, children, family, work, church, etc.). It has required exceptional navigation skills, vigilance, shifting, constant strength, and no time for weakness or vulnerability. It felt like I was walking a tightrope.

While the SBW persona is operationalized in differing degrees and ways for Black women, the key characteristics of strength and total independence are consistent. Further, it has been my experience that my Caucasian friends and colleagues are somewhat baffled at the discussion of my SBW experience, and initially would like to say their experiences and responsibilities are similar. The difference is the *compounding* factors of sexism, racism, micro-aggressions, and cultural norms. This is where the disconnect and inability to understand occurs. As a trained and licensed mental health clinician, educator, self-identified SBW, and often labeled Superwoman, I am fortunate to have keen insight into both the benefits and risks of endorsing the SBW/Superwoman persona. Whereas some women, especially those 35 years of age and younger, appear to find living up to the persona burdensome. For me, it comes quite easily, and I take great pride in the multiple roles that are required of me daily. Even with a doctorate, healthy and successful children, and professional acumen, I actually still feel that I have not and am not accomplishing enough. I have a responsibility to do more!

Although I personally have been able to overcome relationship difficulties often attributed to SBW characteristics, attain professional and personal balance while establishing my career, and learn to express emotion appropriately, it has not been easy. I attribute this primarily to educational insight and years of self-reflection during clinical training, which most strong Black women are simply not privy to. I understand my experience both literally and figuratively. As a result, I clearly see the emotional, psychological, societal, and even cultural struggle of Black women all around me. I see the need to be and appear strong at all times, as well as its impact upon one's mental, physical, and relational health. This is certainly a topic that falls into multicultural sensitivity and should be addressed when counseling women of color.

COUNSELING ASIAN AMERICAN WOMEN

© szefei/Shutterstock.com

What Counselors Need to Know

As attention shifts to Asian Americans, it is noteworthy to highlight that this cultural group is the fastest going racial minority population in the U.S. According to the Pew Research Center, between 2000 and 2015, the Asian American population grew 72% and increased from 11.9 million to 20.4 million (Lopez et al., 2017). The diversity of the U.S. Asian population is also significant to note. "A record 20 million Asian Americans trace their roots to more than 20 countries in East and Southeast Asia and the Indian subcontinent, each with unique histories, cultures, languages and other characteristics" (Lopez et al., 2017, para. 1). As of 2015, 24% of Asian Americans (4.9 million) were of Chinese origin, making them the single largest origin group, followed by those of Indian and Filipino origin (Lopez et al., 2017).

While the Asian American population continues to increase, numerous studies have found that they are the least likely out of all racial minority groups to seek help for mental health issues, due to the stigma surrounding mental illness in their community (Alegria et al., 2005; Augsberger et al., 2015; Keum et al., 2018; Le Meyer et al., 2009; Reyes et al., 2018). Exposing that someone is suffering from a mental illness in the Asian American community has been associated with not living up the model minority myth (the model minority myth assumes that Asian Americans are the "superior minority" in the United States and their educational and financial success is attributed to this exemplary status) and is seen as a sign of weakness, shame, and dishonor (Augsberger et al., 2015; Lin, 2016; Sanchez & Gaw, 2007; Zane et al., 2004; Zane & Yeh, 2002). This myth oversimplifies the Asian American experience, contributing to the false narrative that they do not experience racism and other forms of discrimination (Chou & Feagin, 2015; Kim & Lee, 2014). This proves to be harmful

© Monkey Business Images/Shutterstock.com

COUNSELING WOMEN

when Asian Americans internalize the model minority myth, playing into the role that they "have it all together," which is detrimental to mental health and limits help-seeking behaviors (Chou & Feagin, 2015; Kim & Lee, 2014). These barriers make it hard to treat and diagnose those Asian Americans suffering from mental illnesses (Augsberger et al., 2015; Lin, 2016; Reyes et al., 2018).

Challenges Faced in Counseling

Asian American women (AAW) face a myriad of challenges in their everyday lives. Historically, AAW have been stereotyped as submissive, passive, exotic, apolitical, and are fetishized, which makes them more vulnerable to both racism and sexism (Hahm et al., 2017; Keum et al., 2017). Numerous studies have found that AAW who experience racism and sexism were more susceptible to developing anxiety, depression, and abuse substances (Essed, 1991; Huynh, 2012; Keum et al., 2017; Nadal et al., 2014; Ong et al., 2013; Yoo et al., 2010).

© Maridav/Shutterstock.com

However, studies on AAW experiences as gendered racial minorities have been limited, overlooked, or couched in the experiences of Asian American men or White women (Essed, 1991; Keum et al., 2017; Mukkamla & Suyemoto, 2018).

Furthermore, studies have found that AAW between the ages of 15-24 and over 65 had the second-highest suicide rates and death by suicide across all racial groups (CDC, 2015; Hahm et al., 2017; Ting & Hwang, 2009). AAW experience pressure from their family to be financially independent while upholding traditional family values, which can lead to **fractured identities** (Hahm et al., 2014). *Fractured Identity Model* developed by Hahm et al. (2014) describes what happens to Asian American women caught in a double bind of wanting to please their parents with being the perfect Asian daughter while playing the role of the model minority in a Western society. This conflict coupled with being raised by parents who demonstrate disempowering parenting styles, leads to Asian American women developing low self-worth and believing that they are never "good enough", adopting harmful coping behaviors which include non-suicidal

cutting, drug abuse, suicidal ideation, and suicide attempts. Additionally, AAW who internalize the model minority myth, which values emotional self-control, often do not seek counseling for fear of appearing weak (Kim & Lee, 2014; Lin, 2016). Instead of seeking professional help for mental health issues, AAW may seek out other means to cope, which include abusing substances and isolating themselves from their family (Hahm et al., 2013; Ho et al., 2017; Lin, 2016).

Counseling Considerations

As previously mentioned, the Asian American community's negative perception of mental illnesses and seeking help creates barriers in accessing mental health services (Alegria et al., 2005; Keum et al., 2018; Le Meyer et al., 2009; Reyes et al., 2018). However, studies have begun to explore ways to make mental health services more cultural inclusive and effective with AAW. A 2018 pilot study created a mental health intervention titled *Asian Women's Action for Resilience and Empowerment Intervention* (AWARE) that developed a culturally informed therapeutic group for AAW with a history of interpersonal violence and diagnosed with posttraumatic stress disorder (Hahm et al., 2019). The counseling interventions include gender-specific treatment that neutralizes the gender power dynamic that may exist in therapy, the mind and body connection valued in Asian cultures, and the *Model of Healing*, which helps to empower AAW while healing fractured identities. Participants of the AWARE study expressed feeling empowered, appreciating the culturally informed modalities, learning the connection between their stressors and parental pressures, and having the opportunity to discuss sexual health, which Asian families rarely discuss (Hahm et al., 2019).

Additionally, a 2014 study explored the importance of ethnic and gender matches between Asian American clients (56% of their participants were AAW) and their counselors. Findings suggested that gender matching helped to increase self-disclosure among Asian American clients, specifically regarding their sex-life, but face concern ("Face concern refers to a person's set of socially sanctioned claims concerning one's social character and social

© NATNN/Shutterstock.com

integrity in which this set of claims or this 'line' is largely defined by certain prescribed roles that one carries out as a member or representative of a certain social or reference group" [Zane & Ku, 2014, p. 67]) mitigated self-disclosure (Zane & Ku, 2014). Lastly, remember that not all AAW are the same as they are from different origins, have different levels of acculturation, and have different levels of proficiency in the English language.

Counseling Recommendations

According to Sue et al. (2019), it is important to consider Asian Americans' collectivistic orientation. For example, you may have an AAW who expresses that her parents want her to become a medical doctor, but she aspires to be a dancer. In America's western society, where we value independence and a self-directed life, you may recommend that she choose her own destiny. However, this may lead to increased emotional distress while not resolving the conflict between her parents and her desires to be a dancer.

Sue et al. (2019) recommended that counselors consider how the decisions of an Asian American client will affect their family, their community, and themselves. Recommended questions for the previous scenario

include "How important is becoming a medical doctor to your family and to you?" and "Have you discussed your desire to go to school to be a dancer with your parents and family members?"

Furthermore, Sue et al. (2019) highlighted recommendations that center on cultural norms. First, due to the patriarchal view in Asian Americans, counselors will often be viewed as an authority figure in the counseling relationship, leading them to please the counselor and not express their true feelings. Second, since emotional control is strongly valued in Asian Americans, displays of emotion may produce feelings of shame or discomfort. Counselors should indirectly address emotions, normalizing that disclosure of personal information is part of the counseling process. Lastly, since Asian Americans view the mind and body as a whole not as parts, counselors should take reports of psychosomatic symptoms seriously.

LOOKING THROUGH THE LENS OF CHRISTIANITY: BIBLICAL INTEGRATION WITH ASIAN AMERICAN WOMEN

Religions like Confucianism, Taoism, and Buddhism have played a vital role in Asian cultures for centuries and are deeply embedded in their beliefs and practices (Edara, 2016; Pan et al., 2014; Tan & Dong, 2014). However, many Asian immigrants who come to the United States have converted to Christianity, and 75% of Asian Americans identify as Christian (Tan & Dong, 2014). During the early migration of the Chinese to the United States, Christian churches played a vital role in assisting them in fighting against discriminatory immigration laws (Tseng, 1996 as cited in Tan & Dong, 2014). Missionaries from the Protestant church supported and helped empower

Chinese women and children by teaching English, establishing homes, and providing schools (Tan & Dong, 2014). The Christian church actions align with our instructions from God as stated in Leviticus 19:33-34 (*New American Standard Bible*, 1960/1995), where the Lord instructs the Israelites to love their neighbors as they love themselves: "When a stranger resides with you in your land, you shall not do him wrong. The stranger who resides with you shall be to you as the native among you, and you shall love him as yourself, for you were aliens in the land of Egypt; I am the Lord your God".

As we see the growing population of Asian American Christians, counselors need to utilize best practices with this population. Studies have found that clinicians who work with Asian American Christians should not ignore their religious beliefs nor challenge them (Tan & Dong, 2014). This may invoke shame, guilt, and lead to premature termination of therapy (Kim & Lee, 2014; Lin, 2016; Tan & Dong, 2014; Zane & Ku, 2014). It is also beneficial to work from the religious belief system of the client to understand their Christian worldview while remaining open to learning more about their belief system (Tan & Dong, 2014). Christian counselors can integrate prayer, inner healing meditation, and Scriptures in an ethical manner, which is beneficial (Seamands, 1985 as cited in Tan & Dong, 2014). Integrating Scriptures that demonstrate Jesus' emotional expressions can normalize emotions such as anger, grief, and sadness (Tan & Dong, 2014). As instructed in Ephesians 4:26-28 (*New American Standard Bible*, 1960/1995), "Be angry, and yet do not sin; do not let the sun go down on your anger, and do not give the devil an opportunity" The Scripture points out that it is okay to be angry. Even Jesus displayed righteous anger against the Pharisees (Mark 3:1-5). Overall integrating spiritual interventions with AAW should only be done with informed consent, an understanding of your client's spiritual maturity, and knowing that you agree with the client's Christian beliefs (Tan & Dong, 2014).

CASE STUDY

Racheal, a second-generation Korean American woman, comes to see you for counseling about a family conflict. Racheal has been in a romantic relationship for a year with a White American man, Richard. She reports that her family does not agree with her decision to stay in the relationship with Richard since he lost his high paying job with a Fortune 500 company. Additionally, Richard has been depressed and has lost motivation to find another job. Because of this, her parents have given her an ultimatum to choose them or the "loser" Richard. Since this family conflict began, Racheal has been suffering from daily headaches and disturbed sleep. She is seeking your assistance to tell her what to do.

© pixelheadphoto digitalskillet/Shutterstock.com

Multicultural Considerations for Racheal

Based on the strong family structure in Asian American families, as her counselor, you should ask Racheal how a decision to continue dating Richard would affect her relationship with her parents now and in the long term. Since Racheal's cultural values adhere to a patriarchal and traditional orientation and are in alignment with a collectivistic culture, her decisions not only affect her, but her family as well. Questions that you can ask Racheal include "How will continuing to date Richard against your parent's wishes impact your relationship with them?" or "How important are your parent's decisions in who you date and potentially marry?" Additionally, since Racheal sees you as an authority figure, you should take a directive approach in providing therapeutic guidance. However, also be aware of the shame that is associated with sharing feelings and wanting to please you as her counselor. Lastly, since Asian American cultures value the mind and body connection, explore Racheal's reported psychosomatic complaints and when they began. Providing an opportunity for Racheal to process what is happening with her physically may help to relieve her psychosomatic symptoms.

© Asier Romero/Shutterstock.com

Gendered Racism/Racialized Sexism among Women of Color

Studies have shown that women, and particularly women of color, have a unique status as a racial gendered minority (Essed, 1991; Keum et al., 2017; Hahm et al., 2017; Mukkamla & Suyemoto, 2018). Therefore, it is important for counselors and counseling students to understand the intersectionality of race and gender and its effect on the identity of their female clients of color. You cannot assume that a woman of color is only dealing with racism while ignoring her experiences with sexism and vice versa. It is essential that a counselor consider the whole identity of their female clients of color.

If you are a male counselor or counselor-in-training, what privileges have you experienced as a man? How might your experiences differ from that of a woman? How might your experiences differ from that of a woman of color? What fears and challenges do women face solely because of their gender and ethnicity and/or race?

If you are a female counselor or counselor-in-training, how might your experiences be similar and different? If part of the majority culture, how might your experiences differ from a woman of color? If you are a woman of color, how might your experiences differ from other women who are of a different cultural minority?

CHAPTER SUMMARY

Being a woman of color in America can have its challenges, but resilience has carried these women through the most difficult times. This chapter provides a brief overview of three major cultural groups in America, including the largest minority group (Latinas/os), the second-largest minority group (Blacks), and the fastest-growing minority group (Asian Americans). Women in these minority groups have unique experiences that are not only connected to their ethnic and racial backgrounds, but are also connected to their gender. Latinas face many barriers when seeking treatment, but keep in mind their strong cultural values as you focus to build the therapeutic relationship (*personalismo*), utilize family-based and strength-based approaches (*familismo* and *la familia*), and seek to incorporate spiritual (*espiritualidad)* and religious practices when appropriate. For Black women, consider the numerous experiences of oppression and intersexuality and the need for safety in the counseling relationship. Black women need to feel heard, which is more congruent with a person-centered approach to counseling. Concerning Asian American women, understand the notion behind the minority model myth and highlight their courage to seek counseling, as well as incorporate culturally informed therapeutic modalities, such as AWARE. Above all else, show the love of God by fulfilling his commandment, which is to love others unconditionally (see Matthew 22:39) and to know that we are all children of God, worthy of salvation, and deserving of heaven through Jesus Christ (see Revelation 7:9). "There is neither Jew nor Greek, there is neither slave nor free, there is no male or female, for you are all one in Christ Jesus (*New American Standard Bible*, 1960/1995, Galatians 3:28).

KEY TERMS

Boarding School Era - the most traumatic era for Native Americans as many children never saw their families again, and a lot of them died from the diseases they caught due to the lack of medical treatment. Children were removed from their homes and assimilated with European children in boarding schools

Cultural Humility - incorporates a lifelong commitment to self-evaluation and self-critique, to redressing the power imbalances in the patient-physician dynamic, and to develop mutually beneficial and non-paternalistic clinical and advocacy partnership with communities on behalf of individuals and defined populations

Culturally Responsive Services - the counselor's knowledge of their client's cultural background, beliefs, values, and traditions. It involves making cultural adaptations in their theoretical and therapeutic approaches

Curanderos (folk healers) – integrates present and deceased significant loved ones (i.e., it is a systemic intervention that includes grief processes and family supportive involvement), uses symbols for intuitive connections, and provides experiences of change through the manipulation of symbols (i.e., multi-sensorial and cognitive-symbolic interpretations that lead to the release of personal pain to an object

Face Concern - refers to a person's set of socially sanctioned claims concerning one's social character and social integrity in which this set of claims or this 'line' is largely defined by certain prescribed roles that one carries out as a member or representative of a certain social or reference group

Familismo - a central relational value that represents the importance of familial relationships (including extended family members) and is family-centered, interdependent, and shows concern for others' health and happiness

Fractured Identity Model - describes what happens to Asian American women caught in a double bind of wanting to please their parents with being the perfect Asian daughter while playing the role of the model minority in a Western society

Gendered Racism - the simultaneous experience of both racism and sexism

Intersectionality - an analysis claiming that systems of race, economic class, gender, sexuality, ethnicity, nationality, and age form mutually constructing features of social organization

Micro-Aggressions - indirect, subtle, or unintentional discrimination

Model Minority Myth - assumes that Asian Americans are the "superior minority" in the United States and their educational and financial success is attributed to this exemplary status

Minority Stress - a significant amount of stress faced by individuals of a disparaging minority groups

Strength-Based Therapy (SBT)- is a client-directed approach that invites people to participate in every aspect of care and to apply their indigenous [emphasis added] strengths and resources toward personally meaningful goals...SBT draws from a variety of sources, ideas, and methods

Sunrise Dance - a 4-day ceremony that starts with a blessing from the girl's father followed by traditional Apache songs and dances; setting up wikiups (traditional home); receiving instructions from the Godmother on how to grow spiritually, mentally, and physically; and learning homemaking skills

SUGGESTED RESOURCES

Articles

American Psychological Association. (2012). *Crossroads: The psychology of immigration in the new century*. http://www.apa.org/topics/immigration/executive-summary.pdf

Arredondo, P., Gallardo-Cooper, M., Delgado-Ramero, E. A. & Zapata, A. L. (2014). *Culturally responsive counseling with Latinas/os*. American Counseling Association.

Center for American Progress. (2013). *The state of women of color in the United States*. https://www.americanprogress.org/wp-content/uploads/2013/10/StateOfWomenColor-1.pdf

Keyes, J. (2017, April 2). Put *down your cape: Solving the Black superwoman syndrome*. Ebony. https://www.ebony.com/self_help/black-women-healing-sisterhood-relationships/

Pew Research Center. (2017, September 8). *Asian Americans: A diverse and growing population*. https://www.pewresearch.org/topics/asian-americans/

MultiAsian.Church. (n.d.). *Article re: Asian American Christians*. https://multiasian.church/data/articles/

National Alliance on Mental Illness. (2013). *Compartiendo esperanza: No hay salud sin salud emocional (Sharing hope: There is no health without mental health)*. https://www.nami.org/getattachment/Find-Support/Diverse-Communities/Latinos/ESPERANZAFamilyGuide.pdf

Pulitzer Center. (2016, April 26). *No more saving face: Empowering Asian America women to seek mental health treatment*. https://pulitzercenter.org/reporting/no-more-saving-face-empowering-asian-american-women-seek-mental-health-treatment

Organizations

Asian American Christian Counseling Service. (n.d.). http://aaccs.org/

Office of Ethnic Minority Affairs, American Psychological Association. (n.d.). OEMA resources and publications. https://www.apa.org/pi/oema/resources/index

Videos

AJ+. (2018, May 4). *Is the 'strong Black woman' stereotype hurting Black women?* [Video]. YouTube. https://youtu.be/OlYSzI8fX9o

Al Jazeera. (2017, October 8). *Why do we call Asian Americans the model minority?* [Video file]. YouTube. https://www.youtube.com/watch?v=PrDbvSSbxk8

American Psychiatric Association. (2014, March 7). *Mental health: A guide for Latinos and their families* [Video file]. https://youtu.be/7QgVi7suKvs

American Counseling Association (Producer). (2006). *La conmovisión de Latinos/as en la consjería/Latino worldviews in counseling, hosted by Patricia Arredondo and Jon Carlson* [Film; educational DVD]. American Counseling Association.

American Psychological Association (Producer). (2005). *Counseling Latina/Latino clients with Patricia Arredondo* [Film; educational DVD]. American Psychological Association.

Granite Schools. (2017, December 6). *Counselors share advice for Latino families* [Video]. YouTube. https://youtu.be/preHJUQ6Dek

Good Morning America. (2018, September 11). *New generation of Asian-American women are fighting to normalize mental health treatment* [Video file]. YouTube. https://youtu.be/gWqvI9m-Ync

Microtraining Associates (Producer). (2002). *Mujeres Latinas—santas y marquesas* [Film; educational DVD]. Microtraining Associates.

Microtraining Associates (Producer). (1999). *Innovative approaches for culture-specific counseling* [Film; educational DVD]. Microtraining Associates.

Microtraining Associates (Producer). (2008). *Counseling with immigrants* [Film; educational DVD]. Microtraining Associates.

MTV News. (2016, May 11). *3 Black female stereotypes that need to die* [Video]. YouTube. https://youtu.be/yQO7XoANYb8

TEDx Talks. (2017, April 10). *What being Hispanic and Latinx means in the United States: Fernanda Ponce* [Video]. YouTube. https://youtu.be/Q1A4Vsh5Qas

TED. (2016, December 7). *The urgency of intersectionality: Kimberle Crenshaw* [Video]. YouTube. https://youtu.be/akOe5-UsQ2o

We are mitú. (2018, July 18). *What's the deal with Latinos not talking about mental health? The Kat call S3-mitú* [Video]. YouTube. https://youtu.be/gGBOhQJ9qvY

REFERENCES

Abrams, J. A., Hill, A., & Maxwell, M. (2019). Underneath the mask of the strong Black woman schema: Disentangling influences of strength and self-silencing on depressive symptoms among U.S. Black women. *Sex Roles, 80*(9-10), 517-526. https://doi.org/10.1007/s11199-018-0956-y

Alegría, M., Canino, G., Shrout, P. E., Woo, M., Duan, N., Vila, D., Torres, M., Chin C., & Meng, X. (2008). Prevalence of mental illness in immigrant and non-immigrant U.S. Latino groups. *American Journal of Psychiatry, 165*(3), 359-369. https://doi.org/10.1176/appi.ajp.2007.07040704

American Psychiatric Association. (2017). *Mental health disparities: Hispanics and Latinos*. https://www.psychiatry.org/psychiatrists/cultural-competency/education/mental-health-facts

Arredondo, P., Gallardo-Cooper, M., Delgado-Romero, E. A., & Zapata, A. L. (2014). *Culturally responsive counseling with Latinas/os*. American Counseling Association.

Augsberger, A., Yeung, A., Dougher, M., & Hahm, H. C. (2015). Factors influencing the underutilization of mental health services among Asian American women with a history of depression and suicide. *BMC Health Services Research, 15*(1), 542-552. https://doi.org/10.1186/s12913-015-1191-7

Avent, J. R., & Cahswell, C. C. (2015). The Black church: Theology and implications for counseling African Americans. *The Professional Counselor, 5*(1), 81-90. https://doi.org/10.15241/jra.5.1.81

Cashwell, C. S., & Young, J. S. (Eds.). (2011). *Integrating spirituality and religion into counseling: A guide to competent practice*. American Counseling Association.

Ceballos, P. L., & Bratton, S. C. (2010). Empowering Latino families: Effects of a culturally responsive intervention for low-income immigrant Latino parents on children's behaviors and parental stress. *Psychology in the Schools, 47*(8), 761-775. https://doi.org/10.1002/pits.20502

Centers for Disease Control and Prevention. (2015). *10 leading causes of death, United States, 2014, Asian/Pac Islander, females* [Data set]. https://webappa.cdc.gov/sasweb/ncipc/leadcaus10_us.html

Centers for Disease Control and Prevention. (2019a). *Summary health statistics: National health interview survey, 2018, table A-7a* [Data set]. https://ftp.cdc.gov/pub/Health_Statistics/NCHS/NHIS/SHS/2018_SHS_Table_A-7.pdf

Centers for Disease Control and Prevention. (2019b). *Summary health statistics: National health interview survey, 2018, table A-8a* [Data set]. https://ftp.cdc.gov/pub/Health_Statistics/NCHS/NHIS/SHS/2018_SHS_Table_A-8.pdf

Chou, R. S., & Feagin, J. R. (2015). *Myth of the model minority: Asian Americans facing racism*. Routledge.

Clark, R., Anderson, N. B., Clark, V. R., & Williams, D. R. (1999). Racism as a stressor for African Americans: A biopsychosocial model. *American Psychologist, 54*, 805-816. https://doi.org/10.1037/0003-066X.54.10.805

Coker, A. D. (2002). *Racial tasks of African American clients: Understanding historical cultural values as a means of developing appropriate counseling interventions* [Paper presentation]. Alabama Counseling Association 36th Annual Conference, Mobile, AL, United States.

Coker, A. D. (2003). *African American women and the utilization of counseling services* [Paper presentation]. American Association of Behavioral and Social Sciences 6th Annual Meeting, Las Vegas, NV, United States.

Coker, A. D. (2004). Counseling African American women: Issues, challenges and intervention strategies. In G. Walz & R. Yep (Eds.), *VISTAS: Perspectives and counseling 2004* (pp. 129-136). American Counseling Association and Counseling Outfitters/CAPS Press.

Cokley, K., Garcia, D., Hall-Clark, B., Tran, K., & Rangel, A. (2012). The moderating role of ethnicity in the relation between religiousness and mental health among ethnically diverse college students. *Journal of Religion and Health, 51*(3), 890-907. https://doi.org/10.1007/s10943-010-9406-z

Collins, P. H. (1998). *Fighting words: Black women and the search for justice.* University of Minnesota Press.

D'Angelo, E., Llerena-Quinn, R., Shapiro, R., Colon, F., Rodriguez, P., Gallagher, K., & Beardslee, W. (2009). Adaptations of the preventive intervention program for depression for use with predominantly low-income Latino families. *Family Process, 48*(2), 269-291.

Davis, S. M. (2015). The "strong Black woman collective:" A developing theoretical framework for understanding collective communication practices of Black women. *Women's Studies in Communication, 38,* 20-35. https://doi.org/10.1080/07491409.2014.953714

Davis, A. W., Levant, R. F., & Pryor, S. (2018). Traditional femininity versus strong Black women ideologies and stress among Black women. *Journal of Black Studies, 49*(8), 820-841. https://doi.org/10.1177/0021934718799016

Edara, I. R. (2016). Relation of individualism–collectivism and ethnic identity to spiritual transcendence among European Americans, Asian Indian Americans, and Chinese Americans. *Counseling and Values, 61*(1), 44-63. https://doi.org/10.1002/cvj.12025

Essed, P. (1991). *Understanding everyday racism: An interdisciplinary theory* (Vol. 2). Sage.

Falicov, C. (1998). *Latino families in therapy: A guide to multicultural practice.* Guilford Press.

Garza, Y., Kinsworthy, S., & Watts, R. E. (2009). Child-parent relationship training as experienced by Hispanic parents: A phenomenological study. *International Journal of Play Therapy, 18*(4), 217-228. https://doi.org/10.1037/a0017055

Ghavami, N., & Peplau, L. A. (2012). An intersectional analysis of gender and ethnic stereotypes: Testing three hypotheses. *Psychology of Women Quarterly, 37*(1), 113-127. https://doi.org/10.1177/0361684312464203

Guerrero, E. G., Khachikian, T., Kim, T., Kong, Y., & Vega, W. A. (2013). Spanish language proficiency among providers and Latino clients engagement in substance abuse treatment. *Addictive Behaviors, 33,* 2893-2897. https://doi.org/10.1016/j.addbeh.2013.08.022

Hahm, H., Chang, S. T. H., Lee, G. Y., Tagerman, M. D., Lee, C. S., Trentadue, M. P., & Hien, D. A. (2017). Asian women's action for resilience and empowerment intervention: Stage I pilot study. *Journal of Cross-Cultural Psychology, 48*(10), 1537-1553. https://doi.org/10.1177/0022022117730815

Hahm, H., Gonyea, J. G., Chiao, C., & Koritsanszky, L. A. (2014). Fractured identity: A framework for understanding young Asian American women's self-harm and suicidal behaviors. *Race and Social Problems, 6*, 56-68. https://doi.org/10.1007/s12552-014-9115-4

Hahm, H., Jang, J., Vu, C., Alexander, L. M., Driscoll, K. E., & Lundgren, L. (2013). Drug use and suicidality among Asian American women who are children of immigrants. *Substance Use & Misuse, 48*, 1563-1576. https://doi.org/10.3109/10826084.2013.808219

Hahm, H. C., Zhou, L., Lee, C., Maru, M., Petersen, J. M., & Kolaczyk, E. D. (2019). Feasibility, preliminary efficacy, and safety of a randomized clinical trial for Asian Women's Action for Resilience and Empowerment (AWARE) intervention. *American Journal of Orthopsychiatry, 89*(4), 462.

Hall, E. V., Phillips, K. W., & Townsend, S. M. (2015). A rose by any other name? The consequences of subtyping "African-Americans" from "Blacks." *Journal of Experimental Social Psychology, 56*, 183-190. https://doi.org/10.1016/j.jesp.2014.10.004

Hall, J. C. (2018). It is tough being a Black woman: Intergenerational stress and coping. *Journal of Black Studies, 49*(5), 481-501. https://doi.org/10.1177/0021934718766817

Ho, I. K., Dinh, K. T., & Smith, S. A. (2017). Intimate partner violence and physical health outcomes among Southeast Asian American women. *Journal of Health Psychology, 22*(4), 515-525. https://doi.org/10.1177%2F1359105315603695

Huynh, V. W. (2012). Ethnic microaggressions and the depressive and somatic symptoms of Latino and Asian American adolescents. *Journal of Youth and Adolescence, 41*, 831-846. https://doi.org/10.1007/s10964-012-9756-9

Keum, B. T., Brady, J. L., Sharma, R., Lu, Y., Kim, Y. H., & Thai, C. J. (2018). Gendered Racial Microaggressions Scale for Asian American women: Development and initial validation. *Journal of Counseling Psychology, 65*(5), 571-585. https://doi.org/10.1037/cou0000305

Kim, P. Y., & Lee, D. (2014). Internalized model minority myth, Asian values, and help-seeking attitudes among Asian American students. *Cultural Diversity and Ethnic Minority Psychology, 20*(1), 98-106. https://doi.org/10.1037/a0033351

La Roche, M. J., D'Angelo, E., Gualdron, L., & Leavell, J. (2006). Culturally sensitive guided imagery for allocentric Latinos: A pilot study. *Psychotherapy: Theory, Research, Practice, Training, 43*(2), 555-560. https://doi.org/10.1037/0033-3204.43.4.555

Le Meyer, O., Zane, N., Cho, Y. I., & Takeuchi, D. T. (2009). Use of specialty mental health services by Asian Americans with psychiatric disorders. *Journal of Consulting and Clinical Psychology, 77*(5), 1000-1005.

Lewis, J. A., Mendenhall, R., Harwood, S. A., & Browne Huntt, M. (2016). "Ain't I a woman?": Perceived gendered racial microaggressions experienced by Black women. *The Counseling Psychologist, 44*(5), 758–780. https://doi.org/10.1177/0011000016641193

Lin, K. (2016). Mental health initiatives for Asian American women. *Alpenglow: Binghamton University Undergraduate Journal of Research and Creative Activity, 2*(1), 1-15. https://orb.binghamton.edu/alpenglowjournal/vol2/iss1/5

Longmire-Avital, B., & Robinson, R. (2017). Young, depressed, and Black: A comparative exploration of depressive symptomatology among Black and White collegiate women. *Journal of College Student Psychotherapy, 32*(1), 53-72. https://doi.org/10.1080/87568225.2017.1344114

Lopez, G., Ruiz, N. G., & Patten, E. (2017, September 8). *Key facts about Asian Americans, a diverse and growing population.* Pew Research Center Fact Tank: News in the Numbers. https://www.pewresearch.org/fact-tank/2017/09/08/key-facts-about-asian-americans/

Matos, M., Torres, R., Santiago, R., Jurado, M., & Rodriguez, I. (2006). Adaptation of parent-child interaction therapy for Puerto Rican families: A preliminary study. *Family Process, 45*(2), 205-222. https://doi.org/10.1111/j.1545-5300.2006.00091.x

Meyer, I. H. (1995). Minority stress and mental health in gay men. *Journal of Health and Social Behavior, 36,* 38-56. https://doi.org/10.2307/2137286

Meyer, I. H. (2007). Prejudice and discrimination as social stressors. In I. H. Meyer & M. E.Northridge (Eds.), *The health of sexual minorities* (pp. 242-267). Springer.

Moreno, O., & Cardemil, E. (2013). Religiosity and mental health services: An exploratory study of help seeking among Latinos. *Journal of Latina/o Psychology, 1*(1), 106-118. https://doi.org/10.1037/a0031376

Muir., J. A., Schwartz, S. J., & Szapoczniki, J. (2004). A program of research with Hispanic and African-American families: Three decades of intervention development and testing influenced by the changing cultural context of Miami. *Journal of Marital and Family Therapy, 30*(3), 285-303. https://doi.org/10.1111/j.1752-0606.2004.tb01241.x

Mukkamala, S., & Suyemoto, K. L. (2018). Racialized sexism/sexualized racism: A multimethod study of intersectional experiences of discrimination for Asian American women. *Asian American Journal of Psychology, 9*(1), 32-46. https://doi.org/10.1037/aap0000104

Murphy, J. J., & Sparks, J. A. (2018). *Strengths-based therapy: Distinctive features.* Routledge.

Nadal, K. L., Griffin, K. E., Wong, Y., Hamit, S., & Rasmus, M. (2014). The impact of racial microaggressions on mental health: Counseling implications for clients of color. *Journal of Counseling and Development, 92,* 57-66. https://doi.org/10.1002/j.1556-6676.2014.00130.x

National Alliance on Mental Illness. (2019). *Latino mental health.* https://www.nami.org/Find-Support/Diverse-Communities/Latino-Mental-Health

New American Standard Bible. (1995). New American Standard Bible Online. https://www.biblestudytools.com/nas/ (Original work published 1960)

New International Bible. (2011). New International Bible Online. https://www.thenivbible.com/ (Original work published 1973)

Noe-Bustamante, L. (2019, September 16). *Key facts about U.S. Hispanics and their diverse heritage.* Pew Research Center. https://www.pewresearch.org/fact-tank/2019/09/16/key-facts-about-u-s-hispanics/

Ong, A. D., Burrow, A. L., Fuller-Rowell, T. E., Ja, N. M., & Sue, D. W. (2013). Racial microaggressions and daily well-being among Asian Americans. *Journal of Counseling Psychology, 60,* 188–199. https://doi.org/10.1037/a0031736

Pan, P. J. D., Deng, L. Y. F., Tsai, S. L., Chen, H. Y. J., & Yuan, S. S. J. (2014). Development and validation of a Christian-based Grief Recovery Scale. *British Journal of Guidance & Counselling, 42*(1), 99-114. https://doi.org/10.1080/03069885.2013.852158

Parra Cardona, J. R., Domenech-Rodriguez, M., Forgatch, M., Sullivan, C., Bybee, D., Holtrop, K., Escobar-Chew, A. R., Tams, L., Dates, B., & Bernal, G. (2012). Culturally adapting an evidence-based parenting intervention for Latino immigrants: The need to integrate fidelity and cultural relevance. *Family Process, 51*(1), 56-72. https://doi.org/10.1111/j.1545-5300.2012.01386.x

Parra Cardona, J., Holtrop, K., Córdova, D. R., Escobar-Chew, A. R., Horsford, S., Tams, L, Villarruel, F. A., Villalobos, G., Dates, B., Anthony, J. C., & Fitzgerald, H. (2009). "Queremos aprender": Latino immigrants' call to integrate cultural adaptation with best practice knowledge in a parenting intervention. *Family Process, 48*(2), 211-231. https://doi.org/10.1111/j.1545-5300.2009.01278.x

Pew Hispanic Center. (2007). *Changing faiths: Latinos and the transformation of American religion.* https://www.pewforum.org/2007/04/25/changing-faiths-latinos-and-the-transformation-of-american-religion-2/

Pew Research Center. (2019). *In U.S., decline of Christianity continues at rapid pace: An update on America's changing religious landscape.* https://www.pewforum.org/2019/10/17/in-u-s-decline-of-christianity-continues-at-rapid-pace/

Piedra, L. M., & Byoun, S. (2012). Vida alegre: Preliminary findings of a depression intervention for immigrant Latino mothers. *Research on Social Work Practice, 22*(2), 138-150. https://doi.org/10.1177/1049731511424168

Ramirez, T. L., & Blay, Z. (2017, October 17). *Why people are using the term 'Latinx.'* The Huffpost. https://www.huffpost.com/entry/why-people-are-using-the-term-latinx_n_57753328e4b0cc0fa136a159

Resnicow, K., Baranowski, T., Ahluwalia, J. S., & Braithwaite, R. L. (1999). Cultural sensitivity in public health: Defined and demystified. *Ethnicity & Disease, 9*(1), 10-21.

Reyes, A. T., Serafica, R., Cross, C. L., Constantino, R. E., & Arenas, R. A. (2018). Resilience, acculturative stress, and family norms against disclosure of mental health problems among foreign-born Filipino American women. *Asian/Pacific Island Nursing Journal, 3*(3), 80-92. https://doi.org/10.31372/20180303.1002

Sanchez, F., & Gaw, A. (2007). Mental health care of Filipino Americans. *Psychiatric Services, 58*(6), 810-815.

Santiago-Rivera, A., Kanter, J., Benson, G., Derose, T., Illes, R., & Reyes, W. (2008). Behavioral activation as an alternative treatment approach or Latinos with depression. *Psychotherapy: Theory, Research, Practice, Training, 45*(2), 173-185. https://doi.org/10.1037/0033-3204.45.2.173

Serrata, J. V., Rodriguez, R., Castro, J. E., Hernandez-Martinez, M. (2019). Well-being of Latina survivors of intimate partner violence and sexual assault receiving trauma-informed and culturally-specific services. *Journal of Family Violence.* Advanced online publication. https://doi.org/10.1007/s10896-019-00049-z

Shae, M., Cachelin, F., Uribe, L., Striegel, R. H., Thompson, D., & Wilson, G. T. (2012). Cultural adaptation of a cognitive behavior therapy guided self-help program for Mexican American women with binge eating disorders. *Journal of Counseling & Development, 90*(3), 308-313. https://doi.org/10.1002/j.1556-6676.2012.00039.x

Sharf, R. S. (1996). *Theories of psychotherapy and counseling: Concepts and cases.* Brooks/Cole.

Shavers, M. C., & Moore, J. L. (2014). Black female voices: Self-presentation strategies in doctoral programs at predominantly White institutions. *Journal of College Student Development, 55*(4), 391-407. https://doi.org/10.1353/csd.2014.0040

Shillingford, M. A., Trice-Black, S., & Butler, S. K. (2013). Wellness of minority women counselor educators. *Counselor Education & Supervision, 52*(4), 255-269. https://doi.org/10.1002/j.1556-6978.2013.00041.x

Storlie, C. A., Mostade, S. J., & Duenyas, D. (2016). Cultural trailblazers: Exploring the career development of Latina first-generation college students. *The Career Development Quarterly, 64,* 304-317. https://doi.org/10.1002/cdq.12067

Sue, D. W. (2010). *Microaggressions in everyday life: Race, gender, and sexual orientation.* John Wiley.

Sue, D. W., & Sue, D. (2003). *Counseling the culturally diverse: Theory and practice* (4th ed.). John Wiley.

Sue, D. W., Sue, D., Neville, H. A., & Smith, L. (2019). *Counseling the culturally diverse: Theory and practice* (8th ed.). John Wiley & Sons.

Tan, S. Y., & Dong, N. J. (2014). Psychotherapy with members of Asian-American churches and spiritual traditions. In P. S. Richards & E. Bergin (Eds.), *Handbook of psychotherapy and religious diversity* (2nd ed., pp. 423-450). American Psychological Association. https://doi.org/10.1037/14371-017

Tervalon, M., & Murray-Garcia, J. (1998). Cultural humility versus cultural competence: A critical distinction in defining physician training outcomes in multicultural education. *Journal of Healthcare for the Poor and Underserved, 9*(2), 117-125.

Ting, J. Y., & Hwang, W. C. (2009). Cultural influences on help-seeking attitudes in Asian American students. *American Journal of Orthopsychiatry, 79*(1), 125-132.

U. S. Census Bureau. (2018). *Selected population profile in the United States: 2017 American Community Survey 1-year estimates.* https://factfinder.census.gov/faces/tableservices/jsf/pages/productview.xhtml?src=bkmk

U. S. Census Bureau. (2019). *Hispanic heritage month 2019.* https://www.census.gov/newsroom/facts-for-features/2019/hispanic-heritage-month.html

Versey, H. S., & Curtin, N. (2016). The differential impact of discrimination on health among Black and White women. *Social Science Research, 57,* 99-115. https://doi.org/10.1016/j.ssresearch.2015.12.012

Villarreal, C. E. (2008). *School-based Child Parent Relationship Therapy (CPRT) with Hispanic parents* (Publication No. AAI3302011) [Doctoral dissertation, Regent University]. Dissertation Abstracts International.

Warner, L. R., Settles, I. H., & Shields, S. A. (2018). Intersectionality theory in the psychology of women. In C. B. Travis & J. W. White (Eds.), *APA handbook of the psychology of women: History, theory, and battlegrounds* (Vol 1, pp. 521-539). https://doi.org/10.1037/0000059-000

White Mountain Apache Tribe. (n.d.). *White mountain Apache tribe.* http://whitemountainapache.org/

Woodward, A. T. (2011). Discrimination and help-seeking: Use of professional services and informal support among African Americans, Black Caribbean's, and Non-Hispanic Whites with a mental disorder. *Race and Social Problems, 3,* 146–159. https://doi.org/10.1007/s12552-011-9049-z

Yoo, H. C., Burrola, K. S., & Steger, M. F. (2010). A preliminary report on a new measure: Internalization of the Model Minority Myth Measure (IM-4) and its psychological correlates among Asian American college students. *Journal of Counseling Psychology, 57*(1), 114–127. https://doi.org/10.1037/a0017871

Zane, N., Hall, G. C. N., Sue, S., Young, K., & Nunez, J. (2004). Research on psychotherapy with culturally diverse populations. In M. J. Lambert (Ed.), *Handbook of psychotherapy and behavior change* (5th ed., pp. 767-804). John Wiley & Sons.

Zane, N., & Ku, H. (2014). Effects of ethnic match, gender match, acculturation, cultural identity, and face concern on self-disclosure in counseling for Asian Americans. *Asian American Journal of Psychology, 5*(1), 66-77. https://doi.org/10.1037/a0036078

Zane, N., & Yeh, M. (2002). The use of culturally-based variables in assessment: Studies on loss of face. In K. S. Kurasaki, S. Okazaki, & S. Sue (Eds.), *Asian American mental health: Assessment, theories, and methods* (pp. 123-138). Kluwer Academic/Plenum Press. https://doi.org/10.1007/978-1-4615-0735-2_9

CHAPTER 3
Counseling Active Duty Women

Timothy Crable, Ph.D., Maranda Griffin, Ph.D., & April Crable, Ph.D.

"Over the last 38 years, I have had the opportunity to witness women soldiers jump out of airplanes, hike 10 miles, lead men and women, even endure the toughest circumstances."
~Ann Dunwoody

"With your help I can advance against a troop; with my God I can scale a wall."
(2 Samuel 22:30, NIV)

Wisdom from Above: Standing in His Grace

Gen. Ann Dunwoody saluting in front of Old Guard Soldiers during her retirement ceremony at Joint Base Myer-Henderson Hall, Va., Aug. 15, 2012.

615 collection / Alamy Stock Photo

In the Old Testament, Deborah was a judge, warrior, and prophet. Few women in the Bible had more significance in governmental power, leadership, and wisdom than Deborah (Christianity. com, 2019). In Judges 4:5, we see Judge Deborah, the leader of Israel at the time, holding court below the Palm of Deborah (BibleGateway, n.d.) in the hill country of Ephraim, wisely discerning and resolving Israelite grievances and conflicts. Deborah the warrior, in Judges 4:6, tells Barak son of Abinoam that the Lord has commanded him to lead 10,000 men to Mount Tabor. Barak replies to her, "If you go with me, I will go; but if you don't go with me, I won't go" (*New International Bible*, 1973/2011, Judges 4:8). Warrior Deborah does go to battle

with him but prophesizes that Sisera will not fall by his hand, but by that of a woman. In Judges 4:21, we see God's word through Prophet Deborah come to pass with Sisera falling at the hand of Jael, Heber's wife.

Judge Deborah remained steadfast on the purpose God had for her life, and God blessed her with peaceful assurance. Through Prophet Deborah, God shows us that he will give us favor when we are obedient to his word. In turn, our words will resonate with the masses and those in our charge with wisdom and correct discernment. Finally, when we act in service to others, as Warrior Deborah did so bravely, he will bolster our resolve against adversity, toward victory, and for the glory of God.

CHAPTER LEARNING OBJECTIVES

Upon completing this chapter, you should be able to:

- Articulate the history of women in the military
- Articulate mental health issues as it relates to women in the military
- Articulate the challenges associated with women in the military
- Obtain an understanding of Biblical integration

CHAPTER OVERVIEW

In this chapter, you will gain an understanding and appreciation of military women and the unique mental health challenges they face. The chapter begins with a focus on the history of service and sacrifices military women have contributed to the United States of America from 1775 to present day. Research is provided on a myriad of statistical outcomes to include demographic points of interest. The chapter then spotlights specific challenges faced by women in the United States military. Examples include mental health issues, racism and discrimination, career concerns, family separation and transition, familiarity with terminology, and stigma of mental health. Counseling recommendations are then presented, followed by a focus on Biblical integration of key concepts. Finally, you will be presented with a case study to bolster practical application, followed by a chapter summary.

HISTORY OF WOMEN IN THE MILITARY

The contributions that women have made to the Armed Forces of the United States (US) of America spans over 240 years (The

Women's Memorial, 2019). Since the inception of the United States in 1775, women served in the US Military in harm's way, although in non-combat roles officially. They overcame the gender bias, which existed at the time to serve as nurses, cooks, and even saboteurs (The Women's Memorial, 2019). In the Civil War, between 1861 and 1865, women wore disguises to hide their femininity as they fought valiantly for both the Union and Confederate sides of the conflict (The Women's Memorial, 2019). In

World War I, from 1917 to 1918, over 400 gave their lives in service to the country. In 1942, five women were captured and held as Prisoners of War at the hands of the Japanese in Guam. In the Vietnam War between 1965 and 1975, over 7000 female service members, primarily nurses, participated in Southeast Asia combat support roles (Colonial Williamsburg Foundation, 2008). In 1991 Women were authorized to fly in combat missions and 1992 on combat ships. Women served valiantly in both *Operation Enduring Freedom* and *Operation Iraqi Freedom* with honor and distinction. Women comprised 14% of the forces in those operations cumulatively (Street et al., 2009). Defense Secretary authorized the membership of women in combat units by lifting the Combat Exclusion Policy in 2013 (Londono, 2013). By 2015, women were permitted to serve in all combat roles for which they are qualified (Rosenberg & Philipps, 2015).

FIGURE 3.1

Timeline

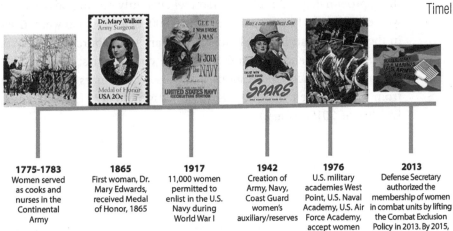

1775-1783	1865	1917	1942	1976	2013
Women served as cooks and nurses in the Continental Army	First woman, Dr. Mary Edwards, received Medal of Honor, 1865	11,000 women permitted to enlist in the U.S. Navy during World War I	Creation of Army, Navy, Coast Guard women's auxiliary/reserves	U.S. military academies West Point, U.S. Naval Academy, U.S. Air Force Academy, accept women	Defense Secretary authorized the membership of women in combat units by lifting the Combat Exclusion Policy in 2013. By 2015, women were permitted to serve in all combat roles for which they are qualified (Rosenberg & Philipps, 2015).

MILITARY WOMEN STATISTICS

Demographics

Today, women proudly serve in every branch of the Armed Forces (Army, Navy, Marines, and Coast Guard) from infantryman on the frontlines of war zones to submariners on fast attack submarines (Lakritz, 2019). Of the approximately 1.3 million personnel currently serving on active duty, women make up 16%, or more than 210,000. Over 150,000 women serve in the Reserve and National Guard (Military One Source, 2017). Women serve in step and alongside their male counterparts; however, "their military experiences and responses to those experiences may be distinct from those of their male counterparts" (Psychological Health Center of Excellence, 2019, para. 2).

Mental Health Statistics

A Department of Defense study found that 1.8 million or 16% of outpatient appointments for active duty military personnel were for mental health needs (Kime, 2019). Across active duty U.S. military personnel in 2018, 8% had a diagnosis of a mental health disorder (Kime, 2019). Although this rate of diagnoses differs from the civilian mental illness prevalence of 20%, the mental health of US military active duty and veteran men and women remains a matter of paramount concern for officials (Kime, 2019). When looking at lifetime prevalence, the same study found that 25% of active duty women were diagnosed with a mental health disorder (Kime, 2019). Comparatively, lifetime prevalence for men on active duty was 16% (Kime, 2019). The aforementioned study highlighted the following mental health disorders:

- Post-traumatic Stress Disorder
- Depression
- Bipolar disorder
- Adjustment disorder
- Substance abuse
- Psychosis
- Bipolar
- Anxiety (Kime, 2018).

CHALLENGES FACED BY WOMEN IN THE MILITARY

As a professional or lay counselor, you may work with women in the military. These clients may enter counseling with a variety of challenges, including mental health issues, racism and discrimination, acculturation, career concerns, and family separation and transition. Counselors must be attuned to the challenges faced by these women. This section offers a foundational introduction to the wide range of problems affecting women as an essential component in counselor competence.

© Master1305/Shutterstock.com

Mental Health Issues

Mental health issues are common among military personnel. Nearly 25% of active duty personnel have symptoms of a mental health disorder (Ursano et al., 2014). Depression, anxiety, post-traumatic stress disorder (PTSD), and substance-related disorders are common. About three-fourths of these disorders were evident before military enlistment. Women are more likely to experience depression. Depression is one of the most common client issues a counselor encounters, and the rate of major depression is five times higher among military personnel compared to civilians. Anxiety, an internalizing disorder, is another commonly encountered issue. When compared to civilians, the rate of anxiety is comparable for military personnel, with a notable difference in a spike of the disorder after enlistment (Ursano et al., 2014). The rate of post-traumatic stress disorder (PTSD) is nearly 15 times as high among military personnel compared to civilians. Women are twice as likely to develop PTSD than men. A large percentage of women experience military sexual trauma due to assaults within the ranks (The Soldiers Project, 2019). A variety of traumatic events lead some to use drugs and alcohol to dull the pain associated with trauma. According to the National Institute on Drug Abuse (2019), more than one in ten veterans are diagnosed with substance use disorder, and the stressors of military service place women at increased risk of substance abuse. Social and emotional support are critical for women seeking mental health treatment. Gender stereotypes contribute to stigma for women who fear backlash and consequences for seeking mental health treatment.

Trauma

A steadily increasing rate of women in the armed forces experience trauma resulting in post-traumatic stress disorder. (Chaumba & Bride, 2010). Navy Cmdr. Paulette Cazares, associate director for mental health at the Naval Medical Center San Diego, stated, "Being in the military can magnify the depression triggers one might experience in the general population," (Military Health Systems Communications Office, 2018, para. 10)." After an injury, military women are more likely to have negative mental health behaviors which contributed to diminished quality of life outcomes (Dye, 2018). The likelihood that military women service members will display symptoms of post-traumatic stress disorder correlates to levels of stress they have prior to and following a deployment (Wooten, 2009). Military women have higher rates of traumatizing events while experiencing less access and availability to mental health resources (Williams, 2015).

Military Sexual Trauma

Veteran males are more likely to be referred to and receive mental health services following a traumatic event (McBratney, 2018). Military women are 90% more likely to suffer from PTSD due to military sexual trauma (MST) (MST is the sexual assault or harassment that occurs while actively serving i.e., active duty, active duty training or inactive duty training [National Guard or Reservist]) than any other trauma, including both combat and prior military service. (White et al., 2018). Women are more likely to report MST at a higher rate than men. According to Kimerling et al., (2010) discussed that while 15.1% of women reported only 0.7% of men reported MST when being assessed. MST is not recognized in the Diagnostic and Statistical Manual of Mental Disorders.

Post-traumatic Stress Disorder (PTSD)

Post-traumatic stress disorder (PTSD) may manifest following a major or minor traumatic event in which the subject victim felt powerless. PTSD "is a long-term reaction to war-zone exposure" (Friedman et al., 1994, p. 1). Common symptoms include hypervigilance, inability for the person to focus their attention, a deficit in memory recall, and startling mental replay of the original traumatic event (Yehuda, 2002). A Post Deployment Health Assessment (PDHA) is a commonly utilized screening tool within the Armed Forces to identify PTSD symptoms (Macera et al., 2014).

Suicide

Military women are approximately 80% more likely to commit suicide than females with no prior active-duty or reserve status (Ghahramanlou-Holloway et al., 2014). A combination of traumatic events experienced throughout a women's life make them more likely to attempt suicide. Military Caucasian women 25 years and younger were 60% of all suicide attempts in 2011. Thirty-three percent of those attempts involved a firearm not connected to their military service. Approximately one half of that group had spouses (Ghahramanlou-Holloway et al., 2014). There were 58 successful suicides by military women from 2008 to 2011 (Ghahramanlou-Holloway et al., 2014).

Research suggested that risk factors which contribute to the likelihood that a military woman will attempt suicide are trifold: 1) Occupational risk factors including but not limited to her participation in combat, mental and physical fitness and access to firearms; 2) Trauma Related Risk Indicators including overall higher rates of trauma throughout their lives, traumatic incidents during childhood, and trauma experienced during military service; 3) Psychiatric risk indicators including an existing mental health problem, a history of mental health disorders, and the combination of currently experienced depression (Ghahramanlou-Holloway et al., 2014).

FIGURE 3.2

Risk Factors Which Contribute to Suicide in Military Women

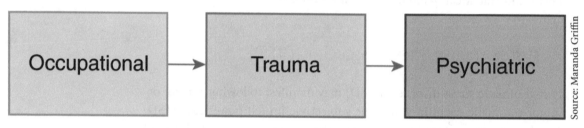

Source: Maranda Griffin

Racism and Discrimination

Despite executive orders, federal laws, and landmark legislation, racism and discrimination persist. Over 68 percent of women who have served or serve in the military have experienced gender discrimination (Monmaney, 2019). Likewise, women of color and ethnic minorities in the military are exposed to racism. Military equal opportunity programs are designed to provide for equal opportunity and treatment for all members based on race, color, religion, sex, national origin, reprisal, disability, age, sexual orientation, and gender identity. Social justice and advocacy are important components of counselor competence. As a mental health professional, you should be willing to address and anticipate these experiences directly by being open, authentic, and empathic.

Acculturation

As with any minority group entering a new environment, women who join the military experience a new culture. Women face a new set of values that might be distinctly different from their own. Women may face new attitudes and behaviors that are inconsistent with their traditional orientation. Military culture is shaped mainly by the dominant group: men. Thus, women enter an environment that has historically conditioned and trained members based on masculine paradigms (Suzuki & Kawakami, 2016). Because the values, attitudes, and beliefs may differ, women may experience acculturation conflicts. This conflict may impact self-identity. Thus, women find themselves vacillating between self-examination, group consciousness, and career choices.

Major Phi Tran, U.S. Air Force

As a first-generation woman in the US, I was born in Vietnam and came to the US when I was 11 years old. Being a female minority, it was challenging joining the military and adapting to the culture norm. The military culture is shaped and surrounded by white, dominant men. Looking back, as a new member in the military, it was difficult to fit in with the "manly" expectations of social and psychological. For instance, one expects to be great at fitness, well versed in sports discussion, be assertive and direct in group activities, have a large network & mentors (such as school affiliation, background, etc). As a leader, you need to appear in control and have everything in order. As a female minority, I did not have all these characteristics as my strengths.

If you don't demonstrate these characteristics, you may be left out of the group. The social and psychological expectations of women in the military culture are quite different than civilian side to some extent. I feel like you are expected to lead, follow, and serve the nation and be strong at all time. However, as a female, you still have the challenge to be soft, caring, and ask for help from the males. If you are strong, bold, dominant, and short, others may look at you negatively (you appear too much/too aggressive/not caring/too rough). It was challenging for me and took a while, but after 4 years, I realized that I'm a creation by God, and I'm enough. I can excel in the military being me. I also learned the system and the importance of soft skills. I act accordingly and adjust in various situations to excel and earn my place as a strong leader. I have to consistently work hard in my job, show the men and leadership that I'm strong and qualify for the position as a minority and female. However, the drive to success in the military caused me not to seek out assistance or help when I needed it. Asking for help and seeking support may look as weak, so I dealt with tough times on my own. For instance, I went to work and returned to work as usual after having an abortion. In another instance, I cried alone with relationship heartbreaks or deaths in my family.

I appear strong and tough in my military life to fit in easier. When trying to fit in to the military culture, I would think twice or three times before asking for help when I needed it. When I ask for help, I would ask another female rather than a male. It delays accessing and reaching out to all the resources available for military members. I realize that I was blessed to be able to continue to do well, with the strong faith in God and a strong support system that other women may not have. After 14 years in the service, I now work hard to share my experience and challenges. I focus on helping to build our military culture to be one that accepts others for who they are, and it is ok to ask for help anytime. It's critical to share the various opportunities and programs the military has to assist others, especially for females and younger airmen to care for and excel where they can. The women need to know that they can be in the military, excel in their life and career, and ask for help, seek advice, and receive counseling. No one is perfect, and it takes a strong leader to know when to seek help, and when to give help and support to your troops.

Contributed by Phi Tran. © Kendall Hunt Publishing Company.

Family Separation and Transition

Work-life balance is a critical barrier to continued service for military women. One of the most mentally and physically challenging aspects of a military career is deployment. **Deployment** refers to a war or mission requirements where military personnel are sent to various locations to support the mission. Deployment poses unique difficulties for women which include separation from children and spouse, isolation, risk of sexual assault, the threat of being taken hostage, and women's health and gynecological issues (Ritchie, 2002). Stress imposed on women and their families as a result of deployment lead some women to separate from the military. Successful adjustment and reintegration into the family, community, and civilian life hinges upon planning, support, resources, and access to mental health services.

© Africa Studio/Shutterstock.com

Career Concerns

Women in the military perceive more obstacles to their career than do male counterparts. Historically, gender has presented significant barriers to women's access to military occupational specialties, both career fields and specific jobs. The underrepresentation of women in certain military occupational specialties is due in part to women being a statistical minority in the military. In 2018, women comprised 16% of the active duty force and, in 2016, women comprised 19% of the Guard and Reserve (Janko et al., 2018). Male-dominated military occupational specialty career fields include maintenance (i.e., engine mechanics), pilots, firefighting, logistics, and engineering. Because women are a minority in these fields, a correlation to high attrition has been cited (Janko et al., 2018). Women often earn less than men when represented in these occupational specialties. Mental health professionals need to be involved in advocating for system level changes to ensure equity.

COUNSELING CONSIDERATIONS

Honoring diversity and embracing a multicultural approach is a core professional value of the counseling profession (American Counseling Association [ACA], 2014). Counselors have an ethical commitment to this value when working with "people within their social and cultural contexts" (ACA, 2014, p. 3). Counselors who work with women in the military should be well informed about military issues, especially as they relate to women. It is important to understand the challenges women in the military face, such as depression, PTSD, racism and discrimination, acculturation, career concerns, and family separation. The needs of this population are unique. Counseling considerations are provided.

Establishing Rapport

Foundational to working with clients is establishing rapport and relationship building. Therapeutic alliance also known as therapeutic relationship is the relationship between counselor and client (Ardito & Rabellino, 2011). Women who serve in the military can be distrustful toward counselors outside of the military (Hartman et al., 2018). The development of trust is crucial to establishing rapport with this population. The use of attending skills, informed consent, and professional disclosure are ways to be intentional in establishing rapport.

Increasing Awareness of Values

Core values are inherent to all of the Armed Forces. Each branch has its own unique set of values. Common to these values are integrity and honor. If you plan on working with this population, then you should be aware

© Kheng Guan Toh/Shutterstock.com

of the values that may influence the client's worldview and perspective. The ACA *Code of Ethics* (2014, §A.2.c.) states that counselors should communicate information in ways that are culturally appropriate. One component of cultural appropriateness is cultural competency related to the values of military clients (McKinzie, 2017). For clients that are actively engaged with the military through employment, these values act as a moral or ethical code, govern how the client lives, and influence how the client conducts herself. In counseling, this is relevant as you may be able to leverage the values as strengths to support the client's goal acquisition or wellness (Myers, 2013). Equally important is the awareness that, at times, the client may feel conflicted by these values as they navigate their life outside of the military. Having an awareness of these values will aid your understanding of the client.

CONCEPT TO CONTEMPLATE

© Asier Romero/Shutterstock.com

As you think about your work with women in the military, it is important to consider any assumptions you have about this population. As you explore your own assumptions, think about how these assumptions shape your worldview. Examining the assumptions can be helpful so your assumptions do not eclipse the ability to establish rapport. Consider: What are the benefits of suspending assumptions when working with clients?

Increasing Familiarity with Terminology

It is important to recognize that the military has its own language across all branches, as well as some specific terminology that is branch specific, as a unique attribute of military culture. As a result, counselors who are working with women in the military must be familiar with military terminology (Forziat et al., 2017). The client has a thorough understanding of the acronyms and phonetic alphabet used within the military community. To address this consideration, counselors should allow clients to educate them on terminology. Equally, counselors can take advantage of cultural competence workshops with an emphasis on the military. Having a familiarity with terminology places the counselor at an advantage so the client can speak comfortably and with ease during sessions without concern for misunderstanding or need for clarity.

Addressing the Stigma of Mental Health

Stigma related to mental health issues, particularly surrounding the potential impact to the client's military career, is a common concern. The stigma may be associated with military values such as strength and a view of themselves as warriors (Forziat et al., 2017). Asking for help may be seen as a weakness. Advocacy efforts have helped to reduce some of this stigma through education and mental health promotion. However, Hartman et al. (2018) found that "the number of soldiers seeking mental health care seems to remain significantly low" (p. 213). The greatest concern around stigma is the fear of a diagnosis that would constitute a member as unfit for duty. Members of the military have to be mission ready at all times. A number of issues can disqualify a member from being fit, to include specific mental health issues. Thus, there may be some hesitation that could easily be labeled as resistance. Combating stigma is an important issue that needs to be understood in order to effectively work with women and/ or their family.

COUNSELING RECOMMENDATIONS

Counselors have an ethical responsibility for increasing cultural competence (ACA, 2014). Within the profession of counseling, you will en-

© BlurryMe/Shutterstock.com

counter diverse cultures which include women in the military. You must be prepared to work with these clients. The following recommendations cover a broad range of considerations to help ensure your preparation for working with these women:

- Collaborate with military mental health and medical providers and military serving community organizations to establish a network of resources (McKinzie, 2017).
- Establish childcare services or supports for childcare to minimize and/or eliminate barriers to accessing face to face counseling (Substance Abuse and Mental Health Services Administration [SAMHSA], 2015a).
- Consider insurance paneling with the military insurance provider, Tri-Care, to help ensure access to services (Myers, 2013).
- Provide gender specific or gender sensitive groups to address issues unique to the needs of women (SAMHSA, 2015b).
- Provide case management, ancillary or supportive services (SAMHSA, 2015a) pre and post deployment to reduce stress associated with deployment and transition.
- Provide telehealth, virtual or remote services to increase access (Wicklund, 2017) and minimize and/or eliminate barriers to face to face counseling.

- Establish peer to peer support networks (Cronk, 2015) for women to address issues related to deployment, changing roles, childcare, being a dual military family, reduce isolation, and assist with readjustment.
- Engage in ongoing professional development (ACA, 2014). For example, attend conferences, workshops, and utilize supervision to increase knowledge about issues related to women in the military.
- Advocate for systems (societal) level changes (ACA, 2014) specific to women in the military.
- Pursue grants that help reduce rates of homelessness (VA, n.d.) for women veterans, especially those with children.
- Contribute to research and publication to advance the topic of women veterans and mental health (Forziat et al., 2017).
- Ensure screening for trauma, including combat, and military sexual trauma in your intake assessment (Kintzle et al., 2015).
- Engage in transparent conversations with clients to learn about their distinct experience being in the military.

Lt Col Theodosia F. Hill

Nearly a month ago, divine intervention saw fit to allow me to see a female Captain out of the corner of my eye not in my chain of command on my way to the base dry cleaners on a Tuesday after 5pm. I have the honor to serve with this Captain at the clinic where I work. Normally I observe her maintaining a look of sheer confidence, strong military bearing combined with gracious humility that shines through at our daily safety huddle meetings and monthly executive committee meetings. Out of the corner of my eye I saw the Captain, but my instinct directed me to stop and ask the Captain walking out of the Air Force exchange a simple question. I asked "are you ok? You don't look like your normal self". She bravely said with tears beginning to form in her eyes, "No ma'am I'm not. I feel so discouraged". I then advised her that we should go to a more private location which was Starbucks nearly 50 feet from us. We walked into Starbucks and fortunately there were plenty of vacant seats. We took chairs near the back of the Starbucks and she went on to express to how she was struggling with understanding how she was not recognized this afternoon at the awards ceremony. She also expressed how she believed that her package was stronger than the person, a male Captain, who won. She told me that she actually saw that person's package and noticed that the other Captain took credit for a project that she actually led. As I was listening to her share her frustrations with me I realized that as a senior leader it was imperative that I encourage her to not be discouraged despite the perceived inequities. I encouraged her by telling her that in the military, even in the medical community, it is important to keep in mind that a lot of decisions are about timing. I reminded her that she had won a major award recently; therefore, the senior leaders may have the mindset that they want to encourage other Captains in the organization to be recognized. I told her that award that she earned is actually much more influential and prestigious than the award that she did not win. My discernment guided me to say, "As a woman of faith, it is important to remember that we all reap what we sow". She then expressed me how she is so grateful that she bumped into me, and how she had not even planned to visit the Air Force exchange that afternoon, but that she was so glad that she did because had she not she would have not received the encouraging word that she needed after feeling so discouraged a few days after the award ceremony. Counselors can best support and understand military women by listening and encouraging.

Contributed by Theodosia Hill. © Kendall Hunt Publishing Company.

LOOKING THROUGH THE LENS OF CHRISTIANITY: BIBLICAL INTEGRATION

Service members of the military take advantage of the same rights to religious freedoms as all Americans. It is among the highest priorities of the Department of Defense (DOD) that personnel are free to worship according to the requirements of their respective faith. More than 200 religions are recognized by the military (Winston, 2017). There are approximately 2,900 active chaplains across all branches of service operating under the Armed Forces Chaplain Board (AFCB; Bailey, 2011). The AFCB reports directly to the Secretary of Defense on moral and religious policy matters. Specific areas of focus include but are not limited to, ensuring religious freedom, maintaining Chaplain force strength levels, and ensuring the necessary resources (tools and equipment) are made available to applicable personnel (Office of the Under Secretary for Personnel Readiness, 2019). At the operational level throughout the military, Chaplains support

© rudall30/Shutterstock.com

DOD personnel by leading religious services and providing spiritual support. In addition, they are essential in "performing religious rites, conducting worship services, providing confidential counseling and advising commanders on religious, spiritual, and moral matters" (Military One Source, 2018, para. 1). Although religious accommodation is a priority, chaplains overwhelmingly "represent Christian denominations" (Harris, 2018, p. 1), likewise more service members identify as Christian than any other faith (Harris, 2018).

The United States of America supports people of faith and Christians specifically because it is important that military personnel have the resources necessary to accomplish the awesome work they are called to perform (Bailey, 2011). Faith serves as an anchor for troops both at their home duty stations and while forward deployed to a foreign land. There are a number of Scriptures which reference the importance of performing works in combination with faith in God. James 2:17 states, "So also faith by itself, if it does not have works, is dead" and James 2:24 (*New King James Bible*, 1982) states, "You see that a person is justified by works and not by faith alone". The awesome work which Christian military women perform toward the success of the mission is honorable and right. It, however, is not without a cost. Military women have unique challenges and outcomes as result of their labor. Their faith in knowing that God will never leave or forsake them in the operation of required duties strengthens their determination.

CASE STUDY

© John Gomez/Shutterstock.com

Felicia is a 37-year-old single Black woman on active duty in the Air Force. At nineteen days before her 38th birthday and six weeks shy of a permanent change in station and in preparation for command, Felicia received a breast cancer diagnosis. At the time, she was over four thousand miles away from her family which included a mother with chronic health issues and a younger brother that she helped to offset financial responsibilities. Sometimes Felicia feels conflicted about jeopardizing her career, caring for her mother, and worrying about financially supporting her college-age brother. She desires to demonstrate strength while experiencing chemotherapy induced menopause symptoms, uncertainty about fertility, and loss of hair, eyebrows, and discolored fingernails. Felicia needs emotional support and has disclosed crying daily for six weeks.

Felicia presents as mildly depressed (exhibits feelings of sadness, fatigue, diminished ability to concentrate, insomnia, and diminished interest in activities). She is experiencing occupational problems and problems related to personal circumstances.

Traditional counseling methods involving individual therapy, cancer support group, and referral for psychopharmacology are warranted. Cognitive behavioral therapy (CBT) can be utilized to raise awareness around the discrepancies that conflict her. It is appropriate to rule in or rule out depression. This may be accomplished through the use of the Beck Depression Inventory or the Patient Health Questionnaire - 9. CBT may be utilized to help reduce the symptoms of depression. However, CBT alone may not be enough. In instances such as this, it is appropriate to recommend client consultation with a physician or psychiatrist for medication assisted therapy. Establishment of rapport is necessary for therapy to be most effective. Opportunities exist to display empathy. Exploring existential themes around meaning could be used to explore strength and life.

If Felicia is a Christian and open to integrating faith in her treatment, asking her to remember the Scripture, "So do not fear, for I am with you; do not be dismayed, for I am your God. I will strengthen you and help you; I will uphold you with my righteous right hand" will remind her that she is not alone and that she can rely on God's strength (*New International Bible*, 1973/2011, Isaiah 41:10). Felicia is also struggling with the uncertainty about her career and the financial stability of her family. Assessing her trust in God and encouraging her to find solace in knowing that God has outlined her plan, so there is no need to worry. In Jeremiah, 29:11, God tells us he knows the plan he has for us. His plan is for our welfare and to give us future and hope. It appears that Felicia is having a hard time seeing a future because of her current medical diagnosis. It is also important to assess whether Felicia's church family can serve as an additional support system because she is living so far from her family. Church members may be able to fill that void.

CHAPTER SUMMARY

In this chapter, you were provided the historical milestones beginning in 1775 and proceeding all the way through to present day success. Military women have met expectations at every turn and even excelled despite the many unique challenges associated with selfless service in the United States Military. We explored the emotional and psychological mindset, military women demographics, and specific mental health concerns, providing a greater awareness of the challenges females face in the armed forces. To address the still present challenges associated with military service and existing mental health disparities, counselors must exhibit an ethical responsibility to cultural competence. Mental health professionals will experience diverse populations which include women in the military. Counselors must be attuned to the challenges faced by these women. We must be mindful to take joy and peace in the service rendered to others, as Judge Deborah did so powerfully, praying that God will bolster our faith and theirs, and strengthen resolve against adversity to encourage one another toward victory for the glory of God.

KEY TERMS

Deployment - refers to war or mission requirements where military personnel are sent to various locations to support the mission

Military Sexual Trauma (MST) - is the sexual assault or harassment that occurs while actively serving i.e., active duty, active duty training or inactive duty training (National Guard or Reservist)

SUGGESTED RESOURCES

Organizations
Military OneSource: https://www.militaryonesource.mil/
Rainn: https://www.rainn.org/
Sexual Assault Prevention and Response: https://www.sapr.mil/
TriCare: https://www.tricare.mil/
Veteran's Affairs: https://www.va.gov/

Scriptures

Fear. (1 John 4:18). 1 John tells us that God is love. His love for us is evident in others. His love is shown through us as we work with clients to help them heal and live in the freedom that he desires for us. There are a number of Scriptures that can be used in counseling and to support the work done in counseling.

Depression. Using Psalms 6:2-7, read aloud to the client or with the client to illustrate how David, a warrior experienced despair and hopelessness. Use this as an opportunity to normalize the experience of depression. Have the client to identify what they identify with from the passage. Emphasize the words of verse 9 as a means to encourage the client. See also Proverbs 12:25; Psalms 30:11

Anxiety. Using 1 Peter 5:7 as a frame of reference, have client to identify all their cares. These can be the things that cause constant concern, worry, and that they are ruminating on. After the list of cares is developed, discuss what it means to cast something. Have the client to describe how they might cast their cares daily. See also Matthew 6:25-34; Philippians 4:6-8

Career concerns. Proverbs 3:5 compels us to trust in the Lord with all of our heart. The second part of the verse encourages us to lean not unto our own understanding. Using this as context, have the client to reflect on how they may be leaning unto their own understanding. Ask the client how their leaning might be influencing their thoughts, emotions and behaviors. You might want to connect this to REBT or CBT and co-construct with the client new thoughts. See also Jeremiah 29:11; Isaiah 55:11; Philippians 1:6

Family separation and transition. In counseling we are trained to not tell clients that everything will be alright. However, Deuteronomy 31:8 reassures believers that in every situation, God has gone before us. The Scripture is comforting as it describes that no matter what we may face, God is with us. While separation and transition are undoubtedly difficult, we are not alone. This verse gives us hope and shares the heart of God. Encourage the client to pray the Scripture daily. See also Matthew 11:28; Romans 8:28

REFERENCES

American Counseling Association. (2014). *2014 ACA code of ethics.* https://www.counseling.org/knowledge-center

Ardito, R. B., & Rabellino, D. (2011). Therapeutic alliance and outcome of psychotherapy: Historical excursus, measurements, and prospects for research. *Frontiers in Psychology, 2*, 270. https://doi.org/10.3389/fpsyg.2011.00270

Bailey, S. P. (2011). *Chaplains watch and wait after DADT ends.* https://www.christianitytoday.com/ct/2011/septemberweb-only/chaplainsdadt.html

BibleGateway. (n.d.). *Judges 4, Deborah.* https://www.biblegateway.com/passage/?search=Judges+4&version=NIV

Chaumba, J., & Bride, B. E. (2010). Trauma experiences and posttraumatic stress disorder among women in the United States military. *Social Work in Mental Health, 8*(3), 280-303. http://dx.doi.org/10.1080/15332980903328557

Christinanity.com. (2019). *Who was Deborah in the Bible?* https://www.christianity.com/wiki/people/who-was-deborah-in-the-bible.html

Colonial Williamsburg Foundation. (2008). *Time line: Women in the U.S. military.* https://www.history.org/history/teaching/enewsletter/volume7/images/nov/womenmilitary_timeline.pdf

Cronk, T. M. (2015). *New peer-to-peer service aims to provide counseling support.* U.S. Department of Defense. https://www.defense.gov/Explore/News/Article/Article/604677/

Dye, J. L. (2018). *Factors that contribute to mental health in combat injured military women.* (Publication No. 10688686) [Doctoral dissertation, The University of Arizona]. ProQuest Dissertations.

Friedman, M. J., Schnurr, P. P., & McDonagh-Coyle, A. M. (1994). *Post-traumatic stress disorder in the military veteran.* https://www.ptsd.va.gov/professional/articles/article-pdf/id12012.pdf

Forziat, K. E., Arcuri, N. M., & Erb, C. (2017). Counseling the military population: The factor of prior military exposure for counselors-in-training. *The Journal of Counselor Preparation and Supervision, 10*(1), 1-36.

Ghahramanlou-Holloway, M., Tucker, J., Neely, L. L., Carreno-Ponce, J. T., Ryan, K., Holloway, K., & George, B. (2014). Suicide risk among military women. *Psychiatric Annals Thorofare, 44*(4), 189-193. https://doi.org/10.3928/00485713-20140403-06

Harris, S. (2018). *As the army grows more diverse, it faces a shortage of chaplains.* https://americanhomefront.wunc.org/post/army-grows-more-diverse-it-faces-shortage-chaplains

Hartman, A., Schuermann, H., & Kenney, J. (2018). Army soliders' trust and confidence in mental health professionals. *The Professional Counselor, 8*(3), 213-225.

Janko, E., Mongtomery, S., & Gaddes, R. (2018). *Women in operational career fields: Lessons learned from male dominated civilian industries.* Insight Policy Research. https://dacowits.defense.gov/Portals/48/Documents/General%20Documents/RFI%20Docs/Sept2018/Literature%20Review%20RFI%2013.pdf?ver=2018-09-06-225106-063

Kime, P. (2018). *Mental health disorders in troops far below national average.* https://www.military.com/daily-news/2019/09/04/mental-health-disorders-troops-far-below-national-average.html

Kimerling, R., Street, A., Pavao, J., Smith, M. W., Cronkite, R. C., Holmes, T. H., et al. (2010). Military-related sexual trauma among veterans health administration patients returning from Iraq and Afghanistan. *American Journal of Public Health*, 100(8), 1409e1412

King James Bible. (2017). King James Bible Online. https://www. kingjamesbibleonline.org/ (Original work published 1769)

Kintzle, S., Schuyler, A. C., Ray-Letourneau, D., Ozuna, S. M., Munch, C., Xintarianos, E., & Castro, C. A. (2015). Sexual trauma in the military: Exploring PTSD and mental health care utilization in female veterans. *Psychological services, 12*(4), 394.

Lakritz, T. (2019). *Then and now: How women's roles have changed in the US military.* https://www.insider.com/women-in-us-military-history-2019-2

Londono, E. (2013). *Pentagon removes ban on women in combat.* Washington Post. https://www.washingtonpost.com/world/national-security/pentagon-to-remove-ban-on-women-in-combat/2013/01/23/6cba86f6-659e-11e2-85f5-a8a9228e55e7_story.html

Lopez, C. T. (2012). *First female four-star general retires from Army.* https://www.army.mil/article/85606/first_female_four_star_general_retires_from_army

Macera, C. A., Aralis, H. J., Highfill-McCoy, R., & Rauh, M. J. (2014). Posttraumatic stress disorder after combat zone deployment among Navy and Marine Corps men and women. *Journal of Women's Health, 23*(6), 499-506.

McBratney, M. A. (2018). *Barriers to treatment for women veterans who have survived military sexual trauma seeking mental health services within the VA: A review of the literature* (Publication No. 10973523) [Doctoral dissertation, Azusa Pacific University]. ProQuest Dissertations.

McKinzie, O. (2017). Ethical considerations when counseling military clients. *Counseling Today, 60*(3), 18-20.

Meadows, S. O., Engel, C. C., Collins, R. L., Beckman, R. L., Cefalu, M., Hawes-Dawson, J., Doyle, M., Kress, A. M., Sontag-Padilla, L., Ramchand, R., & Williams, K. M. (2018). 2015 department of defense health related behaviors survey (HRBS). *Rand Health Quarterly, 8*(2), 5.

Military Health System Communications Office. (2018). *Women and Depression.* Stars and Stripes Guam. https://guam.stripes.com/community-news/women-and-depression

Military One Source. (2017). *2017 demographics: Profile of the military community.* https://download.militaryonesource.mil/12038/MOS/Reports/2017-demographics-report.pdf

Military One Source. (2018). *The unit chaplain: Roles and responsibilities.* https://www.militaryonesource.mil/family-relationships/spouse/getting-married-in-the-military/the-unit-chaplain-roles-and-responsibilities#:~:targetText=Chaplains%20are%20the%20military's%20religious,service%20members%20and%20their%20families.&targetText=Chaplains%20are%20commissioned%20officers%20stationed,military%20members%2C%20including%20combat%20environments.

Monmaney, T. (2019). *New poll of U.S. troops and veterans reveals their thoughts on current military policy.* https://www.smithsonianmag.com/arts-culture/new-poll-us-troops-veterans-reveals-thoughts-current-military-policies-180971134/

Murdoch, M., Bradley, A., Mather, S., Klein, R., Turner, C., & Yano, E. (2006). Women and war: What physicians should know. *Journal of General Internal Medicine, 21*, 5-10. https://doi.org/ 10.1111/j.1525-1497.2006.00368.x

Myers, K. (2013). *Effective treatment of military clients*. Counseling Today. https://ct.counseling.org/2013/08/effective-treatment-of-military-clients/

National Institute on Drug Abuse (2019). *Substance Use and Military Life*. https://www.drugabuse.gov/publications/drugfacts/substance-use-military-life

New International Bible. (2011). New International Bible Online. https://www.thenivbible.com/ (Original work published 1973)

Office of the Under Secretary for Personnel Readiness (2019). Armed Forces Chaplain Board.

Retrieved from https://prhome.defense.gov/M-RA/Inside-M-RA/MPP_ARCHIVE/How-We-Support/Armed-Forces-Chaplains-Board/

Psychological Health Center of Excellence. (2019). *Timeline of women in the U.S. military*. https://www.pdhealth.mil/clinical-guidance/women-s-mental-health

Ritchie, E. (2012). Issues for military women in deployment: An overview. *Military Medicine, 166*(12), 1033-1037. https://doi.org/10.1093/milmed/166.12.1033

Rosenberg, M., & Philipps, D. (2015). *All combat roles now open to women, defense secretary says*. The New York Times. https://www.nytimes.com/2015/12/04/us/politics/combat-military-women-ash-carter.html

Street, A. E., Vogt, D., & Dutra, L. (2009). A new generation of women veterans: Stressors faced by women deployed to Iraq and Afghanistan. *Clinical Psychology Review, 29*, 685-694.

Substance Abuse and Mental Health Services Administration. (2015a). *Comprehensive case management for substance abuse treatment – TIP 27*. https://store.samhsa.gov/product/TIP-27-Comprehensive-Case-Management-for-Substance-Abuse-Treatment/SMA15-4215

Substance Abuse and Mental Health Services Administration. (2015b). *Substance abuse treatment: Group therapy: A treatment improvement protocol – TIP 41*. https://store.samhsa.gov/sites/default/files/d7/priv/sma15-3991.pdf

Suzuki, M., & Kawakami, A. (2016). U.S. military service members' reintegration, culture, and spiritual development. *The Qualitative Report, 21*(11), 2059-2075.

Title 38 USC 1720D. (2012). *Counseling and treatment for sexual trauma. U.S.C. Title 38 - VETERANS' BENEFITS* https://www.govinfo.gov/content/pkg/USCODE-2011-title38/html/USCODE-2011-title38-partII-chap17-subchapII-sec1720D.htm

The Soldiers Project. (2019). *Female veterans and PTSD*. https://www.thesoldiersproject.org/female-veterans-ptsd/

The Women's Memorial. (2019). *Highlights in the history of military women*. https://www.womensmemorial.org/timeline

Ursano, R. J., Colpe, L. J., Heeringa, S. G., Kessler, R. C., Schoenbaum, M., Stein, M. B., & Army STARRS Collaborators. (2014). The Army study to assess risk and resilience in servicemembers (Army STARRS). *Psychiatry: Interpersonal and Biological Processes, 77*(2), 107–119. https://doi.org/10.1521/psyc.2014.77.2.107

VA. (n.d.). *Giving homeless veterans a helping hand*. https://va.org/giving-homeless-veterans-a-helping-hand/

Wicklund, E. (2017). *New telehealth platform offers grief counseling to military survivors*. Telehealth News. https://mhealthintelligence.com/news/new-telehealth-platform-offers-grief-counseling-to-military-survivors

White, K. L., Harris, J. A., Bryan, A. O., Reynolds, M., & Fuessel-Herrmann, D. (2018). Military sexual trauma and suicidal behavior among National Guard personnel. *Comprehensive Psychiatry, 87*, 1-6. https://doi.org/10.1016/j.comppsych.2018.08.008

Williamson, A. (2019). *Ann Dunwoody four-star general, US army*. http://www.quota
belle.com/author/ann-dunwoody

Williams, L. (2015). *Women veterans' perceptions of mental health outpatient services* (Publication No. 3704072) [Doctoral dissertation, University of California]. ProQuest Dissertations.

Winston, K. (2017). *Defense department expands its list of recognized religions*. https://religionnews.com/2017/04/21/defense-department-expands-its-list-of-recognized-religions/

Wooten, N. R. (2009). *Deployment risk and resilience among global war on terrorism army national guard women veterans: Biopsychosocial and mental health outcomes* (Publication No. 33846380 [Doctoral dissertation, University of Maryland]. ProQuest Dissertations.

Yehuda, R. (2002). Post-traumatic stress disorder. *New England Journal of Medicine, 346*(2), 108-114.

CHAPTER 4
Mental Health and the Female Brain

Edward John Kuhnley, M.D. with Anita Knight Kuhnley, Ph.D.

"When a woman understands the uniqueness of the female brain—how to care for it, how to make the most of its strengths, how to overcome its challenges, how to fall in love with it, and ultimately, how to unleash its full power—there is no stopping her."
~Daniel Amen

"Do not conform to the pattern of this world, but be transformed by the renewing of your mind. Then you will be able to test and approve what God's will is--his good, pleasing and perfect will." (Romans 12:2, NIV)

Wisdom from Above: Standing in His Grace

© fizkes/Shutterstock.com

In Isaiah 26 (*New King James Bible*, 1982) we learn, "You will keep him in perfect peace, whose mind is stayed on You, because he trusts in You." Anyone at times may be distracted, lose focus, and experience a wandering of the mind. Many mental health conditions, including depression, anxiety, and Attention-Deficit/Hyperactivity Disorder (ADHD), cause people to experience distraction. This often results in daily and life-long struggles. Counseling and other treatments support the renewing of the mind with healthy cognitive and lifestyle skills. The Bible provides guidance in Romans 12:2 (*English Standard Bible*, 2001) where we learn, "Do not be conformed to this world, but be transformed by the renewal of your mind, that by testing you may discern what is the will of God, what is good and acceptable and perfect." God created us with a beautiful

brain from which springs our minds. You may have heard the term *neuroplasticity*. Plasticity is the ability of the brain to adapt and develop new neurons and neuronal connections throughout life. Science supports the command in the book of Romans, demonstrating that we have the power to renew our minds as we grow, learn, and adapt. This engenders hope, and the instillation of hope is an important therapeutic factor for counselors to utilize in clinical work.

CHAPTER LEARNING OBJECTIVES

Upon completing this chapter, you should be able to:

- Distinguish the different parts of the brain and identify their functions
- Scrutinize literature relevant to the concept of the Female Brain
- Discover the importance of nature and nurture on the development and function of the brain
- Identify the involvement of brain function on a sample of mental illnesses

CHAPTER OVERVIEW

The concept of **The Female Brain** is controversial. While there is abundant literature, there is little consensus. Recent scientists provide compelling evidence that debunks many of the previous established scientific beliefs that the female brain is different from and inferior to the male brain. In this chapter, we will review general aspects about the brain, a sampling of literature regarding differences between the brains of females and males, and a sampling of mental health issues and treatments for women relevant to brain function. Numerous conditions affect the nervous system including traumatic brain injuries, cerebrovascular accidents (strokes and aneurysms), brain tumors, neurodegenerative disorders (dementia), and mental illnesses. Manifestations vary based on the location of impact within the brain and the functions of that area of the brain. Understanding the nervous system and its functions may contribute to a differential diagnosis and specific treatment planning. Treatments target various aspects of the nervous system.

Neuroscience concepts guide lifestyle intervention measures for general health and well-being as well as treatments targeting mental health conditions. A foundational concept is that the nervous system, particularly the brain, is plastic (adaptable) and changes based on life experiences. Dr. Daniel Amen is a board certified psychiatrist and the founder of The Amen Clinics who has pioneered the use of Single-Photon Emission Computed Tomography (SPECT), a type of imaging that allows him to view the activity in the brains of his patients. After reviewing 83,000 brain scans, one of his central messages is the idea that you are not stuck with the brain that you have today. Your brain is adaptive, and you can make changes that improve the health of your brain. The idea that the brain is plastic can bring hope to counselors that we can make a difference and to clients that there is hope for change (TED, 2013). Likewise, life experiences cause changes that may result in improved health or in mental illness. Counselors harness this concept to provide interventions to improve health and overcome or ameliorate mental illness. Counselors have a crucial role in treatment relevant to brain function.

DEFINING THE BRAIN

The Brain is a powerful 3-pound organ. It is soft and squishy with a gel-like consistency. Some authors describe the brain as having the consistency of soft warm butter (Amen, 2013; Potter-Efron, 2012), and this butter-like organ is housed in a very hard skull. It includes masses of neurons (nerve cells) which interconnect with themselves and the body. Using advanced counting techniques, Azevedo et al. (2009) estimated there are 86 billion neurons and 85 billion non-neuronal cells. The distribution of neurons creates various parts of the brain, which have specific and overlapping functions. The brain monitors sensory input; processes, integrates, and coordinates input; stores memory; and determines action. It is involved in most of the functions or activities of the body (Amen, 2013). The three main parts of the brain include the cerebrum, the brainstem, and the cerebellum.

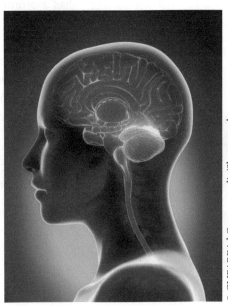

© CLIPAREA l Custom media/Shutterstock.com

The Cerebrum

The **cerebrum** is the largest part of the human brain. "The cerebrum is the crown jewel of creation and evolution. It is a remarkably delicate, intricate, and beautiful structure" (Rhoton, 2007, p. SHC-37). Neuronal cell bodies comprise the grey matter in the brain's outer layer known as the **cerebral cortex**. Understanding how the cortex is organized is still a focus of neuroscience (Shaw et al., 2008), and what we know about the organization of the cortex comes mostly from the analysis of postmortem tissue (Shaw et al., 2008). The cerebral cortex has two hemispheres (right and left). Each hemisphere has four lobes (the frontal lobe, temporal lobe, parietal lobe, and occipital lobe). Neuronal axons or fibers comprise the white matter of the brain. They cross at the **corpus callosum** to provide communication between the hemispheres. This creates laterality. The right side of the brain controls the left side of the body and vice versa. The brain works in an integrated manner with many parts contributing to a particular function or action, but each part of the brain may be predominant in some functions or actions.

The Frontal Lobe

The **frontal lobe** controls cognitive skills. The prefrontal cortex (PFC) has a prominent role in executive function (EF). You can think of this region of the brain as the executive command center of the brain. Functions include attention, reasoning, problem solving, planning, organizing, language and communication, memory, judgment, impulse control, social and sexual behaviors, and personality. Counselors will encounter clients with impairments in EF. Nigg et al. (2017) refer to EF as "top-down, goal directed cognitive processing" (p. 3) which starts with our thoughts (what

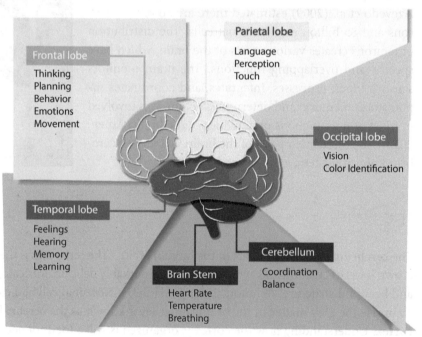

Modified from © Atthapon Raksthaput/Shutterstock.com

we already know) and flows down to our actions or senses. They note psychopathology involving impulse control, problem solving, and emotional regulation in conditions including attention-deficit/hyperactivity disorder (ADHD), depression, anxiety, schizophrenia, learning disorders, and substance use disorders. These challenges in functioning are sometimes referred to as *bottom up* processing (Sibcy & Knight, 2011) where the regions associated with the brain stem and fight or flight responses are activated first (see Chapter 13 for more information).

The Temporal Lobe

The **temporal lobe** is particularly important for counselors because this part of the brain is responsible for listening. The temporal lobe processes sensory input and breaks it down into meaningful bite size pieces that the brain can digest in the form of words, phrases, and other meaningful units. It is the primary auditory cortex. It receives sound input and processes sounds for comprehension including language comprehension. The temporal lobe also places this information in context with other information. It processes visual input for object recognition and meaning. It interprets the emotions and reactions of others. The **hippocampus** is a small organ located in the middle of the temporal lobe. It processes new memory and long-term memory. It is also a major part of the limbic system. It plays a role in learning and emotions. Some researchers using MRI (Magnetic Resonance Imaging) technology have indicated that depression impacts the hippocampus (Sheline et al., 2002). Specifically, in depression, the hippocampus shrinks, and some reports indicate a loss in volume of up to 20% (Sapolsky, 2001). An interesting fact is that some researchers (Teixeira-Machado et al., 2019) have found that ballroom dance can increase hippocampal volume and lead to other positive changes in the brain, including increased neuroplasticity. They screened over one thousand studies, conducted a meta-analysis on eight studies, and concluded, "Based on the evidence, dance practice integrates brain areas to improve neuroplasticity" (Teixeira-Machado et al., 2019, p. 232).

The Parietal Lobe

The parietal lobe processes sensory input for taste, temperature and touch. It is involved in proprioception (spatial sense and navigation). Researchers discovered *proprioception* while studying the senses by which the blind could perceive their environments Charles Sherrington coined the term

This photo shows a group of people learning to dance a form of ballroom dance. Research evidence supports activities such as these may increase the volume of the hippocampus and serve an anti-depressant function.

proprioception, or "perception of one's own" in the year 1906 (Smetacek & Mechsner, 2004, p. 432). Sherrington referred to proprioception, this function of the parietal lobe, as our own *sixth sense*. Input relays through the thalamus (a relay center for sensory and motor information involved in consciousness, alertness and sleep) to the parietal lobe. Some students find it easier to remember that the parietal lobe deals with perception, due to the alliteration of the two words.

The Occipital Lobe

The **occipital lobe** is the visual processing center. It is involved in color recognition, visuospatial processing, motion perception, and reading. Out of the four lobes (frontal, temporal, parietal, and occipital), the occipital lobe is the smallest lobe (Kennedy et al., 1998). Some may find it surprising that even though it processes vision, it is in the posterior region of the brain, under the occipital bone

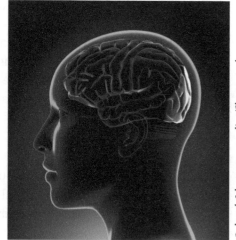

(rather than right behind the eyes). Considering the location of the occipital lobe, the colloquial expression, "Mom has eyes in the back of her head" makes sense. Disruption of connection between the frontal cortex, occipital cortex, and limbic system occurs in social anxiety (Ding et al., 2011). Chang et al. (2020) report findings suggesting that a delay in maturation in the occipital lobe and other posterior brain areas may indicate a possible mechanism for development of the inattentive subtype of ADHD in girls.

The Brain Stem

The **brain stem** is the first region of the brain to develop and controls flow of information between the brain and the rest of the body. It includes the midbrain, the pons, reticular formation, tegmentum and the medulla oblongata. It regulates basic body functions including breathing, heart rate, blood pressure, swallowing, consciousness and wakefulness.

The **limbic system** includes the amygdala (which means almond), the hippocampus (from the Greek hippos for horse and kampos for sea monster), the cingulate gyrus, and mammillary bodies. It is involved in memory, learning, and emotions. Paul Broca (1878), a French neurologist whose name is engraved on the Eiffel Tower in Paris among 72 other scientists, engineers, and mathematicians (Pessoa & Hof, 2015), described "le grand lobe limbique" (p. 2495). Braun (2011) notes that limbic comes from the Latin word limbus (circle) and identifies James Papez as studying involvement with sub-regions of the prefrontal cortex and naming the system the Papez Circuit, followed by Paul McLean who called the functional pathway the limbic system. She notes that facial expression interpretation and dangerous situation evaluation involve areas including the amygdala and prefrontal cortex in determining the fight-flight response. Dysfunction of the limbic system produce conditions including posttraumatic stress disorder, depression, and attention deficit-hyperactivity disorder.

Attachment and the Brain
The hypothalamus plays a role in attachment behaviors (Insel, 1997), and researchers have uncovered interesting neurological patterns associated with attachment responses. For example, based on MRI studies and other research securely attached mothers may experience a pleasure response when they hear their babies cry. Why would they experience pleasure when they hear their infants cry? Perhaps because they are anticipating soothing and caring for their children (Petchtel, 2013) and the reward or oxytocin release associated with the caregiving system. However, those without a secure attachment may experience a very different response. To learn more about how to help clients move toward a secure attachment see *Redeeming Attachment* (2017) by Gary Sibcy and Anita Knight.

The **basal ganglia** include the globus pallidus, caudate nucleus, sub-thalamic nucleus, pallidum, putamen, and substantia nigra. Among numerous functions, they serve to facilitate and coordinate movement and motor learning. The basal ganglia are among the main regions in the brain with sex steroid receptors, and they play a major role in cognitive function (Rijpkema et al., 2011). Gender differences may explain differences in behavior and neuropsychiatric disorders such as ADHD and depression.

The Cerebellum

The **cerebellum** is in the back of the brain. It provides for maintaining balance, and for coordinating eye movements, posture, and smooth body movement. The word *cerebellum* is Latin for *little brain* (Highnam & Bleile, 2011). The **diencephalon** is part of the forebrain. It includes the thalamus, hypothalamus, epithalamus and subthalamus. The **thalamus** is involved in consciousness, sleep and alertness. It is a relay station for all sensory input except olfaction (smell). The **hypothalamus** contains several nuclei and is part of the limbic system. It regulates certain metabolic processes within the autonomic nervous system. It participates in body temperature regulation, sleep, hunger and circadian rhythms (a 24-hour cycle of physiological processes). It plays a role in parenting and attachment behaviors (Insel, 1997). It secretes and releases neuro-hormones involved as releasing factors for stimulation or inhibition of hormones from the pituitary gland for regu-

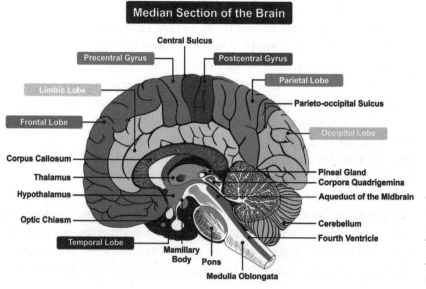

lating other hormones and their activities. The **epithalamus** connects the limbic system to other parts of the brain. It includes the pineal gland and is involved in melatonin secretion and circadian rhythms. The **subthalamus** is one of the major motor regulators related to the basal ganglia.

BRAIN DEVELOPMENT

Numerous factors affect brain development and function including nature (genetics) and nurture (environment). Neural plasticity refers to the phenomenon of change in the form, function, and response of a neuron within a neural circuit. A neural circuit is a population or ensemble of neurons interconnected by synapses that, when activated, perform a function (Purves, 2011, p. 507). Huttenlocher (2002) discusses neural plasticity and the effects of environment on the development of the cerebral cortex over the lifetime. He addresses both positive and negative effects. Stiles (2011) posits that it is "the interaction of genetic factors and the experience of the individual that guides and supports brain development" (p. 3). Nature and nurture intertwine in the life trajectory of an individual. Genetics provides a template and experience alters genetics and its expression over time to shape development including the brain. Biological factors include nutrition, hormones, genetic influences, gene mutation, brain chemistry, and gender.

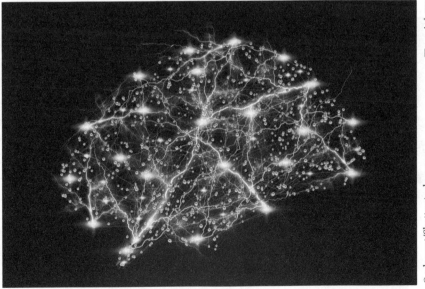

© sdecoret/Shutterstock.com

FIGURE 4.1

This diagram illustrates neural circuits.

Psychosocial factors include life experiences, social interactions, temperament, and culture. Neuroplasticity may be beneficial or harmful. Numerous studies demonstrate that factors may be toxic or protective to the brain. For example, Lipina and Colombo (2009) demonstrated the negative impact of poverty on brain development and patterns of brain activity during childhood. Sheridan et al. (2012) studied the toxic impact of extreme environmental deprivation on brain white matter growth in Romanian orphans and the reversal possible when individuals moved to healthier environments. Arnetz et al. (2020) noted "Persons with trauma-induced disorders have heightened neuro-plastic restructuring of limbic brain circuits (e.g., amygdala and hippocampus), which are critical factors in the pathophysiology of PTSD" (p. 1).

Identification and treatment of toxic effects is a valuable role, which counselors may fulfill for clients. Counselors may assist clients in improving brain function to overcome past adversity and to enhance current function. Counseling techniques and lifestyle measures are effective. For example, Bingaman (2013) notes that "the revolutionary discoveries concerning neuroplasticity challenge the field of pastoral care and counseling to recognize the ability of contemplative-meditational practices to reduce anxiety and to produce long-term, possibly permanent changes in the neural pathways of the human brain" (p. 549).

Gender Differences

© Bonnie Taylor Barry/Shutterstock.com

Sexual dimorphism refers to gender differences between members of the same species. This phenomenon is not limited to humans, but applies to other members of the animal kingdom. For example, the male cardinal has red plumage while the female cardinal has grayish-brown plumage. A number of studies have examined differences between the brains of human males and females. For example, Dekaban and Sadowsky (1978) determined that the weight of the male brain is 9.8% greater than the weight of the male brain is 9.8% greater than the weight of the female brain. Kulynych et al. (1994) reported gender differences in the planum temporale, a region of auditory association cortex. In a study of structural differences in the cerebral cortex of healthy female and male subjects using magnetic resonance imaging (MRI), Schlaepfer et al. (1995) described sexually dimorphic structural differences in the cerebral cortex. They reported that women had "greater gray matter percentages (corrected for overall brain size and age) than men in a language-related cortical region, but not in a more visuospatially related cortical region" (p. 129). Meanwhile, Rabinowicz et al. (1999) indicate that "though human brains lack sexual dimorphism on routine neuro-pathologic examinations, gender-specific brain weight, functional, and morphologic differences exist" (p. 98). Conflicting results as well as differing opinions regarding causation produce debate as to whether there is a true difference in the brains of women and men, as opposed to a differential in development (including the brain) of each individual over a lifetime (Rippon, 2019).

> Cerebral asymmetry refers to differences between the right and left hemisphere of the cerebrum. Differences occur in neuroanatomy and function producing lateralization, which is the tendency for some brain functions to predominate on one side of the brain or the other (Halpern, 2005).

Hormones and the Brain

Hormones have a significant impact on brain development and function and produce patterns of sexual dimorphism and cerebral asymmetries (refers to differences between the right and left hemisphere of the cerebrum. Differences occur in neuroanatomy and function producing lateralization). "Functional cerebral asymmetries (FCAs) refer to the relative differences between the left and the right hemispheres in some neural functions and cognitive processes" (Hausman, 2016, p. 40). Using magnetic resonance imaging, Gilmore et al. (2007) demonstrated that this begins before birth and continues after birth. They suggested that "adult patterns of cerebral asymmetry are the result of ongoing neurodevelopmental processes active after birth, driven by genetic programming as well by experience" (p. 1259). Savic et al. (2017) studied the role of testosterone and Y chromosome genes for the masculinization of the human brain. They concluded that "testosterone has selective, regional effects on cerebral sex dimorphism" (p. 1811). Bao and Swaab (2010) concluded, "The fetal brain develops in the male direction due to a direct effect of

A doctor turns on a Magnetic resonance imaging machine with a patient inside. FMRI detects dynamic patterns of brain activity based on the magnetic properties of deoxyhemoglobin as neural activity increases as blood flow increases more than oxygen metabolism (Buxton, 2013).

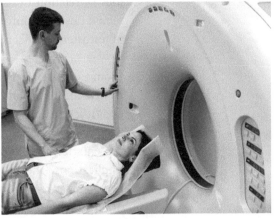

© Garnet Photo/Shutterstock.com

testosterone on the developing neurons, or in the female direction due to the absence of such a testosterone surge" (p. 223). They indicate that differences in the brain affect behaviors and risk for neuropsychiatric disorders. For example, women are more likely to have depression, anxiety disorder, dementia, PTSD and eating disorders, while men are more likely to have autism, attention–deficit/hyperactivity disorder, schizophrenia, and substance abuse. Filová et al. (2013) discussed the effect of testosterone on certain areas of the brain involved in learning and memory including the hippocampus, amygdala, cerebellum, frontal cortex, and midbrain in both males and females. They note the effects do not depend so much on the gender of the individual but more so on the time-period of exposure of the brain to the hormone. Amen (2013) cited literature on the effect of testosterone on the female brain and noted that higher testosterone results in lower eye contact and empathy. The amount of testosterone for males and females at different stages in life determines a positive or negative effect. For a detailed discussion on caring for the female brain, see Dr. Daniel Amen's (2013) book, *Unleash the Power of the Female Brain: Supercharging Yours for Better Health, Energy, Mood, Focus and Sex.*

Hausmann (2016) presented a review of relevant literature and indicated that both biological sex and sex hormones affect functional cerebral asymmetries, which depend upon hormones with dynamic change throughout life. Mitsui et al. (2019) indicated that "prenatal sex hormone exposure may influence the dimorphic brain development and behavior in school-aged girls" (p. 140). In a review of the effects of testosterone on brain behavioral functions, Celec et al. (2015) reported that studies produce controversial and puzzling results. They conclude that "While fMRI results bring interesting data and knowledge on behavioral traits and spatial abilities in relation to testosterone levels and sex differences, the result obtained can show only association or correlation but not causal relationship of testosterone effect on behavior" (p. 13).

From a counseling perspective, it is important to know that many factors, from conception and throughout life, contribute to brain development and function and to illnesses stemming from impairments in brain function. Awareness and knowledge enable a counselor to listen to a client's presentation and consider neurological, biological, social and spiritual implications. The counselor may guide the client in various measures to overcome adverse contributing factors, seek evaluations for identification of targets for treatment, and engage in measures to achieve healthy brain function. Although this is true regardless of whether the client is female or male, there are differences within individuals and relating to gender.

The Female Brain

Is there a *female brain* that is different from a *male brain*? Centuries of research and discussion reveal a predominant view that the brains of women are different from the brains of men. Historically, there are thousands of studies that look at variations in size and function of various areas of the brain, and many interpret the findings to explain the prevailing behaviors of women and men. Until recently, challenges to this notion have been minimal. Rippon (2019) reviewed the literature noting flaws in methodology and conclusions of previous studies, signifying a complex, confusing, and controversial universe of information.

Navigation of the sea of scientific literature on the topic of gender differences is a challenge. The nature versus nurture debate is active. Does genetics dictate female versus male brain development and thus impact gender specific behavior? Do hormones in utero determine brain gender trajectory? Does the environment impact the plasticity of the brain and influence its development in specific directions? The consensus establishes both as influential but variance in opinions occurs in the degree, manner or timing of each influence.

Hyde's (2005) review of 46 meta-analyses of research on gender differences supported the **gender similarities hypothesis**, "which holds that males and females are similar on most, but not all, psychological variables. That is, men and women, as well as boys and girls, are more alike than they are different" (p. 581). In *Gender Similarities and Differences*, she summarizes:

> Domains in which gender differences are small (around d = 0.20) or trivial (d ≤ 0.10) include mathematics performance, verbal skills, some personality dimensions such as gregariousness and conscientiousness, reward sensitivity, the temperament dimension of negative affectivity, relational aggression, tentative speech, some aspects of sexuality (e.g., oral sex experience, attitudes about extramarital sex, attitudes about masturbation), leadership effectiveness, self-esteem, and academic self-concept. Nonetheless, the gender similarities hypothesis

acknowledges exceptions to the general rule. Exceptions to gender similarities, where differences are moderate (d = 0.50) or large (d = 0.80), include 3D mental rotation, the personality dimension of agreeableness/tender-mindedness, sensation seeking, interests in things versus people, physical aggression, some sexual behaviors (masturbation and pornography use), and attitudes about casual sex. (Hyde, 2014, p. 392)

The Female Brain (Brizendine, 2009) and *The Male Brain* (Brizendine, 2011) offered insight into neurobiology and hormones (estrogen, progesterone, testosterone, oxytocin) with impact on female and male brain structure and function, as well as psychological manifestations. She identified differences in the amygdala, hypothalamus, and prefrontal cortex having impact on hormonal regulation and provided explanations for differential behavior of men and women, attributing some of the differences to reproduction, hormones, and puberty.

On her Facebook page, Brizendine refers to a *Science of Success* podcast in which she noted, "The male and female brain are more alike than they are different – but they do have differences" (Dr. Louann Brizendine, 2019). The question is how much of the difference is innate and how much is learned. Her book inspired the movie, *The Female Brain*, released in 2018.

Hines (2005) explored the biological differences between sex and gender. She cautioned that research tends to look at variables and make unsupported assumptions. There are so many factors involved in development that it is unwise to view a structural or behavioral characteristic as indicating a gender difference.

Rippon (2019) reviewed the history of gender and the brain. In a publication called *The Gendered Brain: The New Neuroscience that Shatters the Myth of the Female Brain,* Rippon noted that nature and nurture are entangled. Social expectations alongside how we live our lives create changes in the plastic brain throughout life. She acknowledged gender differences but noted sometimes biology drives development and sometimes development drives biology. She reported that findings of difference receive attention as they reinforce long-standing beliefs of the difference but cautioned regarding the tendency toward confirmation bias. Everybody is unique.

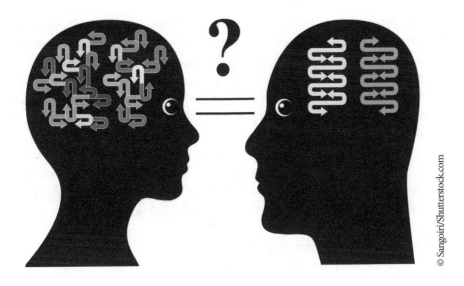

© Sangoiri/Shutterstock.com

Baron-Cohen (2003) describes the female brain as inclined for empathy. He describes the male brain as predominantly inclined for understanding and building systems. In response to Rippon, Baron-Cohen (2019) emphasized that both biology and culture are important in the formation of the brain.

Svedholm-Häkkinen et al. (2018) discussed the Empathizing-Systemizing theory and noted that "the reason for all gender differences lies in the relative weights of two cognitive processes: women empathize more, which is useful in understanding people, while men systemize more, which means interpreting phenomena as rule-based systems" (p. 7). Their study demonstrated that there are men with a female type of brain and women with a male type of brain. They emphasized cognitive type rather than biological sex as a more powerful predictor of the characteristics of a person.

Eliot (2019) conducted research on brain and gender development. From a lifespan perspective, she addressed the role of neuroplasticity in shaping neural circuitry and behavior; innate biology; sociocultural influences; and the life experience of the individual. She wrote, "The hunt for differences between men's and women's brains is full of poor research practice" (Eliot, 2019, p. 453). She added, "The brain is no more gendered than the liver or kidneys or heart" (Eliot, 2019, p. 453). She addressed *social gender learning* as a determinant of differences in males and females, in which society and individuals within society treat males and females differently with a major influence on their development.

The debate continues. Is there a female brain and a male brain? Are structural differences significant and do they amount to functional differences? One answer appears to be that the brains of females and males are alike, but differences occur in indivduals as everyone is unique—no two brains are exactly alike. Each cell is unique and changes over time by internal mutations. Rohrback et al. (2018) noted that the neurons of an individual may experience changes in the actual DNA nucleotide sequences that are divergent from the original cells "and almost certainly contribute to the remarkably diverse phenotypes of single brain cells," (p. 1026). This "may underlie fundamental brain activities including complex behaviors and long term memory" (Rohrback et al., 2018, p. 1041).

Refer to the infographic at https://www.developinghumanbrain.org/brain-structure/ as you read the following discussion.

A consistent finding of differences between the brains of males and females is size – the brains of males tend to be 8-10% larger. Recent literature indicates this has no functional significance. It does not relate to intelligence, executive function, or any other aspect of brain function. Rippon (2019) noted that males on average are larger than females and so are their organs, including the brain. Wierenga et al. (2019) suggested that sex differences in executive function were unrelated to biological development, but rather to the experiences and strategies of an individual.

Numerous studies suggest that males have six times more grey matter (neuronal cell bodies) than females. Females have nearly ten times more white matter (bundles that connect grey matter areas). This is thought to account for men being very task-focused and women being better at multitasking. Kurth et al. (2018) investigated differential contributions of sex and brain size to gray matter asymmetry. They indicated, "Brain size may produce sex differences that do not truly reflect a sex specific characteristic, but rather a size-specific characteristic" (p. 239).

In the largest single-sample study of structural, diffusion, and functional MRI measures, Ritchie et al. (2018) reported "neuroanatomical sex differences in brain volume, surface area, cortical thickness, white matter microstructure, and functional connectivity between adult males and females in the range between middle- and older-age" (p. 2971). Zhang et al. (2018) reported, "Gender can be reliably predicted using rfMRI data and highlights the importance of controlling for gender in brain imaging studies" (p. 1765).

Using magnetic resonance imaging, Goldstein et al. (2001) demonstrated that "there was a significantly greater magnitude of adult sexual dimorphism among the group of brain areas with developmentally high levels of sex steroid hormone receptors than among the other regions" (p. 492). She noted that women have larger brain volume in the frontal and medial paralimbic cortices, while men had larger volumes in the frontomedial cortex, the amygdala and hypothalamus.

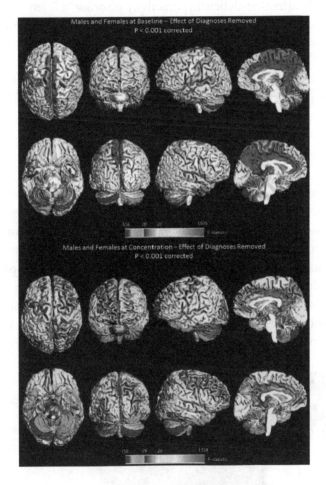

FIGURE 4.2

Republished with permission of IOS Press B.V. provided by Copyright Clearance Center, from "Gender-Based Cerebral Perfusion Differences in 46,034 Functional Neuroimaging Scans," Amen et al., 60(2):605-614, 2017; permission conveyed through Copyright Clearance Center, Inc.

Amen et al. (2017) used single-photon emission computerized tomography (SPECT) to study gender-based cerebral blood flow differences. In 46,034 scans of both clinical and healthy men and women, they demonstrated significant gender differences which they noted "lays a foundation for understanding the neurophysiological basis of differential gender risk for psychiatric and neurodegenerative disease" (p. 8) (see Figure 4.2).

In summary, males and females appear to have brains that are more similar than they are different. The brain of each individual is unique. Nature and nurture intertwine and exert impact over a lifetime. To define a brain as female or male appears insignificant in terms of any individual. However, differences, whether the result of nature or nurture, may provide some understanding of the differential frequency between genders of some illnesses, and this may guide research on treatment options. These illnesses include attention-deficit/hyperactivity disorder, anxiety disorders and depression, posttraumatic stress disorder, schizophrenia, autism, Alzheimer's disease and many others (Cahill, 2006).

MENTAL HEALTH AND THE FEMALE BRAIN

Depression and Anxiety Disorder and the Brain

When counseling women with depression or anxiety disorders, it is helpful for counselors to have knowledge of the brain. This knowledge may guide the counselor's choice of interventions for these common mental health conditions. In addition, family history may provide important information. Pagliaccio et al. (2019) report that children of parents with major depression are two to three times more likely than children of parents without history of major depression to have symptoms of major depression themselves. They documented smaller **putamen** volume (the putamen is a structure at the base of the forebrain that is involved in sever-

al functions but is especially implicated in motor behaviors and autonomic behaviors) in children, with potential impact on affect reward learning processes, resulting in an increased risk for major depressive disorder. A counselor may have a client who has children who are at risk or who are experiencing a current major depression. This provides an opportunity for identification and early intervention, which would benefit both the child and the mother.

The American Psychiatric Association's (2013) *Diagnostic and Statistical Manual of Mental Disorders* (5th ed.; *DSM-5*) reports a twelve-month prevalence of 7% for major depressive disorder in the United States with the rate in females being 1.5- to 3-fold higher than males. The ratio of female to males with anxiety disorders is two to one. The *DSM-5* cites 12-month prevalence rates of 7% for social anxiety disorder, 7% for phobia, 2-3% for panic disorder, 11% for panic attacks, 1.7% for agoraphobia and 2.9% for generalized anxiety disorder.

Brain-Based Evaluation and Treatment in Anxiety and Depression

In clients with major depression, disruption in functional brain networks contribute to disturbances in mood and cognition (Zhang et al., 2011). Rappaport et al. (2020) indicated depression as correlated with and predicted by dysfunction or hypo-reactivity in the brain reward system, which involves areas that include the nucleus accumbens, putamen, caudate, insula and anterior cingulate cortex. The reward system includes motivation, learning, and pleasant emotions.

Serotonin, norepinephrine, and dopamine are neurotransmitters that regulate physiological functions including mood, sleep, appetite, aggression, and sexual behavior. Dysfunction of the neurotransmitter systems contributes to symptoms of mental illnesses including depression and anxiety. A study by Nishizawa et al. (1997) noted that the serotonin synthesis rate was 52% higher in males than females and indicated this may relate to the lower incidence of major depression in males.

While brain and body systems impact brain and body functions and manifest as illnesses, many factors, including culture and socialization, impact brain development and function. In an extensive review of the literature on gender differences in fear and anxiety, McLean and Anderson (2009) concluded, gender differences at each level of analysis are likely moderated by socialization processes that prescribe gender-specific expectations regarding the expression of anxiety and the acceptable means of coping with anxiety. These socialization factors influence expression of traits by shaping patterns of reinforcement that cultivate and promote processes related to anxiety. (p. 503)

The hypothalamus in the brain interacts with the nearby pituitary gland to produce factors which stimulate glands (including the adrenal glands located above the kidneys) to regulate body functions. The hypothalamic-pituitary-adrenal axis (HPA axis) is the major stress response system known as fight-or-flight. Taylor et al. (2000) noted that the fight-or-flight response to stress is typical in females and males, but they proposed that women might also respond with "tend and-befriend", a more social, nurturing process. They offered neuroendocrine evidence suggesting involvement of estrogen, endogenous opioid mechanisms, and oxytocin, a neuropeptide hormone produced in the hypothalamus and released in the pituitary gland.

Oxytocin is known as the *cuddle hormone* or the *love hormone*. It is involved in reproduction and social bonding.

Oxytocin plays a role in social bonding. They suggested that, under stress, women tend to seek social groups to reduce vulnerability. The aggression in fight-or-flight may involve activation by testosterone, whereas "sympathetic and HPA responses may be downregulated by oxytocin under stressful circumstances and that oxytocin, coupled with endogenous opioid mechanisms and other sex-linked hormones, may foster maternal and affiliative behavior in response to stress" (Taylor et al., 2000, p. 422).

In addition, Quintana et al. (2019) conducted fMRI meta-analysis to reveal oxytocin-pathway gene maps, which correspond with processing of anticipation, appetite, and aversive cognition.

Martin et al. (2010) noted, "A primary alteration in brain structure or function or in neurotransmitter signaling may result from environmental experiences and underlying genetic predisposition; such alterations can increase the risk for psychopathology" (p. 550). This applies to depression and anxiety disorders. Many areas of the brain are known to be involved in depression, most notably the amygdala, hippocampus, and thalamus, along with connections to the cerebral cortex, especially the prefrontal cortex. The areas of the brain that influence symptoms of anxiety include the amygdala and the hippocampus, both part of the limbic system. The amygdala plays an important role in controlling fears and the hippocampus has a role in controlling memories.

Dusi et al. (2015) reviewed literature on brain volume reductions in the hippocampus, putamen, caudate, anterior cingulate, amygdala and frontal cortical regions, which correlate with cognitive and emotional processes implicated with symptoms of depression including hopelessness, guilt, despair and heightened response to

Neurogenesis is the development of new nerve cells.

negative emotions. They noted, "Alterations in hypothalamus, locus coeruleus and periaqueductal grey matter may be involved in neuro-vegetative and neuroendocrine alterations, such as sleep and appetite disturbances, loss of weight, psychomotor retardation or agitation" (p. 458). They discussed antidepressant treatment as having possible neuroprotective effects, meaning medications produce changes in the nerve cells that result in improved function and reduced chance of damage. They also discussed neuro-modulatory effects, meaning the impact of medications on how neurons communicate with each other. They included discussion of the enhancement of brain derived neurotrophic factor (BDNF), a compound produced in the brain to generate new neurons (neurogenesis).

Kim et al. (2015) determined that the prefrontal cortex, the amygdala, and the hippocampus (involved in memory and learning) are highly susceptible to stress. The hypothalamic-pituitary-adrenal (HPA) axis is well known for involvement in the stress response (fight, flight, or freeze). Prolonged stress produces changes in these areas of the brain and in their function.

Neuromodulation is a process by which neurons use chemicals to regulate other neurons.
Neuroprotection refers to the preservation of the structure and function of neurons.

Counselors may assist clients in the reduction and management of stress to reduce impact upon the brain. Relaxation techniques, meditation, and breathing exercises can be helpful. Dodich et al. (2018) reported that brief meditation training impacted brain regions involved in self-control, attention, and self-awareness.

Using MRI scanning, Sheline et al. (1996) observed hippocampal atrophy (a wasting away resulting from a reduction in size and number of cells) in women with recurrent major depression. With further review, Sheline et al. (1999) noted that duration of depression, but not age, affected the amount of reduction in size. They concluded, "Repeated stress during recurrent depressive episodes may result in cumulative hippocampal injury as reflected in volume loss" (p. 5034). Counselors play a crucial role in reducing the duration and impact of depression on the brains of their clients. Treating current episodes and preventing occurrence and/or impact of future episodes may preserve and possibly restore some brain function.

A meta-analysis of 226 task-related functional imaging studies by Janiri and colleagues (2019) reported trans-diagnostic clusters of hypo-activation in the inferior prefrontal cortex/insula, inferior parietal lobule, and putamen of individuals with mood and anxiety disorders. These regions are associated with inhibitory control and salience processing (determining importance). They suggest potential clinical relevance of these areas as targets for intervention. Counselors may assist clients in development of these skills.

Neurotransmitters serve as targets for medication treatment and psychotherapy. Derubeis et al. (2008) compared cognitive therapy versus medication for depression. They looked at treatment outcomes and neural mechanisms. In clients with depression, repetitive negative thinking is associated with increased limbic activity and decreased activity in the prefrontal cortex based on neuroimaging including positron-emission tomography (PET) and functional MRI (fMRI).

Cognitive therapy prompts clients to improve their emotion-regulation skills, targeting brain circuits involved in emotion processing. Antidepressant medication targets limbic activity and may exert effects through neurotransmitter mechanisms initially and neurogenesis in the long-term. Some clients are more suited for cognitive therapy and others for medication. Many respond to the combination. The difference is likely based on brain regions affected in the individual client in addition to other factors. Current research seeks to elucidate differences and provide guidance for treatment.

> Some clients are more suited for cognitive therapy and others for medication. Many respond to the combination.

Many neuromodulation techniques are available to treat depression. High-frequency repetitive transcranial magnetic stimulation (rTMS) uses magnets to stimulate targeted areas of the brain. Zrenner et al. (2019) discuss the impact of rTMS on the left dorsolateral prefrontal cortex (DLPFC) as potentially useful in the treatment of major depression. Electroconvulsive therapy (ECT) passes small electric currents through the brain to trigger a brief seizure, which may cause changes in brain chemistry to impact symptoms of depression and anxiety. However, in some clients, it may worsen anxiety and/or impact memory (Sigström et al., 2020). ECT may benefit clients who are unresponsive to other treatment measures. Surgical interventions include deep-brain stimulation (DBS) and vagus nerve stimulation (VNS). Schlaepfer et al. (2014) present the clinical benefits of DBS in treatment-resistant depression (TRD), and particularly involvement of the reward system.

In mood disorders, posttraumatic stress disorder, and anxiety disorders, the most consistent trans-diagnostic abnormalities in task-related brain activity converge in regions that are primarily associated with inhibitory control and salience processing. Targeting these shared neural phenotypes could potentially mitigate the risk of affective morbidity in the general population and improve outcomes in clinical populations. Jeon and Kim (2015) provide a detailed review of the effects of psychotherapy on brain function relevant to major depressive disorder.

Resources are available for counselors to offer clients support for improving brain function to overcome anxiety and depression. Please see the recommended resources for more information.

In *Unleash the Power of the Female Brain: Supercharging Yours for Better Health, Energy, Mood, Focus, and Sex*, Daniel Amen (2013) offers guidance with a practical program for women. Regardless of whether the female brain is distinct from the male brain, women may improve their brain function and harness the power of their brain for greater energy, happiness and health. This is a valuable resource for counselors to expand understanding of the brain and brain-health for themselves and for clients.

Russell-Chapin (2016) provides an overview of neuro-counseling techniques, which involve physiological self-regulation as in neuro-feedback, skin temperature control, diaphragmatic breathing and therapeutic life changes such as nutrition and exercise. She addresses how to integrate these techniques into counseling practice. Field et al. (2017) presented neuro-counseling as a brain-based perspective by which counselors may understand the concerns of clients, conceptualize their cases, and plan treatment.

CONCEPT TO CONTEMPLATE

Given what we have learned about neuroplasticity and the capacity of the brain to heal and grow, how may a counselor use knowledge of neuroanatomy to engender hope in a client?

Attention-Deficit Hyperactivity Disorder (ADHD) and the Brain

We know that neurotransmitter (dopamine and norepinephrine) function is involved in the brains of individuals with ADHD. Imaging studies demonstrate areas of the brain involved. The frontal cortex maintains executive functions including memory, problem solving, motivation, decision-making, ability to delay gratification, impulse control, judgment, planning, organization, perception of time, social behavior and sustaining attention. The limbic system regulates emotions, and impairment in this area may cause lower frustration tolerance, restlessness and inattention. Impairment in the basal ganglia, which control communication within the brain, may result in poor impulse control. Impairment in the reticular activating system, which is a major relay system within the brain, may contribute to hyperactivity, inattention and poor impulse control. The cerebellum is involved in the pathophysiology of ADHD (Wyciszkiewicz et al., 2017), including risk within executive control. "Structural alterations of cerebellar circuitry have emerged as a neural nexus of this broad risk, highlighting the cerebellum's importance for executive control" (Hariri, 2019, p. 17).

These functions within the various areas of the brain may manifest in various ways in individuals with ADHD. Behavioral and skill-building measures may affect the functions of the brain and reduce impairment associated with ADHD. Medications target neurotransmitter functions in these brain areas to improve function. Counselors may guide individuals with ADHD in obtaining necessary assessments and interventions.

ADHD in Women

"ADHD is a neurodevelopmental disorder defined by impairing levels of inattention, disorganization, and/or hyperactivity-impulsivity." (American Psychiatric Association [APA], 2013, p. 32). The *DSM-5* manual provides diagnostic criteria including nine symptoms of inattention and nine symptoms of hyperactivity-impulsivity for a diagnosis of ADHD. Weissenberger et al. (2017) note, "As of 2013, with the introduction of *DSM-5*, it is no longer classified as a childhood disorder but as a chronic lifelong disorder" (p. 1). While the condition most often begins in childhood, it continues into adulthood for roughly 2 out of 3 individuals (Faraone et al., 2005), resulting in impact for 4.4% of adults (Kessler et al., 2006). "ADHD is more frequent in males than in females in the general population, with a ratio of approximately 2:1 in children and 1.6:1 in adults. Females are more likely than males to present primarily with inattentive features" (APA, 2013, p. 63). They may be considered daydreamers, couch potatoes, or space cadets (Amen, 2013).

Counselors are important in the treatment of individuals with ADHD, and especially in the identification and treatment of women with ADHD. The life course of girls and women with ADHD may be different from that of males with the condition in many ways. It is common that there is a delay in the diagnosis of females, often missed or misdiagnosed prior to adulthood.

Depression and anxiety are common comorbid conditions and many women undergo treatment for these conditions with limited results prior to obtaining diagnosis and treatment for the core symptoms of ADHD. Many

"As of 2013, with the introduction of *DSM*-5, it (ADHD) is no longer classi-fied as a childhood disorder but as a chronic lifelong disorder."
(Weissenberger et al., 2017, p. 1)

women achieve accurate diagnosis when they obtain evaluation and treatment for their child with ADHD, a highly genetic condition. They study the condition relevant to their child, realize they may have the condition, and seek evaluation for themselves. Other women reach a point where they can no longer compensate or cope with their circumstances and seek help, happening upon a clinician knowledgeable about ADHD and able to recognize it in the life story and suffering of the woman.

Without an accurate diagnosis and understanding of their condition and facing life day after day with impairment from the symptoms of ADHD, women with ADHD experience daily stress, shame, self-doubt, a sense of failure, low self-esteem, helplessness, anxiety, depression, and rejection sensitivity. They tend to struggle with organization, life management skills, and interpersonal issues (with family, friends, co-workers and acquaintances) at home and at work. They believe something is wrong with them but are unable to determine what it is. As a result, women often develop guilt and shame stemming from their impairment. These emotions involve activation of the frontal lobe, the temporal lobe, and the amygdala within the limbic system (Michl et al., 2012). This may drive maladaptive and self-injurious behaviors including suicidal inclinations.

Counselors may develop interventions to help women with ADHD to address these issues. The first step is to obtain an accurate diagnosis and identification of any comorbid conditions co-occurring with ADHD. This may require a referral to an additional professional versed in identification and treatment of ADHD, and especially a professional capable of prescribing medication if deemed medically necessary. A list of the impairments and impacts on daily life serve as foci for interventions. The next step is to help the client understand their condition(s) are the result of brain function and not their fault. This often provides considerable relief to the client and sets the stage for engagement in intervention. Cognitive behavioral and rehabilitation approaches are important for improving cognitive functions, self-awareness, self-acceptance, self-esteem, self-regulation, organization, problem solving, stress-reduction, anxiety management, life management skills, and environmental restructuring. They also help in overcoming self-blame and shame.

Many clients with ADHD, depression, and/or anxiety disorders struggle with a self-view that they are "not good enough." They have low self-esteem or self-evaluation. Macdonald et al. (2003) discussed humanistic approaches, which "viewed self-esteem as a personal evaluation of one's goodness or worth" (p. 24). Using neuroimaging, Yang et al. (2016) studied neural responses to self-reflection and attitude toward social feedback. They noted that self-esteem involves neural activity in the orbitofrontal cortex (OFC) which is part of the network involved in emotional processing. The medial prefrontal cortex (PFC) and posterior cingulate cortex (PCC) are involved in cognitive processing relevant to self-evaluation with connections to memory-related brain regions. "Self-esteem is shaped by the appraisals we receive from others" (Will et al., 2017, p. 1). Brain imaging demonstrated enhanced connectivity between the insular cortex (involved in sensory experience from the environment and the emotional valence as to the goodness or badness of the experience) and the vmPFC (ventromedial prefrontal cortex) which processes risk and fear, inhibits emotional responses, and produces decision making. Will et al. (2017) suggested that this increased connectivity during updating beliefs about the self might represent a marker for psychiatric vulnerability.

Counselors may intervene to assist clients in re-evaluating their self-esteem and reducing vulnerability. It takes time and effort to overcome existing maladaptive brain patterns of thought and emotions to develop new and healthier beliefs. There are many ways to improve self-esteem. If clients indicate or demonstrate that they believe they are "not good enough", consider an approach I (John) developed in 1981 at a personal level and offered to clients since then with positive results. Assist the client in acknowledging (accepting) and affirming (asserting strongly), the following statement and repeating it many times daily: "What I am today is good enough [acceptance], what I will be tomorrow—even better [growth]." Clients may remind themselves of this powerful truth every time they experience diminished confidence or worth. It is the foundation of building a better self-image and self-worth.

A Radical Guide for Women with ADHD: Embrace Neurodiversity, Live Boldly, and Break through Barriers (Solden & Frank, 2019) is a valuable resource for counselors to share with clients. Another resource is *Healing ADD: The Breakthrough Program That Allows You to See and Heal the Seven Types of Attention Deficit Disorder* (Amen, 2013).

Active review of the literature for new studies is valuable. Some studies identify brain connections and the impact upon an individual's development and function. For example, on December 26, 2019, an online publication provided exciting promise for early identification and intervention.

© pathdoc/Shutterstock.com

COUNSELING WOMEN

Whitfield-Gabrieli et al. (2019) reported that brain measurements at age 7 predict future ADHD and major depressive disorder risk. They noted,

> less positive coupling at age 7 years between the dorsolateral prefrontal cortex (DLPFC) and the medial prefrontal cortex was associated with decreased attentional symptoms by age 11 years. A less positive coupling between the subgenual anterior cortex (sgACC) — a brain region implicated in mood — and the DLPFC at age 7 years was associated with an increase in internalizing behaviors, such as anxiety and depression, by age 11 years. (p. E2)

CASE STUDY

A 28-year-old woman presented to the counselor. She reported recent diagnosis of ADHD which she realized had been present without recognition since her early childhood. Although a prescriber provided medication which helped her to focus her attention and sustain effort in activities to achieve completion, she continued to experience the impact of the ADHD on her sense of self and self-esteem, as well as daily living activities. She reported shame over not meeting the expectations of her family and herself and she blamed herself. She continued to have difficulty with life management skills.

Using a narrative therapy approach, the counselor guided the woman toward separating her identity as an individual, deserving of respect, from the condition. With a focus on self-acceptance and elimination of blame, the counselor empowered the client to deconstruct larger issues into smaller, manageable problems for which she could develop skills. The client was a Christian, therefore, they explored how her symptoms had impacted her faith, and her spiritual life. For example, they discussed if it was harder to focus during prayer, or to pay attention while reading Scripture. They then determined ways to manage the distraction. The result was improved self-esteem, relationships, and cognitive functions including organization, memory and problem solving.

© wavebreakmedia/Shutterstock.com

The Life Journey and Spiritual Discovery of a Woman with ADHD
Melissa McGinness, LPC

Melissa McGinness, LPC is the owner and a clinical Counselor at Wild Heart Counseling, LLC in Lynchburg, VA. She provided the following account of her experience as a woman with ADHD:

ADHD was a factor in me to have to repeat first grade as I would constantly daydream and "leave" the classroom through my imagination. My continuous creativity, overwhelming assault of continuous thoughts, and difficulty with focus and follow through have been in constant conflict throughout my life. My internal dialogue turned towards frustration with myself and self-hatred. I would say to myself, "What the hell is wrong with you?!? Why can't you just do this, just get your act together!" Impulsive food choices and purchase decisions lead to consequences and further cause to not like myself. And, in being a counselor, this was not good. I needed to change so I started allowing others and finally, Jesus to pour truth into me. Jesus had the kindest intentions towards me, and I slowly learned that my ADHD, anxiety, and negative self-talk did not disqualify me from being able to help others. Often now, I hear Him speak into my heart that a negative thought about myself is "not an option" as that is not HIS truth about ME. In one particular encounter with Jesus, I was on a solitude retreat with my church and I saw in my heart a recurrent image that had come to my mind many times in the past. In this image, there are two of me and one of me is completely beating up and physically assaulting myself until there is nothing left of the "beat up" me. The hostile version then proceeds to smooth out the body of the other version to look for what was wrong with me and why I kept making mistakes or had not been able to, "just get it together". Jesus then asked me if I had ever found anything wrong or any tumor, mass, or spot. I replied that I had found nothing whenever I had looked through myself. And then it came to me, there was nothing wrong with me, Jesus found nothing wrong with me. If He does not find anything wrong with me then I have no right to keep tormenting myself over not being perfect. He covers my imperfections and He knows what I can and can't do, and He accepts me and 100% loves me (M. McGinness, personal communication, November 11, 2019).

Like Melissa, we all may struggle with negative self-talk and being our own worst critic from time to time. Bringing the thoughts we have before the Lord and asking him to prune us so we can have more fruitful and helpful thoughts is a great practice to adopt to care for our minds. It has been my experience (Anita) that counselors in training often disqualify themselves, asking professors if they have too many problems to help others, and on the other hand, others ask if they can help others having not struggled with major loss and addiction. However, consider the Scriptures below from the book of John that remind us that the Father is bringing forth fruit and pruning us:

"I am the true vine, and my Father is the gardener. He cuts off every branch in me that bears no fruit, while every branch that does bear fruit he prunes so that it will be even more fruitful. You are already clean because of the word I have spoken to you. Remain in me, as I also remain in you. No branch can bear fruit by itself; it must remain in the vine. Neither can you bear fruit unless you remain in me. I am the vine; you are the branches. If you remain in me and I in you, you will bear much fruit; apart from me you can do nothing. If you do not remain in me, you are like a branch that is thrown away and withers; such branches are picked up, thrown into the fire and burned. If you remain in me and my words remain in you, ask whatever you wish, and it will be done for you." (New International Bible, 1973/2011, John 15:1-7)

CHAPTER SUMMARY

In summary, every individual is different. Everyone has a brain unique from all others. The plasticity of the brain causes continuous development and adaptability throughout the lifespan of a person, because of the impact of biology, life circumstances, and choices by the individual. As experiences affect the development of the brain, the person affects her or his life circumstances, which further impacts brain development. There does not appear to be a "Female Brain", but rather females experience biological and life circumstances that create likely changes in the brain and their behaviors, many of which may be different from males.

Counselors provide care to individuals. An understanding of the individual, including life circumstances, psychological factors, behaviors and brain functions involved, places counselors in a position to guide the individual to improved health and well-being. This may involve lifestyle measures and cognitive behavioral strategies, which may overcome previous toxic influences and past adversity upon brain function while enhancing skills for healthy brain development in a manner that is protective and improves overall function.

Counselors could approach women in counseling from a brain perspective by counseling them in brain healthy habits and guiding them towards treatment to address any conditions they have developed that involve the brain. For example, EMDR could help individuals with PTSD. Cognitive behavioral therapy has tremendous effects upon the brain and its function. Referral to prescribers of psychotropic medication provides access to medications that may improve brain function and produce new nerve cells and nerve tracks.

Christian counselors can address the spirituality of the client and the power of prayer on brain function. Neubauer (2013) presents an fMRI study which suggests that the brain areas associated with theory of mind (the ability to attribute mental states to oneself and to others) treat both prayer and speaking to a loved one as an interpersonal relationship. Grafman et al. (2020) described the neural basis of religion and noted, "Religious cognition involves a complex interplay among the brain regions underpinning cognitive control, social reasoning, social motivations, and ideological beliefs" (p. 126).

KEY TERMS

Brain - a powerful 3-pound organ. It is soft and squishy with a gel-like consistency. Some authors describe the brain as having the consistency of soft warm butter

Cerebral Asymmetries - refers to differences between the right and left hemisphere of the cerebrum. Differences occur in neuroanatomy and function producing lateralization

Functional Cerebral Asymmetries (FCAs) – involve the relative distinctions between the left and the right hemispheres of the brain associated with various types of cognitive processes

Neurogenesis – the development of new nerve cells

Neuromodulation - a process by which neurons use chemicals to regulate other neurons

Neuroprotection - the preservation of the structure and function of neurons

Oxytocin - known as the "cuddle hormone" or the "love hormone." It is involved in reproduction and social bonding

Parietal Lobe - processes sensory input for taste, temperature and touch. It is involved in proprioception (spatial sense and navigation)

Prefrontal Cortex (PFC) - a structure located in the temporal lobe that has a prominent role in executive function (EF)

Putamen - a structure at the base of the forebrain that is involved in several functions; especially implicated in motor behaviors and autonomic behaviors

Sexual Dimorphism - refers to gender differences between members of the same species. This phenomenon is not limited to humans, but applies to other members of the animal kingdom. For example, the male cardinal has red plumage while the female cardinal has grayish-brown plumage

SUGGESTED RESOURCES

Books

Healing ADD: The Breakthrough Program that Allows you to See and Heal the Seven Types of Attention Deficit Disorder by Daniel Amen

Unleash the Power of the Female Brain: Supercharging yours for Better Health, Energy, Mood, Focus, and Sex by Daniel Amen

Change your Brain, Change your Life: The Breakthrough Program for Conquering Anxiety, Depression, Obsessiveness, Lack of Focus, Anger, and Memory Problems by Daniel Amen

The Female Brain by Louann Brizendine

Pink Brain, Blue Brain: How Small Differences Grow into Troublesome Gaps--and What We Can do About it by Lise Eliot

Redeeming Attachment: A Counselor's Guide to Facilitating Attachment to God and Earned Security by Anita Knight & Gary Sibcy

Neurocounseling: Brain-Based Clinical Approaches by Thomas Field, Laura Jones, & Lori Russell-Chapin

Brain Gender by Melissa Hines

DBT Skills Training Handouts and Worksheets by Marsha Linehan

Treating Chronic Depression with Disciplined Personal Involvement by James McCullough

Gender and our Brains: How New Neuroscience Explodes the Myths of the Male and Female Minds by Gina Rippon

Podcasts

Goodman, I. (Host). (2019, March 15). *Gina Rippon on the myth of the gendered brain* [Audio podcast]. NOUS. http://nousthepodcast.libsyn.com/gina-rippon-on-the-myth-of-the-gendered-brain

Videos

Developing Human Brain. (2019, February 7). *Male brain vs female brain: What is the big difference?* [Video]. YouTube. https://www.youtube.com/watch?v=q9EbaIOSSzk

Perry, B. D. [The ChildTrauma Academy.] (2013). *Sevenslideseries: The human brain* [Video]. YouTube. https://www.youtube.com/watch?v=uOsgDkeH52o

Websites

ADHD resources and education: https://www.additudemag.com/

REFERENCES

Amen, D. G. (2013). *Healing ADD from the inside out: The breakthrough program that allows you to see and heal the seven types of attention deficit disorder.* Berkley Books.

Amen, D. G. (2013). *Unleash the power of the female brain: Supercharging yours for better health, energy, mood, focus, and sex.* Random House.

Amen, D. G., Trujillo, M. V., Keator, D. A., Taylor, D., Willeumier, K., Meysami, S., & Raji, C. (2017). Gender-Based cerebral perfusion differences in 46,034 functional neuroimaging scans. *Journal of Alzheimer's Disease, 60*(2), 605–614. https://doi.org/10.3233/jad-170432

American Psychiatric Association. (2013). *Diagnostic and statistical manual of mental disorders* (5th ed.). https://doi.org/10.1176/appi.books.9780890425596

Arnetz, B. B., Sudan, S., Arnetz, J. E., Yamin, J. B., Lumley, M. A., Beck, J. S., Stemmer, P. M., Burghardt, P., Counts, S. E., & Jamil, H. (2020). Dysfunctional neuroplasticity in newly arrived Middle Eastern refugees in the U.S.: Association with environmental exposures and mental health symptoms. *Plos One, 15*(3). https://doi.org/10.1371/journal.pone.0230030

Azevedo, F. A., Carvalho, L. R., Grinberg, L. T., Farfel, J. M., Ferretti, R. E., Leite, R. E., Filho, W. J., Lent, R., & Herculano-Houzel, S. (2009). Equal numbers of neuronal and nonneuronal cells make the human brain an isometrically scaled-up primate brain. *The Journal of Comparative Neurology, 513*(5), 532–541. https://doi:.org/10.1002/cne.21974

Bao, A.-M., & Swaab, D. F. (2010). Sex differences in the brain, behavior, and neuropsychiatric disorders. *The Neuroscientist, 16*(5), 550–565. https://doi.org/10.1177/1073858410377005

Baron-Cohen. (2003). *The essential difference: The truth about the male and female brain*. Penguin.

Baron-Cohen, S. (2019, Mar 09). So why do women remember birthdays? *The Times* Retrieved from http://ezproxy.liberty.edu/login?url=https://search-proquest-com.ezproxy.liberty.edu/docview/2189181363?accountid=12085

Bingaman, K. (2013). The promise of neuroplasticity for pastoral care and counseling. *Pastoral Psychology, 62,* 549-560. https://doi.org/10.1007/s11089-013-0513-0.

Braun, K. (2011). The Prefrontal-Limbic system: Development, neuroanatomy, function, and implications for socioemotional development. *Clinics in Perinatology, 38*(4), 685–702. https://doi.org/10.1016/j.clp.2011.08.013

Brizendine, L. (2009). *The female brain*. Bantam.

Brizendine, L. (2011). *The male brain*. Bantam.

Broca, P. (1878) Anatomie comparée des circonvolutions cérébrales: Le grand lobe limbique et la scissure limbique dans la série des mammifères. *Rev Anthropol,* (1), 385-498.

Buxton, R. B. (2013). The physics of functional magnetic resonance imaging (fMRI). *Reports on Progress in Physics, 76*(9), 096601. https://doi.org/10.1088/0034-4885/76/9/096601

Cahill, L. (2006). Why sex matters for neuroscience. *Nature Reviews Neuroscience, 7*(6), 477–484. https://doi.org/10.1038/nrn1909

Celec, P., Ostatnãkovã¡, D., & Hodosy, J. (2015). On the effects of testosterone on brain behavioral functions. *Frontiers in Neuroscience, 9*(12), 1-17. https://doi.org/10.3389/fnins.2015.00012

Chang, T.-M., Yang, R.-C., Chiang, C.-T., Ouyang, C.-S., Wu, R.-C., Yu, S., & Lin, L.-C. (2020). Delay maturation in occipital lobe in girls with inattention subtype of attention-deficit hyperactivity disorder. *Clinical EEG and Neuroscience, 00*(0), 1-6. https://doi.org/10.1177/1550059419899328

Dekaban, A. S., & Sadowsky, D. (1978). Changes in brain weights during the span of human life: Relation of brain weights to body heights and body weights. *Annals of Neurology, 4*(4), 345–356. https://doi: 10.1002/ana.410040410

Derubeis, R. J., Siegle, G. J., & Hollon, S. D. (2008). Cognitive therapy versus medication for depression: Treatment outcomes and neural mechanisms. *Nature Reviews Neuroscience, 9*(10), 788–796. https://doi.org/10.1038/nrn2345

Ding, J., Chen, H., Qiu, C., Liao, W., Warwick, J. M., Duan, X., Zhang, W., & Gong, Q. (2011). Disrupted functional connectivity in social anxiety disorder: A resting-state fMRI study. *Magnetic Resonance Imaging, 29*(5), 701–711. https://doi.org/10.1016/j.mri.2011.02.013

Dodich, A., Zollo, M., Crespi, C., Cappa, S. F., Martinez, D. L., Falini, A., & Canessa, N. (2018). Short-term Sahaja Yoga meditation training modulates brain structure and spontaneous activity in the executive control network. *Brain and Behavior, 9*(1), 1-11. https://doi.org/10.1002/brb3.1159

Dr. Louann Brizendine. (2019, May 2). *Home* [Facebook page]. Facebook. Retrieved May 25, 2020 from https://www.facebook.com/DrLouannBrizendine/

Dusi, N., Barlati, S., Vita, A., & Brambilla, P. (2015). Brain structural effects of antidepressant treatment in major depression. *Current Neuropharmacology, 13*(4), 458–465. https://doi.org/10.2174/157015 9x1304150831121909

Eliot, L. (2019). Bad science and the unisex brain. *Nature, 566*, 453–454.

English Standard Bible. (2001). English Standard Bible Online. https://www.esv.org/

Faraone, S. V., Biederman, J., & Mick, E. (2005). The age-dependent decline of attention deficit hyperactivity disorder: A meta-analysis of follow-up studies. *Psychological Medicine, 36*(2), 159–165. https://doi.org/10.1017/s003329170500471x

Field, T. A., Jones, L. K., & Russell-Chapin, L. A. (2017). *Neurocounseling: Brain-based clinical approaches*. American Counseling Association.

Filová, B., Ostatníková, D., Celec, P., & Hodosy, J. (2013). The effect of testosterone on the formation of brain structures. *Cells Tissues Organs, 197*(3), 169–177. https://doi.org/10.1159/000345567

Gilmore, J. H., Lin, W., Prastawa, M. W., Looney, C. B., Vetsa, Y. S., Knickmeyer, R. C., Evans, D. D., Smith, J. K., Hamer, R. M., & Gerig, G. (2007). Regional gray matter growth, sexual dimorphism, and cerebral asymmetry in the neonatal brain. *The Journal of Neuroscience: The Official Journal of the Society for Neuroscience, 27*(6), 1255–1260. https://doi.org/10.1523/jneurosci.3339-06.2007

Goldstein, J. M., Seidman, L. J., Horton, N. J., Makris, N., Kennedy, D. N., Caviness, V. S., Jr., Faraone, S. V., & Tsuang, M. T. (2001). Normal sexual dimorphism of the adult human brain assessed by in vivo magnetic resonance imaging. *Cerebral Cortex, 11*(6), 490–497. https://doi.org/10.1093/cercor/11.6.490

Goodman, I. (Host). (2019, March 15). *Gina Rippon on the myth of the gendered brain* [Audio podcast]. NOUS. http://nousthepodcast.libsyn.com/gina-rippon-on-the-myth-of-the-gendered-brain

Grafman, J., Cristofori, I., Zhong, W., & Bulbulia, J. (2020). The neural basis of religious cognition. *Current Directions in Psychological Science, 29*(2), 126–133. https://doi.org/10.1177/0963721419898183

Halpern, M. E. (2005). Lateralization of the vertebrate brain: Taking the side of model systems. *Journal of Neuroscience, 25*(45), 10351–10357. https://doi.org/10.1523/jneurosci.3439-05.2005

Hariri, A. R. (2019). The emerging importance of the cerebellum in broad risk for psychopathology. *Neuron, 102*(1), 17-20.

Hausmann, M. (2016). Why sex hormones matter for neuroscience: A very short review on sex, sex hormones, and functional brain asymmetries. *Journal of Neuroscience Research, 95*(1-2), 40–49. https://doi.org/10.1002/jnr.23857

Highnam, C. L., & Bleile, K. M. (2011). Language in the cerebellum. *American Journal of Speech-Language Pathology Review,* (20), 4. https://doi.org/10.1044/1058-0360(2011/10-0096)

Hines, M. (2005). *Brain gender.* Oxford University Press.

Huttenlocher, P. R. (2002). *Neural plasticity: The effects of environment on the development of the cerebral cortex.* Harvard University Press.

Hyde, J. S. (2005). The gender similarities hypothesis. *American Psychologist, 60*(6), 581-592. https://doi.org/10.1037/0003-066x.60.6.581

Hyde, J. S. (2014). Gender similarities and differences. *Annual Review of Psychology, 65*(1), 373–398. https://doi.org/10.1146/annurev-psych-010213-115057

Insel, T. (1997). A neurobiological basis of social attachment. *American Journal of Psychiatry, 154*(6), 726-735. https://doi.org/10.1176/ajp.154.6.726

Janiri, D., Moser, D. A., Doucet, G. E., Luber, M. J., Rasgon, A., Lee, W. H., Murrough, J. W., Sani, G., Eickhoff, S. B., & Frangou, S. (2019). Shared neural phenotypes for mood and anxiety disorders. *JAMA Psychiatry, 1, 1-8.* https://doi.org/10.1001/jamapsychiatry.2019.3351

Jeon, S. W., & Kim, Y.-K. (2015). The effects of psychotherapy on brain function — major depressive disorder. *Major Depressive Disorder - Cognitive and Neurobiological Mechanisms.* https://doi.org/10.5772/59405

Kennedy, D., Lange, N., Makris, N., Bates, J., Meyer, J., & Caviness, V. S. (1998). Gyri of the human neocortex: An MRI-based analysis of volume and variance. *Cerebral Cortex, 8*(4), 372–384. https://doi.org/10.1093/cercor/8.4.372

Kessler, R. C., Adler, L., Barkley, R., Biederman, J., Conners, C. K., Demler, O., Faraone, S. V., Greenhill, L. L., Howes, M. J., Secnik, K., Spencer, T., Ustun, T. B., Walters, E. E., & Zaslavsky, A. M. (2006). The prevalence and correlates of adult ADHD in the United States: Results from the national comorbidity survey replication. *American Journal of Psychiatry, 163*(4), 716–723. https://doi.org/10.1176/ajp.2006.163.4.716

Kim, E. J., Pellman, B., & Kim, J. J. (2015). Stress effects on the hippocampus: A critical review. *Learning & Memory, 22*(9), 411–416. https://doi.org/10.1101/lm.037291.114

Kulynych, J. J., Vladar, K., Jones, D. W., & Weinberger, D. R. (1994). Gender differences in the normal lateralization of the supratemporal cortex: MRI surface-rendering morphometry of heschls hyrus and the planum temporale. *Cerebral Cortex, 4*(2), 107–118. https://doi.org/10.1093/cercor/4.2.107

Kurth, F., Thompson, P. M., & Luders, E. (2018). Investigating the differential contributions of sex and brain size to gray matter asymmetry. *Cortex, 99*, 235-242. https://doi.org/10.1016/j.cortex.2017.11.017

Lipina, S., & Colombo, J. (2009). *Poverty and brain development during childhood: an approach from cognitive psychology and neuroscience* (First edition.). American Psychological Association.

Macdonald, G., Saltzman, J. L., & Leary, M. R. (2003). Social approval and trait self-esteem. *Journal of Research in Personality, 37*(2), 23–40. https://doi.org/10.1016/s0092-6566(02)00531-7

Martin, E. I., Ressler, K. J., Binder, E., & Nemeroff, C. B. (2010). The neurobiology of anxiety disorders: Brain imaging, genetics, and psychoneuroendocrinology. *Clinics in Laboratory Medicine, 30*(4), 865–891. https://doi.org/10.1016/j.cll.2010.07.006

Mclean, C. P., & Anderson, E. R. (2009). Brave men and timid women? A review of the gender differences in fear and anxiety. *Clinical Psychology Review, 29*(6), 496–505. https://doi.org/10.1016/j.cpr.2009.05.003

Michl, P., Meindl, T., Meister, F., Born, C., Engel, R. R., Reiser, M., & Hennig-Fast, K. (2012). Neurobiological underpinnings of shame and guilt: A pilot fMRI study. *Social Cognitive and Affective Neuroscience, 9*(2), 150–157. https://doi.org/10.1093/scan/nss114

Mitsui, T., Araki, A., Miyashita, C., Ito, S., Ikeno, T., Sasaki, S., Kitta, T., Moriya, K., Cho, K., Morioka, K., Kishi, R., Shinohara, N., Takeda, M., & Nonomura, K. (2019). Effects of prenatal sex hormones on behavioral sexual dimorphism. *Pediatrics International, 61*(2), 140–146. https://doi.org/10.1111/ped.13756

Neubauer, R. L. (2013). Prayer as an interpersonal relationship: A neuroimaging study. *Religion, Brain & Behavior, 4*(2), 92–103. https://doi.org/10.1080/2153599x.2013.768288

New International Bible. (2011). New International Bible Online. https://www.thenivbible.com/ (Original work published 1973)

New King James Bible. (1982). New King James Bible Online. https://www.biblestudytools.com/nkjv/

Nigg, J., Jester, J., Stavro, G., Ip, K., Puttler, L., & Zucker, R. (2017). Specificity of executive functioning and processing speed problems in common psychopathology. *Neuropsychology, 31*(4), 448–466. https://doi.org/10.1037/neu0000343

Nishizawa, S., Benkelfat, C., Young, S. N., Leyton, M., Mzengeza, S., Montigny, C. D., Blier, P., & Diksic, M. (1997). Differences between males and females in rates of serotonin synthesis in human brain. *Proceedings of the National Academy of Sciences, 94*(10), 5308–5313. https://doi.org/10.1073/pnas.94.10.5308

Pagliaccio, D., Alqueza, K. L., Marsh, R., & Auerbach, R. P. (in press). (2019). Brain volume abnormalities in youth at high risk for depression: Adolescent brain and cognitive development study. *Journal of the American Academy of Child & Adolescent Psychiatry.* https://doi: 10.1016/j.jaac.2019.09.032

Pessoa, L., & Hof, P. R. (2015). From Paul Brocas great limbic lobe to the limbic system. *Journal of Comparative Neurology, 523*(17), 2495–2500. https://doi.org/10.1002/cne.23840

Potter-Efron, R. (2012). *Healing the angry brain: How understanding the way your brain works can help you control anger and aggression.* New Harbinger Publications. https://books.google.com/books?hl=en&lr=&id=IknhPaMyPkkC&oi=fnd&pg=PR7&dq=your+brain+is+consistency+of+butter&ots=BFmD7SZ3Ym&sig=JJprNQFnpc2DEb9BIHORTHdL1q4#v=onepage&q=your%20brain%20is%20consistency%20of%20butter&f=false

Purves, D. (2011). *Neuroscience* (5th ed.). Sinauer.

Quintana, D. S., Rokicki, J., Meer, D. V. D., Alnæs, D., Kaufmann, T., Córdova-Palomera, A., Dieset, I., Andreassen, O. A., & Westlye, L. T. (2019). Oxytocin pathway gene networks in the human brain. *Nature Communications, 10*(1), 1-12. https://doi.org/10.1038/s41467-019-08503-8

Rabinowicz, T., Dean, D. E., McDonald-Comber Petetot, J., & de Courten-Myers, G. M. (1999). Gender differences in the human cerebral cortex: More neurons in males; More processes in females. *Journal of Child Neurology, 14*(2), 98-107.

Rappaport, B. I., Kandala, S., Luby, J. L., & Barch, D. M. (2020). Brain reward system dysfunction in adolescence: Current, cumulative, and developmental periods of depression. *American Journal of Psychiatry.* Advance online publication. https://doi.org/10.1176/appi.ajp.2019.19030281

Rhoton, A. L. (2007). THE CEREBRUM. *Neurosurgery, 61*(suppl_1), SHC-37-SHC-119. https://doi.org/10.1227/01.neu.0000255490.88321.ce

Rijpkema, M., Everaerd, D., Pol, C. V. D., Franke, B., Tendolkar, I., & Fernández, G. (2011). Normal sexual dimorphism in the human basal ganglia. *Human Brain Mapping, 33*(5), 1246–1252. https://doi.org/10.1002/hbm.21283

Rippon, G. (2019). *Gender and our brains: How new neuroscience explodes the myths of the male and female minds.* Pantheon Books.

Rippon, G. (2019). *The gendered brain: The new neuroscience that shatters the myth of the female brain.* The Bodley Head.

Ritchie, S. J., Cox, S. R., Shen, X., Lombardo, M. V., Reus, L. M., Alloza, C., Harris, M. A., Alderson, H. L., Hunter, S., Neilson, E., Liewald, D. C. M., Auyeung, B., Whalley, H. C., Lawrie, S. M., Gale, C. R., Bastin, M. E., McIntosh, A. M., & Deary, I. J. (2018). Sex differences in the adult human brain: Evidence from 5216 UK biobank participants. *Cerebral Cortex, 28*(8), 2959–2975. https://doi.org/10.1093/cercor/bhy109

Rohrback, S., Siddoway, B., Liu, C. S., & Chun, J. (2018). Genomic mosaicism in the developing and adult brain. *Developmental Neurobiology, 78*(11), 1026–1048. https://doi.org/10.1002/dneu.22626

Russell-Chapin, L. A. (2016). Integrating neurocounseling into the counseling profession: An introduction. *Journal of Mental Health Counseling, 38*(2), 93–102. https://doi.org/10.17744/mehc.38.2.01

Sapolsky, R. M. (2001). Depression, antidepressants, and the shrinking hippocampus. *Proceedings of the National Academy of Sciences of the United States of America, 98*(22), 12320–12322. https://doi.org/10.1073/pnas.231475998

Savic, I., Frisen, L., Manzouri, A., Nordenstrom, A., & Hirschberg, A. L. (2017). Role of testosterone and Y chromosome genes for the masculinization of the human brain. *Human Brain Mapping, 38*(4), 1801–1814. https://doi.org/10.1002/hbm.23483

Schlaepfer, T. E., Harris, G. J., Tien, A. Y., Peng, L., Lee, S., & Pearlson, G. D. (1995). Structural differences in the cerebral cortex of healthy female and male subjects: A magnetic resonance imaging study. *Psychiatry Research: Neuroimaging, 61*(3), 129–135. https://doi.org/10.1016/0925-4927(95)02634-a

Schlaepfer, T. E., Bewernick, B. H., Kayser, S., Hurlemann, R., & Coenen, V. A. (2014). Deep brain stimulation of the human reward system for major depression—Rationale, outcomes and outlook. *Neuropsychopharmacology, 39*(6), 1303–1314. https://doi.org/10.1038/npp.2014.28

Shaw, S., Kabani, N. J., Lerch, J. P., Eckstrand, K., Lenroot, R., Gogtay, N., Greenstein, D., Clasen, L., Evans, A., Rapoport, J. L. L., Giedd, J. N., & Wise, S. P. (2008). Neurodevelopmental trajectories of the human cerebral cortex. *Journal of Neuroscience, 28*(14), 3586-3594. https://doi.org/10.1523/JNEUROSCI.5309-07.2008

Sheline, Y. I., Mittler, B. L., Mintum, M. A. (2002). The hippocampus and depression. *European Psychiatry, 17*(S3), 300-305. https://doi.org/10.1016/S0924-9338(02)00655-7

Sheline, Y. I., Sanghavi, M., Mintun, M. A., & Gado, M. H. (1999). Depression duration but not age predicts hippocampal volume loss in medically healthy women with recurrent major depression. *The Journal of Neuroscience, 19*(12), 5034–5043. https://doi.org/10.1523/jneurosci.19-12-05034.1999

Sheline, Y. I., Wang, P. W., Gado, M. H., Csernansky, J. G., & Vannier, M. W. (1996). Hippocampal atrophy in recurrent major depression. *Proceedings of the National Academy of Sciences, 93*(9), 3908–3913. https://doi.org/10.1073/pnas.93.9.3908

Sheridan, M. A., Fox, N. A., Zeanah, C. H., McLaughlin, K. A., & Nelson, C. A., 3rd (2012). Variation in neural development as a result of exposure to institutionalization early in childhood. *Proceedings of the National Academy of Sciences of the United States of America, 109*(32), 12927–12932. https://doi.org/10.1073/pnas.1200041109

Sibcy, G., & Knight, A. (2011). *Attachment, neurobiology, and emotional intelligence* [Workshop]. World Conference on Christian Counseling, Nashville, TN, United States.

Sibcy, G. & Knight, A. (2017). *Redeeming attachment: A counselor's guide to facilitating attachment to God and earned security.* Kendall Hunt Publishing.

Sigström, R., Nordenskjöld, A., Juréus, A., Clements, C., Joas, E., Pålsson, E., & Landén, M. (2020). Long-term subjective memory after electroconvulsive therapy. *BJPsych Open, 6*(2), e26. https://doi.org/10.1192/bjo.2020.9

Smetacek, V., Mechsner, F. (2004). Making sense. *Nature, 432*, 21. https://doi.org/10.1038/432021a

Solden, S., & Frank, M. (2019). *A radical guide for women with ADHD: Embrace neurodiversity, live boldly, and break through barriers.* New Harbinger Publications, Inc.

Stiles, J. (2011). Brain development and the nature versus nurture debate. *Progress in Brain Research Gene Expression to Neurobiology and Behavior: Human Brain Development and Developmental Disorders*, 3–22. https://doi.org/10.1016/b978-0-444-53884-0.00015-4

Svedholm-Häkkinen, A. M., Ojala, S. J., & Lindeman, M. (2018). Male brain type women and female brain type men: Gender atypical cognitive profiles and their correlates. *Personality and Individual Differences*, *122*, 7–12. https://doi.org/10.1016/j.paid.2017.09.041

Taylor, S. E., Klein, L. C., Lewis, B. P., Gruenewald, T. L., Gurung, R. A. R., & Updegraff, J. A. (2000). Biobehavioral responses to stress in females: Tend-and-befriend, not fight-or-flight. *Psychological Review*, *107*(3), 411–429. https://doi.org/10.1037//0033-295x.107.3.411

TED. (2013, October 16). *The most important less from 83,000 brain scans | Daniel Amen | TEDxOrangeCoast* [Video]. YouTube. https://www.youtube.com/watch?v=esPRsT-lmw8

Teixeira-Machado, L., Arida, R. M., & Mari, J. J., (2019). Dance for neuroplasticity: A descriptive systematic review. *Neuroscience & Behavioral Reviews*, (96), 232-240. https://doi.org/10.1016/j.neubiorev.2018.12.010

Weissenberger, S., Ptacek, R., Klicperova-Baker, M., Erman, A., Schonova, K., Raboch, J., & Goetz, M. (2017). ADHD, lifestyles and comorbidities: A call for an holistic perspective – from medical to societal intervening factors. *Frontiers in Psychology*, *8*. https://doi.org/10.3389/fpsyg.2017.00454

Whitfield-Gabrieli, S., Wendelken, C., Nieto-Castañón, A., Bailey, S. K., Anteraper, S. A., Lee, Y. J., Chai, X., Hirshfeld-Becker, D. R., Biederman, J., Cutting, L. E., & Bunge, S. A. (2019). Association of Intrinsic Brain Architecture With Changes in Attentional and Mood Symptoms During Development. *JAMA Psychiatry*, *77*(4), 378-386. https://doi.org/10.1001/jamapsychiatry.2019.4208

Wierenga, L. M., Bos, M. G. N., Rossenberg, F. V., & Crone, E. A. (2019). Sex effects on development of brain structure and executive functions: Greater variance than mean effects. *Journal of Cognitive Neuroscience*, *31*(5), 730–753. https://doi.org/10.1162/jocn_a_01375

Will, G.-J., Rutledge, R. B., Moutoussis, M., & Dolan, R. J. (2017). Neural and computational processes underlying dynamic changes in self-esteem. *ELife*, *6*. https://doi.org/10.7554/elife.28098

Wyciszkiewicz, A., Pawlak, M. A., & Krawiec, K. (2017). Cerebellar volume in children with attention-deficit hyperactivity disorder (ADHD). *Journal of Child Neurology*, *32*(2), 215–221.

Yang, J., Xu, X., Chen, Y., Shi, Z., & Han, S. (2016). Trait self-esteem and neural activities related to self-evaluation and social feedback. *Scientific Reports (Nature Publisher Group)*, *6*, 20274. http://dx.doi.org.ezproxy.liberty.edu/10.1038/srep20274

Zhang, C., Dougherty, C. C., Baum, S. A., White, T., & Michael, A. M. (2018). Functional connectivity predicts gender: Evidence for gender differences in resting brain connectivity. *Human Brain Mapping*, *39*(4), 1765–1776. https://doi.org/10.1002/hbm.23950

Zhang, J., Wang, J., Wu, Q., Kuang, W., Huang, X., He, Y., & Gong, Q. (2011). Disrupted brain connectivity networks in drug-naive, first-episode major depressive disorder. *Biological Psychiatry*, *70*(4), 334–342. https://doi. org/10.1016/j.biopsych.2011.05.018

Zrenner, B., Gordon, P., Kempf, A., Belardinelli, P., Mcdermott, E., Soekadar, S., Fallgatter, A., Zrenner, C., Ziemann, U., & Dahlhaus, F. M. (2019). Alpha-synchronized stimulation of the left DLPFC in depression using real-time EEG-triggered TMS. *Brain Stimulation*, *12*(2), 532. https://doi.org/10.1016/j. brs.2018.12.753

CHAPTER 5

Developmental Considerations in Counseling Women

> "It takes courage to grow up and become who you really are."
> ~E. E. Cummings

> "Before I formed you in the womb I knew you, and before you were born I consecrated you...."
> (Jeremiah 1:5, ESV)

Wisdom from Above: Standing in His Grace

© Evellean/Shutterstock.com

Imagine what Mary must have experienced emotionally and physically, to carry the Son of God in her womb (Matthew 1:18). In human form, the newborn Jesus was delivered in a modest manger and wrapped in cloth to protect his fragile skin (Luke 2:7, 10, 11). Nourished from his Mother's breast, Mary witnessed her beautiful child soon become a toddler, walking, playing, and napping just like any other little boy. In a family with siblings, in the city of Nazareth (Matthew 2:23), Jesus as a young boy was socialized in the Jewish traditions and learned the trade of carpentry (Luke 1:31-35). Mary watched her precious baby boy grow taller and more independent. In human form Jesus developed as a teen into a young man. As an adult, Christ began his career in full-time ministry. Only three short years later, Mary watched as her perfect son, Jesus was nailed to a cross to die (John 19:25). The Son of God, in human physical form, must have experienced excruciating pain as his inflicted wounds bled freely. Despite his immense pain, he still looked lovingly down at his mother and his followers, as well as those

143

CHAPTER LEARNING OBJECTIVES

Upon completing this chapter, you should be able to:

- Identify the interaction between biological (nature) and environmental (nurture) factors influencing development
- Differentiate common developmental periods of life that occur in an orderly process for all
- Understand an intervention that enhances self-awareness
- Articulate the importance for counselors to be able to identify developmental issues that are age related

who had persecuted him (John 19:25). As any parent, Mary had the joy of witnessing Jesus transition from baby to child, child to an adolescent, and adolescent to adulthood. However, she had to witness his lifespan cut short—something no mother should have to experience.

Scripture tells us "But Mary treasured up all these things and pondered them in her heart" (*New International Bible*, 1973/2011, Luke 2:19). As counselors, we too should spend time reflecting on this incredible gift that Jesus gave to us. Do you understand at a heartfelt level how Christ suffered and died for you? Can you allow yourself to hold onto that incredible sense of peace that comes from comprehending how cherished you are as one of God's children (Luke 20:36)? Now, consider your client, for they too share this precious gift and this common history. Created by God, they grew from birth to their current age, physically, emotionally, and cognitively experiencing what it means to live as a human in a broken world, just as Jesus encountered so many years ago (Romans 3:23). Like you, clients also have their own specific experiences that have shaped and influenced their own constructed view of the world. While you may be different from one another, you and your client also share a great deal. From this point of equality, as fellow children of God, allow these thoughts to humble you as a therapist. You are encouraged to be like Mary and deeply ponder the lifespan of her son Jesus, knowing that both client and counselor, and even Christ himself, are each affected by the brokenness of this world.

CHAPTER OVERVIEW

Human development is the process of change that occurs from conception to the moment of death. Complex multi-dimensional biological and environmental factors combine and are experienced in a state of constant movement and adaptation. While all humans are unique, there are also areas of commonality that everyone shares. Thus, the term lifespan development is utilized to represent the passage of time, as individuals change through similar sequential stages of life. This chapter will explore the developmental periods of young adulthood, middle adulthood, and later adulthood. Various theories of human development will be presented. Major concepts and terminology related to the growth process will be defined and discussed. The chapter material will be applied to three case studies. Interventions are included to assist individuals in self-discovery and provide a therapeutic activity for counseling. A Biblical integration of the material is included, as spirituality is considered. A conclusion summarizing the major aspects in the chapter brings closure.

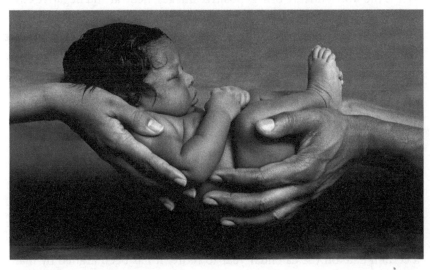

© In The Light Photography/Shutterstock.com

How does normal development occur? How does abnormal development occur? If parents do a "good" job of parenting, will their children become contributing members of society? If children grow up in poverty, attend an underachieving school district with poor graduation rates, experience violence in the home, or live in a drug saturated neighborhood, are they doomed to remain in such a lifestyle? Ask any parent of two or more children, and they can describe different personalities, temperaments, interests, and the need to apply various styles of disciplining. What about children raised in the same household, under indistinguishable parenting styles, incurring duplicate life events, and attending the same schools, yet, grow up to be such differing adults? These are the types of questions that developmentalists explore. Since the focus of this chapter is on women and not on those early years of development, a brief synopsis of developmental theories and concepts is presented that form the foundation for fully conceptualizing the life of a woman.

COMPONENTS OF DEVELOPMENT

Nature versus Nurture

Nature refers to those characteristics, predispositions, and traits of biological genetic origins. Nurture refers to all exposure to environmental factors, such as opportunities for learning, socioeconomic status, parenting styles, and exposure to the behaviors of others (Brofenbrenner, 2005). While the word nurture brings positive images, neutral and negative environmental influences also exist. Negative examples include violence, trauma experiences, all types of abuse, and toxic substances (Bell Holleran et al., 2016). Here the terminology of *genetic versus environmental* will be utilized, as it better illustrates the complexity of what is heritable and what influences a human being after conception (Gordon & Greene, 2018).

Age

Chronological age is the period between one's birth and the number of years lived. Moreira (2016) explains chronological age is utilized by institutional quantitative standards to determine eligibility for services. Some examples include the age to get a license to drive a car, legal age to vote, or a certain date on the calendar year to retire. It has been argued by many that different standards of measurement should be utilized (Del Barrio et al., 2018; Marshall & Rahman, 2015; Moreira, 2016). One's biological age relates to health and functioning of the body (Santrock, 2019). Social age refers to the roles of an individual and how active the person is with others (Beauvais, 2016; Whitbourne, 2012). Psychological age may refer to the cognitive abilities to think clearly and control one's emotions appropriately (Beauvais, 2016; Whitbourne, 2012). Chronological age may no longer be a good measure of one's ability to function well in the community.

Cognitive Development

This is a broad concept that involves the maturing of the brain's ability to obtain knowledge. This knowledge can be awareness, perceptions, beliefs that form, the ability to problem solve, reason, and decision-making skills. The American Psychological Association defines cognitive development as "the skills involved in performing the tasks associated with perception, learning, memory, understanding, awareness, reasoning, judgment, intuition, and language" (VandenBos, 2015, p. 202).

Physical Development

Beginning at the moment of conception when cell division begins to the moment of death, when all bodily systems shut down, physical development is in a constant flux of change (Kyriazis, 2020). In prenatal care, medical professionals carefully monitor the growth of vital organs, comparing size and shape to that of healthy humans in the womb (Ickovics et al., 2019). Blood work can check for optimal maternal hormonal levels that can prevent problems from arising within the pregnancy. At birth babies are measured in length, weight, and head circumference to compare to the percentile norm. Children from 2 to 20 are also measured in terms of weight, height, and body mass index (Center for Disease Control and Prevention, 2017). From peak growth periods to the aging deterioration of various bodily components, internal and external physical development should continue to be monitored to ensure a healthy lifestyle.

Social Development

The process of obtaining skills and competency to relate to others in a culturally appropriate behavior is social development. In infants, social development is usually stimulated by caretakers and siblings. As others respond in a positive manner or meet their needs, the child is reinforced to repeat the behavior. In what is believed to be a process rooted in instinct, sensitive caregivers responding with consistent warmth to a child's behavioral expression of needs, leads to a secure **attachment** (an emotional and psychological bond that forms between a young child and a caregiver as a result of basic needs being met. This significant bond may result in a range of emotions from security when needs are predictably met

© fizkes/Shutterstock.com

to distress when separation occurs or needs are met with inconsistency) bond (van Rosmalen et al., 2016). John Bowlby's Attachment Theory, along with Mary Ainsworth's research support, suggest that this secure bond carries into future relationships through childhood into adulthood (Schröder et al., 2019; van Rosmalen et al., 2016). The quality of the attachment impacts the ability to emotionally self-regulate and develop trust, stimulates the central nervous system's functioning, and increases social competency (Black, 2019). Infants and young children who experience maltreatment, prolonged separation from the primary caregiver, or significant trauma, may form other types of patterns of attachment bonding, such as disorganized, anxious resistant, anxious avoidant, and ambivalent styles of connection (Black, 2019). Unhealthy attachment bonding is a predictor of possible personality issues, poor self-esteem, instability in relationships, and poor health outcomes (Black, 2019; Schröder et al., 2019; van Rosmalen et al., 2016). Individuals with various mental health issues have been found to respond to enhanced attachment security in treatment (Black, 2019; Marcia & Josselson, 2013). Group therapy has been found to build positive attachment connections that may lead clients to improved emotional ability to self-regulate, to learn to trust more, and to experience enhanced functioning of the central nervous system (Black, 2019).

Social development continues from infancy to adult relationships. Toddlers engage in imitative play (Schumacher et al., 2019) and preschoolers in parallel play where they play in the same area as another child, but not really interacting cooperatively (Meland et al., 2019). As children age, they begin to interact through playing games and team activities. Children often play out adult roles, such as in playing house or dressing up. Skills such as sharing, taking turns, remaining seated (Sewell, 2019), using inside voices and keeping one's hands to themselves, are all examples of skills children develop. Communication skills are contextually and culturally determined, such as being able to read social cues, which involves understanding how our behavior influences and is perceived (Freeman, 2015). Growth continues in social development as older children learn to develop friendships and teens begin to date, with the possibility of eventually sharing an intimate relationship with a lifelong spouse. Conflict resolution and compromise are higher levels of social skills that are utilized in relationships in various settings, including work, church, family, and in marriage (Freeman, 2015).

© Rawpixel.com/Shutterstock.com

Emotional Development

This type of development involves a biological system that increasingly differentiates, involving the ability to experience feeling sensations and express them to get one's own desires met. Both a sender and a receiver are involved, as one reacts with a physical reaction expressing a feeling, while another interprets the expression with a contextual and culturally socialized perception (Holodynski & Seger, 2019). Emotions are subjective internal reactions that may involve bodily functions, such as an increase in breathing rate and blood pressure (Holodynski & Seger, 2019). This process of an increasing emotional repertoire interplays with the learning of self-regulation, where one can control the expression of a feeling (Holodynski et al., 2013). Hoemann et al. (2019) points out that sensory input from the environment are cues to be interpreted by the brain and are constantly being updated through language.

Spiritual Development

The Association for Spiritual, Ethical, and Religious Values in Counseling (ASERVIC), defines spirituality as "a capacity and tendency that is innate and unique to all persons. This spiritual tendency moves the individual toward knowledge, love, meaning, peace, hope, transcendence, connect-

> "Most of the issues and problems individuals face in life are developmental in nature and understanding the dynamics of human growth and development is essential to success as a helper." (Remley & Herlihy, 2010, p. 26).

edness, compassion, wellness, and wholeness" (2010, p. 1). The process of growing spiritually involves an intrinsic motivation to find meaning that can sustain individuals in times of prolonged suffering (Frankl, 2006; Ganea, 2019). Spiritual growth incorporates developing an awareness of the existence of something greater than ourselves (Love & Talbot, 2009). Spirituality may or may not involve organized religions. Spiritual growth can lead to fulfillment and balance between one's thoughts and actions, as values are solidified (Love & Talbot, 2009).

IMPORTANCE TO COUNSELORS

Imagine you are a counselor in training. You have just been handed the intake file of a new female client. How do you begin to conceptualize the new client's issues and work towards a treatment plan? You plan to listen with unconditional positive regard and show empathy, as a means of relationship building. Questions begin to form as you read through her file. What might some of your questions be?

One beginning step to case conceptualizing is to mentally contemplate the developmental aspects of a client's current and past development, as it applies to their current symptoms. Over time, a great deal of information can be gained by counselors about social, cognitive, emotional, physical, cultural, and spiritual aspects, allowing the counselor to better understand a client's life story. What would it be like to be her? How does one client differ from another client? If the client is cognitively challenged, the therapeutic treatment plan may be very different. A 53-year-old female client might physically be experiencing menopause. Would menopause impact her current issues? What about the client who has experienced traumatic events throughout her life? Why does one client show a tremendous amount of resiliency in dealing with a crisis, while another client with the same trauma experiences, might need to be hospitalized due to her inability to function daily? You might be considering if there are any referral services or resources in the community that may be helpful, especially if limited social support systems exist. Past and present developmental components, taken in culmination, will impact how your client progresses.

© Digital Storm/Shutterstock.com

Galatians 6:5 (*New International Bible,* 1973/2011) states, "for each should carry their own load". What load are you carrying? How does it relate to your past development and where you are currently in life? What relationships have influenced you? How has your world view been formed given the cultural background you have? Using the various aspects of development, think about what you were like socially, cognitively, spiritually, emotionally, and physically at the age of 4, 10, 16, 20…. Given your own developmental experiences physically, socially, cognitively, spiritually, emotionally, and even culturally, what might get in your way of successfully counseling with a client?

The more you understand about yourself, the better able you are to assist in carrying another's load appropriately, until the client learns the skills or clarifies their needs and seeks out resources to be able to carry on with their own life. Numerous scholars have written on the need to deal with one's own **ethnocentrism** (involves viewing others through the self-lens of one's own, entrenched socialization, culture, and values from a homogenizing moral stance. Whether through ignorance or purposeful behavior, one's in-group culture is viewed as superior to that of out-group cultural differences) to be an effective therapist (Corey et al., 2019; Merrill-James et al., 2019; Rosin, 2015; Sue et al., 2019). In addition, Rosin points out that such self-reflection is a lifelong process that counselors must journey upon throughout their career and encourages counselors to intentionally foster such growth. If not, counselors run the risk of engaging in potentially harmful transference and countertransference (Corey et al., 2019; Cureton & Clemens, 2015; Rosin, 2015).

THEORIES OF DEVELOPMENT

Another way to build on our conceptualization skills is to examine a client through the lens of one or more developmental theories. In this section an overview of five overall classifications of theories will be presented. These developmental theories include Psychoanalytic Theory, Psychosocial Development Theory, Behavioral Theories, Cognitive Theories, and Ecological Systems Theory.

Psychoanalytic Theory

Sigmund Freud believed that humans were driven by biological instinctual drives. Infants are driven to gratify their wishes and develop strategies to succeed or tolerate the emotions of the inability to accomplish their wishes (Redekop et al., 2017). A heavy emphasis was placed on the type of parenting/caregiving that young children experienced. Freud's Psychosexual Stages (Santrock, 2019; Wong et al., 2015) focused on instinctual sexual drive, where pleasure was initially oral, then anal, proceeding to a phallic period, on to a time of latency period of repression, and ending with a genital reawaking of the sexual drive (libido).

FIGURE 5.1

Freud's Psychosexual Stages

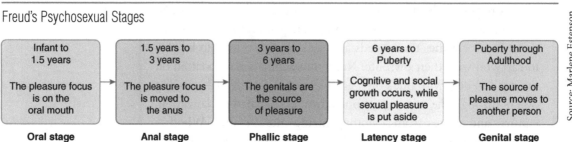

Source: Marlene Estenson

Freud indicated that each stage involved conflict which needed to be resolved, or the individual could become fixated (Rizzolo, 2018). These drives, conflicts, and sources of pleasure are experienced for the most part, unconsciously. Freud believed that defense mechanisms, such as repression, rationalization, and projecting, were unconsciously created to protect the individual from conscious emotional turmoil over unresolved issues from the early stages (Santrock, 2019). Adult neurosis is consequently seen as a result of fixation within the unresolved conflicts of childhood (Rizzolo, 2018).

The counselor's job is to safely assist the client in bringing the unconscious to the conscious. Strategies utilized by therapists include free association, dream interpretation (Cherry, 2019b), and the processing of transference and countertransference (Cureton & Clemens, 2015) in the client-counselor relationship (Redekop et al., 2017). The past relationships of conflict, such as with one's parent, can be reconstructed in the therapy relationship, so that a corrective experience may occur (Redekop et al., 2017).

While aspects of Freud's Theory have been criticized over the years, the emphasis on the unconscious and the influence of relationships in early childhood, continue to be accepted in developmental research. One of the criticisms is how negatively women were portrayed by psychoanalysts. For additional reading on Psychoanalytic Theory and women see suggested resources information on Balsam (2015) and Gilligan (1982).

Erikson's Psychosocial Theory

Erik Erikson was also a Psychoanalyst who trained under Anna Freud. Where Freud saw personality development as having arrived by the time one reached adulthood and focused more on pathology, Erikson presented a lifespan narrative of stages, focusing more on healthy development (Cherry, 2019a). While conflict still occurs within the stages, sexuality is not the focus. Individuals are influenced by additional social interactions with peers and other adults, as well as by the immediate family. In addition, Erikson acknowledged genetics and environmental interaction (Dunkel & Harbke, 2017). Thus, Erikson described all the parts integrated with the eight stages of life as forming the whole of one's life (Dunkel & Harbke, 2017). Stages are chronological periods of life, such as childhood and adolescence. Each stage involves an integration of balance between contradictory dispositions that result in a psychosocial strength or virtue when accomplished successfully (Knight, 2017). However, the opposites are both experienced by the person and integrated into their personality. Individuals can become *stuck* in aspects of the conflict within any one stage and carry issues into the next. Each stage begins with a *crisis*, an intense time of exploration of oneself (Wong et al., 2015). This reassessment may emerge as a varied way of looking at oneself and one's place in the world (Cherry, 2019a; Knight, 2017). Personality and identity development are shaped throughout life, and subject to change, as one reworks identity within each new stage (Marcia & Josselson, 2013). Thus, a client might have aspects of earlier conflicts that were not totally resolved, but the therapist would assist them within the broader context of their current stage in life.

FIGURE 5.2

Erikson's Developmental Stages

Diagram source: Anita Kuhnley. Icons from top, going clockwise: © Visual Generation/Shutterstock. com, © Premiumvectors/ Shutterstock.com, © Nice Illustration/Shutterstock. com, © Blan-k/Shutterstock. com, © Blan-k/Shutterstock. com, © lukpedclub/Shutter-stock.com, © Alluvion Stock/ Shutterstock.com, © natrot/ Shutterstock.com

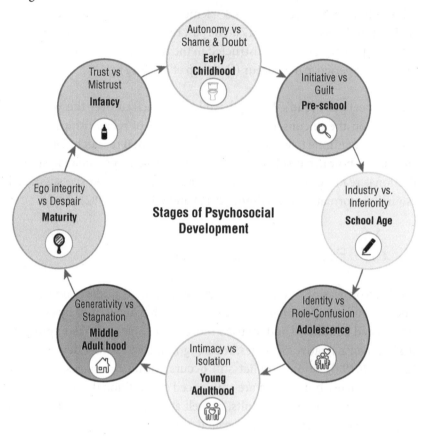

A brief review of the chronological stages follows (see Figure 5.2). It should be noted that the age of beginning and ending are approximated and not fixed in stone. During infancy through approximately 1.5 years of age, the newborn, if well cared for, develops a sense that the world is a safe, trust-worthy place and the psychosocial strength/virtue of hope is formed. If needs are not met, the baby will see the world with a sense of mistrust (Mar-cia & Josselson, 2013). From 1.5 to 3 years of age, the child's personality is influenced by a crisis of *autonomy vs. shame and doubt*. Here the toddler pursues aspects of independence, and yet fears failure. Parents allow the child to have some control and make choices, which results in the formation of the psychosocial strength/virtue of willpower (Knight, 2017). Children whose parents do everything for them, stifle the child's motivation to try new experiences and gain determination. Parents recognize this as a time of independence, where the toddler wants to do things themselves even if they are not always capable of the task (Helming, 2015). This need to develop a sense of control is even stronger in the next stage of initiative vs. guilt between the ages of 3 to 5 years of age. Control over appropriate choices can allow the child to develop the virtue of purpose (Dunkel & Harbke, 2017). Guilt is experienced if caretakers stifle this independence by showing disapproval. Success at this stage allows the child to advance into the next period with a stronger identity to face the outside world (Helming, 2015).

The previous stages involved the oversight of the primary caretakers. Now the influence of peers and other adults plays a major role in development. Children ages 6 to 12 experience *industry vs. inferiority*, a time where the child interacts with other children and may feel inadequate socially and academically compared to their peers (Wong et al., 2015). They may avoid feelings of failure and not explore their own strengths. However, with the support and guidance of caring adults, children can be successful and form a sense of competence. These previous ego identity strengths are foundational as the child enters the period of identity vs. role confusion between the ages of 12 to 18 (Knight, 2017). The beginning of this stage corresponds with the onset of puberty. This is a time where teens try out various behaviors, roles, ways of looking at oneself, and beliefs in their journey to determine identity (Dunkel & Harbke, 2017). Identity formation leaves the teen feeling more secure in their future direction and in relationships with others. A lack of success in this stage results in the teen

© Africa Studio/Shutterstock.com

feeling confused in how they fit into the world with others and possibly a loss of future career direction (Marcia & Josselson, 2013). Confusion may result in the inability to form the strength/virtue of fidelity, which is needed to form committed, nurturing relationships with others in the next period. Dunkel and Harbke (2017) indicate that the development of a strong sense of self-understanding and self-identity is needed before one can truly know others in an authentic way.

Stages six, seven, and eight occur during the adult years. The sixth stage is the period of young adulthood where *intimacy vs. isolation* occurs in the years between 19 and 40. The ability to form healthy friendships and focus on intimacy in relationships is key to avoiding isolation (Dunkel & Harbke 2017). It is during this period that selecting a mate, having children, and developing a career are usually seen. Feelings of affiliation and connectedness to others, such as partners, family, and in friendships mark the success of this stage. The virtue developed in this period is the abili-

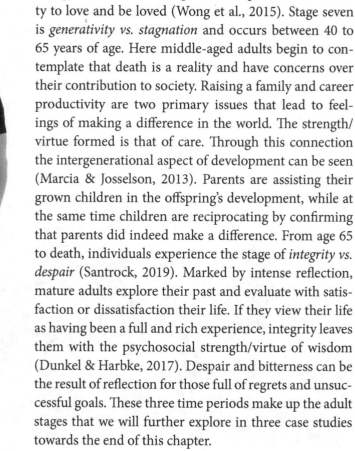

ty to love and be loved (Wong et al., 2015). Stage seven is *generativity vs. stagnation* and occurs between 40 to 65 years of age. Here middle-aged adults begin to contemplate that death is a reality and have concerns over their contribution to society. Raising a family and career productivity are two primary issues that lead to feelings of making a difference in the world. The strength/virtue formed is that of care. Through this connection the intergenerational aspect of development can be seen (Marcia & Josselson, 2013). Parents are assisting their grown children in the offspring's development, while at the same time children are reciprocating by confirming that parents did indeed make a difference. From age 65 to death, individuals experience the stage of *integrity vs. despair* (Santrock, 2019). Marked by intense reflection, mature adults explore their past and evaluate with satisfaction or dissatisfaction their life. If they view their life as having been a full and rich experience, integrity leaves them with the psychosocial strength/virtue of wisdom (Dunkel & Harbke, 2017). Despair and bitterness can be the result of reflection for those full of regrets and unsuccessful goals. These three time periods make up the adult stages that we will further explore in three case studies towards the end of this chapter.

© OoddySmile Studio/Shutterstock.com

Behavioral Theory of Development

Evolving over time, the Behavioral Theory of Development involved several theorists. Starting with Ivan Pavlov's classical conditioning experiments on dogs, it was demonstrated that behavior could be manipulated (Jarius & Wildemann, 2017). John Watson demonstrated that behavior could be anticipated and controlled through classical conditioning that included a behavioral stimulus and response process paired with a neutral stimulus. The neutral stimulus through the pairing would then be converted through repetition to cause the conditioned response (Watson, 2017). Watson asserted that he could take a group of children and condition them into working at any profession he chose. (Moore, 2017). In fact, he did indeed experiment on a child of nine months to a year of age. Little Albert, as he was referred to in the literature, was shown a white rat, that he displayed no fear towards. Watson then paired a loud noise with Albert's reaching for the rodent (Watson, 2017). Fear of the rat was the result of the experiment, and the emotional fear was later generalized to another white animal, a rabbit. Watson wanted to prove that learned habits were what caused emotional reactions and not biological instincts (Moore, 2017).

Similar to Watson, Skinner also believed in the science of behavior that could serve in social activism to create a better world (Moore, 2017). However, Skinner emphasized contingencies and consequences that were more complex than just stimulus-response conditioning. Skinner acknowledged classical conditioning but felt operant conditioning also led to behavioral changes. Thoughts and feelings were not focused upon, rather reinforcement and negative consequences resulted in the increase and reduction of behavior (Santrock, 2019). "In assuming that human behavior is learned, behaviorists also hold that all behaviors can also be unlearned, and replaced by new behaviors; that is, when a behavior becomes unacceptable, it can be replaced by an acceptable one" (Zhou & Brown, 2015, p. 1). By modifying the environment with the appropriate reinforcement, problem behavior learned in one's early years can be altered. Behaviorists are criticized for not focusing on factors such as creativity of an individual and for not giving credence to cognitive thoughts (Zhou & Brown, 2015).

Albert Bandura built upon the Behaviorist concepts, and the Social Cognitive Theory was formulated. This theory is considered to be transitional between Behavioral Theories and Cognitive Theories. Bandura (1977) was convinced that much of behavior is the result of social modeling. However, he believed cognitive processes played a role in learning from response consequences. He also included self-efficacy (one's confidence in their capacity to perform and accomplish distinctive outcomes) as an important determinant (Bandura, 1977). Past accomplishments were very important to how engrained one's belief were in the expectation of succeeding. Internal physical responses from emotions, such as fear, were caused by provoking thoughts, which could serve as a motivator to continuing or discontinuing efforts. Thoughts could be internally generated or presented through persuasion from others in the external environment. Aspects of behavioral modification can be seen today in various educational settings, residential centers, and in out-patient facilities, where variations of a token economy process are utilized to reward desired behavior and reduce negative behavior (Moore, 2017). Thus, from Behaviorism to Social Learning, we can see how components of the various theories serve to build upon knowledge. This building process can also be seen in the next theory.

Cognitive Theories

There are two theorists to review in this section, Piaget and Vygotsky. While Piaget focused on the healthy development of young children, several of his concepts can be utilized by therapists to better understand how an adult female client may view the world and how to introduce new information. Piaget believed children were not blank slates, as described by some Behaviorists, rather children were born with a network of basic structures that all future learning would build upon (Wong et al., 2015). Four sequential stages, age related, were presented by Piaget: Sensorimotor, Preoperational, Concrete Operational, and Formal Operational (see Figure 5.3). These distinct stages involve a biological readiness and are not dependent on the quantity of knowledge, rather they represent abilities to process information. As one ages, the abilities become more sophisticated and more complex processing of information can occur. For example, children do not achieve the ability to think abstractly until they reach the stage of Formal Operations between the approximate ages of 11 and 15 (Santrock, 2019).

FIGURE 5.3

Piaget's Four Stages of Cognitive Development

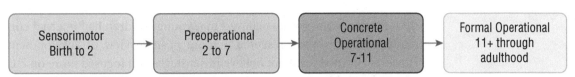

Source: Marlene Estenson

Individuals are introduced to new stimuli, and to understand the meaning of the stimuli, they form schemata. Schemata (a structured set of cognitions stored in memory that impact expectations and interpretation of new data) are cognitive structures in the brain that allow one to organize and classify stimuli from their environment. New information is processed through a system of either assimilation or accommodating the knowledge. Assimilation (takes new information and fits the data into pre-existing schema. New learning is adapted to fit into previous knowledge without revision) takes new information and fits the construct into pre-existing schemata. For example, a child recognizes from their toy farm, what a white and black cow looks like. When visiting a farm, she sees a brown cow. Here a discomfort occurs that requires an adaptation. The child can process that cows do come in other colors. This is an example of assimilation. However, what if the child is at a zoo and sees a white and black zebra? She may refer to the zebra as a cow, but her parent may point out that zebras have stripes and do not give milk. Now the equilibrium is more confusing. To adapt the information, the child accommodates the knowledge. Accommodation (the modification of old schema to form a new schema that accounts for the expanded information. As

Cherry (2019c) in her discussion of Piaget, shares this information: "Albert Einstein once described Piaget's observations on children's intellectual growth and thought process as a discovery 'so simple that only a genius could have thought of it'" (para. 7).

new information is constructed, the individual is unable to fit the data into existing knowledge and must revise existing schema) involves a modification of the old schema to form a new schema that accounts for the expanded information. Now the child understands that other animals besides cows can be white and black. It is clear why Piaget's Cognitive Theory is utilized in educational settings focusing on learning. Over time, Piaget's work has been the source of a great deal of research, much of which has been confirmed (Bormanaki & Khoshhal, 2017). One criticism that has been found is that the ages may not be completely accurate for everyone. For example, infants may form concepts earlier than Piaget ever imagined (Barrouillet, 2015), and language and culture were not part of Piaget's Theory (Bormanaki & Khoshhal, 2017).

Both Piaget and Vygotsky believed that young children had internal cognitive structures and presented a more positive view of development. However, Vygotsky did not believe in set stages and focused more on culture and social interaction with adults and more skilled peers. Vygotsky's Sociocultural Cognitive Theory has been referred to as a social constructivist approach, as he viewed meaning as being constructed through social interaction (Santrock, 2019). Language and symbols are tools serving the ability to communicate socially and allow the child to adapt to their culture/environment. Interaction with others was a process of reciprocal socialization and collaboration. Children could develop meanings on their own, which were referred to as spontaneous. More important, were the nonspontaneous meanings that came from the guidance of adults or peers with more mature abilities. Two terms that have had tremendous importance to educators are scaffolding and zone of proximal development (Santrock, 2019). Scaffolding (an interactive process between a more knowledgeable person and one less skilled at a task, where support is adapted based on the learner's current level of ability, and guidance is decreased as increasing competency is achieved) involves the level of support that reduces, as the individual's ability increases for a given task/skill. The zone of proximal development (the range between the point where a learner is unable to comprehend cognitively or perform a skill without supportive interactive guidance of a more knowledgeable person, and between the point where independent mastery is achieved) is the range just at the tip of the child's abilities to learn on their own, and the upper level of what the individual is capable of mastering with assistance (Karimi-Aghdam, 2017). The zone of proximal development not only involves a relationship between the adult and child, but also a relationship between meanings, as the child's less mature conception of meaning grows to be closer to that of the adult's more mature meaning (Clarà, 2017).

CONCEPT TO CONTEMPLATE

© ImageFlow/Shutterstock.com

Is there something you wish to learn more about or a new skill you want to master, but perhaps doubt your own abilities? How could the concepts of zone of proximal development and scaffolding assist you in learning a new skill?

Ecological Systems Theory

Urie Brofenbrenner (2005) went further with interactions and influence on the child to include layers of various systems that could enhance or inhibit a child's development. As well, the child could mutually accommodate with the environment (Wong et al., 2015) through reciprocal complex interactions (Brofenbrenner, 2005). Nancy Darling (2007) points out that Bronfenbrenner was responsible for human development professionals to move towards paying more attention to contextual differences. Brofenbrenner was also credited for changing developmental research from artificial studies to *ecologically valid* studies with individuals in normal experiences, interacting reciprocally within their own natural environmental systems (Darling, 2007; Brofenbrenner, 2005). The environment consisting of social and cultural practices, for the most part within institutions, make up most of an individual's experiences (Brofenbrenner, 2005). Brofenbrenner conceptualized the interacting-systems as layering, as seen in Figure 5.4.

Brofenbrenner (2005) defines five layers that interact to impact the development of a specific individual over a period of time. The layers move from the person's innermost immediate interactions to the outside. These five are described by Brofenbrenner (2005):

Microsystems - A microsystem is a pattern of activities, social roles, and interpersonal relations experienced by the developing person in a given face-to-face setting with particular physical, social, and symbolic features that invite, permit, or inhibit engagement in sustained, more progressively complex interactions with, and activity in, the immediate environment. Examples include such settings as family, school, peer group, and workplace.

Mesosystems – The mesosystem comprises the linkage and processes taking place between two or more settings containing the developing person (e.g., the relations between home and school and workplace, etc.). In other words, mesosystems are a system of microsystems.

Exosystems – The exosystem comprises the linkage and processes taking place between two or more settings, at least one of which does not contain the developing person, but in which events occur that indirectly influence processes within the immediate setting in which the developing person lives (e.g., for a child, the relation between the home and the parent's workplace...).

Macrosystems – The macrosystems consists of the overarching pattern of micro, meso-, and exosystems characteristic of a given culture or subculture, with particular references to the belief systems, bodies of knowledge, material resources, customs, lifestyles, hazards, and life course options that are embedded in each of these broader systems.

Chronosystems - Chronosystems are the final systems parameter [which] extends the environment into a third dimension... A Chronosystem encompasses change or consistency over time not only in the characteristics of the person but also of the environment in which that person lives (pp. 5-6).

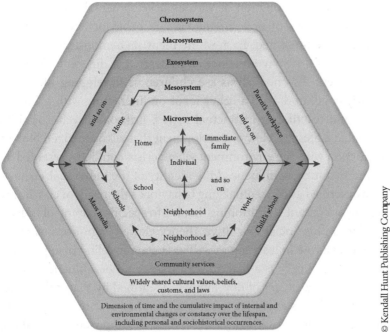

© Kendall Hunt Publishing Company

FIGURE 5.4

Ecological Systems
Theory

In his later years, Bronfenbrenner added to the model and referred to it as a bioecological model, since he acknowledged that heredity and genetic differences vary in environmental enhancement of potential. Thus, Bronfenbrenner (2005) encouraged social programs and funding to provide resources that would assist those in less than ideal developmental situations/environments.

Darling (2007) in her analysis of Bronfenbrenner's 1961 work focusing on gender, describes how Bronfenbrenner conceptualized the differences seen in males versus females. Girls were presented as receiving more loving discipline that promoted compliance and sensitivity to social cues in the environment. Parents demonstrating more overall warmth for daughters, giving affection and nurturance that included less leadership enhancement, dependence, and attention to adult expectations, resulting in less autonomy and self-expression in female children (Darling, 2007). Males were seen as receiving more punishment type discipline that resulted in inadequate compliance with community norms. In addition, Bronfenbrenner felt parents fostered more autonomy and independence in males (Darling, 2007). Thus, gender differences in adolescent male and females were not defined by biology, but rather by the meaning that tasks were given by males versus females from their interactions with their various systems.

Through this examination of various developmental theorists, differing conceptual views of how an individual's behavior and personality are shaped, were presented. Each of the theorists demonstrate the complexity of factors that may influence an individual at different points in their development. Psychoanalysts see children as developing life-long traits in early childhood, with a heavy focus on interacting with primary caregivers and reacting to instinctual drives. Erikson's Psychosocial Theory presented a lifespan view of development that acknowledged biology and interaction with the environment where crisis/conflicts presented at each period that further influenced the identity of the individual. Behaviorists were described as conceptualizing behavior as the result of classical conditioning or operant conditioning that led to specific shaping of individuals. Bandura in his Social Cognitive Theory viewed cognitions as important in playing a role in learning as well as social modeling of appropriate behavior. Self-efficacy is a determinant that could be influenced by others. Four sequential stages of development identified by Piaget illustrated the maturing of one's cognitive processing abilities over time. Vygotsky's Sociocultural Cognitive Theory emphasized the importance in culture and social interactions with adults or more skilled peers. The zone of proximal development and scaffolding were explained as important in the learning process between a child and a guiding adult. Bronfenbrenner's Ecological Theory explained the mutual accommodating that occurs between an individual and a number of interacting layered systems that can enhance or inhibit development. These theories presented lay a foundational examination of factors that influence an individual's development, socially, physically, cognitively, emotionally, and spiritually. Through the developmental foundation presented, application to the lives of three women in different periods of lifespan development will be discussed: young adulthood, middle adulthood, and older adulthood. At the end of the chapter, a list of resources is given.

CONTEXTUAL INTEGRATION OF DEVELOPMENT OF THREE ADULT WOMEN

It should be noted that various theorists indicate minor differences in ages for when periods of development begin and end. Some refer to young adolescence as beginning with the onset of puberty. If the average for females starting to menstruate is 11 years of age (Wong et al., 2015), would one then be identified as a teen? When do the teenage years end? Legally, the age of 18 is usually seen as the age where one is held responsible as an adult in the United States courts, when one can vote, and join the armed services. However, over the last decade, MRI based structural studies and functional studies have demonstrated that various areas of the brain mature at different rates and have been mapped to behavioral domains (Breiner et al., 2018; Herringa, 2019). The prefrontal circuitry, amygdala, and orbitofrontal region in particular have been explored, demonstrating that areas that impact decision-making and higher risk behavior may not be fully mature until into the 20's (Breiner et al., 2018; Li et al., 2019). Society has changed in ways that impact the roles of teens, where taking on adult roles may be delayed. Thus, the age of beginning the periods of late adolescence and young adulthood are not clearly differentiated. For the purpose of this first case study, Samantha will be viewed at the age of 20 as a young adult. The following two case studies focus on Carla, age 45 in the period of middle age, and Dorothy, at age 70 in late adulthood.

Young Adulthood

Samantha, a Caucasian twenty-year-old woman had been instructed by her university's Student Affairs Department to attend counseling, before she would be allowed to return to college. Her mom, Carla, and stepfather, Tom, attended the first session with Samantha, at the community counseling center in Bakerstown, Kansas. The parents stated that they came for the first session to be sure that Samantha "gave accurate information, since she lies constantly." Since Samantha was twelve and her biological father and her mom divorced, Samantha blamed her mother for her father's leaving and moving far away. Since then, there had been no contact with her dad, except for a yearly birthday card. The mom and stepfather married when Samantha was fourteen. Currently, they live in New York City, where Tom owns a successful business. What they did not tell the counselor was that Tom worked long hours, and Carla would drink to numb her feelings of loneliness and anxiety. During most of Samantha's youth she had come home from school to fend for herself, as her mother was usually intoxicated. Carla indicates that Samantha has been caught drinking alcohol and using drugs on several occasions since the sixth grade. After graduating from high school, Samantha attended her freshman year at an Ivy League university. However, Samantha recently was placed on behavioral probation and asked to sit out a semester, as a form of university discipline for having been caught smoking marijuana in her honors dorm room. Samantha has agreed to the counseling and to having her parents at the first session because they have threatened her with not paying for college if Samantha did not attend therapy while living in Kansas. Recently, Samantha sold an expensive diamond necklace that had been given to her by her stepfather to keep as an heirloom. Tired of dealing with her behavior, the frustrated parents decided to send her to Bakerstown, to live with her maternal grandmother, Dorothy. Samantha has not seen her grandmother since she was a little girl. The only thing she really knew about the older woman was that Carla avoided contact with Dorothy, as they did not get along. The plan was for the parents to spend a few nights in a hotel, having dropped Samantha off at Dorothy's, before returning home to New York City. Later, they would return for Samantha right before the following Ivy League university semester begins. Samantha shared that she has been at her grandmother's home for two days, and knew that she did not want to live with Dorothy, because the grandmother has very rigid routines about what time meals are served, when bedtime is, cleaning up after themselves, doing chores, and insists on upholding a curfew. Dorothy made it clear on the first day that her twenty-year-old granddaughter must work and pay rent while living under her roof. Samantha appeared very uncooperative and disrespectful, resenting the entire situation.

Over the next few weeks, Samantha began to warm up to the predictableness of Dorothy's schedule. She even tolerated Dorothy praying out loud before meals. Dorothy noticed how often Samantha chose to dress provocatively, and she even bragged about being sexually suggestive with males she had met in the small town. Assuming Samantha was just testing her to get an argument started, Dorothy chose not to respond to such comments. Slowly, Samantha began to enjoy her Grandmother's company. Dorothy insisted Samantha attend Sunday church services together with her. Soon, Samantha was dating a young man at their church named Jerry. Things in the household seemed to be going well. Then, one day as they were talking, Samantha shared with her grandmother that her stepfather had regularly molested her from the ages of fifteen to seventeen. She indicated that the abuse stopped after Samantha threatened to share a secret diary which she had been keeping with her mother and his co-workers. The diary allegedly contained details of each abuse occurrence. The threat had scared the stepfather enough that he had temporarily stopped. Samantha claimed that the recent gift of the heirloom necklace was really a bribe to coerce her to begin having sex with him, and to keep her quiet about the abuse. Instead, Samantha reported that she sold the necklace to the "sleaziest pawn shop she could find." According to Samantha, Carla did not know about the abuse. Dorothy later called Carla to tell her about what her granddaughter had shared. Samantha was furious that her grandmother had told her mom. Carla left her husband and came to stay at Dorothy's house. A conflicted Samantha went back and forth over the next few weeks, stating she had lied about her stepfather, and at other times she would say the abuse had occurred. Tensions were high, as Samantha fought verbally with Carla, Carla fought with Dorothy, and Tom continued by phone to say he was innocent.

The more tense things became, the more promiscuous Samantha behaved with Jerry. Samantha's behavior made Jerry uncomfortable, as he had chosen not to be sexually active before marriage. Having Jerry say no to her was utterly perplexing to Samantha. The more he resisted the more outrageous her advances became. Finally, Samantha realized Jerry was serious about his beliefs. This had never happened before. She had always been able to get affection from men through sex. Samantha began to reconsider how she related to others. Could some people really be genuinely trustworthy and love others without ulterior motives? Thank goodness her time in Bakerstown was only half over, as it would give her time to discuss her thoughts and feelings with her counselor.

Middle Adulthood

Again, age differentiations vary among theorists. Here middle adulthood will be viewed as a period of life from approximately 40 to 65. Carla, at age 45, is married for the second time and lives in New York. She is married to Tom, a successful owner of his own business. Socially and economically they live an upper-class lifestyle. Carla grew up as an only child with her parents in a small town in Kansas. She felt very close to her father and enjoyed being her daddy's little girl. However, Carla was constantly angry at her mother, Dorothy. Carla's father drank too much, which led to constant fighting among her parents. Carla always doubted that her mother loved her, as she showed little affection and never said I love you. Carla was a good student and dated some in high school. During her junior year, her father died of a sudden heart attack. Carla blamed her mother for always fighting with him and nagging. As soon as Carla was of age, she eloped with a young man that her mother had forbidden her to date. He had promised her a wonderful and exciting life. Instead, her husband could not keep a job and bought things they could not afford, resulting in creditors constantly calling. Her unplanned pregnancy, with daughter Samantha, only added to the stress. Her husband left her when Samantha was twelve. As a single mom, she struggled economically to pay the bills, which left Carla feeling anxious and all alone. She began to drink to stop the emotional pain. Carla refused to consider moving back to Kansas to live with her mother. She avoided talking with her mother on the phone. Dorothy would give unsolicited advice, which only led to more resentment and anger. Carla had promised herself that she would never be like her mother. Then, she had met Tom, and soon they were married. Living the lifestyle she had always dreamed of, she no longer had to struggle to pay her bills. Tom worked long hours and traveled a great deal for his business. Surprisingly, she found herself once again feeling lonely, so she would drink. As a teen, Samantha often came home from school, only to find her mother passed out drunk.

Carla found motherhood quite a challenge, especially when Samantha was a teenager. She often felt inadequate as a mother. Samantha constantly pushed Carla's emotional buttons. They constantly fought over everything. Yet, her husband Tom seemed to bond with Samantha in a way she could not understand. He was always doting on the girl and buying her expensive gifts, even when Samantha began to get into trouble with drugs and alcohol. It had proven to be a constant battle of the wills, which had left Carla even more exhausted than usual. Through the years she had experienced periods of depression where it was even hard to get out of bed in the morning. She had found some guidance self-help books and tapes that promised to center her energy from within. She was actually glad when Samantha had left for her Ivy League university, and yet, she felt unexplainably guilty at the same time. However, it did not last as Samantha had once again gotten into trouble, and this time was being sent home. For two weeks they had yelled at one another, until Samantha had finally crossed the line. Carla could not believe that once Samantha had been gifted the necklace, she had sold the treasured heirloom. How could her child not be grateful for everything they had done for her? Carla had reached her limit.

Now, she finds that Samantha has accused her stepfather of molestation. Her marriage could be ripped apart once again. She was caught between wanting to believe and protect her daughter, and then, wanting to trust the man who had provided for them financially. It just could not be true she thought. She remembered all the times he and Samantha had gone off to have fun at the ballgames and the amusement park. Carla had been happy to see them go together, as she herself disliked such activities. Now she finds herself faced with having to come face to face with Dorothy, as she confronts Samantha for lying. However, Dorothy had sounded genuinely concerned when she had called. Perhaps, this time they could listen to one another. Could it be possible to view her mother from a different lens? After all, she needed to rethink her trust in Tom. As she packed her bags, her thoughts raced. Her husband had not been interested in sex for a long time. Then, she considered the gift of the heirloom necklace. If it was true how could she not have known? What kind of a mother would that make her? What kind of a woman was she, if her husband had chosen her daughter over his own wife? How would she survive, if it proved to be true? She grabbed her suitcase and headed to Kansas.

Older Adulthood

Dorothy is 70 years old, and in her "golden years". Bakerstown had been her home for her entire life. She has several friends, enjoys her home, and feels useful in her volunteer job, as the church custodian twice a week. Cleaning had always given her pleasure, so why not serve at church? People were always complimenting how she made everything shine. While she lived alone, she still had lots of company since she became known as the neighborhood pet sitter. Gardening was her favorite activity, but lately her arthritis in her back made it hard to sit on the ground for any period of time. It was just as well, she thought, as her cataracts had led her to use the wrong fertilizer on her cherished pink roses. Since her husband's death many years ago, Dorothy's life has actually been better. Her marriage of twenty-five years had been miserable once her husband had gotten injured at work, and they were forced to live off his disability check. He spent his days drinking and spending all their food money on one bottle of liquor after another. She was grateful to God that she was able to hold down two jobs to keep them afloat. Her husband's alcoholism had hurt Carla the most. She worshipped the ground her father walked on. Carla had dealt with her Dad's injury by pretending his drinking was not a problem.

Her daughter was always blaming Dorothy, as if she could keep him from drinking. Despite her difficult relationship with Carla, she still felt happy that her granddaughter was coming to stay. She had not seen Samantha since she was a little girl. She planned to introduce her granddaughter to all her friends. Of course, she would ask for a minimum amount of rent from Samantha, so she could learn the importance of being an independent woman, capable of taking care of herself. She would not tell Samantha her plan till the end of her visit. All the rent money would be put away and returned to her, to put towards college. Truth be told, she was a little envious, as she had never had such an opportunity, as she had grown up the only girl in a family of nine children.

However, things immediately become chaotic when her daughter, Carla arrived with Samantha. Within minutes, there is obviously tension between Samantha and her mother. Both are yelling and arguing over something. Carla stays five minutes and leaves to go back to the hotel. How nice it would have been if both Carla and Samantha had stayed. Dorothy imagined herself fixing a pot roast dinner with all the fixings. She guessed that neither of them had enjoyed a good pot roast in a long time. However, if it meant yelling and screaming, they both would have to leave. Dorothy would not allow such ugly language to be used in her home. God demanded better language than what she had just heard her daughter and granddaughter use. Carla did not want such chaos in her peaceful home. Together, she and Samantha walked into the house to have a cup of coffee. As soon as Samantha heard the expectations that Dorothy had for her, the ungodly language began again. Dorothy picked up her fly swatter and chased Samantha out the screen door, off the porch, and out of her yard. She calmly said, "You can come back when you learn some manners. Dinner is at 6:00 sharp." Samantha did return with a different attitude, and the two of them had dinner together. Dorothy could not remember when she had been this happy. While she enjoyed her life, this was her granddaughter eating at her table. A few weeks later, Samantha casually mentions that her stepfather had molested her over a two-year period. Dorothy felt like she had been punched in the stomach. Afterwards, Samantha went for a walk. Dorothy sat with tears in her eyes and prayed. Finally, she stood up to go to the phone and call Carla.

From the limited information, what do you know about each woman?

© Digital Storm/Shutterstock.com

What inferences can you make about each woman's physical, social, cognitive, emotional, and spiritual development given their lives at different developmental stages, such as at age 4, 10, 16, 25, 45, and at age 70?

Which theory of development helps you to best conceptualize the women's' lives?

What are some of the schemata beliefs that each may have learned about trust, relationships, and themselves?

Draw Brofenbrenner's Ecological Model and label one of the women's microsystem, mesosystem, exosystem, macrosystem, and chronosystem. Think about who and what may have influenced their development.

What specific developmental issues might each woman be currently facing at their current stage? How do you see each woman's sense of identity strength?

As a counselor trainee or practicing professional, what are the issues you feel should be addressed in a treatment plan for each woman?

LOOKING THROUGH THE LENS OF CHRISTIANITY: BIBLICAL INTEGRATION

Having applied questions to contemplate theories and concepts to examine the lives of three women of different ages, a focus on spiritual integration is now explored. An integration of spirituality in the lives of the three women will first be discussed. Secondly, a bridge of connection will be made to that of the reader's life. While a Christian belief system is an integral part of each chapter, there exists the possibility that some readers may have other religious backgrounds. Yet, all humans have a spiritual need to search out their place in the universe and to find meaning in life and experiences (Frankl, 2006; Negru-Subtirica et al., 2016).

Consideration is first given to Dorothy's rigid structure around time and tasks. It is clear to Dorothy that the Lord's name should never be taken in vain. From these situations, it is evident that Dorothy has had some experience in being taught messages from the Bible. Given her age, it can be hypothesized that living in a small town with conservative values, she probably attended church regularly. Over her lifespan she had the influence of many relationships within her immediate microsystem, mesosystem, exosystem, macrosystem, and chronosystem, (Brofenbrenner, 2005). Society may have changed in how Christian values are viewed, however, Dorothy's earlier development had stronger expectations that probably shaped her cultural meaning about God, faith, prayer, and church attendance. Perhaps, her faith is what is responsible for her contribution to the community, pet sitting for neighbors, and cleaning the church as an act of service. She has strong feelings about the use of substances, such as alcohol, that could harm her Christian witness. One could argue that her sense of caring for others was the virtue that forms from the balance found in the integration of integrity vs. despair, in women in her age range (Dundel & Harbke, 2017). It is likely that her integration included the acceptance of God's grace and love, which brought her true peace. Churches vary in their sense of rules and appropriate ways of behaving. However, Dorothy may have been drawn to the church that provided the security of boundaries set in rules (Krause, 2016). While a life full of structure and routine assisted her in coping when things had been out of her control, it could have been solidified by her faith, bringing her to a place where she could love others.

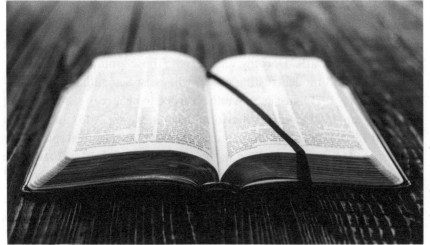

It is not to suggest that Dorothy always acted Christ-like, especially in her interactions with her daughter Carla. So, what can be made of Carla's apparent lack of faith? She obviously was searching, as we see her listening to motivational tapes giving instruction to harness her internal energy to reduce stress. Out of Carla's anger at her mother, she not only rejected Dorothy but also rejected her mother's teachings about faith. Carla's anger blinded her to many areas of her life, including not seeing the signs that her husband was molesting their daughter. It is when her existential crisis of having lost what must have felt like all control that she reaches out for a genuine connection with her mother. Krause (2016) reports that individuals who struggle with forgiving others who have hurt them, need to forgive the other person, forgive themselves, and address their forgiveness with God. Religion can be seen as a social phenomenon that allows one to be influenced by the surrounding community (Brofenbrenner, 2005). Through this social support that Carla so needs, the possibility exists for this middle-aged woman to reconstruct her worldview. Krause (2016) found that as individuals grow older, they are more willing to forgive others. Perhaps, as they struggle to reconcile and find new ways of interacting, Carla will find the ability to connect with God.

Samantha, the youngest of the women, clearly has confusion about religious faith. However, it appears that her future may include relationships with more people of faith as she stays with her grandmother. Thus, the possibility of her finding a different meaning in her search than that which her mom found at Samantha's age is quite possible. By the various unpleasant interactions with her mother and those of her stepfather, she has been motivated to reject trust and avoids close relationships, since no relationship feels safe to her. However, there is even greater prognosis for Samantha, as she will experience the healing indirectly and directly that occurs between Carla, Dorothy, and herself. Those around her who show compassion and model trusting others will assist Samantha in this journey (Bandura, 1977). Just as Samantha learned to behave in self-damaging ways, she can unlearn those behaviors (Zhou & Brown, 2015). Individuals between 18-29 years of age were found to seek a more personal spirituality that assisted in finding meaning in their life (Negro-Subtirica, 2016). The more she interacts with safe people, the more her identity may be shaped to trust others and eventually, to accept God's loving grace.

© Asier Romero/Shutterstock.com

CONCEPT TO CONTEMPLATE

What personal lessons can be learned from these three? As Brofenbrenner's model demonstrates, all interactions directly and to a large part indirectly, impact the systems and thus, the individuals within. Christ called us to love one another (John 13:34) and to feed His sheep (John 21:17). Are there parts of your past development that have taught you messages and left you with emotions that get in your way of understanding God's love? It is up to you to change through the process of assimilating and accommodating information. Will you interact with environments that enhance your life? While not everything can be controlled by you, God knows the heart's desire. Do not underestimate the impact of your life.

INTERVENTION ACTIVITY: CIRCLE OF ROLES

This activity is called a Circle of Roles. It is useful to assist women in identifying their personal needs, which often they are unaware of or unable to communicate effectively to others. Take a few minutes and do this for yourself. Remember the Scripture Galatians 6:5 (*New International Bible*, 1973/2011) states, "for each should carry their own load". How do you know what that load is if you are unaware of your own needs? This is not an activity about selfishness, but rather to assist in being more authentic in your own communication with others. Circle of Roles has been found to be a very therapeutic activity for various women's groups and in dealing with anger issues in individual therapy with clients.

These are the instructions and possible scenarios that arise. Draw a large circle on the page and divide the circle into segments, one for each role you have in your life (see Figure 5.5). First, reflect on what a role might entail. Think of a role as a labeled position that you and society have expectations regarding. For example, some of your roles might be a mom, employee, sister, daughter, church member, student, teacher, aunt, grandmother, and others. If you have not participated in the role behaviorally or actively thought about it over the last two weeks, do not include that role. Here you want only those roles that are important aspects of your identity. Select one or two of the most important roles and ask yourself these questions:

1. **What are your emotional needs within that role?** Often, clients are unable to verbalize needs and will list tasks, such as "well as a mom, I have to take the kids to school, pick up the groceries, and such". Help the client understand what an emotional need a mom might have, such as affection or appreciation from her children. Usually, the need can be found by asking "tell me the last time you were frustrated as a mom". Probing questions can assist the client to clarify what the actual need might be. For example, if a client says, "I need them to do their chores without being told over and over", assist her in identifying what the actual need is behind her frustration. Perhaps, it is a desire to be appreciated for all the things she does for the children.

2. **What happens if your needs are not met?** Really explore the thoughts you might be saying to yourself or the behavior you display. Often, it may be helpful to ask how another individual would know what they were feeling.

3. **How could you start getting your needs met?** You can see how this can lead into discussing assertive and honest communication, with 'I statements', owning personal needs, and clarifying realistic expectations. Needs are God given, like emotions, and are natural. "Who is responsible for meeting that need" is often a helpful prompt.

4. **What would it be like if your needs were met?** This activity also often moves to identifying unrealistic expectations; it does not mean the need is not valid. It is also possible some needs will never be met in the way the person desires. An illustration of this can be seen for Carla, who needed to know her mom loved her and to feel nurtured by her showing affection. If Dorothy had been unable or unwilling to genuinely hear and respond to Carla, what would be a healthy way for Carla to address her own need? It is at this point, that clients often begin to realize that they have a great deal of sadness under the anger they have experienced by not having emotional needs met and then can begin to grieve. Then, they can decide what that means in terms of healthy boundaries for the relationships in their current life. The counselor can assist in clarifying the needs, emotions, options, and assist in preparing for possible consequences of actions the client may select.

FIGURE 5.5

Circle of Roles

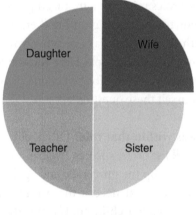

Write your roles on the empty circle below similar to this circle, and then answer the following questions for each role.

What are your emotional needs within that role?
What happens if your needs are not met?
How could you start to get your needs met?
What would it be like if your needs were met?

Source: Anita Kuhnley

Template for you to complete:

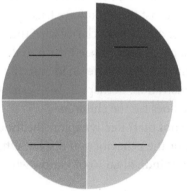

Write your roles on the empty circle below similar to this circle, and then answer the following questions for each role.

What are your emotional needs within that role?
What happens if your needs are not met?
How could you start to get your needs met?
What would it be like if your needs were met?

Source: Anita Kuhnley

CHAPTER SUMMARY

In this chapter, the complexity of human development has been examined by discussing the interaction between biology-genes (nature) and environmental factors (that nurture). Theories and concepts were presented to provide a foundation in which to conceptualize individual differences in behavior. Through interaction with pieces of the various theories presented and additional ones to be encountered in the future, you will continue to integrate your conceptual understanding of human development. Through the lives of the three women, application for counseling was demonstrated. The Circle of Roles activity was shared to illustrate one additional way to assist clients. By owning one's own thoughts, emotions, and behaviors, there is increased space in one's life to be an authentic individual taking responsibility for getting needs met appropriately. Spiritual integration is an essential part of how we influence systems and are influenced by environments. As researchers continue to explore real life situations and advances continue in neurobiology and genetics, knowledge will continue to be processed by humans. Development is proof that individuals are unique while the same in some ways, and active participants in their learning within their lifespan. In addition, with greater understanding and awareness of your impact on others, individuals may advocate for social change that will improve issues that currently inhibit healthy development.

KEY TERMS

Accommodation – the modification of old schema to form a new schema that accounts for the expanded information; as new information is constructed, the individual is unable to fit the data into existing knowledge and must revise existing schema

Assimilation – takes new information and fits the data into pre-existing schema; new learning is adapted to fit into previous knowledge without revision

Attachment – an emotional and psychological bond that forms between a young child and a caregiver as a result of basic needs being met. This significant bond may result in a range of emotions from security when needs are predictably met to distress when separation occurs or needs are met with inconsistency

Ethnocentricism – involves viewing others through the self-lens of one's own, entrenched socialization, culture, and values from a homogenizing moral stance. Whether through ignorance or purposeful behavior, one's in-group culture is viewed as superior to that of out-group cultural differences

Scaffolding – an interactive process between a more knowledgeable person and one less skilled at a task, where support is adapted based on the learner's current level of ability, and guidance is decreased as increasing competency is achieved

Schema or Schemata (plural) – a structured set of cognitions stored in memory that impact expectations and interpretation of new data

Self-Efficacy – involves one's confidence in their capacity to perform and accomplish distinctive outcomes

Zone of Proximal Development (ZPD) – the range between the point where a learner is unable to comprehend cognitively or perform a skill without supportive interactive guidance of a more knowledgeable person, and between the point where independent mastery is achieved

SUGGESTED RESOURCES

Books

In a Different Voice: Psychological Theory and Women's Development by Carole Gilligan

Life-Span Development (17th ed.) by John Santrock

Counseling Individuals through the Lifespan (3rd ed.) by Daniel W. Wong, Kimberly R. Hall, Cheryl A. Justice, and Lucy Wong Hernandez

Articles

The War on Women in Psychoanalytic Theory Building: Past to Present by Balsam, R. H. (2015). *The Psychoanalytic Study of the Child, 69*(1), 83-107.

Journals

Fortune Journals. *Journal of Women's Health and Development.*

http://www.fortunejournals.com/journal-of-womens-health-and-development-home-fjwhd.php

Organizations

U.S. Department of State. Office of Global Women's Issues: https://www.state.gov/bureaus-offices/bureaus-and-offices-reporting-directly-to-the-secretary/office-of-global-womens-issues

World Health Organization. *Women's and girl's health across the life course.* https://www.who.int/life-course/news/women-and-girls-health-across-life-course-top-facts/en/

REFERENCES

Association for Spiritual, Ethical, and Religious Values in Counseling. (2010). *ASERVIC white paper.* http://www.aservic.org/wp-content/uploads/2015/02/ASERVIC-WHITE-PAPER.pdf

Balsam, R. H. (2015). The war on women in Psychoanalytic Theory building: Past to present. *The Psychoanalytic Study of the Child, 69*(1), 83-107.

Bandura, A. (1977). Self-efficacy: Toward a unifying theory of behavioral change. *Psychology Review, 84*(2), 191-215.

Barrouillet, P. (2015). Theories of cognitive development: From Piaget to today. *Developmental Review 38,* 1-12. https://doi.org/10.1016/j.dr.2015.07.004

Beauvais, C. (2016) Ages and ages: The multiplication of children's 'ages' in early twentieth-century child psychology, *History of Education, 45*(3), 304-318. https://doi.org/10.1080/0046760X.2015

Bell Holleran, L. L., Vaughan, T. J., & Vandiver, D. M. (2016). Juror decision-making in death penalty sentencing when presented with defendant's history of child abuse or neglect. *Behavioral Sciences and the Law, 34,* 742–766. https://doi.org/10.1002/bsl.2271

Black, A. E. (2019). Treating attachment in Group Therapy: Attachment Theory meets modern sychoanac technique. *International Journal of Group Psychotherapy, 69*(3), 259-286.

Bormanaki, H. B., & Khoshhal, Y. (2017). The role of equilibration in Piaget's Theory of Cognitive Development and its implication for receptive skills: A theoretical study. *Journal of Language Teaching and Research, 8*(5), 996. https://doi.org/10.1016/j.dr.2015.07.004

Breiner, K., Li, A., Cohen, A. O., Steinberg, L., Bonnie, R. J., Scott, E. S., Taylor-Thompson, K., Rudolph, M. D., Chein, J., Richeson, J. A., Dellarco, D. V., Fair, D. A., Casey, B. J., & Galván, A. (2018). Combined effect of peer presence, social cues, and rewards on cognitive control in adolescents. *Developmental Psychology 60*(3), 292-302.

Brofenbrenner, U. (2005). Ecological models of human development. In M. Gauvain, & M. Cole (Eds.). *Readings on the development of children* (4th ed., pp. 3-8). Worth Publishers.

Center for Disease Control and Prevention in the United States. (2017). *CDC growth charts.* National Center for Health Statistics. https://www.cdc.gov/growthcharts/clinical_charts.htm

Cherry, K. (2019a). *Biography of Erik Erikson (1902-1994).* https://www.verywellmind.com/erik-erikson-biography-1902-1994-2795538

Cherry, K. (2019b). *The influence of Psychoanalysis on the field of psychology.* https://www.verywellmind.com/what-is-psychoanalysis-2795246

Cherry, K. (2019c). *Quote by Einstein regarding Piaget in 10 influential psychologists.* https://www.verywellmind.com/most-influential-psychologists-2795264

Clarà, M. (2017). How instruction influences conceptual development: Vygotsky's Theory revisited. *Educational Psychologist, 52*(1), 50-62. https://doi.org/10.1080/00461520.2016.1221765

Corey, G., Corey., M. S., & Corey, C. (2019). *Issues and ethics in the helping professions.* (10th ed.). Cengage Learning.

Cummings, E. E., (n.d.). *Quote on courage.* Brainy Quotes. https://www.brainyquote.com/search_results?q=e+e+cummings+growing+up

Cureton, J. L., & Clemens, E. V. (2015). Affective constellations for counter transference awareness following a client's suicide attempt. *Journal of Counseling & Development, 93*(3), 352-360. https://doi-org.ezproxy.liberty.edu/10.4324/9780203080719.ch3

Darling, N. (2007). Ecological Systems Theory: The person in the center of the circles. *Research in Human Development, 4*(3-4), 203-217.

Del Barrio, E., Marsillas, S., Buffel, T., Smetcoren, A. S., & Mayte, S. (2018). From active aging to active citizenship: The role of (age) friendliness. *Social Sciences, 7*(8). https://doi.org/10.3390/socsci7080134

Dunkel, C. S., & Harbke, C. (2017). A review of measures of Erikson's stages of psychosocial development: Evidence for a general factor. *Journal of Adult Development, 24*, 58-76.

Frankl, V. (2006). *Man's search for meaning.* Beacon Press.

Freeman, J. (2015). Developing social skills and relationships. *Reclaiming Children and Youth, 23*(4), 48-51. http://ezproxy.liberty.edu/login?url=https://searchproquest-com.ezproxy.liberty.edu/docview/1655359264?accountid=12085

Ganea, I. (2019). Review of man's search for meaning, by Victor E. Frankl. *Euromentor Journal (Bucharest), 10*(3), 150-155.

Gilligan, C. (1982). *In a different voice.* Harvard University Press.

Gordon, N., & Greene, E. (2018). Nature, nurture, and capital punishment: How evidence of a genetic-environment interaction, future dangerousness, and deliberation affect sentencing decisions. *Behavioral Sciences & The Law, 36*(1), 65-83.

Helming, L. (2015). *God's plan for the terrible-twos.* https://digitalcollections.Dordt.edu/faculty_work/139

Herringa, R. (2019). Commentary: Pediatric post-traumatic stress disorder from a neurodevelopmental network perspective: Reflection on Weems et al. (2019). *The Journal of Child Psychology and Psychiatry, 60*(4), 409-411. https://doi-org.ezproxy.liberty.edu/10.1111/jcpp.13049

Hoemann, K., Xu, F., & Barrett L. F. (2019). Emotion words, emotion concepts, and emotional development in children: A constructionist hypothesis. *Developmental Psychology, 55*(9), 1830-1849.

Holodynski, M., & Seeger, D. (2019). Expressions as signs and their significance for emotional development. *Developmental Psychology, 55*(9), 1812-1829.

Holodynski, M., Seeger, D., Kortas-Hartmann, P., & Wörmann, V. (2013). Placing emotion regulation in a developmental framework of self-regulation. In K. C. Barett, N. A. Fox, G. A. Morgan, D. J. Fidler, & L. A. Daunhauer (Eds.), *Handbook of self-regulatory processes in new directions and international perspective.* (pp. 27-59). https://doi-org.ezproxy.liberty.edu/10.4324/9780203080719.ch3

Ickovics, J. R., Lewis, J. B., Cunningham, S. D., Thomas, J., & Magriples, U. (2019). Transforming prenatal care: Multidisciplinary team science improves a broad range of maternal-child outcomes. *American Psychologist, 74*(3), 343-355. https://doi.org/10.1037/amp0000435

Jarius, S., & Wildemann, B. (2017). Pavlov's reflex before Pavlov: Early accounts from the English, French, and German classic literature. *European Neurology, 77*(5-6), 322-326.

Karimi-Aghdam, S. (2017). Zone of proximal development. *Integrative Psychology and Behavioral Sciences, 51*(1), 76-93.

Knight, Z. G. (2017). A proposed model of Psychodynamic Psychotherapy linked to Erik Erikson's eight stages of psychosocial development. *Clinical Psychology and Psychotherapy 24,* 1047-1058. https://doi.org/1002cpp2066

Krause, N. (2016). Compassion, acts of contrition and forgiveness in middle and late life. *Pastoral Psychology, 65,* 127-141. https://doi-org.ezproxy.liberty.edu/10.1007/s11089-015-0669-x

Kyriazis, M. (2020). Ageing throughout history: The evolution of human lifespan. *Journal of Molecular Evolution, 88,* 57-65.

Li, J.- B., Willems, Y., Stok, F. M., Deković , M., Bartels, M., & Finkenauer, C. (2019). Parenting and self-control across early to late adolescence: A three-level meta-analysis. https://doi-org.ezproxy.liberty.edu/10.1177/1745691619863046

Love, P., & Talbot, D. (2009). Defining spiritual development: A missing consideration for student affairs. *National Association of Student Personnel Administrators (NASPA) Journal, 46*(4), 614-628.

Marcia, J., & Josselson, R. (2013). Eriksonian personality research and its implications for psychotherapy. *Journal of Personality, 81*(6) 617- 629.

Marshall, B. L., & Rahman, M. (2015). Celebrity, ageing and the construction of 'third age' identities. *International Journal of Cultural Studies, 18*(6), 577-593.

Meland, A. T., Kaltvedt, E., & Reikerås, E. (2019). Toddlers' play in ECEC institutions from a gender perspective. *European Early Childhood Education Research Journal, 27*(2), 241-256.

Merrill-James, R. H., Douglass, M. J., & Shupp, M. R. (2019). Promoting awareness of self: Cultural immersion and service-learning experiences of counselors-n-training. *Journal of Counselor Preparation and Supervision, 12*(2), 95-103.

Moore, J. (2017). John B. Watson's classical S-R behaviorism. *The Journal of Mind and Behavior, 38*(1), 1-34.

Moreira, T. (2016). De-standardising aging? Shifting regimes of age measurement. *Ageing and Society, 36*(7), 1407-1433. https://doi.org/10.1017/S0144686X15000458

Negru-Subtirical, O., Tiganasu, A., Dezutter, J., & Luyckx, K. (2017). A cultural take on the links between religiosity, identity, and meaning in life in religious emerging adults. *British Journal of Developmental Psychology, 35*, 106-126.

New International Bible. (2011). New International Bible Online. https://www.thenivbible.com/ (Original work published 1973).

Redekop, F., Luke, C., & Malone, F. (2017). From the couch to the chair: Applying Psychoanalytic Theory and practice in counseling. *Journal of Counseling & Development,* 95(2), 100-109.

Remley, T. P., & Herlihy, B. (2010). *Ethical, legal, and professional issues in counseling* (6th ed.). Pearson Education. https://doi.org/10.1002/jcad.1212

Rizzolo, G. S. (2018). The specter of the primitive. *Journal of The American Psychoanalytic Association, 65*(6), 945-977.

Rosin, J. (2015). The necessity of counselor individuation for fostering reflective practice. *Journal of Counseling & Development, 93*(1), 88-95. https://doi.org/10.1002/j.1556-6676.2015.00184.x

Santrock, J. (2019). *Life-Span development* (17th ed.). McGraw Hill.

Schröder, M., Ludtke, J., Fux, E., Izat, Y., & Bolten, M., Gloger-Tippelt, G., Suess, G. J., & Schmid, M. (2019). Attachment disorder and Attachment Theory – Two sides of one medal or two different coins? *Comprehensive Psychiatry, 95*, 152139. https://doi.org/10.1016/j.comppsych.2019.152139

Schumacher, N., Köster, M., & Kärtner, J. (2019). Modeling prosocial behavior increases helping in 16-month-olds. *Child Development, 90*(5), 1789-1801. https://doi.org/10.1111/cdev.13054

Sewell, A. (2019). An adaption of the Good Behaviour Game to promote social skill development at the whole-class level. *Educational Psychology in Practice, 35*(4). https://doi.org/101080/02667363.2019.1695583

Sue, D. W., Sue, D., Neville, H. A., & Smith, L. (2019). *Counseling the culturally diverse: Theory and Practice* (8th ed.). https://www.wiley.com/en-us/978111944824

VandenBos, G. R. (2015). *APA Dictionary of Psychology* (2nd ed.). American Psychology Association. http://dx.doi.org.ezproxy.liberty.edu/10.1037/dev0000698

Van Rosmalen, L., Van Der Horst, F. C. P., & Van Der Veer, R. (2016). From secure dependency to attachment: Mary Ainsworth's integration of Blatz's security theory into Bowlby's Attachment Theory. *History of Psychology, 19*(1) 22-39.

Watson, J. (2017, September). *Behaviorism.* https://doi-org.ezproxy.liberty.edu/10.4324/9781351314329

Whitbourne, S. K. (2012, June 23). *What's your true age?* Psychology Today. https://www.psychologytoday.com/us/blog/fulfillment-any-age/201206/what-s-your true age

Wong, D. W., Hall, K. R., Justice, C. A., & Hernandez, L. W. (2015). *Counseling individuals Through the lifespan* (3rd ed.). Sage.

Zhou, M., & Brown, D. (Eds.). (2015). *Educational learning theories* (2nd ed.). Online Open Textbooks. https://oer.galileo.usg.edu/education-textbooks/1/

CHAPTER 6
Self-Identity Issues Facing Women

HOLLY JOHNSON, PH.D.

"Be who you are and say what you feel because those who mind don't matter and those who matter don't mind." ~ Dr. Seuss

"I praise you because I am fearfully and wonderfully made; your works are wonderful, I know that full well." (Psalm 139:14, NIV)

Wisdom from Above: Standing in His Grace

There are times in life when we may feel insecure, worthless, and irredeemable. Satan wants us to find our identity in the things that we do, and he tries to ensure that we measure our perceived value based upon our jobs, our social status, our financial worth, or our relationships. When those things falter or fail, we often lose our sense of self-worth and feel like a failure. However, as a Christian, we have received a new identity in Christ. In that new identity, we do not lose our true self, but instead, we become the true self that God has created us to be – His chosen and beloved child of the Most High. John 1:12 (*New International Bible*, 1973/2011) says, "Yet to all who did receive him, to those who believed in his name, he gave the right to become children of God". Our acceptance as a child of God, thus our new identity in Christ, means that we are working to free ourselves of the negative labels placed by ourselves or by others.

CHAPTER LEARNING OBJECTIVES

Upon completing this chapter, you should be able to:

- Identify the factors that shape identity development
- Differentiate the way that roles and relationships shape identity
- Evaluate how societal factors and external influences may be detrimental to self-identity
- Explore important evidenced-based treatment options for self-identity issues
- Formulate Biblical insights related to self-identity

God desires for us to know that we are loved, unique, and worth celebrating.

As a young child reads a storybook and watches her adult role models, she begins a search of who she will become when she grows up. However, we do not find our identity; we grow into it through our experiences and our relationships. There is a continual seeking for purpose and belonging, and often when things do not work out as planned and life challenges occur, there is a search to discover who the person you call "I" is after all. Self-identity is about an awareness of who you are becoming and an understanding that you are in the driver's seat in spite of the bumps in the road and the obstacles along the way.

CHAPTER OVERVIEW

This chapter will explore the facets of the development of self-identity through internal and external factors. The material seeks to provide a guide for helping women to understand their sense of self, realize and embrace their purpose, and assign meaning to their lives. The discussion will begin by focusing on how relationships, cultural factors, gender considerations, and media sources influence a woman's sense of self. The chapter ends with a case study application and resources to use when counseling women with self-identity issues.

SELF-IDENTITY ISSUES

A woman's identity is rooted in her identifications and associations. Developing a strong positive self-identity is essential to overall well-being. A woman's identity may be influenced by things such as gender, religion, ethnicity, relationship changes, social comparisons, and more. Many great theorists including Jung, Adler, Erikson, and Maslow have written works about how we view ourselves. Carl Rogers

(1959) posited that there were three main concepts to the development of self-identity. These concepts are:

- **self-image** – the way that we see ourselves, including body image
- **self-esteem** – the way that we think about ourselves or our perceived value
- **ideal self** – who we wish we were

Within Roger's overarching concepts, Bracken (2009) further broke down the concepts to relate to the following eight dimensions:

- physical (how we look)
- social (how we interact with others)
- family (how we interact or relate to family)
- competence (how we manage the basic needs of our lives)
- academic (how we learn; our intelligence)
- affect (how we interpret and understand our emotions)

Identity development is on a continuum and can be challenged by many environmental forces. Not having a strong self-identity may lead to difficulties such as insecurity, anxiety, and depression.

© Prostock-studio/Shutterstock.com

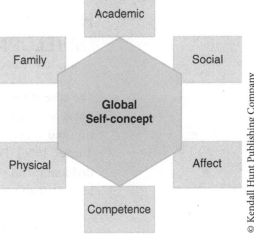

© Kendall Hunt Publishing Company

Symptoms Resulting from Identity Issues

Identity issues for women can result in questioning who they are in regards to various life aspects. There can be internal conflicts related to relationships, age, career, or role in society as a whole. In addition, questioning your beliefs, religious interpretations, interests, and values can all have a major impact on your self-concept. Low self-concept can lead to depressive symptoms (Lee-Flynn et al., 2011) and is correlated with lower subjective well-being (Ritchie et al., 2011; Slotter et al., 2010). Low self-concept is attributed to body dissatisfaction, lower academic and professional performance, and lower self-esteem (Błażek, & Besta, 2012; Hoeve et al., 2014; Willows et al., 2013).

Components of Self-Identity

The Barna Research Group (2015) found that family is the most significant component of personal identity followed by "being an American" and "religious faith". Career and ethnicity were also noted as significant components of identity. Other factors include appearance, culture, relationships, age, gender, education, income, and media (Byrne, 1996; Cash, 2011; Orenstein, 1995). Our self-identity is influenced by our feelings, sights, thoughts, experiences, judgments, and interactions. As we work to recognize detriments to our self-concept and strive to see ourselves as Christ sees us, we can improve our self-concepts and become all that the Lord has created us to be!

HISTORY AND BACKGROUND OF IDENTITY DEVELOPMENT

The core of identity is the understanding of who we are in all life aspects. This understanding is comprised of two fundamental parts, personal identity, and social identity (the story that society tells about you) (Tajfel & Turner, 1986). Personal identity is the understanding of who you are individually, and social identity is who you are in relation to others. Social identity is about the labels that you feel are projected onto you by society.

A woman's journey for self-identity is a challenging process of identifying and acknowledging the positive and negative experiences that shape who she is as a person. Entwined in the process are times of happiness, fear, clarity, doubt, disenchantment, gratitude, understanding, and misunderstanding. As we look at the process of identity, Abraham Maslow (1963) argues that we have both a need to know and a need to understand, and curiosity is the driving force, which helps to meet these cognitive needs and validate our existence. However, the driving force of curiosity often fades when one's reality

© Dmitri Ma/Shutterstock.com

is counter to their expectations, hopes, and dreams. The journey to self-identity is a process of what Jung (1936) calls individuation which is a progression of integrating the conscious and the unconscious to form your own personal sense of self. Erik Erikson (1980) proposed that self-identity is an evolving process which takes place of the entire course of your lifetime.

> "All those psychological and social factors that increase fear will cut our impulse to know; all factors that permit courage, freedom, and boldness will thereby also free our need to know"
> (Maslow, 2013, p. 67)

Influence of the Stages of Development

Erikson (1980) viewed the transition between childhood and adolescence as important in the development of self-identity. As adolescents begin to feel responsible for their future, these changes in perspective and new feelings of vulnerability set the stage for identity exploration. Erikson (1980) states:

> The period can be viewed as a psychosocial moratorium during which the individual, through free role experimentation, may find a niche in some section of his society ... In finding it the young adult gains an assured sense of inner continuity and social sameness which will bridge what he was as a child and what he is about to become (p. 111).

As adolescents emerge into adults, the experiences of the childhood years and the interpretations of those experiences shape their preferences and beliefs and contribute to the development of a positive or a negative self-identity. According to Habermas and Bluck (2000), the interpretive process, which is ever evolving, is the product of what they call autobiographical reasoning. **Autobiographical reasoning** is the process of drafting your life story by connecting the parts of your past, present, and future life with your personality throughout your development. It "embeds personal memories in a culturally, temporally, causally, and thematically coherent life story" (Habermas, 2010, p. 1). When you see your life experience as a process that promotes personal growth and self-transformation, this predicts positive psychological well-being following those experiences (Banks & Salmon, 2013; Lilgendahl & McAdams, 2011; Pals, 2006). Further information about developmental considerations in counseling women can be found in Chapter 5.

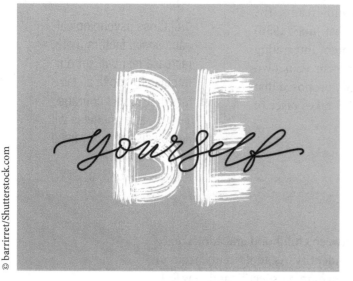
© barrirret/Shutterstock.com

Desired, Expected, Actual, or Ideal Self

As women review their life narratives, they often consider the expectations of the world around them in their construction of self-identity. Women often make comparisons of their actual self to the internalized views that they hold about who they *ought* to be or who they are *expected* to be. Personal identity is dependent upon the overview of your past, present, and future self. It is a combination of remembering experiences and considering social and relationship roles in the construction of the current, desired, expected, or ideal self (Erikson, 1968).

The real self is who we are in the present, and our ideal self is the image of what we would like to become. When the real self is inconsistent with the ideal self, there can be emotional discomfort. The ideal self can be influenced by the things that we have been taught, our life experiences, what we are told by media and entertainment, and by what we admire in others.

CULTURAL FACTORS SHAPING IDENTITY

Cultural identity is shaped through a dynamic interplay of factors such as
- Race
- Ethnicity
- Familial roles
- Gender roles
- Language
- Religion
- Political attitudes

Cultural Identity

Cultural identity (the connection and identification you have with a particular group or groups) relates to the connection and identification that an individual has with a particular group or groups. Cultural groups establish the norms for a group member's behavior and conduct. All individuals develop a cultural identity (Helms, 1995). Cultural identity is not static and is shaped through a dynamic interplay of factors such as race, ethnicity, familial roles, gender roles, language, religion, and political attitudes. Changes in cultural identity can be influenced by social, political, economic, or contextual factors and can be strongly affected and often reshaped by pervasive media systems (Lee, 2002; Varan, 1998). Cultural identity is an important contributor to overall well-being, and belonging to a cultural group provides social networks and connections to people with shared values, ambitions, desires, and beliefs. Having a strong cultural identity has been linked with positive outcomes in health, education, and overall well-being (Smith & Silva, 2011; Usborne & Taylor, 2010).

An important aspect in the journey to a strong self-identity (the story that you tell about yourself) is the clarity of one's cultural identity. The way that an individual embraces and/or relates to their cultural practices can significantly correlate to their feelings about themselves (Usborne & Taylor, 2010). When a person's cultural surroundings are altered or shifted, it can positively or negatively affect their personal outlook. A women's sense of cultural identity is changed not only by how she views herself, but by how she perceives that she is viewed by others. Her opinions, practices, self-image, and self-concept are affected by daily environmental influences. Learning to embrace the varying aspects of one's culture, heritage, and core beliefs can lead women to experience self-love and gain more self-acceptance.

Self-Identity vs Social Identity

From job interviews, public speeches, and corporate engagements, to interactions at dinner parties, exercise classes, and church activities, we continually face situations where we evaluate our performance or consider our perceptions of the evaluations of others. Social identity is the story that society tells about you, while self-identity is the story that you tell about yourself. Often, one's self-identity may change with the contexts of their social surroundings (Crocetti et al., 2018). Individuals may become fused with a group, and their perception of self is equated to the perception of their place within the group (Swann et al., 2009). This can be common in familial relationships, work relationships, social clubs, political affiliations, friendship circles, and educational settings. When the social group dissolves, often the individual is left unsure of who they are.

Social Conditioning and Social Modeling

Individuals are shaped through many processes including environmental influences, social modeling (the practice of mimicking the behaviors

of those around you), and social supports (Friedkin & Johnsen, 2011). Social modeling theory, according to Bandura et al. (1961) posits that individuals mimic the behaviors of those around them. They learn through observing, imitating, and then modeling the behaviors. Modeling positive traits such as kindness, politeness, respect, and morality can be beneficial to a women's self-identity. However, mimicking negative behaviors can be detrimental to self and to others. Growing up, a child may hear her mother talking about the need to lose weight, and she may begin doing the same thing creating an identity of shame and dissatisfaction with her appearance. Examining your identity through the lens of your experiences can provide much insight into your positive and negative core beliefs.

Sexuality – Negotiating Gender Roles

Gender roles pertain to how we are expected to behave, dress, speak, and conduct ourselves based upon our assigned sex. These gender role expectations can differ related to society, ethnicity, culture, and religion. In recent years, changes in laws, policies, and public opinion have brought about much cultural discourse related to gender (Smith & Smith, 2016), and perceptions and expectations can change within the same society over time. During development, the assimilation of images, objects, interactions, and influences provide a foundation for identity development related to gender roles. Social interactions influence the way that a woman internalizes views, opinions, and perceptions as she forms her self-identity. Maccoby (2000) explained how children internalize cultural beliefs and environmental influences to define their personal definition of gender roles and expectations. Children learn what is appropriate and what is taboo based upon the social reinforcement they receive from parents and society. Family is the most significant agent in social reinforcement (Lindsey, 2015). The family is paramount in the development of a child's personality, self-concept, and self-esteem including familial messages about expectations related to gender roles. Family norms are reinforced by other social relationships and experiences, and enforced gender messages are predictors of future behavior and attitudes.

Society upholds an ever-evolving pressure for women to adhere to stereotypical standards of beauty, sexuality, and gender roles. Contradicting standards may exist, leading to dissatisfaction and confusion. However, when women have a strong, healthy, and positive self-identity, we have confidence to follow our life goals, attain education, and pursue the dreams to change our worlds in spite of any negative gender-related messages that come from others. The Bible provides us with many messages to counter the world's message that we do not measure up to the standards, talents, or abilities of others. The following Scriptures provide us with the truth that we are all accepted and created equal:

© EtiAmmos/Shutterstock.com

- "For God does not show favoritism" (*New International Bible*, 1973/2011, Romans 2:11).
- "There is neither Jew nor Gentile, slave nor free, male nor female, for you are all one in Christ Jesus" (*New International Bible*, 1973/2011, Galatians 3:28).
- "For there is no difference between Jew and Gentile—the same Lord is Lord of all and richly blesses all who call on him" (*New International Bible*, 1973/2011, Romans 10:12).
- "So God created mankind in his own image, in the image of God he created them; male and female he created them" (*New International Bible,* 1973/2011, Genesis 1:27).

Positive identity development is often hindered by stereotyped messages (Heilman, 2012; Martiny et al., 2015). Children demonstrate stereotyped beliefs regarding their gender roles at an early age and these can be beneficial in identity development (Caldera et al., 1989; Golombok et al., 2008). However, stereotypes can produce faulty and harmful assumptions which negatively impact women's career opportunities, self-esteem, and self-identity (Heilman, 2012; Hentschel et al., 2018). A gendered stereotype is a preconceived view concerning the characteristics, expectations, or roles that should be endorsed by women and men (Cook & Cusack, 2011). These stereotypes are harmful for women when they limit the ability to pursue a chosen career, hinder the development of their personal talents and abilities, or inhibit their freedom or ability to make personal choices. Wrongful gender stereotyping can create discrimination against women and may affect overall well-being, living standards, or educational attainment. Gender stereotypes can be particularly harmful when they excuse or even justify abuse and violate human rights.

© asife/Shutterstock.com

Relationships

Surrey's (1985) self-in-relation theory posits that women define their sense of self through the relationships that they maintain with others. Theorists suggest that a woman's self-identity is strongly influenced by interactions with other individuals (Jordan, 1992; Miller, 1976; Surrey, 1985). God created us to be relational beings, and the Bible emphasizes the importance of interdependence (Romans 12:4-50). Our self is structured and developed in the context of our important relationships. During the course of a woman's life, she develops and maintains many relationships. Women wear many hats during their lifetime related to these relationship roles: daughter, friend, girlfriend, wife, mother, chef, professional, grandmother, teacher, supporter, and many more. With all of the roles and expectations, relationship trials are inevitable, and these trials can often challenge a woman's self-concept.

Self-Identity and Partnership Status

Every little girl has dreams of living happily ever after, but most often those fairy tale wishes are confronted by the villains of the story. We have an innate desire to belong and be engaged in meaningful relationships (Baumeister & Leary, 1995). Relationships take a great deal of work, and a women's identity is often intertwined with her idea of what is personally and socially expected for her

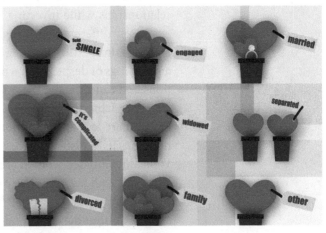

intimate relationship development. It is beyond the scope of this book to talk about all the various relationship statuses that have an effect on women's self-identity. However, we will discuss some of the ways that marriage, singlehood, divorce, motherhood, and trauma affect a women's identity.

Self-Identity and Marriage. When a martial partnership begins, there is beauty as two people become one. A healthy marital relationship celebrates and values the unique contributions of each person's sense of self and the combination of who they become in togetherness. However, as the relationship progresses and compromises occur, women may begin to feel as if their independent self is being lost. Important concepts to consider when working with women are the differentiation of self within a marital relationship and the need for authenticity as an individual.

Differentiation of Self. Differentiation of self is defined as "the ability to emotionally self-regulate and to maintain a sense of autonomy within a deep intimate relationship" (Ferreira et al., 2014, p. 390). Well-differentiated women are able to manage their emotions (Bowen, 1978) and remain connected to self while maintaining a deep connection to their marital partner.

Bowen (1978) purported that individuals who are highly differentiated have a fully developed sense of self that allows them to securely invest in relationships while investing in themselves. In contrast, individuals who are poorly differentiated struggle to maintain individuality within a stable relationship. Getting lost in a relationship can create anxiety, resentment, and feelings of desperation which can be expressed in exaggerated interactions and can threaten the quality of a martial relationship (Kerr & Bowen, 1988; Schnarch & Regas, 2012). Whereas, women who are well-differentiated are less anxious, more resilient to the effects of stress, and have more marital satisfaction (Kerr & Bowen, 1988; Schnarch & Regas, 2012). Well-differentiated women are able to maintain autonomy in a marital relationship and act from their core values and sense of self without negatively responding to a spouse's demands or reactive emotions (Sheikh et al., 2013). Boundaries can be established around an individual's sense of self that allows room for the marriage to flourish and the marital commitment to deepen. Proper differentiation of self may provide a bridge between a woman's identity development within her family of origin (Kerr & Bowen, 1988), and the identity development that she experiences within an intimate relationship (Ferreira et al., 2012). Positive identity development within the marital relationship results as you to give of yourself while your partner respects your need for individuality and vice versa.

> "Managing your emotions doesn't mean you don't express yourself; it means you stop short of hurting others and sabotaging yourself."
> ~Sue Fitzmaurice

Authenticity. Within any intimate relationship, an important part of self-identity is remaining authentic. Authenticity provides an opportunity for you to remain genuine and true to yourself while building a new life together with your spouse. It is often challenging to balance a strong sense of self while being purposeful in building a strong marital relationship. However, authenticity is not eliminating the filter for what we think or what we speak (Jordan, 2010). It is about remaining honest while maintaining a strong realization that our words powerfully impact our marital relationship.

Self-Identity and Singlehood. As noted above, self-identity can be strongly influenced by relationship status. Research has indicated that happiness is positively correlated to being involved in romantic relationships (Day et al., 2011; Diener & Seligman, 2002). As a whole, society expects individual members to adhere to social norms and those who do not may be labeled or considered deviant (Jacobsen & Van Der Voordt, 1980; Rimal & Lapinski, 2015). Western societal beliefs promote expectations for individuals to form intimate relationships that are legalized through the institution of marriage. These expectations are idealized, and those not married are identified as being single. The term single implies a deficiency. DePaulo and Morris (2005) purport that individuals who are single face what they term as singlism, which is a form of stigmatization and discrimination related to the lack of being married or coupled. Even though being single is suggested to be a woman's choice and is becoming more common in the Western world, when that choice is made, single women are often negatively viewed as being lonely, miserable, unhealthy or a failure (Lahad, 2013; Lahad, 2014; Sharp & Ganong, 2011; Slonim et al., 2015). Women who remain single are often viewed as being in a waiting period to be married (Lahad, 2012), and counselors report that female clients aged 30 to 45 often commonly experience distress related to remaining single (Shachar et al., 2013).

In spite of the stereotypes and discrimination against single women, some women who choose to be single have found peace and happiness in their identity status of singlehood and are found to be as happy as those in mar-

© Antonio Guillem/Shutterstock.com

ital relationships (Timonen & Doyle, 2014). In current research it is found that strong personal relationships, whether romantic or not, are positively correlated with an increase in happiness (Demir et al., 2017; Diener et al., 2018). Social support from family and friends seems to be one of the mitigating factors between remaining single and avoiding loneliness and shame (Adamczyk, 2016; Demir et al., 2017).

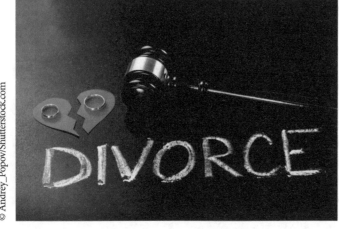

© Andrey_Popow/Shutterstock.com

Self-Identity and Divorce. Divorce requires a major reassessment of a woman's values, roles, choices, assumptions, activities, and relationships which often lead to changes in self-identity (Sakraida, 2005; Wiseman, 1975). Many studies have provided evidence for these identified changes (Gregson & Ceynar, 2009; Lewandowski et al., 2006; Slotter et al., 2010). Many women see a significant loss of friendships after divorce (Greif & Deal, 2012; Mc-Dermott et al., 2013), lose health insurance (Lavelle & Smock, 2012), and often find significant decreases in their financial resources and overall socioeconomic status (Gadalla, 2009; Thomas & Ryan, 2008).

Women often face negative self-concept post-divorce (Mason et al., 2012; Slotter et al., 2010) and these decreased perceptions of the self may increase depressive symptoms (Slotter et al., 2010) and lead to lower self-esteem, increased stress, and overall poor health (Dare, 2011; Symoens et al., 2014). These negative effects can be countered by religious orientation (Błażek, & Besta, 2012), positive self-talk, and social support (Papa & Lancaster, 2016).

Self-Identity and Motherhood

Motherhood can be a time that brings about powerful changes to a woman's identity and contributes to a vast array of all-consuming emotions that range from love and protectiveness to exhaustion and confusion. Life transitions theory notes that transition periods such as motherhood require an individual's goals and behaviors to be restructured while a new self-concept is being established (Barba & Selder, 1995). Motherhood can

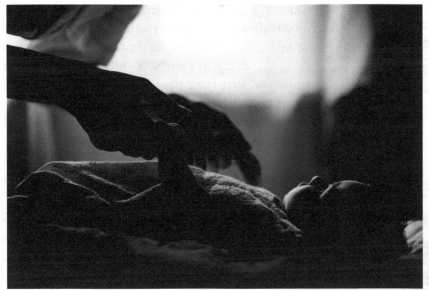

be such a busy and demanding period of life that women find themselves with no time to consider how the transition into this phase of life affects their own personal identity and how their new identity should be defined and maintained. Women often struggle with vulnerability and find it difficult to establish total peace with their new role which often conflicts with the established norms of their identity (Elliott et al., 2009). There is often a raging conflict between the loss of identity and the expansion of identity (Hollway, 2010). During this time, women reevaluate their appearance, sexuality, occupation, and relationships (Elliott et al., 2009), and many women suffer with postpartum depression (Shorey et al., 2018). Women may feel that their self-identity does not measure up to the ideal motherhood identity, and they may feel guilt or feel like a failure. Many new mothers feel a sense of loss as they define their new identity by motherhood. Most individuals who experience a healthy transition do so by maintaining a core sense of their pre-motherhood self while making space for their children's needs as they expand their core identity (Laney et al., 2015).

Becoming a mother means being open to allowing a new expanded identity to have a pervasive influence, not only on your sense of self, but also on your life choices as a whole (Ali et al., 2013). When women do not see motherhood as limiting, but instead view it as growth-inducing, they are able to develop an expansion of their identity personally, generationally,

> "Everything has changed, and yet, I'm more me than I've ever been." ~Iain Thomas

relationally, and even professionally (Laney et al., 2014). Women who did not view motherhood and career as competing commitments but instead viewed them as having the ability to exercise a "broader panorama of themselves" were more positive and felt more authentic in their new identities (p. 18). During this period of life transition, social support is paramount for a woman's mental health and overall well-being (Warren et al., 2012).

Self-Identity and Relationship Trauma

Numerous research studies have proposed that partner abuse negatively impacts the self-identity of women (Crawford et al., 2009; Lynch, 2013; O'Doherty et al., 2016). According to the traumatic bonding theory, it is purported that abused women focus on the abusive partner's needs rather than their own in an attempt to avoid future violent acts (Dutton & Painter, 1981). The failure to no longer attend to her own needs and the negative feedback received from the abusive partner creates changes to identity and the woman's "sense of self self comes to be experienced through the eyes of the abuser" (Graham & Rawlings, 1991, p. 122). The erosion of self-esteem by the abuse creates feelings of loss of self and may lead to depression and substance use disorders (Carlyle et al., 2008; Follingstad & Rogers, 2014). Shame, stigmatization, and the negative effects to women's self-concept related to the abuse may cause victims of partner violence to conceal the abuse and to live in fear (Murray, Crowe & Brinkley, 2015; Murray, Crowe & Overstreet, 2015). The threat of violence creates emotional stress and may shift a woman's cognitive schema of herself and of others (Lynch, 2013; O'Doherty et al., 2016). Women suffering from partner abuse have decreased self-worth, inferior self-image, lower self-confidence, and other negative self-perceptions (Lynch, 2013).

In spite of the loss of identity while living in an abusive relationship, women may find increased strength, empowerment, and healing when they break free from an abusive relationship (Matheson et al., 2015; Song 2012). Support, recovery programs, and self-efficacy are key factors in facilitating healing and change. Self-care practices such as participation in yoga can facilitate improvement in self-concept post abuse (Dale et al., 2011). More information regarding verbal/emotional abuse and partner violence can be found in Chapter 20.

SOCIETAL FACTORS, EXTERNAL INFLUENCES, AND SOCIAL COMPARISON

Self-identity or self-concept relates to the all-encompassing ideas that we hold about who we are including our emotional, spiritual, physical, and social aspects. Baumeister (1999) defines self-concept as what an individual both knows and believes about herself. Rosenberg (1979) defines self-concept as "...the totality of an individual's thoughts and feelings having reference to himself as an object" (p. 7). These thoughts and feelings

© Sapunkele/Shutterstock.com

can be influenced by social factors. Research shows that media narratives and life events can influence and alter self-identity (Ward & Harrison, 2005; McAdams & Olson, 2010; Richter et al., 2014). Our self-identity has meaning within our social context, and our social environment can shape not only who we are but can guide what we think about ourselves and how we act upon our thoughts (Haslam et al., 2009).

Cooley's (1902) concept of the *looking-glass self* claims that our perceptions of how others see us often guide how we see ourselves. Research has supported this concept that our self-identity often mirrors others' perceptions (Beer et al., 2013). As we find ourselves evaluated by others, then we may find ourselves adopting those evaluations as truth. Women often perform social comparisons, which is when you compare yourself to another person to gain insight to your sense of self and your position in life (Festinger, 1954). Celebrity culture and the prevalence of carefully crafted social-media feeds increase the concerns related to social comparison and expose women to endless comparisons of themselves to individuals who appear to be perfect. Research shows that social comparison influences self-evaluations (Zell & Balcetis, 2012) and can even negatively impact both mental and physical health (Pham-Kanter, 2009). Many women make unreasonable comparisons of their self to others and are more likely to compare *up* (people better off than themselves) rather than to compare *down* (people worse off than themselves) (Gerber et al., 2018). Social comparisons may correlate with higher levels of anxiety and depression (Seabrook et al., 2016).

Professional Self-Identity

Since the mid-1970s, there have been major shifts in the numbers of women who are employed outside the home. During the mid-70s, less than half of all women with children under 18 were employed outside the home. The numbers of women joining the labor force rose and peaked in 1999 at 60.0% (Bureau of Labor Statistics, 2019). In 2018, nearly half of the total labor force was made of women (Bureau of Labor Statistics, 2019). Combining career and family can often be stressful and problematic. Hence, in recent years, the numbers of women in the workforce have begun to decline as women are deciding to "opt-out" of careers and assume a role of a stay at home mom (Tossi, 2016). The percentage of women in the labor force is projected to decrease to be 55.4% in 2024 and 51.9% in 2060 (Tossi, 2016).

In addition to the challenges of combining career and family, women suffer from inequality in the workforce. In spite of progress for women at senior levels, women remain significantly underrepresented in senior management, and the majority of corporate boards are dominated by men (Deloitte and Alliance for Board Diversity, 2019). In 2018, men held 77.5% of the Fortune 500 company board seats while only 22.5% were held by women, and only 4.6% of those were held by women of color. In addition, there is a great pay disparity for women as compared to men with women earning approximately 80% of what men earn (National Women's Law Center, 2018).

Research indicates that motherhood further exacerbates the gender inequality in today's labor force. Women assume the bulk of the responsibility in parenting, and even though parental leave is available to both genders, the majority of family leave is taken by women rather than men (Han et al., 2009). Women who have children have lower salaries and performance reviews following family leave (Bernard & Correll, 2010; Budig et al., 2012; Kahn et al., 2014). In addition, mothers are perceived to have less competency and commitment than similar workers (Bernard & Correll, 2010), and women in general are often perceived as less competent than men (Cikara & Fiske, 2009). Research has found that women who are equally competent as men are more likely to adopt the gender stereotypes and underestimate their performance and abilities (Ehrlinger & Dunning, 2003; Bench et al., 2015; Patzak et al., 2017). Additionally, women who adopt a role of being traditionally feminine in appearance and actions are more at risk of gender harassment (Leskinen et al., 2015). These factors can negatively affect a woman's self-concept.

Finally, self-identity can be affected by social comparisons in the workplace. According to research, social comparisons have a strong impact on self-evaluations (Strickhouse & Zell, 2015). Balancing the personal and professional life can be a struggle, and identity shifts related to career can be stressful and challenging (Hoffnung & Williams, 2013).

Although career is highly esteemed among women, many feel that career benefits do not outweigh the benefits and importance of family. Over identifying with a professional career can be problematic when you equate your self-worth with your career. However, it is challenging to separate the idea of meaning from work and meaning from life. In a culture that is hyper-connected, finding life-balance and inner peace requires the ability to set boundaries and equate your success with the values of your authentic self, not with negative thoughts or your perceptions of the negative thoughts of others. Positive professional identity is contingent upon your self-value or how you treat yourself. Work-life balance comes from maintaining an internal locus of control, sustaining strong supporting relationships, maintaining boundaries, and letting go of the fear of asking for help.

Marketing and Self-Identity

Throughout the years, women have been instructed about what makes an ideal self and how they should represent their gender (Hirschman, 1993;

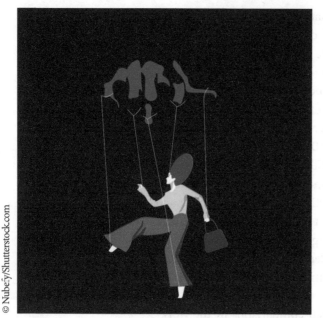

Zukin & McGuire, 2004; Ranjitha & Unnithan, 2018). A study by Zell and Balcetis (2012) noted that individual's self-evaluations can be strongly affected by social comparison processes. Marketing and advertising not only communicate which product to buy, but work as a means of influencing an individual's identity development throughout the lifespan (Tuncay-Zayer & Coleman, 2015). Objectification theory is based upon how a woman internalizes the perceptions of how others see her as she constructs her sense of self (Fredrickson & Roberts, 1997). Women may become obsessed with how their physical being matches up with the social representation of what is ideal.

Marketing and advertising often promotes a standard of beauty for women that is not normal and often unattainable by most (APA, 2007). Exposure to sexual objectification of women in the media promotes the importance of physical appearance (Gordon, 2008) and contributes to body dissatisfaction, eating disorders, shame, and low self-worth (Manago et al., 2015). Festinger (1954) purported that individuals have an inherent drive to perform self-evaluations and to determine their social and personal worth based upon how their abilities, skills, appearance, or talents measure up against others. Marketing and advertising often creates an unattainable picture of what is ideal, and this can produce discouragement, anxiety, and depression for women who have low self-confidence (Gurrieri et al., 2013). The research shows links between advertising and negative body image (Robinson et al., 2017). A social climate that provides marketing of objectification of women and unrealistic images of the ideal self threatens the psyche of women which can lead to threats to a women's sense of self (Manago et al., 2015).

Social Media and Self-Identity

Social media has become an easy way to build virtual relationships and keep in contact with family and friends. However, attitudes about one's self can be impacted by the use of social media networks (Pempek et al., 2009).

© Rawpixel.com/Shutterstock.com

Social media can be used to make oneself appear to be attractive and increase social capital (Urista et al., 2009). Research has shown that individuals are often selective in their self-presentation in an effort to impress others (Jiang et al., 2011; Urista et al., 2009). This can create a paradox effect for women as they present themselves in a way that is incongruent with how they really are and this may lead to the creation of what Winnicott (1967) termed as the "false self". This "false self" is a defensive, protective identity that works to hide the "true self". Low degrees of falseness are natural and may not harm one's self-identity (Goffman, 1959; Rogers, 1959; Winnicott, 1967). However, the more time spent practicing a false self, the more difficult it becomes to be satisfied with your true identity, and the comparison of the realistic self to the online self can be detrimental to self-esteem and overall psychological well-being (Vogel et al., 2014).

Social comparison on social media platforms can also be problematic to a woman's self-concept. Festinger (1954) posited that self-perceptions may be based partly on how one compares themselves to others. Social media magnifies the impact of social comparison and provides an impression that other people are happier, more adjusted, and have better lives (Chou & Edge, 2012). These social comparisons may foster negative self-perceptions (De Vries, & Kühne, 2015), lead to depressive symptoms (Feinstein et al., 2013), increase body dissatisfaction (Fardouly & Vartanian, 2015), and increase negative relational experiences (Fox & Moreland, 2015). Social comparisons can lead to envy which can exacerbate depressive symptoms (Appel et al., 2016). Envy is one of the seven deadly sins, and as social media creates a rise in envy, narcissism and the desire for self-promotion intensifies (Taylor & Strutton, 2016).

COUNSELING RECOMMENDATIONS FOR SELF-IDENTITY ISSUES

> The essential self is comprised of spirituality, self-care, gender identity and cultural identity.
> ~Myers and Sweeney (2005)

When counseling women, remember that self-identity is a process. It is a journey of self-discovery to find purpose and meaning in life. It involves examining feelings, reactions, and motives. It is about discovering the contrast between a woman's individual experiences and her experiences with others. Competing interpretations of self-identity may exist during one's lifetime. Those interpretations may be evaluated, judged, and reinterpreted many times. With each interpretation and reevaluation, it is important to work toward discovering what Myers and Sweeney (2005) call the essential self. The essential self is comprised of the four components: spirituality, self-care, gender identity, and cultural identity. Each of these components are important considerations in counseling.

Gender and culture provide women with filters through which they view their relationships and experiences. Healthy self-identity is rooted in self-awareness. It is about letting go of habituated thoughts and beliefs and holding close to those thoughts and beliefs which resonate with your deepest self – that self that aligns with your God given identity.

Because of multiple roles and external pressures, women often find themselves under a great deal of stress. When identity changes are prevalent such as in a new career, changing relationships, or life changes such as motherhood, resilience training is important as resilience reduces stress (Troy & Mauss, 2011; Loprinzi et al., 2011). Effective coping strategies during life transitions include spirituality, critical reflection, and support from positive social networks (Rajan-Rankin, 2014). Developing affirmative networks of friends and sharing communication surrounding interests and goals provides a platform for constructing positive self-identities throughout a woman's lifespan (Anthony & McCabe, 2015).

Finding mentors and role models help women in professional careers to improve self-efficacy and to increase a more positive professional self-identity (Chemers et al., 2011; Ronett et al., 2015). Cognitive-Behavioral Therapy (CBT), Gestalt Therapy, and Person-Centered Therapy may help to promote self-awareness, growth, and increase self-efficacy which correlates with positive self-identity (O'Mahen et al., 2012; Saadati & Lashani, 2013). In addition to improving self-awareness and self-efficacy, relationship satisfaction with colleagues and co-workers provide improved professional identity and overall improvement in mental well-being (Canrinus et al., 2012).

Relationship therapy is important to aid women in probing deeper into their self-understanding of relational connections so that each role, interaction, and decision is more congruent with their true self (Motschnig-Pitrik & Barrett-Lennard, 2010). Helping women to improve self-compassion provides them with motivation to improve health and provides a more positive outlook on life and improved body image (Albertson et al., 2015; Breines, & Chen, 2012). Mindfulness, acceptance commitment therapy, and CBT have been noted to aid improvement in self-compassion (DeBruin et al., 2016; Yadavaia et al., 2014). In addition, therapeutic techniques such as EMDR and hypnosis have shown to increase unconditional self-acceptance, self-confidence, and self-efficacy; mitigate the effects of shame and self-criticism; and provide overall improvements in self-identity (Hensley, 2012; Kennedy, 2014; Milburn, 2011).

Helping women to focus on their internal self-worth instead of comparing themselves to others can increase self-assurance and help them to find comfort in who God has created them to become. This self-assurance provides women the ability to heal from feelings of worthlessness and helps them to exercise greater control over their personal and professional lives. As a counselor, you can help a woman to change the story of who she is and explore the person that she is becoming, allowing her to take charge of her life, make active choices for a better future, and embrace the path to a more authentic and positive sense of self. Counselors can help women navigate the transitions in life and be free to adapt and integrate their life changes to become everything that God has created them to be.

Featured Practitioner
Dr. Sylvia Hart Frejd

© Sylvia Frejd

Dr. Sylvia Hart Frejd has a master's degree specializing in Christian counseling, a doctorate in leadership, and is an ICF Professional Life Coach, Certified Spiritual Director (CSD), author, and speaker. She has co-authored the book: *The Digital Invasion: How Technology Shapes You and Your Relationships* with her father Dr. Archibald Hart. She is a featured presenter and trainer with the American Association of Christian Counselors and has invaluable experience and expertise to share on the topic of women's self-identity.

What societal and external factors most influence women's self-identity?

Our digital world has given us so much, the ability to communicate with anyone, anywhere, at any time. But, it has also taken a toll on our self-identity as women. I believe that one of the most important ways that technology is changing our self-identity is by shifting us from being internally to externally driven. Today our self-identity is no longer self-identity (meaning derived from the self). Instead it is an identity which is projected onto us by our popular culture and does not accurately reflect who we really are. Social Media plays a large part in this change. The goal has become how many likes, and good responses can I get on Social Media. Our worth and value is being determined by the number of friends, followers, and likes we receive. Our identity becomes what we would like to have or want people to see rather than the reality of who we really are. The very nature of social media breeds envy, fear, and the comparing, competing and contrasting game. Social Media can also exacerbate feelings of depression. In fact, one study found that the more social platforms people are actively engaged on, the more likely they'll feel depressed and anxious (Dibb, 2019).

Today our increase in Social Media use is producing an epidemic of anxiety and depression in women. This comes on the heels of a new study from the University of Surrey, which found that Facebook has a negative effect on some user's physical and mental health, particularly in women (Primack et al., 2017). The study found that those who compared themselves to their Facebook "friends" were more likely to experience physical ailments such as sleep problems, change in weight and muscle tension. The findings revealed that women in particular, and those experiencing anxiety or depression, also perceived more symptoms of these ailments, though they did not specify why. Participants in the study who were more satisfied with their lives to begin with and had higher self-esteem, on the other hand, were associated with fewer physical symptoms.

As I sit with women each week in counseling and coaching, I see many who lack a strong spiritual core. This age of digital distraction is keeping us from going deep in God, in ourselves and with others. Without this strong spiritual core women will not know their true identity in Christ and have the resources they need to navigate life's struggles, pain and disappointments.

What are some ways that women can rediscover their identity after a major life event?

When I work with women rebuilding their life after a major event, I focus on growing their life systems. This involves their spiritual, emotional, physical, and relational system. I believe it is important that when we work with women we deal with the whole person. I assess all areas of a woman's life to see how she can rebuild each of these systems. It is imperative to help a woman see herself the way Christ sees her. Encourage her to meditate on Scriptures that remind her of her worth. Challenge her to daily have her mind renewed from the contamination of the world's system, so that her mind will be changed, and she will start living out of a place that is congruent with her identity in Christ.

What advice would you offer to Christian counselors in working with women who are struggling with self-identity issues?

As I mentioned before, the first thing I do with every female client is help her to build a strong spiritual core, help her find her true identity in Christ, and to build a support system. I also encourage her to use Social Media in a positive way to connect with friends she doesn't get to see a lot, but then learn how to log off when it is causing her to feel depressed. The research is clear, no more than an hour on Social Media, any more than that and it starts to pull you down.

CONCEPT TO CONTEMPLATE

An important commitment in promoting a positive sense of self is to believe in your own true value and reject the lies you have been told about yourself. Before you can help others to discover their self-identity, it is imperative that you work on your own self-concept and understand the process of becoming everything that God has created you to become. As you think about your work with clients, think about the following questions. How can you help clients to take responsibility for their own choices which may contribute to a negative self-identity while granting themselves unconditional love and acceptance? How can a Christian woman maintain a strong sense of self without countering the Biblical commands to refrain from pride or arrogance?

BIBLICAL INSIGHTS ON SELF-IDENTITY

Finding Our Identity in Christ

Society can provide a very confusing depiction of the role of women. Throughout much of history, women have been viewed as second-class, have been sexually objectified, and made to feel unimportant. However, that was not the role that God intended for women. Genesis 1:27 (*New International Bible, 1973/2011*) tells us that "…God created mankind in his own image, in the image of God he created them; male and female he created them". Just as man, woman is created in the image and likeness of God. God described women as being strong, resilient, wise, resourceful, tender, nurturing, and loving.

God's greatest commandment declares that you are to "Love the Lord your God with all your heart and with all your soul and with all your mind" (*New International Bible, 1973/2011*, Mark 12:30) while the second greatest is to "Love your neighbor as yourself" (*New International Bible, 1973/2011*, Mark 12:31). The love relationship that we have with God teaches us how to love ourselves unconditionally as He loves us, and this gives us the basis for our self-worth and for our identity. With God, we do not have to pretend to be anything that we are not.

© Olga Gold/Shutterstock.com

We can be our self and rest in the unconditional acceptance that He affords. That kind of love and acceptance is the only security in our lives that is invulnerable and can never be shaken. The Psalmist declares, "When I felt secure, I said, I will never be shaken" (*New International Bible, 1973/2011*, Psalm 30:6). Every woman must establish first and foremost her relationship with God as her Creator and Redeemer. If God is preeminent in our lives, that will provide the foundation for a healthy self-identity as we see ourselves as He sees us, and we understand who we are in Christ. Adopting our identity from the world will make us insecure and weak. However, when we receive our identity through Christ, we find everything that we need to face any circumstance and conquer any fear. God never intended for women to have a self-centered identity, instead He desired that we have a God-centered identity. If our identity is self-centered, then we will always find ourselves dependent upon others for our happiness and well-being. In contrast, if our identity is God-centered we will find the ultimate fulfillment in living for God's glory which is the purpose for which we are created.

© De Visu/Shutterstock.com

What do you think about yourself? As you counsel women regarding their self-identity, it is important to understand how you feel about yourself. Self-awareness is a key factor in being an effective counselor. In the fairy tale Snow White, the vain queen continuously gazed into her mirror stating the words, ""Mirror, mirror on the wall, who's the fairest of them all?" As long as the report came back that she was the fairest, then all was well. However, when the mirror displayed that Snow White was fairer than she, then the queen became enraged (Hand et al., 1937). Social comparison can create envy, shame, and a sense of dissatisfaction with who we are. However, at some deep level, we realize that self-awareness and accurate judgement reveals our strengths and our weaknesses which allow us to see clearly into who and what we truly are.

> "Even before he made the world, God loved us and chose us in Christ to be holy and without fault in his eyes" (*New Living Bible*, 1996, Ephesians 1:4).

Our emotional state and overall sense of self can be affected by the environment we are in, the people that we associate with, our physical health, and much more. When we become a Christian, we receive a new identity in Christ (2 Corinthians 5:17). However, Satan is always present, tempting us to forget that identity and to live in a state of inferiority, doubt, and failure. To overcome Satan's plots to undermine our identity, we must see ourselves as God sees us. A wonderful reminder of that is provided in the book of Ephesians. The Apostle Paul tells us that we are blessed, chosen, redeemed, forgiven, provided grace, and loved unconditionally by the Lord. We have been given wisdom and understanding to live a live that is for His glory! As counselors, know who you are in Christ and receive the gifts of wisdom and understanding to help women become all that that have been created to be and to believe that they truly are "fearfully and wonderfully made" (*New International Bible*, 1973/2011, Psalm 139:14). Remember that God loved each one of your clients before they were born and created them to be amazing vessels of honor for His glory. He loves them with an extravagant love and entrusts them to you to help guide them in their journey to believe in His plans and purposes for their lives. In addition to helping clients find themselves, work to know yourself in light of one created in God's image, and search for the invisible essentials in yourself, as our beloved neighbor Mister Rogers would say (Kuhnley, 2020).

CONCEPT TO CONTEMPLATE

© Digital Storm/Shutterstock.com

God created each woman to have a unique purpose. He also created us to be in relationship with others and live through His divine will. The more closely we are drawn to God, the more we discover our true identity and divine purpose. These verses help to understand who we are destined to be and to embrace our identity in Christ.

- The Lord delights in you: Isaiah 62:3-5; Psalms 149:4; Psalms 18:19; Zephaniah 3:17
- God made you Himself and you have a specific purpose: Psalm 138:8; Isaiah 44:2; Isaiah 43:7; Jeremiah 1:5; Ephesians 2:10
- Your past does not define you: Romans 5:8; I John 1:9; I Timothy 1:15; Romans 15:7; John 6:37
- You are loved, honored, and accepted by God: Isaiah 43:4; John 3:16; Psalm 136:26; Romans 5:8; Romans 8:37-39; I John 4:9-11

"For I am convinced that neither death nor life, neither angels nor demons, neither the present nor the future, nor any powers, neither height nor depth, nor anything else in all creation, will be able to separate us from the love of God that is in Christ Jesus our Lord."
(*New International Bible*, 1973/2011, Romans 8:38-39).

Kiera is a single mother with a two-year-old daughter. She shares custody with her ex-husband Luke. Kiera described her ex-husband as verbally and emotionally abusive. They were married for three years before she became pregnant. She never felt supported by him when they were married. Luke left Kiera for another woman. He told her that she was "fat and no longer desirable."

Kiera's father died when she was born, and she grew up with an alcoholic step-father and a mother who worked two jobs to support the family. Kiera was the oldest of five children and spent a good deal of her childhood helping to care for her younger step-siblings. Kiera's step-father always put her down and made her feel unloved and unimportant. Kiera's mother worked so much that she did not have time to give Kiera any positive reinforcement. Kiera struggled with weight issues all of her life and was bullied in school due to her weight and her flaming red hair. The taunting continued through high school, and Kiera found it difficult to make friends. She rarely participated in social events and was mostly isolated.

During college, things began to change for Kiera. Kiera's mother had wanted her to be a doctor, but Kiera had always dreamed of being a teacher. After speaking with a vocational counselor, Kiera decided that for once, she would make her own decisions and become a teacher. After her first year of college, Kiera began to make friends. Then she met Luke. Luke was a star football player and was very handsome. They met in the library when Luke asked Kiera for help with homework. Luke's persistent charm broke down Kiera's walls, and they were inseparable for the remainder of college. Kiera began to exercise and managed to lose 50 pounds. Just after graduation, Kiera and Luke were married, and Kiera began a new job as a high school math teacher. Kiera said that she began to finally feel like she really was "somebody". She described her experiences in the classroom as a time when she felt "in control" and "confident about her abilities". She had a good rapport with her students and received praise from her colleagues and superiors. Kiera enjoyed hiking and biking and went with a group of friends to the gym every afternoon. She also began attending a local church and was involved in teaching children in Sunday school. Luke would never attend, but told Kiera that he would "allow her to go".

After Kiera and Luke had been married for several years, Luke took a position with a prestigious law firm. Luke began to work late every night, and he barely spent any time with Kiera. He began to make negative comments about her clothing and appearance, and asked her to "go shopping to look more like an attorney's wife instead of a school teacher". He pressured her daily about quitting her job and being more supportive of his career since it was more lucrative. He emphasized that her job was not as important, and anyone could do the work that she did. He gave Kiera many administrative tasks to do for him which seemed to always need to be done on Sundays. This caused Kiera to have to give up her volunteer work with the church, and she rarely got to attend worship services. When she would go with Luke to company parties, Luke would leave her sitting by herself while he socialized. She said that it seemed like he was "ashamed of her". Kiera worked on her appearance and wardrobe to try and please her husband and make him "love her more". Kiera gave up her teaching job and did everything that she could to support her husband.

After Kiera and Luke's third year anniversary, Kiera found out that she was pregnant. Luke seemed excited, and Kiera felt that maybe the baby would help her to feel more secure in their marriage and more confident in herself. During the pregnancy, Kiera gained a great deal of weight, and Luke became more and more distant. He worked later and barely spoke to Kiera when he came home. Kiera was not allowed to go to any of the company parties because she was "too fat and ugly". Kiera became increasingly more isolated from everyone, and she said that she felt "lost and alone". Just after the baby was born, Luke left her for another woman.

Kiera has struggled with motherhood. She feels guilty that she is not as bonded to her baby as she thinks that she should be. She stated, "I am no good at anything. I can't keep a husband, I don't have a job, and I am a terrible mother. I really am worthless. I don't even know who I am without Luke. When I was with him, it was the only time that I felt like somebody important."

Counseling sessions with Kiera should begin with building a strong therapeutic relationship and identifying and emphasizing Kiera's strengths. Erikson (1968) posited that experiences during the childhood years are instrumental in forming the sense of self, and Kiera did not receive what was needed to construct a strong self-identity during her adolescent years. However, noting that Kiera thrived when she was in a teaching position shows that she has strong resilience and strengths to build upon as she gains a more positive sense of her inner self that is waiting to

be discovered. The therapeutic relationship can build a supportive environment that is non-judgmental and unbiased which will help Kiera to discover her own desires and needs and begin to embrace her own likes and dislikes.

Cognitive behavioral therapy could be used to challenge Kiera's beliefs of being unimportant and the thought that everyone else's needs are more important than her own. Helping Kiera to view her irrational beliefs from different angles and construct new, more appropriate beliefs about herself will enable her to see her strengths and focus on her talents and abilities. For homework, Kiera could maintain a log of her negative thoughts and self-defeating beliefs and begin challenging them with positive thoughts about her abilities and strengths. For clients who request Biblical integration, focusing on changing negative thoughts with truths from Scripture is encouraged. Helping Kiera to realize that even though the foundations for her low self-esteem and self-concept were laid down early in her life, as an adult, she has control over making the changes needed to improve her sense of self. Allowing Kiera to see her power of setting her own standards will help her not to allow others to control her values, her morality, or her destiny. Positive affirmations can be beneficial for Kiera to recognize her worth and embrace her value. Solution focused therapy could allow Kiera to problem solve about how she can care for her child, re-establish her social interactions, attend church again, and return to the career that she loves will be valuable to her success.

The strong therapeutic relationship built with Kiera will help her to believe in herself; to cultivate her self-awareness and self-confidence; and to help her to break free from the past and move forward to achieve her goals and dreams.

CHAPTER SUMMARY

As we see in this chapter, self-identity forms through a complex combination of genes, experiences, and environmental factors. As you help women to look beyond any culturally, personally, or socially imposed identities, remember that the authentic self is not limited to the constraints of the imagined self and is not bound by labels. Remind yourselves and the women that you counsel to acknowledge limitations, let go of beliefs and destructive emotions which hinder positive progress, and acknowledge the Biblical truths that we are indeed "fearfully and wonderfully made" (*New International Bible*, 1973/2011, Psalm 129:14).

KEY TERMS

Autobiographical Reasoning - is the process of drafting your life story by connecting the parts of your past, present, and future life with your personality throughout your development

Cultural Identity - the connection and identification you have with a particular group or groups

Differentiation of Self - the capacity to self-regulate emotions and to sustain a sense of independence within a deep intimate relationship

Ideal Self - who we wish we were

Self-Esteem - the way that we think about ourselves or our perceived value

Self-Identity - the story that you tell about yourself

Self-Image - the way that we see ourselves, including body image

Social Identity - the story that society tells about you

Social Modeling - the practice of mimicking the behaviors of those around you

SUGGESTED RESOURCES

Books

The Six Pillars of Self-Esteem by Nathaniel Branden

The Gifts of Imperfection: Let Go of Who You Think You're Supposed to Be and Embrace Who You Are by Brene Brown

Lies Women Believe: And the Truth that Sets Them Free by Nancy DeMoss Wolgemuth

Emotional Intelligence: Why it can matter more than IQ by Daniel Goleman

Get Out of Your Mind and Into Your Life: The New Acceptance and Commitment Therapy by Steven C. Hayes

Negative Self-Talk & How to Change It by Shad Helmstetter

The Self-Confidence Workbook: A Guide to Overcoming Self-Doubt and Improving Self-Esteem by Barbara Markway and Celia Ampel

Approval Addiction: Overcoming Your Need to Please Everyone by Joyce Meyer

The Purpose Driven Life: What on Earth am I Here For? by Rick Warren

REFERENCES

Adamczyk, K. (2016). An investigation of loneliness and perceived social support among single and partnered young adults. *Current Psychology, 35*(4), 674-689. https://doi.org/10.1007/s12144-015-9337-7

Albertson, E. R., Neff, K. D., & Dill-Shackleford, K. E. (2015). Self-compassion and body dissatisfaction in women: A randomized controlled trial of a brief meditation intervention. *Mindfulness, 6*(3), 444-454. https://doi.org/10.1007/s12671-014-0277-3

Ali, D. S., Hall, M. E. L., Anderson, T. L., & Willingham, M. M. (2013). 'I became a mom': Identity changes in mothers receiving public assistance. *Journal of Social Service Research, 39*(5), 587-605. https://doi.org/10.1080/01488376.2013.801391

American Psychological Association. (2007). *Report of the APA task force on the sexualization of girls.* https://www.apa.org/pi/women/programs/girls/report-full.pdf

Anthony, A. K., & McCabe, J. (2015). Friendship talk as identity work: Defining the self through friend relationships. *Symbolic Interaction, 38*(1), 64-82. https://doi.org/10.1002/symb.138

Appel, H., Gerlach, A. L., & Crusius, J. (2016). The interplay between Facebook use, social comparison, envy, and depression. *Current Opinion in Psychology, 9,* 44-49. https://doi.org/10.1016/j.copsyc.2015.10.006

Bandura, A., Ross, D., & Ross, S. A. (1961). Transmission of aggression through imitation of aggressive models. *Journal of Abnormal and Social Psychology, 63,* 575-82. https://doi.org/10.1037/h0045925

Banks, M. V., & Salmon, K. (2013). Reasoning about the self in positive and negative ways: Relationship to psychological functioning in young adulthood. *Memory, 21,* 126. https://doi.org/10.1080/09658211.2012.707213

Barba, E., & Selder, F. (1995). Life transitions theory. *Nursing Leadership Forum, 1*(1), 4-11.

Barna Research Group. (2015). *Atheists and agnostics invading Christian churches.* Barna Research Group.

Baumeister, R. F. (1999). *The nature and structure of the self: An overview.* In R. Baumeister (Ed.), The self in social psychology (pp. 1-20). Psychology Press (Taylor & Francis).

Baumeister, R., & Leary, M. R. (1995). The need to belong: Desire for interpersonal attachments as a fundamental human motivation. *Psychological Bulletin, 117,* 497-529. https://doi-org.ezproxy.liberty.edu/10.1037/0033-2909.117.3.497

Beer, A., Watson, D., & McDade-Montez, E. (2013). Self–other agreement and assumed similarity in neuroticism, extraversion, and trait affect: Distinguishing the effects of form and content. *Assessment, 20,* 723-737. https://doi.org/10.1177/1073191113500521

Bench, S. W., Lench, H. C., Liew, J., Miner, K., & Flores, S. A. (2015). Gender gaps in overestimation of math performance. *Sex Roles, 72,* 536-546. https://doi.org/10.1007/s11199-015-0486-9

Bernard, S., & Correll, S. J. (2010). Normative discrimination and the motherhood penalty. *Gender & Society, 24,* 616-646. https://doi.org/10.1177/0891243210383142

Błażek, M., & Besta, T. (2012). Self-concept clarity and religious orientations: Prediction of purpose in life and self-esteem. *Journal of Religion and Health, 51*(3), 947-960. https://www.jstor.org/stable/41653880

Bowen, M. (1978). *Family therapy in clinical practice.* Jason Aronson.

Bracken, B. A. (2009). Positive self-concepts. In *Handbook of positive psychology in schools* (pp. 107-124). Routledge.

Breines, J. G., & Chen, S. (2012). Self-compassion increases self-improvement motivation. *Personality and Social Psychology Bulletin, 38*(9), 1133-1143. https://doi.org/10.1037/e512142015-364

Budig, M. J., Misra, J., & Boeckmann, I. (2012). The motherhood penalty in cross-national perspective: The importance of work–family policies and cultural attitudes. *Social Politics, 19*(2), 163-193. https://doi.org/10.1093/sp/jxs006

Bureau of Labor Statistics. (2019). *Table 3: Employment status of the civilian noninstitutional population by age, sex, and race, current population survey.* https://www.bls.gov/cps/cpsaat03.htm

Byrne, B. M. (1996). *Measuring self-concept across the life span: Issues and instrumentation.* American Psychologist Association.

Caldera, Y., Huston, A., & O'Brien, M. (1989). Social interactions and play patterns of parents and toddlers with feminine, masculine, and neutral toys. *Child Development, 60,* 70–76. https://www.jstor.org/stable/1131072

Canrinus, E. T., Helms-Lorenz, M., Beijaard, D., Buitink, J., & Hofman, A. (2012). Self-efficacy, job satisfaction, motivation and commitment: Exploring the relationships between indicators of teachers' professional identity. *European journal of psychology of education, 27*(1), 115-132. https://doi.org/10.1007/s10212-011-0069-2

Carlyle, K. E., Slater, M. D., & Chakroff, J. L. (2008). Newspaper coverage of intimate partner violence: Skewing representations of risk. *Journal of Communication, 58,* 168–186. https://doi.org/10.1111/j.1460-2466.2007.00379.x

Cash, T. F. (Ed.). (2011). *Body image: A handbook of science, practice and prevention.* The Guilford Press.

Chemers, M. M., Zurbriggen, E. L., Syed, M., Goza, B. K., & Bearman, S. (2011). The role of efficacy and identity in science career commitment among underrepresented minority students. *Journal of Social Issues, 67*(3), 469-491. https://doi.org/10.1111/j.1540-4560.2011.01710.x

Chou, H. T. G., & Edge, N. (2012). "They are happier and having better lives than I am": the impact of using Facebook on perceptions of others' lives. *Cyberpsychology, Behavior, and Social Networking, 15*(2), 117-121. https://doi.org/10.1089/cyber.2011.0324

Cikara, M., Fiske, S. T. (2009). Warmth, competence and ambivalent sexism: Vertical assault and collateral damage. In Barreto, M., Ryan, M. K., Schmitt, M. T. (Eds.), *The glass ceiling in the 21st century: Understanding barriers to gender equality* (pp. 73–96). American Psychological Association.

Cook, R., & Cusack, S. (2011). *Gender stereotyping: Transnational legal perspectives.* University of Pennsylvania Press.

Cooley, C. H. (1902). *Human nature and social order.* Scribner's.

Crawford, E., Liebling-Kalifani, H., & Hill, V. (2009). Women's understanding of the effects of domestic abuse: The impact on their identity, sense of self and resilience. A grounded theory approach. *Journal of International Women's Studies, 11*(2), 63–82. https://link-galecom.ezproxy.liberty.edu/apps/doc/A229530798/GIC?u=vic_liberty&sid=GIC&xid=f1e667fe.

Crocetti, E., Prati, F., & Rubini, M. (2018). The interplay of personal and social identity. *European Psychologist, 23*(4), 300. https://doi.org/10.1027/1016-9040/a000336

Dale, L. P., Carroll, L. E., Galen, G. C., Schein, R., Bliss, A., Mattison, A. M., & Neace, W. P. (2011). Yoga practice may buffer the deleterious effects of abuse on women's self-concept and dysfunctional coping. *Journal of Aggression, Maltreatment & Trauma, 20*(1), 90-102. https://doi.org/10.1080/10926771.2011.538005

Dare, J. S. (2011). Transitions in midlife women's lives: Contemporary experiences. *Health Care for Women International, 32*(2), 111-133. https://doi.org/10.1080/07399332.2010.500753

Day, M. V., Kay, A. C., Holmes, J. G., & Napier, J. L. (2011). System justification and the defense of committed relationship ideology. *Journal of Personality and Social Psychology, 101*(2), 291. https://doi.org/10.1037/a0023197

DeBruin, E. I., Van der Zwan, J. E., & Bögels, S. M. (2016). A RCT comparing daily mindfulness meditations, biofeedback exercises, and daily physical exercise on attention control, executive functioning, mindful awareness, self-compassion, and worrying in stressed young adults. *Mindfulness, 7*(5), 1182-1192. https://doi.org/10.1007/s12671-016-0561-5

Deloitte and Alliance for Board Diversity (2019). *Missing pieces report: The 2018 board diversity census of women and minorities on fortune 500 boards.* https://www.catalyst.org/research/missing-pieces-report-the-2018-board-diversity-census-of-women-and-minorities-on-fortune-500-boards/

Demir, M., Haynes, A., & Potts, S. K. (2017). My friends are my estate: Friendship experiences mediate the relationship between perceived responses to capitalization attempts and happiness. *Journal of Happiness Studies, 18*, 1161-1190. https://doi-org.ezproxy.liberty.edu/10.1007/s10902-016-9762-9

DePaulo, B. M., & Morris, W. L. (2005). Singles in society and in science. *Psychological Inquiry, 16,*57–83. https://doi.org/10.1080/104784 0X.2005.9682918

De Vries, D. A., & Kühne, R. (2015). Facebook and self-perception: Individual susceptibility to negative social comparison on Facebook. *Personality and Individual Differences, 86,* 217-221. https://doi.org/10.1016/j.paid.2015.05.029

Dibb, B. (2019). Social media use and perceptions of physical health. *Heliyon, 5*(1), e00989.

Diener, E., & Seligman, M. E. P. (2002). Very happy people. *Psychological Science, 13*(1), 81–84. https://doi.org/10.1111/1467-9280.00415

Diener, E., Seligman, M. E., Choi, H., & Oishi, S. (2018). Happiest people revisited. *Perspectives on Psychological Science, 13*(2), 176-184. https://doi.org/10.1177/1745691617697077

Dutton, D. G., & Painter, S. L. (1981). Traumatic bonding: The development of emotional attachments in battered women and other relationships of intermittent abuse. *Victimology: An International Journal, 6*(1-4), 139-155.

Elliott, H., Gunaratnam., Y., Hollway, W., & Phoenix, A. (2009). Practices, identification, and identity change in the transition to motherhood. In M. Wetherell, (Ed.), *Theorizing identities and social action* (pp. 19-37). Palgrave.

Erikson, E. H. (1968). *Identity, youth, and crisis.* Norton.

Erikson, E. H. (1980). *Identity and the life cycle.* Norton.

Ehrlinger, J., & Dunning, D. (2003). How chronic self-views influence (and potentially mislead) estimates of performance. *Journal of personality and social psychology, 84*(1), 5. https://doi.org/10.1037/0022-3514.84.1.5

Fardouly, J., & Vartanian, L. R. (2015). Negative comparisons about one's appearance mediate
the relationship between Facebook usage and body image concerns. *Body Image, 12,* 82-88. https://doi.org/10.1016/j.bodyim.2014.10.004

Feinstein, B. A., Hershenberg, R., Bhatia, V., Latack, J. A., Meuwly, N., & Davila, J. (2013). Negative social comparison on Facebook and depressive symptoms: Rumination as a mechanism. *Psychology of Popular Media Culture, 2*(3), 161. https://doi.org/10.1037/a0033111

Ferreira, L. C., Narciso, I., & Novo, R. F. (2012). Intimacy, sexual desire and differentiation in couplehood: A theoretical and methodological review. *Journal of Sex & Marital Therapy, 38*(3), 263-280. https://doi.org/10.1080/009262 3X.2011.606885

Ferreira, L. C., Narciso, I., Novo, R. F., & Pereira, C. R. (2014). Predicting couple satisfaction: The role of differentiation of self, sexual desire and intimacy in heterosexual individuals. *Sexual and Relationship Therapy, 29*(4), 390-404. https://doi.org/10.1080/14681994.2014.957498

Festinger, L. (1954). A theory of social comparison processes. *Human Relations, 7*(2), 117–140. https://doi.org/10.1177/001872675400700202

Follingstad, D. R., & Rogers, M. J. (2014). The nature and prevalence of partner psychological abuse in a national sample of adults. *Violence and Victims, 29*(1), 3-23. https://doi.org/10.1891/0886-6708.09-160

Fox, J., & Moreland, J. J. (2015). The dark side of social networking sites: An exploration of the relational and psychological stressors associated with

Facebook use and affordances. *Computers in Human Behavior, 45*, 168-176. https://doi.org/10.1016/j.chb.2014.11.083

Fredrickson, B. L., & Roberts, T. A. (1997). Objectification theory: Toward understanding women's lived experiences and mental health risks. *Psychology of Women Quarterly, 21*(2), 173-206. https://doi.org/10.1111/j.1471-6402.1997.tb00108.x

Friedkin, N. E., & Johnsen, E. C. (2011). *Social influence network theory: A sociological examination of small group dynamics.* Cambridge University Press.

Gadalla, T. (2009). Impact of marital dissolution on men's and women's incomes: A longitudinal study. *Journal of Divorce & Remarriage, 50*(1), 55–65.

Gerber, J. P., Wheeler, L., & Suls, J. (2018). A social comparison theory meta-analysis 60+ years on. *Psychological Bulletin, 144*(2), 177. https://doi.org/10.1037/bul0000127

Goffman, E. (1959). *The presentation of self in everyday life.* Anchor Books.

Golombok, S., Rust, J., Zervoulis, K., Croudace, T., Golding, J., &Hines, M. (2008). Developmental trajectories of sex-typed behavior in boys and girls: A longitudinal general population study of children aged 2.5–8 years. *Child Development, 79*, 1583–1593. https://doi.org/10.1111/j.1467-8624.2008.01207.x

Gordon, M. K. (2008). Media contributions to African American girls' focus on beauty and appearance: Exploring the consequences of sexual objectification. *Psychology of Women Quarterly, 32*(3), 245-256. https://doi.org/10.1111/j.1471-6402.2008.00433.x

Graham, D. L., & Rawlings, E. (1991). Bonding with abusive dating partners: Dynamics of Stockholm Syndrome. In B. Levy (Ed.), *Dating violence: Young women in danger* (pp. 119-135). Seal Press.

Gregson, J., & Ceynar, M. L. (2009). Finding "me" again: Women's postdivorce identity shifts. *Journal of Divorce & Remarriage, 50*, 564–582. https://doi.org/10.1080/10502550902970546

Greif, G. L., & Deal, K. H. (2012). The impact of divorce on friendships with couples and individuals. *Journal of Divorce & Remarriage, 53*(6), 421-435. https://doi.org/10.1080/10502556.2012.682894

Gurrieri, L., Previte, J., & Brace-Govan, J. (2013). Women's bodies as sites of control: Inadvertent stigma and exclusion in social marketing. *Journal of Macromarketing, 33*(2), 128-143. https://doi.org/10.1177/0276146712469971

Habermas, T., & Bluck, S. (2000). Getting a life: the emergence of the life story in adolescence. *Psychological Bulletin, 126*(5), 748. https://doi.org/10.1037/0033-2909.126.5.748

Habermas, T. (2010). Autobiographical reasoning: Arguing and narrating from a biographical perspective. In T. Habermas (Ed.) *The development of autobiographical reasoning in adolescence and beyond. New Directions for Child and Adolescent Development, 131*, 1–17. https://doi.org/10.1002/cd.285

Han, W. J., Ruhm, C., & Waldfogel, J. (2009). Parental leave policies and parents' employment and leave-taking. *Journal of Policy Analysis and Management: The Journal of the Association for Public Policy Analysis and Management, 28*(1), 29-54. https://doi.org/10.1002/pam.20398

Hand, D., Jackson, W., Sharpsteen, B., Morey, L., Cottrell, W., & Pearce, Perce. (Directors). (1937). *Snow white and the seven dwarfs* [Film]. Walt Disney Productions.

Haslam, S. A., Jetten, J., Postmes, T., & Haslam, C. (2009). Social identity, health and well-being: An emerging agenda for applied psychology. *Applied Psychology,58*(1), 1–23.

Heilman, M. E. (2012). Gender stereotypes and workplace bias. *Research in organizational Behavior, 32*, 113-135. https://doi.org/10.1016/j.riob.2012.11.003

Helms, J. E. (1995). An update of Helms's White and people of color racial identity models. In J. G. Ponterotto, J. M. Casas, L. A. Suzuki, & C. M. Alexander (Eds.), *Handbook of multicultural counseling*. Sage.

Hensley, B. J. (2012). Adaptive information processing, targeting, the standard protocol, and strategies for successful outcomes in EMDR reprocessing. *Journal of EMDR Practice and Research, 6*(3), 92-100. https://doi.org/10.1891/1933-3196.6.3.92

Hentschel, T., Braun, S., Peus, C., & Frey, D. (2018). The communality-bonus effect for male transformational leaders–leadership style, gender, and promotability. *European Journal of Work and Organizational Psychology, 27*(1), 112-125. https://doi.org/10.1080/1359432X.2017.1402759

Hirschman, E. C. (1993). Ideology in consumer research, 1980 and 1990: A Marxist and feminist critique. *Journal of consumer research, 19*(4), 537-555. https://doi.org/10.1086/209321

Hoeve, Y. T., Jansen, G., & Roodbol, P. (2014). The nursing profession: Public image, self-concept and professional identity. A discussion paper. *Journal of Advanced Nursing, 70*(2), 295-309. https://doi.org/10.1111/jan.12177

Hoffnung, M., & Williams, M. A. (2013). Balancing act: Career and family during college-educated women's 30s. *Sex Roles, 68*(5-6), 321-334.

Hollway, W. (2010). Conflict in the transitions to becoming a mother: A psycho-social approach. *Psychoanalysis, Culture & Society, 15*, 136-155. http://doi.org/10.1057/pcs.2009.34

Jacobsen, C., & Van Der Voordt, T. J. (1980). Interpreting modal frequencies to measure social norms. *Sociological Methods & Research, 8*(4), 470-486. https://doi.org/10.1177/004912418000800407

Jiang, L. C., Bazarova, N. N., & Hancock, J. T. (2011). The disclosure–intimacy link in computer-mediated communication: An attributional extension of the hyperpersonal model. *Human Communication Research, 37*(1), 58-77. https://doi.org/10.1111/j.1468-2958.2010.01393.x

Jordan, J. V. (1992). The relational self: A new understanding for women's development. *Contemporary Psychotherapy Review, 7*, 56-71. https://doi.org/10.1007/978-1-4684-8264-5_8

Jordan, J. V. (2010). *Relational-cultural therapy*. American Psychological Association.

Jung, C. G. (1936). The concept of the collective unconscious. *Collected works, 9*(1), 42.

Kahn, J. R., García-Manglano, J., & Bianchi, S. M. (2014). The motherhood penalty at midlife: Long-term effects of children on women's careers. *Journal of Marriage and Family, 76*(1), 56-72. https://doi.org/10.1111/jomf.12086

Kennedy, A. (2014). Compassion-focused EMDR. *Journal of EMDR practice and research, 8*(3), 135-146. https://doi.org/10.1891/1933-3196.8.3.135

Kerr, M. E., & Bowen, M. (1988). *Family evaluation.* Norton.

Kuhnley, A. K. (2020). *The Mister Rogers Effect: 7 secrets to bringing out the best in yourself and others.* Baker Books.

Lahad, K. (2012). Singlehood, waiting, and the sociology of time. *Sociological Forum, 27*(1), 163-186. https://doi.org/10.1111/j.1573-7861.2011.01306.x

Lahad, K. (2013). "Am I asking for too much?" The selective single woman as a new social problem. *Women's Studies International Forum, 40,* 23-32. https://doi.org/10.1016/j.wsif.2013.04.009

Lahad, K. (2014). The single woman's choice as a zero-sum game. *Cultural Studies, 28*(2), 240-266. https://doi.org/10.1080/09502386.2013.798341

Laney, E. K., Carruthers, L., Hall, M. E. L., & Anderson, T. (2014). Expanding the self: Motherhood and identity development in faculty women. *Journal of Family Issues, 35*(9), 1227-1251. https://doi.org/10.1177/0192513x13479573

Laney, E. K., Hall, M. E. L., Anderson, T. L., & Willingham, M. M. (2015). Becoming a mother: The influence of motherhood on women's identity development. *Identity, 15*(2), 126-145. https://doi.org/10.1080/15283488.2015.1023440

Lavelle, B., & Smock, P. J. (2012). Divorce and women's risk of health insurance loss. *Journal of Health and Social Behavior, 53*(4), 413-431. https://doi.org/10.1177/0022146512465758

Lee, J. S. (2002). The Korean language in America: The role of cultural identity in heritage language learning. Language. *Culture and Curriculum, 15*(2), 117–133. https://doi.org/10.1080/07908310208666638

Lee, K. S., & Ono, H. (2012). Marriage, cohabitation, and happiness: A cross-national analysis of 27 countries. *Journal of Marriage and Family, 74*(5), 953-972. https://doi.org/10.1111/j.1741-3737.2012.01001.x

Lee-Flynn, S. C., Pomaki, G., DeLongis, A., Biesanz, J. C., & Puterman, E. (2011). Daily cognitive appraisals, daily affect, and long-term depressive symptoms: The role of self-esteem and self-concept clarity in the stress process. *Personality and Social Psychology Bulletin, 37*(2), 255-268. https://doi.org/10.1177/0146167210394204

Leskinen, E. A., Rabelo, V. C., & Cortina, L. M. (2015). Gender stereotyping and harassment: A "catch-22" for women in the workplace. *Psychology, Public Policy, and Law, 21*(2), 192. https://doi.org/10.1037/law0000040

Lewandowski, G. W. Jr., Aron, A., Bassis, S., & Kunak, J. (2006). Losing a self-expanding relationship: Implications for the self-concept. *Personal Relationships, 13,* 317–331. https://doi.org/10.1111/j.1475-6811.2006.00120.x

Lilgendahl, J. P., & McAdams, D. P. (2011). Constructing stories of self-growth: How individual differences in patterns of autobiographical reasoning relate to well-being in midlife. *Journal of Personality, 79,* 391-428. https://doi.org/10.1111/j.1467-6494.2010.00688.x

Lindsey, L. L. (2015). *Gender roles: A sociological perspective.* Routledge.

Loprinzi, C. E., Prasad, K., Schroeder, D. R., & Sood, A. (2011). Stress Management and Resilience Training (SMART) program to decrease stress and enhance resilience among breast cancer survivors: A pilot randomized clinical trial. *Clinical Breast Cancer, 11*(6), 364-368. https://doi.org/10.1016/j.clbc.2011.06.008

Lynch, S. M. (2013). Not good enough and on a tether: Exploring how violent relationships impact women's sense of self. *Psychodynamic Psychiatry*, *41*(2), 219-246. https://doi.org/10.1521/pdps.2013.41.2.219

Maccoby, E. E. (2000). Perspectives on gender development. *International Journal of Behavioral Development. 24*, 398-406.

Manago, A. M., Ward, L. M., Lemm, K. M., Reed, L., & Seabrook, R. (2015). Facebook involvement, objectified body consciousness, body shame, and sexual assertiveness in college women and men. *Sex Roles, 72*(1-2), 1-14.

Martiny, S. E., Gleibs, I. H., Parks-Stamm, E. J., Martiny-Huenger, T., Froehlich, L., Harter, A. L., & Roth, J. (2015). Dealing with negative stereotypes in sports: The role of cognitive anxiety when multiple identities are activated in sensorimotor tasks. *Journal of Sport and Exercise Psychology*, *37*(4), 379-392. https://doi.org/10.1123/jsep.2014-0284

Mason, A. E., Law, R. W., Bryan, A. E., Portley, R. M., & Sbarra, D. A. (2012). Facing a breakup: Electromyographic responses moderate self-concept recovery following a romantic separation. *Personal Relationships, 19*(3), 551–568. https://doi.org/10.1111/j.1475-6811.2011.01378.xdoi:10.1111/j.1475-6811.2011.01378.x

Maslow, A. H. (1963). The need to know and the fear of knowing. *The Journal of General Psychology*, *68*(1), 111-125. https://doi.org/10.1080/00221309.1963.9920516

Maslow, A. H. (2013). *Toward a psychology of being.* Simon and Schuster.

Matheson, F. I., Daoud, N., Hamilton-Wright, S., Borenstein, H., Pedersen, C., & O'Campo, P. (2015). Where did she go? The transformation of self-esteem, self-identity, and mental well-being among women who have experienced intimate partner violence. *Women's Health Issues, 25*(5), 561-569. https://doi.org/10.1016/j.whi.2015.04.006

McAdams, D. P., & Olson, B. D. (2010). Personality development: Continuity and changeover the life course. *Annual Review of Psychology, 61*, 517–542. https://doi.org/10.1146/annurev.psych.093008.100507

McDermott, R., Fowler, J., & Christakis, N. (2013). Breaking up is hard to do, unless everyone else is doing it too: Social network effects on divorce in a longitudinal sample. *Social Forces, 92*(2), 491–519. https://doi.org/10.1093/sf/sot096

Milburn, M. C. (2011). Cognitive-behavior therapy and change: Unconditional self- acceptance and hypnosis in CBT. *Journal of Rational-Emotive & Cognitive-Behavior Therapy, 29*(3), 177-191. https://doi.org/10.1007/s10942-010-0121-1

Miller, J. B. (1976). *Toward a new psychology of women.* Beacon Press.

Motschnig-Pitrik, R., & Barrett-Lennard, G. (2010). Co-actualization: A new construct in understanding well-functioning relationships. *Journal of Humanistic Psychology, 50*(3), 374-398. https://doi.org/10.1177/0022167809348017

Murray, C. E., Crowe, A., & Brinkley, J. (2015). The stigma surrounding intimate partner violence: A cluster analysis study. *Partner Abuse, 6*(3), 320-336.

Murray, C. E., Crowe, A., & Overstreet, N. M. (2015). Sources and components of stigma experienced by survivors of intimate partner violence. *Journal of Interpersonal Violence, 33*(3), 515-536. https://doi.org/10.1177/0886260515609565

Myers, J. E., & Sweeney, T. J. (2004). The indivisible Self: An evidence-based model of wellness. *Journal of Individual Psychology, 61*(3). 234-245.

National Women's Law Center. (2018). *Fact sheet: Frequently asked questions about the wage gap.* https://nwlc.org/resources/faq-about-the-wage-gap/

New International Bible. (2011). New International Bible Online. https://www.thenivbible.com/ (Original work published 1973).

New Living Bible (1996). New Living Bible. https://www.biblegateway.com/versions/New-Living-Translation-NLT-Bible/

O'Doherty, L. J., Taft, A., McNair, R., & Hegarty, K. (2016). Fractured identity in the context of intimate partner violence: Barriers to and opportunities for seeking help in health settings. *Violence Against Women, 22*(2), 225-248. https://doi.org/10.1177/1077801215601248

O'Mahen, H., Fedock, G., Henshaw, E., Himle, J. A., Forman, J., & Flynn, H. A. (2012). Modifying CBT for perinatal depression: what do women want?: A qualitative study. *Cognitive and Behavioral Practice, 19*(2), 359-371. https://doi.org/10.1016/j.cbpra.2011.05.005

Orenstein, P. (1995). *School girls: Young women, self-esteem and the confidence gap.* Anchor.

Pals, J. L. (2006). Narrative identity processing of difficult life experiences: Pathways of personality development and positive self-transformation in adulthood. *Journal of Personality, 74,* 1079-1110. https://doi.org/10.1111/j.1467-6494.2006.00403.x

Papa, A., & Lancaster, N. (2016). Identity continuity and loss after death, divorce, and job loss. *Self and Identity, 15*(1), 47-61. https://doi.org/10.1080/15298868.2015.1079551

Patzak, A., Kollmayer, M., & Schober, B. (2017). Buffering impostor feelings with kindness: The mediating role of self-compassion between gender-role orientation and the impostor phenomenon. *Frontiers in Psychology, 8,* 1289. https://doi.org/10.3389/fpsyg.2017.01289

Pempek, T. A., Yermolayeva, Y. A., & Calvert, S. L. (2009). College students' social networking experiences on Facebook. *Journal of Applied Developmental Psychology, 30*(3), 227-238. https://doi.org/10.1016/j.appdev.2008.12.010

Pham-Kanter, G. (2009). Social comparisons and health: Can having richer friends and neighbors make you sick? *Social Science & Medicine, 69*(3), 335-344. https://doi.org/10.1016/j.socscimed.2009.05.017

Primack, B. A., Shensa, A., Escobar-Viera, C. G., Barrett, E. L., Sidani, J. E., Colditz, J. B., & James, A. E. (2017). Use of multiple social media platforms and symptoms of depression and anxiety: A nationally-representative study among US young adults. *Computers in human behavior, 69,* 1-9. https://doi.org/10.1016/j.chb.2016.11.013

Ranjitha, G. P., & Unnithan, A. B. (2018). Self and identity of being an ideal woman: An exploratory qualitative study. *IIM Kozhikode Society & Management Review, 7*(1), 33-44. https://doi.org/10.1177/2277975217733883

Rajan-Rankin, S. (2014). Self-identity, embodiment and the development of emotional resilience. *The British Journal of Social Work, 44*(8), 2426-2442. https://doi.org/10.1093/bjsw/bct083

Richter, T., Appel, M., & Calio, F. (2014). Stories can influence the self-concept. *Social Influence, 9*(3), 172-188. https://doi.org/10.1080/15534510.2013.799099

Rimal, R. N., & Lapinski, M. K. (2015). A re-explication of social norms, ten years later. *Communication Theory, 25*(4), 393-409. https://doi.org/10.1111/comt.12080

Ritchie, T. D., Sedikides, C., Wildschut, T., Arndt, J., & Gidron, Y. (2011). Self-concept clarity mediates the relation between stress and subjective well-being. *Self and Identity, 10*(4), 493-508. https://doi.org/10.1080/15298868.2010.493066

Robinson, L., Prichard, I., Nikolaidis, A., Drummond, C., Drummond, M., & Tiggemann, M. (2017). Idealised media images: The effect of fitspiration imagery on body satisfaction and exercise behaviour. *Body Image, 22,* 65-71. https://doi.org/10.1016/j.bodyim.2017.06.001

Rogers, C. R. (1959). A theory of therapy, personality, and interpersonal relationships: As developed in the client-centered framework. In S. Koch (Ed.), *Psychology: A study of a science: Vol 3. Formulations of the person and the social context* (pp. 184-256). McGraw-Hill.

Rosenberg, M. (1979). *Conceiving the self.* Basic Books.

Saadati, H., & Lashani, L. (2013). Effectiveness of gestalt therapy on self-efficacy of divorced women. *Procedia-Social and Behavioral Sciences, 84,* 1171-1174. https://doi.org/10.1016/j.sbspro.2013.06.721

Sakraida, T. J. (2005). Common themes in the divorce transition experience of midlife women. *Journal of Divorce and Remarriage, 43*(1–2), 69–88. https://doi.org/10.1300/J087v43n01_04

Schnarch, D., & Regas, S. (2012). The crucible differentiation scale: Assessing differentiation in human relationships. *Journal of Marital and Family Therapy, 38*(4), 639-652. https://doi.org/10.1111/j.1752-0606.2011.00259.x

Seabrook, E. M., Kern, M. L., & Rickard, N. S. (2016). Social networking sites, depression, and anxiety: A systematic review. *JMIR Mental Health, 3*(4), e50. https://doi.org/10.2196/mental.5842

Shachar, R., Leshem, T., Nasim, R., Rosenberg, J., Schmidt, A., & Schmuely, V. (2013). Exploring discourses that affect therapists regarding single women. *Journal of Feminist Family Therapy, 25*(4), 257-280. https://doi.org/10.1080/08952833.2013.777887

Sharp, E. A., & Ganong, L. (2011). "I'm a loser, I'm not married, let's just all look at me": Ever-single women's perceptions of their social environment. *Journal of Family Issues, 32*(7), 956-980. https://doi.org/10.1177/0192513X10392537

Sheikh, F., Koolaee, A. K., & Zadeh, M. R. (2013). The comparison of self-differentiation and self-concept in divorced and non-divorced women who experience domestic violence. *International Journal of High Risk Behaviors & Addiction, 2*(2), 66. https://doi.org/10.5812/ijhrba.10029

Shorey, S., Chee, C. Y. I., Ng, E. D., Chan, Y. H., San Tam, W. W., & Chong, Y. S. (2018). Prevalence and incidence of postpartum depression among healthy mothers: A systematic review and meta-analysis. *Journal of Psychiatric Research, 104,* 235-248. https://doi.org/10.1016/j.jpsychires.2018.08.001

Slonim, G., Gur-Yaish, N., & Katz, R. (2015). By choice or by circumstance?: Stereotypes of and feelings about single people. *Studia Psychologica, 57*(1), 35.

Slotter, E. B., Gardner, W. L., & Finkel, E. J. (2010). Who am I without you? The influence of romantic breakup on the self-concept. *Personality and Social Psychology Bulletin, 36*(2), 147-160. https://doi.org/10.1177/0146167209352250

Smith, T. B., & Silva, L. (2011). Ethnic identity and personal well-being of people of color: A meta-analysis. *Journal of Counseling Psychology, 58*(1), 42. https://doi.org/10.1037/a0021528

Smith, J. S., & Smith, K. E. (2016). What it means to do gender differently: Understanding identity, perceptions and accomplishments in a gendered world. *Humboldt Journal of Social Relations, 1*(38), 8. https://www.jstor.org/stable/humjsocrel.38.62

Song, L. Y. (2012). Service utilization, perceived changes of self, and life satisfaction among women who experienced intimate partner abuse: The mediation effect of empowerment. *Journal of Interpersonal Violence, 27*(6), 1112-1136. https://doi.org/10.1177/0886260511424495

Strickhouser, J. E., & Zell, E. (2015). Self-evaluative effects of dimensional and social comparison. *Journal of Experimental Social Psychology, 59,* 60-66. https://doi.org/10.1016/j.jesp.2015.03.001

Surrey, J. L. (1985). *The" self-in-relation": A theory of women's development.* Wellesley College, Stone Center for Developmental Services and Studies.

Swann Jr, W. B., Gómez, Á., Seyle, D. C., Morales, J., & Huici, C. (2009). Identity fusion: The interplay of personal and social identities in extreme group behavior. *Journal of Personality and Social Psychology, 96*(5), 995. https://doi.org/10.1037/a0013668

Symoens, S., Van de Velde, S., Colman, E., & Bracke, P. (2014). Divorce and the multidimensionality of men and women's mental health: The role of social-relational and socio-economic conditions. *Applied Research in Quality of Life, 9*(2), 197-214. https://doi.org/10.1007/s11482-013-9239-5

Tajfel, H., & Turner, J. C. (1986). The social identity theory of intergroup behavior. *Psychology of Intergroup Relations, 2,* 7-24. https://doi.org/10.4324/9780203505984-16

Taylor, D. G., & Strutton, D. (2016). Does Facebook usage lead to conspicuous consumption? The role of envy, narcissism and self-promotion. *Journal of Research in Interactive Marketing, 10*(3), 231-248.

Thomas, C., & Ryan, M. (2008). Women's perception of the divorce experience: A qualitative study. *Journal of Divorce & Remarriage., 49*(3-4), 210–224. https://doi.org/10.1080/10502550802222394

Timonen, V., & Doyle, M. (2014). Life-long singlehood: Intersections of the past and the present. *Ageing & Society, 34*(10), 1749-1770. https://doi.org/10.1017/S0144686X13000500

Tossi, M. (2016, September). *A look at the future of the U.S. labor force to 2060: Spotlight on statistics.* Bureau of Labor Statistics. https://www.bls.gov/spotlight/2016/a-look-at-the-future-of-the-us-labor-force-to-2060/home.htm

Troy, A. S., & Mauss, I. B. (2011). Resilience in the face of stress: Emotion regulation ability as a protective factor. In S. Southwick, D. Charney, M. Friedman, & B. Litz (Eds.), *Resilience to stress* (pp. 30–44). Cambridge University Press.

Tuncay-Zayer, L., & Coleman, C. A. (2015). Advertising professionals' perceptions of the impact of gender portrayals on men and women: A question of ethics?.

Journal of Advertising, 44(3), 1-12. https://doi.org/10.1080/00913367.2014.9758 78

Urista, M.A., Dong, Q., & Day, K. D. (2009). Explaining why young adults use myspace and facebook through uses and gratifications theory. *Human Communication, 12*(2), 215-229.

Usborne, E., & Taylor, D. M. (2010). The role of cultural identity clarity for self-concept clarity, self-esteem, and subjective well-being. *Personality and Social Psychology Bulletin, 36*(7), 883-897. https://doi.org/10.1177/0146167210372215

Varan, D. (1998). The cultural erosion metaphor and the transcultural impact of media. *Journal of Communication, 48,* 58–85. https://doi.org/10.1111/j.1460-2466.1998.tb02748.x

Vogel, E. A., Rose, J. P., Roberts, L. R., & Eckles, K. (2014). Social comparison, social media, and self-esteem. *Psychology of Popular Media Culture, 3*(4), 206.

Ward, L. M., & Harrison, K. (2005). The impact of media use on girls' beliefs about gender roles, their bodies, and sexual relationships: A research synthesis. In E. Cole, & J. H.Daniel (Eds.), *Featuring females: Feminist analyses of media* (pp. 3–23). APA Books.

Willows, N. D., Ridley, D., Raine, K. D., & Maximova, K. (2013). High adiposity is associated cross-sectionally with low self-concept and body size dissatisfaction among indigenous Cree schoolchildren in Canada. *BMC pediatrics, 13*(1), 118. https://doi.org/10.1186/1471-2431-13-118

Winnicott, D. W. (1967). The location of cultural experience. *International Journal of Psycho-Analysis, 48,* 368-372. https://doi.org/10.1093/med:psych/9780190271398.003.0075

Wiseman, R. S. (1975). Crisis theory and the process of divorce. *Social Casework, 56,* 205-212. https://doi.org/10.1177/104438947505600402

Yadavaia, J. E., Hayes, S. C., & Vilardaga, R. (2014). Using acceptance and commitment therapy to increase self-compassion: A randomized controlled trial. *Journal of contextual behavioral science, 3*(4), 248-257. https://doi.org/10.1016/j.jcbs.2014.09.002

Zell, E., & Balcetis, E. (2012). The influence of social comparison on visual representation of one's face. *PloS one, 7*(5), e36742. https://doi.org/10.1371/journal.pone.0036742

Zukin, S., & Maguire, J. S. (2004). Consumers and consumption. *Annual Review of Sociology, 30,* 173-197. https://doi.org/10.1146/annurev.soc.30.012703.110553

CHAPTER 7
The Marriage Relationship

JENNIFER J. BERES, PH.D.

"To be fully seen by somebody, then, and be loved anyhow—this is a human offering that can border on miraculous." ~ Elizabeth Gilbert, Committed: A Skeptic Makes Peace with Marriage

"Be always humble, gentle, and patient. Show your love by being tolerant with one another. Do your best to preserve the unity which the Spirit gives by means of the peace that binds you together." (Ephesians 4:2-3, GNB).

Wisdom from Above: Standing in His Grace

© Inked Pixels/ Shutterstock.com

A man married a beautiful girl. He loved her very much. One day, she developed a skin disease. Slowly, she started to lose her beauty. It so happened that one day her husband left for a tour. While returning, he met with an accident and lost his eyesight. However, their married life continued as usual. But as days passed, she lost her beauty gradually. Blind husband did not know this and there was not any difference in their married life. He continued to love her and she also loved him very much. One day she died. Her death brought him much sorrow. He finished all her last rites and wanted to leave that town. A man from behind called and said, 'Now how will you be able to walk all alone? All these days your wife used to help you'. He replied, 'I am not blind. I was acting because I knew if she knew I could see her skin condition due to a disease, it would have pained her more than her disease. I didn't love her for her beauty alone, but I fell in love with her caring and loving nature. So, I pretended to be blind. I only wanted to keep her happy' (Moral Stories, 2019, para.1)

We all know the moral of this story, don't we? Love is sacrificial. Love is compassionate. As 1 Corinthians 13: 4, *New International al Bible* (1973/2011) indicates, "Love is patient, love is kind. It does not envy, it does not boast, it is not proud." It is the offering of grace and protecting of the spirit for the purpose of providing a safe place for someone to be loved for who they are, on good days and bad. It is the creation of a relationship that is unlike any other, and because of that, marriage holds the ability to influence us in unique and powerful ways.

CHAPTER OVERVIEW

The challenges that arise in marriage counseling can be complex. Fortunately, a wealth of research offers us powerful information, solid theories, and thriving practices that are yielding promising results in couples counseling. While there is no way to review all of these approaches, or even exhaustively cover the few that are included, this chapter will address some of the most common pitfalls in marriages, effective and modern theories of practice, and successful therapeutic interventions for marriage counseling, as well as some general facts and statistics on marriage and divorce. As it often helps to make application of what we read to a real-life scenario, a case study will be provided to apply the counseling principles discussed in the chapter.

CHAPTER LEARNING OBJECTIVES

Upon completing this chapter, you should be able to:

- Identify causes of marital problems
- Symptoms, diagnosis, and statistics of marital problems
- Evidence-based interventions for marriage counseling
- Biblical understanding of the marriage relationship

© GANNA MARTYSHEVA/Shutterstock.com

MARITAL COUNSELING

Counseling individuals is not an easy task by any means. It requires skill, practice, compassion and excellent planning skills. Marriage counseling can be even more challenging - for both clients and counselors - as not just one person's thoughts and feelings are being expressed, but

two, often of which are at odds. The role of a counselor must be to support both parties in communicating their concerns and identifying areas of dysfunction, while working to find common ground and effective ways to problem-solve.

Research indicates that, even more so than the selected theoretical approach, the development of rapport is crucial in counseling (Rogers, 1951). Clients must believe that their counselor is working for them, with them, and seeking their best interest, without judgment, taking sides or attempting to force a client to change (Meier & Davis, 2019). Perhaps secondary to rapport is the importance of offering clients hope. We find this through a hope-focused counseling relationship where identity development is supported and clients gain a different perspective once they are offered new information (Larsen & Stege, 2012). Most counselors today

© Jane0606/Shutterstock.com

believe that the fundamental aspects of counseling first posed by Carl Rogers (1951) of empathy, warmth and genuineness are the core elements that create a positive working alliance within the counseling relationship and that change is most possible when these conditions exist.

Statistics

How appealing is marriage these days? Is it still the modern American dream to have one marriage, 2.5 children and a house with a white picket fence? Perhaps for some, but the American dream seems to have been overhauled over the years. In the past few decades, a popular area of study for scholars in the field of counseling and human services is that of marriage and divorce trends. These trends tend to point out how social, economic, and moral changes that have developed over the last few decades impact individuals and families and can begin to explain changes in marriage and divorce rates over time. Throughout the 21st century, we have found that trends are not stable or constant but instead, are impacted by various factors at different times in American history. For example, increased educational and employment options for women in the past 30 to 40 years has resulted in a greater level of independence as well as being tied to changing the perception of marriage as an economic advantage and influencing divorce behavior (Mokhtari et al., 2019).

The divorce rate in the United States still hovers slightly below the 50% mark with suggestions that the number is currently declining (Kennedy & Ruggles, 2014). Marriage has historically been shown to offer physical, emotional, and financial protective factors (Woods et al., 2018). Generally speaking, married adults will live longer, healthier, more stable lives. However, research also indicates that men benefit more from marriage than women, perhaps due in part to inequality of role workload. Women are reporting more responsibility for the upkeep of the home (even when employed herself), more childcare responsibilities, and more effort put into maintaining the emotional connections required to sustain a healthy friendship and intimate relationship with her spouse (Doan & Quadlin, 2018). It is not surprising to see recent research reporting that while 75% of divorced people will remarry, men are three times more likely to get remarried than are women, many of whom appear to be choosing to remain single (Lewis & Kreider, 2015).

Over the past few decades, the rates of marriage and divorce have not been as predictable, because as our culture changes, so does our perception of what would make us content or offer us the most benefits. The stability of family trends, particularly when it comes to marriage and divorce rates, seems to be heavily influenced by cultural expectations, acceptable social norms, governmental policies, and economic benefits and drawbacks (Mokhtari et al., 2019). Ultimately, it appears that the values and beliefs that we hold and the lifestyles that we subscribe to impacts our perspective on marriage, family, divorce, remarriage and singlehood.

Symptoms and Criteria

Counselors use screening tools and interviews to assess for symptoms that align with the *Diagnostic and Statistical Manual of Mental Disorders* (*DSM-5*; American Psychiatric Association [APA], 2013), which provides the criteria for various psychological disorders. The *DSM-5* has listed marital relationship issues as a z-code, a classification of disorders that are separated from other psychological conditions that might exist, such as depression or anxiety. Z-codes are used when the presenting problem is not better defined by another primary diagnosis. Symptoms of intimate partner relationship distress include impaired cognitive, behavioral or emotional functioning and are likely to become evident in difficulty with communication and conflict resolution. Clients struggling with relationship problems will often display withdrawal or over-involvement in activities and report chronic sadness, apathy, or anger (APA, 2013). There can be a tendency for couples who are struggling to blame one another for past personal relationship disappointments and have difficulty planning for the future or wanting to stay in the present relationship because of arguments or distance in the relationship (O'Leary et al., 1998).

WHY DO COUPLES SEEK COUNSELING?

When do you choose to fill up your gas tank in your car? For some, it is as soon as the red line hits the half-way mark. For others, it may not be until the dashboard is threatening to leave them stranded on the side of the road! Both types of drivers know that at some point, their car will need a fill-up. But the first may be at less risk than the second, or the second was simply willing to wait until the situation was desperate enough to require immediate attention. In counseling couples, we see a similar pattern. Some couples will seek professional help when they notice that they have not been connecting well lately, when they seem to feel more distant than usual, or when they have additional stressors, such as a new baby, a job, or are entering a new phase of life. However, and perhaps more often than not, couples will wait until the air is so thick with frustration, disillusionment, and even resentment that they are unable to course-correct and, only then, are willing to seek out a counselor for help.

While there are a host of reasons why couples seek counseling, research has shown a handful of issues that seem to be the most common. The following sections will review five of them as well as identify the key factors of each, the way in which they impact couples, and the impaired marital functioning that typically follows.

Communication Issues

Part of the joy of being in an intimate relationship is having someone that we feel we can talk to, share things with, and depend on for input, support, and understanding. Our desire for connection and belonging is often fulfilled when we can communicate on a deeper level that fosters closeness and allows for us to be vulnerable without risking being rejected or judged. Most of the time, communication does serve as an effective way to build and sustain good relationships. However, communication is often harder and more complex than people believe it to be. In any relationship, communication can be thwarted by the intentional or unintentional use of words or behaviors that raise concerns and confusion or cause pain. It was about the late 1960s when researchers began to look at the dynamics of communication and identified that while verbal communication skills were central in relationships, so were non-verbal skills (Stewart, 2012). In fact, the two could not be independently studied as factors in communication because of the connection between the two and the psy-

chological ability to perceive both when communicating with another person. Things like facial expressions, eye contact and gaze, proximity of space, touch, and body gestures all have a significant impact on how our words will be processed and understood. Compare the pictures below and consider the difference between the words, "Wow, I'm amazed by you!" with a smile on your partner's face versus "Wow, I'm amazed by you" with a look of disgust. The words are the same, but the difference in meaning is immediately clear.

Dr. John Gottman, a leading expert and researcher in the study of relationships, has demonstrated the power of unhealthy interpersonal communication through numerous empirical studies conducted with many couples across a variety of stages of marriage (Gottman, 1999). Much of his research focuses on the specific aspects of verbal and nonverbal communication that cause the most destruction in marriage. The Four Horsemen of the Apocalypse is a concept found in the New Testament to describe what end times will be like (Revelation 6:2-8). Gottman uses the metaphor to identify what he believes is most likely to cause devastation in relationships and an end to marriages. These horsemen include Criticism, Contempt, Defensiveness, and Stonewalling (Gottman, 1999; Lisitsa, 2013). Let us take a moment to review each of these as they relate to ineffective or harmful communication.

Criticism

In any relationship, there will be times when we are frustrated and, in our frustration, we will complain. But complaining is quite a bit different than criticism. For example, consider the difference between "I get frustrated when you say you will call and then don't. I am left to worry about what may have happened and the rest of my day is spent feeling anxious and alone" versus "You never think about anyone but yourself. What does it matter if other people are upset? As long as things are fine for you!" Criticizing almost always uses character assassination to communicate the hurt that we might be feeling about a certain situation. It removes the most important message, "I am worried, I am lonely, and I need this from you", and replaces it with an emotionally charged message that attaches the more permanent message of "you are a selfish, thoughtless person". We lose the focus on the unwanted behavior - a valid issue - to the personal deficits of the other individual, which is often not valid at all. Criticism can be damaging enough on its own, but the bigger problem with criticism is that it also paves the way for the more dangerous horseman to follow (Gottman, 1999; Lisitsa, 2013).

Contempt

> "Contempt is the sulfuric acid of love." ~John Gottman

Perhaps the cruelest horseman we see in unhealthy relationships is that of contempt (utterly worthless or despicable). Contempt, according to Gottman's research, is the "*single most corruptive behavior in a couple relationship*" (Dashnaw, 2017, para.1). One powerful definition of contempt was made by a 19th century philosopher in his book "The Art of Controversy" when he explained contempt as the unsullied conviction of the worthlessness of another (Schopenhauer, 2007). Interestingly, contempt is a method of communication that can be identified universally and is often the best predictor of divorce (Gottman & Gottman, 2015). It is characterized by disrespect, sarcasm, mockery, ridicule, eye-rolling and scoffing at a partner. While criticism can damage a relationship by ascribing negative character qualities to a person unfairly, contempt assumes their inherent lack of worth and takes on a position of moral superiority over them (Lisitsa, 2013). Consider the following example and its counterpart:

© VGstockstudio/Shutterstock.com

You are tired? Cry me a river. I've been with the kids all day, running around like mad to keep this house going, and all you do when you come home from work is flop down on that sofa like a child and play those idiotic video games. I don't have time to deal with another kid. Could you be any more pathetic? (Lisitsa, 2013, para.6)

I know work has been tiring for you lately, and that when you come home you just want to relax. But I have been exhausted all day taking care of the kids, fixing meals, cleaning up messes, going to doctor's appointments and potty-training our toddler, so when you come home and sit in front of the t.v., I get angry and feel even more alone than I did when you were at work and not available to help me out. I need a partner and I feel like I don't have one (Lisitsa, 2013, para.6).

We can hear the dramatic difference in tone and meaning of these two messages, even though they both address the same foundational issue: a wife feels there is a lack of partnership present and a lack of appreciation for her needs by her husband. We have all heard the phrase, "It is not what you said, it is how you said it": a great example of how powerful our choice of words and tone can be in communication!

Defensiveness

The third horseman is defensiveness. It is easy to see how this horseman follows that of criticism. The natural response to being criticized by someone is to defend ourselves with excuses or what we may like to see as a valid rationale for our behavior. Rarely, however, does defensiveness result in changing the perspective of the other person or bridging an emotional gap between people. Lisitsa (2013) provided these examples:

> *"Did you call Betty and Ralph to let them know that we are not coming tonight as you promised this morning?"*
> ***Defensive response:*** *"I was just too darn busy today. As a matter of fact, you know just how busy my schedule was. Why didn't you just do it?"*
> ***Relational response:*** *"Oops, I forgot. I should have asked you this morning to do it because I knew my day would be packed. That's my fault. Let me call them right now"* (Defensiveness section).

In this example, we can see the defensive posturing as well as a tendency to turn the blame around. This horseman lives by the old adage, "the best defense is a good offense" and pulls double-duty in both not accepting responsibility for causing a relational rift while at the same time pointing out the flaws in another that may be contributing to one.

Stonewalling

Lastly is the horseman of **stonewalling**. (This is when a spouse withdraws and shuts down, often because of feeling overwhelmed.) It could also be

© fizkes/Shutterstock.com

© fizkes/Shutterstock.com

COUNSELING WOMEN

referred to as "the silent killer", since the purpose of stonewalling is to shut down communication entirely and use behavioral cues to send the message that "you are not worthy of my words or empathy". This is commonly a response to contempt, signaling back that we have reached our limit. We no longer are allowing the other person to have access to our thoughts or emotions, and are unwilling to try to communicate or respond rationally to our partner (Lisitsa, 2013). Intimate relationships depend upon the concept of give-and-receive, but when couples see that their efforts are met with resistance or worse yet, disdain, we easily slip into a pattern of demand-withdraw, and stonewalling becomes an easy way to tune out our spouse's criticism, nagging, and disrespect (Haase et al., 2016). Perhaps one of the scariest parts about this horseman is that it quickly becomes habitual, as it serves to protect us from being willing to engage vulnerably and authentically, which are qualities that are fundamentally necessary for a healthy marriage.

The "Roommate" Situation

Love and marriage may go together like a horse and carriage, but what about intimacy and marriage? In many instances, these two things are not a guaranteed link, leaving love in marriages to fade into something more along the lines of friendship in marriage or a state of being "roommates". Consider the following narrative:

> "We just do not connect romantically anymore. We talk about the events of the day, the kids, our schedule for the week. We sleep in different bedrooms. We have our own social calendars and interests. We do not hate each other... we do not even fight! But we do not have an intimate relationship at all. It is like we are just roommates".

It is a story many marriage counselors have heard in their office, coming from women and men alike. The story does not lack distress, but it does not present with the same fury and passion that some marital issues do. Recent research suggested approximately 20% of couples have not had sex in the past year, and other couples report engaging in occasional sex, but because they lack critical elements of intimacy with their spouse, they function more as platonic partners than lovers (Kuster, 2016). We also find research that points to intimacy as both the quality of communication that is most likely to lead to happiness or fulfillment as well as the one that is most capable of causing destruction of a relationship (Pourmousa et al., 2018).

What is missing in these roommate type marriages? How do couples move from being in love to being friendly companions at best? While many factors may be at play, unintentional neglect and diminishing interest in a partner may be the starting point, while disillusionment and anger may be a more solidifying factor over time (Moschetta & Moschetta, 2010). Instead of the passionate vision they originally had of marriage, it becomes a dull routine. Couples get busy with jobs, raising kids and keeping up with the daily grind, and in the process, lose the art of intimacy: sharing deep feelings, dreams, concerns, and joys. Interestingly, intimacy also requires awareness of self, knowing what we are feeling, and being able to consider those feelings in regard to what we need to communicate or change (Naddaf & Heidari, 2017). Without this aspect of personal growth and development, couples are more likely to settle into a roommate relationship over time.

An Affair

Mignon McLaughlin once said, "A successful marriage requires falling in the love many times, always with the same person" (Gavazzi, 2015, p.152). If couples could find a way to heed this advice, we may not need to include this section. Unfortunately, affairs are one of the top reasons that couples do seek marriage counseling, and why many marriages fail. Studies are now suggesting that approximately 22% to 25% of married men and 12% to 15% of married women in the United States have engaged in some form of sexual infidelity during their lifetimes (Fife, 2016). But physical affairs are not the only type of affair that can erode a marriage. While men are more likely to engage in sexual relationships outside of marriage, women are more likely to engage in emotional affairs. Emotional infidelity, often given less attention than physical infidelity, can be just as damaging and can occur more often than physical affairs. In the past decade, we have also begun to see a new type of affair resulting from relationships that develop online.

Research on the damage pornography can do in a marriage indicates it is powerful and disturbing. Kirk and Price (2014) noted that not only do individuals perceive the involvement of their partner in pornography as infidelity, but that being involved in pornography places a colossal risk on the likelihood of an affair in marriage. According to a study conducted with over 20,000 married couples, "individuals who reported seeing an X-rated movie in the last year were 25% more likely to be divorced and 101% more likely to have had an extramarital affair. They were also 12% less likely to report having a very happy marriage (if they were still married) and 7% less likely to report being very happy with life in general" (Kirk & Price, 2014, pp. 495-496).

Fife (2016) explained that across each of these types of infidelity, couples would experience a breakdown of the vital aspects that have built and sustained their marriage from the start. Trust, loyalty, empathy and respect are lost in the pursuit of excitement, change, passion, even a sense of risk or danger in a new and forbidden romance. But neither the partner, the offender, nor the betrayed are without emotional fall-out. The offending partner will usually experience distress from trying to hide their activities from their spouse while the betrayed, prior to confirming an affair, is likely to feel doubt, growing mistrust, and a fear of finding out about an affair. Once an affair has been uncovered, the offending partner may experience guilt, shame, or remorse, while their spouse is often first shocked, confused and angry and later plagued with intense emotions of grief, betrayal and an intense need to know more information about the details of the affair. The processing period often results in symptoms of depression and anxiety, even post-traumatic stress disorder.

© Antonio Guillem/Shutterstock.com

When an affair has occurred, couples are faced with the decision to either repair the damage in the marriage or end the relationship. Whether or not the offending partner feels guilt and remorse about the affair will often be a pivotal point in this decision, with the willingness of the betrayed partner to reconcile and forgive his or her spouse as another critical factor. Counseling can be a welcomed first step when reconciliation is the goal. If the cheating partner does not want to end the affair or displays signs of lacking empathy, patience, or remorse for their actions, reconciliation is not likely to occur (Atkins et al., 2005).

Unsolvable Problems

Years ago, in order to file for divorce, couples had to provide a rationale for the request. Judges were more likely to weigh in on the morality of why a marriage had failed. Over time, states developed "no fault" divorce, leading the nation toward a having a more casual, laissez-faire attitude toward divorce. Modern divorce forms will often list "irreconcilable differences" as a legal reason for the dissolution of a marriage. The term seems almost juvenile – "I just can't get along with that person, and I don't feel like living with them anymore". And yet, this final section covers one of the most common reasons we see couples struggling within their marriages: unsolvable problems. LMFT Jeff Herring (2005) explained

> Unsolvable relationship problems are generally related to what are called your requirements. Whether you are aware of it or not, whether you know them or not, you do have non-negotiable requirements. These requirements have to be met in order for a relationship to work for you. If even one of these requirements is missing, the relationship will not work for you (para. 5).

Issues often labeled as "unsolvable problems" usually stem from perceptions, expectations, and demands of each partner.

This breakdown of what is "unsolvable" outlines what may be the most important aspect of this relational problem: personal expectations and demands. The downside to this is that rarely do our personal expectations change in reaction to what our spouse is capable of offering. Instead, the bar we set remains in place, and frustration, disillusionment, even bitterness will develop when our partner does not clear the bar. Cue the four horsemen. It is easy to see how this issue would quickly develop into a cycle encompassing other common destructive behaviors in marriage.

The Gottman Institute expanded on this concept of "unsolvable problems" noting that according to their research, 69% of relationship problems are perceptual problems, or the fundamental differences between two people (Fulwiler, 2012). This suggests that, in fact, most problems are *not* unsolvable, but rather are issues that one partner feels are non-negotiable, requiring compliance from their partner in order to commit to staying in the relationship. Adding to this research, it was found that unsolvable problems had less to do with what differences existed in a marriage and more to do with whether a couple was willing and capable of communicating these needs effectively. Fulwiler (2012) wrote, "If they cannot establish such a dialogue, the conflict becomes gridlocked, and gridlocked conflict eventually leads to emotional disengagement" (para. 2). Not surprisingly, many couples will possess more than one of the top problems listed in this chapter, which certainly add to the need for an effective intervention process.

MARRIAGE COUNSELING TECHNIQUES

An old, married couple was being interviewed on the news recently and were asked, "What's the secret to a successful marriage?" It is the million-dollar question that captures the attention of people everywhere. For marriage counselors, the million-dollar question is, "What is the most effective way to save a marriage that's falling apart?" If we figure it out,

© fizkes/Shutterstock.com

we have a billion-dollar answer! As practitioners, we want to know what works, what is tried and true, what shows the most promise and best outcomes. Often, we refer to this as *best practice,* and if the practice has been tested against other practices and evaluated for its effectiveness, it is then referred to as *evidence-based practice.* Every therapist wants to be able to help their clients. They not only want to be able to answer the million-dollar question but implement it successfully. So, what is the most efficient route to success? Turns out that generally speaking, no one therapeutic approach stands out as offering better results than any other. Mulhauser (2014) noted, "Despite clear evidence demonstrating the effectiveness of counseling and psychotherapy, pinning down specific reasons for effectiveness or identifying particularly effective approaches remains tricky" (para.1). Tricky as this task may be, we do know that some approaches yield very promising results. Below are a few of the models that offer counselors the tools to do their job well.

Collaborative Couples Therapy

The collaborative counseling approach has two basic premises: that language shapes reality, and that reality is socially constructed (Dvorak, 2013). The goal of this approach is meaning-making (in counseling, meaning-making is the process of how people interpret and make sense of their life events and relationships. It is their ability to find purpose or value in their experiences, positive or negative) within communication based on an individual's reality and experiences (Prasad, 2016). Narrowing this approach to the framework of working with couples, Wile (2011) found that once reality is perceived to be conflictual, couples either turned to fighting or they would withdraw. Intimacy suffered as a result of not being able to work through either approach to dealing with conflict. Seeing how this pattern prevented communication and relational connection, he developed a treatment approach that would address it: Collaborative Couples Therapy (CCT). When Wile developed this model, he did so with the belief that conflict is only seen as a negative thing in relationships because we train ourselves to fear its outcome. Our past experiences have wired us to anticipate disaster, which leads to avoidance. Wile (2011) also believed that conflict actually provides an opportunity for couples to develop intimacy. His research pointed to the fact that when partners are unable to express their true thoughts and feelings, they leaned either toward aggression or withdrawal in the relationship. However, if they were given the opportunity to share these things within a safe climate where they would be heard and valued, there would be an increased sense of connection and bonding.

Wile (2011) expanded the importance of this relational response even to the role of the therapist with a client. In an interview, he stated, "A big problem in couple therapy is that we react to clients in the same way partners do with each other when they fight. When clients act in an arrogant, bullying, or other off-putting way, we get angry at them—though, of course, in a much milder way than the partners do with each other. Being angry, we think of these clients in pejorative terms, make pejorative interventions, and lose the ability to look at things from their point of view" (Wetheford, 2009, para. 4). If we, as counselors, can make this error, how much easier is it for an emotionally invested couple? In order to lay the right foundation for marriage counseling, Wile (2011) suggested that the following three hallmark qualities of collaborative couples therapy must be present: Empathy, the Leading-Edge, and finally, the Relationship Atmosphere.

Empathy

The role of empathy is so crucial that Wile (2011) suggested that counseling cannot occur without it being present. The inability to feel empathy for one's partner results in undermining their perspective and their value as a worthy human being. One's feelings, thoughts, and experiences are often what fuels the way in which they respond, so invalidating responses do not just tell a partner "I disagree with you", but "you are not acceptable". Wethford (2009) suggested that one of the precursors to effective couples counseling was being able to consider what it would be like to be the other person. He suggested it was important to find *hidden reasonableness* in their seemingly unreasonable behavior. Of equal importance is the client's ability to work to avoid reacting to their partner and instead, responding to what it is they might be needing to know, what they need their partner to understand, or something they need to process with the other person's help.

> Teaching and modeling empathy are essential and lays the groundwork for creating a safe space for expression of emotion.

Empathy also takes the form of a sedative in conflict. When we can respond in an empathic way, not only does that take us out of our own state of defensiveness, but it takes our partner out of their adversarial state. Communication can now ensue, as each person is able to hear what the other has to say without the fear of being shot down, shamed, or discredited.

The Leading Edge

Identifying *leading-edge* emotions is another hallmark quality of this model. The therapeutic task of this aspect of the model is to solve the *moment* rather than the entire *problem* (Wile, 2011). Solving the moment is perhaps the most empowering way to solve the couple's problem, since it encourages practical solutions and creates exactly what couples need to be able to solve any future problem: a collaborative spirit. In fact, Wile (2011) concluded that in many cases, the absence of this spirit is responsible for the problem in the first place. However, identifying leading-edge emotions may be more difficult for clients than we might expect. In Wile's (2009) interview, he suggested that if we see a client struggling to identify, for example, something other than anger (a common default emotion), we might offer multiple-choice options for other feelings we believe may be the leading edge emotion in that moment.

Sometimes, the counselor can serve as a mouthpiece for the other partner, who may have less power or permission to make such suggestions. Wile (2009) went on to provide the following example:

> At times withdrawing or being angry is a leading-edge feeling. So, I would help people capture that. I might help them express their anger in a way that is more satisfying to them and easier for their partners to hear. Moving over and speaking for them, I might say, 'I'm still fuming about what you said ten minutes ago. I'm not even listening to anything you are saying. It wiped me out.' I'm hoping that the person I'm speaking for will express a sigh of relief and, when I ask whether I got her feelings right, will improve what I said to make it more accurate (para. 15).

Along with the importance of using words to identify leading-edge emotions is the value of non-verbal communication. Facial expressions and body language are vital to what is happening internally so they are crucial to observe and address, as they will often flush out what people will hesitate to verbalize.

The Relationship Atmosphere

The last element of this model includes the need to establish the relationship atmosphere. Wile (2013) referred to this as the aspect of *sensibility*.

Initially, we may hear these terms and believe that it is the atmosphere created by or for the clients, but the bigger focus in CCT is to develop a sensible approach on the part of the counselor to create an atmosphere that is free from judgment or taking sides when working with a couple. More often than not, a marriage counselor will find themselves *taking sides*, even if they do not want or mean to. It can be difficult to remain empathetic and neutral when we witness one partner blaming, nagging, or yelling at the other.

Our internal reactions are also based on our own experiences, beliefs or values and can create countertransference issues. The inherent problem with this is that personal judgment slips in and reduces one's ability to create a space where each person is being fully heard and knows their meaning-making is equal to that of their partner's. As challenging as this component may be, it is crucial for the counselor to help their client make their case, especially if it is evident that they are not especially skilled at doing so themselves. Helping clients to identify their thoughts and feelings and communicate that in a way that elicits an empathic response from a partner creates an atmosphere of safety, respect, and productivity and is a crucial aspect of the counselor's role in facilitating a collaborative approach to therapy.

Emotionally-Focused Couples Therapy

One of the most validated forms of relational therapy is emotionally-focused couples therapy, or EFCT, reporting rates of a 70-73% recovery rate (Dalglish et al., 2015). This approach looks at relationships through the lens of insecure attachment styles and separation distress (Johnson, 2015) and uses attachment theory to understand the underlying needs and emotions of each partner (Daglish et al., 2015). Over the past 40 years, EFCT has gained a great deal of exposure and experiential analysis (experiential analysis is the process of gathering real-world data and results through the direct experiences and reports of individuals rather than by depending solely on theoretical concepts) that has been tied to additional research about why couples struggle. As research evolved, it was determined that couples respond to one another based on primary and secondary emotions. For example, a woman who was emotionally or physically abandoned by her father in

> Primary emotions may be more difficult to identify or display than the self-protective nature of secondary emotions.

her youth may have primary emotions of fear and pain, but her secondary emotion may be anger and resentment.

Attachment Theory

> Formation of attachments early on impacts quality of relational connections later in life.

Attachment theory is essential to understand when working with couples, as identifying unresolved issues in a client's childhood directly impacts their ability to relate and connect in an intimate way with their present partner. It theorizes that all human beings seek to establish strong bonds with significant people in their lives as a young child, and that those bonds then go on to influence the way the child feels about himself and others with whom they develop relationships. When the messages we gather from a young age are, "you are not safe", "you are not worthy", or "you are stupid", schemas (schema refers to a pattern of thought or a belief system that categorizes information we gather over time) are developed that will continue to be accessed when future situations mirrors one from our youth. All the emotions and reactions that a child had when they first experienced these messages will be called up by automatic neurological processes, and the person will respond as if they are in the same situation, even if many years have passed. What appears to be a current issue is instantly no longer only about the current situation, but perhaps hundreds of others that have trained a person to respond in a manner of fight or flight. It is easy to see, then, how quickly that person's spouse may scratch their head and say, "Wait a minute, what just happened here?", or something worse yet. Two key factors in EFCT are 1) the ability to pick up on one's partner's attachment cues, and 2) the presence of relationship trust. Let us take a moment to look at each of these in the context of conducting EFCT.

Relationship distress occurs when partners are either not able to identify attachment cues or they are unwilling to respond to them. Failing to address these cues results in an uptick in harmful emotions and a further deterioration of the security of attachment bonds. Not surprisingly, individuals with attachment issues tend to have a higher level of anxiety when it comes to relationships. They have exaggerated needs for emotional support and tend to either downplay those needs by repressing negative feelings and by avoiding disclosing their more intimate thoughts and emotions (Moser et al., 2018). Their history has become proof that this behavior is simply too risky and results in pain. When we compare this with people who have attachment security, we see that they are lacking the anxiety that comes with intimate relationships, conversations and conflict management and report higher levels of trust, intimacy and satisfaction (Moser et al., 2018).

Attachment theorists posit that counselors can do a great deal of therapeutic work just in responding to a client with an attachment disorder in a way that is unlike most people have ever offered in the past. They serve as an example for the client's partner on how to do the same. One notable component in reducing attachment anxiety was that of *blamer-softening*, or the process of substituting a default mode of finding fault for the more difficult practice of vulnerability and engagement (Moser et al., 2018). In blamer-softening, both partners are emotionally available and engaged, resulting in reduced attachment avoidance. Their primary fears, which are the root source of their need for acceptance and care, can be safely communicated and their partner begins to see the whole picture. Gaining that kind of understanding generates empathy, another core need of their partner. This allows them to then respond in an empathetic and proactive way, resulting in reduced attachment anxiety. Over time, with these behaviors in place, the client begins to function and behave in a way that is more similarly aligned with those who have not experienced attachment issues.

Relationship Trust

Relationship trust is also a central principle of EFCT. Psychoeducation, modeling and facilitation of trust-building exercises are all a part of the counselor's objectives at the start of treatment. Once partners have been shown how to pick up on attachment cues, they must also establish a relationship where trust is the norm. As adults, those we have the closest relationships with become our attachment figures. In a marriage, that is often our spouse. When an attachment figure is emotionally available and quick to respond with authenticity and compassion during times of need, trust is developed (Moser et al., 2018). Trust provides partners with the ability to ask for their attachment needs to be met, and for them to be able to ex-

press their thoughts or feelings without fear of rejection. EFCT is simply not possible in the absence of couples trusting each other and having some faith that their partner still cares for them when they are beginning to open up and share their more primary emotions and attachment longings. The counselor's facilitating role in this aspect of treatment is three-fold: De-escalation, Re-Engagement and Blame-Softening. The first step is to de-escalate, or help the couple to redirect their criticism and focus on their partner's underlying and unmet attachment needs and to recognize the cycle that exists in their relationship. The second is to re-engage with new patterns of relating to one another in non-threatening ways. More specifically, a partner that tends to withdrawal learns to engage instead, identifying and expressing basic attachment needs for love, acceptance, and commitment from their partner. Lastly, the partner who tends to engage in fault-finding employs blame-softening, or the willingness to step away from pointing the finger, and instead takes the risk of sharing their own desire for security or significance in the relationship (Moser et al., 2018). Ultimately, the counselor engaging in EFCT must continue to educate and remind couples that all human beings are dependent on others for emotional connection, safety, security, and well-being and that the greatest gift they can bring to a marriage is the ability to offer those qualities to one another (Hardy & Fisher, 2018).

The Gottman Method

Imagine creating a theoretical approach to solving relationship problems based on watching a reality television show. Could you do it? For the past 40 years, John Gottman has been doing something of the sort. His work has focused on researching couples first-hand, observing their communication and problem-solving patterns in real-time. Dubbed "The Love Lab" (Gottman, 2019; Gottman & Gottman, 2008), Gottman created a workshop where he reviewed countless hours of video witnessing how couples interacted naturally and in their own element (rather than a counseling office). This long-time empirical research led him to develop his own theory on conflict in relationships and the most common culprits of dissatisfaction within them. He became so skilled at it, he made the bold claim that he could predict with 90% accuracy which couples will divorce and which will stay married (Gottman, 2015). As we reviewed earlier in the chapter, Gottman developed the concept of the Four Horsemen in communication and conflict resolution. He also developed what is known as the *Sound Re-*

lationship House, which incorporated the elements that predict relationship success. Take a moment to review the adjacent diagram before we discuss the therapeutic goals of the Gottman Method below.

The Pillars of Trust and Commitment

In order to establish a romantic relationship, partners must believe that trust and commitment are present and valued. These two elements represent the *pillars* of the relationship that hold it together. Nothing can be added if these two qualities fail to exist. The sound house diagram then points to the fact that there is a hierarchy of needs in a relationship.

The First Three Levels

The first three levels include elements that create a strong base: friendship, fondness and admiration, and the holding of a positive emotional bank account. Partners who seek to maintain a friendship might ask each other, "What things are making you worry or feel stressed out right now?" or "Tell me about your hopes and dreams for the next five years". Questions bring about a desire to share and sharing brings about friendship and intimacy. They look for qualities they admire and respect in the other and find opportunities to bring those things up in communication rather than only thinking it. Working to maintain fondness and admiration, they may state, "I am just so proud of what terrific work you are doing for your new company" or "Your commitment to the well-being of our children is incredible. It is a hard job and you do it well". They also look for ways to turn toward, rather than away from their partner's bid for an emotional connection. For example, "Wow honey, look at that boat" can be met with no response at all (most damaging), with "Huh!" (minimal connection), or with "Now THAT's a boat! We should get one of those and sail around the globe, what do you say?" Emotional connection quickly forms the bond that places a deposit in one's emotional bank account (Gottman & Gottman, 2013). These three levels are crucial to being able to support the additional levels of the house.

The Fourth Level

The fourth level includes positive sentiment override (PSO), which refers to couples who are able to see negative emotions expressed by their partner as neutral rather than aggressive or meant for harm. When couples see their partner as their friend, they tend to assume the best about them, resulting in offering more grace and less blaming behaviors. For example, seeing clothes left in the dryer could be perceived as one's partner being lazy and unsupportive, or, using PSO, he or she may choose to believe that their partner was late to work and forgot to take them out before they left.

The Fifth Level

The fifth level is the ability to manage (not solve) conflict. Managing conflict means being gentle toward one another, softening one's tone, knowing when a reparative word is needed (soothing the other) and knowing how to self-soothe when things escalate (Gottman & Gottman, 2013). It is the ability to say gently, "Okay, hey, take a breath. I can tell you are overwhelmed and angry about this. Let me help with dinner and we can talk while we work. Even if we can't solve it, we can come up with a plan together to manage it".

The Two Top Levels

The final top two levels of the house focus on dreams and shared meaning. Couples functioning at these levels create an atmosphere where intimacy about who they are, who they want to be, and what dreams or goals they have are all not only safe to share, but are shared because the other person asks about them regularly and regards their answer as valuable. Couples may ask one another "How are you feeling about this new opportunity?" or "Tell me about what you most wish for when it comes to our kids". These two levels point to the importance not only of shared meaning in communication, but also in traditions, rituals and other activities that help form the couple's identity, making it unique and valuable to them (Gottman & Gottman, 2013; Henderson et al., 2013).

Evaluating the Relational House

Counselors working from the Gottman Method will start by evaluating how sound their client's *relational house* is at the time they start therapy. Because conflict in relationships is unavoidable, this method focuses on conflict

> Conflict is unavoidable but reparative interventions can prevent escalation.

management rather than conflict resolution. The message counselors share is that couples can and do make choices when they engage with one another that will escalate or de-escalate negative emotions (Gottman, 1999; Gottman & Gottman, 2008) and that making an effort to engage in a way that is reparative goes a long way in mending and maintaining the intimacy of the relationship. Henderson et al. (2013) notes that repair attempts include anything a partner does with the intent to de-escalate the conflict and reduce the painful emotions that exist. A repair might include a silly gesture or facial expression. Whatever the repair action might be, "It seems what may matter most is the ability to repair things when they go wrong" (Gottman, 1999, p. 7). Couples need to be able to learn how to be intentional when involved in tough conversations rather than reacting from a gut-level emotion, which is often rooted in self-protection or preservation.

Gottman's (1999) approach is packed with valuable insights and tools for counselors working with couples. It is an approach that is still being developed and expanded upon, with trainings unique to those who desire to use it in therapy, but counselors using this approach will serve more as observers and teachers rather than psychoanalysts. The focus is on observation and re-routing of behaviors that gridlock the relational process. Clinicians might ask, "How is that accomplished?" The answer is, by following a three-step process: Assessment (couples share their relationship history, philosophy and goals), Therapeutic Framework (determining frequency of meetings, length of sessions and duration of treatment), and Therapeutic Interventions (couples learn specific techniques that build the crucial levels of a sound relationship house). Counselors empower and encourage couples to: Reaffirm commitment to the relationship, deepen trust, build love maps, share fondness and admiration, turn towards instead of away, develop a positive view of their partner, manage conflict effectively, ask about life dreams and goals, and create a shared meaning as a couple (Gottman, 2017). Preventative and healing in nature, these actions represent the essence of the Sound Relationship House theory and directly impact the degree to which positive change is likely to occur in a couple's relationship.

BIBLICAL INSIGHTS ON MARRIAGE

One of God's first designs recorded in the Bible is the creation of marriage. He saw that it was not good for man to be alone, so a helper was created for Adam, and in turn, Adam would serve as a provider and protector for Eve. Not only are the benefits of marriage made clear in secular research, but the Bible also speaks to how valuable this relationship can be and presents us with the mystery that unlike any other relationship, two people become one in the eyes of God when they choose to marry (Ephesians 5:31-32). Their thoughts, decisions, and ability to care for one another the way they would care for themselves is a central part of how God intended the marriage bond to work. The Bible portrays marriage as sacred, and the one relationship besides our relationship with God that, aside from rare exceptions, we are instructed to commit to permanently. Intimacy in marriage is also unique and provides safety and connection to both partners. This alone can explain why infidelity and marital distress can be more painful than struggles we experience in other relationships. Ask any Christian couple who has been married for a decade or longer and they are likely to tell you that marriage has offered them both the greatest blessings in life as well as some of the hardest lessons that can be experienced in human relationships. It is a relationship that requires tremendous self-awareness, humility, patience, tenderness, self-sacrifice, and perhaps most importantly, unconditional love (I Corinthians 13:8). Each mate needs to be prepared to care for the unique needs of their spouse. Without the Biblical structure for a healthy marriage, couples can quickly begin to doubt their ability to make their marriage work. Incorporating scriptural principles for both personal and marital growth offers a tremendous amount of structure, meaningful order, and a hope-focused approach to unlocking the blessings that God intended in His creation of the marriage relationship.

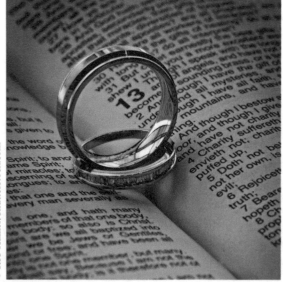

CASE STUDY

Jane and John have come in for counseling. Their first comment was, "Something has to change if we are going to stay married". In the initial interview, it was found that John works full time, is going to school for a master's degree, and is committed to the elder board at his church, while Jane works part time but is the primary caretaker of their three young children when she is not working. For the past two years, they have struggled with their multiple roles, workload distribution, parenting disagreements, lack of intimacy in their emotional and sexual relationship, and have begun to argue so often in the evenings that John has moved into their son's bedroom to sleep. They state that they want to stay together, but their situation is starting to feel unbearable. Jane has some concerns that John is spending a good deal of time traveling for work with a younger woman employed at his company who is single and even according to John, flirtatious. John has admitted that her attention is flattering, but states that he has not been unfaithful to his wife.

© wavebreakmedia/Shutterstock.com

The first few sessions focused on gathering current presenting problems and family of origin information. As the couple described their families, it was found that John grew up in a strict, but secular home where your value was based on what you achieved. His parents divorced when he was 14 and expected John to pick up the extra work around each of their homes, including helping raise his younger siblings. Jane grew up in a Christian home where faith and family was a priority. Jane's parents had a strong marriage, but her mom stayed at home and her dad worked jobs that paid less but offered the flexibility of being home in the evenings to help his

children with homework and have dinner with the family. Throughout these opening sessions, the counselor observed how the couple discussed their struggles, noticing that Jane often used sarcasm in the way she described John's efforts to work hard or improve their family's situation by continuing his education, and John had the tendency to disengage and when this occurred, even stopping mid-sentence and refusing to continue if Jane interrupted. The counselor used this as an opportunity to review the 4 horsemen of the apocalypse and the impact of words and non-verbal communication in the way they handled conflict and differences in perspective.

After identifying the couple's primary problems, beliefs and values, therapy goals, and measurable objectives for meeting those goals, the counselor spent the next few sessions reviewing what she noticed was occurring in their communication patterns when they discussed difficult or emotionally-charged topics. Both parties were asked to complete a family history assignment that pointed out the attachment styles and love languages learned as they were growing up. Initially, the response to their results was cynical laughter followed by comments like, "Yep, that would be why you are who you are!", but was eventually met with appreciation for the reason their partner might see things or respond to things the way he or she did. Both John and Jane were starting to see that these motivations, behaviors and belief systems were rooted in who they had always been told they must be to earn love or respect. In addition, they discussed Biblical approaches to strengthening marriage, addressing conflict in marriage, and a Christian's call to forgiveness and reconciliation in relationships.

The sessions that followed allowed the couple to identify areas of mistrust that existed and foundational areas of their relationship that had been cracked for some time. Jane learned that John's attempt to work harder meant longer work hours which she translated to his lack of love and desire to be with her and the kids. She did not trust that he was not choosing work over their marriage, and perhaps was even interested in another woman. In John's mind, if you love someone, you work hard to make sure that they have all that they need and set yourself up for professional success so that they will never have to worry about a lack of provision. John learned that Jane's attempts to talk him into coming home, asking him to put additional education on hold and taking time off of being a deacon at the church was due to her view of a healthy family including the husband and father being at the dinner table every night, having meaningful connection time with her, and being available to tuck his children into bed at night. In Jane's mind, loving one's family meant being willing to live on less money, willing to have less luxuries, and not worrying about the future, in favor of spending quality time together as a family.

Throughout the remainder of the sessions, John and Jane's counselor spent time reviewing with them how to build the levels of a "sound relational house", how to de-escalate, re-engage and soften blame when they attempt to communicate how they are feeling, and how to work toward a common goal (staying married, prioritizing family) without either partner feeling they are sacrificing the meaning they attach to giving and receiving love. She also helped them to identify areas where they felt spiritually depleted and selected Scriptures that they could pray over together and for one another as they worked to improve their relationship; Ephesians 4:2, "Be always humble, gentle, and patient. Show your love by being tolerant with one another", (*Good New Bible*, 1966/1976); Romans 12:10, "Be devoted to one another in love. Honor one another above yourselves" (*New International Bible*, 1973/2011); Ephesians 4:32 "Be gentle with one another, sensitive. Forgive one another as quickly and thoroughly as God in Christ forgave you", (*The Message Bible*, 1993/2002). John and Jane's counselor chose to implement these therapeutic interventions as a supportive guide, teacher, and accountability partner. Her role was to observe the areas of disconnection that stemmed from the couple's individual way of thinking, perceiving, feeling and communicating, and identify the underlying reasons why those differences existed. She provided psychoeducation regarding how nature and nurture builds us into unique individuals with powerful needs and expectations, pointed out the importance of key relational skills and common pitfalls in marriage, and supported the development of a new, healthy, and effective approach to conflict management and expression of love within the relationship.

© ImageFlow/Shutterstock.com

Marital therapy can stir up strong feelings for any counselor. How might you handle counseling sessions where you feel more aligned with one partner than the other? If you were to recognize feelings of frustration or anger toward a client, what proactive approaches might you use in order to maintain a healthy rapport, empathic response, and an objective clinical approach to your sessions? Unconditional positive regard is essential!

CHAPTER SUMMARY

The role of the counselor in marital counseling is multifaceted. Unlike counseling an individual, counseling couples requires the clinician to be mindful of two sets of emotions, needs, and personalities as well as being able to observe and address complex patterns of interaction. Counselors must be familiar with current resources and approaches used for relational counseling and be comfortable implementing various techniques that would best serve the couple with whom they are working. While not all couples are exactly alike, many trends do exist. We see that communication is a critical aspect to consider in every marriage, that empathy is a necessary character trait for couples to develop and employ, and that both words and behaviors must demonstrate that each party is committed to the marriage relationship in order for trust to exist. Counselors must acknowledge the degree to which they may relate more to one mate than another and work to avoid issues of transference or unfair treatment of one partner in marriage counseling sessions. They must also serve as a supportive guide, allowing the couple to do most of the therapeutic work. Finally, counselors must keep in mind that even more important than the theoretical approach or specific interventions used is the development of rapport and the ability to express confidence, hope, and an authentic desire to assist couples in improving the state of their marriage.

KEY TERMS

Blame-Softening - the willingness to step away from pointing the finger, and instead take the risk of sharing their own desire for security or significance in the relationship

Contempt - feeling utterly worthless or despicable

De-escalate - redirect criticism and focus on their partner's underlying and unmet attachment needs and to recognize the cycle that exists in their relationship

Experiential Analysis - experiential analysis is the process of gathering real-world data and results through the direct experiences and reports of individuals rather than by depending solely on theoretical concepts

Meaning-Making – the process of how people interpret and make sense of their life events and relationships. It is their ability to find purpose or value in their experiences, positive or negative

Schema - refers to a pattern of thought or a belief system that categorizes information we gather over time

Stonewall - this happens when a spouse withdraws and shuts down, often because of feeling overwhelmed

SUGGESTED RESOURCES

Books
Love & Respect by Emerson Eggrichs
Marriage Mentor Training Manual for Wives by Les and Leslie Parrott
Marriage Mentor Training Manual for Husbands by Les and Leslie Parrott
The Seven Principles for Making Marriage Work by John Gottman
A Couples Guide to Communication by John Gottman

Marriage Counseling
Hope Restored: A Marriage Intensive Experience - (866) 875-2915

Focus on the Family Resources
Focus on the Family Marriage Articles (topical): https://www.focusonthe-family.com/topic/marriage/
Focus on the Family Marriage Shows (video/audio): https://www.focuson-thefamily.com/shows/
Focus on the Family Marriage Assessment: https://assessments.focuson-thefamily.com/s3/focus-on-marriage-assessment?utm_source=www.focusonthefamily.com&utm_medium=referral&utm_campaign=ar-ticle_cta_foma&refcd=662001

REFERENCES

Atkins, D. C., Eldridge, K. A., Baucom, D. H., & Christensen, A. (2005). Extramarital affair and behavioral couple counseling: Optimism in the face of betrayal. *Journal of Consulting and Clinical Psychology, 73*, 144–150.

Dalgleish, T. L., Johnson, S. M., Moser, M. B., Lafountaine, M., & Weibe, S. A. (2015). Predicting change in marital satisfaction throughout emotionally focused couple therapy. *Journal of Marital and Family Therapy, 41*(3), 276-291.

Dashnaw, D. (2017). *The problem of contempt in relationships.* https://couplestherapyinc.com.

Doan, L., & Quadlin, N. (2018). Partner characteristics and perceptions of responsibility for housework and child care. *Journal of Marriage and Family, 81*(1), 145-163.

Dvorak, K. B. (2013). Collaborative therapy: Relationships and conversations that make a difference. *Journal of Community and Applied Social Psychology, 23*(5), 451-452.

Fife, S. T. (2016). Extramarital affairs and infidelity. In J. Carlson & S. Dermer (Eds.), *The SAGE encyclopedia of marriage, family, and couples counseling* (pp. 584-588). SAGE Publications.

Fulwiler, M. (2012, July 2). *Managing conflict: Solvable vs. perceptual problems.* The Gottman Relationship Blog. https://www.gottman.com/blog/managing-conflict-solvable-vs-perpetual-problems/

Gavazzi, S. M. (2015). For better and for worse: Understanding optimal campus-community relationships through the lens of marriage. *Metropolitan Universities, 26*(1), 147-154.

Good News Bible. (1976). Good News Bible Online. https://www.biblegateway.com/versions/Good-News-Translation-GNT-Bible/

Gottman, J. M. (1999). *The marriage clinic: A scientifically based marital therapy.* Norton & Company.

Gottman, J., & Gottman, J. (2008). Gottman method couple therapy. In A. S. Gurman (Ed.), *Clinical handbook of couple therapy* (4th ed., pp. 138-164). Guilford Press.

Gottman, J. M., & Gottman, J. S. (2013). Difficulties with clients in Gottman method couples therapy. In A. W. Wolf, M. R. Goldfried, & J. C. Muran (Eds.), *Transforming negative reactions to clients: From frustration to compassion* (pp. 91–112). American Psychological Association. https://doi.org/10.1037/13940-004

Gottman, J. M., & Gottman, J. S. (2015). Gottman method couple therapy. In A. S. Gurman, J. L. Lebow, & D. K. Snyder (Eds.), *Clinical handbook of couple therapy* (5th pp. 129-157). Guilford Press.

Gottman, J. M., & Gottman, J. S. (2017). The natural principles of love. *Journal of Family Theory and Review, 9*(1), 7-26.

Gottman, J. (2019). *Love lab.* https://www.gottman.com/love-lab/

Haase, C. M., Holley, S. R., Bloch, L., Verstaen, A., & Levenson, R. W. (2016). Interpersonal emotional behaviors and physical health: A 20-year longitudinal study of long-term married couples. *Emotion, 16*(7), 965-977.

Hardy, N. R., & Fisher, A. R. (2018). Attachment vs. differentiation: The contemporary couple therapy debate. *Family Process, 57*(2), 557-571.

Henderson, A., Robey, P. A., Dunham, S. M., & Dermer, S. B. (2013). Change, choice and home: An integration of the work of Glasser and Gottman. *Journal of Choice Theory and Reality Therapy, 32*(2), 36-47.

Herring, J. (2005, May 23). *Relationship problems: Solvable or unsolvable?* Knight Rider Tribune News Service.

Johnson, S. M. (2015). *Emotionally focused couple therapy. Clinical handbook of couple therapy.* https://www.psychotherapy.net/

Kennedy, S., & Ruggles, S. (2014). Breaking up is hard to count: The rise of divorce in the United States, 1890-2010. *Demography, 51*(2), 587-98.

Kirk, D., & Price, J. (2014). Pornography and marriage. *Journal of Family and Economic Issues, 35*(4), 489-498.

Kuster, E. (2016). The cure for sexless marriages. *Prevention, 68*(7), 070.

Larsen, D. J., & Stege, R. (2012). Client accounts of hope in early counseling sessions: A qualitative study. *Journal of Counseling and Development, 90*(1), 45-54.

Lewis, J. M., & Kreider, R. M. (2015). *Remarriage in the United States.* https://www.healthymarriageinfo.org/wp-content/uploads/2017/12/acs-30.pdf

Lisitsa, E. (2013). *The four horseman: Criticism, contempt, defensiveness, and stonewalling.* The Gottman Institute. https://www.gottman.com.

Meier, S. T., & Davis, S. R. (2019). *The elements of counseling* (8th ed.). Waveland Press, Inc.

The Message Bible (2002). The Message Online. https://messagebible.com/read-the-message/

Mokhtari, M., Pollock, E., & Ashtari, M. (2019). Implications of unstable trends in marriage, birth, and divorce. *Journal of Divorce and Remarriage, 61*(1), 1-19.

Moral Stories. (2019). A blind man's love. https://www.moralstories.org/blind-mans-love/

Moschetta, P., & Moschetta, E. (2010). *Are you roommates or soulmates?* On Hot Two Press.

Moser, M. B., Johnson, S. M., Dalgleish, T. L., Weibe, S. A., & Tasca, G. A. (2018). The impact of blamer-softening on romantic attachment in emotionally focused couples therapy. *Journal of Marriage and Family Therapy, 44*(4), 640-654.

Mulhauser, G. (2014). *Evaluating therapeutic effectiveness in counselling and psychotherapy.* https://counsellingresource.com/therapy/types/effectivness.

Naddaf, S., & Heidari, A. (2017). The relationship between marital intimacy and quality of life. *Indian Journal of Public Health Research and Development, 8*(4), 63-67.

New International Bible. (2011). New International Bible Online. https://www.thenivbible.com/ (Original work published 1973)

O'Leary, K. D., Heyman, R., & Jongsma, A. E. (1998). *The couples therapy treatment planner.* Wiley.

Pourmousa, H., Mohammadifar, M. A., Pesand, S. T., & Rezaei, A. M. (2018). The effectiveness of intimacy training with cognitive-behavioral approach on couples' life quality and happiness. *Electronic Journal of General Medicine, 15*(6), 1-9.

Prasad, V. (2016). Collaborative language systems. In J. Carlson, & S. B. Dermer (Eds.), *The SAGE encyclopedia of marriage, family, and couples counseling.* SAGE Publications, Inc. http://dx.doi.org/10.4135/9781483369532.n90

Rogers, C. (1951). *Client-centered therapy: Its current practice, implications and theory.* Constable.

Schopenhauer, A. (2007). The art of controversy. (T. B. Saunders, Trans.). Cosimo Classics, Inc. (Original work published 1896)

Stewart, J. (2012). *Bridges not walls* (11th ed.). McGraw Hill.

Wetheford, R. (2009). *Dan Wile on collaborative couples therapy.* https://www.psychotherapy.net/interview/couples/dan-wile

Wile, D. B. (2011). Collaborative couple therapy. In D. K. Carson & M. Casado-Kehoe (Eds.), *Case studies in couples therapy: Theory-based approaches* (pp. 303-316). Routledge.

Wile, D. B. (2013). *The three defining elements of collaborative couple therapy.* http://danwile.com/2013/01/the-three-defining-elements-of-collaborative-couple-therapy.

Woods, S. B., Priest, J. B., Signs, T. L., & Maier, C. A. (2018). In sickness and in health: The longitudinal associations between marital dissatisfaction, depression and spousal health. *Journal of Family Therapy, 41*(1), 102-125.

CHAPTER 8
Coping with Divorce

Jennifer J. Beres, Ph.D.

"It is better to light a candle than curse the darkness."
~Eleanor Roosevelt

"The LORD is close to the brokenhearted and saves those who are crushed in spirit."
(Psalm 34:18, NIV)

Wisdom from Above:
Standing in His Grace

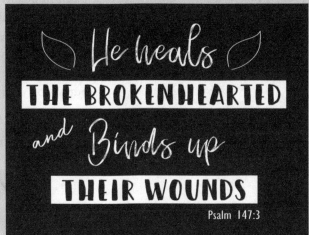

He heals THE BROKENHEARTED and Binds up THEIR WOUNDS
Psalm 147:3

© PaintZz/Shutterstock.com

One day, a donkey fell into a pit. The animal cried and whined for hours while his owner tried to figure out what to do. Finally, the farmer decided that since the animal was old, and the pit needed to be covered up anyway, he would just bury the old donkey right there. He got a shovel and started filling in the pit. The donkey kept up its wailing, but then fell silent. After an hour of furious shoveling, the farmer paused to rest. To his amazement, he saw his old donkey jump out of the pit and trot away! At first, when the donkey realized what was happening, he cried even more piteously. But then the wise animal hit on a plan. As each spade-full of dirt hit his back, the donkey would shake it off and take a step up on the growing mound of earth. Eventually, the mound grew high enough for him to jump out of the pit" (Lieder, n.d. Para. 6-7).

CHAPTER LEARNING OBJECTIVES

Upon completing this chapter, you should be able to:

- Evaluate causes of relational failure and divorce
- Appraise symptoms, diagnosis, and statistics of divorce
- Apply evidence-based interventions and recovery from divorce
- Articulate a Biblical understanding of divorce

Life can be cruel, can seem impossible to manage, and may even lead us to believe that we are not able to survive our current circumstances. Nevertheless, hope is a powerful thing. The trick to getting out of the pit is to shake off the dirt and take a step up. God will help us, and the Scriptures remind us that He has a long arm and can reach us even in a deep pit. Consider the Scripture which says, "Surely the arm of the LORD is not too short to save, nor his ear too dull to hear" (*New International Bible*, 1973/2011, Isaiah 59:1). We can make it out of our deepest, darkest pits when we refuse to succumb to the belief that we have been defeated. The Psalmist shared his experience saying, "He lifted me out of the slimy pit, out of the mud and mire; he set my feet on a rock and gave me a firm place to stand" (*New International Bible*, 1973/2011, Psalm 40:2).

CHAPTER OVERVIEW

All of us will have suffered through the pain of loss at some point in our lives: The loss of someone we loved, the loss of a job we treasured, the loss of our health or our finances, or the loss of a dream. There is a unique aspect to the pain that comes from having to let go of an expectation about what our life would look like, and it can be heart wrenching to watch our vision of the future dying before our very eyes with no

© Orla/Shutterstock.com

ability to save it. The loss of a dream is often the experience that women who are facing divorce will express throughout their grieving process. The load is heavy, and the fight is unfair. As the donkey in the story above, they may feel that the very person they trusted the most is trying to bury them along with every dream and hope they had for their future. What a painful human experience – that of not only loss, but of betrayal and fear caused by the person you most believed would always work to rescue you from harm.

If we consider the many layers of grief, we see that human connection, empathy, and support are a critical component. However, we also know that divorce often creates a tendency not to trust, to fear being open or vulnerable again – even with friends. Yet, healing requires us to learn how to trust and who to trust, to know when trust has been earned, and how to use healing experiences in our daily lives to take the broken pieces of our hearts and use them to build a stronger version of ourselves that we never knew we could be.

Thankfully, we do not face these challenges alone. God not only promises to be close to us when we are in pain, but also, He promises a plan for our lives, no matter what life itself throws at us. Jeremiah 29:11, *New International Bible* (1973/2011) states, "For I know the plans I have for you, declares the Lord, plans to prosper you and not to harm you, plans to give you a hope and a future." The hope we cling to when we face those trials in life that threaten to crush our very spirit comes from the reassurance of the God who knew us before we were born, who walks with us through unforeseen storms and who promises that our future will be fully restored.

This chapter will focus on the physical, emotional, cognitive, and spiritual impact of divorce on women, stages of grief involved in the process of divorce, coping skills that have been found to help prevent impairment, and effective counseling interventions for women who have experienced or are coping with divorce. We will also review Biblical insights on divorce and wrap up with a case study where these interventions can be viewed from an application-based perspective.

EXPERIENCING DIVORCE

The concept of "shaking off the dirt" and stepping up to a brighter future sounds easy enough, but we know it is not. The experience of finding our-

© Eetu Mustonen/Shutterstock.com

selves in a pit without a quick or easy way to the top, knowing that we must make the climb on our own, can be overwhelming. Not surprisingly, research indicates that divorce can be devastating. According to the Social Readjustment Rating Scale (SRRS) which identifies what life events create the most disturbance for those who experience it, divorce is listed as one of life's most severe stressors (Abrams, 2019). The fallout from dissolving a marriage is multi-faceted. Couples will face a grieving or 'letting go' process, a mix of emotions, new responsibilities, financial changes, parenting challenges, and expanding needs for social support. Divorce has been tied to a number of physical and psychological challenges such as reduced health, increased mortality, lower levels of psychological well-being, and high levels of anxiety and depression (Emery et al., 2012). Depending on the state of the marriage and the partner who initiated the divorce, it can also be tied to a feeling of excitement about new experiences or relief in terms of escaping an unhealthy relationship (Lebow, 2019). However, research indicated that even for the initiating partner, there are still negative emotions and identity issues of "Who am I now?" associated with divorce (Lebow, 2019).

Statistics

As discussed in the marriage chapter of this book, we know that divorce impacts a little less than 50% of those who marry (Kennedy & Ruggles, 2014). What may be more surprising is the fact that more women than men are choosing to end their marriages. According to the National Center for Health Statistics (2017), almost 80% of divorces are initiated by women. The most common reasons for divorce vary but research suggested that most of them fall under the umbrella of sociocultural changes, shifts from a nuclear to a more individualized family style, educational and economic empowerment of women, changes in personal or cultural values, and personality traits of couples (Ariplackala & Georgea, 2015). This list may point to a powerful change in the way women view the benefits of marriage, their ability to take care of themselves apart from a spouse, and their ability to walk away from a relationship in which their partner is disconnected or lacking interest in keeping intimacy alive. Women are approximately 70% more likely than their male counterpart to seek out counseling when relationships begin to deteriorate and are more likely to become disillusioned with an unhealthy marriage or a disinterested partner (Doss et al., 2007). In addition to that, they may have a greater support network already developed outside of their spouse, with 82% of women reporting that they share their serious psychological or emotional concerns with their friends, and only 2% of men reporting the same (Doss et al., 2007). We also see that psychological pain holds a direct correlation to losing something that we perceive as an asset, which includes intimacy in a marriage and not just the marriage itself. The impact of divorce is often tied to the quality of the marital relationship prior to separation. This follows the contextual approach that stressful life conditions result in a sense of relief or at a bare minimum, an easier transition to the next phase of life, once they come to an end (Bourassa et al., 2015). Generally speaking, married couples are happier and healthier than those who divorce, but women in unhealthy or dissatisfying relationships have been shown to experience less distress than men following the dissolution of a marriage. This may point to the fact that a fulfilling relationship is more of a priority of women and that women are more sensitive to changes in marital quality (Kiecolt-Glaser & Newton, 2001). Nevertheless, divorce does present with emotional risks and challenges, including reduced coping skills, difficulty adjusting to being single, diminished emotional intelligence, and various psychiatric symptoms, including PTSD (Slanbekova et al., 2017).

> Women prioritize fulfilling relationships, are sensitive to changes in quality of relationships, and are more likely to walk away from relationships that are unrewarding.

Symptoms and Criteria

The *DSM-5* (2013) discusses divorce as a z-code, much the same as if a couple is seeking marriage counseling. It is considered relationship distress with a spouse or intimate partner and symptoms include impaired functioning in a person's thinking, behavior, or mood. They may display difficulty with conflict resolution, a desire to withdrawal, or conversely, over-involvement. It is common to see these problems result in feelings of negativity, chronic sadness, apathy or anger toward their partner. Women going through a divorce may also meet the criteria for other diagnoses like depression or anxiety which present with hopelessness, diminished interest in activities normally enjoyed, difficulty sleeping well, maintaining a normal appetite, or being able to concentrate as well as agitation, irritability, excessive fear and worry, being easily fatigued, muscle tension and restlessness.

GRIEF STAGES IN DIVORCE

People approach grief very differently, depending on the loss they have experienced. Death has a cultural expectation of how we should respond, a set of rituals that are well-respected and meant to offer support and closure. But what about when it comes to grieving the loss of a relationship? Divorce can feel like a death to a person going through it, but rarely do others react to a divorce the way they do when someone dies. No one

© Gergely Zsolnai/Shutterstock.com

gasps or cries along with the bereaved at the news. No one puts together an article honoring the life of the marriage. There are no divorce casseroles brought, no final services to say goodbye and find closure. Well-meaning friends may even tell divorcees to be happy, to celebrate, and to engage in new relationships and social activities for singles. No one ever celebrates the death of a spouse by pointing out how much fun it will be to have less responsibility or engage in a new romance.

Divorce seems to be viewed through the lens of hope for new opportunities rather than the realization that years of once joy-filled memories will become bittersweet, or that precious visions and expectations of one's future will crumble and rebuilding will have to be done alone. Some women have experienced abuse and have chosen to leave a marriage. Others may have experienced long-standing unhealthy patterns in a marriage and choose to walk away from the perpetual dysfunction. While this decision may be necessary for

© studioarz/Shutterstock.com

their mental, emotional, physical and spiritual health, it is not without difficulty, pain, guilt, or grief. For those who did not want a divorce, there is the stinging awareness that this devastating loss is not because their partner died, but because they chose to leave the relationship. Equally as upsetting, this decision was made by the person they may have loved and trusted more than anyone else in their lives.

Disengaging from a relationship that was once the most meaningful, and the one that provided physical, social, mental and emotional support, is a palpable loss. For some, this loss brings with it a host of additional losses: parenting time or custody issues if children are involved, loss of friendships previously held as a couple, financial status, freedom of employment status, and one's identity or sense of self. It may also impact a person's faith and spiritual well-being. It is not uncommon for people to become angry with God as a result of a painful loss, even giving up on their relationship with Him entirely. However, just as people react in various ways to their

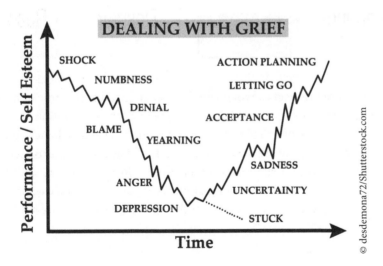

© desdemona72/Shutterstock.com

grief, people respond differently to God in their pain. Some report feelings that they deepened the roots of their faith and that their relationship with God was what helped them to navigate painful periods of unrest (Mercer & Evans, 2006). The grieving process has become well-known in the field of counseling since Elizabeth Kubler-Ross first introduced the five stages of grief in 1969. Her model of grief included a set of five stages that, while linear overall, could be experienced in or out of order at different points in the grieving process. These stages included *Denial, Anger, Bargaining, Depression* and *Acceptance*. This model primarily aimed toward understanding the grief process after the death of a loved one.

Although we may be more familiar with Kubler-Ross' stages of grief, her model was preceded by Bowlby's (1961) model of grief built upon his theory of attachment. Attachment theory emphasizes the need for a safe, long-lasting psychological connection with a meaningful person who gives feelings of pleasure in interaction and who soothes us in times of stress (Bowlby, 2008). This theory focuses on the impact and importance of secure attachment styles in our primary relationships as well as what happens when that secure attachment is not present. When it came to the stages of grief, Bowlby put more emphasis on how powerful human attachments and bonds are and provided an explanation of how the involuntary severing of those bonds with significant others creates tremendous emotional distress, attachment trauma, and a challenging grief process. His stages of grief included *Shock, Yearning and Protest, Despair,* and *Recovery* (Buglass, 2010).

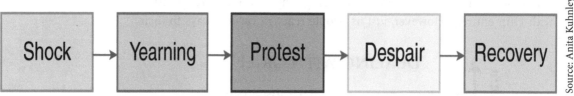

Source: Anita Kuhnley

While grief impacts anyone who has experienced a loss, research indicated that the loss of a marriage is unique in both the emotions felt as well as the process of grieving that is experienced (Papa & Lancaster, 2016). Below, we will review Bowlby's stages of grief as they relate to divorce and detaching from a significant other. Kubler-Ross' stages are addressed as well. As you read the sections below, see if you can identify where the two models are different from one another and where they share similarities.

© Antonio Guillem/Shutterstock.com

Shock

Take a moment to consider a time in your life when you received devastating news that you did not expect. What were the emotions you felt in those first few minutes, hours, and days? Most of us have experienced this at some point in our lives. Perhaps you can recall the shock of the news, the inability to process it all at once, and the crushing feeling of an incredibly painful reality pressing down on you. Now change the scenario a bit: Can you recall a time when you were the one who had to break bad news to someone else, knowing it would create this same experience for him or her? What differences of emotion were present in that instance? For many, there can be a sense of dread but also of some degree of dissociation – having to remove ourselves from the emotional impact of what we are about to do. Bowlby (1973) suggested that shock may occur in situations like these because it protects us from the emotional devastation of being forcibly removed from an attachment figure that has become central to our overall well-being. The human spirit naturally rejects the idea of permanent separation, viewing it instead as intolerable even if there may be a good reason for it. This is also seen in Kubler-Ross' (1969) first stage of grief, denial. One woman might think, "This is not happening to me. It is a huge misunderstanding. Surely, we can work this out!" while another might think, "I cannot believe I am going to go through with this, but there is no option to stay. I have to move

> Initially, denial can be a method of self-protection.

on from where I am in this relationship." Women who experience divorce will find themselves on one side or the other of this coin, and the shock or denial of ending a marriage will be present even if it shows up in slightly different ways. Denial serves as a protective factor of sorts, allowing someone to avoid fully embracing what a new, harrowing situation will mean for them, and how it will affect their daily life, their needs, their abilities, and their responsibilities (Sher & Noth, 2013). Understandably, this initial stage can be anxiety provoking and can even result in symptoms of trauma. The grief and recovery process are comprised of many stages. The processing of grief and sorrow may seem endless, but the confusion and distress that comes with separation and divorce do eventually fade. For most people, this occurs over a period of 18 months to a few years' time, depending on their ability to process the event, rebuild a new, independent life, and develop healthy coping strategies (Tesler & Thompson, 2006).

Yearning and Protest

Perhaps one of the most troubling parts of divorce is the realization that life will change dramatically when a marriage ends. The length of a woman's marriage, whether she has children with her spouse, whether she is educated and/or employed, and her financial ability to support herself are

© fizkes/Shutterstock.com

COUNSELING WOMEN

all dynamics that have a significant impact on the degree of fear and anxiety she may experience due to a divorce. Bowlby (1973) suggested that when people feel that there is a high level of risk in losing a critical relationship, they will yearn for stability and fight to keep the relationship safe by protesting change. Kubler-Ross (1969) called this *bargaining*, or a willingness to do something extraordinary if God or someone else will just prevent a catastrophe from occurring. In either model, we might see a person pleading, "If you will just stay, I will change, I promise", or "If I agree to (fill in the blank), can we get back together?" The underlying message is "I am scared. This is not something I want to sign up for, and I will do just about anything to reverse where I see this going". It is also not hard to see the emotional manipulation that this stage of grief can create for someone who is facing a crisis that demands logical thinking and emotional stability. While Bowlby (1973) does not expressly address anger in his model, Kubler-Ross' (1969) *anger* stage of grief may also fit here. The bereaved might lament, "I cannot believe he would do this to me! What did I ever do to deserve this? What a terrible person he is!" The primary emotion here may be a desire to save the marriage (yearning) but anger fuels the secondary emotion, which is what we see or hear (protest). The psychological process of displacement allows the bereaved to focus on an emotion that is more tolerable (anger) rather than dealing with the primary issue (unsuccessful yearning or bargaining) that creates cognitive dissonance and personal discomfort. This defense mechanism is also present in *blaming* within a marriage, including the inability to take ownership for one's own part in a failed marriage (Tesler & Thompson, 2006).

> Yearning and protest can be present at the same time, with one often fueled by the other.

Despair and Disorganization

Experiencing despair is a normal part of the emotional journey tied to ending any relationship, particularly a marriage. Our personal views about marriage and our expectation or vision of what our life would look like certainly impacts the degree of hopelessness we may feel about an impending divorce. Our families, society and churches all have something to say on this topic, which can have a

© pathdoc/Shutterstock.com

powerful impact on our perception of our role and responsibility in a divorce. A woman may feel guilt for not fulfilling the promises she made to a spouse, shame that she may be viewed differently by society as a divorced woman or as part of a broken family, or shame that she is a failure for not being able to make her marriage work. Christian women often feel they have disappointed God by not honoring the sanctity of marriage, even when extremely unhealthy circumstances exist (White & Berghuis, 2016). To complicate matters, some women also have a history of marital infidelity, betrayal, and deceit, which can exacerbate feelings of guilt and shame when a marriage ends. Regardless of whether these emotions exist for good reasons or are a product of a faulty belief of not measuring up to what others expect, they can be painful and create serious distress. Women can quickly transform them into other emotions, such as depression or anger, without awareness of the primary emotions (guilt and shame) that created these feelings.

> Hopelessness arises when a person fails to work successfully through their despair and disorganization.

Authentic healing can be difficult when emotional insight is minimal and accountability for behavior is absent. Typically, however, by the final stage in the grief process, a person begins to accept the changes that have taken place as well as the fact that things will never go back to the way they used to be. Throughout each stage, women must come to grips with the fact that things may never quite look the way they had imagined, which can be an even harder loss to process. In this third stage, however, there is often an overwhelming sense of despair or hopelessness, along with anger and questioning. Life feels like it may never improve, the world seems unfair, and people seem untrustworthy. Bowlby (1973) suggested that if we do not progress through this stage successfully, we will continue to struggle with depression and anger, leading to an attitude that reinforces negativity and hopelessness.

Re-organization and Recovery

In this final stage, a grieving individual will begin to find healing, meaning, and purpose. A woman realizes that while her past life is gone, and her future is changed forever, not all is lost. She is moving toward accepting her *new normal*. Kubler-Ross (1969) described this stage as *acceptance*, and while Bowlby's version is similar, he used the terms *re-organization* and *recovery* to highlight the idea that there is more than acceptance needed in this final stage of grief. He surmised what would lend itself best to the resolution of grief was the ability for someone to restructure their life, dreams, expectations, and plans for their future, indicating that women would recover only when they were able to move not only into a new way of thinking, but of living. Each stage of grief can take some time, and it may be a slow process to accept that there are positive aspects of their life after loss. We begin to see someone gradually re-engaging in the things they previously enjoyed, a higher energy level, joy in their daily activities, and more positive emotions overall. Of course, other factors influence the development and outcome of this final phase. These factors may include her attachment style, the value she places on the marriage, the ability to see hope in her future as an individual, the ability to care for herself emotionally, financially and psychologically, and her capacity to understand that, while the pain of a significant loss may never disappear entirely, she will experience less pain as time moves on and a new identity is established (Williams & Haley, 2017).

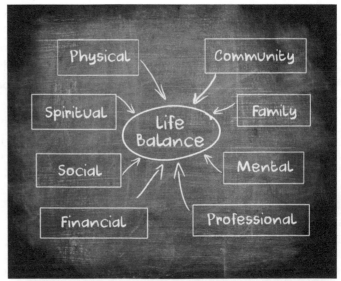

© Take Photo/Shutterstock.com

© Illustration Forest/Shutterstock.com

COUNSELING INTERVENTIONS FOR DIVORCE RECOVERY

Ask those who have been through a divorce, "What does it feel like?" and the answers will pour in: "Like a tornado came in and demolished everything about my life"; "Like freedom and sorrow"; "I am so tired, I did not know an exhaustion like this was possible"; "It feels like shame. It feels like failing. It feels unnatural"; "Like I have no idea where to go from here". The sentiment is repetitive and clear: divorce is incredibly hard, emotionally, and otherwise. In counseling, we must be able to address not only the issues of grief that accompany divorce, but the numerous struggles that emerge from that loss. Depression, anxiety, and even a diagnosis of trauma can be common in treating women going through a divorce. Below, we will review a couple of the most effective therapeutic interventions for helping a woman cope with the transition from marriage to singlehood. While it is not an easy one, with the right support, she can find meaning, hope, and purpose in her journey.

Cognitive-Behavioral Therapy

Bereavement at its best is a meaning-making process. At its worst, it is a recurring process of rumination. Both ends of this spectrum involve our thoughts and behaviors. We can use them for growth and moving forward with our lives, or we can choose to remain stuck in the past, where memories are all we have left and represent the only place we find comfort.

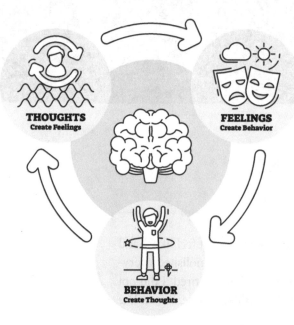

In time, however, it becomes harder and harder to recover that sense of comfort from that which we can no longer physically enjoy. Cognitive-behavioral therapy (CBT) identifies negative or self-defeating thought patterns and unhealthy, unproductive behaviors that often accompany emotional pain (Dobson & Dobson, 2017). In the case of divorce, this may mean helping a client to identify the areas of her life where her fears, confusion, anger, or sadness have begun to shape her thoughts accordingly but inaccurately. It may mean identifying what choices she is making on a regular basis and evaluating how her daily decisions in her personal, social, professional, or spiritual life are impacting her overall health and her healing process. The process that occurs between thoughts, behaviors, and emotions is interrelated. What we allow ourselves to think will shape the way we feel, and the way we feel will often shape the decisions we make.

The cognitive aspect of CBT is perhaps the most crucial because thoughts are the first 'check point' of mood regulation. Imagine a person walking a dog. The dog represents a person's emotions. The person represents a person's thoughts and behaviors. Have you ever seen a person walking a dog that was untrained and out of control? It may have appeared that the dog was the one walking the person! In much the same way, when a person's emotions are taking the lead, sometimes thoughts and behaviors will follow powerlessly. Cognitive restructuring, which includes becoming aware of cognitive distortions, allows us to reconsider how true or helpful our thinking may be in light of our situation. Common distorted patterns of thinking include all-or-nothing thinking, overgeneralizations, disqualifying the positive, jumping to conclusions (mind-reading or fortune telling), catastrophizing, and emotional reasoning, among others (Assen, 2016; Dobson & Dobson, 2017). To combat these tendencies, we might encourage a client to list their thoughts about their problems, identify the nature of those thoughts, and alter them to reflect a more truthful and positive outlook. For example, the thought that "I am unlovable" (a generalization) may be re-stated as "John told me I am unlovable" (John's opinion). As another example, "I will never be happy again" (fortune telling) may be replaced first with "It feels like this pain will never end" (client's emotion), and eventually with "I will find joy in my life again, even if my future looks different from my past" (hope-focused belief).

Behavior is the powerful sidekick to thoughts. If thoughts are the brain of the person walking the dog, behaviors are the hand that controls the leash. Behaviors take our thoughts and put them into action. Much like cognitive restructuring, behavioral restructuring is essential to altering the way in which we feel and how we manage our situation. It is often more challenging to alter our behavior than our thoughts because it requires being proactive and making the decision to do something that we do not yet feel like doing. Clients who have struggled with isolating may cringe at the idea of committing to a social activity, even if they know logically that it would be good for them. Because of this, we want to set small, measurable, realistic goals in behavioral therapy plans. For example, we might encourage a client who finds herself disen-

> Reframing negative thoughts and following through with healthy choices can improve mood.

gaging, feeling apathetic or lacking motivation to redirect her thoughts and then intentionally connect with other people for support and encouragement. Her goal may be to follow a more structured routine, meditate, set daily attainable personal goals, incorporate specific activities back into their schedule a little at a time, and be aware of her emotional state (improvements and ongoing needs) while implementing these changes (Dobson & Dobson, 2017).

Interestingly, some studies have shown that behaviors alone (even when thoughts are not on board) can be enough to change one's mood. Have you ever been in a bad mood and run into an acquaintance in public where you struck up a pleasant conversation? Chances are you were not capable of feeling as angry after that interaction as you were feeling prior to it. Smiling or amiably conversing with others even when we are angry (or sad) makes it much more difficult to feel or display anger (or sadness). When our behaviors trump our emotions, even temporarily, we see a shift in the emotions we experience. More powerful yet, when our thoughts and behaviors are aligned, emotions have little option but to follow suit.

Narrative Therapy

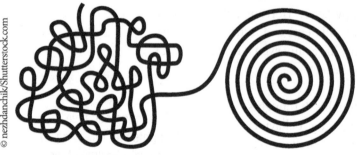

Brene Brown, a present-day social worker and researcher, stated in her book, *The Gifts of Imperfection*, "Owning our story and loving ourselves through that process is the bravest thing that we will ever do" (Brown, 2010, p. xiv). Narrative therapy is a clinical approach to allowing clients to do just that – tell their story and learn to love, trust, and appreciate their journey, along with who they have become through that process. Pietsch (2002) described it as a conversation between the counselor and client that consists of a series of questions and answers about how the current problem or story in their life is affecting their perception of themselves and the world around them. The client shares her reality, her experiences, and the ways in which those experiences have shaped her thoughts, emotions and behaviors. The process is collaborative in nature, with the counselor being non-judgmental and capable of asking relevant questions about the client's story, and in turn, the client finds meaning in her struggle as well as what is needed to

© nezhdanchik/Shutterstock.com

move past those struggles (Pietsch, 2002). Therapy is successful when the client, in collaboration with the therapist, creates a new narrative with different meanings that change her perspective and improve her emotional health.

© ESB Professional/Shutterstock.com

Women experience divorce in various stages, each of which may come with a different narrative and therapeutic struggle. Some clients will seek counseling in the pre-divorce stage, some during a divorce, and still others in the post-divorce stage (Bogolub, 1995). Across these three stages, a shared therapeutic process includes: 1) creating an autonomous self, 2) changing negative view of self, 3) changing negative views of divorce, and 4) creating and using resources (Pietsch, 2002). In the first stage, the client has two goals: first, she needs to be able to see herself as a single capable person, and second, she needs to be able to find meaning beyond the life she lived with her spouse. In this stage, a counselor may choose to ask relevant questions that either assist the client in these goals or use confrontation to point out areas that will prevent her from meeting them. These are referred to as relational identity questions (Combs & Freedman, 2016). For instance, a counselor may ask, "How did you manage to stop that urge to talk to your ex-spouse about the relationship, or more than necessary?", "How does having an image of yourself as married or your identity as 'Mrs. X' stop you from moving ahead with the life you now have?", or "How were you able to decide to keep the house when previously you were unsure about what to do?" Asking questions such as these encourages a client to move from simply sharing her current story to seeing how that story may be preventing her from creating a new narrative that is separate from her past. Clients in this stage may be utterly unaware of who they now are, how to make important decisions, or how others may see them if they are no longer married. This may be so overwhelming (and depressing) that they may choose to withdraw or isolate. Counselors may ask, "How does your fear of not knowing how to handle certain situations stop you from doing the things that would make you happy?" Clients may need to be able to talk through their feelings of insecurity or address identity issues through the lens of what they can do rather than what they have always done in the past.

> Insight, empowerment, and goal setting are critical aspects of narrative work. Helping to build a client's sense of confidence and self-efficacy results in the development of a healthy new identity.

In the second and third stages of this therapeutic approach, clients are working to change their negative perspective of themselves or their divorce. When a marriage ends, a damaged identity has usually been formed. A former spouse may have labeled their wife as demanding, incompetent, or simply not enough. Comments that were once just someone's opinion (or even a heated emotional reaction) can quickly become the primary source of one's sense of identity, and a client can get stuck viewing themselves this way (Pietsch, 2002). Counselors may help a client to differentiate the past and present by asking, "How has the story of you as incompetent affected the way in which you view yourself since the divorce?" or "How has your ex-husband's narrative of you being demanding impacted your relationships with friends now that you are single?" As a client shares her story about new daily responsibilities or tasks, we may take the opportunity to challenge the idea that she is not capable, along with the idea that divorce will mean she will forever be handicapped in one way or another. One way to do this is to set goals as the client's narrative unfolds. For example, she may tearfully explain that her husband always used to take care of things around the house that needed fixing. In turn, a counselor may take that opportunity to validate the fear of having to manage this alone, and brainstorm options to learn to do some of these things herself or find assistance when needed.

After a successful attempt at managing one of these tasks, counselors might ask, "What does it say about you that you can physically take care of your home on your own?" The answer can serve to point out the client's strengths and abilities, replacing her fears and self-doubt. The new message is that "I am competent and capable" despite what a previous partner may have otherwise claimed. Taking this further, counselors may tie her newly found confidence in her work, her parenting, or priorities into the ways in which divorce can grow a person. For example, asking questions such as "How has the divorce affected your self-esteem and confidence?" or "What does it mean to you that you were able to hold on to your values and priorities during such a time of chaos?" reinforces the idea that while divorce can be emotionally devastating, it can also present an opportunity to reveal powerful, positive character qualities that were previously obscure or unknown to the client (Combs & Freedman, 2016; Pietsch, 2002).

In the final stage of narrative work, we want to help a client create and use the resources they have, whether internal (positive traits and abilities) or external (social support, problem-solving skills). We move from "How has not being able to depend on your ex-spouse affected your life?" (addressing emotion) to "What can you do when you are not able to depend on your ex-spouse to do something for you?" (addressing an action plan), and eventually to "What does it say about you as a person that you were able to do something without your ex-spouse's help?" (addressing positive change). In this stage, each piece of the client's story becomes an important part in fully understanding why they feel or act the way they do, and creates a shift from where

they have been or what their current circumstances may be toward something more hope-focused and meaningful. The client needs to be able to see that *perception is reality*, and that what she chooses to believe and embody, or what she aspires to and work towards, will influence her ability to perceive her future in a positive light, laying the foundation for the direction she desires to go. We could think of narrative therapy as a process of intentional training. Imagine a woman who decides she wants to become a champion swimmer. At first, she is unsure of the most effective strokes, her muscles are undefined, and her lungs are unfamiliar with the breath control needed to swim long distances. However, with training and education, exercise, practice, and perseverance, she discovers that she had the ability all along. Her skills just needed to be developed. Ultimately, clients need to create a narrative based on a workable plan, not on chance. They need permission to let go of how they have seen themselves in the past and develop the confidence to be who they desire to be in the present. This approach fosters genuine hope. Ask yourself if you were a client: Would you rather agonize over every character flaw and mistake you have ever made with the hope that someday things might be different, or would you explore all of your possible strengths, abilities and positive qualities knowing that those are what will give you the greatest possible future? The message of narrative therapy is clear: What we focus on will be what we will develop!

Interpersonal Therapy

> Our roles and relationships help to form our identity. Losing a primary role results in painful adjustments.

If someone were to ask you, "Who are you?" how might you answer? Most people answer based on the roles they play in life: "I am a wife", "I am a mother", or "I am an employee". These roles create what becomes our identity. When one or more of those core roles changes, the impact can be devastating. The sheer number of transitions that will take place after a divorce can be difficult just to sort out, much less experience. For women who may have married in their early 20's, there really is not much of a baseline for how to live as a single adult. Marriage is all they have known. For those who have children, there is a transition from being a married parent to a single parent. Some women have taken on the role of primarily caring for the home or the children, working part time or not at all. The transition to working full time may be taxing on its own, but taking on 100% of the roles in the home while working full-time can add insult to injury. Friendships developed as a couple may also change after a marriage dissolves. Loyalties of friends may lie with a woman's partner, leaving her to grieve the loss of peer relationships and activities as well. Interpersonal therapy (IPT) addresses the issues of complicated bereavement, role transitions, role disputes, and interpersonal deficits and is rooted in both relational theory and attachment theory (Lipsitz & Markowitz, 2013).

Counselors who employ IPT work to tie their client's diagnosis to their treatment plan and outcome (Markowitz & Weissman, 2004). For instance, a counselor may say, "As we have discussed, your divorce has led to a depressive disorder. You have been struggling with eating, sleeping, decision-making, and mood disturbances. My recommendation is that we spend the next 12 weeks working on the bereavement process and related interpersonal problems you are experiencing. Grief is natural and can feel consuming, but it does not last forever. As grief subsides, conditions change, and our mood improves." The connection between life events and mood is important to define, as it sets the stage for clients to recognize that while their feelings are valid, they have the power to alter their circumstances for the better and, consequently, will feel more at peace, experience joy again, and develop an improved sense of self-confidence and self-efficacy (Markowitz & Weissman, 2004).

It is also crucial that clients are empowered to regain healthy social ties after a divorce. Bowlby (1961) asserted that interpersonal bonding is cru-

cial in developing meaningful attachments and, while these attachments start with the parent-child relationship, they expand to include making meaningful connections with others, an individual's relational style, and their roles within society. These social roles serve as a protective layer over our need to connect and attach with others. They also provide meaningful responsibilities to fulfill, which result in increases in self-efficacy and self-esteem (Bandura, 1977). Role transitions such as a divorce, a career change, parenting only part time, or a financial status change often interfere with these social ties. Consider these scenarios: What used to be date night for a handful of couples is no longer an appropriate environment for the newly divorced woman, even though she enjoyed the company of the other couples for so long. The moms group that met every Saturday served as a time to share the joys and burdens of parenting while kids played together, but the newly divorced mom will miss out every other Saturday because her kids are with their father for the weekend. The newly divorced woman who has no children desires to go on an annual vacation, but without her spouse, she has no one to go with. How lonely for each of these women as they yearn for what once offered security and connection! Her previous social engagements have morphed into bittersweet events, or worse yet, can serve as a reminder of the loss she has experienced. In the counseling office, these issues present as grief. The client has lost a primary social tie that previously provided support and a sense of social connection and belongingness. After such a loss, there may be difficulty investing in relationships or being able to draw benefits from engaging with others. After all, trust is hard to build, easy to break, and difficult to place in others once betrayed.

Consequently, IPT suggests offering psychoeducation and support, and encourages the resolving of interpersonal problems through 1) increasing social support, 2) decreasing interpersonal stress, and 3) improving interpersonal skills (Lipsitz & Markowitz, 2013). Counselors work to help clients identify their options for social support outside of their past marriage and any relationships that suffered when the marriage ended. The counseling office also becomes a source of trustworthy support and safety, as well as a place where a client can talk through what relational fears or challenges, they are experiencing. Counselors may use role-play with clients to improve their interpersonal communication and interactive skills with others. One of the primary factors found to be helpful in increasing social support is to validate for a client that the struggles she is facing are not due to her own lack of social skills, but simple role insecurity as she faces new and unfamiliar situations due to her life circumstances. While not all stressful life events are interpersonal, those that are create both more distress and a unique type of distress compared to those that are impersonal, correlating with the symptoms seen in post-traumatic stress disorder (Bolger et al., 1989; Dorahy et al., 2009).

> Clients gain a sense of confidence when they successfully master new and challenging skills.

Decreasing interpersonal stress for women facing a divorce might include reducing her interactions with her former spouse, reducing daily hassles, increasing options for various types of needed support, stabilizing physical health, and maintaining positive social relationships that meet emotional needs. IPT invites, accepts, and validates the expression of emotion, simultaneously stressing the impact of emotions, including how they may train us to respond to others in the future. It is crucial for clients to process their feelings, losses, and changes in order to decrease interpersonal stress. In weekly sessions, this may mean allowing negative feelings to increase in order to talk through any ongoing hostility, friction, anger, shame, helplessness, and/or alienation (Lipsitz & Markowitz, 2013). We also see that interpersonal stress is reduced when a client begins to gain mastery over challenges they previously never had to face. Intentional inclusion of new personal, social, developmental, or professional goals may be a wise addition to the treatment planning process in IPT (Horowitz, 2004). Once a client has begun to increase their social support and decrease their interpersonal stressors, they can learn ways to improve their interpersonal skills.

Nearly all theories of counseling focus on the need to nurture and enhance interpersonal skills and the inclusion of healthy social functioning, interaction, and support ranks among the most universal goals in psychotherapy (Follette & Greenberg, 2005). IPT recognizes that situational crises in a client's life can lead to the development or exacerbation of unhealthy interpersonal skills, which, in turn, can increase vulnerability to additional psychological disorders. Counselors work with clients to communicate their feelings more concretely, develop assertiveness skills, learn how to diffuse tension, and insight on how to best adapt to their new role. In addition to working through their interpersonal problem, a client needs to acquire new skills. These may include boundary setting, learning how to do things their spouse used to do for them, recognize personality traits that contribute to communication or relational problems, and gain awareness of healthy conflict management skills (Lipsitz & Markowitz, 2013).

LOOKING THROUGH THE LENS OF CHRISTIANITY: BIBLICAL INTEGRATION

grace

© HowLettery/Shutterstock.com

Historically, divorce has been a complicated topic for the church to address. Highly emotionally charged and difficult to know the details of each person's situation, the issue of divorce becomes a balancing act between what is made clear in Scripture on the breaking of the marriage bond and the expectation that we would place the value of every human life over even the sacred commitment to a marriage. Over the years, many clients in my office have expressed disillusionment with the way the Christian community responded to their news of an impending divorce. Some were shamed, while others felt chastised for not making more of an effort. Others were simply alienated from their peer group now that they would no longer be a part of a married group. Some of these women were survivors of their spouse's physical or emotional abuse or had been betrayed by an affair, and yet judgement was clear, as was the message: "Divorce is wrong, hence you should not get a divorce." How incredibly damaging when the impact of divorce is already so overwhelmingly difficult, and the need for support, companionship, unconditional love and acceptance is higher than perhaps ever before. Conversely, the secular worldview on divorce often leans too far in the opposite direction. Those contemplating or facing divorce may be encouraged to do whatever makes them happy and to put their own needs first. Often, the concept of the sanctity of marriage, commitment, perseverance, and fidelity are discounted or disregarded. Neither approach is therapeutic or spiritually appropriate.

In Matthew 19, *New International Bible* (1973/2011), we see the Pharisees deciding to corner Jesus on this topic, asking Him "Is it legal for a man to divorce his wife for any reason?" At that time in history, men were able to divorce their spouses for just about any reason, including trading their wife in for "younger, newer model". Jesus replied by reminding them that a man and woman were designed to leave their family of origin to create their own by becoming "one flesh", and that no one should ruin this God-designed plan by tearing a marriage apart. The Pharisees shot back in rebuttal, "If that's so, why did Moses give instructions for divorce papers and procedures?" The answer Jesus gives is so important to understand how we should handle this issue as well. He responded by explaining that while divorce was never part of God's original plan for marriage, the hard-heartedness of some married people was a greater tragedy and

represented a greater risk than divorce, despite the fact that God hates it. Consider that God hates divorce, but that He would rather see a divorce take place than the harm that can come from a hardened heart of a husband toward his wife or a wife toward her husband. Jesus showed compassion for those who are in a marriage where love is not present or infidelity is, and where woundedness would continue to occur. As counselors, we must consider Jesus' words here. While our calling is to value and hold marriage in high regard, we must hold the value of one's humanity and dignity higher still.

There may also be times when we do not have the whole story. Counseling is full of one-sided, emotional narratives. Sometimes the perspective someone has is the one that serves him or her best in the moment, and we may never know all the details accurately. The Bible speaks to us about both wise judgment and staying out of judgment as well. While we are called to be wise and show discernment (John 7:24), we are also called to avoid judging others for their sins when we have sin in our lives (Matthew 7:1). The late Billy Graham said, "It is the Holy Spirit's job to convict, God's job to judge, and my job to love". He had the wisdom to know that Jesus left us with the commandment to love one another and told us that people would know we are Christians by how we love others, regardless of who they are, what sin they are struggling with, or how their values align with our own. For those clients who are open to Biblical integration in their counseling sessions, counselors have the ability to speak the truth in a loving way and direct clients to what Jesus had to say about many tough topics, divorce included, but the journey should be the client's and our compassion should be unconditional.

Lauren, a 43-year-old mother of two, arrived at her first session in tears, stating that six weeks ago her husband of 18 years had told her "out of the blue" that he was filing for divorce. He moved out the next day and has rarely been back to the house or even called to check in on the children. Since then, she had learned that he had been having an affair with a co-worker for the past year. She stated, "I am absolutely heartsick. My life has turned upside down. I do not even feel like I know who I am now, and I have no idea how I am going to make it on my own". In the initial interview, Lauren disclosed that she was a stay-at-home mom caring for her 10-year-old son and 7-year-old daughter. She acknowledged that while she grew up in a Christian home, her husband had not. Throughout their marriage, they had attended church sporadically due to his reluctance to attend and get involved in a church setting. She did report having a marketable degree and had enjoyed working in the past for a well-known company before her first child was born. She had just recently begun to send out resumes in search of a new job but was concerned that her work hours may leave her needing to find afternoon childcare. Lauren's counselor reviewed the history of her marital relationship, changes that had occurred over the past year, and asked about her social support system, which included a small group of close friends and her two sisters who live 30 minutes from her home.

In the first half of Lauren's therapy sessions, the counselor worked to develop rapport with Lauren, listening carefully to what she shared, reflecting back what he heard in the content and emotion she presented, asking relevant questions and

© Nikki Zalewski/Shutterstock.com

remaining neutral or supportive as she told her story. He reviewed with his client Bowlby's stages of grief and asked her to consider where she was at the current point in time, as well as asking her to consider what the future stages might look like for her. He also encouraged Lauren to consider the impact of spiritual support and the opportunity to reconnect to God and her local church family. The client and counselor worked to put together a treatment plan that included: (1) identifying and working through her grief process, (2) coping with the pain of infidelity, (3) understanding how betrayal can impact current and future relationships, (4) telling her story of the marriage, and (5) creating the narrative she would like to see unfold for her future and the future of her children. Her counselor discussed

© stoatphoto/Shutterstock.com

self-care strategies and encouraged her to identify what thoughts or behaviors may be keeping her from healing or healthy living, and how she might best create a new identity for herself outside of her previous marriage.

Throughout the remainder of Lauren's therapy, the counselor validated and normalized her feelings of shock and disbelief that her husband had truly left the marriage and the excruciating heartache and anger that stemmed from her husband's infidelity. She was able to express her struggle with why God had allowed this to happen to her family and how the Christian community may respond to her failed marriage. The counselor worked to help Lauren identify the reasons she had been attempting to try to repair the marriage and talk her husband into returning home, allowing her to process aloud what that would look like, what both parties would need to commit to, and the need for forgiveness and restoration if he were to agree to it. As Lauren talked through the despair she often experienced in trying to manage her life and her home alone, her counselor taught her how crucial her thinking process and choices would be going forward, and the value of avoiding a number of common cognitive distortions. Using psychoeducation, ways were suggested in which she could stay on top of her own health and daily responsibilities, including connecting with her social and spiritual support system and seeking stability and meaning through a career she once enjoyed. Every week, Lauren's counselor would review with her what she had accomplished without the help of her husband and asked her to process how that felt, how it

was empowering her, and what she was learning about her ability to trust herself to be the woman and mother she wanted to be and who God called her to be.

Lauren began working with her counselor on how to keep conversations with her ex-husband brief, polite and focused on the best interest of the children. She accepted a job offer that would provide her with an adequate income, connected with other working moms, and joined a co-op of parents who helped with after-school care, which reduced her stress about having to return to work. She began attending church with her children weekly and talking with them about what they were learning together. She and her children memorized Isaiah 43:18-19, *Good News Bible*, (1966/1976) But the Lord says, "Do not cling to events of the past or dwell on what happened long ago" and Romans 8:28, *New Living Bible* (1996) "And we know that God causes everything to work together for the good of those who love God and are called according to his purpose" to remind them that God does new, restorative things in life all the time. Through the process of reframing her thoughts, being intentional about her choices, telling her story fully and vulnerably, and working through the relational issues she uncovered in the process, Lauren began to find that despite her grief and the challenges she faced, she was, in fact, capable of things she never believed possible before. In time, she found that her story could be one of faith and courage in the midst of chaos and realized that hope exists even in the midst of our darkest hour.

© Asier Romero/Shutterstock.com

What is your personal perspective on divorce? How might this perspective influence your ability to counsel someone who is considering initiating a divorce? Empathy is often easier to display when we are working with the sufferer. Are you able to see past which partner asked for a divorce in order to attend to the presenting woundedness?

Empathy, compassion, and lack of judgment are critical counselor traits!

CHAPTER SUMMARY

My hope is that you have now gained a better understanding of the complex issues that accompany the experience of divorce and have a working idea of the factors that should be addressed with clients who are seeking to effectively cope with this life crisis. Counselors working with women facing divorce need to understand that the grieving process is unique. In the event that a spouse dies, a woman may experience Kubler-Ross' (1969) stages of grief, experience the void that comes with that kind of a loss, and need to restructure her life to continue to have her emotional needs met through other relationships. However, her spouse did not choose to leave the marriage, and she did not have to make the decision to leave her spouse. Women facing the loss of a spouse to divorce, on the other hand, are forced to work through this truth which can add the distress of abandonment, guilt, resentment and mistrust to the grief process. As Bowlby (1961) noted, the loss of a central attachment can create a pattern of intimacy problems that are difficult to recognize and even more difficult to correct over time and years of ingrained behavior.

While divorce represents a risk to women emotionally, physically, socially, financially, and otherwise, we know that it can also present an opportunity for meaning-making and personal as well as spiritual growth. The way a person thinks and the choices that they make will often account for most of whether they are successful in resolving their grief and situational crisis. Research points to how important it is to identify the areas of a woman's life that have been or will be negatively impacted by a divorce. Identity development commonly lies in our assumed roles, so as our roles change, our identity can be difficult to stabilize. Through psychoeducation and various therapeutic approaches, counselors help clients identify stressors in their interpersonal relationships and daily responsibilities, as well as areas in their life that they will need to pay special attention to social connectedness, emotion regulation, healthy communication, self-care and the learning of new practical skills. As clients begin to recognize areas of life that they can control, they can set goals based on what they are learning about and processing in therapy. When mastery occurs, they are likely to experience improved mood, self-confidence, and self-efficacy.

SUGGESTED RESOURCES

Books

Attachments: Why You Love, Feel, and Act the Way You Do by Tim Clinton and Gary Sibcy

Redeeming Attachment: A Counselor's Guide to Facilitating Attachment to God and Earned Security by Anita Kuhnley and Gary Sibcy

Where is God When It Hurts? by Phillip Yancy

The Problem of Pain by C.S. Lewis

Walking with God through Pain and Suffering by Timothy Keller

Before the Last Resort by George Kenworthy

New Life After Divorce by Bill Butterworth

Growing Through Divorce by Jim Smoke

When Happily Ever Shatters by Sue Birdseye

My Single Mom Life by Angela Thomas

REFERENCES

Abrams, A. (2019). *Post-divorce trauma and PTSD.* https://www.verywellmind.com/post-divorce-trauma-4583824

Ariplackala, R., & Georgea, T. S. (2015). Psychological components for marital distress and divorce in newlywed Indian couples. *Journal of Divorce & Remarriage, 56*(1), 1–24.

Assen, A. (2016). Emotional disorders and the wounded self. *American Journal of Clinical Hypnosis, 59*(1), 1-3.

Bandura, A. (1977). Self-efficacy: Toward a unifying theory of behavioral change *Psychological Review, 84*(2), pp. 191-215.

Bogolub, E. B. (1995). *Helping families through divorce: An eclectic approach.* Springer Publishing Company.

Bolger, N., DeLongis, A., Kessler, R. C., & Schilling, E. A. (1989). Effects of daily stress on negative mood. *Journal of Personality and Social Psychology, 57*(5), 808-818.

Bourassa, K. J., Sbarra, D. A., & Whisman, M. A. (2015). Women in very low quality marriages gain life satisfaction following divorce. *Journal of Family Psychology, 29*(3), 490-499.

Bowlby, J. (1961). Processes of mourning. *International Journal of Psychoanalysis, 42,* 317-339.

Bowlby, J. (1973). *Attachment and loss.* Basic Books.

Bowlby, J. (2008). *Attachment.* Basic Books.

Brown, B. (2010). *The gifts of imperfection.* Hazelden.

Buglass, E. (2010). Grief and bereavement theories. *Nursing Standard, 24*(41), 44-47.

Combs, G. & Freedman, J. (2016). Narrative therapy's relational understanding of identity. *Family Process, 55*(2), 211-224.

Dobson, D. & Dobson, K. S. (2017). *Evidence-based practice of cognitive behavioral therapy.* Guilford Press.

Dorahy, M. J., Corry, M., Shannon, M., MacSherry, A., Hamilton, G., & McRobert, G. (2009). Complex PTSD, interpersonal trauma and relational consequences: Findings from a treatment-receiving Northern Irish sample. *Journal of Affective Disorders, 112*(1), 71-80.

Doss, B. D., Atkins, D. C., & Christensen, A. (2007). Who's dragging their feet? Husbands and wives seeking marital therapy. *Journal of Marital & Family Therapy, 29*(2), 165-177.

Emery, R. E., Shim, H., & Horn, E. (2012). Examining divorce consequences and policies and the question: Is marriage more than a piece of paper? In L. Campbell & T. J. Loving (Eds.), *Interdisciplinary research on close relationships: The case for integration* (pp. 227–250). American Psychological Association.

Follette, W. E. & Greenberg, L. S. (2005). *Technique factors in dysphoric disorders: Principles of therapeutic change that work.* Oxford University Press.

Good News Bible. (1976). Good New Bible Online. https://www.biblegateway.com/versions/Good-News-Translation-GNT-Bible/

Horowitz, L. M. (2004). *Interpersonal foundations of psychopathology* (1st ed.). American Psychological Association.

Kennedy, S. & Ruggles, S. (2014). Breaking up is hard to count: The rise of divorce in the United States, 1890-2010. *Demography, 51*(2), 587-98.

Kiecolt-Glaser, J. K., & Newton, T. L. (2001). Marriage and health: His and hers. *Psychological Bulletin, 127*, 472–503.

Lebow, J. L. (2019). *Treating the difficult divorce: A practical guide for psychotherapists.* American Psychological Association.

Lieder, Y. (n.d). *The donkey in the pit: A parable on pain and* gain. https://www.chabad.org/library/article_cdo/aid/217529/jewish/The-Donkey-in-the-Pit.htm

Lipsitz, J. D. & Markowitz, J. C. (2013). Mechanisms of change in interpersonal therapy. *Clinical Psychology Review, 33*(8), 1134-1147.

Markowitz, J. C., & Weissman, M. M. (2004). Interpersonal psychotherapy: principles and applications. *World Psychiatry, 3*(3), 136–139.

Mercer, D., & Evans, J. (2006). The impact of multiple losses on the grieving process: An exploratory study. *Journal of Loss & Trauma, 11*(3), 219–227.

National Center for Health Statistics (2017). *Marriage and divorce.* https://www.cdc.gov/nchs/fastats/marriage-divorce.htm

New International Bible. (2011). New International Bible Online. https://www.thenivbible.com/ (Original work published 1973)

Papa, A., & Lancaster, N. (2016). Identity continuity and loss after death, divorce, and job loss. *Self & Identity, 15*(1), 47–61.

Pietsch, U. (2002). Facilitating post-divorce transition using narrative therapy. *Journal of Couple & Relationship Therapy, 1*(1), 65-81.

Sher, T. G. & Noth, K. (2013) Divorce and health. In M. D. Gellman, & J. R. Turner (Eds.), *Encyclopedia of behavioral medicine.* Springer Publishing.

Slanbekova, G., Chung, M. C., Abildina, S., Sabirova, R., Kapbasova, G., & Karipbaev, B. (2017). The impact of coping and emotional intelligence on the relationship between posttraumatic stress disorder from past trauma, adjustment difficulty, and psychological distress following divorce. *Journal of Mental Health, 26*(4), 334-341.

Tesler, P. H. & Thompson, P. (2006). *Collaborative divorce: the revolutionary new way to restructure your family, resolve legal issues, and move on with your life.* ReganBooks.

White, G. M. & Berghuis, D. M. (2016). Self-Identified Christian women and divorce: The recovery and discovery of self. *Journal of Psychology & Christianity, 35*(2), 175-186.

Williams, L., & Haley, E. (2017). *Before the five stages were the FOUR stages of grief.* https://whatsyourgrief.com/bowlby-four-stages-of-grief/

CHAPTER 9
Counseling Women through Motherhood

CAPRI BROOKS, PH.D., SARAH KITCHENS, PH.D., & SUMMER KUBA, PH.D.

"There's no way to be a perfect mother and a million ways to be a good one."
~Jill Churchill

"As a mother comforts her child, so will I comfort you;
and you will be comforted over Jerusalem." (Isaiah 66:13, NIV)

Wisdom from Above: Standing in His Grace

© Veronika_Decart/Shutterstock.com

One of the best examples of motherhood in Scripture is Mary, the mother of Jesus. Throughout her journey, we see examples of unwavering obedience, love of family, trust, vibrant prayer, and total dependence upon the Lord. All mothers can identify with the desirability of these traits. In the first chapter of the gospel of Luke, Mary was described as "highly favored" and "blessed among women." She was chosen by God to be the mother of the Kings of Kings, and the angel reassured her that "the Lord is with you." She was given the amazing task of being the mother of the Messiah, the very Son of God…no pressure at all! Despite what had to be incredible stress, Mary handled her calling with grace and humility by willingly answering God's call with "I am the Lord's servant," and "May your word to me be fulfilled." Her special call no doubt came with many challenges, but she did not stop to think them over or take time to consider her options. Instead, she modeled immediate obedience to God's calling in the midst of uncertainty.

CHAPTER LEARNING OBJECTIVES

Upon completing this chapter, you should be able to:

- Define infertility and miscarriage and evaluate the impact on women
- Recall facts about foster-care and adoption
- Recognize the psychological impact of pregnancy, childbirth, and postpartum depression
- Identify varying parenting styles and family structures
- Investigate evidenced-based treatment options while also incorporating Biblical insights

In Luke 1:39-42, Mary went to visit her cousin Elizabeth who was also expecting a child. She maintained focus on her family rather than simply her own personal challenges. Elizabeth attested to the strength of Mary's character during this time in Luke 1:42 (*New International Bible,* 1973/2011): "In a loud voice she exclaimed: 'Blessed are you among women, and blessed is the child you will bear!'" We also see Mary's value of prayer in Luke 1:46-55 which provides a magnificent example of the necessity of praying and praising God during times of trial. Shortly after the birth of Jesus, Mary began to care for him and his needs: "and she gave birth to her firstborn, a son. She wrapped him in cloths and placed him in a manager, because there was no guest room available for them" (*New International Bible,* 1973/2011, Luke 2:7). Furthermore, In Luke 2:22-24, Mary dedicated Jesus to the Lord as evidence that she was surrendering to God's plan for her baby. That attitude of surrender would mark Mary's guidance of her son Jesus the rest of his life (Luke 2:41, 4:16).

Mary's unconditional love for her son would go the very end of his life. John 19:25 (*New International Bible,* 1973/2011) reads, "Near the cross of Jesus stood his mother…" Her presence by her son's side in the hardest moments of his life shows the never-ending love and support of a mother. She did not abandon him or leave when things were difficult, rather she stood by him in the worst of times. Mary's life is truly a picture of a mother's love and devotion to both God and her child.

CHAPTER OVERVIEW

Being a mother is often considered one of the most rewarding experiences of a woman's life. Psalm 127:3-5, *New American Standard Bible* (1960/1995) states: "Behold, children are a gift of the Lord, the fruit of the womb is a reward. Like arrows in the hand of a warrior, so are the children of one's youth. How blessed is the man whose quiver is full of them; they will not be asked when they speak with their enemies in the gate". Although motherhood is a blessing, it can become "all too easily idealized" (Loewen, 2016, p. 32). This idealization leads to misconceptions about motherhood that ultimately shape the thinking, whether conscious or unconscious, of women. One of the most common misconceptions is that when a woman becomes a mother, she becomes an instant expert on all things regarding her child and motherhood. While there are instances where mothering comes naturally, there is a learning curve for many. The reality is that mothering often comes with daily challenges that may lead women into counseling. As such, counselors have a unique opportunity to assist women with the various challenges they may face. This chapter gives an overview of various issues mothers face regarding infertility (a woman's inability to become pregnant after having unprotected intercourse for at least a period of one year), miscarriage, pregnancy, postpartum, adoption (the process by which a person takes legal permanent custody of a child not biologically born to them) , fostering (a temporary arrangement where adults provide care for a child or children whose biological parents are unable to care for them), parenting, and balancing work and home life.

INFERTILITY AND MISCARRIAGE

© Lopolo/Shutterstock.com

Infertility is typically defined as a woman's inability to become pregnant after having unprotected intercourse for at least a period of one year (Clinton & Langberg, 2011; Vetriselvi & Kalavathi, 2013). Secondary Infertility is a woman's inability to become pregnant after previously giving birth (Coddington, 2017). It is estimated that in the United States approximately 6% of married women aged 15 to 44 are faced with infertility while approximately 12% of women in this same age range have difficulty getting pregnant and staying pregnant (The Centers for Disease Control and Prevention [CDC], 2019). Miscarriage (the loss of pregnancy in a woman up to twenty-three weeks) is typically defined as the loss of pregnancy in women up to twenty-three weeks (Mutiso et al., 2018). It is estimated that approximately 10-15% of all pregnancies end in miscarriage (Mutiso et al., 2018) and approximately one in four women will experience miscarriage during the first trimester (Rogers et al., 2019).

> "There is virtually no area of our existence that remains untouched when baby hunger makes its unwelcomed entrance." (Forbus, 2011, p. 2)

Recurrent miscarriage (two or more miscarriages) is defined as two or more miscarriages (American College of Obstetricians and Gynecologists, 2015). There are numerous causal factors and treatments of infertility and miscarriage. However, emotional impacts can extend well beyond the physical treatments. Women struggling with infertility and miscarriage often experience shame, depression, anxiety, social isolation, grief, and jealousy (Kalu, 2019; Markin, 2016; Ramamurthi et al., 2016). Beth Forbus (2011) sums up the totality of the effects of such trauma in that "infertility causes crisis in so many areas of our lives" (p. 2). She goes on to write that "there is virtually no area of our existence that remains untouched when baby hunger makes its unwelcomed entrance" (Forbus, 2011, p. 2).

Psychological Factors

There are numerous psychological factors facing women who experience infertility and miscarriage. Infertility is often considered a major crisis and has a considerable impact on a person's quality of life (Vetriselvi & Kalavathi, 2013). Women facing infertility experience many different feelings. Oftentimes they are ashamed of their condition, experience guilt that they cannot become pregnant, and blame themselves for their lack of fertility (Kalu, 2019; Markin, 2016). They may feel inferior to those around them who can have children and sometimes even fear being stigmatized (Ried & Alfred, 2013; Vetriselvi & Kalavathi, 2013). Furthermore, feelings of stress, anxiety, and depression are common (Luk & Loke, 2015; Nieuwenhuis et al., 2009), as well as deep emotional feelings of sadness, disappointment, and grief (Kalu, 2019; Sohr-Preston et al., 2018). Women who deal with miscarriage often experience similar negative emotions including guilt, isolation, shame, anxiety and depression (Bardos et al., 2015; Randolph et al., 2015). Such feelings are often perpetuated due to the cultural standards of silence and minimization of pregnancy loss (Rogers et al., 2019). Moreover, grief from pregnancy loss differs from other types of grief. Women who lose a child to miscarriage grieve the loss of a dream of who a child would be and what they would become just as much as the physical loss of the child (Betz & Thorngren, 2006; Gerber-Epstein et al., 2008). "In times of crisis, we must grapple with the fact that we are called to trust the God who sometimes, at least for a time, says 'No'" (Forbus, 2011, p. 4). God understands this pain and provides comfort: "When doubt filled my mind, your comfort gave me renewed hope and cheer" (*New Living Bible*, 1996, Psalm 94:19).

> "In times of crisis, we must grapple with the fact that we are called to trust the God who sometimes, at least for a time, says 'No.'"
> (Forbus, 2011, p. 4)

Other Factors

The myriad of feelings associated with infertility are not only related to women but can also affect both partners. The stressors related to infertility can cause anxiety and discord in marriage, including issues with intimacy, sexual satisfaction and sexual functioning (Lu & Loke, 2019; Luk & Loke, 2016; Drosdzol & Skrzypulec, 2009; Greil, 1997). In addition, women facing infertility may feel social and cultural pressure. Expectations of family and friends to have a baby can lead to avoiding social events, which in turn can lead to feelings of isolation (Loke et al., 2012). Also, there is a general lack of knowledge about miscarriage in American culture (Reiheld, 2015) that likely perpetuates the silence surrounding the topic (Sohr-Preston et al., 2018).

Furthermore, religion and spirituality can have a great impact on how women face their journey (Roudsari et al., 2007). Some women dealing with infertility find comfort in spirituality and religion and look to God for meaning during the struggle (Greil et al., 1989; Roudsari et al., 2007).

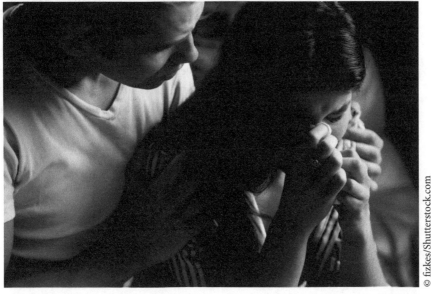

© fizkes/Shutterstock.com

However, others look to God as someone to blame for the struggle they are facing. Religious beliefs may also bring about turmoil in determining medical procedures and confronting religious objections from others (Hynie & Burns, 2006; Klitzman, 2018). As a result, women are often led to remain secretive about their medical choices related to infertility. Thus, while spiritual and religious focus may help women cope, it can also create internal conflict and limit treatment options (Klitzman, 2018). The impact of faith and religion on an individual should be considered to fully understand their infertility journey (Thorn, 2009). Perhaps no one in Scripture had a journey of faith and infertility as unique as Abraham's wife, Sarah.

Sarah's Journey

The first account of infertility in the Bible is found in the book of Genesis and centers on a couple named Abraham and Sarah. Scripture communicates that Sarah was "childless because she was not able to conceive" (*New International Bible*, 1973/2011, Genesis 11:30). Despite the many generations that have come and gone since Sarah's struggles, many of the same thoughts and emotions apply to women struggling with infertility today. In Genesis 21:2, *New International Bible* (1973/2011) "Sarah became pregnant and bore a son to Abraham in his old age, at the very time God had promised him." Sarah's journey is one that ends the way she always wanted it to – with a little baby boy. However, not every longing couple is blessed with the same result. The path of infertility is long and hard, but what God shows us through Abraham and Sarah's struggle is that He is faithful to walk right beside His people through their struggles. He has a faithful promise and plan for all His children, even if those plans are different from those we would make for ourselves. The critical requirements for women walking through trials such as infertility are to submit every day to the Lord's will and to trust in His plans. The road may be hard, even seemingly unbearable, but God is faithful and worthy to be trusted.

Infertility and Miscarriage

Emily P. Meyer

© David Meyer

Emily P. Meyer is a writer, based out of Virginia, where she lives happily with her husband, miracle baby son, and their sweet dog. She writes about finding hope in the unexpected picture of you at www.emilypmeyer.com.

Like a majority of women, I've longed to be a mother for as long as I can remember. My story of motherhood was not as simple as I had hoped. My story included a diagnosis with Polycystic Ovarian Syndrome (PCOS), taking fertility drugs and unsuccessful (expensive) fertility treatments, and finally being told after more testing for both my husband and me that it would be nearly impossible for us to have a biological child. In the midst of processing all of this, I tried to celebrate with others for their joyful news and deflect questions from loved ones trying to pry into our very tender circumstances.

Two years after we were told this and were actively pursuing adoption, I was at a routine yearly appointment with my OBGYN. The pregnancy test they had me take at the beginning of the appointment was unexpectedly declared positive by the end of my appointment. We were shocked. The impossible had happened. We were elated. However, about 40 days later, we were grieving as the ultrasound told us that there was no heartbeat. After we passed through the waiting room and went to the exam room, the doctor came in, leaned against the wall and said, "It isn't fair. It just isn't fair." I felt the need to say something. I thought it was for him and that I was bravely not wasting my platform for Christ. But in actuality, I needed the truth preached from God's Word even if it was from my own lips. "No, it isn't fair," I responded. "But the Lord gives and the Lord takes away. My heart will choose to say, 'Blessed be the name of the Lord.'"

After a second ultrasound, I was given medication to deliver my baby at home. For eight hours, I labored with contractions (even at 8-9 weeks gestation) and delivered our precious baby's body. In the background, my husband had a live stream of the Tower Bridge in London. It gave me hope for tomorrow as I cried out, "God help me!" between contractions. I needed to know it was tomorrow some-where and that I would get there, too. For some reason, the name of my great grandfather, whom I had never met was impressed on my heart: "Manuel Elias." I looked up the meaning of his name and knew beyond a shadow of a doubt that was to be this baby's name. His name means "*God is with us*" and "*Jehovah is God.*" A week later, my husband and I privately buried our baby under a rose bush in our backyard, with our dog standing guard as we sang "Amazing Grace" ever so softly and read from Isaiah 65:20, *English Standard Bible*, (2001), "No more shall there be an infant who lives but a few days."

People have often asked me through the years what I needed during my times of infertility and miscarriage. Both seasons were difficult, and the season that followed for the year after our miscarriage made it especially difficult to get out of bed every day.

What I needed most during our longest stretch (7 years!) of infer-tility was for people to honor me as a woman with purpose and not pressure me in the mom department. The deepest moments of pain occurred when people either pried, asking when we were going to have a baby or if we even wanted one. It was as if it never crossed their minds that we might be silently suffering. God was doing a work in our own hearts to help us navigate through that season of profound uncertainty and anxiety.

Many of these instances of pain overlapped with our season of mis-carriage. Many insensitive (no matter how well meaning) questions and comments were offered that dug at the scabs of our wounds. I also had to come to terms with how I would answer the question, "So, do you have any kids?" Even now, years later with a miracle child in my arms, Mother's Day is still a tender day because I remem-ber so well the ache of our hearts during those seasons and I think about the little one I won't get to hold until Heaven one day. One baby does not solve the ache of the loss of another baby. Each life has a unique purpose and has been fearfully and wonderfully made. If we are going to be pro-life as Christians, this is something we all need to embrace a little more. A life is a life. A loss is a loss. Even so, once we shared what we were going through with fertility problems and the loss of a child, we did experience more empathy. The biggest things that helped during this season were times of space to process our loss, people bringing meals during the first week of the miscarriage, reading books by others who have experienced such loss, talking with a trusted few —some who had been in our shoes, some who we were just doing life with — about the rawness of it all, having something on the calendar to actually show up for to prompt me to get out of the bed every day, and going to a Christian counselor.

Through my time in counseling, I have been reminded of the hope and promise of Psalm 139:16 (*New International Bible,* 1973/2011) over and over, "Your eyes saw my unformed body; all the days ordained for me were written in your book before one of them came to be." My first baby's life was given purpose for all of the some 45 days God ordained for him before he was ever even made. And his purpose lives on, even with him in Heaven with Jesus, because as his mother, I continue to give dignity to the life he had and to let God redeem our story of loss into one of sharing the same comfort from Christ that we received with others who are going through a similar loss. Counseling gave me a safe place to start working through this loss and to realize that there were other areas of my life that I needed to process as well. Having the tender, listening ear of my counselor always pointing me back to the truth and hope of God's Word, not in a preachy way, but a gentle way was one of the greatest tools for processing my pain.

My greatest encouragement for anyone who is going through infertility and/or miscarriage is this: God sees, God hears, and God remembers. Even if you do finally experience the miracle of a baby in your arms, there is still the reality of the loss you have experienced. God never intended for us to experience such loss, but because sin entered the world, things broke. It's ok to curse the darkness. It's ok to acknowledge the shadows. And, it's ok to bless the light. Jesus is with you through it all. He is Emmanuel. And He will guide you through it all with a compassion and empathy that no one else can because He knows you and loves you better than anyone else ever could.

ADOPTION AND FOSTERING

Adoption and foster care are both a means for women to become mothers. Adoption is the process by which a person takes legal permanent custody of a child not biologically born to them (Adoption Center, n.d.) while fostering is a temporary arrangement where adults provide care for a child or children whose biological parents are unable to care for them (Adoption Center, n.d.). Foster care, a temporary arrangement where adults provide care for a child/children whose biological parents are unable to care for them, may be either informal or arranged through a court order or a social service agency with the end goal being reunification with the birth family (Adoption Center, n.d.). Children who are unable to be reunited with their birth family may be placed for adoption if it is ruled that it is in the child's best interest (Adoption Center, n.d.). Approximately 135,000 children are adopted in the United States each year and one out of every 25 families in the United States have an adopted child (Adoption Network, 2019; Fogle, 2018).

Approximately 135,000 children are adopted in the United States each year (Adoption Network, 2019).

For many mothers, fostering and/or adoption is part of their journey into motherhood and for some, it represents their only chance of becoming a mother. Moth-

© Yuriy Golub/Shutterstock.com

ers may decide to adopt or foster for a variety of reasons including infertility, feeling as though they may be saving a child, lack of an appropriate partner, or a stepparent adopting their spouse's biological child (Mental Help, n.d.). Through adoption, dreams of having a child become reality. Adoption and foster care are a reflection of God's love. The Bible tells us in James 1:27 (*New International Bible*, 1973/2011) that true religion is taking care of orphans: "Religion that God our Father accepts as pure and faultless is this: to look after orphans and widows in their distress and to keep oneself from being polluted by the world."

© SewCream/Shutterstock.com

Mothers experience a variety of feelings as they journey through this process. While adoption and foster care can be a joyous time for many mothers, there are also challenges. Depending on the reason behind this choice, these challenges can be significant. If a mother has been facing infertility or repeated miscarriages that leads them into fostering or adoption, they may experience feelings of guilt, shame, inadequacy, loss of control, and even jealousy of others who have been able to have biological children (Goldberg et al., 2009; Kupecky & Anderson, 2001, as cited in Child Welfare Information Gateway, 2015). During this process, mothers may also face many challenging life-changing decisions that can be both stressful and exciting (Child Welfare Information Gateway, 2015).

Once the foster placement is made or the adoption is complete, mothers face stresses similar to biological mothers. Post-placement/post-adoption depression may occur for mothers due to the realities of parenthood, including lack of sleep and the weight of parental responsibilities (Child Welfare Information Gateway, 2015). In addition, many adoptive or foster mothers struggle with their new identity while also trying to dedicate time to develop a bond between them and their new child. While fostering or adoption allows women to have an impact on the lives of children in a significant way, it can be difficult for foster mothers to give their heart and develop strong bonds with children who may either be in their life for only a short time or who are not biologically their own (Child Welfare Information Gateway, 2016). These feelings of uncertainty and guilt may cause women to experience significant stress and anxiety leading them to seek counseling.

Pregnancy, Childbirth, and Postpartum

29% of children will spend at least three years in foster care and six percent of children have been in foster care for five or more years (Adoption Network, 2019).

© Kaya Shelest/Shutterstock.com

Pregnancy is one of the most pivotal times in a mother's life. It is filled with physical, emotional, and interpersonal changes and often involves a great deal of stress (Kopala & Keitel, 2003). Many women experience psychosocial stress during this time which can have negative outcomes for both the baby and mother (Woods et al., 2010; Witt et al., 2014; Su et al., 2015). During pregnancy, women also experience some physiological changes that often involve changes in sleep, digestion, appetite, weight gain, and mood; such changes are expected to be managed while balancing the stress of work and family demands (Kopala & Keitel, 2003) and dealing with financial strains and role changes (Baffour et al., 2009; DiPietro et al., 2004; DiPietro et al., 2015). "Individuals deal with stress in different ways, and how a woman views her pregnancy and its concomitant physiological and psychosocial challenges will determine to a great extent how adaptive she will be to the circumstances she encounters" (Kopala & Keitel, 2003, p. 258). This is important because approximately 10-25% of pregnant women deal with stress and depression related to pregnancy (Accortt et al., 2015).

While some women have a wonderful experience with childbirth, others can be traumatized by the process (Baston et al., 2015). In either case, there are potential physical, psychological and social impacts (Held, 1989). Research indicates that women can suffer from a range of psychological problems during this time (Kennedy et al., 2002). Among these are situations in which women experience traumatic childbirth and feel a lack or loss of control (Baston et al., 2015). Furthermore, if new mothers are unable to cope with the resulting stresses of the experience after a one-month period, they may actually suffer from "postnatal posttraumatic stress disorder" (Beck, 2004; Grekin & O'Hara, 2014). Finally, it is important to remember that a mother's perception of the traumatic event may be different from that of the doctor. In this scenario, her perception becomes reality and must be addressed (Beck, 2004).

Depression is not uncommon surrounding pregnancy and childbirth. However, the degree of depressive symptoms varies widely (Kopala & Keitel, 2003). There are three main types of depressive conditions associated with pregnancy and childbirth. The first is postpartum blues or baby blues. Baby blues affect approximately 50% of women after childbirth (Clinton & Trent, 2009).

> Approximately 10-25%
> of pregnant women deal
> with stress and depression
> (Accortt et al., 2015).

Symptoms typically begin soon after birth, continue for up to a week and include being overly emotional, tearful, and experiencing loss of appetite (Clinton & Trent, 2009). The Mayo Clinic provides a further inclusive list of signs and symptoms: "Mood swings, anxiety, sadness, irritability, feeling overwhelmed, crying, reduced concentration, appetite problems, and trouble sleeping" (2018, Baby Blues section, para. 1). The most common of the depressive episodes is peripartum or postpartum depression which affects between 10% and 15% of mothers (Miller, 2002). This diagnosable depression is defined by the *Diagnostic and Statistical Manual of Mental Disorders* (5th ed.; *DSM-5*; American Psychiatric Association, 2013) as a major depressive episode or major depression that can be qualified as peripartum when onset occurs during pregnancy or within 4 weeks of delivery. However, The American College of Obstetricians and Gynecologists (ACOG) notes that perinatal depression can occur within 12 months of delivery (2018). These symptoms may interfere with a mother's ability to care for her baby, and symptoms may include:

> Depressed mood or severe mood swings, Excessive crying, Difficulty bonding with your baby, Withdrawing from family and friends, Loss of appetite or eating much more than usual, Inability to sleep (insomnia) or sleeping too much, Overwhelming fatigue or loss of energy, Reduced interest and pleasure in activities you used to enjoy, Intense irritability and anger, Fear that you're not a good mother, Hopelessness, Feelings of worthlessness, shame, guilt or inadequacy, Diminished ability to think clearly, concentrate or make decisions, Restlessness, Severe anxiety and panic attacks, Thoughts of harming yourself or your baby, and Recurrent thoughts of death or suicide. (Mayo Clinic, 2018, Postpartum Depression section, para. 2)

Postpartum psychosis is a rare disorder that affects one to two women out of every one thousand women giving birth (Clinton & Trent, 2009). It is characterized by severe symptoms of "confusion and disorientation, obsessive thoughts about the baby, hallucinations and delusions, sleep disturbances, excessive energy and agitation, paranoia, and attempts to harm yourself or your baby" (Mayo Clinic, 2018, Postpartum Psychosis section, para. 1). Unfortunately, many symptoms of postpartum depression often go unnoticed during and after pregnancy (Clinton, & Trent, 2009; Murray & Cooper, 1997). However, such struggles do not go unnoticed by God, "God remembers those who suffer; he does not forget their cry" (Psalm 9:12, *Good News Bible, 1976*). Scripture also promises hope in Psalm 43:5 (*New American Standard Bible*, 1960/1995) "Why are you in despair, O my soul? And why are you disturbed within me? Hope in God, for I shall again praise Him, the help of my countenance and my God."

> There are three types of depressive conditions that are common during and after pregnancy: baby blues, peripartum or postpartum depression and postpartum psychosis (Clinton & Trent, 2009).

FAMILY STRUCTURE

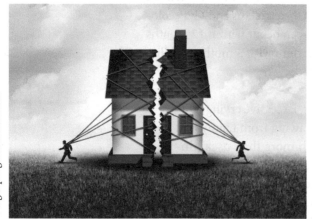

© Lightspring/Shutterstock.com

The complexities related to family structure must also be considered when counseling women. Unfortunately, God's plan for the family unit has been subverted and shifted by man to a much less stable structure, namely through the rise of the popularity of divorce. Divorce is much more socially acceptable today than ever, which results in fewer two-parent households (Dugan, 2017). For example, in the early 60's, 73% of children were living in a home with their two married parents whereas today, less than 46% of children live with two married parents (American Psychological Association, n.d.-b).

Divorce has significant effects on women, leaving them with higher rates of depression, anxiety, and self-esteem issues (Barnhart et al., 2018; Clinton & Langberg, 2011; Liang et al., 2019). The complexity of divorce intensifies for women when children are involved, especially when they are left to carry the full financial and emotional burden of raising children on their own in a single-parent home (Leahy-Warren et al., 2012). Single mothers make up 12% of households in America, and, when caring for children on their own, their views of motherhood may become distorted due to lack of support (Barnhart et al., 2018; Clinton & Langberg, 2011). As mother's navigate the intricacies of motherhood through these emotionally taxing times, they may seek counseling to navigate their changing world and deal with unmet social and emotional needs (Barnhart et al., 2018; Clinton & Langberg, 2011; Liang et al., 2019).

© Lapina/Shutterstock.com

According to the Centers for Disease Control and Prevention (2016), the divorce rate is actually declining in the United States and has dropped approximately 18% in the last 10 years. Along with the decline in divorce numbers there is also a decline in the number of marriages due to couples choosing cohabitation over marriage. It is estimated that 1 in 4 parents are unmarried but cohabitating (Livingston, 2018). Although divorce was not part of God's divine plan, there is an offering of grace, hope, restoration and healing when divorce happens. "I will give you back your health and heal your wounds," says the Lord" (*New International Bible*, 1973/2011, Jeremiah 30:17).

There are approximately 43.5 million mothers, between the ages of 15 and 50, in the United States who have given birth to approximately 96 million children (U.S. Census Bureau, 2017).

PARENTING STYLES

As we begin to define parenting and outline the four parenting styles, it is important to remember that the word parent, *in this section*, is synonymous with mother and parenting with mothering. With that said, the definition of parenting has evolved over the years, and with the accelerated pace of modern life, it is becoming almost impossible to define. According to Meyers (2018), parents are faced with a list of unrealistic expectations, among which are to "not only attend to, but anticipate, their child's every need, orchestrate their child's academic success, provide their child with all the best experiences and most useful activities, and make home an oasis of peace and harmony for the family" (para. 1). Modern day parenting has become more about what society deems as valuable, important, and moral (Medina & Magnuson, 2009). As such, teaching Christian values is increasingly delegated to Sunday morning church services rather than the home. Unfortunately, esteeming God above all else is oftentimes devalued, and, despite the charge of Deuteronomy 6:6-9 to teach children Godly values in the home, the priorities of society and the secular world take precedence.

Baumrind (1966), the pioneer of parenting research, defined three parenting styles (authoritative, authoritarian, and permissive) and also noticed that they had an impact on the behavior of children (Baumrind, 1966, 1967, 1971). His work led other researchers to define what we now know as the four key parenting styles: authoritative, authoritarian, permissive, and uninvolved (Baumrind, 1966, 1967, 1971, 1989, 1991; Maccoby & Martin, 1983). These parenting styles demonstrate how parents express love, exercise authority, and deal with their child's needs. Furthermore, each of the four styles are classified as either responsive or unresponsive, demanding or undemanding and have implications on the outcome of children's lives (Baumrind, 1991; Berk, 2001).

CONCEPT TO CONTEMPLATE

© Asier Romero/Shutterstock.com

Proverbs 13:24, *English Standard Bible* (2001) states, "Whoever spares the rod hates his son, but he who loves him is diligent to discipline him." How do you interpret the meaning of 'discipline' in this verse?

Authoritative Parenting

The first parenting style is authoritative parenting. Authoritative parenting is the most highly recommended and effective style and is defined as the style of parenting which allows for a child's emotional needs to be met while also setting and maintaining standards by which to live (Kuppens et al., 2019). Demands in this style are high, yet reasonable, and expectations are both clear and consistent (Larzelere et al., 2013). **Emotional responsiveness** (the degree that parents are sensitive and accepting to their child's developmental and emotional needs) is evident through love and support (Kuppens et al., 2019), and discipline is firm, fair, and consistent rather than punitive (Ingram, 2006). The authoritative parent is flexible and welcomes open communication when solving problems (Morin, 2019). These characteristics have the potential to lead to more mature children who are resilient and optimistic and who have greater self-esteem, social competence and academic achievement (Kuppens et al., 2019). This parenting style is reflected in 1 Peter 5:3 with the instructions to be "examples to the flock" instead of being domineering "over those in your charge."

© Yuganov Konstantin/Shutterstock.com

> Parental responsiveness is a predictor of social competence and psychosocial functioning (Poon et al., 2017).

Authoritarian Parenting

Unlike the authoritative parent, the authoritarian parent is far more domineering (Larzelere et al., 2013). This style is often defined by a 'tough love' type of parenting with rigidity being prevalent. These parents typically have a "because I said so" type of response to their children (Morin, 2019). Parents with an authoritarian style have placed extremely high, even unrealistic, expectations on their children (Ingram, 2006). While they tend to want what is best for their child, they provide very little in regards to nurturing or positive feedback and also inflict punishment (not discipline) for misbehavior as well as innocent mistakes (Kuppens et al., 2019; Morin, 2019). Discipline is described as punitive and often presents moral conflict for Christian mothers who "spare the road, spoil the child" as they navigate God's word in regards to parenting. Proverbs 13:24 (*New International*

© wavebreakmedia/Shutterstock.com

Bible, 1973/2011) states, "Whoever spares the rod hates their children, but the one who loves their children is careful to discipline them."

Parents often ask, "Does God intend for this passage to be taken literally?" In response to this question, it is important to remember Paul's warning to the Ephesians not to raise children who would reject the faith completely (Ephesians 6:4). Although the strictest environments may be thought of as the most effective way to train a child, this is not necessarily the case. Research shows that children raised with this type of parenting are not necessarily better behaved or more successful (Hoeve et al., 2008). In actuality, it may be the exact opposite as children present with more aggressive and delinquent behaviors as well as anxiety and negative developmental outcomes (Hoeve et al., 2008; Kuppens et al., 2018). Power struggles between adults and children often begin to surface as children rebel against such oppressive authority.

Permissive Parenting

Unlike authoritarian parenting, permissive parenting is the least rigid of the four parenting styles (American Psychological Association, n.d.-a; Baumrind, 1966, 1967, 1971, 1989, 1991; Maccoby & Martin, 1983). Permissive parents expect very little from their children and are often

© New Africa/Shutterstock.com

heard saying, "kids will be kids" (Morin, 2019). They are loving and responsive to their child's needs, yet do not impose discipline. Rather, bribery is employed as a means to foster positive behavior (Kuppens et al., 2019). The lack of consistency and structure lead to a friendship type of relationship as opposed to a parent-child relationship (Morin, 2019). When permissive parenting is used, children oftentimes display more aggressive behavior, less emotional understanding, are less mature than their peers, and struggle in decision-making and problem-solving (American Psychological Association, n.d.a; Hoeve et al., 2008).

Uninvolved Parenting

Finally, uninvolved parenting, albeit included as a parenting style, is ultimately defined by the lack thereof. It is often referred to as neglectful parenting and is the most detrimental of all the parenting styles (Hoskins, 2014; Maccoby & Martin, 1983). Uninvolved parents allow children to lead themselves with little to no guidance in any area of life (Ingram, 2006). Uninvolved parenting is low in both responsiveness and demandingness (the degree that parents demand the maturity of their child or are controlling of their child's behavior) and has significant negative effects on children (Hoeve et al., 2008). It can lead to feelings of rejection as well as depression, anxiety, low self-esteem, poor academic competence, inability to self-regulate and antisocial behavior (American Psychological Association, n.d.).

© Marcos Mesa Sam Wordley/Shutterstock.com

TABLE 9.1

Characteristics of Parenting Styles

	Authoritarian	Authoritative	Permissive	Uninvolved
Parent Demandingness	High, Lacks flexibility	Reasonable	Set but not followed	None
Discipline	Punitive Punishment	Consistent	Bribery	None
Control	Must obey authority	Encourages autonomy	Indulgent	Indifferent
Parent Responsiveness	Cold	Warm/Nurturing	Warm/Nurturing	Aloof/Neglectful
Child's Typical Response	Power struggle	Cooperative	Demanding	Attention Seeking

Mothering (parenting) brings with it uncertainty, worry and self-doubt even when Biblical principles are applied. Listen to one mother's story about how she purposefully chose authoritative parenting rooted in Bib-

© Carson Hatch

lical values and also prayed without ceasing but still faced battles. This is a clear example of how women must not lose sight of their blessings but embrace what God is teaching them through their battles while also recognizing that despite their best efforts, there will be times when children choose to go their own way and veer from the path their mother modeled for them. Carol Mularski, mother of two and pastor's wife states (C. Mularski, personal communication, November 13, 2019),

> My advice for all the mothers out there is this, pray about everything, and worry about nothing. The bigger your faith, the smaller your worries. God provides a way daily for us to live above the cares of this world and not focus on what can't be or what might never change. Even when things don't look good, God is good and He is always working all things out for the good, and that includes the good of our children. After all, He loves our kids more than we do!

Balancing Work and Mothering

A common theme in motherhood is guilt. **Mom guilt** (feelings of guilt and uncertainty when mothers worry they may be not meeting expectations) can strike at any time and can happen for a variety of reasons related

© MicroOne/Shutterstock.com

to motherhood and everyday life. Often, mothers are triggered with guilt as they grapple with such decisions as whether to breastfeed or bottle feed, use cloth diapers or disposable, work full time, part time or stay at home completely. Mothers may also feel guilty because they feel they are too strict, not strict enough, put their kids to bed too early or too late, feed them unhealthy food, yell too much, lack quality time together, and a myriad of other subjects.

Collier (n.d., What is Mom Guilt" section) states "Mom guilt is the feeling of guilt, doubt, anxiousness or uncertainty by mothers when they worry they're failing or falling short of expectations in some way". Mom guilt develops when mothers compare themselves both with others (Collier, n.d.) and with expectations established from society, media, family and friends (Mihalich-Levin, 2017). The choices mothers make regarding various facets of life can create a feeling that they are not doing enough or that they could do better (Lindholm, 2019a). Mihalich-Levin (2017) suggests mom guilt, as well as the feelings, thoughts and behaviors associated with guilt, may be displayed through depression, anxiety, negative thoughts, overuse of social media, overworking, overscheduling, addictive behaviors, and perfectionism. When contemplating "mom guilt" the following Scripture may offer, comfort, "But he said to me, 'My grace is sufficient for you, for my power is made perfect in weakness.' Therefore I will boast all the more gladly about my weaknesses, so that Christ's power may rest on me" (*New International Bible*, 1973/2011, 2 Corinthians 12:9). Likewise, we are invited to take comfort in the idea of God's care. Consider 1 Peter 5:7 (*New International Bible*, 1973/2011) which indicates, "Cast all your anxiety on him because he cares for you."

> "Mom guilt is the feeling of guilt, doubt, anxiousness or uncertainty by mothers when they worry they're failing or falling short of expectations in some way."
> (Collier, n.d.)

TABLE 9.2

Characteristics of Mom Guilt

Moms who struggle with *depression and anxiety* may be filled with constant worry, stress, exhaustion, anger, low self-worth, etc.
Moms who struggle with *negative thoughts* are often saying things to herself like: "I am a bad mom." "My child's behavior is my fault." "I am neglecting my child by going to work."
Moms who are addicted to *social media* are constantly engaged in social media attempting to showcase they're a "good mom" while comparing themselves to everyone else.
Moms who *overdo, overwork, and overschedule* often have a "more is better" mentality. They are involved in everything and constantly exhausted. This leads to burnout.
Moms who struggle with *addictive behaviors* may turn to substances such as alcohol, drugs, overspending, overeating, etc.
Moms who struggle with *perfectionism* appear to have it all together on the outside, yet she fears judgement and failure while inside she's falling apart.

Source: Mihalich-Levin, L. (2017). *What Exactly IS Mom Guilt Anyway? A Clinical Psychotherapist Explains.* https://www.mindfulreturn.com/mom-guilt/

Balancing both work and family can be a challenging task. One third of working women in the United States have children 18 years of age or younger (Lamar et al., 2019). Currently in the United States, approximately 71% of mothers work outside of the home, while 27% stay at home (U.S.

Department of Labor, 2019). There are various opinions when it comes to whether or not a mom should work outside of the home. Sixty percent of Americans believe children are better off when a parent stays at home, while 35% believe children are just as well off if both parents work (Cohn & Caumont, 2014). Some mothers may need to work because they are the sole provider of their family. Other moms struggle with high childcare costs and determining whether childcare is worth the cost. Still others may love their job and find meaning in what they do. Ultimately, no matter the opinions of others regarding childcare, each mother has to decide what is best for her family and personal circumstances.

© goodluz/Shutterstock.com

Working mothers are often expected to be successful at work while also carrying 60% to 90% of childcare and housework responsibilities (Coogan & Chen, 2007). Studies have shown conflicts arise when work and family collide to prevent mothers from fulfilling their duties both at home and at work (Lamar et al., 2019). On the home-front, moms may miss dinner, bedtime, and school activities due to obligations at work. Conversely, working moms may miss work in order to attend school conferences or to stay at home with their sick children. Lindholm (2019, para. 6) states, "one of the most psychologically destabilizing realities of modern motherhood is that we are expected to care for entire families at home, as if we don't have careers, and that our employers expect us to work in the office as if we don't have children." Lamar et al. (2019) also find mothers are more likely to experience gaps of employment or career development challenges due to motherhood and the need to care for their children. Sleep deprivation resulting from the work/home balance is also a problem for mothers and can increase depression, anxiety, stress, panic attacks and other health issues (Lindholm, 2019b). As a result, working moms may desire to seek out more flexible jobs or possibly even part-time work in order to find a better balance between family and work (Lamar et al., 2019). Finally, working mothers also face special challenges such as the possibility of unequal pay, discrimination, barriers to upward mobility, and other inappropriate behaviors such as sexual harassment, body shaming, and sexual assault (Lindholm, 2019b).

© Kaspars Grinvalds/Shutterstock.com

Working from home is a growing trend for mothers seeking to balance work and family. Currently, 3.9 million employees in the United States work from home at least part time (Reynolds, 2018). Landrum (2018) states flexibility is a top reason ninety percent of moms desire to work from home. Being a work-from-home mom allows women to both make money and contribute to the household while taking care of the children. However, working from home brings its own challenges as there is often little to no physical separation between a mom's personal and professional life. Moms may find it difficult to juggle two full time jobs (work and family) without a specific time set aside for each task.

Over the last decade there has been a rise in mothers who stay at home with their children (Cohn & Caumont, 2014). Currently, approximately 27% of moms stay at home with their children full time (U.S. Department of Labor, 2019). Stay at home mothers are often perceived to have the easy road. People may say things to such moms as, "So, what did you do all day?, "It must be so nice to get to stay home and relax all day." "It must be nice not to have to work!" However, staying at home can be isolating, and mothers may feel added pressure to both raise their children and keep up with household duties (Bean et al., 2015). Stay at home moms have also been shown to have higher levels of worry, sadness, stress, anger, and depression than those who work outside of the home (Mendes et al., 2012).

Featured Practitioner
Kristina M. Nelson, Ph.D., NCC

© Kristina Nelson

In my clinical experience, I have worked with women who struggle with challenges related to balancing work and family life, particularly those trying to balance motherhood and a career. Many women have reported wanting to "have it all," meaning being a mother and also having a career outside of their home. Although grateful for these opportunities, some women feel overextended, and physically and emotionally exhausted much of the time; never feeling like they are meeting all the expectations that they have for themselves, or that others have of them. As a result, they may also battle feelings of shame, guilt and frustration.

Finding a "balance" between work and family life is not always easy. When counseling women with such concerns, I believe it is important to recognize that "balance" is different for everyone, and it is important to gain an understanding of the system in which the client lives and works. Overall, I tend to conceptualize cases through a systemic lens; however, I intentionally and strategically choose interventions from various theoretical orientations to help meet the needs of each individual client.

From a family systems theoretical approach to counseling, clients may explore family roles, patterns, and beliefs that have shaped their perspective about both family and career, and thus, better understand their experience. As a result, they may begin to restructure their own system to help achieve the "balance" they desire. Additionally, an Existential approach to counseling can help clients examine the significance and meaning in their life regarding both family and career. Some clients have reported searching for their purpose, and God's purpose, in their role(s) within their family unit as well as their career, which some feel "called" to do. When clients examine and identify the significance and meaning in their various roles, they may be able to obtain peace about their choices or begin the process of recreating themselves, leading to the balance between work and family that they have sought to achieve.

While some clients enjoy the process of exploring generational influences in their life, or searching for meaning, others desire specific suggestions or steps to help them achieve balance. One approach that I have found to be particularly useful is helping clients to strategically establish boundaries with their time; allowing for family, work, and much needed self-care time in their daily or weekly schedule. This process usually requires some flexibility and frequent restructuring of one's schedule before establishing the desired balance.

There are various counseling theories and interventions that may be helpful to address issues and concerns related to trying to achieve balance between work and family life. Regardless of the theoretical approach, it is important to intentionally and strategically incorporate appropriate interventions that will best meet the needs of our clients. Having a thorough understanding of the whole person as well as the system in which they live and work can help the counselor better understand how to help their client.

COUNSELING MOTHERS

Women present with complex needs due to the social and cultural shifts that have taken place over the last decade. As they journey through modern motherhood, the need for support is crucial which may be what ultimately leads mothers into counseling. It is extremely beneficial for mothers to connect with those who can empathize with their struggles (Lamar et al., 2019). Emotional support is also very important during trying times, and counselors are in a position to provide full emotional support (Vetriselvi & Kalavathi, 2013). The counseling process can help mothers feel less alone and empower them to find solutions to deal with the various challenges they face (Lindholm, 2019).

Lamar et al. (2019) encourage counselors to remain unbiased and to refrain from stereotypical gender roles while working with mothers. As mothers strive to understand their role, societal expectations should be confronted rather than ignored through the counseling process (Lamar et al., 2019). By confronting unrealistic expectations, counselors can then help mothers deal with misconceptions directly. Counselors can help bring awareness to expectations placed on mothers from the client themselves and the culture around them. Once these misconceptions are exposed, counselors can incorporate Biblical truths. By turning to God's Word, one example counselors can highlight is that of Eunice, Timothy's mother. Although Eunice does not have a Biblical narrative of her own, she was commended by Paul in 2 Timothy 1:5 (*English Standard Bible,* 2001) as he said, "I am reminded of your sincere faith, a faith that dwelt first in your grandmother Lois and your mother Eunice and now, I am sure dwells in you as well." Just as Eunice prayed for her child and demonstrated unwavering faith, today's mothers must pray without ceasing and raise their children up in the way they should go. By doing so, mothers hold the course set forth in God's Word.

During the different phases of motherhood, counseling can help women work through feelings of anxiety, anger, fear, worry, sadness, depression, and shame. Person-centered therapy can be utilized to help women simply process the emotions they are feeling in different stages of their motherhood journey (Monach, 2013; Vetriselvi & Kalavathi, 2013). The use of therapeutic skills such as reflection, validation, and open-ended questions may help mothers explore their beliefs regarding parenting and their life roles (Lamar et al., 2019). In addition, Cognitive-behavioral therapy (CBT) may also be an effective approach when mothers are experiencing symptoms of depression and anxiety (Lamar et al., 2019). Second Corinthians 12:9 (*New American Standard Bible,* 1960/1995) gives hope in light of such a trial: "And he has said to me, 'My grace is sufficient for you, for power is perfected in weakness.' Most gladly, therefore, I will rather boast about my weakness, so that the power of Christ may dwell in me."

Featured Practitioner

Teshunda Hannor-Walker, PhD, LPC, NCC, CPCS
Author of *How to Raise a Successful Child with ADD*

As a therapist in private practice, I have the fortunate opportunity to work with mothers from all walks of life with various experiences.

While being a mother is one of the most rewarding experiences a woman could imagine, a mother must never forget that before she was a wife and mother, God created her first to be a woman. As women, mothers, and wives, we must intentionally cultivate (nurture) the seeds (babies, dreams, destinies) God has placed within us if we are to live out Proverbs 31:28-29, *English Standard Bible* (2001), which reads, " Her children rise up and call her blessed; her husband also, and he praises her: Many women have done excellently, but you surpass them all." Therefore, women were uniquely created to carry seeds -not just babies -within their womb. God has blessed women with the capacity to birth babies, dreams, and destinies. If we limit ourselves to motherhood only, we may never truly discover the true destiny within us as a woman. I believe we are a multi-faceted jewel with many possibilities within us (T. Hannor-Walker, personal communication, December 7, 2019).

© AE Jenkins, Jr.

CONCEPT TO CONTEMPLATE

© ImageFlow/Shutterstock.com

Women juggle multiple responsibilities and roles at the same time and often feel as if they need to do and be everything to everyone. Because of this, they may begin to experience burnout. How might you counsel a woman through a season of burnout?

CASE STUDY

Jill is a 32-year-old, married Caucasian woman with one child. After college, she started to climb the career ladder. She quickly became a very well-respected lawyer in a large firm. She worked long hours and rarely made time for social events. Jill began dating another attorney she met through her work. They quickly fell in love and were married when Jill was 29 years old. Jill continued to work hard as she and her husband decided to wait to have children. However, about a year after their decision, Jill became pregnant. She and her husband were very excited about becoming parents. She decided she would continue to work at her firm as she was very close to becoming partner. After baby Thomas was born, Jill took her scheduled maternity leave of 6 weeks and then went back to work. Once she got back to work, Jill began to experience anxiety about leaving the baby. She felt guilty for working long hours, and oftentimes only saw Thomas a couple of hours a day. She was torn between wanting to work hard at fulfilling her job responsibilities and wanting to spend time with Thomas and being present in his life. She felt guilty while at work for not being with Thomas but felt guilty for not working when she was with Thomas. The struggle felt like it would never end, and Jill's husband suggested that she seek counseling. Hesitantly, she decided something had to change and agreed to see a counselor. During the intake, Jill reported that she "cried almost every day" and "had difficulty getting to sleep at night." She also said she had been struggling with focusing on her work and that she just "feels torn all the time." She said "I feel so guilty and stressed all the time." Jill reported praying about how to balance work and home life, but feeling like she is lost and unable to figure out how to be both a good mother and a good employee.

During the initial sessions, the counselor used reflection, validation and open-ended questions to help Jill explore her beliefs about her role as a mother and employee. The counselor encouraged Jill to talk about her feelings both in and out of session, knowing that having a safe person in whom to confide could help her to not feel so alone in the journey. The therapist also worked with Jill to set some goals to help reduce the guilt she was feeling. One of these goals was that Jill would delay working after coming home each day until putting Thomas to bed for the night. This was difficult, but something Jill felt would help her focus on Thomas more during the few hours she had with him each day. The therapist also talked to Jill about balancing life with work and a baby. They made a plan that helped Jill achieve more balance in her life, including quality time with God incorporating spiritual disciplines (reading Bible, praying) to help her lean on him for wisdom and strength. She slowly began to cope more efficiently with her stress while learning to find balance in her beautiful new reality.

© ImageFlow/Shutterstock.com

What other interventions might you consider to help Jill find balance in her life? Consider which theoretical approach might be most effective in working with Jill.

CHAPTER SUMMARY

"No language can express the power and beauty and heroism of a mother's love" (Chapin, n.d., as cited in Newmarks Chicken Soup for the Soul: Messages from Heaven and Other Miracles, 2019, p 2). Motherhood is one of the most difficult yet rewarding jobs that women can have. It is a journey filled with blessings, battles, and a lifetime of learning that requires support, love and grace. As counselors work with mothers, they help them recognize the strength they possess as they journey through this uncharted territory. While facing these challenges, Scripture confirms the blessing and gift of motherhood: "Behold, children are a gift of the Lord, the fruit of the womb is a reward. Like arrows in the hand of a warrior, so are the children of one's youth. How blessed is the man whose quiver is full of them; they will not be ashamed when they speak with their enemies in the age" (*New American Standard Bible*, 1960/1995, Psalm 127:3-5).

KEY TERMS

Adoption - the process by which a person takes legal permanent custody of a child not biologically born to them

Demandingness - the degree that parents demand the maturity of their child or are controlling of their child's behavior

Emotional Responsiveness - the degree that parents are sensitive and accepting to their child's developmental and emotional needs

Fostering - a temporary arrangement where adults provide care for a child or children whose biological parents are unable to care for them

Infertility - a woman's inability to become pregnant after having unprotected intercourse for at least a period of one year

Mom Guilt - feelings of guilt and uncertainty when mothers worry they may be not meeting expectations

Miscarriage - the loss of pregnancy in a woman up to twenty-three weeks

Recurrent Miscarriage - two or more miscarriages

Secondary Infertility - a woman's inability to become pregnant after previously giving birth

SUGGESTED RESOURCES

Books

All on One Plate: Cultural Expectations on American Mothers by Solveig Brown

Balancing it All: My Story of Juggling Priorities and Purpose by Candace Cameron Bure and Dana Wilkerson

The New Dare to Discipline by James Dobson

Win at Home First: An Inspirational Guide to Work-life Balance by Cory Carlson

Loving Your Child too Much: Raising Your Kids Without Overprotecting, Overindulging, or Overcontrolling by Tim Clinton and Gary Sibcy

I Call You Mine: Embracing God's Gift of Adoption by Kimberly de Blecourt

Surviving Infertility: What the Bible says about your Baby Hunger by Beth Forbus

Love Lost: Living Beyond a Broken Marriage by David Hawkins

Adopted for Life: The Priority of Adoption for Christian Families and Churches by Russell Moore

Understanding Your Moods When You're Expecting: Emotions, Mental Health, and Happiness by Lucy Puryear

The Unseen Companion: God with the Single Mother by Michelle Senters

Taking Charge of Your Fertility by Toni Weschler

Mayo Clinic Guide to a Healthy Pregnancy (2nd ed.) by Myra Wick

Organizations

Center for Adoption Support and Education:
http://www.adoptionsupport.org

Sarah's Laughter Christian Support Group for Infertility and Child Loss:
https://www.sarahs-laughter.com/

REFERENCES

Accortt, E. E., Cheadle, A. C., & Schetter, C. D. (2015). Prenatal depression and adverse birth outcomes: An updated systematic review. *Maternal Child Health, 19*, 1306–1337. https://doi.org/10.1007/s10995-014-1637-2

Adoption Center. (n.d.). *Adoption laws.* http://www.adopt.org/adoption-laws

Adoption Network. (2019). *U.S. adoption statistics.* https://adoptionnetwork.com/adoption-statistics

American College of Obstetricians & Gynecologists. (2015, August). *Repeated miscarriages: Frequently asked questions.* https://www.acog.org/Patients/FAQs/Repeated-Miscarriages

American College of Obstetricians & Gynecologists. (2018). ACOG committee opinion No. 757: Screening for perinatal depression. *American College of Obstetricians and Gynecologists, 132*(5), e208-e212. https://doi.org/ 10.1097/AOG.0000000000002927

American Psychiatric Association. (2013). *Diagnostic and statistical manual of mental disorders* (5th ed.). https://doi.org/10.1176/appi.books.9780890425596

American Psychological Association (n.d.a). *Parenting styles.* https://www.apa.org/act/resources/fact-sheets/parenting-styles

American Psychological Association. (n.d.b). *Marriage and divorce.* https://www.apa.org/topics/divorce/

Baffour, T. D., Gourdine, R. M., Domingo, C., & Boone, K. (2009). Rural hassles and coping strategies among pregnant and parenting African American women. Families in society. *Journal of Contemporary Social Services, 90*(2), 183–188. https://doi.org/10.1606/1044-3894.3866

Ballard, M. R. (n.d.). *Daughters of God.* https://www.churchofjesuschrist.org/study/general-conference/2008/04/daughters-of-god?lang=eng

Bardos, J., Hercz, D., Friedenthal, J., Missmer, S. A., & Williams, Z. (2015). A national survey on public perceptions of miscarriage. *Obstetrics and Gynecology, 125*, 1313–1320. https://doi.org/10.1097/OG.0000000000000859

Barnhart, S., Gearhart, M. C., & Maguire-Jack, K. (2018). Perceptions of collective efficacy among single mothers: Insights for conceptualization and measurement. *Journal of Family Issues, 39*(17), 4019-4040. https://doi.org/10.1177/0192513X18804285

Baumrind, D. (1966). Effects of authoritative parental control on child behavior. *Child Development, 37*(4), 887-907. https://doi.org/10.2307/1126611

Baumrind, D. (1967). Child care practices anteceding three patterns of preschool behaviour. *Genetic Psychology Monographs, 75*, 43–88.

Baumrind, D. (1971). Current patterns of parental authority. *Developmental Psychology, 4*, 1–103. https://doi.org/10.1037/h0030372

Baumrind, D. (1989). Rearing competent children. In W. Damon (Ed.), *Child Development Today and Tomorrow* (pp. 349–378). Jossey-Bass.

Baumrind, D. (1991). The influence of parenting style on adolescent competence and substance abuse. *Journal of Early Adolescence, 11*, 56–95. https://doi.org/10.1177/0272431691111004

Bean, H., Softas-Nall, L., Eberle, K. M., & Paul, J. A. (2015). Can we talk about stay-at-home moms? Empirical findings and implications for counseling. *The Family Journal, 24*(1), 23–30. https://doi.org/10.1177/1066480715615631

Beck C. T. (2004). Post-traumatic stress disorder due to childbirth: The aftermath. *Nursing Research, 53*(4), 216-24. https://doi.org/10.1097/00006199-200407000-00004.

Berk, L. E. (2001). *Development through the lifespan* (2nd ed.). Allyn & Bacon.

Betz, G., & Thorngren, J. M. (2006). Ambiguous loss and the family grieving process. *The Family Journal, 14*(4), 359–365. https://doi.org/10.1177/1066480706290052

Centers for Disease Control and Prevention. (2016). *Marriage and divorce*. https://www.cdc.gov/nchs/fastats/marriage-divorce.htm

Centers for Disease Control and Prevention. (2019). *Infertility*. https://www.cdc.gov/reproductivehealth/Infertility/

Child Welfare Information Gateway. (2015). *Impact of adoption on adoptive parents*. https://www.childwelfare.gov/pubPDFs/impactparent.pdf#page=2&view=Impact%20of%20the%20%20decision%20to%20adopt

Child Welfare Information Gateway. (2016). *Reunification: Bringing your children home from foster care*. https://www.childwelfare.gov/pubPDFs/reunification.pdf

Clinton, T., & Langberg, D. (2011). *The quick-reference guide to counseling women*. Baker Books.

Clinton, T., & Trent, J. (2009). *The quick-reference guide to marriage & family counseling*. Baker Books.

Coddington, C. (2017, February 8). *Secondary infertility: Why does it happen* https://www.mayoclinic.org/diseases-conditions/infertility/expert-answers/secondary-infertility/faq-20058272.

Cohn, D., & Caumont, A. (2014). *7 key findings about stay-at-home-moms*. https://www.pewresearch.org/fact-tank/2014/04/08/7-key-findings-about-stay-at-home-moms/

Collier, T. (n.d.). *Mom guilt is real. Here's how to beat it*. https://www.activekids.com/parenting-and-family/articles/mom-guilt-is-real-here-s-how-to-beat-it.

Coogan, P. A., & Chen, C. P. (2007). Career development and counselling for women: Connecting theories to practice. *Counselling Psychology Quarterly, 20*(2), 191–204. https://doi.org/10.1080/09515070701391171

Day2Day Parenting. (2015). *The challenges and rewards of foster parenting*. https://day2dayparenting.com/foster-parenting/

DiPietro, J. A., Goldshore, M. A., Kivlighan, K. T., Pater, H. A., & Costigan, K. A. (2015). The ups and downs of early mothering. *Journal of Psychosomatic Obstetrics and Gynecology, 36*(3), 94–102. https://doi.org/10.3109/0167482X.2015.1034269.

DiPietro, J., Ghera, M., Costigan, K., & Hawkins, M. (2004). Measuring the ups and downs of pregnancy stress. *Journal of Psychosomatic Obstetrics and Gynecology, 25*(3/4), 189–201. https://doi.org/10.1080/01674820400017830.

Drosdzol, A., & Skrzypulec, V. (2009). Depression and anxiety among Polish infertile couples – an evaluative prevalence study. *Journal of Psychosomatic Obstetrics & Gynecology, 30*(1), 11–20. https://doi.org/10.1080/01674820902830276

Dugan, A. (2017). *U.S. divorce rate dips, but moral acceptability hits new high*. https://news.gallup.com/poll/213677/divorce-rate-dips-moral-acceptability-hits-new-high.aspx.

*English Standard Bible. (*2001). English Standard Bible Online. https://www.esv.org/

Fogle, A. (2018). *Surprising facts you may not know about adoption.* https://www.goodhousekeeping.com/life/parenting/a35860/adoption-statistics/.

Forbus, B. (2011). *Surviving infertility: What the Bible says about your baby hunger.* Crossbooks.

Children's Rights. (2019). *Foster care.* https://www.childrensrights.org/newsroom/fact-sheets/foster-care/.

Gerber-Epstein, P., Leichtentritt, R. D., & Benyamini, Y. (2008). The experience of miscarriage in first pregnancy: The womens voices. *Death Studies, 33*(1), 1–29. https://doi.org/10.1080/07481180802494032

Greil, A. L., Porter, K. L., Leitko, T. A., & Riscilli, C. (1989). Why me? Theodicies of infertile women and men. *Sociology of Health & Illness, 11*(3), 213–229. https://doi.org/10.1023/A:1022347729368

Greil, A. L. (1997). Infertility and psychological distress: A critical review of the literature. *Social Science and Medicine, 45,* 1679–1704. https://doi.org/10.1016/s0277-9536(97)00102-0

Grekin, R., O'Hara, M. W. (2004). Prevalence and risk factors of postpartum posttraumatic stress disorder: A meta-analysis. *Clinical Psychology Review, 34*(5), 389-401. https://doi.org/10.1016/j.cpr.2014.05.003.

Held, V. (1989). Birth and death. *Ethics, 99*(2), 362–388. https://doi.org/10.1086/293070

Hoeve, M., Blokland, A., Dubas, J. S., Loeber, R., Gerris, J. R. M., & van der Laan, P. H. (2008). Trajectories of delinquency and parenting styles. *Journal of Abnormal Child Psychology, 36,* 223–235. https://doi.org/10.1007/s10802-007-9172-x

Hoskins, D. (2014). Consequences of parenting on adolescent outcomes. *Societies, 4*(3), 506-531. https://doi.org/10.3390/soc4030506

Hynie, M., & Burns, L. H. (2006). Cross-cultural issues in infertility counseling. In *Covington SN, Infertility counselling: A comprehensive handbook for clinicians* (pp. 61-82). Cambridge University Press.

Ingram, C. (2006). *4 parenting styles and effective child discipline.* https://www.focusonthefamily.com/parenting/4-parenting-styles-and-effective-child-discipline/

Kalu, F. (2019). Women's experiences of utilizing religious and spiritual beliefs as coping resources after miscarriage. *Religions, 10*(3), 185. https://doi.org/10.3390/rel10030185

Kennedy, H. P., Beck, C. T., & Driscoll, J. W. (2002). A light in the fog: Caring for women with postpartum depression. *Journal of Midwifery and Women's Health, 47*(5), 318–330. https://search-ebscohost-com.ezproxy.liberty.edu/login.aspx?direct=true&db=mnh&AN=12361343&site=ehost-live&scope=site

Klitzman, R. (2018). How infertility patients and providers view and confront religious and spiritual issues. *Journal of Religion and Health, 57*(1), 223–239. https://doi-org.ezproxy.liberty.edu/10.1007/s10943-017-0528-4

Kopala, M., & Keitel, M. A. (2003). *Handbook of counseling women* (1st ed.). SAGE.

Kuppens, S., & Ceulemans, E. (2018). Parenting styles: A closer look at a well-known concept. *Journal of Child and Family Studies, 28*(1), 168-181. https://doi.org/10.1007/s10826-018-1242-x

Kuppens, S., Kuppens, S., Ceulemans, E., & Ceulemans, E. (2019). Parenting styles: A closer look at a well-known concept. *Journal of Child and Family Studies, 28*(1), 168-181. https://doi.org/10.1007/s10826-018-1242-x

Lamar, M., Forbes, L., & Capasso, L. (2019). Helping working mothers face the challenges of an intensive mothering culture. *Journal of Mental Health Counseling, 41.* https://doi.org/10.17744/mehc.41.3.02.

Landrum, S. (2018). *More millennial women are becoming stay-at-home moms- Here's why.* https://www.forbes.com/sites/sarahlandrum/2018/02/09/more-millennial-women-are-becoming-stay-at-home-moms-heres-why/#67107cf26a2b.

Larzelere, R., Morris, A., & Harrist, A. (2013). *Authoritative parenting: Synthesizing nurturance and discipline for optimal child development.* American Psychological Association. https://doi.org/10.1037/13948-000

Leahy-Warren, P., McCarthy, G., & Corcoran, P. (2012). First-time mothers: Social support, maternal parental self-efficacy and postnatal depression. *Journal of Clinical Nursing, 21,* 388-397. https://doi.org/10.1111/j.1365-2702.2011.03701.x.

Liang, L. A., Berger, U., & Brand, C. (2019). Psychosocial factors associated with symptoms of depression, anxiety and stress among single mothers with young children: A population-based study. *Journal of Affective Disorders, 242,* 255-264. https://doi.org/10.1016/j.jad.2018.08.013

Lindholm, M. (2019a). *Don't let "mom guilt" make you a worse parent: Ten things to remember when coping with contradictory reality of mom guilt.* https://www.psychologytoday.com/us/blog/more-women-s-work/201902/don-t-let-mom-guilt-make-you-worse-parent

Lindholm, M. (2019b). *Moms need wide-ranging mental health care.* https://msmagazine.com/2019/09/20/moms-need-wide-ranging-mental-health-care/

Livingston, G. (2018). *The changing profile of unmarried parents: A growing share are living with a partner.* https://www.pewsocialtrends.org/2018/04/25/the-changing-profile-of-unmarried-parents/.

Loewen, S. G. (2016). "We are all meant to be mothers of God": Mothering as embodied peacemaking. *Vision (Winnipeg, Man.), 17*(2), 32–43.

Loke, A. Y., Yu, P. L., & Hayter, M. (2012). Experiences of sub-fertility among Chinese couples in Hong Kong: A qualitative study. *Journal of Clinical Nursing, 21*(3–4), 504–512. https://doi.org/10.1111/j.1365-2702.2010.03632.x.

Luk, B. H. K., & Loke, A. Y. (2015). The impact of infertility on the psychological well-being, marital relationships, sexual relationships, and quality of life of couples: A systematic review. *Journal of Sex & Marital Therapy, 41*(6), 610–625. https://doi.org/10.1080/0092623X.2014.958789

Luk, B. H.-K., & Loke, A. Y. (2016). A review of supportive interventions targeting individuals or couples undergoing infertility treatment: Directions for the development of interventions. *Journal of Sex & Marital Therapy*, *42*(6), 515–533. https://doi.org/10.1080/0092623x.2015.1074133

Luk, B. H. K., & Loke, A. Y. (2019). Sexual satisfaction, intimacy and relationship of couples undergoing infertility treatment. *Journal of Reproductive & Infant Psychology*, *37*(2), 108–122.

Maccoby, E. E., & Martin, J. A. (1983). Socialization in the context of the family: Parent-child interaction. In P. H. Mussen, & E. M. Hetherington (Eds.), *Handbook of child psychology: Vol. 4. Socialization, personality, and social development* (4th ed., pp. 1-101). Wiley.

Markin, R. D. (2016). What clinicians miss about miscarriages: Clinical errors in the treatment of early term perinatal loss. *Psychotherapy*, *53*(3), 347–353.

Mayo Clinic. (2018). *Postpartum depression*. https://www.mayoclinic.org/diseases-conditions/postpartum-depression/symptoms-causes/syc-20376617

Medina, S., & Magnuson, S. (2009). Motherhood in the 21st century: Implications for counselors. *Journal of Counseling & Development*, *87*(1), 90-96. https://doi.org/10.1002/j.1556-6678.2009.tb00553.

Mendes, E., Saad, L., & McGeeney, K. (2012). *Stay-at-home moms report more depression, sadness, anger*. https://news.gallup.com/poll/154685/stay-home-moms-report-depression-sadness-anger.aspx.

Mental Help. (n.d.). *Choosing to adopt*. https://www.mentalhelp.net/adoption/choosing-to-adopt/

Meyers, L. (2018). *Parenting in the 21st century*. https://ct.counseling.org/2018/02/parenting-21st-century/

Mihalich-Levin, L. (2017). *What exactly is mom guilt anyway? A clinical psychotherapist explains*. Retrieved from https://www.mindfulreturn.com/mom-guilt/

Miller, L. J. (2002). Postpartum depression. *JAMA: Journal of the American Medical Association*, *287*(6), 762.

Morin, A. (2019). *4 types of parenting styles and their effects on kids*. https://www.verywellfamily.com/types-of-parenting-styles-1095045

Murray, L., & Cooper, P. (1997). Effects of postnatal depression on infant development. *Archives Of Disease In Childhood*, *77*(2), 99–101.

Mutiso, S. K., Murage, A., & Mukaindo, A. M. (2018). Prevalence of positive depression screen among post miscarriage women- A cross sectional study. *BMC Psychiatry*, *18*(1), 32.

New American Standard Bible. (1995). New American Standard Bible Online. https://www.biblestudytools.com/nas/ (Original work published 1960).

New International Bible. (2011). New International Bible Online. https://www.thenivbible.com/ (Original work published 1973).

New Living Bible (1996). New Living Bible. https://www.biblegateway.com/versions/New-Living-Translation-NLT-Bible/

Newmarks, A. (2019). *Chicken soup for the soul: Messages from heaven and other miracles.* Simon and Schuster.

Nieuwenhuis, S. L., Odukogbe, A.-T. A., Theobald, S., & Liu, X. (2009). The impact of infertility on infertile men and women in Ibadan, Oyo State, Nigeria: A qualitative study. *African Journal Of Reproductive Health, 13*(3), 85–98.

Ramamurthi, R., Kavitha, G., & Pounraj, D. S. (2016). Psychological impact and coping strategies among women with infertility - A hospital based cross sectional study. *IAIM, 3*(2), 114-118.

Randolph, A. L., Hruby, B. T., & Sharif, S. (2015). Counseling women who have experienced pregnancy loss: A review of the literature. *Adultspan Journal, 14,* 2–10. https://doi.org/10.1002/j.2161-0029.2015.00032.x

Reiheld, A. (2015). "The event that was nothing": Miscarriage as a liminal event. *Journal of Social Philosophy, 46*(1), 9–26. https://doi.org/10.1111/josp.12084

Reynolds, B. W. (2018). *The state of the remote job marketplace.* https://www.flexjobs.com/blog/post/state-of-the-remote-job-marketplace/.

Rogers, J. L., Crocket, J. E., & Suess, E. (2019). Miscarriage: An ecological examination. *Professional Counselor, 9*(1), 51–66.

Roudsari, R. L., Allan, H. T., & Smith, P. A. (2007). Looking at infertility through the lens of religion and spirituality: A review of the literature. *Human Fertility, 10*(3), 141–149. https://doi.org/10.1080/14647270601182677.

Sohr-Preston, S. L., Morain, S., Chapman, A., Pardue, S., & Ford, S. (2018). Examining misperceptions about miscarriage in U.S. adults. *Journal of Prenatal & Perinatal Psychology & Health, 32*(4), 285–305.

Su, Q., Zhang, H., Zhang, Y., Zhang, H., Ding, D., Zeng, J., & Li, H. (2015). Maternal stress in gestation: Birth outcomes and stress related hormone response of the neonates. *Pediatrics & Neonatology, 56*(6), 376–381. https://doi.org/10.1016/j.pedneo.2015.02.002

Thorn, P. (2009). Infertility counselling: Alleviating the emotional burden of infertility and infertility treatment. *Int J Fertil Steril, 3*(1), 1-4. https://doi.org/10.1007/s10815-011-9701-y

U.S. Census Bureau. (2017). *Facts for features: Mother's day.* https://www.census.gov/newsroom/facts-for-features/2017/cb17-ff09-mothers-day.html

U.S. Department of Labor, Bureau of Labor Statistics. (2019, April 18). *Employment status of the population by sex, marital status, and presence and age of own children under 18, 2017-2018 annual averages.* https://www.bls.gov/news.release/famee.t05.htm.

Vetriselvi, V., & Kalavathi, (2013). Infertility & counselling. *International Journal of Nursing Education, 5*(2), 229–232.

Witt, W. P., Litzelman, K., Cheng, E. R., Wakeel, F., & Barker, E. S. (2014). Measuring stress before and during pregnancy: A review of population-based studies of obstetric outcomes. *Maternal and Child Health Journal, 18*(1), 52–63. https://doi.org/10.1007/s10995-013-1233-x

Woods, S. M., Melville, J. L., Guo, Y., Fan, M. Y., & Gavin, A. (2010). Psychosocial stress during pregnancy. *American Journal of Obstetrics and Gynecology, 202*(1), E1-61.E7. https://doi.org/10.1016/j.ajog.2009.07.041

CHAPTER 10
Counseling Women and Caregivers

Sheila W. Speight, Ph.D. & Dallas E. Speight, Ed.D.

"Some days there won't be a song in your heart. Sing anyway."
~Emory Austin

"Do not merely look out for your own personal interests, but also for the interests of others." (Philippians 2:4, NASB)

Wisdom from Above: Standing in His Grace

Austin's quote is a great reminder of both the challenges and the rewards associated with the task of caregiving. There will be those days when the sun will shine brightly, days filled with hope and peace, but there will also come those days when darkness may prevail. It is in those moments that one is reminded of the Apostle Paul's admonition, "Do not merely look out for your own personal interests, but also for the interests of others" (*New American Standard Bible, 1960/1995*, Philippians 2:4). It is in the spirit of this

© Nikki Zalewski/Shutterstock.com

high calling to which individuals are called to be caregivers – a calling that will most certainly include days when one must sing despite having a heavy heart.

CHAPTER OVERVIEW

The number of caregivers in the United States and other countries may be underreported due to some persons who are in need refusing or neglecting to ask for assistance or provision of care in private homes. Despite this, the number of caregivers is a growing phenomenon ranging from caring for children to senior adults. Those being served may present with any number of physical, mental and even emotional diagnoses, and may come from an array of sources: friends, children, spouses, parents, and siblings. Whereas some individuals may have agreed to take on this responsibility, others may be forced into this role because of the need or because it is being unmet by others. Regardless of the reason, it is important that counselors be prepared to address the needs of caregivers through a meaningful counseling relationship. In preparation for this role, this chapter will address different types of caregivers as well as their various roles and responsibilities. Additionally, insights as to the many challenges that caregivers may experience, how to assess their needs, evidence-based treatment options and Biblical principles will be addressed. Finally, this chapter integrates a case study using the treatment options and provides additional resources.

A BIBLICAL ACCOUNT OF CAREGIVING

Though the term caregiver may appear to be a relatively new phrase, it may be surprising how dated it is. One of the first accounts of caregiving is found in the book of John chapter 11 in the home of Mary, Martha and Lazarus. Capper (2006) concluded that Bethany, the hometown for Mary, Martha and Lazarus, was identified as a place for the poor and a place

CHAPTER LEARNING OBJECTIVES

Upon completing this chapter, you should be able to:

- Differentiate the different types of caregivers
- Evaluate the roles and responsibilities of informal and formal caregivers
- Identify the emotional, physical, and spiritual challenges faced by caregivers
- Describe evidenced-based treatment options while also incorporating Biblical insights

to care for the sick. It was the city of Simon the Leper as well as where we find Lazarus who was suffering a sickness that would eventually lead to his death (Daly-Denton, 2017). Lazarus' story has many important theological implications for caregivers.

What do we know about Mary and Martha? Perhaps more important to this study of caregivers, how might their lives provide insight into the lives of caregivers? Mary is described as the devoted follower of Christ who was apparently quiet, reflective, and sensitive to recognize Jesus, whereas Martha was more active and busied herself with activities around the home. It is because of their unique personalities that we gain insight into the lives of caregivers and the role of caregiving. Like the situation with Lazarus, no two situations are the same, nor are any two caregivers the same. Yet many of the challenges faced by Mary and Martha will present themselves in the lives of those providing care.

CAREGIVERS: WHO ARE THEY?

Who are the caregivers? From this brief encounter of Mary and Martha, it is clear that caregivers present themselves in a variety of ways. Mary, the quiet, reserved and reflective individual may respond to Lazarus' needs by sitting calmly by his bedside, echoing prayers and words of solace. Martha, whose caregiving qualities are just as important, may busy herself with changing his bed, cleaning the room, and preparing his meals. Is one approach any better than the other? Does one need to have a certain personality or specific training to be an effective caregiver? These are questions we may ponder, but the truth is that anyone can serve as a caregiver.

Those who serve in a caregiving capacity include a variety of personal and professional individuals and are typically described as either formal or informal caregivers (Family Caregiver Alliance, Caregiver Statistics, 2019). **Formal caregivers** are defined as those who are paid for their services whether in the home or in a caregiving facility. **Informal caregivers** are typically unpaid and may include family members, friends, or others who desire to assist. It may not be uncommon for many of the informal caregivers to be forced into this role due to the relationship with the care recipient, the lack of resources, and the fact that others are not willing to be involved or take on the responsibilities.

Formal Caregivers

Types of Caregivers
- Informal
- Formal

As noted earlier, this group of caregivers represent those individuals who are paid for their services. Formal caregivers might include nursing personnel, aides, sitters and others. According to Caregiving in the US (2015) the list of medical issues formal caregivers might address include patients suffering from Alzheimer's, dementia, surgery and wound care, cancer, heart issues, diabetes, stroke, arthritis, fractured bones, and the list continues. Among this list, Alzheimer's and dementia appear to be the most prevalent concerns (Caregiving in the US, 2015).

Informal Caregivers

Informal Biblical Caregivers
Mary – the Quiet and
Reflective Caregiver
&
Martha – the Active and
Demanding Caregiver

The field of family caregivers is burgeoning with the many economic, demographic, and even social changes that have emerged over the past few years. With an increase in an aging population and a decrease of resources, many family members are being called to serve in the role as informal caregivers. These new responsibilities have resulted in significant challenges. It is estimated that approximately 69% of family caregivers must modify their work schedules as well as their work hours. This is not to mention the loss of wages and the use of leave time (Caregiving in the US, 2015).

The types of responsibilities vary according to the needs of the family member. According to one study, approximately 43% assisted their person receiving care getting in and out of bed or a chair; 32% reported helping someone dress; 26% assisted with bathing and showering needs; 25% provided help to the care recipient getting on and off the toilet; and another 19% reported helping with feeding responsibilities (National Alliance for Caregiving, 2009). It may not be uncommon for the informal caregiver to provide some of the same medical needs as formal caregivers.

Demographics

Traditionally, females have served as caregivers, although it has been suggested that with the increase of baby boomers the number of men will increase (Swanberg et al., 2006). Despite this projection, the prevalence of caregivers has remained somewhat consistent. Edwards et al. (2017) reported demographics from a 2009 study which noted that among caregivers, roughly 67.5% were women and 32.5% were men (p. 387). Caregiving in the US (2015) reported similar results with the number of female caregivers at 65% and males 35%. The largest number of caregivers, approximately 85% provide care to a relative, with 49% of that number providing care to a parent or parent-in-law (Caregiving in the US, 2015).

Just as there are gender differences, there are also age and racial/ethnic differences among caregivers. According to Caregiver Statistics (2019), the average age of caregivers is 49.2, with approximately 48% between the ages of 18-49, and 34% of caregivers 65 years or older.

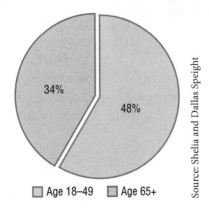

FIGURE 10.1

Ages of Caregivers

Among this group, approximately 62% are white and 13% are Hispanic. African Americans represent approximately 20.3%, and Asian Americans represent 19.7% (Caregiver Statistics, 2019). However, these numbers could be underrepresented due to a failure to self-report by some caregivers.

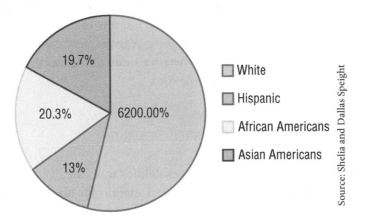

FIGURE 10.2

Racial Background of Caregivers

The roles and responsibilities for caregivers vary significantly. Whether the caregiver is in a formal or informal role, the challenges continue to flourish. It has even been described as the new normal (Gaugler & Kane, 2015, p. 7).

Both formal and informal caregivers may be burdened with other concerns and responsibilities outside their given roles. In addition to what is referred to as activities of daily living (ADLs), commonly described as bathing, dressing, etc., other responsibilities may include tasks such as running errands, shopping, etc. Caregivers may also perform medical, emotional and even spiritual support (Caregiving in the US, 2015; Giovannetti et al., 2012).

Medical Support

Caregivers participate in a broad range of medical or healthcare related activities, which include tasks such as medication management or treatment protocols, coordinating health related information and services, and/or operating medical equipment (Rosland et al., 2013; Wolff & Jacobs, 2015). The number of individuals working in this area appear to have increased significantly over the last few years. Rosland et al. (2013) reported approximately 44% of the caregivers were involved in some type of medical caregiving tasks; whereas a study conducted by Lee et al. (2017) saw this number increase to 63.6%.

Social and Emotional Support

Despite the multitude of responsibilities that caregivers may provide to care recipients, social and emotional support are also a common responsibility. Social support includes tasks such as supporting, encouraging, and maintaining a level of social engagement (Cooper et al., 2013; Off et al., 2019). According to Tippy (2016), psychosocial support is an essential part of providing care for cancer patients. Emotional support involves acts such as listening to the worries and concerns of the care recipient, demonstrating love for the person, or in some cases providing spiritual support and resources (Cooper, 2013).

The Institute of Medicine advocated for high quality of care for their cancer patients, but also suggested the spiritual and social support needs of the patients be addressed (Kelly et al., 2019). Four types of social support were identified: emotional, informational, appraisal, and instrumental (Kelly et al., 2019). Accordingly, emotional support was the one mentioned most often and included feeling supported and cared for. Informational support was described as providing support via support groups or in some cases social media. Patients identified appraisal support as providing social support and the opportunity to discuss spirituality and religion. Instrumental support referred to the tasks taken on by the caregiver/spouse. These tasks were typically related to issues such as managing home and family affairs or arranging logistics for treatment purposes.

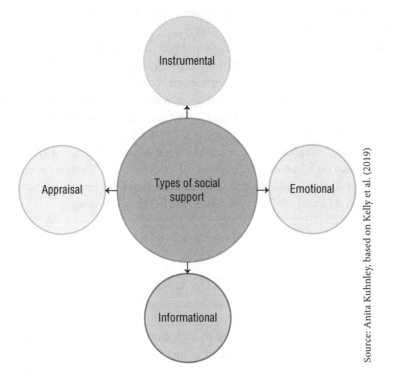

FIGURE 10.3

Types of Social Support

Source: Anita Kuhnley, based on Kelly et al. (2019)

CASE STUDY: MEET THE SMITHS

The Smith family consists of Richard, a 64-year-old, his wife, Susan, age 63, and Richard's mother, Eudora, an 89-year-old. For several years, Eudora lived on the same property in her private residence but has since moved into the home with her son, Richard and his wife, Susan. During the earlier years, Richard visited in his mother's home regularly, ate meals with her, and provided ongoing support as needed. However, since she fell and broke her leg two-years prior, the care provided has increased significantly. As informal caregivers, Richard and Susan ensure she makes and attends her medical appointments, organizes and administers her daily medication, morning, noon and evening, prepares her meals. When a formal caregiver such as a sitter is not available, Susan assists with her personal needs such as bathing. Formal caregiving services are provided on a very limited basis only because Richard and Susan are both retired and can provide fulltime care.

© Photographee.eu/Shutterstock.com

Though Richard would not want to admit it, the stress of providing care for his mother as well as giving attention to his wife has been challenging. Adding to the stress of not being able to take many breaks due to the ongoing caregiving responsibilities, Richard and Susan each have their own medical issues. Although Richard's siblings assist as much as possible several factors prohibit them in providing more time in care. All three live several hours away and are all currently employed. Although Eudora has been willing to make visits as she feels up to it for a period of one-two weeks, her increased frailty and symptoms of dementia cause her anxiety to increase significantly when her routine is interrupted.

As you might discern, the stressors that the Smiths' experience are numerous. Yet, it is in this environment that Richard and Susan are being called upon to extend all levels of support - emotional, informational, appraisal and instrumental (Kelly et al., 2019). It seems clear that caregivers, whether formal or informal, have a tremendous amount of responsibility. Further attention is needed to understand the impact of these many duties on the health of caregivers.

CHALLENGES FACING CAREGIVERS

Caregivers may not be aware of the emotional, mental, physical and spiritual impact that can result because of caring for another. The type of needs presented by care recipients vary and impact the caregivers in a variety of ways, yet caregivers working with terminally ill patients will often face their own set of challenges. For example, they are tasked with ensuring the patient is made comfortable, helping with interpersonal relationships, and living with the uncertainty of when the patient will die (Ray et al., 2013). Care duration is also a challenge, since the need to care for a terminally ill patient can last weeks, months or even years. Of course, not all care recipients are terminally ill, yet the impact of these and other factors can lead to overwhelming stress and **burnout** (a syndrome of emotional exhaustion, depersonalization and decreased personal satisfaction in one's accomplishments).

Caregiver Burnout

Caregiver burnout has been well-documented, with as high as 50% indicating psychological stress which can lead to burnout (Toledo & Akinyemi, 2017). Despite what has been described as disagreement as to the cause of burnout, stress has certainly been identified as a contributing factor (Levy & Gordon, 2013; Maslach, 2003; Nunn & Isaacs, 2019). Burnout has been described as "a syndrome of emotional exhaustion, depersonalization, and reduced personal accomplishment that can occur among individuals who do 'people work' of some kind" (Maslach, 2003, p. 2). Six sources of stress that can lead to burnout include: 1) work overload, 2) lack of control, 3) insufficient reward, 4) breakdown of community, 5) unfairness, 6) significant value conflicts (Maslach, 2003, pp. 109-110). See Figure 10.4 below.

FIGURE 10.4

Stress Sources of Burnout

Should these not be dealt with in a timely manner, burnout can become a reality. The following tables provide a useful look at the key signs and symptoms of burnout (Table 10.1) and (Table 10.2) list some steps for dealing with daily burnout (Wicks, 2010, pp. 32-33).

TABLE 10.1

Key Signs and Symptoms

- Mentally fatigued at the end of the day
- Feeling unappreciated, frustrated, bored, tense, or angry as a result of contact(s) with family, colleagues, supervisors, superiors, assistants or others
- Experiencing physical symptoms (headache, backache, upset stomach, etc.)
- Pace of day's activities or requirements of tasks seem greater than personal or professional resources available.
- Tasks required on the job are repetitious, beyond one's ability, or require intensity on a continuous basis.

The possibility of caregivers experiencing burnout is a known reality; however, there are also steps that can be taken for responding to it (Ammar et al., 2017; Staloff et al., 2018).

TABLE 10.2

Steps for Dealing with Daily Burnout

- Correcting errors in thinking so there is greater recognition of when one is exaggerating or personalizing situations in an inappropriate or negative way
- Having a variety of activities in one's daily schedule
- Getting sufficient rest
- Faithfully incorporating meditation (or quiet reflective time) into one's daily schedule
- Interacting on a regular basis with supportive friends
- Being assertive
- Getting proper nourishment and exercise

Compassion Fatigue

It is not uncommon for some caregivers to experience what is referred to as compassion fatigue. **Compassion fatigue** has been defined as a "state of exhaustion and dysfunction—biologically, psychologically, and socially—as a result of prolonged exposure to compassion stress and all that it evokes" (Figley, 1995, p. 253). Compassion fatigue can affect caregivers over time, and has been associated with a gradual desensitization to patient stories, a decrease in quality care for patients and clients sometimes described as 'poor bedside manners,' an increase in clinical errors, and higher rates of depression and anxiety disorders among helpers (Figley, 2012; Mathieu, 2012). It is important for caregivers to understand the concept of compassion fatigue as it may lead to the implementation of more effective prevention strategies (Lynch, 2018).

Strategies to address compassion fatigue vary; however, McNutt and Watson (2015) suggested the most important aspect of managing compassion fatigue is self-awareness. The following list can be useful in helping caregivers renew their lives emotionally, physically and spiritually:

- Seeking an appropriate support system: a safe space to vent
- Seeking group counseling (weekly, semi-weekly or monthly basis) to provide a structure for feedback and support
- Finding time for solitude and reflection
- Finding time to rediscover the spiritual realm of the helping profession: to see compassion as a spiritual entity and not merely an emotional investment
- Scrutinizing and assessing the appropriateness of belief systems, God-images and basic convictions as to why and for what purpose
- Being generous to oneself: do something different, such as things that are enjoyable such as a vacation, recreation, reading a good book, etc.
- Revisiting existing paradigms in order to create an accommodative stance in life: what can be changed by setting new goals and what cannot be changed and needs to be accepted
- Undergoing a paradigm shift: move from Mr. or Mrs. Fixit to Mr. or Mrs. Support (helping is to be there with ...). Be available and do not try to fix everything; move from doing functions into being functions
- Maintaining resilience: a non-anxious presence; gracious patience and courage; concentrating on being-functions
- Developing a sense of humor: being a fulltime caregiver can rob one of their joy and the ability to find humor in events. Spending time watching a humorous movie or television show or spending time with a friend can help to alleviate the stress related to caregiving (Louw, 2015).

Bereavement and Grief Issues

Just as caregivers may be subject to burnout and compassion fatigue, it is also a matter of reality that they will experience some level of grief in their caregiving responsibilities. Grief has been described as an internal response to a loss which may manifest itself in the bereaved person as an emotional response such as sadness, numbness, and possibly guilt, and "may be evidenced by sleep disturbances, chest tightness, confusion, dry

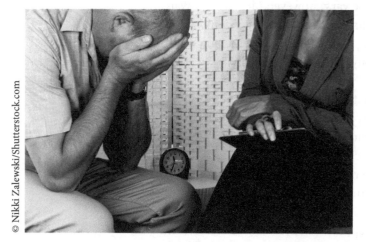

mouth, social withdrawal, and searching for meaning" (D'Antonio, 2014, p. 99). No one is exempt from bereavement and grief issues; therefore, it is important that counselors understand how experiencing a loss can impact the lives of caregivers. For example, formal caregivers may face multiple patient deaths during their times of providing care and may not always have the necessary time to reflect on their grief before another patient death occurs. Certainly not all deaths will impact caregivers the same, yet over a period of time, having to respond to numerous deaths can take its toll on the healthiest of caregivers.

Kübler-Ross's (1969) initial work regarding death and dying provided counselors with a new way of thinking about grieving and the various stages that she observed. Though other theoretical approaches for understanding grief and the grief process have emerged, for our purposes Kübler-Ross's insight along with Kessler's work provides a useful perspective (Stroebe et al., 2017). Kessler (2019), building on the work of Kübler-Ross and her stages of grief including denial, anger, bargaining, depression, acceptance, added a sixth stage: finding meaning. This additional stage came about after Kessler experienced the death of his twenty-one-year-old son and struggled to make meaning of his experience, which is an important issue for caregivers (Kessler, 2019).

The following suggestions for responding to grief have been offered by Elizabeth Kübler-Ross and David Kessler. Those who are grieving need their grief to be witnessed, meaning having someone be fully present without attempting to reframe, lessen or point out the silver lining (Kessler, 2019, p. 29). This process allows a grieving person to feel her grief is being reflected and acknowledged by others (p. 30). The process of listening without advising, judging, or questioning may be important to the caregiver. Allowing the individual to get to the depths of her grief by just espousing her hurt, pain or suffering as a result of this loss is important.

Caregivers may begin to question their faith or life's meaning when they repeatedly face various forms of grief. Grief for a spouse, sibling, or family member is much different from that of a formal caregiver who has a different type of relationship with the care-recipient. In such experiences it is appropriate that the counselor also assess the caregivers' grief responses. The following questions have been modified from the work of Jeffreys (2015) as a means for helping caregivers probe their grief (p. 110).

- Task 1: Ask the caregiver to rate the extent to which the loss has impacted her conscious awareness.
- Task 2: Ask the caregiver to rate the extent it has impacted her emotional pain.
- Task 3: Ask the caregiver to consider and rate her cognitive, behavioral and spiritual reactions to the loss.
- Task 4: Ask the caregiver to consider and rate her ability to create and integrate a new image of the deceased into her worldview as noted by Kessler (2019) by creating a new meaning as it relates to one's life.

Walking the individual through the stages of grief is important, as well as reminding her that these stages can recycle again, such as finding new reasons to be angry or feel guilty. However, the primary goal is to achieve some form of acceptance and, as Kessler (2019) mentioned, find meaning through this process. Jesus was our greatest example of how to grieve in the smallest verse in the Bible, John 11:35 (*New International Bible*, 1973/ 2011), which says simply that "Jesus wept". Jesus wept over the death of Lazarus even though He knew He could raise him from the dead. Being free to express grief is important to the healing process. For further insights into grief and loss, review Chapter 12.

Grief can be experienced outside the physical loss of death. The caregiver may experience layers of grief particularly when she has lost her job, withdrawn from involvement in church, or is struggling to redefine her identity as a person. She can also experience the loss of control regarding her previous life such as time for self, activities, events, and so forth. An important question that such caregivers need to explore involves asking themselves – "who am I?" It is important to address this type of grief with the caregiver as she may experience similar stages of grief as identified by Kübler -Ross and Kessler (2019).

Guilt

Guilt is a term that is often used in Christianity and focuses on one's transgressions, yet for our purposes guilt will be viewed from the caregiver's perspective. Caregivers may express guilt in the following ways.

- Guilt over having or expressing negative emotions such as anger or resentment toward the care-recipient.
- Guilt for not having done enough, feeling that they could have done a better job.
- Guilt over neglecting their own family members.
- Guilt over having to place a family member or care-recipient in a long-term care facility (Prunity & Folie, 2019).
- Guilt overlapping with grief as related to the issues above.

© Andrew Rybalko/Shutterstock.com

Although guilt is associated as a potential symptom of depression, typically negative caregiver emotions are not addressed clinically until depression develops (Prunity & Folie, 2019). In most cases, the suggested treatment interventions such as Cognitive Behavioral Therapy (CBT) and Narrative Therapy (NT) are useful strategies.

INTERVENTIONS FOR CAREGIVERS

"Rejoice with those who rejoice, and weep with those who weep" (*King James Bible*, 1769/2017, Romans 12:15). It is one thing to identify a multitude of challenges for caregivers, yet if one fails to intervene, typically little will change. Baldwin (2017) echoed a similar reminder, "Not everything that is faced can be changed. But nothing can be changed until it is faced" (para. 8). And as noted, caregivers will experience a multitude of challenges – emotional, physical, social, and even spiritual. Therefore, what are potential treatment options, interventions and resources for addressing these challenges?

CONCEPT TO CONTEMPLATE

© Asier Romero/Shutterstock.com

How important is it to assess the needs of caregivers? How often do you think they should be assessed? Can you think of someone in your life now who is a caregiver? Is there something that comes to mind that you could do to help meet a need for them?

Assessing Needs

Determining the needs and issues presented by the caregiver is a significant issue for the counselor. It may involve the ability to identify, analyze, evaluate, and address the problems presented. A significant part of this role involves active listening.

Active listening allows the care-recipient the opportunity to verbalize her feelings without judgment or interruption. Individuals may carry around bottled up emotions that have not been expressed for a variety of reasons, such as guilt, fear of criticism, anger, grief, or feeling that it is not spiritual to express such emotions. For example, one may experience guilt that she is not doing enough for the patient, or anger at self, others and even God. In other experiences, well-meaning caregivers may begin to feel resentful due to having to watch the care-recipient suffer.

Thus, it is during these moments that the counselor needs to listen attentively, but also begin to assess the situation through observation, a series of questions, and even written assessments. Some basic questions that can be asked of the caregiver might include:

1. What has been going on?
2. What kind of changes would you like to see?
3. What steps have you already taken to resolve some of your concerns?
4. What worked? What has not worked?
5. What brought you to counseling at this point in time?

While assessing the needs of the caregiver, an intake interview will be beneficial. The Caregiver Intake Interview may differ from a typical assessment in which psychopathology or distress may exist (American Psychological Association, 2019). Not only is it important to determine the challenges facing the caregiver, it is equally important to determine the nature of the caregiving situation and the diagnosis or developmental stage of the care recipient. The Family Caregiver's Alliance (FCA) Nation-

© Tashatuvango/Shutterstock.com

al Center on Caregiving identified seven important domains to assess in relationship to the caregiver:

1. Background of the caregiver and the caregiving situation
2. Caregiver's perception of health and functional state of the care recipient
3. Caregiver's values and preferences with respect to everyday living and care provision
4. Health and well-being of the caregiver
5. Consequences of caregiving on the caregiver
6. Care-provision requirements (skills, abilities, and knowledge)
7. Resources to support the caregiver, asking specifically about emotional, social and spiritual resources. (para. 2)

Certainly, other questions might be posed to the caregiver, but the goal is to determine the basic needs, determine what steps have been taken to resolve the caregivers' concerns, and identify appropriate goals and intervention strategies. Perhaps the stress has reached a point that one's usual coping skills and strategies have reached their limits. Whatever the reasons, it is important to gain some understanding of the pressing needs and issues surrounding the caregivers desire to seek help.

Assessment Instruments

Not everyone will find assessments useful, but in some cases, they might provide the counselor insight that might have otherwise been overlooked. The Caregiver Self-Assessment Questionnaire (American Psychological Association, 2019) is a self-report measure devised by the American Medical Association to provide physicians a way to assess the stress-levels of family caregivers accompanying chronically ill older adult patients to their medical visits. There are 18-items where the caregiver responds either "yes" or no" to a series of statements addressing how they might have felt during the last week. Two helpful questions in this assessment may provide more depth regarding the caregivers needs. For question #17, family caregivers are asked to rate their level of stress on a 1-10 basis. For question #18, they are asked to rate their perception of their current health in comparison to their health one-year ago. This may provide a baseline in understanding the caregivers' immediate needs.

The Beck Depression Inventory (BDI) is useful in assessing the level of depression that a caregiver may be experiencing. The inventory is a 21-item, self-report that measures primary symptoms of depression and has been validated for reliability and consistency.

Treatment Options, Interventions and Resources

Treatment Options
- Counseling/psychotherapy
- Behavioral therapy
- Education/information
- Social support
- Alternative forms

Five unique treatment options for caregivers were suggested by Barsevick et al. (2002): counseling/psychotherapy, behavioral therapy, education/information, social support and other forms, which included alternative forms of interventions such as music therapy. Regardless of the approach, Zarit and Lewis (2008) suggested that effective treatment options have at least four overlapping characteristics: "a psychological rather than purely educational approach, multidimensionality, flexibility, and sufficiency in the amount or dosage of treatment" (p. 47). Whether the need is to address psychoeducational needs or possibly a more acute diagnosis, the important aspect is to match the treatment intervention with the needs of the caregiver.

COUNSELING INTERVENTIONS

Two interventions, Cognitive Behavioral Therapy (a form of therapy which relates primarily to one's thinking and thoughts processes) and Narrative Therapy (a form of therapy in which individuals experience life through stories and people give meaning to their lives and relationships through stories) have each been proven effective in treating the challenges that caregivers may experience. Although other counseling interventions are available, the counselor is encouraged to select one that fits the need(s) of the caregiver and is within the counselor's area of expertise or training. The following case study involving Beth will be used with two different therapy methods.

CASE STUDY: COGNITIVE BEHAVIORAL THERAPY WITH BETH

Beth is a 60-year-old, widowed female caregiver providing care for her aging mother who is in overall good health, although she cannot be left alone. Beth provides care daily without the assistance of family or friends as she has no siblings, and her friendships have diminished after the death of her spouse and her inability to remain active in church. She reported feeling exhausted, emotionally drained, and stated a lack of joy and meaning in everyday activities. She also expressed guilt as she recognized that her duty as a Christian was to honor her mother but acknowledged that knowing this Biblical truth did not leave her feeling comforted. She further acknowledged becoming increasingly irritable and short with her mother.

Cognitive Behavioral Therapy

Cognitive-Behavioral Therapy (CBT) was founded in the 1960s by Aaron Beck when he theorized that one's thoughts were keenly associated with one's behaviors. A central theme of CBT is related to thinking and the way in which one's thought process is activated, and associated with mood, physiological and behavioral changes (Wenzel et al., 2011). Two persons can experience the same phenomena, yet because of the way they think, different reactions can be evidenced. Thoughts that arise are referred to as automatic thoughts, which are thoughts that occur quickly and are often overlooked or not recognized at the time (Wenzel et al., 2011). Automatic thoughts, over time, develop into schemas, which are enduring and stored information. Schemas give rise as to what one believes about themselves, others and the world (Beck, 2011). A basic principle at work in CBT is to target emotions by changing thoughts and behaviors, which ultimately contribute to distressing emotions (Cully & Teten, 2008).

CONCEPT TO CONTEMPLATE

What makes Cognitive Behavioral Therapy (CBT) such a strong therapeutic approach for working with caregivers?

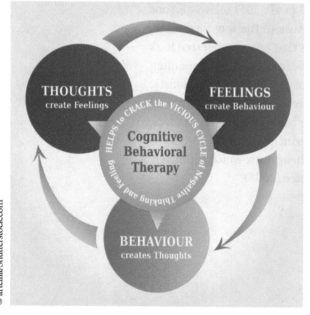

Basic Tenants of Cognitive Behavioral Therapy

Although the basic tenants of CBT may vary somewhat as one implements it in treating different types of clients, there are several defining features:

- Forming a Collaborative Relationship and Case Conceptualization
- Formulating a Clinical Plan and Treatment Options
- Fostering Intentionality and Accountability

Forming a Collaborative Relationship and Case Conceptualization

According to CBT theory, one of the most important steps in this process is that of establishing a warm, genuine and empathic response with the caregiver which assists the counselor in formulating a case conceptualization. The case conceptualization serves to 1) assist in understanding the caregiver and her initial problems, 2) to identify potential treatment and intervention techniques, and 3) to provide a foundation for assessing the caregiver's progress (Cully & Teten, 2008). Information gathered in this session is useful in establishing a plan and treatment goals, and can be collected from a variety of sources such as the caregiver's self-assessment, the Beck Depression Scale, the Beck Anxiety Inventory or even a problem list developed by the caregiver.

The following problem list might provide insight into Beth's situation. In using this problem list, four categories are identified: 1) *Problem or Activating Event(s):* what are some of the key problems or activating event identified by the caregiver? 2) *Belief:* what does the caregiver believe about the problem or activating event? 3) *Consequences or Severity:* the caregiver describes what she perceives as the consequences or severity of her emotional pain. A question might be, "Using a scale of 1 (low) to 10 (high), can you rate your mood?" 4) *Impact:* What are the potential results of this continued behavior?

TABLE 10.3

Assessing the Caregiver's Activity Event and Consequences

Activating Event	Belief	Consequences	Impact
A friend called and asked Beth to go to the movies.	"There is no one to help."	On a scale of 1-10, Beth identified 9.	Feeling estranged from friends, and enjoyable activities.
Feeling emotionally drained.	"I never feel good anymore."	Very high most days-9.	Decreased energy level with a desire for increased naps.
Feeling my life lacks a sense of meaning and purpose.	"God must not love me to saddle me with this responsibility and no help."	When it occurs, the caregiver assessed it as a 6.	Feeling guilty for having these feelings.

Formulating a Clinical Plan and Treatment Options

Additional problems may be identified throughout the therapeutic relationship, which is perfectly acceptable. Also, the treatment goals and process ought to be reviewed regularly. Although the ongoing alliance between the counselor and the caregiver is extremely important, ultimately, it is the responsibility of the caregiver to assume responsibility for improvement. In this stage of the relationship, the counselor shares with the caregiver her impressions or clinical plan, which might be as follows:

Clinical Impressions/Plan with Beth

Beth, in our brief amount of time together, I have noticed that some of your thoughts and beliefs have helped to form what is typically referred to as burnout. This is not an uncommon issue for caregivers, yet I believe you can overcome this and live a healthy and hopeful life. I would like to review with you some of the problems that I have noticed, treatment goals and plan. Is that acceptable? Remember that your response/belief to the activating event in your life will usually determine the outcome; therefore, practical changes are required.

TABLE 10.4

Proposed Treatment Plan

Problem	Treatment Goals	Treatment Intervention/Plan
Feels increasingly depressed, which has resulted in a diminished desire to provide the care needed for her mother.	"I want to feel like I did last year. I had energy."	Engage client in a collaborative and involved therapeutic relationship by identifying ongoing behavioral actions and cognitive thoughts completing homework assignments and taking responsibility for her changes. Create an exercise program and log participation.
I have no friends or social activities.	"I would like to attend church at least once a month and renew my friendships."	Maintain a log of negative thoughts (depressive and anxiousness) and when they occur. Identify a list of community and/or church resources available to assist you in a time of respite. Identify a list of church or social activities that you can engage in monthly.
Life has no meaning or purpose.	"I would like to stop feeling guilty for caring for my mother and rediscover something meaningful for me."	Client will maintain a list of automatic thoughts, which interrupt her behaviors. Train client to utilize relaxation techniques.

Fostering Intentionality and Accountability

As part of a counselor's ongoing responsibility to Beth, it is important to continue educating her about automatic thoughts and distorted thinking patterns such as blaming, all or nothing thinking, jumping to conclusions, etc. Based on Beth's openness, it is important to integrate appropriate Christian principles to assist her in relying on her faith to address her thinking. For example, one of Beth's challenges is the guilt she experiences in caring for her mother. It might be helpful to remind Beth that in Christ we are given a spirit of freedom, and though Scripture reminds us to honor our mother and father, it is certainly acceptable to find a way to moderate the pressure that she has placed on herself. According to Pearce (2015), "We are made OK with God simply by grace, not by our pressured determination to keep all the 'shoulds' in one life" (p. 22).

It also important to continue reevaluating the treatment goals and outcomes and involve Beth in any possible solutions. Beth will also be expected to complete homework assignments as a means of tracking her reactions to different situations. Below is an example of one such tracking method. The caregiver completes this and returns during follow up visits with the counselor.

TABLE 10.5

Dysfunctional Thought Record Worksheet Example

Situation *What was the context? What was happening at the time?*	Automatic Thought *Describe your immediate thought.*	Emotion *What feelings came to you at the time?*	Cognitive Distortion *Blaming, all or nothing thinking…*	Alternative Thought *What is a more useful way to think about this?*	Outcome *Now evaluate your thoughts. Have they changed? If so, how?*

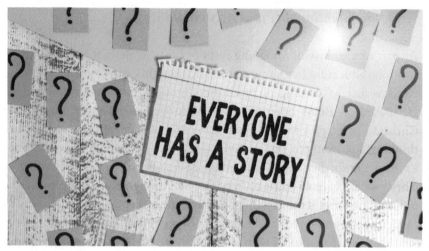
© Artur Szczybylo/Shutterstock.com

Narrative Therapy

Narrative therapy was developed in the 1980's by Michael White and David Epston, two therapists, who believed that it was important to separate people from their problems. Key principles related to narrative therapy suggest that individuals experience life through stories and people give meaning to their lives and relationships through stories (Combs & Freedman, 2012). McAdams (2013), posited, "stories do many things: they entertain, educate, inspire, persuade, and motivate, but above all, they make sense of our lives, they convey meaning" (p. 55).

Although narrative therapy provides a helpful alternative, it is prudent to acknowledge that it is founded on a post-modern principle, which in part emphasizes that truth is subjective. Essentially, narrative therapy promotes the idea that there is no objective reality or absolute truth (Hankle, 2016). However, truth as we know it is grounded in Scripture, and it is through life stories that we can discern "the intersection of human stories and God's story in the context of community and culture" (Scheib, 2016, Chapter 1, Section 1, para. 3).

Therapeutic Principles and Narrative Therapy

According to narrative therapy the following are key principles which guide the process.
- Stories told are the organizing principles which help to shape and form one's behavior (Hankle, 2016).

- The therapist functions as a co-author or consultant by drawing out key aspects of one's story to help shift the client's core ideas and create a new sense of meaning and purpose (Hankle, 2016).
- The problem one faces does not define the person.

"A central purpose of the Christian church is to proclaim, interpret, and live out this story of God's profound healing and redeeming love, which restores our brokenness and invites us to respond through continued growth in love" (Scheib, 2016, Chapter 1, Section 1, p. 3).

Application of Narrative Therapy

Stories have a way of helping to view past experiences, make sense of the present, and provide the opportunity to view the future with a renewed sense of hope. In working with Beth, it is important to allow her to share her story in full.

Narrative Therapy with Beth

Beth: "I am a 60-year-old, widowed female caring for my aging mother. She will soon be 85 years old. Overall, her health has been good, but she cannot be left alone. Mom has not been diagnosed with dementia, although she does present with some limited symptoms. She tends to forget things and tends to open the door and walk down the street if I am not paying attention. I never seem to get a break."

Counselor Pauses and Listens:

Beth: "The problem is that I have not had a break for almost two years now. I know it is not fair to complain because I know we are to honor our father and mother, but prior to me caring for my mother, my husband was diagnosed with a terminal illness. Even though I didn't want to stop working, he continued to insist so I stopped working. It has been almost 18 months since I have been able to go to church. Initially the pastor and few friends would stop by to check on me, but since my mother appears in good health the visits have stopped. I suppose they think I could get away if I really want to."

Beth: "I am just so tired. I no longer have any friends. I feel guilt for feeling this way. It seems as though God has totally abandoned me."

Counselor Interjects: "You certainly have had a difficult 18 months. What else?"

In this case, Beth shared a new narrative regarding her husband's passing after a period in which she was his caregiver. He was diagnosed at the age of 59 with terminal cancer and lived for about six months. At his request, Beth ceased working outside the home to care for him. Once again, she felt guilty for not having time to herself, but also felt it was a privilege to care for her spouse to whom she had been married for 40 years. Shortly after his passing, Beth became the caregiver to her mother, which interrupted her plans to return to work, and limited her ability to attend church. She had little time to grieve her husband's loss and adjust to a new life when her life changed once again by caring for her mother.

The sudden changes in Beth's life had brought about significant conflict in how she saw herself, how she constructed meaning and interpreted her future. For example, she and her husband had already been discussing retirement plans, which were suddenly crushed. Beth enjoyed work and her church activities, yet both had come to a halt. Finally, the more withdrawn she had become, she began to give herself messages such "no one cares," "I am all alone," "God must be punishing me," and "life no longer has any meaning."

In working with Beth, it is important to allow her to share her story and to maintain notes of how she has constructed her worldview. McAdams (2006) proposed six steps for evaluating one's life story: (1) coherence – the story holds together and makes sense, (2) openness- the story unfolds freely, (3) credibility – all major parts of the story are included, (4) differentiation- life-stories are rich and complex, which need to be explored, (5) reconciliation-the place where challenges and contradictions are exposed in one's story, and (6) generative imagination- one's life story is not simply focused inward, but also outward (p. 54). These steps will assist in interpreting and helping Beth to re-create her life story.

Guided by these key steps, the counselor would assist or coach Beth to share her story fully and freely. Sometimes it is easy to leave out important aspects of one's story, particularly if it is too painful. Beth is to be commended for the courage to share the rich and complex aspects of her story, but also to recognize that it is saturated with significant contradictions and when addressed can allow her to re-create her story.

In Beth's case, it is critical to remind her of how her story might conflict with what her faith allows. For example, Beth has allowed stress of her story to turn inward, and as a result she has begun to experience feelings of anger, guilt and blame. A careful and conscious reminder of God's promise might help her to re-envision her future as we are reminded to, "trust in the Lord with all your heart and lean not on your own understanding; in all your ways submit to him, and he will make your paths straight" (*New International Bible*, 1973/2011, Proverbs 3:5-6).

It is also important to remind Beth that she is co-creator with God in her life-story. In other words, God has given us a freedom of choice and will and she is greater than the sum of her story, which at this point in her life-story has been defined by the grief and caregiving problems she is experiencing. Although this process cannot be rushed, the sensitive counselor understands that we are called by God to be in a relationship with Him and others which fosters healing.

CONCEPT TO CONTEMPLATE

© ImageFlow/Shutterstock.com

Are you aware of additional therapies that might aid you in caring for caregivers?

CHAPTER SUMMARY

Caregivers may be the unsung and unknown heroes in our society. More people are becoming caregivers to those who cannot care for themselves. People are living longer and in some cases are healthier than in times past. Caregivers are not limited to family members, but extend to friends, siblings, paid professionals, strangers, and more. As the need continues to increase for caregivers, the need for qualified counselors will also increase. We need to be cognizant of these needs and our training as we seek to support the mental and emotional health of caregivers, especially for long-term caregivers with family members suffering from cancer, dementia, Alzheimer's, physical limitations, and other issues. This chapter in no way addressed every need of the caregiver but presented a variety of important topics related to caregiving that are important for counselors to discern, including formal and informal caregivers, demographics, roles and responsibilities, various challenges, and the importance of assessment and treatment interventions.

KEY TERMS

Burnout - a syndrome of emotional exhaustion, depersonalization and decreased personal satisfaction in one's accomplishments

Compassion Fatigue - the state of exhaustion and dysfunction—biologically, psychologically, and socially—as a result of prolonged exposure to compassion stress

Cognitive Behavioral Therapy - a form of therapy which relates primarily to one's thinking and thoughts processes

Formal Caregivers - represents the group of caregivers who are paid for their services

Informal Caregivers - typically represents the group of caregivers who are not paid for their services. These may include family members and friends

Narrative Therapy - a form of therapy in which individuals experience life through stories and people give meaning to their lives and relationships through stories

SUGGESTED RESOURCES

Organizations and Support Groups

Caregivers Guide to Medication and Aging: https://www.caregiver.org/caregiver%CA%BCs-guide-medications-and-aging

Caregiver Policy and Advocacy: https://www.caregiver.org/policy-advocacy

CarePredict: Top Online Communities for caregivers and family members: https://www.carepredict.com/blog/online-caregiver-support-groups/

Dementia Caregivers Support Group: https://www.facebook.com/groups/672984902717938/

Grief Care Fellowship: https://www.griefcarefellowship.org/

National Center for Caregiving (NCC) works to advance the development of high-quality, cost-effective policies and programs for caregivers in every state in the country. Uniting research, public policy and services, the NCC serves as a central source of information on caregiving and long-term care issues for policy makers, service providers, media, funders and family caregivers throughout the country: https://www.caregiver.org/national-center-caregiving

Resources by Health Issue or Condition: https://www.caregiver.org/resources-health-issue-or-condition

State by State Help for Caregivers: https://www.caregiver.org/family-care-navigator/

REFERENCES

American Psychological Association. (2019). *Assessment tools.* https://www.apa.org/pi/about/publications/caregivers/practice-settings/assessment/tools

American Psychological Association. (2019). *Beck depression inventory.* https://www.apa.org/pi/about/publications/caregivers/practice-settings/assessment/tools/beck-depression

Ammar, B. H., Hamdi, G., & Hechmi, Z. L. (2017). Burnout of caregivers in geriatric institutions: Coping strategies. *European Psychiatry, 41,* S608-S608.

Baldwin, J. (2017, April 21). *27 quotes to change how you think about problems.* https://www.entrepreneur.com/article/288957

Barsevick, A. M., Sweeney, C., Haney, E., & Chung, E. (2002). A systematic qualitative analysis of psychoeducational interventions for depression in patients with cancer. *Oncology Nursing Forum, 29*(1), 73–87.

Beck, A. T., Steer, R. A., & Garbin, M. G. (1988). Psychometric properties of the Beck Depression Inventory: Twenty-five years of evaluation. *Clinical Psychology Review, 8*(1), 77-100.

Beck, J. S. (2011). *Cognitive Behavior Therapy: Basics and beyond* (2nd ed.). The Guilford Press.

Capper, B. J. (2006). Essene community houses and Jesus' early community. In J. H. Charlesworth (Ed.), *Jesus and archaeology* (pp. 474–502). Wm. B. Eerdmans Publishing

Caregiving in the U.S. (2015, June). https://www.aarp.org/content/dam/aarp/ppi/2015/caregiving-in-the-united-states-2015-report-revised.pdf

Combs, G., & Freedman, J. (2012). Narrative, poststructuralism, and social justice: Current practices in narrative therapy. *The Counseling Psychologist, 40*(7), 1033-1060.

Cooper, D. L., Powe, B. D., & Smith, T. (2013). Social support provided by strain experienced by African-American cancer caregivers. *Support Care Cancer, 21*, 2719-2725.

Cully, J. A., & Teten, A. L. (2008). *A therapist's guide to brief Cognitive Behavioral Therapy.* Department of Veterans Affairs.

Daly-Denton, M. (2017). From Bethany to Jerusalem. In *John: An Earth Bible Commentary: Supposing Him to Be the Gardener* (pp. 147–160). Bloomsbury Academic. http://dx.doi.org.ezproxy.liberty.edu/10.5040/9780567674531.0017

D'Antonio, J. (2014). Caregiver grief and anticipatory mourning. *Journal of Hospice and Palliative Nursing, 16*(2), 99-104.

Edwards, V. J., Anderson, L. A., Thompson, W. W., & Deokar, A. J. (2017). Mental health differences between men and women caregivers, BRFSS 2009. *Journal of Women & Aging, 29*(5), 385-391.

Family Caregiver Alliance: National Center on Caregiving (n.d.). *What should family caregiver assessments include?* https://www.caregiver.org/caregivers-count-too-section-3-what-should-family-caregiver-assessments-include

Figley, C. R. (1995). *Compassion fatigue: Coping with secondary traumatic stress disorder*. Routledge.

Figley, C. R. (Ed.). (2012). *Treating compassion fatigue*. Routledge.

Gaugler, J. E., & Kane, R. L. (Eds.). (2015). *Family caregiving: The new normal*. Elsevier Inc.

Giovannetti, E. R., Wolff, J. L., Xue, Q. L., Weiss, C. O., Leff, B., Boult, C., Hughes, T., & Boyd, C. M. (2012). Difficulty assisting with health care tasks among caregivers of multimorbid older adults. *Journal of General Internal Medicine, 27*(1), 37–44. https://doi.org/10.1007/s11606-011-1831-5

Hankle, D. D. (2016). Christian worldview and the use of Narrative Therapy in the Christian counseling setting. *The Journal of Christian Healing, 32*(1), 5-14.

Jeffreys, J. S. (2015). Self-assessment of tasks of mourning. In R. A. Neimeyer (Ed.), *Techniques in grief therapy: Assessment and intervention.* (p. 110). Routledge.

Kelly, E. P., Meara, A., Hyer, M., Payne, N., & Pawlik, T. M. (2019). Understanding the type of support offered within the caregiver, family, and spiritual/religious contexts of cancer patients. *Journal of Pain and Symptom Management, 58*(1), 56-64.

Kessler, D. (2019). *Finding meaning: The sixth stage of grief.* Scribner.

Kübler-Ross, E. (1969). *On death and dying.* Macmillian.

Lee, A. A., Piette, J. D., Heisler, M., Janevic, M. R., Langa, K. M., & Rosland, A. M. (2017). Family members' experiences supporting adults with chronic illness: A national survey. *Families, Systems, & Health, 35*(4), 463-473.

Levy, J. A., & Gordon, A. K. (2013). Stress and burnout in the social world of Hospice. In L. F. Paradis (Ed.), *Stress and burnout among providers caring for the terminally ill and their families.* Routledge.

Louw, D. J. (2015). Compassion fatigue: Spiritual exhaustion and the cost of caring in the pastoral ministry. Towards a "pastoral diagnosis" in caregiving. *HTS Teologiese Studies/ Theological Studies, 71*(2), 1-10.

Lynch, S. H. (2018). Looking at compassion fatigue differently: Application to family caregivers. *American Journal of Health Education, 49*(1), 9-11.

Maslach, C. (2003). *Burnout the cost of caring.* Malor Books.

Mathieu, F. (2012). *The compassion fatigue workbook.* Taylor & Francis Group.

McAdams, D. (2006). *The person: A new introduction to personality psychology* (4th ed.). Wiley.

McAdams, D. (2013). *The redemptive self.* Oxford University Press.

McNutt, L., & Watson, M. (2015). Self-care: Managing compassion fatigue. *InnovAiT, 8*(6), 364-367.

National Alliance for Caregiving (2009). *Caregiving in the U.S.* https://www.caregiving.org/data/Caregiving_in_the_US_2009_full_report.pdf

New American Standard Bible. (1995). New American Standard Bible Online. https://www.biblestudytools.com/nas/ (Original work published 1960).

New International Bible. (2011). New International Bible Online. https://www.thenivbible.com/ (Original work published 1973).

New King James Bible. (1982). New King James Bible Online. https://www.biblestudytools.com/nkjv/

Nunn, K., & Isaacs, D. (2019). Burnout. *Journal of Pediatrics and Child Health, 55*, 5-6.

Off, C. A., Griffin, J. R., Murray, K.W., & Milman, L. (2019). Interprofessional caregiver education, training, and wellness in the context of a cohort model for aphasia rehabilitation. *Topics in Language Disorders, 39*(1), 5-28.

Pearce, M. J. (2015). Religiously integrated Cognitive Behavioral Therapy: A new method of treatment for major depression in patients with chronic medical illness. *Psychotherapy (Chic), 52*(1), 1-19.

Prunity, M., & Folie, K. J. (2019). Guilt experienced by caregivers to individuals with dementia: A concept analysis. *International Journal of Older People Nursing, 14*, 1-13.

Ray, E. B., Nichols, M. R., & Perritt, L. J. (2013). A model of job stress and burnout. In L. F. Paradis (Ed.), *Stress and burnout among providers caring for the terminally ill and their families*. Routledge.

Rosland, A. M., Heisler, M., Janevic, M. R., Connell, C. M., Langa, K. M., ... Kerr, E. A. (2013). Current and potential support for chronic disease management in the United States: The perspective of family and friends of chronically ill adults. *Families, Systems & Health, 31*(2), 119–131.

Scheib, K. (2016). *Pastoral care: Telling the stories of our lives*. Abingdon Press.

Staloff, J., Diop, M., Matuk, R., Riese, A., & White, J. (2018). Caring for caregivers: Burnout and resources for caregivers in Rhode Island. *Rhode Island Medical Journal, 101*(9), 10-11.

Stroebe, M., Schut, H., & Boerner, K. (2017). Cautioning health-care professionals: Bereaved persons misguided through the stages of grief. *OMEGA: Journal of Death and Dying, 74*(4), 455-473.

Swanberg, J. E., Kanatzar, T., Mendiondo, M., & McCoskey, M. (2006). Caring for our elders: A contemporary conundrum for working people. *Families in Society, 87*(3), 417-426.

Tippy, M. (2016). Psychosocial aspects of cancer for children and their families. In P. Lanzkowky, J. M., Lipton, J. M., & J. D. Fish (Eds.), *Lanzkowsky's manual of pediatric hematology and oncology* (6th ed., pp. 676-687). Elsevier Inc.

Toledo, T., & Akinyemi, E. (2017). Caregiver burnout: Application of Dialectical Behavioral Therapy. *American Journal of Geriatric Psychiatry, 25*(3), S88-S89.

Wenzel, A., Brown, G. K., & Karlin, B. E. (2011). *Cognitive Behavioral Therapy for depression in veterans and military servicemembers: Therapist Manual*. U.S. Department of Veterans Affairs. http://www.mirecc.va.gov/docs/cbt-d_manual_depression.pdf

Wicks, R. J. (2010). *Bounce: Living a resilient life*. Oxford Press.

Wolff, J. L., & Jacobs, B. J. (2015). Chronic illness trends and the challenges to family caregivers: Organizational and health system barriers. In J.E. Gaugler & R. L. Kane (Eds.), *Family caregiving: The new normal.* (pp. 79-94). Elsevier Inc.

Zarit, S., & Lewis, L. (2008). Behavioral and psychosocial interventions for family caregivers. *The American Journal of Nursing, 108*, 47-53.

CHAPTER 11

Counseling Women Facing Chronic Illness

DARIA WHITE, PH.D. & CHRISTINA VILLARREAL-DAVIS, PH.D.

> "When you have exhausted all possibilities, remember this: you haven't."
> ~Thomas Edison

> "She had suffered a great deal overall demoralization and anxiety the care of many doctors and had spent all that she had. Yet instead of getting better, she grew worse."
> (Mark 5:26, NIV)

Wisdom from Above: Standing in His Grace

You may be familiar with the story of the woman who had suffered for twelve long years from internal bleeding (Mark 5: 24-34). We do not know what the cause was, but that she had gone to many doctors and yet, instead of getting better, she grew worse. This is a recognizable story for chronic illness and for women who have to deal with the burden of taking care of

failing health while trying to hold many other responsibilities. The passage in Mark chapter 5 goes on to describe how the woman came closer to Jesus in the crowd so that she could touch his cloak. Imagine yourself in that crowd when Jesus asked, "Who touched me?" (*New International Bible*, 1973/2011, Mark 5:30) and the incredulous response of the disciples, "There are so many people here pressing together" (*New International Bible*, 1973/2011, Mark 5:31). However, Jesus knew the intention of this woman was different, and that healing power had come out from him. The woman trembled at His feet and shared

her story, and Jesus' response was simply, "Your faith has healed you" (*New International Bible*, 1973/2011, Mark 5:34). Seeking healing through proximity to Jesus and being in His presence has been a source of hope for many through the ages. Counselors have the opportunity to be a source of care and comfort by being fully present with their clients. As we take this journey to explore some of the most common chronic illnesses and the roadblocks for women who live with them, remember the Great Physician and Healer of all. Our desire is to bring our clients into close proximity of His healing presence!

CHAPTER LEARNING OBJECTIVES

Upon completing this chapter, you should be able to:

- Define chronic illness and contrast with chronic disease
- Describe common chronic illnesses seen in counseling, the psychological impact on mental wellbeing, and related DSM-5 diagnoses in women
- Identify evidence-based treatments, tools, and techniques used in counseling women suffering from a chronic illness
- Integrate a Biblical perspective of chronic illness in women

CHAPTER OVERVIEW

In this chapter, we will discuss some of the most common chronic illnesses. With millions impacted by one or two chronic conditions, such as heart disease, diabetes, cancer, and autoimmune disorders, illness will be either the primary concern or the unaddressed issue in the background of your client's problems. We will look at diagnosis and causation. We will address factors to consider such as **Adverse Childhood Experiences** (early experiences measured by a short test that assesses for traumatic early experiences), **Allostatic Load** (the body's response to adversarial environmental factors), and the current **Culture of Healthism** (a belief that people are responsible for their wellbeing and health).

Research often considers evidence-based treatments as they relate to specific chronic diseases. Overall, researchers have found motivational interviewing, cognitive behavioral therapy, narrative therapy, emotion-focused therapy, and self-compassion work useful in the increase of well-being and self-care for clients with chronic illness. The personal stories shared here are to serve as examples of the journey and counseling help that could promote hope, greater resilience, and mastery over situations that seem out of control to the individual. A case study will give you a chance to apply the chapter discussion, considering potential uses for the interventions.

Finally, remember that the search for answers often takes years. Learning to be patient with the process and holding hope for the client could be the most valuable of gifts to offer. In the fantasy trilogy *The Lord of the Rings,* Galadriel gave the light of Earendil to Frodo with the words: "May it be a light to you in dark places, when all other lights go out" (Tolkien, 1991, p. 397).

DEFINITIONS AND STATISTICS

What is chronic illness and how does this differ from chronic disease? According to Martin (2007), "*chronic illness* (long term illness that typically is unable to be cured) is the personal experience of living with the affliction that often accompanies chronic disease" (p. 2086) while the definition of chronic disease (medical condition that is long term and often progressive, lasting over one year or more while requiring continuing medical care, limit day-to-day activities, or both)is based on symptomatology described from the biomedical disease classification system. Chronic diseases are also conditions that last over one year or more and require continuing medical care, or limit day-to-day activities, or both (National Center for Chronic Disease Prevention and Health Promotion [NCCD-PHP], 2019). For this section, the term *chronic illness* will be used since the focus is on lived experiences with chronic disease.

More than 40% of people in the USA, or about 133 million, struggle with chronic illnesses, with the population projected to grow to 157 million in

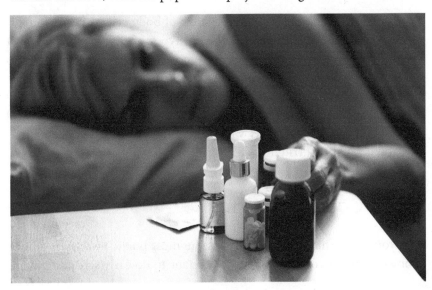

© fizkes/Shutterstock.com

2020 and 81 million of these currently living with multiple chronic conditions (National Health Council, 2014). The research literature also adds diabetes, depression, fibromyalgia, rheumatoid arthritis, inflammatory bowel diseases (IBD), and other autoimmune illnesses in the category of diseases that cannot be cured and are chronic in nature. With more than 40% of the population impacted by chronic illness, many of the women you see in counseling will bring mental health issues directly related to coping with common chronic conditions.

COMMON CHRONIC ILLNESSES SEEN IN COUNSELING

Cardiac Disease

Cardiac disease is the most common chronic disease and leading cause of death. In treating clients, the counselor should be aware of the different types of cardiac disease including angina, arrhythmia, heart failure, myocardial infarction, coronary artery disease, coronary heart disease, hypertension, and stroke. It is important to note that gender, age, and ethnicity are predictors for the types of symptoms and severity of the disease (Sperry, 2009).

Cancer

Cancer refers to the mutation and change of body cells that grow rapidly and out of control. There are different types of cancer with the most common being breast cancer. Once diagnosed, the patient is rushed into immediate decisions they might not be ready to make including surgery, chemotherapy, radiation, hormone therapy, and biological therapy (American Cancer Society, n.d.). It is the fear and the way the medical profession treats the diagnosis, which could lead to increased stress, anxiety, and depression (Tritter & Calnan, 2002).

Breast Cancer in Women

Did you know that breast cancer has the most public awareness among women, with a strong push from physicians to do early screening mammograms? Mammograms are the best way to screen for cancer, but doctors use Magnetic Resonance Imagining (MRI) and ultrasound to determine the presence of tumors and the best line of treatment. Women's self-administered monthly breast exams could lead to early detection and higher survival rates. A critical voice in the field (Tritter & Calnan, 2002) suggests that cancer should not be included in the list of chronic illnesses, since it entails intense treatment time and seasons of remission.

© Little Hand Creations/Shutterstock.com

Autoimmune Diseases

If you have a healthy immune system, then you are capable of fighting off invading microorganisms, such as bacteria and viruses, by creating antibodies or sensitized lymphocytes (types of white blood cells). So, what happens when you cannot fight off those invaders? This is called autoimmunity, when the immune system attacks the body itself, leading to an autoimmune disease (Rose, 2018). According to the American Autoimmune Related Diseases Association, Inc. (2018; AARDA), there are 151 autoimmune diseases (ADs). Some common ADs include Addison's disease, celiac disease, Crohn's disease, fibromyalgia, Graves' disease, Hashimoto's thyroiditis, lupus, multiple sclerosis, myasthenia gravis, pediatric autoimmune neuropsychiatric disorders associated (PANDAS), pernicious anemia, psoriatic arthritis, rheumatoid arthritis, Sjögren's syndrome, Type 1 diabetes, and ulcerative colitis. Although there is no one single cause that leads to an autoimmune disease diagnosis, genetics and the environment are two common factors triggering ADs (Rose, 2018). Depression and anxiety have also been associated with ADs in several research investigations (Kheirandish et al., 2015; Marrie et al., 2018; Muscatello et al., 2017) and there is growing evidence revealing that the association could be bidirectional, meaning that autoimmunity could be potentially leading to certain mental health disorders (Andersson et al., 2015; Euesden et al., 2017; Lu et al., 2016).

Diabetes

Currently 422 million worldwide and 46 million Americans live with diabetes (International Diabetes Federation, 2017). Diabetes is an autoimmune disease, with type 2 being highly preventable and 80% of diabetes found in low- and middle-income countries.

Living with Fibromyalgia and Chronic Fatigue
Marquita Wooley

© Marquita Wooley

Marquita Wooley is a 45-year-old Black woman diagnosed with fibromyalgia, a chronic illness that affects the muscles in the body with chronic muscle pain and tenderness throughout the entire body and chronic fatigue. Although this condition is not fatal, it can have serious, lifelong effects. When she was first diagnosed, Marquita experienced some symptoms and feelings associated with grief, including feeling shocked, denial, bargaining with God, depression, and anger towards the doctors who did not have any answers for five years.

Marquita describes the journey of living with fibromyalgia as a "humbling experience" (M. Wooley, personal communication, November 25, 2019). The chronic fatigue and exhaustion experienced throughout her day is the hardest part of living with this chronic illness. It affects her daily functioning and she has to choose what tasks she will complete for each day. The best way to grasp and understand what it is like living with fibromyalgia is through the ***spoon theory*** created by Christine Miserandino (2003). Marquita had this author (Christina Villarreal-Davis) grab a handful of spoons and then had her describe her typical day. Each task, such as getting out of bed, taking a shower, putting on clothes, and brushing her teeth, represented a spoon. By the end of this author's typical day, she had used up 27 spoons. Next, Marquita pointed out that living with fibromyalgia is like having only ten spoons to choose from daily. She had this author pick out her ten tasks for the day, which visually illustrated the point that women with fibromyalgia are limited in their daily tasks due to the effects of this illness on the body. She also pointed out that if she pushed herself to complete more than the ten tasks for that day, she would have to borrow some spoons from the next day as the exhaustion would lead to even less energy and spoons available for that next day. Lastly, Marquita emphasized that healthy women have the luxury of unlimited choices for their day.

Marquita also emphasized that most people do not understand fibromyalgia since those who suffer from it might look "normal" to others. For example, one day she drove to her local Walmart, parked in a handicapped parking space with her handicapped decal displayed. Upon returning, she found a hurtful note that was left on her windshield (see picture to the right). This uninformed and naive comment had such a profound ef-

© Marquita Wooley

fect on her that she holds on to this note even till today. Because of this, she refers to fibromyalgia as the "invisible handicap" (M. Wooley, personal communication, November 25, 2019).

Marquita is also a Licensed Professional Counselor and views her treatment from a clinical and holistic perspective. Her personal experience has given her a bird's eye view of medical and mental health treatment, which also provides recommendations for counselors working with this population. Marquita believes that her first step in healing was "acknowledging and accepting there is no cure for fibromyalgia" (M. Wooley, personal communication, November 25, 2019). She also incorporates Tia Chi (gentle and slow movements with deep paradigm breathing), mindfulness, cognitive behavioral therapy, self-hypnosis, and aquatic therapy. Furthermore, Marquita encourages women to educate themselves about fibromyalgia so that they can become their own advocate and health care manager. For example, she took a course that gave her an extensive medical and psychology view of fibromyalgia, which used Devin Starlanyl's (1999) book *The Fibromyalgia Advocate: Getting the Support You Need to Cope with Fibromyalgia and Myofascial Pain Syndrome*. Additionally, Marquita explained that the stress of not being able to work as much, which resulted in a decrease of income and her inability to complete daily chores, had a significant impact on her family members as well as her relationships with them. She recommends that spouses attend doctor appointments so they can learn more about the medical condition. She also encourages family therapy to help address the stress and psychological aftermath of the diagnosis on family dynamics. Lastly, as a woman of Christian faith, Marquita relies heavily on prayer and meditation. She often meditates on her favorite scriptures (Psalm 91:6; Hebrews 11:1; Psalm 103) and stated, "My constant source of spiritual inspiration is my sustainable, unshakable faith in God" (M. Wooley, personal communication, November 25, 2019).

DSM-5 DIAGNOSES RELATED TO CHRONIC ILLNESS

Diagnostically, Somatic Symptom Disorder (F45.1) is characterized by excessive thoughts, feelings, and behaviors associated with the person's health concerns, worrying about the seriousness of the disease, high levels of anxiety, and time spent thinking about and devoting to the symptoms (American Psychiatric Association [APA], 2013). Illness Anxiety Disorder (F45.21) is characterized by the fear and preoccupation with serious illness (APA, 2013). Psychological and Behavioral Factors Associated with Disorders or Diseases Classified Elsewhere (F54) follow the presence of a medical condition and could influence the course of the illness by exacerbating symptoms, delaying recovery, and interfering with treatment (APA, 2013). Diagnosis of one of these disorders is generally caused by the person's inability to manage the emotional stress and aftermath once diagnosed with a chronic disease (APA, 2013). There is also a high comorbidity between chronic illnesses and mental health disorders, especially those who are severe and difficult to manage while considering the person's experience of stress, anxiety, and depression. Patients with cancer meet the strict diagnostic criteria for mental health disorders at 31%, while women with breast cancer have the highest percentage of comorbidity at 42% exhibiting depression and anxiety primarily (Connolly-Zubot et al., 2019). In coronary disease, Sperry (2009) found that 1 in 5 patients experienced anger. Furthermore, as the individual ages and resources become limited, negative emotions could become more prominent (Kunzmann et al., 2019).

FACTORS TO CONSIDER WITH CHRONIC ILLNESS

Adverse Childhood Experiences

Given that there are many specific conditions that are chronic, but varied in their causes, symptomatology, and impact on daily life, it is difficult to make general statements on best practices. Most of the research focuses on one illness and its management and treatment. In recent years, there has been growing evidence that adverse childhood experiences (ACEs) have a direct impact on chronic health conditions and serious illnesses such as coronary disease, cancer, and diabetes. Researchers found that when childhood trauma was more extensive, these could lead to early death and twenty years shorter lifespan (Felitti et al., 1998).

Allostasis is the body's response to adversarial environmental factors. Allostasis (Groer & Nursing, 2010) explains how stress may produce illness. Psychological and behavioral states change in response to external developmental forces and, with the progression of time, could become more evident. Counselors should pay attention to both adverse childhood experiences and the allostatic load, which could affect the success of medical and psychological treatment and a woman's chances for thriving and surviving.

> **Allostatic load** is a measurement of multisystemic risk that is influenced by stress. Our body responds to adversarial environmental factors and stress that could produce chronic illness (Groër & Nursing, 2010).

© Papa Annur/Shutterstock.com

FIGURE 11.1

An allostatic model of women's health. CVD = cardiovascular disease; HPA = hypothalamic-pituitary-adrenal; HTN = hypertension; SNS = sympathetic nervous system; STD = sexually transmitted disease.

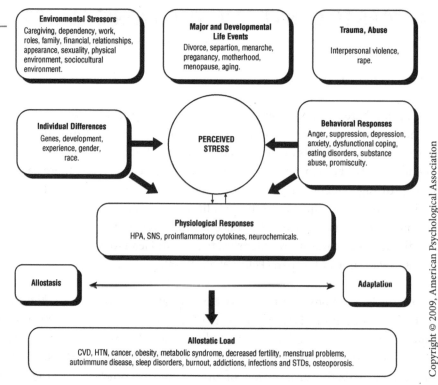

Environmental Stressors
Caregiving, dependency, work, roles, family, financial, relationships, appearance, sexuality, physical environment, sociocultural environment.

Major and Developmental Life Events
Divorce, separtion, menarche, preganancy, motherhood, menopause, aging.

Trauma, Abuse
Interpersonal violence, rape.

Individual Differences
Genes, development, experience, gender, race.

PERCEIVED STRESS

Behavioral Responses
Anger, suppression, depression, anxiety, dysfunctional coping, eating disorders, substance abuse, promiscuity.

Physiological Responses
HPA, SNS, proinflammatory cytokines, neurochemicals.

Allostasis

Adaptation

Allostatic Load
CVD, HTN, cancer, obesity, metabolic syndrome, decreased fertility, menstrual problems, autoimmune disease, sleep disorders, burnout, addictions, infections and STDs, osteoporosis.

What Do Adverse Childhood Experiences Have to Do with Chronic Illness?

In 1985, Dr. Felitti treated patients in an obesity clinic. Many of the women gave up after having great success in losing weight. Felitti noticed the connection between early sexual and physical abuse and obesity. These women consciously wanted to lose the extra pounds that subconsciously were a barrier and defense against intimate relationships. Dr. Felitti created the ACEs test to measure the impact of early childhood experiences and discovered the astounding increase in depression, suicide, and chronic illness when the ACE score was over 3 points. A score of 4 or higher led to 260% increase of chronic obtrusive pulmonary disease, 460% higher likelihood of depression, and 1,220% higher chance for attempted suicide (see Appendix, Figure 11.2 and Felitti (2002) for more information).

The ACE test can be located online and introduced to a client in one of your sessions. It consists of 10 questions and can be taken in a couple of minutes. One point is calculated for each question that is responded with a "yes." The ACE score could provide useful information about your client's background and the specific challenges they might have faced before they got to this point. It should also be noted that this questionnaire does not include all traumas, such as witnessing domestic violence, experiencing or witnessing community violence, placed in foster care, displaced by a natural disaster, and death of a family member or loved one.

View the ACE test here:
https://www.ncjfcj.org/sites/default/files/Finding%20Your%20ACE%20Score.pdf

Illness Severity

When studying women with fibromyalgia, those with lower levels of illness severity perceived the illness as peripheral to their core self and had better subjective well-being (Asbring, 2001). Check in the suggested resources at the end of this chapter for the *Illness Intrusiveness Scale* that can help you determine the current impact chronic illness has on a client. Chronic illness often leads to a changed perception of the personal identity of a woman referred to as an identity transformation (Asbring, 2001). For example, a woman with a stronger perceived competence would have a weaker illness identity, stronger control, and less severe consequences whereas a woman with a lower perceived competence would have a strong illness identity, less control, and more severe consequences (Sperry, 2009, see also Devins & Deckert, 2018).

> **Illness Intrusiveness Scale:** identifies instrumental functioning, intimacy, relationships, and personal development (Asbring, 2001).

Culture of Healthism

Current cultural attitudes focus on the responsibility of the person to achieve a great state of body function and better life. This could lead to shaming people for not trying hard enough (Chrisler & Johnson-Robledo, 2018). Self-blame for one's condition could lead to body distrust, which means the individual will never again return to the pre-illness sense of self, of options, of invulnerability, of obliviousness to the body's functioning. Her own body is seen as the enemy. Furthermore, a woman is also socialized to be the primary nurturer, a role much harder to achieve when she cannot perform simple tasks and fulfill needs for herself (Moss & Dyck, 1996).

© Tashatuvango/Shutterstock.com

Illness Causation

Type 2 diabetes "is a lifelong disease that prevents your body from using insulin the right way...It's the most common type of diabetes... Your pancreas makes a hormone called insulin. It helps your cells turn glucose from the food you eat into energy. People with type 2 diabetes make insulin, but their cells don't use it as well as they should. Doctors call this insulin resistance" (WebMD, n.d., para. 1-4).

It is important to remember that many current chronic conditions might have been caused or might have been exacerbated by life choices. Rapid urbanization, unhealthy diets, and increasingly sedentary lifestyles have resulted in previously unheard higher rates of obesity and diabetes, and many countries do not have adequate resources to provide preventive or medical care for their populations (International Diabetes Federation, 2017). For example, type 2 diabetes is highly preventable. Women diagnosed with hyperglycemia (seriously elevated blood sugar levels) during pregnancy can control blood sugar levels through diet, exercise, and blood glucose monitoring (International Diabetes Federation, 2017). However, cancer can be caused by both external factors (e.g. tobacco, infectious organisms, chemicals, and radiation) and internal factors (e.g. inherited mutations, hormones, immune conditions, and mutations that occur from metabolism; American Cancer Society, n.d.).

EVIDENCE-BASED TREATMENTS FOR CHRONIC ILLNESS

When we meet with someone who presents with chronic illness as a main problem in counseling, we must consider what is under the power of the individual to control and change. There are three categories to consider when working with people with chronic illness including lifestyle change, psychosocial treatment, and medication (Sperry, 2009). Mutual trust and bond with their doctor are also predictors of better outcomes (Yaghmaian & Miller Smedema, 2019).

Motivational Interviewing

When it comes to change, motivational interviewing and the four stages of change is one evidence-based approach in working with this population. How ready are they for changing radically certain aspects of their lives? Are they in the precontemplation, contemplation, preparation, or action stage? Do they need more information as they begin to contemplate what this diagnosis means, how it will impact their life, and what they have under control already? Can they begin preparing with your support for some major shifts in priorities and beliefs about what makes a good mom, an excellent worker, a contributing member of a community and a church? The place to start is always wherever the client is in the journey. In one study on asymptomatic heart failure patients, Mills et al. (2015) found that four weeks of gratitude journals improved mood and decreased the current stress. Furthermore, these investigators found that introducing daily gratitude could lead to better mood and sleep, less fatigue, more-self efficacy, and a lower cellular inflammatory index.

> "Our lives have become like that of a pensioner. You just can't cope with having guests at the house, at least very rarely. And you can't plan for it as you may feel so awful that you can't face seeing anyone."
> (Asbring, 2011, p. 316)

CONCEPT TO CONTEMPLATE

© Asier Romero/Shutterstock.com

Motivational Interviewing in Action

Consider the following questions when working with a client diagnosed with a chronic illness. What would be the stumbling blocks to improved mental well-being? How can you prevent a sense of defeat and disappointment when you enact the desired change? Counselors should keep in mind that when setting these types of goals, it should be small and attainable goals, avoiding bigger and unrealistic goals.

Cognitive Behavioral Therapy

Another evidence-based treatment when working with chronic illness is cognitive behavioral therapy (CBT). Sperry's (2009) study revealed that exposure therapy is a useful adjunct in working with Implantable Cardioverter Defibrillator (ICD) patients by addressing psychosocial risk factors, treatment-interfering representations of the illness, angina (chest pain, pressure, and discomfort) thoughts, illness perception, and non-cardiac chest pain. Counselors who are interested in using CBT to treat the psychological effects of chronic illness may find Renee Taylor's (2006) book helpful (see suggested resources). She offers specific case examples, CBT techniques, and guidance throughout sessions that address different medical conditions. Group work with CBT should be considered as part of the treatment of many clients with chronic illness (Sperry, 2009). Although not evidence-based, local (or online) support groups for women with breast cancer, multiple sclerosis (MS), fibromyalgia, and other chronic illnesses are great places to feel supported and to exchange valuable information about treatments, resources and services.

Narrative Therapy

Narrative therapy, which views clients as separate from their problems and helps them rewrite their story, is another evidence-based intervention. According to Adams (2015), reflection with clients on the changes that have occurred as a result of the illness will help create a revised schema that is more fitting to their current life situation and functioning. When a client finds out what the **illness intrusiveness** (the impact an illness has on one's lifestyle, activities, and interests) is and how the client has made sense of the illness, then they are able to identify unhealthy thought patterns in order to recreate their narrative. Processing, rumination, and reflection on the early days after diagnosis by looking at its impact and severity with a newfound, healthier perspective can help clients create a revised schema that better fits their current lives. This is a perfect example of post-traumatic growth (PTG) that has occurred and is a direct result of that revision. Clients can grow in relating to others, find new possibilities, increase personal strength, improve spirituality, and display appreciation for life (Adams, 2015). However, repeated failure to revise the schema of previous life could take months or years until the person is ready to revise (Adams, 2015). Furthermore, the timing for growth is diverse and appears different among individuals and their chronic illness diagnosis.

CONCEPT TO CONTEMPLATE

Narrative Therapy in Action

Adams (2015) proposed intentional questions when utilizing narrative therapy with chronic illness clients:

- What does your illness mean to you?
- When was the illness particularly important to you and when was it not important to you?
- How do you experience it?

Emotion Focused Therapy

Emotion focused therapy (EFT) helps clients to be more in touch with their emotions and experience them viscerally (Psychology Tools, n.d.). Connolly-Zabbot et al. (2019) suggest the use of EFT to treat women with breast cancer. The authors emphasize dealing with the depression and anx-

iety that results from the cancer diagnosis (see the figure here: https://link-springer-com.ezproxy.liberty.edu/article/10.1007/s10879-019-09439-2/figures/1). Triggers could be things from the past or the current cancer and existential threat. Global distress is a woman's overall presentation of demoralization and anxiety when she begins counseling. Women can attempt to self-treat by going to one of two extremes: staying positive and strong avoiding emotions or placing impossible expectations on self, not feeling "good enough". Avoidance of emotions would lead to further triggers and increase in fear. Once these emotions are identified and dealt with, the client is faced with core pain: loss being felt as ambiguous and/or realistically concrete. Focusing on the unmet needs will help clients to begin processing their current situation with self-compassion, release anger, let go and discover the places where they have agency and power.

Self-Compassion Work

Self-blame can play a big role in the internal dialogue of someone at the onset of their illness (Callebaut et al., 2017). Self-compassion brings better behavioral, clinical and emotional results with diabetes' patients (Ventura et al., 2019). It is associated with self-managing behaviors, more motivation for healthier choices, and better clinical outcomes (Callebaut et al., 2017). A client could be encouraged to write a self-compassion journal for one week or more. She would include the things she felt bad about during the day and then address them mindfully with an understanding of common humanity, with phrases such as "everyone goes through difficult times" and "I am not alone" (see self-compassion exercises to use with clients at Self-Compassion.org by Kristen Neff). Moreover, mothers with chronic illness may struggle to engage in parenting activities without self-blame. Farber et al. (2015) found that self-acceptance and a defined purpose in life brought about positive results in mothers diagnosed with multiple sclerosis. This study indicates the importance of helping mothers reframe their chronic illness and limitations to see mentally healthier possibilities for the future to reduce feelings of victimization to the forces outside them. Resiliency, agentic identity, and social support are key! Encouraging your client to develop a better positive relationship with herself and better attitude toward herself supports reduced symptoms of anxiety and depression and may increase overall quality of life (Chrisler & Johnston-Robledo, 2018).

ENGAGING THE BODY IN THERAPY

Given the fact that Adverse Childhood Experiences (ACEs) are associated with a much higher rate of chronic illnesses and poorer life-prognosis, addressing the trauma in a woman's life could bring significant positive change. The clinician can complete the ACE test with the client and use it in discussing further the major shaping events. Because trauma impacts the whole body, many approaches combine mindfulness, intention, and body work. Though not yet defined as evidence-based, the following approaches have been beneficial in the author's practice with clients who struggle with chronic illness.

Emotional Freedom Technique

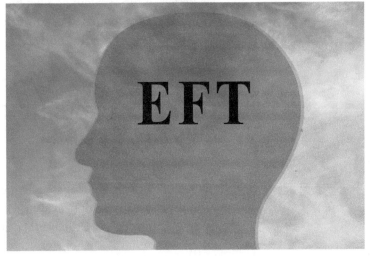

© hafakot/Shutterstock.com

The Emotional Freedom Technique (EFT) involves tapping on meridian points to release stress, and is utilized with veterans and clients with PTSD. It helps pair the stressor a person is experiencing with a validation in the beginning of the tapping process, acknowledging the current problem and the commitment to self through statements such as, "Even though I am feeling sick today, I deeply and completely love, honor, and accept myself." The person proceeds through tapping 12 meridian points while simply naming how she feels in statements such as, "I feel sick today, I feel sick today, I feel sick today." This approach helps the client express the negative emotion freely, breathing through the frustration and pain and continuing to hold the reality of self-acceptance and love. It is easy to use one of the numerous YouTube videos to explain to the client what the technique does. Here is an easy one to try (Gonick, 2010): https://www.youtube.com/watch?v=TRq8o1MEUtU. There is very little published research in the psychological literature to suggest that this is effective. The last one is from 2009 (McCaslin). EFT might not be the miracle cure the video shared above claims, but it is a concrete and easy way to name emotion daily.

Trauma Release Exercises

Trauma Release Exercises (TRE) are based on the premise that when animals escape danger they shake involuntarily to release the trauma. The exercises are to be practiced at home, and they help create involuntary tremors to unlock past trauma. Here is a video (TRE for all, 2019) you could share with your client if she is interested in trying out TRE: https://www.youtube.com/watch?v=FeUioDuJjFI.

Peter Levine's (2005) small book, *Healing Trauma: A Pioneering Program for Restoring the Wisdom of Your Body,* contains a CD to use in sessions with your client to guide her through feeling safe inside her body, create healthy bodily boundaries, and ability to relate to the world without compromising her core self.

LOOKING THROUGH THE LENS OF CHRISTIANITY: BIBLICAL INTEGRATION

In the current cultural climate of America being sick, disabled, or old are realities that do not connect well with the great ideal of staying young, energetic, and happy. Unlike other cultures, the American prefers high

© Alice TK/Shutterstock.com

positive emotions, such as enthusiasm, cheerfulness, friendliness, and fun (Tsai, 2007). Not only are positive emotions preferred, but negative emotions are to be avoided. Even though the Bible speaks both to the low (serene, peaceful) and high positive emotions, current American Christians strive for high positive states and experiences (Tsai et al., 2007). To grapple with the impact and heaviness of chronic illness, counselors and clients must both face the challenge in leaving the cultural expectations of healthism and remember that we follow "a crucified Savior" (personal communication with a student recently diagnosed with rheumatoid arthritis).

From a Christian perspective, instead of using the words *happiness* and *optimism*, substitute the words *joy* and *hope*! If happiness and optimism are fake assumptions and impossible goals this side of Heaven, especially when one faces darkness, fear, hopelessness, and uncertainty, then joy and hope are God's promises. Remember Job's exclamation in the midst of his physical and emotional pain when he said, "Even if He slays me, I shall hope in Him" (*New English Bible,* 1996/2017, Job 13:15). Leading clients to hope and trust no matter what, and to encourage them to express all their sadness, frustration, and anger to God directly ("How long, O Lord? Will you forget me forever?", *English Standard Bible*, 2001, Psalm 13:1), is to offer them the one secure place in the world when faced with illness and loss, like a safe haven with a loving Father who would not give a stone when a child asks for bread.

Living with Ulcerative Colitis, Breast Cancer, and Chronic Fatigue

Daria White

© Andrew White

I still remember the day 14 years ago when my doctor informed me that I had ulcerative colitis. Initially I felt shocked and devastated. I had lots of questions for my doctor including, "Is there a cure?" and "Will I have to live with this for the rest of my life?" In colitis, the autoimmune system begins attacking the colon causing ulcerations in parts or in its entirety. Some of the symptoms I experienced included persistent, often severe diarrhea and bleeding, from several times to 20-30 times a day. After several years of relative calm, the disease began creeping further and further up the colon. At its worst I could not leave the house, had a hard time climbing up the stairs to the second floor, and slept for 16 hours a day. At the end of that dark journey I was given another major medical blow, I was diagnosed with Stage 1 breast cancer.

Like the woman healed by touching Jesus who had been bleeding for many years and "suffered under the care of many doctors," I could say I tried it all - conventional medicine, herbs, vegan and paleo diets, homeopathy, holistic treatment, counseling, meditation, massage treatments, juice and water fasts, hypnotherapy, and prayer! My efforts for getting well often came from despair, and something must be done and must be done now!

Three years ago, when diagnosed with breast cancer, I went to a Christian healer. The three hours spent with him and his wife brought something invaluable into my life - HOPE! Scripture became alive again, God's promises and care for me - reality! With that hope I had the lumpectomy and radiation, miraculously began recovering from colitis and a year after cancer wrote and defended a dissertation.

This story is not over. Stress still is my enemy. I became sick again this year with the colitis and my initial response was not one of hope, but fear! My family, friends, and church surrounded me with love and care. This time it took two months instead of years to recover. I have learned in the last three years to engage in self-compassion and gratitude daily. My main focus when working with the chronically ill is the recovery of hope!

© Awardimages/Shutterstock.com

CASE STUDY

Stella is an African American woman who has come for counseling after a referral from the Health Clinic. The first thing you notice in her file is the long list of medications. During her first appointment, she is holding on to her jacket even though it is warm in the room. She says she is easily chilled. By the end of the session, she explains she had a very hard time getting up and coming in, so that she has only a house shirt under the coat, this is why she will not take it off.

The conversation moves back and forth between the people she cares for – there are two children she calls her daughters, but you find out that they are not her biological daughters, one is her granddaughter she takes care of, because her daughter is dealing with addiction, another is a daughter of a younger sister. Stella has multiple health complaints, the main diagnoses she reports to you are: high blood pressure and diabetes. Stella reports a childhood in an abusive family, neglecting mother,

and broken relationships. She is not used to being taken care of or considered by others.

How could you help her given everything you know now about chronic illness and treatment approaches? Because this is an African American client, the authenticity of the therapeutic alliance will be tested and Stella might need proof that you care. Given that she is overwhelmed by taking care of others, a phone call before sessions could be a good way to check in and remind her to be there. Creating a genogram with her will help to understand better the family system and the challenges she deals with daily.

You will have some long-term and short-term work to do: sorting through the past trauma and focusing each time on daily function. When you discuss health, it would be important to know Stella's overall functioning. Is she sleeping enough, does she have any exercise in her daily routine, what kind of food does she eat, what does she find restful, are there any spiritual practices she engages in? You know now that both type 2 diabetes and high blood pressure could respond favorably to life-style changes. You could begin talking about small measurable goals for Stella to complete. Could she take a 5-min walk outside when she feels particularly stressed out? Does she have a friend she could go out with once a week? Sleeping enough and feeling rested could be key to showing up for the counseling sessions and having enough resilience to believe in progress and keep trying. You could introduce breathing and grounding techniques, self-compassion, and gratitude exercises.

Begin working on Stella's understanding of the illness and its impact. The Illness Intrusiveness Scale could be utilized to see how much the illness is part of Stella's identity. You could choose one of the theories we discussed to engage with her. Narrative therapy could guide her to rewrite her story considering how if tomorrow things were different in her managing of the illness and how that would change her world. You could explore Cognitive Behavioral Therapy and work on the schemas she has about what normal functioning looks like and what she believes is possible or not possible for her.

For the trauma work, the ACE test can be completed with her and utilized in discussing further the major shaping events in her life. You might want to use the Emotional-focused therapy to explore core pain and unmet needs. Because trauma impacts the whole body you might want to consider approaches we discussed earlier in the chapter: Emotional Freedom Technique, (EFT), Trauma Release Exercises (TRE), or the simple exercises from Levine's book (2005) on how to heal trauma. The CD from Levine's book you could use in sessions with Stella to guide her to create healthier boundaries and say no to the demands of others.

The case provided is from working in a State institution where sharing of faith is considered inappropriate. What this author does in such cases is to check with the spiritual awareness and desires of the client. The client was an African American woman of deep faith who attended a strong Christian community. Questions on spirituality could be asked during assessment and informed consent obtained. This gives permission to the clinician to work with the faith of the client. Once you know that this is a Christian woman who values faith, you could ask her how Scripture supports her resolve to take care of herself and what God might be saying to her through this experience. As mentioned earlier, you could use the Christian terms hope and joy to promote a stronger vision of the future and commitment to work through the hardships.

CHAPTER SUMMARY

Women who live with chronic illness require courage and grace to live through each day, especially when illness is out of control with few answers and solutions. This chapter provided an overview of what counselors need to know in working with this population, understanding the impact of ACEs and life choices on those suffering from a chronic illness. Evidence-based treatments were also reviewed to shed light on best practices. Motivational interviewing, CBT, narrative therapy, emotional-focused therapy, and self-compassion work have revealed positive clinical outcomes for those living with a chronic illness. Because chronic illness is in the body, using therapies that impact the whole body could have an impact on the illness progression and severity.

Remember, you might be the presence of Jesus in many of these lives, to hold hope where there is none and to believe in the goodness of God in the darkness of current challenges. Pray and ask the God of comfort to sustain both you and the woman you help through the times of uncertainty and pain.

KEY TERMS

Chronic Illness - long term illness that typically is unable to be cured

Chronic Disease - medical condition that is long term and often progressive, lasting over one year or more while requiring continuing medical care, limit day-to-day activities, or both

Adverse Childhood Experiences - early experiences measured by a short test that assesses for traumatic early experiences

Allostatic Load - the body's response to adversarial environmental factors

Culture of Healthism - a belief that people are responsible for their well-being and health

Illness Intrusiveness - the impact an illness has on one's lifestyle, activities, and interests

SUGGESTED RESOURCES

Assessments

Adapted Illness Intrusiveness Ratings to go over with clients (IIRS): https://www.selfmanagementresource.com/docs/pdfs/English_-_illnessintrusiveness.pdf

International Classification of Functioning, Disability, and Health- IDF Diabetes Atlas: https://www.who.int/classifications/icf/en/

Post Traumatic Growth Inventory (PTGI): https://www.emdrhap.org/content/wp-content/uploads/2014/07/VIII-B_Post-Traumatic-Growth-Inventory.pdf

The Functional Assessment of Chronic Illness Therapy Spiritual Well-Being Scale (FACIT-SP12): https://www.facit.org/FACITOrg/Questionnaires

The Gratitude Questionnaire (GQ-6): http://www.midss.org/content/gratitude-questionaire-gq-6

Books

Cognitive Behavioral Therapy for Chronic Illness and Disability by Renee R. Taylor

Grief and the Expressive Arts: Practices for Creating Meaning by Barbara E. Thompson and Robert A. Neimeyer

Organizations

American Cancer Society: http://www.cancer.org/cancer.html

International Diabetes Federation: https://www.idf.org/e-library/epidemiology-research/diabetes-atlas.html

Self-Compassion.org: https://self-compassion.org

Training

Emotion Focused Therapy: https://www.youtube.com/watch?v=TRq8o1MEUtU

Trauma Releasing Exercises: https://www.youtube.com/watch?v=FeUioDuJjFI

REFERENCES

Adams, H. L. (2015). Insights into processes of posttraumatic growth through narrative analysis of chronic illness stories. *Qualitative Psychology, 2*(2), 111-129.

American Autoimmune Related Diseases Association. (2018). *Autoimmune disease list.* https://www.aarda.org/diseaselist/

American Cancer Society. (n.d.). *Cancer basics.* http://www.cancer.org/cancer.html

American Psychiatric Association. (2013). *Diagnostic and statistical manual of mental disorders* (5th ed.). https://doi.org/10.1176/appi.books.9780890425596

Andersson, N. W., Gustafsson, L. M., Okkels, N., Taha, R., Cole, S. W., Munk-Jørgensen, P., & Goodwin, R. D. (2015). Depression and the risk of autoimmune disease: A nationally representative, prospective longitudinal study. *Psychological Medicine, 45*(16), 3559-3569. https://doi.org/10.1017/S0033291715001488

Asbring, P. (2001). Chronic illness – a disruption in life: Identity transformation among women with chronic fatigue syndrome and fibromyalgia. *Journal of Advanced Nursing, 34*, 312–319. https://doi.org/10.1046/j.1365-2648.2001.01767.x

Callebaut, L., Molyneux, P., & Alexander, T. (2017). The relationship between self-blame for the onset of a chronic physical health condition and emotional distress: A systematic literature review. *Clinical Psychology & Psychotherapy, 24*(4), 965-986.

Chrisler, J. C., & Johnston-Robledo, I. (2018). The (un)healthy body. In J. C. Chrisler & I. Johnston-Robledo (Eds.), *Psychology of women book series. Woman's embodied self: Feminist perspectives on identity and image* (pp. 123-140). American Psychological Association.

Connolly-Zubot, A., Timulak, L., Hession, N., & Coleman, N. (2019). Emotion-focused therapy for anxiety and depression in women with breast cancer. *Journal of Contemporary Psychotherapy: On the Cutting Edge of Modern Developments in Psychotherapy.* Advance online publication.

Devins, G. M., & Deckert, A. (2018). Illness intrusiveness and self-management of medical conditions. In E. Martz (Ed.), *Promoting self-management of chronic health conditions: Theories and practice* (pp. 80-125). Oxford University Press.

Euesden, J., Danese, A., Lewis, C. M., & Maughan, N. (2017). A bidirectional relationship between depression and the autoimmune disorders: New perspectives from the National Child Development Study. *PLoS ONE, 12*(3), 1-14. http://dx.doi.org/10.1371/journal.pone.0173015

Farber, R. S., Kern, M. L., & Brusilovsky, E. (2015). Integrating the ICF with positive psychology: Factors predicting role participation for mothers with multiple sclerosis. *Rehabilitation Psychology, 60*(2), 169-178.

Felitti, V. J., Anda, R. F., Nordenberg, D., Williamson, D. F., Spitz, A. M., Edwards, V., Koss, M. P., & Marks, J. S. (1998). Relationship of childhood abuse and household dysfunction to many of the leading causes of death in adults: The adverse childhood experiences (ACE) study. *American Journal of Preventive Medicine, 14*(4), 245-258.

Felitti, V. J. (2002). The relationship between adverse childhood experiences and adult health: Turning gold into lead. *Permanente Journal, 6*(1), 44-47. https://dx.doi.org/10.13109/zptm.2002.48.4.359

Gonick, S. (2010, December 11). *How to do EET* [Video]. YouTube. https://www.youtube.com/watch?v=TRq8o1MEUtU

Groër, M., & Nursing, W. H. R. G. (2010). Allostasis: A model for women's health. In K. Kendall-Tackett (Ed.), *The psychoneuroimmunology of chronic disease: Exploring the links between inflammation, stress, and illness* (pp. 183-218). American Psychological Association.

International Diabetes Federation. (2017). *IDG diabetes atlas* (8th ed.). Retrieved November 4, 2019 from https://www.idf.org/e-library/epidemiology-research/diabetes-atlas.html

Kheirandish, M., Faezi, S. T., Paragomi, P., Akhlaghi, M., Gharibdoost, F., Shahali, A., Fini, M. E., & Akbarian, M. (2015). Prevalence and severity of depression and anxiety in patients with systemic lupus erythematosus: An epidemiologic study in Iranian patients. *Modern Rheumatology, 25*(3), 405-409. https://doi.org/10.3109/14397595.2014.962241

Kunzmann, U., Schilling, O., Wrosch, C., Siebert, J. S., Katzorreck, M., Wahl, H. W., & Gerstorf, D. (2019). Negative emotions and chronic physical illness: A lifespan developmental perspective. *Health Psychology, 38*(11), 949-959.

Levine, P. A. (1997). *Waking the tiger: Healing trauma.* North Atlantic Books.

Levine, P. A. (2005). *Healing trauma: A pioneering program for restoring the wisdom of your body.* Sounds True.

Lu, M., Guo, H., Lin, M., Livneh, H., Lai, N., & Tsai, T. (2016). Bidirectional associations between rheumatoid arthritis and depression: A nationwide longitudinal study. *Scientific Reports (Nature Publisher Group), 6*, 1-7. http://dx.doi.org/10.1038/srep20647

Marrie, R. A., Hitchon, C. A., Walld, R., Patten, S. B., Bolton, J. M., Sareen, J., Walker, J. R., Singer, A., Lix, L. M., El-Gabalawy, R., Katz, A., Fisk, J. D., Bernstein, C. N., & Canadian Institutes of Health Research Ream in Defining the Burden and Managing the Effects of Psychiatric Comorbidity in Chronic Immunoinflammatory Disease. (2018). Increased burden of psychiatric disorders in rheumatoid arthritis. *Arthritis Care & Research, 70*(7), 970–978. https://doi.org/10.1002/acr.23539

Martin, C. M. (2007). Chronic disease and illness care: Adding principles of family medicine to address ongoing health system redesign. *Canadian Family Physician, 53,* 2086-2091.

McCaslin, D. L. (2009). A review of efficacy claims in energy psychology. *Psychotherapy: Theory, Research, Practice, Training, 46*(2), 249-256.

Mills, P. J., Redwine, L., Wilson, K., Pung, M. A., Chinh, K., Greenberg, B. H., Lunde, O., Maisel, A., Raisinghani, A., Wood, A., & Chopra, D. (2015). The role of gratitude in spiritual well-being in asymptomatic heart failure patients. *Spirituality in Clinical Practice, 2*(1), 5-17.

Miserandino, C. (2003). *The spoon theory.* https://www.butyoudontlooksick. com/the_spoon_theory

Moss, P., & Dyck, I. (1996). Inquiry into body and environment: Women, work and chronic illness. *Environment and Planning D: Society and Space, 14,* 737–753.

Muscatello, M. R., Troili, G. M., Pandolfo, G., Mento, C., Gallo, G., Lanza, G., Pintaudi, B., Di Vieste, G., Di Benedetto, A., Zoccali, R. A., & Bruno, A. (2017). Depression, anxiety and anger in patients with type 1 diabetes mellitus. *Recenti Progressi in Medicina, 108*(2), 77-82. http://dx.doi. org/10.1701/2636.27098

National Center for Chronic Disease Prevention and Health Promotion (NCCDPHP). (2019, October 23). *About chronic diseases.* https://www.cdc. gov/chronicdisease/about/index.htm

National Center for Health Statistics, Centers for Disease Control and Prevention. (2013). *Summary Health Statistics for the U.S. Population: National Health Interview Survey, 2012.* http://www.cdc.gov/nchs/data/ series/sr_10/sr10_259.pdf

National Health Council. (2014, July 29). *About chronic diseases.* https://www. nationalhealthcouncil.org/sites/default/files/AboutChronicDisease.pdf

New English Bible (2017) New English Bible Online. https://netbible.org/ (Original work published 1996).

New International Bible. (2011). New International Bible Online. https://www. thenivbible.com/ (Original work published 1973).

Psychology Tools (n.d.). *Emotion focused therapy (EFT).* https://www. psychologytools.com/professional/therapies/emotion-focused-therapy/

Rose, N. R. (2018). *The common thread: How autoimmune diseases are related.* https://www.aarda.org/who-we-help/patients/common-thread/

Sperry, L. (2009). Cardiac disease. In L. Sperry (Ed.), *Treatment of chronic medical conditions: Cognitive-behavioral therapy strategies and integrative treatment protocols* (pp. 135-152). American Psychological Association.

Starlanyl, D. (1999). *The fibromyalgia advocate: Getting the support you need to cope with fibromyalgia and myofascial pain syndrome.* New Harbinger Publication, Inc.

Taylor, R. R. (2006). *Cognitive behavioral therapy for chronic illness and disability*. Springer.

TRE. (2019, November 26). *TRE® (Tension & Trauma Releasing Exercises): Full instructions with Dr. David Berceli (Official)*. [Video]. YouTube. https://www.youtube.com/watch?v=FeUioDuJjFI

Tolkien. R. R. (1991). *The Lord of the rings*. Houghton Mifflin Company.

Tritter, J. Q., & Calnan, M. (2002). Cancer as a chronic illness? Reconsidering categorization and exploring experience. *European Journal of Cancer Care*, *11*(3), 161-5.

Tsai, J. L. (2007). Ideal affect: Cultural causes and behavioral consequences. *Perspectives on Psychological Science, 2*, 242–259. https://doi.org/10.1111/j.1745-6916.2007.00043.

Tsai, J. L., Miao, F., & Seppala, E. (2007). Good feelings in Christianity and Buddhism: Religious differences in ideal affect. *Personality and Social Psychology Bulletin, 33*, 409-421.

Ventura, A. D., Nefs, G., Browne, J. L., Friis, A. M., Pouwer, F., & Speight, J. (2019). Is self-compassion related to behavioural, clinical and emotional outcomes in adults with diabetes? Results from the second diabetes MILES—Australia (MILES-2) study. *Mindfulness, 10*(7), 1222-1231.

Yaghmaian, R., & Miller Smedema, S. (2019). A feminist, biopsychosocial subjective well-being framework for women with fibromyalgia. *Rehabilitation Psychology, 64*(2), 154-166.

FIGURE 11.2

The Truth about ACEs

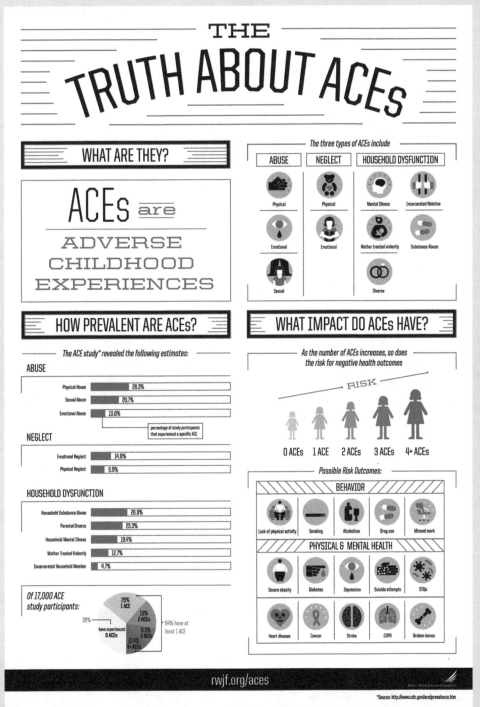

CHAPTER 12
Counseling Women Facing Grief and Loss

CHRISTINA VILLARREAL-DAVIS, PH.D. & DEBORAH BRABOY, PH.D.

"There is a sacredness in tears. They are not a mark of weakness, but of power. They speak more eloquently than ten thousand tongues. They are the messengers of overwhelming grief, of deep contrition, and of unspeakable love."
~Washington Irving

"And God shall wipe away all tears from their eyes; and there shall be no more death, neither sorrow, nor crying, neither shall there be any more pain..."
(Revelation 21:4, KJV)

Wisdom from Above: Standing in His Grace

© ibreakstock/Shutterstock.com

When you first think about the story of Ruth, you most likely recall her story of God's redemption through a kinsmen redeemer. However, what you may not realize is that this book of the Bible also eloquently portrays the grief experiences of two women, Naomi and Ruth. Naomi, who had moved to a foreign country due to famine in her land, which was mostly likely her first loss we read about, also experienced the loss of her husband and two sons (Ruth 1: 3-5). She seemed to even blame God for her losses and you can sense the depth of her grief and pain when she stated, "the hand of the Lord has gone out against me!" (*English Standard Bible*, 2001, Ruth 1:13) and "Do not call me Naomi; call me Mara, for the Almighty has dealt very bitterly with me. I went

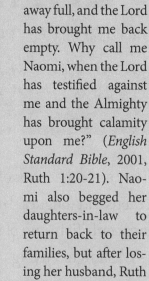

CHAPTER LEARNING OBJECTIVES

Upon completing this chapter, you should be able to:

- Define grief and loss and how grief uniquely affects women
- Explain the difference between grief and mourning
- Describe the common symptoms of grief seen in counseling and the psychological impact on mental wellbeing as it relates to *DSM-5* diagnosis
- Discuss evidence-based treatments, tools, and techniques used in counseling women suffering from grief and loss
- Evaluate grief and loss in women from a Biblical perspective

away full, and the Lord has brought me back empty. Why call me Naomi, when the Lord has testified against me and the Almighty has brought calamity upon me?" (*English Standard Bible*, 2001, Ruth 1:20-21). Naomi also begged her daughters-in-law to return back to their families, but after losing her husband, Ruth could not imagine another loss and leaving Naomi, "Do not urge me to leave you or to return from following you. For where you go I will go, and where you lodge I will lodge. Your people shall be my people, and your God my God. Where you die I will die, and there will I be buried. May the Lord do so to me and more also if anything but death parts me from you" (*English Standard Bible*, 2001, Ruth 1:16-18).

These two women's experiences of grief, loss, and weeping sadness (Ruth 1:9, 14) give the reader a glimpse into the emotional impact of death, loss, and separation. These symptoms are not only seen in the death of a loved one, but also in the many other experiences of loss, such as the loss of a job or marriage.

CHAPTER OVERVIEW

In this chapter, the topics of grief and loss in women are explored. First, each topic is defined along with an explanation of facts that counselors need to know when working with women facing these experiences of loss. Second, evidence-based treatments and interventions are discussed to promote effective and ethical counseling practices. Next, an examination of grief and loss through a Biblical lens is presented. Lastly, a case study is provided to promote further insight, understanding, and Biblical integration.

GRIEF AND LOSS IN WOMEN

Definitions and Statistics

What is grief? **Grief** (the emotional reaction to any type of loss) is the emotional reaction to a loss – it can be a death, or it can be a non-death loss such as loss of a job, friendship, or marriage, as discussed in Chapter 8. Worden (2009) describes grief as "the personal experience of the loss" (p. 37). Anderson (2010) describes grief as "the normal but bewildering cluster of ordinary human emotions arising in response to significant loss, intensified and complicated by the relationship to the person or object lost, and by the way the person dies" (p. 128). **Mourning** (adjusting to the new reality after a loss in an intensely personal manner) is the process wherein the griever adjusts to their new reality or world in which their loved one no longer lives. Grief is an intensely personal, unpredictable, and lonely journey. Grief is as unique as a fingerprint.

According to the 2015 U.S. Census Bureau, 800,000 people are widowed each year, and of those, almost 700,000 of them are women, who will then be widows for an average of 14 years. There are over 11 million widows in the United States.

In order to help them "grieve well," we must help clients learn to find a way of living with a reality that they do not want to be true. They would like to wake up from the nightmare that is now their reality. Julia Samuel (2017) explains it well: "Grief forces us to face our own mortality, which we have spent an entire lifetime denying, often through the creation of order – because, if we have order, we have predictability and, most importantly, control" (p. xvii). She goes on to add, "Death shatters control; it is brutal in its ultimate power over us, and it is this fact that we find so impossible to accept" (p. xvi).

It is important to respect and understand the process of grief and recognize how important it is to acknowledge and validate that experience for those

> What does it mean to "***hold space***" for a client? **Holding space** means that you are willing to walk alongside another person in their journey without judging them, making them feel inadequate, trying to fix them, or trying to impact the outcome. When counselors hold space for their clients, they open their own hearts, offer unconditional support, and let go of judgment and control.

> According to Randolph et al. (2015), one in four pregnancies ends in miscarriage. There are about 216,000 stillbirths each year. On average, 23,215 infant deaths occur in each year. Some 10,000 child deaths occur every year for children between 1 and 14 years old.

who are grieving. The medical model suggests that something can be treated, even battled, and then recovered. But that is not the case with grief. Women, and men as well, naturally avoid suffering, but to heal grief, it is important to allow women to *feel their pain* because it cannot be escaped. Therefore, when counseling a grieving woman, counselors need to "*hold space*" for their clients.

There are gender differences that influence the expression of grief (Polatinsky & Esprey, 2000). These gender role expectations are part of the socialization process of our society (Worden, 2009). When a child dies, mothers tend to be preoccupied with the loss longer than fathers, and they are also reported to experience higher levels of anxiety, intrusive thoughts, and disrupted sleep (Samuel, 2017).

Women who experience pregnancy loss (either a miscarriage or a stillbirth) typically experience grief accompanied with feelings of guilt, emptiness, abandonment, and emotional attachment (Randolph et al., 2015). This is also the experience for women who experience the death of a child. The role of social support is crucial for the grieving process to be successful, but what often happens instead is women experience isolation, silence, and insensitivity (Randolph et al., 2015). Women also report feeling that others avoid them after their loss which is often attributed to the overall discomfort with the subject and feelings of death, grief, and loss.

Ambiguous Loss

When most people hear the term *grief*, they immediately think about a death. However, there are many situations, losses, and relationships that are grieved without the presence of a physical death. **Ambiguous loss** is defined as "a situation of unclear loss that remains unverified and thus without resolution" (Boss, 2007; Boss, 2016, p. 269). The different types of ambiguous loss are physical and psychological. With physical ambiguous losses, a person may not know where their loved ones are or whether they are dead or alive. Their loved one is physically absent, yet they are kept psy-

chologically present because there is no evidence of their death – or their location may be known but the loss is still felt deeply. Examples of this type of ambiguous loss include war, terrorism (missing soldiers, for example), a natural disaster with missing persons (think of 9/11 or even earthquakes, tornados, flooding, etc.), kidnapping, desertion or disappearance (a wayward child), a missing body/person (plane crash, murder), incarceration, immigration, foster care and/or adoption, divorce, work relocation, military deployment, and even young adults leaving home (Boss, 2016).

A psychological ambiguous loss is when a loved one is present, yet psychologically they are missing (think of someone living with Alzheimer's or dementia, addiction, a traumatic brain injury, illness, or injury, etc.). Other examples of this type of ambiguous loss include family members in a coma, chronic mental illness, autism, and even obsessions. With ambiguous loss, there is no official verification of the loss and therefore, no finality with support or rituals such as a funeral (Boss, 2016). Instead, people are often criticized for not finding closure and left on their own to cope with no validation for the loss they are experiencing.

Primary Losses and Secondary Losses

The initial death or loss is often referred to as the *primary loss* and subsequent losses are identified as *secondary losses*. Secondary losses are not any less important, intense, or difficult, they all emerge out of, or are a consequence of the primary loss -- basically it is everything else (Worden, 2018). Sometimes secondary losses are described as *hidden losses* because they are not quite as obvious, or they are not realized immediately following a loss. It is a chain reaction and can feel like a train wreck with one car running into the next, and the next, etc., until you have a big pile up. One would ask, "Isn't one grief enough?" but rarely is any person grieving just one loss.

When the loss is the death of a spouse, the grieving spouse has not only lost her life partner, she has also lost her role as being part of a couple, her travel partner, her co-parent, and her lover. She is also grieving the loss of companionship, her role as a wife, and hopes and dreams for their future of growing old together. It is important to ask grieving clients what are some of the possible secondary losses they are grieving? They could be related to household responsibilities such as taking care of the lawn, paying the bills, or caring for the pets. Secondary losses could also be the loss of material things such as loss of income or financial stability, a change in lifestyle, or the need to move and relocate as a result of the primary loss. Other loss categories to explore include: loss of relationship (e.g. things they used to do together, opportunities or activities they had planned for), loss of material things, loss of functional ability (e.g. things they miss doing for the deceased loved one, chores they now have to assume), loss of roles (e.g. couple role, wife role, caregiver role, roles within their community), loss of support system, and the loss of hopes, dreams, and expectations. These secondary losses are not felt all at once. Oftentimes however, grieving individuals feel as if they are losing parts of themselves every day as these begin to become more apparent in their life.

FIGURE 12.1

Secondary Losses

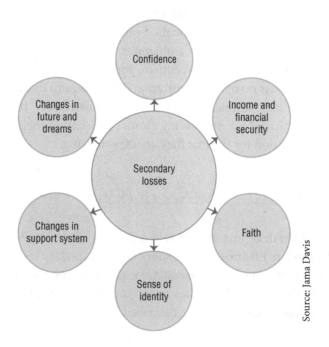

Source: Jama Davis

The same can be true when the loss is a job, an older parent diagnosed with dementia or Alzheimer's, or becoming an empty nester. The primary loss is obvious, but then there are also secondary losses which can complicate the grieving process (Worden, 2018). All of these losses cause grief and need to be mourned. It is important to help those grieving explore and process all they have lost so they can adjust and make the necessary changes to cope.

When the Death Is a Suicide

There is a stigma with *suicide* – even though the culture in the United States is more open to conversations about suicide, the stigma remains. When a loved one dies by suicide, the family members who are left to grieve are often faced with social disapproval (Lindsey, 2015). The survivors are at times suspected to have some blame or ownership in the suicide death and at times face being shunned and/or isolated. Perhaps some people think they should have seen some signs or suspected that something was wrong and sought help.

The stigma of suicide can be subtle and can be manifested in overt ways toward loved ones, such as blaming the spouse or other family members, or by omitted actions, such as not receiving benefits including life insurance (Lindsey, 2015). When women face the experience of an untimely death of a loved one, particularly when it is by suicide, their grief process can be more complicated. The complexity results in a different type of mourning. Four primary factors that distinguish the complexities of suicide bereavement for families include "stigma, questions about reasons, issues of remorse and guilt, and various logistical and legal factors unique to suicide that necessarily influence the events and processes following the death" (Lindsey, 2015, p. 444; Minois, 1999). The question that most often comes up is "Why?", because the suicide event is often seen as preventable. These questions are seldom answered and this thought process then often defines and complicates the grief process.

The culture in the United States is moving away from saying one "committed suicide" to instead using the phrase that the individual "died by sui-

> In 2018, there were 48,344 recorded **suicides**, and 1,400,000 attempts according to the American Foundation for Suicide Prevention. On average, adjusted for age, the annual U.S. **suicide rate** increased 24% between 1999 and 2014. White males accounted for 69.67% of suicide deaths in 2018. The rate of suicide is highest in middle-age white men in particular. On average, there are 132 suicides per day (American Foundation for Suicide Prevention, 2020).

cide". This distinction shows that the person who died was suffering from a mental illness and the death is just as if they had a medical condition that prompted the death. When one says a person "committed suicide", it is as if they had a choice, they were within their right mind, and they could control the outcome. This slight adjustment in describing the death is one step towards removing the stigma.

Symptoms, General Causes, and *DSM-5* Diagnosis

According to the *Diagnostic and Statistical Manual of Mental Disorders* (*DSM-5*; American Psychiatric Association [APA], 2013), grief is not defined as a *disorder*. Over the past couple of decades, awareness and discussion have increased regarding whether Prolonged Grief Disorder (PGD) constitutes a mental disorder. PGD is defined as intense, prolonged symptoms of grief, coupled with some form of functional impairment beyond 6 months post loss (Maciejewski et al., 2016). It was not adopted into the *DSM-5*. Instead, the diagnostic code V62.82, Uncomplicated Bereavement, is the diagnosis used when the focus of counseling is on the normal grief reactions to the death of a loved one. Grieving clients may present with symptoms that include feelings of sadness, insomnia, poor appetite, and weight loss. Although these symptoms are also characteristic of a major depressive disorder, when there is a loss, these symptoms can be considered a normal response to the loss, and the individual may seek counseling for help to relieve some of the symptoms and process the loss. The main distinctions between grief and depression are that while a grieving individual may experience some depressive symptoms, there is not the loss of self-esteem or intense feelings of guilt and/or shame (Worden, 2018). Grief is typically preceded by a loss and depression can develop at any time. Symptoms of grief usually improve on their own over time whereas women who experience depression often need medication and treatment to recover.

Traumatic, Disenfranchised, and Complicated Grief

Dr. Renee Turner

Dr. Renee Turner is an Assistant Professor at the University of Mary Hardin-Baylor, a Licensed Professional Counselor-Supervisor, and a Registered Play Therapy-Supervisor who specializes in the areas of grief and loss, bereavement, complex trauma, and identity and spiritual issues. She integrates mind-body-spirit and expressive therapies to create an experimental form of therapy. However, she did not just stumble into these specializations. Her interests come from her very own personal experiences of traumatic losses.

© Renee Turner

At the young age of only 7-years-old the unimaginable occurred, her father died by suicide, and her whole world forever changed. The **ruptured attachment** (a break and disconnect of a nurturing and loving relationship) from her father led to difficulties in developing a healthy attachment with others, especially her mother who had become less available, physically and emotionally (The Ainsworth Attachment Clinic, 2017). This traumatic loss also significantly impacted her future relationships, ability to trust others, and faith in God. Dr. Turner stated, "I questioned why God would allow this. I felt betrayed and angry towards God" (R. Turner, personal communication, November 22, 2019).

It was not until early adulthood when Dr. Turner eventually sought professional counseling to cope with her symptoms of complicated and **disenfranchised grief** (grief that is not socially accepted or recognized, and where the griever is not identified as someone who should be grieving). **Complicated grief** (prolonged grief symptoms that become pathological resulting in the impact of one's daily functioning, leading to significant psychological impairment) is a term used to describe prolonged grief symptoms that become pathological and impact one's daily functioning and lead to significant psychological impairment (Worden, 2009). It "is distinguished from acute grief by intensity and duration" (Knight, 2011, p. 20). Disenfranchised grief is a term used to describe grief that is not socially accepted or recognized, and where

© bellerebelle_n/Shutterstock.com

the griever is not recognized as someone who should grieve (Doka, 1989). Examples include death by suicide, the loss of a pet, or the death of a secret partner. Her first counseling experience was with a professional counselor who used traditional talk therapy. Although this two-year experience was helpful in realizing her spiritual disconnect, it was **Integral Breath Therapy** (IBT) (an experiential form of therapy that uses breathwork to work through various inner experiences and/or traumas) that had a profound healing effect and facilitated the post-traumatic growth she needed to heal herself physically, mentally, emotionally, and spiritually. She recalls, "It wasn't in my head, but part of my embodied experience and very spiritual. Through IBT, I found new spiritual meaning and made meaning of my traumatic loss. I needed the embodied grief process to understand my whole self: mind, body, and spirit" (R. Turner, personal communication, November 22, 2019). IBT uses breathing techniques to remove physical, mental, emotional, and spiritual blocks or stresses in the body. IBT incorporates conscious connected breathing, a circular breathing pattern where there is no pause between an inhale and an exhale, which facilitates healing and insight in the body (physically), emotions (emotionally), mind (mentally), and spirit (spiritually) (Lampman, 2010).

Unfortunately, losing her father was not Dr. Turner's only experience of traumatic loss. After years of trying to conceive, Dr. Turner became pregnant with twins but experienced a late term loss at 21 weeks gestation that devastated her world and impacted her identity as a woman and mother. She commented on the differences between her two traumatic losses, "When my Dad died, I felt like God had betrayed me, but with my twins, I felt like my body had betrayed me" (R. Turner, personal communication, November 22, 2019). Dr. Turner strongly felt that her previous and continued work in IBT, along with her spiritual faith in God and prayer, carried her through these difficult times. Additionally, she found Peter Levine's (1997) book *Waking the Tiger: Healing Trauma* informative as it helped her reconnect with her body, which was in a state of confusion. She indicated, "I needed to give my body a corrective experience and how it would have worked if it hadn't been in the fight/flight/freeze response mode. It helped me regain attunement with my body" (R. Turner, personal communication, November 22, 2019).

Today, Dr. Turner continues her professional work in grief/loss and provides the following suggestions:
- Grief is so complex and as such, there is no template for how grief is experienced
- Some women might compare themselves with someone else's grief template, which can impede the healing process or lead to shame
- Grief is a privilege, meaning not all women have the ability to take time off, take care of themselves, and seek professional help

She also provides the following recommendations for counselors working with this population:
- Show acceptance for how each woman copes with her grief since she is doing the best they can do
- Consider an embodied approach as this will lead to a body and whole brain experience that incorporates the right (where grief emotions, sensations, and relationship responses are stored) and left hemispheres (where cognitive, narrative, and making meaning of the loss occur)
- Address the woman's identity of being a mother, daughter, and spouse as this often drives who they were, who they are now, and who they will become throughout their lifespan
- Discuss any secondary losses, such as the woman having to take on her spouse's responsibilities or losing a house due to the loss of a dual income
- Utilize the woman's spiritual beliefs to help facilitate the healing process

In her dissertation research, Dr. Turner discovered that "all but one of my participants experienced a reduction in complicated grief symptoms. This one participant was also the only one that did not lean towards any spirituality and considered herself agnostic" (R. Turner, personal communication, November 22, 2019). Lastly, Dr. Turner provided this challenge for counselors to consider: What spiritual gifts come from the pain you have experienced and what will you do with those gifts?

TREATMENT OF GRIEF AND LOSS

© pixelheadphoto digitalskillet/Shutterstock.com

Grief is described as a process and has been seen by different theorists in various ways, primarily as phases, stages, or tasks. The stage approaches imply that people go through the stages in a linear fashion; and consequently, there is a tendency for some to take the stages very literally. The tasks concept suggests that grieving can be influenced from the outside. This gives the person grieving some sense of leverage and hope that there is something she can actively do to adapt to the death of a loved one. Much like developmental tasks that children master as they grow, someone grieving can address the issues of the tasks in order to adapt to their loss.

Kubler-Ross Model

© sirtravelalot/Shutterstock.com

Probably the most widely known stage model of grief is one that was introduced by Elizabeth Kubler-Ross (Kubler-Ross, 1969; Worden, 2009). This five-stage model was initially developed for the dying but soon was adopted by counselors trying to understand and describe grief. The five stages of denial, anger, bargaining, depression, and acceptance were expected to be experienced in that exact order (Smit, 2015). Kubler-Ross' model has been criticized because bereavement research has shown that grief is anything but a linear and predictable experience (Hall, 2011; Stroebe et al., 2017).

The Task Model

In *Grief Counseling and Grief Therapy: A Handbook for the Mental Health Practitioner* (4th ed.), Worden (2009) proposes that the grieving person address four tasks in order to adapt to the loss. Although the tasks do not need to be attended to in a specific order, some ordering is suggested by the definitions. These tasks each require effort – hence the term *grief work*. "Grief is a cognitive process involving confrontation with and restructuring of thoughts about the deceased, the loss experience, and the changed world within which the bereaved must now live" (Worden, 2009, p. 39). Grief is a fluid process and Worden suggests identifying many different mediating factors that need to be considered when working with a grieving person, such as who the person was who died and their relationship to the one grieving, the nature of the attachment, how the person died, historical antecedents, personality variables, social variables, and concurrent stresses (Smit, 2015).

FIGURE 12.2

Worden's Four Tasks of Mourning

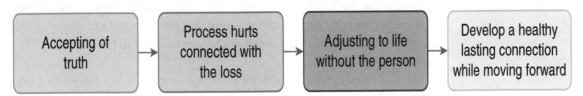

Source: Jama Davis, based on Worden's (2009) Four Tasks of Mourning

The first task is accepting the reality of the loss. People tend to struggle with this the most, particularly during the earlier days and months when there is a tendency to question whether their loved one is really gone and they are having to face the reality that they will not return. Bowlby (1980) and Parkes (2001) have written extensively about the *searching behavior*, which directly correlates with accomplishing this task. People who have experienced the death of a loved one find themselves waiting for them to return, or they may think they see them in a crowd (misidentify) and then have to remind themselves that they are gone. There are several ways people protect themselves from the reality of the loss through different types or levels of denial, but it most often involves either the facts of the loss, the meaning of the loss, or the irreversibility of the loss (Worden, 2009).

The second task is processing the pain of grief. Many have described the pain as a physical ache or sharp pain that they experience that goes along with the emotional pain of the loss. The intensity of the pain is different for everyone, and it also depends on the relationship that they had with the person who is now gone. Depending on cultural differences, women may have become accustomed to avoiding any negative emotions, so this task can be complicated by cutting off feelings and pretending that everything is okay. Some people simply stop themselves from feeling the discomfort, sadness, and dysphoria, and others use alcohol or drugs (or other unhealthy coping strategies) to numb their pain. Worden (2009) believes that helping people so that they do not carry the intensity of the grief and pain throughout the rest of their lives is one of the primary goals of grief counseling.

Adjusting to a world without the deceased is the third task. Worden (2009) identifies three areas of adjustment that need to be addressed after the loss of a loved one: external adjustments (how the death affects one's everyday functioning in the world), internal adjustments (how the death affects one's sense of self), and spiritual adjustments (how the death affects one's beliefs, values, and assumptions about the world). During this task, people try to make sense of the world. Death can shake the foundations of one's assumptive world (Worden, 2009). For many people, there are no answers and the question then becomes, "How do I live with not knowing?" If this task is not completed, the result is a failure to adapt to the loss.

The fourth task, which has been rewritten since Worden (2009) first proposed the four tasks of mourning, is to find an enduring connection with the deceased in the midst of embarking on a new life. He explains that people need "to find ways to memorialize, that is, to remember dead loved ones – keeping them with us but still going on with life" (p. 50). The counselor's role in this task is NOT to help the grieving client give up their relationship with the deceased, but to help them find an appropriate place for them in their emotional lives – a place that will enable them to go on living effectively in the world. This last task is usually the most difficult to accomplish. Many people get stuck at this point in the grieving process and later discover that they stopped living at the point the loss occurred.

The Dual-Process Model

The Dual-Process model introduced a key concept, which says that people oscillate between two dimensions, a *loss-oriented response* and a *restoration-oriented response*, and was developed by Stroebe and Schut (Smit, 2015). The loss-oriented response includes the grief work (such as separation distress, appraisal of the meaning of the loss, and relocation of the deceased in a world without the deceased's presence). However, during restoration-orienting, the griever shifts focus to the external changes caused by the loss in their life, such as focusing on skill mastery, identity change, and other psychosocial transitions, which could include the rebuilding of shattered assumptions of themselves and the world. Stroebe and Schut believe that it is not possible to attend to both loss and restoration components at the same time (Worden, 2009). This model also highlights the importance of determining factors such as the circumstances behind the death, culture influences, and gender differences. Smit (2015) added that an important element of the dual-process model is that it takes into consideration the effect of cultural and religious beliefs on the grieving process, which highlights the individuality of how loss and grief are experienced.

The Meaning-Making Model

Niemeyer introduced the meaning-making model as a tool to use with people who were suffering from life-threatening illnesses (Smit, 2015). It has already been noted that death challenges personal assumptions about the world, making women question what they previously knew to be true. Research supports the claim that the ability to find meaning in the experience of loss predicts positive adaptation, while a persistent and unsuccessful struggle or an inability to make sense of the loss is associated with more complicated forms of grief (Hall, 2011). The death of a loved one (or even other varieties of loss) can challenge the basic narrative of our lives, which then propels the griever to make every effort to make sense of what has happened and who they now are. *Meaning-making* allows the griever to process the event story of the death itself and gives them access to the backstory of the relationship to the deceased in a healing fashion (Neimeyer & Sands, 2011).

Grieving individuals have memories related to their loved ones. Some memories that are related to the lost relationship are often associated with feelings (emotional states) including sadness, longing, searching, and apathy. Some relational memories can be seen as *unfinished business*, such as the need to express gratitude or forgiveness, frequently appearing associated with an intense emotional response such as feelings of abandonment, guilt, and even anger (Jeffreys, 2011). Unprocessed unfinished business can result in chronic depression and prolonged longing and yearning for the deceased loved one over time and is often manifested by talking about him/her repetitively or ruminating (Puigarnau & Morales, 2017). Whatever techniques the counselor may use to help clients deal with grief related memories, healing ultimately comes through the bereaved person's capacity to establish and maintain contact with themselves and their loss experience. This contact is gained through a process of integrative meaning reconstruction of the loss experience (Puigarnau & Morales, 2017).

Interventions and Tools for Grief Work

It is not uncommon for grieving clients to struggle to find the words to express what they are feeling. Grief runs deep and touches the soul in ways that are difficult to express verbally, and creativity serves as a tool to allow people to express what may often seem as inexpressible. Creativity allows individuals to dig deep into the unconscious, and art therapy is one form of creativity that blends therapy and creative expression (Arellano et al., 2018).

© zimmytws/Shutterstock.com

Expressive or visual art modalities are often incorporated into grief therapy work. It is reported by Weiskittle and Gramling (2018) that more than 80% of trained art therapists work with grief clients. They go on to report, "Art therapists' orientation toward externalizing processes and facilitating insight meld naturally with meaning-focused therapeutic practice" (p. 11). The spontaneous creation of art or writing in session offers the one who is grieving an opportunity to memorialize the relationship and thus facilitates *continued bonds*. Different modalities of art therapy have been used in grief therapy, such as drawing, painting, photography, clay/sculpture, and photography. Creating mandalas, scrapbooks, and thematic collages are some of the more frequently implemented expressive art techniques used by grieving individuals. This often begins as early as the funeral service with the creation of a slide show of photographs depicting the deceased one's life.

> "Attachments to the deceased that are maintained rather than relinquished have been called **continuing bonds**." (Worden, 2009, p. 3)

One art technique that clients find insightful, innovative, and fun is based on the Japanese tradition of repairing broken ceramics with gold, silver, or platinum lacquer. *Kintsukuroi* or *kintsugi* treats the breakage in the ceramic as part of the object's history instead of seeing it as a flaw, error, or failure to be covered up or discarded (Witt, 2018). *Kintsukuroi* dates back to the late 15th century and means *to repair with gold*. The artisan would put the pieces back together to create something stronger and more beautiful than it was before. We live in a society with a *disposable* mentality. When something is broken, we throw it away; but beauty, strength, growth, and resilience can come from brokenness. Using this modality, clients break a clay pot, paint the pieces, and glue them back together with metallic gold glue. The end result is a piece that shows the growth and beauty that can be created from the pain and brokenness. A song written and released by Emily Anderson in December 2019 titled *Gold* speaks to the feelings experienced and proposes an answer to the question of, "What do I do with the spaces that used to be me?" Listen to it here: https://emilyandersonak.bandcamp.com/track/gold

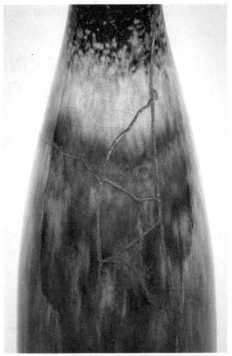

© photoBeard/Shutterstock.com

Journaling is used in grief work to help clients tell their story and journey. It can be done in the form of writing stories, poetry, and songs. Those who have a strong connection with music find that it offers them a way to express their thoughts and emotions. Music therapy interventions such as singing, playing, and songwriting have been found to reduce grief symptoms (Myers-Coffman et al., 2019). Using a combination of different expressive interventions, including art, music, and writing, along with traditional talk therapy, allows clients opportunities to express their emotions, including those they can articulate and those that are deeper and are beyond their ability to verbalize.

Therapeutic silence is very important in grief work. Sometimes this is the first-time clients have told the entire story, or specific parts of the story. Other times, they have repeated it so often that it sounds rote. Letting them tell their story without interruption is important. Non-verbal communication to let them know you hear them, you see them, and you feel their pain is essential. Equally important is using the basic counseling skills of reflecting back the *content* and the *emotion* you sense the grieving client is feeling (and may not have yet identified). This is also very valuable in sessions. Make sure to have an open body posture and reaffirm non-verbal communication so that grieving clients feel heard.

It is also critical that counselors can discern the difference between, "I just don't want to live without them" and "I want to kill myself." Grief clients are often inaccurately assessed as suicidal. Although they make comments about feeling dead inside and wishing they did not have to go on living, these words do not mean that they are having suicidal ideation. Using a suicide assessment, such as the SIMPLE STEPS suicide tool (McGlothlin et al., 2016), would be helpful to determine whether the individual is suicidal or merely grieving. It is important to avoid pathologizing grief. It is also recommended to have grief clients seen by a psychiatrist or their primary care physician to determine whether medication, such as an antidepressant, would be helpful to them during the first months or year of grief.

LOOKING THROUGH THE LENS OF CHRISTIANITY: BIBLICAL INTEGRATION

"Happiness has gone out of our lives; grief has taken the place of our dances" (*Good News Bible,* 1966 (NT)/1976 (OT/NT), 1992, Lamentations 5:15). Even though death is a natural event that everyone will eventually experience, it can feel extremely unnatural because it goes against every instinct and urge that we have. We live in a time when doctors and medicine have both training and technology to sustain and prolong life. The average life expectancy in the United States for men is now 76.1 years and 81.1 years for women! We cling to life, sometimes even to the extent that the quality of life is severely lacking (U.S. Census Bureau, 2015).

But do you ever wonder how God views death? What does the Bible say is the truth about death, and how can that truth influence our thoughts and

feelings when it comes to death? The apostle Paul wrote in Philippians 1:21-24, *New Living Bible* (1996) "For me, living is for Christ, and dying is even better. But if I live, I can do more fruitful work for Christ. So I really don't know which is better. I'm torn between two desires: I long to go and be with Christ, which would be far better for me. But for your sakes, it is better that I continue to live." Furthermore, Hebrews 2:14-15, *New Living Bible* (1996) says, "... only by dying could He break the power of the devil, who had the power of death. Only in this way could He deliver those who have lived all their lives as slaves to the fear of dying." The reality is that most of us are scared to death of death. Why are we so afraid? What is the basis of this fear? It seems that a big reason is the fear of the unknown. We do not know what it will feel like: Will we be in pain? Will we have to suffer? What can we expect? And, what happens after death, after we die? Jesus recognized this fear and offered the comfort that He is going to prepare a place for us (John 14:2). The old saying, "It's not what you know, but *who* you know" holds even more true in death. Knowing Jesus and having faith in Him calms some of the fears of the unknowns surrounding death.

We also fear the separation from those we love and the loss of control that death brings. We fear what it will be like for those we leave behind. These are realistic and practical things to think about, but they do not need to enslave or consume us. Sometimes it feels like death has won – with the feeling like you do not think you can go on, the gripping fear, and the bitter sting of death. Paul offered this encouragement to the Corinthians: "Then, when our dying bodies have been transformed into bodies that will never die—this Scripture be fulfilled: 'Death is swallowed up in victory. O death, where is your victory? O death, where is your sting?'" (*New Living Bible*, 1996, 1 Corinthians 15:54-55). He wrote this because death is not the end of the story. In the life of believers, physical death does not have the final word. But, because of Jesus' victory over death, those who place their faith in Him will live eternally with Him in heaven. On the day of a believer's death, they enter a pain-free, perfect place where there will be "no more death or mourning or crying or pain" (*New International Bible*, 1973/2011, Revelation 21:4). A perfected eternity that is the believer's greatest hope is the counselor's greatest truth with which to enable the client to process their grief.

Joel Jueckstock (2018) conducted a study to examine an individual's grief experience through the lens of relational spirituality or their attachment to God. A secure attachment to God is described as the practice of prayer and their ability to trust God to provide peace and calm during the difficult emotional response to grief. All of the participants in the study reported an increased emphasis on relationships with God and family, which is described as a primary source of purpose and meaning. Even though some reported "not being religious", they identified a personal connection with God or a higher power. The study was a deductive qualitative analysis of parents who lost a child to death. The results showed that those with a secure attachment to God were able to be more gracious with themselves, to be able to process the difficult emotions of grief, and to explore ways to continue with their lives after the death. The study suggested that secure attachment to God may be more likely to result in a grief experience that results in resilience and recovery.

© Marjan Apostolovic/Shutterstock.com

Kristen came into the office and was smiling nervously. She was in her mid-thirties, too young to be a widow. Her husband died unexpectedly two months earlier after having a routine medical procedure. She kept smiling but she struggled to keep eye contact in an effort to keep from crying. She had a 4-year old daughter, now a fatherless little girl. Her general appearance exuded confidence and professionalism yet when she spoke, it was apparent she completely lacked confidence and she seemed apprehensive. She said it was difficult to know whether she could trust that I would understand her pain.

She sighed and began to tell her story of how they had met, of their wedding, and first couple of years of marriage, and then what had occurred that led to his death. She was not with him when he died but she instead received a call from the hospital chaplain saying they were "working on him" and that she needed to get to the hospital as soon as she could. She admitted to me that she felt intense guilt for not being there with him when he died. She drove to the hospital and was told she could go in to see him. She decided not to go in though; she reasoned that she could not live with the memory of him lying in the hospital bed when he was really no longer "there". She also did not see him at the funeral home for the viewing or at the funeral. She explained that they had a strong connection and whenever one of them entered a room, they would reach out with some form of physical touch to connect – he may touch her on the shoulder or lovingly caress her hand. Her fear, she stated, was, "If I saw him, I would want to touch him, and if I touched him and he does not respond, well, I just can't live with that

the rest of my life." She claimed she does not regret not seeing him after he died though.

Kristen's grief was taking a toll on her body. She was having trouble sleeping and she lacked an appetite, so she was also not eating. She had lost about 25 pounds since his death a few months ago. She did not have any family living nearby but said she had church friends who were supportive. She had also noticed that some of her friendships had changed. Because she was no longer part of a "couple," she was the "third wheel" at events. She found herself becoming more isolated and withdrawing from attending activities in an effort to avoid having to answer the inevitable question, "How are you doing?" She said there were a few times she answered honestly, but that only made people avoid her.

She stated she was struggling to manage all of her responsibilities (keeping the house clean, taking care of the children, laundry, cooking, paying the bills, etc.) and now she had HIS responsibilities to handle as well (mowing the lawn, feeding the animals, fixing things that break, taking care of the cars, etc.). It was overwhelming. She said multiple times, "I just don't think I can do this alone."

Kristen attended counseling weekly for over 2 years. She navigated a lot of changes that took place following her husband's death, such as returning to work, moving (she could no longer afford or maintain her home with just one income), coordinating her child's schedule, establishing new holiday traditions, navigating relationships with friends and family, and being a single parent. She found her counseling sessions to be her "safe place" to feel and process her grief. It also allowed her to brainstorm who she was after her husband's death and what her future could and would look like.

The first few meetings with Kristen were opportunities for her to tell and retell her story. Each telling of the story brought out different details about her experience. During these sessions, she identified not only the obvious loss of her "husband" but also the many different secondary losses she experienced (her best friend, partner in parenting their children, the one who took care of the cars and the yard, the bill payer, the spiritual head of their family, and on and on). In emphasizing and validating her loss, it was important to give her permission to grieve all of those losses! When working with women who are widowed, or any woman who experiences grief and loss, exploring what resilience is and how life can/will look after their loss is important to incorporate into counseling. They are entering a new chapter of their life and it is often scary with much uncertainty.

It was important to assess the role spirituality played in Kristen's life (as it is with all grieving clients). Faith has a big influence on how one processes their loved one's death. What do they believe about afterlife, heaven and hell? What or where do they believe their loved one is now? Do they believe their loved one is in heaven and will be there

when they die and they will be reunited one day? Or, is there no spiritual foundation and therefore no belief in an afterlife so this life is all there is? Kristen was a professing Christian and believed her husband took his last breath here on earth and his next breath in heaven with Jesus. This gave her immense comfort – most of the time. However, there were times that even though she "knew he was in paradise", she would rather have him here with her. This led to feelings of guilt because she felt that she was "being selfish". Her life after his death was forever changed and although she didn't question God or her faith, it made her question a lot of other things. Ultimately though, she believes her faith is what got her through.

Some things to consider when providing grief counseling: What role does therapeutic silence play in grief work? How would you utilize that in counseling with Kristen? What types of non-verbal communication and posturing are most helpful?

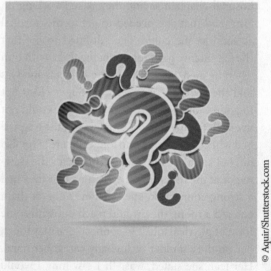

CONCEPT TO CONTEMPLATE

Worden's Tasks of Mourning and the Counselor's Own Grief

Take a closer look and personally examine Worden's (2009, pp. 39-53) tasks of mourning below.

© Digital Storm/Shutterstock.com

Task I	To accept the reality of the loss
Task II	To process the pain of grief
Task III	To adjust to a world without the deceased
Task IV	To find an enduring connection with the deceased in the midst of embarking on a new life

Consider the following questions as it relates to counseling women experiencing grief and loss:

1. Which task stands out to you the most and why?
2. What do these tasks look like in a counseling session?
3. Worden felt that "task IV is the most difficult one to accomplish" (p. 52). Do you agree? Why or why not?
4. How might these "tasks" of mourning differ from "stages" or "phases" of grief?
5. How have you experienced these tasks in your own experiences of grief and loss?
6. Have you looked into your own loss history? If not, consider exploring your own history of loss (see Worden, 2009, pp. 254-255).

CHAPTER SUMMARY

Women experiencing grief and loss experience a deep sense of loss that is revealed in the many signs and symptoms of grief. This chapter provided an overview of what counselors need to know in working with this population, such as encouraging grieving women to feel their pain, counselors holding space for their grieving clients, and the powerful impact of therapeutic silence. Evidence based treatments were also reviewed to shed light on best practices when counseling women experiencing grief and loss. Creative and expressive interventions (i.e., art therapy, journaling, creative writing/poetry) for meaning making in grief work have shown to have a significant impact on grief symptoms. Lastly, counselors should consider the spiritual impact on grief and loss and utilize spiritual resources to help women better cope with the life and family changes grief experiences bring.

KEY TERMS

Ambiguous Loss - when loss is unclear and unverified resulting in a lack of resolution

Complicated Grief - prolonged grief symptoms that become pathological resulting in the impact of one's daily functioning, leading to significant psychological impairment

Disenfranchised Grief - grief that is not socially accepted or recognized, and where the griever is not identified as someone who should be grieving

Grief - the emotional reaction to any type of loss

Holding Space – a willingness to walk alongside someone in their journey without judging them, making them feel inadequate, trying to fix them or trying to impact the outcome

Integral Breath Therapy - an experiential form of therapy that uses breathwork to work through various inner experiences and/or traumas

Mourning - adjusting to the new reality after a loss in an intensely personal manner

Ruptured Attachment - a break and disconnect of a nurturing and loving relationship

SUGGESTED RESOURCES

Books

Grief and the Expressive Arts: Practices for Creating Meaning by Barbara Thompson and Robert Neimeyer

Grief Counseling and Grief Therapy: A Handbook for the Mental Health Practitioner (5th ed.) by J. William Worden

Websites

Modern Widows Club: http://ModernWidowsClub.com

Post Traumatic Growth Inventory (PTGI): https://www.emdrhap.org/content/wp-content/uploads/2014/07/VIII-B_Post-Traumatic-Growth-Inventory.pdf

Self-Compassion: https://self-compassion.org

REFERENCES

American Foundation for Suicide Prevention. (2020). *Suicide statistics*. https://afsp.org/about-suicide/suicide-statistics/

American Psychiatric Association. (2013). *Diagnostic and statistical manual of mental disorders* (5th ed.). https://doi.org/10.1176/appi.books.9780890425596

Anderson, H. (2010). Common grief, complex grieving. *Pastoral Psychology, 59(2)*, 127-136. https://doi.org/10.1007/s11089-009-0243-5.

Arellano, Y., Graham, M. A., & Sauerheber, J. D. (2018). Grieving through art expression and choice theory: A group approach for young adults. *International Journal of Choice Theory and Reality Therapy, 38*(1), 47-57.

Boss, P. (2007). Ambiguous loss theory: Challenges for scholars and practitioners. *Family Relations, 56*(2), 105-111.

Boss, P. (2016). The context and process of theory development: The story of ambiguous loss. *Journal of Family Theory & Review, 8*, 269-286. https://doi.org/10.1111/jftr.12152.

Bowlby, J. (1980). *Attachment and loss: Vol. 3. Loss, sadness, and depression*. Basic Books.

Doka, K. J. (1989). *Disenfranchised grief: Recognizing hidden sorrow*. Lexington Books.

English Standard Bible. (2001). English Standard Bible Online. https://www.esv.org/

Good News Bible. (1992). Good News Bible Online. https://www.biblestudytools.com/gnt/. (Original work published 1976).

Hall, C. (2011). Beyond Kubler-Ross: Recent developments in our understanding of grief and bereavement. *InPsych, 33*(6), 8-11.

Jeffreys, J. S. (2011) *Helping grieving people–When tears are not enough: A handbook for care Providers.* Routledge.

Jueckstock, J. A. (2018). Relational spirituality and grief: A qualitative analysis of bereaved parents. *Journal of Psychology and Theology, 46(1)*, 38-51. https://doi.org/10.1177/0091647117753902

Knight, A. (2011). The popular encyclopedia of Christian counseling. In T. Clinton, & R. Hawkins (Ed.), *Grief, crisis, and trauma intervention* (pp. 393-406). Harvest House Publishers.

Kubler-Ross, E. (1969). *On death and dying.* The MacMillan Company.

Lampman, C. A. (2010). *What is integral breath therapy?* https://www.integrationconcepts.net/s/What-is-Integral-Breath-Therapy.pdf

Levine, P. A. (1997). *Waking the tiger: Healing trauma.* North Atlantic Books.

Lindsey, M. (2015). Bereavement experience of female military spousal suicide survivors: Utilizing Lazarus' cognitive stress theory. *The Professional Counselor, 5*(4), 442-457. https://doi.org/0009972786;10.15241/lm

Maciejewski, P. K., Maercker, A., Boelen, P. A., & Prigerson, H. G., (2016). "Prolonged grief disorder" and "persistent complex bereavement disorder", but not "complicated grief," are one and the same diagnostic entity: An analysis of data from the Yale bereavement study. *World Psychiatry, 15*, 266-275. https://doi.org/10.1002/wps.20348.

McGlothlin, J., Page, B., & Jager, K. (2016). Validation of the SIMPLE STEPS model of suicide assessment. *Journal of Mental Health Counseling, 38*(4), 298-307.

Minois, G. (1999). *History of suicide: Voluntary death in western culture.* John Hopkins University Press.

Myers-Coffman, K., Baker, F. A., Daly, B. P., Palisano, R., & Bradt, J., (2019). The resilience songwriting program for adolescent bereavement: A mixed methods exploratory study. *Journal of Music Therapy, 56*(4), 348-380. https://doi.org/10.1093/jmt/thz011.

Neimeyer, R. A., & Sands, D. C. (2011). Meaning reconstruction in bereavement: From principles to practice. In R. A. Neimeyer, H. Winokuer, D. Harris, & G. Thornton (Eds.), *Grief and bereavement in contemporary society: Bridging research and practice* (pp. 9-22). Routledge.

New International Bible. (2011). New International Bible Online. https://www.thenivbible.com/ (Original work published 1973).

New Living Bible (1996). New Living Bible. https://www.biblegateway.com/versions/New-Living-Translation-NLT-Bible/

Parkes, C. M. (2001). *Bereavement: Studies of grief in adult life* (3rd ed.). Taylor & Francis.

Polatinsky, S., & Esprey, Y. (2000). An assessment of gender differences in the perception of benefit resulting from the loss of a child. *Journal of Traumatic Stress, 13*, 709-718. https://doi.org/10.1023/A:1008980419116

Puigarnau, A. P. & Morales, A. C. (2017). Unfolding meaning from memories: An integrative meaning reconstruction method for counseling the bereaved. *Illness, Crisis & Loss, 27(3)*, 209-225. https://doi.org/10.1177/1054137316687954

Randolph, A. L., Hurby, B. T., & Sharif, S. (2015). Counseling women who have experienced pregnancy loss: A review of the literature. *Adultspan Journal, 14*(1), 2-10. https://doi.org/10.1002/j.2161-0029.2015.00032.x

Samuel, J. (2017). *Grief works: Stories of life, death, and surviving.* Simon Schuster, Inc.

Smit, C. (2015). Theories and models of grief: Applications to professional practice. *Whitireia Nursing & Health Journal, 22,* 33-37.

Stroebe, M., Schut, H., & Boerner, K. (2017). Cautioning health-care professionals: Bereaved persons are misguided through the stages of grief. *Omega – Journal of Death and Dying, 74*(4), 455-473. https://doi.org/10.1177/0030222817691870

The Ainsworth Attachment Clinic and the Circle of Security. (2017). *Circle of security/attachment theory terminology.* http://theattachmentclinic.org/AboutUs/terminology.html

U.S. Census Bureau. (2015). *Recent population trends for the U.S.: 2000-2010.* Retrieved March 3, 2020, from https://www.census.gov/newsroom/blogs/random-samplings/2011/03/population-distribution-and-change-2000-to-2010.html

Weiskittle, R. E., & Gramling, S. E. (2018). The therapeutic effectiveness of using visual art modalities with the bereaved: A systematic review. *Psychology Research and Behavior Management, 11*, 9-24. https://doi.org/10.2147/PRBM.S131993

Witt, A. (2018). Kitsugi. *Issues in Science and Technology, 34*(4), 55-66.

Worden, J. W. (2009). *Grief counseling and grief therapy: A handbook for the mental health practitioner* (4th ed.). Springer Publishing Company.

Worden, J. W. (2018). *Grief counseling and grief therapy: A handbook for the mental health practitioner* (5th ed.). Springer Publishing Company.

CHAPTER 13
Counseling Women with Anxiety Disorders

PATTI HINKLEY, ED.D. & APRIL CRABLE, PH.D.

"Anxiety is a thin stream of fear trickling through the mind. If encouraged, it cuts a channel into which all other thoughts are drained."
~Robert Albert Bloch

"When I am afraid, I put my trust in you." (Psalms 56:3, NLT)

Wisdom from Above: Standing in His Grace

© arloo/Shutterstock.com

What are you anxious about today? Yes, as counselors, we also face our own anxiety-filled days. Like every human, we face problems, make decisions, and are hurt in relationships. At times we get stuck and have a hard time determining how to move forward. To top it off, we carry anxiety over our clients. We can be flooded with questions like "Is there more I could have done to help?" or "Will my client be alright this week?" Consider the words of Paul as he wrote to the Philippians:

> Don't be pulled in different directions or worried about a thing. Be saturated in prayer throughout each day, offering your faith-filled requests before God with overflowing gratitude. Tell him every detail of your life, then God's wonderful peace that transcends human understanding will make the answers known to you through Jesus Christ. (*The Passion Translation Bible*, 2017, Philippians 4:6-7)

© pixelheadphoto digitalskillet/Shutterstock.com

CHAPTER LEARNING OBJECTIVES

Upon completing this chapter, you should be able to:

- Recognize the causes and maintaining factors involved in anxiety
- Distinguish the different anxiety disorders and their identifying characteristics as provided in the *DSM-5*
- Apply assessment options for determining how to treat anxiety disorders
- Construct evidenced-based treatment options while also incorporating Biblical insights

Paul encourages us to saturate our lives in prayer, taking even the details of our uncertainty to God. He will supply answers as well as provide a haven of peace from anxiety. As a Christian counselor, it is important to regularly fill your own soul with Bible study, prayer, and church attendance, along with other spiritual disciplines to prepare your mind and heart prior to counseling. We should then approach each counseling session submitted to God and His insight while doing our best. There will be times we may look back at a session and wish we could do it over, however, God does not expect us to be perfect. As counselors, we need to live responsibly and do our best to help, yet we are not responsible for change in the client. We are just one "tool" God uses in the life of a client. God is able to overcome our weaknesses and even use them for His glory. Take your concerns to God, and then rest in His peace, unless He prompts you to take necessary action. "*As you walk through the valley of the unknown, you will find the footprints of Jesus both in front of you and beside you*" (Stanley, 2012, p. 45).

CHAPTER OVERVIEW

Anxiety is inevitable and is a natural part of being human. God has designed our bodies to respond in a "fight or flight" response to danger (Taylor et al., 2000). While this is necessary to preserve our lives, sometimes the fear of danger can run rampant in our minds and take control of our thoughts and actions. Even in day-to-day living, most people will feel a bit anxious about simply making a decision. Facing the consequences of a poor choice can lead to feelings of anxiety or even avoidance. In all reality, most problems and psychiatric disorders will cause a level of anxiety. It is only normal to feel anxious when presented with a problem or a struggle to overcome. This chapter will address all types of anxiety, from minor issues to the profound, including psychiatric disorders provided in the *Diagnostic and Statistical Manual of Mental Disorders* (5th ed.; *DSM-5*). The causes of anxiety are considered along with a look at how the brain operates when faced with an anxious event or thought. Properly assessing for anxiety, along with the best evidence-based treatment options, are provided. Biblical principles and their application are also included. The chapter closes with a case study application, along with valuable counseling resources.

WHAT IS ANXIETY?

Anxiety is complex, as it can rear its ugly head in multiple contexts. It can be felt as an eagerness or excitement facing a new opportunity like a job interview or going on a first date. Anxiety can also be evident when a sense of failure is anticipated or experienced, such as failing an exam or being overlooked in a job promotion. A deep sense of paralyzing anxiety can be experienced when faced with traumatic experiences. These are all reactions to life events, however, there are times when individuals experience ongoing, excessive anxiety on a daily basis. This type of anxiety has no factual or logical explanation to the one experiencing it and can become debilitating if not treated. Typically, when the feeling of anxiety

© Motortion Films/Shutterstock.com

significantly impairs our ability to cope with the demands of everyday life, the symptoms are described as clinical (Dailey et al., 2014). Mental health professionals talk about anxiety as a state of alarm in response to a vague sense of threat or danger. While fear is an immediate alarm response to a serious or known threat (Comer, 2014), it is important to note that the term *anxiety disorder* refers to specific psychiatric disorders found in the *DSM-5* (American Psychiatric Association [APA], 2013) and involves extreme fear or worry that causes distress or impairment in functioning.

Symptoms

Anxiety symptoms include one or more of the following: Feeling nervous, irritable or on edge, increased heart rate, a sense of impending panic or doom, breathing rapidly, sweating, trembling, difficulty concentrating, feeling weak, difficulty sleeping, or gastrointestinal problems (Anxiety and Depression Association of America, n.d.; APA, 2013). Since many of the symptoms are experienced as physical, it often comes first to the attention of physicians rather than mental health professionals.

Statistics

Anxiety is the most common form of mental disorder in Western societies. *Our World in Data* (n.d.) estimated in 2017 that 264 million people worldwide have an anxiety disorder. The prevalence of anxiety disorders is at 18% in the United States (Kessler et al., 2005). In healthy populations, 25% of all individuals will become "clinically anxious" at least once in their lifetime (Comer, 2014; Scully et al., 1990). Women have consistently higher prevalence rates and are twice as likely as men to be diagnosed with an anxiety disorder in their lifetime (Anxiety and Depression Association of America, n.d.; McLean et al., 2011). They are also at more risk of receiving a lifetime anxiety disorder diagnosis for all anxiety disorders than men (Kessler et al., 2005). McLean et al. (2011) also found that one in three women met criteria for an anxiety disorder at some point in her lifetime, compared to 22% of men. However, social anxiety disorder has shown the least amount of gender difference in prevalence with one study indicating no gender difference in prevalence (McLean et al., 2011).

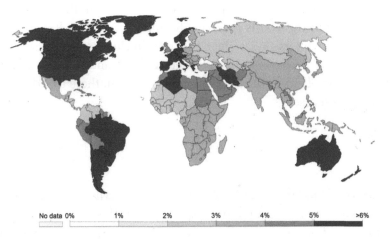

Source: Our World in Data, CC BY 4.0, https://our-worldindata.org/grapher/share-with-anxiety-disorders?time=1990..2017

Share of population with anxiety disorders, 2017.

TYPES OF ANXIETY DISORDERS

As was mentioned earlier, there are many types of anxiety that may need to be addressed in the counseling office. Anxiety that is caused by daily stressors or that accompanies many of the *DSM-5* disorders need to be addressed in counseling treatment, however, this particular section will focus on the description of the specific clinical anxiety disorders presented in the *DSM-5*.

The Diagnostic and Statistical Manual of Mental Disorders (APA, 2013) identifies five general types of anxiety disorders including specific phobia, social phobia, agoraphobia, panic disorder, and generalized anxiety disorder. Obsessive-compulsive disorder (OCD), as well as posttraumatic stress disorder (PTSD), have been given their own chapters in the *DSM-5*, while in former editions they were included in the anxiety chapter. OCD and PTSD clearly exhibit anxiety; however, since they are not currently classified under

© pathdoc/Shutterstock.com

Women have consistently higher prevalence rates and are twice as likely as men to be diagnosed with an anxiety disorder in their lifetime.

anxiety disorders, they will only be briefly mentioned in this chapter. An entire section in this text is dedicated to trauma, therefore PTSD will be discussed in Chapters 18-21. The *DSM-5* also includes two anxiety disorders found in children, separation anxiety disorder and selective mutism. Since this text places a focus on counseling women, these two disorders will not be discussed.

Generalized Anxiety Disorder

Generalized Anxiety Disorder (GAD) is best described as uncontrollable, excessive worry about multiple aspects of life. The anxiety can be over health issues, finances, weather, family members, work, and various other life events or activities (APA, 2013). Restlessness, irritability, fatigue, irritability, sleep disturbance, muscle tension, as well as difficulty concentrating are all symptoms. An individual would report having three or more of these symptoms for a majority of the days for the past six months to receive a diagnosis of GAD (APA, 2013). It is important to note that context is important as the anxiety experienced should be disproportionate to the likelihood of the dreaded outcome. Individuals with GAD have a hard time understanding what it means to relax. They also often engage in rumination of thoughts and experience chronic muscular tension (McRay et al., 2016). Research also strongly suggests that maladaptive or dysfunctional thinking is a primary cause of GAD. People with GAD are prone

© Stock-Asso/Shutterstock.com

to tune in on social or situational cues that they perceive as threatening. They also have irrational beliefs about the world, leading to exaggerated feelings of danger (McRay et al., 2016).

Prevalence among Women

Around 4% of the adult population of the United States suffer with GAD on a regular basis (Comer, 2014). Women are twice as likely as men to be diagnosed with GAD, while the overall 12-month prevalence of GAD among adults in the United States is 2.9% (Kopala & Keitel, 2017; McRay et al., 2016). Women may have a higher level of impairment in areas such as missing work and overall level of disability (McLean et al., 2011). Women are also more likely to have a comorbid depressive disorder or another additional anxiety disorder. A woman's menstrual cycle has also been found to increase the level of severity in some women (Howell et al., 2001). Symptoms typically appear first in childhood and adolescence which could suggest a developmental influence as well (McRay et al., 2016).

> "Suffering with GAD is like being flushed with regular injections of adrenaline. Sooner or later the person is wasted—all available resources are spent." (McRay et al., 2016, p. 167)

Specific Phobia

Specific Phobia (SP) is one of the most common mental disorders in the general population, marked by extreme and irrational fear or anxiety about a specific object or situation (APA, 2013). When confronted with the fear the individual will experience intense anxiety and often bodily sensations such as respiration, heart palpitations, and perspiration. Where a phobia becomes a concern is when it causes distress or impairment in daily functioning. The *DSM* distinguishes between the subtypes of animal (spiders, snakes), natural environment (e.g. heights, weather), blood-injection-injury (e.g. needles, blood), situational (e.g. flying on a plane, elevators) and other (e.g. vomiting, choking) (APA, 2013, 2013; Wardenaar et al., 2017). Specific phobias can cause functional impair-

© lassedesignen/Shutterstock.com

ment due to a restricted lifestyle resulting from the avoidance of the object or situation that produces fear (Wardenaar et al., 2017).

Prevalence among Women

Approximately 10% of adults experience a phobia at least once annually, while 14% experience a phobia at some point in their life (Comer, 2014). Rarely do individuals seek treatment for phobia; however, social phobia has been found to be strongly associated with other anxiety disorders (Lebeau et al., 2010; Stinson et al., 2007). Research studies have found that there is a higher prevalence in women. One study by Fredrikson et al. (1996) found that 26.5% of all women and 12.4% of all men met criteria for SP. Lebeau et al. (2010) found that animal phobia, height phobia, and situational phobia had a higher prevalence for women than men. In a study conducted by Stinson et al. (2007), fears of animals and heights were the most common with 50% of all individuals with SP reporting them. They also found that most specific phobias involve multiple fears with only 28.9% of individuals with SP reporting only a single specific fear. In one study women had a prevalence of 12.1% for animal phobia versus 3.3% in men (Fredrikson et al., 1996).

Social Anxiety Disorder

Social Anxiety Disorder (SAD or SANXD) is associated with a persistent and intense fear of social situations, especially where the individual may be exposed to the scrutiny of others (APA, 2013). A few examples may include meeting unfamiliar people, being observed eating or interacting with others, or performing in front of people. The individual is fearful of embarrassment, humiliation, or rejection; therefore, social situations are avoided or are endured with intense anxiety. In order to meet the diagnostic criteria for social anxiety disorder, the symptoms must be present for six months or more, the anxiety must be out of proportion to the actual threat, the avoidance behavior must cause significant impairment or distress to the individual, and the anxiety must not be better explained by the effects of a medical condition or another psychological disorder (APA, 2013). These difficulties in interpersonal interactions can result in significant impairment in almost all facets of daily life. The impairment caused by SANXD is very high, with SANXD being among the five most impairing psychiatric disorders (Alonso et al., 2004).

Prevalence among Women

The 12-month prevalence rate for SANXD in the United States is around 7%, with women meeting the criteria slightly more often than men. The most prevalent age of onset is between the ages of 8 and 15 years, which can emerge from social inhibition or shyness as a child (APA, 2013). Research indicates that there is no difference in the overall course of social anxiety disorder between the genders; however, women have a greater number of social fears as well as situational panic attacks (Xu et al., 2012). Women are more likely to

experience anxiety while eating and drinking in front of others, speaking up at a meeting, being the center of attention, expressing disapproval, speaking to authority figures, and being interviewed. Men are more likely to experience anxiety in dating, returning goods to stores, or urinating in public bathrooms (Xu et al., 2012). Women were found to be more likely to have comorbid internalizing disorders (i.e., other anxiety disorders and depression), while men were more likely to have comorbid externalizing disorders such as conduct disorder and substance abuse (Asher & Aderka, 2018; Xu et al., 2012).

Panic Disorder

Panic Disorder is best described as the experience of reoccurring panic attacks that happen unexpectedly without having an obvious trigger causing the panic reaction. Four out of the following symptoms must occur in order to meet the diagnosis of panic disorder: Sweating, heart palpitations, trembling, chest pain or discomfort, shortness of breath, feelings of choking, chest pain, dizzy sensations, nausea, chills or heat sensations, derealization (feelings of unreality), numbness or tingling sensations, fear of losing control, or fear of dying (APA, 2013). Panic attacks are also a

symptom of a variety of other mental health disorders; therefore, experiencing panic attacks alone does not constitute a diagnosis of panic disorder. Therefore, to fully diagnose panic disorder, at least one of the attacks should be followed by 1) one month or more of either persistent concern about having additional panic attacks or 2) the individual experiences a significant maladaptive change in behavior related to the attacks. It is also important to confirm that the panic attacks are not caused by a substance such as a drug or medication or a medical condition (APA, 2013). Individuals who experience a panic attack often worry about reoccurrences and what may happen if a panic attack happens in public (Frances, 2013). This fear of reoccurrence can eventually lead to Agoraphobia where one fears leaving home.

Prevalence among Women

The overall 12-month prevalence rate is 2% to 3% in adults and adolescents with the median age of onset being around 20-24 years (APA, 2013). Women have significantly higher rates of panic disorder and are twice as likely to be diagnosed as men. The *DSM-5* indicates that these gender differences may take place as early as 14 years, and in girls, there is a gradual increase in panic disorder diagnoses through adolescence (APA, 2013). Panic disorder often has comorbidity with other disorders, with the most common being depressive disorders, substance use disorders, as well as additional anxiety disorders. Research studies also indicate that women with panic disorder are more likely to experience increased symptoms during menstruation, as well as more panic attacks during the premenstrual phase (Haigh et al., 2018). Panic disorder has also been found to be more prevalent in postpartum women, along with depression comorbidity (Kessler et al., 1998; Matsumoto et al., 2019).

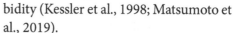

Agoraphobia

Agoraphobia is an anxiety about being in places or situations from which escape might be difficult or embarrassing or where help may not be available if something bad were to happen. To meet the clinical diagnosis, the anxiety

involves feeling fear in two or more of the following situations: Being in open spaces, being in enclosed spaces (e.g., shopping mall, theatre), standing in line or being in a crowd, or just being outside of the home alone (APA, 2013; Substance Abuse and Mental Health Services Administration, 2016). Agoraphobia often develops after having one or more **panic attacks**. (Symptoms of rapid heartbeat, rapid breathing, shaking, sweating, chest pain, dizziness, nausea, and various other symptoms that often continue for 15 seconds up to 30 minutes.)

Prevalence among Women

Women are twice as likely to experience symptoms of agoraphobia compared to men. In most cases, the initial onset begins before the age of 35 (APA, 2013). Tibi et al., (2015) determined the median age of onset for agoraphobia is 24 years of age versus 20 for panic disorder. They also indicated an early onset is considered 27 years or younger, while a late onset is older than 27. Individuals with an early onset had a family history of anxiety disorders, while those with a late onset also had increased psychosocial severity (Tibi et al., 2015).

CONCEPT TO CONTEMPLATE

© ImageFlow/Shutterstock.com

As noted in the chapter, women have consistently higher prevalence rates and are twice as likely as men to be diagnosed with an anxiety disorder in their lifetime. What are your thoughts regarding the prevalence rates? Are women more prone to anxiety or is it possible that men are being misdiagnosed or just not seeking treatment?

EFFECTS OF ANXIETY ON THE BODY

Since anxious thoughts often result in biological reactions it is important for counselors to be aware that there often are medical comorbidities as well. Excess anxiety wears on the body and can lead to a myriad of medical disorders, especially if there is a genetic vulnerability (Sternberg & Gold, 2002). The rates of gastrointestinal disorders, migraine headaches, cardiac disorders, and respiratory disorders are very high among individuals with anxiety (Culpepper, 2009). The figure below provides a quick review of all the interactions taking place within the body as the body experiences anxiety.

FIGURE 13.1

Effects of Anxiety on the Body

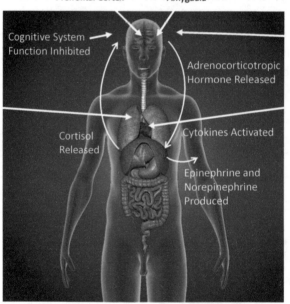

Hypothalamic-pituitary-adrenal axis

Prefrontal Cortex   Amygdala

Cognitive System Function Inhibited

Somatosensory/Emotional Stimulus

Adrenocorticotropic Hormone Released

Respiratory Rate Increased

Cardiovascular System Outflow Increased

Cortisol Released

Cytokines Activated

Epinephrine and Norepinephrine Produced

Modified from © sciencepics/Shutterstock.com

ASSESSMENT OF ANXIETY

Counselors assess clients for anxiety disorders both quantitatively and qualitatively. They gather information from clients by using evidence-based screening tools and self-reports, by reviewing previous medical and mental health history, and by conducting clinical interviews (Jones, 2010). The clinical interview is usually conducted during the first

© Yeexin Richelle/Shutterstock.com

session. Counselors use the clinical interview as an opportunity to build rapport and gather information about the client by asking relevant questions to identify the client's current problems or issues (Tomas-Aragones, et al., 2017). These can include questions such as: What type of symptoms have you been experiencing?; How long have you been experiencing your current symptoms?; Have you seen a counselor in the past?; What do you believe may be causing your current symptoms?; and What made you decide to come in for counseling? Additionally, the clinical interview helps the counselor determine the treatment plan, assess the client's progress, and the client's satisfaction with counseling throughout the therapeutic relationship (Drill et al., 2015).

The purpose of this section is to provide a review of the different types of the most commonly used, reliable, and valid screening tools available to assist in diagnosing specific types of anxiety disorder. Furthermore, counselors are responsible for using appropriate assessments based on the client's culture and the client's personal history (American Counseling Association [ACA], 2014). The tools presented are not an exhaustive list of what is available; however, it is a glimpse of what other counselors are using in treatment. The instruments presented in this section are all valid and reliable for adults. Most of these do offer a version for children.

TABLE 13.1

Common Screening Tools for Anxiety Disorders

Anxiety Disorder	Screening Tool	Brief Description
Generalized Anxiety Disorder (GAD)	**GAD7** (Generalized Anxiety Disorder 7) & **GADSS** (Generalized Anxiety Disorder Severity Scale)	**GAD7** – a 7-question tool to determine if a complete assessment for anxiety is warranted (Spitzer et al., 2006). **GADSS** – a 6-item interview rating scale that measures the severity of symptoms of GAD (Shear et al., 2006).
Specific Phobia	**BAT** (Behavioral Approach Test) & **Severity Measure for Specific Phobia-Adult**	**BAT** – measures the severity of the symptoms by exposing the client to the identified fear (Cochrane et al., 2008; Ollendick et al., 2011.) **Severity Measure for Specific Phobia-Adult** is a 10-item screening tool to assess severity in adults (Craske et al., 2013).
Social Anxiety Disorder	**LSAS** (Liebowitz Social Anxiety Scale) **SPIN** (Social Phobia Inventory) **SPAI** (Social Phobia & Anxiety Inventory) Severity	**LSAS** – is most widely used to measure social anxiety and phobia (Heimberg et al., 1999). **SPIN** – contains 17 items to assess the symptom domains of social anxiety disorder (Connor et al., 2000). **SPAI** – is successful in determining the difference between social and non-social phobias (Beidel et al., 1989).
Panic Disorder & Agoraphobia	**PAQ** (Panic Attack Questionnaire) **PDSS** (Panic Disorder Severity Scale) **PAS** (Panic and Agoraphobia Scale) **AS** (Agoraphobia Scale)	**PAQ** – is a self-report of open-ended questions that is a commonly used tool to assess for panic attacks (Norton et al., 1985). **PDSS** – assesses the frequency and severity of panic attacks. It is also used for agoraphobia (FuruKawa et al., 2009; Shear et al., 1997). **PAS** – measures the severity and intensity of panic attacks and can be used to monitor the client's progress (Bandelow, 1995). **AS** – is a 20-item tool that rates symptoms that are common to agoraphobia (Ost, 1990).

There are specific tools that measure the severity of anxiety, such as the *Beck Anxiety Inventory* (BAI; Beck et al., 1988) and the *State-Trait Anxiety Inventory* (STAI; Spielberger, 1983). The *Beck Anxiety Inventory* is a 21-question multiple-choice instrument that measures the severity of anxiety in children as well as adults (Beck et al., 1988). The *State-Trait Anxiety Inventory* is a 40 question self-report that measures two different types of anxiety. It measures state anxiety which is anxiety related to a specific event and trait anxiety which is the level of anxiety based on personal characteristics (Spielberger, 1983).

Women Specific Anxiety Screening Tools

The screening tools presented in this chapter are all normed to be used with women. However, there is evidence in the research (Phipps et al., 2019) that supports that some are more accurate in identifying anxiety in women than others. The GAD 7, HADS, and the BAI are recommended as the best tools for measuring anxiety in women as well as the Edinburgh Postnatal Depression Scale (EPDS; Phipps et al., 2019). The EPDS is a 10-item screening used to identify depression and anxiety in prenatal and a year after the birth of the child. The recommendation is that the screening should be administered by a health professional (Cox et al., 1987). The screening tools are specific to women or normed for prenatal or postnatal women. The questions are related to anxiety before, during, and after childbirth. Here is a list of screening tools used for screening anxiety in pre and postnatal women:

© Black Kings/Shutterstock.com

- Edinburg Postnatal Depression (EPDS; Cox et al., 1987).
- Pregnancy Anxiety Scale (PAS; Levin, 1991)
- Delivery Fear Scale (DFS; Wijma et al., 2002).
- Perinatal Anxiety Screening Scale (PASS; Somerville et al., 2014)

TREATMENT OF ANXIETY

Evidence-based treatment for anxiety disorders includes psychotropic medication, psychotherapy, or an integration of both (Bandelow et al., 2017). This section will begin with describing psychotherapy approaches, leading into an introduction on psychotropic medications. While counselors do not prescribe medications, it is helpful to have an awareness of the medications often prescribed by psychiatrists and doctors.

Psychotherapy

Cognitive Behavior Therapy (CBT) is an evidence-based psychotherapeutic treatment for mental health and addiction disorders, including anxiety disorders (Beck et al., 2005). There is research evidence to suggest CBT is more effective, or just as effective, as any other form of therapy or medication. Although it was initially developed to treat depression, CBT is extremely useful in the treatment of anxiety disorders. It is the first-line therapy for generalized anxiety disorder, panic disorder, agoraphobia, and social phobia (Hofmann & Smits, 2008; Hoffman et al., 2012; Kaczkurkin & Foa, 2015; Lang, 2004).

The premise of CBT is that a person's thoughts and feelings drive their behaviors and/or play a role in the development of psychological disorders (Beck et al., 2005; Hollon & Beck, 2013). CBT acknowledges that there is a strong link between thoughts, feelings, and behaviors. The goal of CBT is to change automatic negative thoughts or cognitive distortions to improve emotional difficulties and negative behaviors. Counselors and clients work together to learn skills to recognize and change maladaptive thoughts and negative behaviors (Beck et al., 2005; Hollan & Beck, 2013). Counselors identify specific CBT interventions and techniques based on the client's full assessment and identified disorder.

Focused on Emotions · Problem-Focused · Focused on Thoughts · Focused on Behaviors · Cognitive Behavioral Therapy · Client-Centered · Collaborative · Present-Centered

© arka38/Shutterstock.com

CBT interventions and techniques are specific to treating anxiety disorders through cognitive restructuring, exposure therapy, social skills and relaxation training, and journaling (Beck et al., 2005). The key is to help the client with emotional regulation.

Cognitive Restructuring (the therapeutic process of identifying and challenging cognitive distortions (negative and irrational thoughts) is a central component of CBT (Beck & Dozois, 2011). There are four steps to cognitive restructuring: 1) clients identify negative automatic thoughts; 2) clients are taught how to recognize cognitive distortions within the automatic thoughts that happen before, during, or after experiencing an anxiety-provoking incident. Additionally, clients should have an understanding of how powerful cognitive distortions affect their emotions and behaviors; 3) clients increase awareness and learn how to challenge irrational thoughts by using data; and 4) clients develop rational thoughts by relying on gathered information (Heimburg, 2002; Hope et al., 2010). Cognitive restructuring is a collaborative process between the client and the counselor. There needs to be a strong therapeutic relationship for this to be effective (Beck & Dozois, 2011). When helping a client with cognitive restructuring, an excellent technique to use is journaling or thought journaling. Thought journaling allows the client to track and combat their cognitive distortions by collecting opposing facts and evidence. For example, a counselor may assign a client to journal about a cognitive distortion and then replace it with rational thought.

Exposure Therapy is an evidence-based behavioral therapy approach. It is a central component of CBT used to treat anxiety disorders (Kaczkurkin & Foa, 2015). The premise of exposure therapy is to minimize a person's irrational feelings towards an event or object by safely and slowly exposing the person to different variations of the fear while teaching coping strategies (Craske et al., 2014). For example, a counselor may show a client who has a phobia of frogs a picture of frogs to measure the client's level of fear of frogs and to also slowly expose the client to frogs. The counselor may do these for several sessions, along with teaching skills. Exposure therapy is used in collaboration with other techniques such as relaxation, guided imagery, and mindfulness (Grohol, 2018). When the counselor has assessed a reduction in symptoms or level of distress and the client's ability to apply coping skills successfully, the counselor may expose the client to a real frog. The treatment is done in a safe therapeutic environment. The counselor must build a trusting relationship with the client and prepare the client for what to expect in the upcoming sessions. The licensed counselor must be trained in exposure therapy to prevent re-traumatizing the client.

There are different types of exposure therapies: imaginal, in vivo, and virtual exposure therapy that are effective for treating anxiety disorders, particularly phobias, generalized anxiety disorder, and panic attacks (Craske et al., 2008; Parsons & Rizzo, 2008). Imaginal Exposure Therapy is the mode in which the client confronts the fear by mentally thinking about the situation or object that causes the distress. Imaginal exposure therapy can be directed by the client or the counselor (Wiederhold et al., 2002). In Vivo Exposure Therapy is the process of exposing the client to the actual object or situation that he or she fears. In vivo exposure therapy is guided by the therapist in a safe therapeutic environment combination of imaginal and in vivo therapies is known as virtual exposure therapy. Virtual Exposure Therapy consists of the counselor exposing the client to feared object or situation by using virtual reality. Research has shown that virtual reality seems to be a preferred treatment for clients with various mental health diagnoses because it is less fearful than in vivo (Wilson et al., 2008; Freedman et al., 2010).

Social Skills Training is an evidence-based technique used in CBT to treat anxiety disorders. Counselors working with clients who suffer from social anxiety teach the client how to minimize the anxiety by using counselor modeling, homework, social reinforcement, and behavior rehearsal (Heimburg, 2002). Social skills training has been found to be useful as an individual treatment or as combined with others like cognitive restructuring and exposure therapy (Franklin et al., 2001; Herbert et al., 2002).

Relaxation Training is an evidence-based intervention used in CBT to teach clients relaxation strategies to help reduce anxiety and start to experience changes in their bodies (Kanji & Ernest, 2000; Manzoni et al., 2008; Rowa & Anthony, 2005). Clients who often experience anxiety for extended periods may

© LightField Studios/Shutterstock.com

© mimagephotography/Shutterstock.com

start to experience headaches, back pain or muscle tension, and various other somatic symptoms (Snaith, 2003). Somatic symptoms are the body's way of alerting that something is going on, and it needs intervention. **Systematic Desensitization** is a form of behavioral therapy that teaches clients to replace a fear response with a relaxation response by applying deep muscle relaxation and deep breathing exercises. Additionally, guided imagery and soothing sounds may also be incorporated (Wolpe, 1958).

Journaling is an effective cognitive-behavioral intervention used to help clients reduce or alleviate anxiety through writing. Additionally, journaling is an effective way to reduce stress, foster personal growth, and gain clarity (Smith et al., 2005; Smyth et al., 2018). Clients often gain insight regarding their everyday thoughts, feelings, and behaviors through journaling. Counselors will often ask clients to share their journals in session to help clients make connections to what is the underlying cause of their anxiety. There are numerous ways to use journaling in practice. Counselors assign journal assignments based on the client's treatment goals. Journaling can be used as a stand-alone intervention or as a complement to another intervention. Additionally, counselors may assign journaling as a way to have open communication with clients, as a way to assess the client's progress, and as a client's own safe space to express their emotions.

1. **Reflective journaling** is commonly assigned to clients to write or use visuals to reflect on their thoughts, feelings, and behaviors related to a specific event (Kennison & Misselwitz, 2002). Reflective journaling is a great way to allow the client to write freely without any particular format or an opportunity for the client's writing to be intentional by assigning a specific journal topic.

2. **Gratitude journaling** provides the client with an opportunity to reflect on the things that are going well in their current lives or recent experiences (Watkins et al., 2003). Clients who suffer from anxiety often worry about the things that are not going well or have a negative view of the present. It is often a challenge to get clients to focus on the areas that are going well or to identify the things that they are presently grateful for in their lives. To address this, counselors may assign the client to write a gratitude journal.

Additional Therapies

Cognitive Behavioral Therapy (CBT) is the most empirically supported therapy for treating psychological disorders, including anxiety disorders; however, other emerging therapies and interventions should be considered when treating anxiety disorders (David et al., 2018; Hoffman et al., 2012). CBT may not work well for all clients, so it is good to have basic knowledge of alternative approaches. Therefore, it is essential to review these interventions in this chapter.

© fizkes/Shutterstock.com

Mindfulness-Based Interventions (MBIs) is an approach shown to be effective in treating anxiety, specifically generalized anxiety disorder (GAD), and the treatment principles are well-matched with CBT (Hofmann & Gomez, 2017; Vollestad et al., 2011; Evans et al., 2007). Research on MBIs has increased for the last ten years. The most common of mindfulness-based interventions are **Mindfulness-Based Stress Reduction (MBSR)** and **Mindfulness-Based Cognitive Therapy (MBCT)**.

Mindfulness-based therapies incorporate the practice of mindfulness to help promote good mental health. Mindfulness is the practice of having an awareness of our thoughts, sensations, consciousness, body state, and our environment in the present moment without judgment. The premise is that by teaching clients mindfulness, they will remain in the present and become less reactive to experiences in the past or focusing on the future (Bishop et al., 2004). Interventions include mindfulness meditation, walking meditation, deep breathing, body scans, journaling, and yoga (Kabat-Zinn, 1990; Zoogman et al., 2015).

Dialectical Behavior Therapy (DBT) is a form of cognitive-behavioral therapy with an emphasis on mindfulness and dialectical thinking. It was developed initially to treat clients with Borderline Personality Disorder but has been found efficacious with other mental health disorders, including anxiety-related symptoms (Gratz et al., 2005; Lothes & Mochrie, 2017). Counselors use DBT to teach clients four sets of skills: mindfulness; distress tolerance, interpersonal effectiveness; and emotional regulation. Like other mindfulness-based therapies, DBT teaches skills that promote non-judgment, acceptance, and focuses on the present moment. The standard of practice of DBT is that the client engages in weekly individual and weekly group sessions (Linehan, 1993).

> "I honestly didn't realize at the time that I was dealing with myself. But I suppose it's true that I developed a therapy that provides the things I needed for so many years and never got." ~Marsha Linehan (Carey, 2011, p. 2).

Although **Eye Movement Desensitization and Reprocessing (EMDR)** was developed to treat symptoms of distress from traumatizing memories, it has become a standard treatment for anxiety disorders specifically panic disorders and stress from other life experiences (Shapiro & Maxfield, 2002). According to Horst and colleagues (2017), the results of their study showed that EMDR is just as effective as CBT in treating symptoms of panic disorders. Additionally, EMDR demonstrated efficacy in treating anxiety disorders (Valient-Gomez et al., 2017). EMDR focuses on the client's past, present, and future. It pulls elements from CBT, person-centered, psychodynamic, and other therapies (Shapiro, 2001). It is an eight-phase approach that helps address emotional distress and trauma and teach coping skills to help manage any future stress or trauma. A trained EMDR therapist utilizes eye-movements, taps, or tones to help the client resolve emotional distress associated with a specific traumatizing memory (Shapiro & Maxfield, 2002).

Psychotropic Medications

Clients may have a need for psychotropic medication; however, counselors recommend and refer clients to seek a psychiatric evaluation by a psychiatrist to determine if medication is indicated. When making the rec-

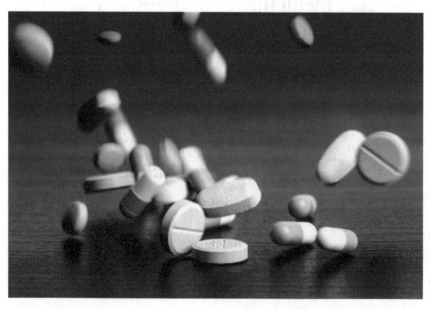

© Tibor Duris/Shutterstock.com

ommendation, it is not within the counselor's scope of practice to inform a client that medication is needed or to recommend any medications (ACA, 2014). It is our responsibility to be familiar with commonly prescribed medications to have the ability to monitor any side effects a client may experience while taking medication.

The commonly used medications to treat anxiety are benzodiazepines, selective serotonin reuptake inhibitors (SSRIs), serotonin and non-norepinephrine reuptake inhibitors (SNRIs), tricyclic antidepressants, beta-blockers, and Buspar (Bandelow et al., 2017).

TABLE 13.2

Commonly Used Medications for Anxiety

Commonly Used Medications for Anxiety	Description
Benzodiazepines	Treats anxiety by working on the neurotransmitters in the brain that suppresses the activity in the nerve. • Short-term use as can cause dependence • Typically used as first-line of treatment for anxiety • More likely to be prescribed to women than to men (Furbish et al., 2017; National Institute of Mental Health, 2018)
Selective Serotonin Reuptake Inhibitors (SSRIs)	Increases the amount of serotonin in the brain. Commonly used for GAD. (Masand & Gupta, 2003; American College of Obstetricians and Gynecologists, 2019)
Serotonin & Non-norepinephrine Reuptake Inhibitors (SNRIs)	Treats anxiety by inhibiting the reuptake of both serotonin and norepinephrine in the brain. • These are often used when SSRI's are not effective. • Commonly used for PD, GAD, and SANXD (Dell'Osso et al., 2010)
Tricyclic Antidepressants	A class of older drugs that increases serotonin and norepinephrine. Commonly used for panic disorder. (American College of Obstetricians and Gynecologists, 2019; Zohar & Westenberg, 2000)
Beta Blockers	Stops adrenaline from making contact with the heart's beta receptors. Often used to reduce rapid heartbeat, sweating, and shaking. (Brudkowska et al., 2018; Butt et al., 2017)
Buspar	A serotonin receptor agonist that works by increasing action at the serotonin receptors in the brain. It has been shown to be effective with GAD. (Locke et al., 2015)

NEUROSCIENCE AND ANXIETY: WHY IS IT IMPORTANT FOR COUNSELORS TO KNOW THIS?

The brain uses two pathways that lead to anxiety.

Did you know that many counselors misinterpret how to treat anxiety due to a lack of understanding of how the brain works? The brain uses two pathways that lead to anxiety. One is the cortex (the outermost layer of the brain that is responsible for thinking and processing information), which is the "pathway of sensations, thoughts, logic, imagination, intuition, conscious memory, and planning" (Pittman & Karle, 2015, p 14.). This part of the brain is aware of what is happening in the present and also includes memories. If you have thoughts or images that run through your mind while you experience anxiety or become obsessed with anxious thoughts, your cortex is producing these thoughts. The second pathway is the amygdala (located in the medial temporal lobe of the brain, and primarily processes emotions) which is the part of your brain that takes charge to protect you when you feel threatened (Pittman & Karle, 2015). It sends messages directly to your body's sympathetic nervous system to react instantly. This immediate reaction sends an adrenaline rush through your body, increases your blood pressure and heart rate, as well as causes muscle tension. For instance, if you open the door and see a snake on the ground, you may immediately jump back without even thinking about it. This is your amygdala going directly into action sending messages to your body for survival purposes. While the amygdala can act alone without the cortex to produce anxiety, the cortex works in conjunction with the amygdala to produce the physical sensations of anxiety (Pittman & Karle, 2015).

Amygdala-Driven Anxiety

To understand the amygdala's role in anxiety, it is good to know that the amygdala is like a radar noticing sights, sounds, smells, and other various situations throughout the day, even though you may not be consciously focused on them. When it detects danger, it can then put off the alarm response to prepare your body to fight or flee. This is what happens with panic attacks. Often when trauma or a severely unpleasant experience takes place in one's life the amygdala forms an emotional memory of that event. Therefore, when it picks up on a smell, sight, or sound that *triggers*

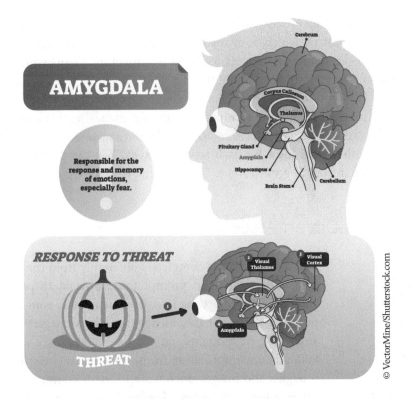

the emotional memory, it can automatically cause an anxiety reaction, even though there is no real threat at the present time (Pittman & Karle, 2015). For example, a young boy who is bit by a dog may immediately experience stress reactions whenever he sees a dog, even though the present dog may be very friendly and harmless. His brain reacts in alarm before his mind can process the reality of what is happening.

Individuals have little control over the amygdala's rapid responses, meaning they experience fear and anxiety rather than having conscious control over the response (Pittman & Karle, 2015). Many clients report that they feel like they are going crazy when a panic attack happens out of the blue. They may even drive themselves to the emergency room, thinking they are having a heart

Limbic system

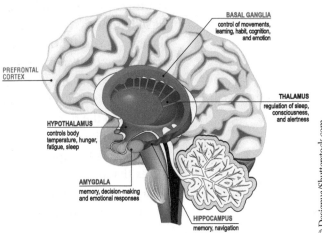

attack. When they find out they really are alright, they may then sense a loss of control, which is disturbing as it does not make logical sense to them. Therefore, an important part of treatment for clients with panic attacks is to educate them about this automatic reaction in the brain and body. By doing so, it will help clients to be less troubled about their panic attacks. There are specific techniques to use for managing this amygdala driven anxiety. *Rewire Your Anxious Brain* by Pittman and Karle is a great book with several ideas for each type of anxiety. You can find the book provided in your *Suggested Resources* at the end of this chapter.

Cortex-Driven Anxiety

"While people may think that rumination will lead to a solution, what appears to happen instead is a strengthening of the circuitry in the cortex that produces the anxiety." (Nolen-Hoeksema, 2000)

The cortex operates completely differently from the amygdala; however, it can prompt the amygdala to produce anxiety. Without getting into too much detail, your cortex produces thought-based anxiety as well as imagery-based anxiety. These thoughts and images can take place without taking in any information from your senses. However, the thoughts and images often work together communicating information to the amygdala often leading to anxiety reactions in the body (Pittman & Karle, 2015). For example, a counseling graduate receives a letter in the mail from the state licensure board after completing all the requirements. Imagining it is a rejection letter, the graduate becomes anxious and may even set it aside. However, once opened the anxiety dissipates as he realizes he was granted licensure. In this case, the cortex interpreted the letter as a threat of rejection leading to distressing thoughts. Another point to make here is that cortex driven anxiety can also be caused by thoughts alone, as in **rumination** (repeatedly mulling over negative thoughts). For example, a client may report that she heard there may be layoffs at work over the next few months. She mentions that she is unable to stop worrying about this and spends much of her day and night focused on a possible layoff in the future. Dwelling on these thoughts only makes her more anxious. While people may think that rumination will lead to a solution, what appears to happen instead is a strengthening of the circuitry in the cortex that produces the anxiety (Nolen-Hoeksema, 2000). Schwartz and Begley (2003) call this the *survival of the busiest*, meaning that whatever circuitry is used repetitively is likely to be activated easier in the future.

LOOKING THROUGH THE LENS OF CHRISTIANITY: BIBLICAL INSIGHTS ON ANXIETY

The first account of anxiety can be found in the book of Genesis where Adam and Eve hid from God out of fear after disobeying God's orders. From that day on anxiety has been a part of daily life for humanity. It is important to note that fear itself is not sinful as God created us to experience the feeling of anxiety when we are faced with a threat or danger. After all, it is important for our own survival. However, when anxiety takes control of us impairing our ability to function in a healthy and productive manner it alerts us of the need to address it.

Matthew 6:25-32 (*King James Bible*, 1769/2017) instructs us to be anxious for nothing, but rather to put our faith in God's sovereignty. Paul is also reminding the Philippians to be anxious about nothing, and instead take everything to God in prayer, which then leads to a peace that only God can provide (*King James Bible*, 1769/2017, Philippians 4:6-7). These verses are great reminders of God's sovereignty and promise to help us in our anxiety. However, at the same time as counselors, we should use these Scriptures to teach and encourage rather than invoke shame to those who are afraid and vulnerable. It becomes challenging to trust in God or to keep things in perspective when we feel anxious and vulnerable as it drains us of our courage (Collins, 2007). Therefore, we should apply the knowledge we gain in treating anxiety while also applying Biblical principles. Meditation on Scriptures alone rarely *fixes* serious anxiety struggles. Instead, God's grace and the truth of Scripture must be integrated into the context of daily living (McRay et al., 2016).

I CAN DO *all things* through Christ WHICH STRENGTHENETH ME

Philippians 4.13

© Solomnikov/Shutterstock.com

CASE STUDY

Josie is a 79-year-old widow who lives alone with her two cats and one dog. She has never remarried or dated anyone since her husband died twenty years ago. She does not see her family often because they have all moved away from their hometown. Josie decided to seek counseling at the recommendation of her primary care physician because of several recent visits in the last year. During the initial consultation, Josie shared that her visits to her primary care physician were due to her feeling like she was experiencing symptoms of a heart attack. She described on each occasion breaking out in cold sweats, experiencing heart palpitations, and tightening in her chest. She has denied taking any medication or substance abuse that could explain any of these symptoms.

Josie reported that the doctor has given her a "clean" bill of health. Additionally, Josie expressed worrying about her children and grandchildren daily. She stated that she has difficulty sleeping because she is up late at night, thinking that something terrible will happen to them despite their weekly reports that they are all in good health. Josie disclosed that she excessively worries about finances, losing friendships, and dying. She stated that she finds it difficult to relax and concentrate on her daily responsibilities. Josie reported that she is becoming anxious about continuing counseling services.

Based on the information given in the case study, it appears that Josie may meet the criteria for Generalized Anxiety Disorder (APA, 2013). However, it is vital to continue the assessment by gathering information and utilizing the assessment tools to make an accurate diagnosis, identify additional symptoms, and to develop a treatment plan. Because Josie has anxiety about continuing with counseling, it is imperative to not only explore her concerns but also to affirm her decision to come despite her anxiety. Affirmation will help build rapport by creating a safe environment for Josie to open up other concerns. In addition, educating her about panic attacks and how the brain often goes into an automatic response when an emotional memory is triggered (see previous section on *Amygdala-Driven Anxiety*), may help her gain understanding and realize she can take action to reduce those symptoms.

Due to Josie's age, being a widow, current isolation from her family, lack of finances, and her loss of friends, it is important to conduct a suicide risk assessment. This assessment should include questions regarding past psychiatric history, previous suicide attempts, and direct questions such as, "Do you have thoughts of killing yourself?" and "Have you ever had any previous suicide attempts?" It is essential to inquire about Josie's current support system. Josie may benefit from establishing connections and building a community. Teaching Josie techniques such as mindfulness exercises, deep breathing, and relaxation may be an excellent place to start to address her anxiety symptoms. If Josie is a Christian, reminding her of 2 Corinthians 10:3-5 ("For though we walk in the flesh, we do not war after the flesh; [for the weapons of our warfare are not carnal, but mighty through God to the pulling down of strongholds], casting down imaginations, and every high thing that exalteth itself against the knowledge of God, and bringing into captivity every thought to the obedience of Christ" [*King James Bible*, 1769/2017]) would provide a foundation for tackling her irrational beliefs and cognitive distortions. In these verses Paul encourages believers to take every thought captive to the obedience of Christ.

Discussing her level of trust in God, while helping her to submit to God for comfort, wisdom, and strength would be important as Isaiah 26:3 ("You keep him in perfect peace whose mind is stayed on you, because he trusts in you" [*King James Bible*, 1769/2017]) talks about how God provides perfect peace for those who trust in him. Incorporating appropriate Scripture passages and prayer into relaxation techniques would be a good coping skill to recommend as well. There are other areas to explore such as grief and loss due to her husband passing away and her current loss of friends, referral for psychiatric evaluation, and her finances.

Sample CBT Treatment Plan for Josie

Problem: Generalized Anxiety Disorder. **Rationale:** Josie meets the DSM-5 (2013) criteria for Generalized Anxiety Disorder: Josie has experienced excessive anxiety and worry about various topics, events, and activities for more than six months. Josie's topics can shift from one topic to the other; she has difficulty controlling her anxiety; Josie also has physical and cognitive symptoms (pain in her chest, restlessness, sweating difficulty sleeping, and impaired concentration) that cannot be explained by a medical disorder.

Assessment Measures: Beck Anxiety Inventory; Generalized Anxiety Disorder 7 (GAD7); Generalized Anxiety Disorder Scale (GADSS).

Long-Term Goals: Josie will learn and implement healthy coping skills that result in a reduction of anxiety and worry, and improved daily functioning. Josie will reduce the overall frequency, intensity, and duration of the anxiety so that daily functioning is not impaired.

Objective: 1: Josie will participate in counseling 1x per week and schedule an appointment with a psychiatrist for a psychological evaluation.
Intervention 1: The counselor will focus on developing a therapeutic trust with Josie and build a safe place for the client by using psychoeducation to explain the counseling process. The counselor will provide Josie with several referrals for psychiatrists in her area.

Objective 2: Josie will learn and practice two healthy coping skills at least 4x a week to help reduce her anxiety.
Intervention 2: The counselor will teach Josie coping skills (e.g., relaxation techniques, journaling, deep breathing) that she can apply to her daily life. The counselor will assign Josie weekly homework assignments to practice and assess progress.

Objective 3: Josie will learn to identify and to eliminate irrational beliefs/ or cognitive distortions that contribute to her anxiety at least once per week.
Intervention 3: The counselor will explain the concept of cognitive therapy and help Josie identify triggers, irrational beliefs, and consequences followed by rationally disputing those dysfunctional. If Josie has Christian values, she would be encouraged to evaluate and dispute her thoughts and beliefs based on Biblical principles.

CHAPTER SUMMARY

As indicated throughout this chapter, women experience anxiety and seek out treatment more often than men. Hopefully, you have gained practical knowledge regarding the types of anxiety disorders, prevalence, symptoms, assessment, Biblical principles as well as evidence-based treatment options to assist you in counseling women who are coping with anxiety in some form or another. In all reality, anxiety is experienced by all clients regardless of the problem or disorder. Seeking treatment from a counselor in itself can be very anxiety-provoking. Therefore, you most likely will counsel clients who suffer from minimal to severe anxiety. While there are various treatment approaches provided, the research supports Cognitive Behavioral Therapy as the most commonly used treatment modality for clinical anxiety disorders. In addition, it is wise to have a good knowledge base of tools and Scriptural application to assist clients with this issue. The authors hope that you walk away from this chapter equipped with an understanding of the clinical and spiritual needs of women who suffer from anxiety.

KEY TERMS

Amygdala - located in the medial temporal lobe of the brain, and primarily processes emotions

Cognitive Restructuring - the therapeutic process of identifying and challenging cognitive distortions (negative and irrational thoughts)

Cortex - the outermost layer of the brain that is responsible for thinking and processing information

Imaginal Exposure Therapy - the mode in which the client confronts the fear by mentally thinking about the situation or object that causes the distress

In Vivo Exposure Therapy - the process of exposing the client to the actual object or situation that he or she fears

Panic Attacks - symptoms of rapid heartbeat, rapid breathing, shaking, sweating, chest pain, dizziness, nausea, and various other symptoms that often continue for 15 seconds up to 30 minutes

"Survival of the Busiest" - whatever circuitry is used repetitively is likely to be activated easier in the future

Virtual Exposure Therapy - consists of the counselor exposing the client to feared object or situation by using virtual reality

SUGGESTED RESOURCES

Books

Making the Best of Stress: How Life's Hassles Can Form the Fruit of the Spirit by Mark McMinn

Rewire Your Anxious Brain by Catherine Pittman and Elizabeth Karle

The Anxiety and Phobia Workbook by Edmund Bourne

The Stress-Proof Brain by Melanie Greenberg

The Anxiety Toolkit by Alice Boyes

Outsmart Your Anxious Brain: Ten Simple Ways to Beat the Worry Trick by David Carbonell

Organizations/Websites

Anxiety and Depression Association of America: https://adaa.org/living-with-anxiety/ask-and-learn/resources

National Institute of Mental Health: https://www.nimh.nih.gov/health/topics/anxiety-disorders/index.shtml

Substance Abuse and Mental Health Services Administration (SAMHSA): https://www.samhsa.gov/search_results?k=anxiety

REFERENCES

Alonso, J., Angermeyer, M., & Lepine, J. (2004). The European study of epidemiology of mental disorders (ESEMeD) project: An epidemiological basis for informing mental health policies in Europe. *Acta Psychiatrica Scandinavica, 109*, 38-46. https://doi.org/10.1111/j.1600-0047.2004.00325.x.

American College of Obstetricians and Gynecologist. (2019). *Women's preventive services initiative report.* https://www.womenspreventivehealth.org/recommendations/final-report/

American Counseling Association. (2014). *2014 ACA code of ethics.* https://www.counseling.org/knowledge-center

American Psychiatric Association. (2013). *Diagnostic and statistical manual of mental disorders* (5th ed.). https://doi.org/10.1176/appi.books.9780890425596

Anxiety and Depression Association of America. (n.d.). *Anxiety and depression association of America.* https://adaa.org/

Asher, M., & Aderka, I. (2018). Gender differences in social anxiety disorder. *Journal of Clinical Psychology, 74*, 1730-1741. https://doi.org/10.1002/jclp.22624

Bandelow, B. (1995). Assessing the efficacy of treatments for panic disorder and agoraphobia: II. The Panic and Agoraphobia Scale. *International Clinical Psychopharmacology, 2*, 73-81. https://doi.org/10.1097/00004850-199506000-00003

Bandelow, B., Michaelis, S., & Wedekind, D. (2017). Treatment of anxiety disorders. *Dialogues in Clinical Neuroscience, 19*(2), 93.

Beck, A. T., & Dozois, D. J. (2011). Cognitive therapy: Current status and future directions. *Annual Review of Medicine, 62, 397-409.*

Beck, A. T., Emery, G., & Greenberg, R. L. (2005). *Anxiety disorders and phobias: A cognitive perspective.* Basic Books.

Beck, A. T., Epstein, N., Brown, G., & Steer, R. A. (1988). An inventory for measuring clinical anxiety: Psychometric properties. *Journal of Consulting and Clinical Psychology, 56*(6), 893.

Beidel, D. C., Turner, S. M., Stanley, M. A., & Dancu, C. V. (1989). The social phobia and anxiety inventory: Concurrent and external validity. *Behavior Therapy, 20*(3), 417-427.

Bishop, S. R., Lau, M., Shapiro, S., Carlson, L., Anderson, N. D., Carmody, J., Segal, Z. V., Abbey, S., Speca, M., Velting, D., & Devins, G. (2004). Mindfulness: A proposed operational definition. *Clinical psychology: Science and Practice, 11*(3), 230-241.

Brudkowska, Ż., Tomczyk, M., Jusiak, K., Karakuła-Juchnowicz, H., & Rudnicka-Drożak, E. (2018). The role of beta-adrenolytic drugs in treating anxiety disorders. *Current Problems of Psychiatry, 19*(3), 209–224.

Butt, J. H., Dalsgaard, S., Torp-Pedersen, C., Køber, L., Gislason, G. H., Kruuse, C., & Fosbøl, E. L. (2017). Beta-blockers for exams identify students at high risk of psychiatric morbidity. *Journal of Child and Adolescent Psychopharmacology, 27*(3), 266-273.

Carey, B. (2011). *Expert on mental illness reveals her own fight.* The New York Times. https://www.nytimes.com/2011/06/23/health/23lives.html

Cochrane, A., Barnes-Holmes, D., & Barnes-Holmes, Y. (2008). The perceived-threat behavioral approach test (PT-BAT): Measuring avoidance in high-, mid-, and low-spider-fearful participants. *The Psychological Record, 58*(4), 585-596.

Collins, G. (2007). *Christian counseling: A comprehensive guide.* Thomas Nelson.

Comer, R. (2014). *Abnormal psychology* (8th ed.). Worth.

Connor, K. M., Davidson, J. R., Churchill, L. E., Sherwood, A., Weisler, R. H., & Foa, E. (2000). Psychometric properties of the Social Phobia Inventory (SPIN): New self-rating scale. *The British Journal of Psychiatry, 176*(4), 379-386.

Cox, J. L., Holden, J. M., & Sagovsky, R. (1987). Detection of postnatal depression: Development of the 10-item Edinburgh Postnatal Depression Scale. *The British Journal of Psychiatry, 150*(6), 782-786.

Craske, M. G., Kircanski, K., Zelikowsky, M., Mystkowski, J., Chowdhury, N., & Baker, A. (2008). Optimizing inhibitory learning during exposure therapy. *Behaviour Research and Therapy, 46*(1), 5-27.

Craske, M. G., Treanor, M., Conway, C. C., Zbozinec, T., & Vervliet, V. (2014). Maximizing exposure therapy: An inhibitory learning approach. *Behavior Research and Therapy, 58,* 10-23.

Craske, M., Wittchen, U., Bogels, S., Stein, M., Andrews, G., & Lebeu, R. (2013). *Severity Measure for Specific Phobia-Adult [Measurement instrument].* https://www.psychiatry.org/psychiatrists/practice/dsm/educational-resources/assessment-measures

Culpepper, L. (2009). Generalized anxiety disorder and medical illness. *Journal of Clinical Psychiatry, 70*(2), 20-14.

Dailey, S., Gill, C., Karl, S. l., Barrio Minton, C. (2014). *DSM-5 learning companion for counselors.* American Counseling Association.

David, D., Cristea, I., & Hofmann, S. G. (2018). Why cognitive behavioral therapy is the current gold standard of psychotherapy. *Frontiers in Psychiatry, 9*, 4. https://doi.org/10.3389/fpsyt.2018.00004

Dell'Osso, B., Buoli, M., Baldwin, D. S., & Altamura, A. C. (2010). Serotonin norepinephrine reuptake inhibitors (SNRIs) in anxiety disorders: A comprehensive review of their clinical efficacy. *Human Psychopharmacology: Clinical and Experimental, 25*(1), 17-29.

Drill, R., Nakash, O., DeFife, J. A., & Westen, D. (2015). Assessment of clinical information: Comparison of the validity of a Structured Clinical Interview (the SCID) and the Clinical Diagnostic Interview. *The Journal of Nervous and Mental Disease, 203*(6), 459–462.

Evans, S., Ferrando, S., Findler, M., Stowell, C., Smart, C., & Haglin, D. (2007). Mindfulness based cognitive therapy for generalized anxiety disorder. *Journal of Anxiety Disorders, 22,* 716-721.

Frances, A. (2013). *Essentials of psychiatric diagnosis.* Guilford.

Franklin, M. E., Feeny, N. C., Abramowitz, J. S., Zoellner, L. A., & Bux, D. A. (2001). Comprehensive cognitive behavior therapy: A multi-component treatment for generalized social phobia. *Psicoterapia Cognitiva e Comportamentale, 7,* 211–221.

Fredrikson, M., Annas, P., Fischer, H., & Wik, G. (1996). Gender and age differences in the prevalence of specific fears and phobias. *Behavior Research Therapy, 34,* 33–39.

Freedman, S. A., Hoffman, H. G., Garcia-Palacios, A., Weiss, P., Avitzour, S., & Josman, N. (2010). Prolonged exposure and virtual reality-enhanced imaginal exposure for PTSD following a terrorist bulldozer attack: A case study. *Cyberpsychology, Behavior, and Social Networking, 13*(1), 95-101. https://doi.org/10.1089/cyber.2009.0271

Furbish, S. M., Kroehl, M. E., Loeb, D. F., Lam, H. M., Lewis, C. L., Nelson, J., Chow, Z., & Trinkley, K. E. (2017). A pharmacist–physician collaboration to optimize benzodiazepine use for anxiety and sleep symptom control in primary care. *Journal of Pharmacy Practice, 30*(4), 425-433.

Furukawa, T. A., Katherine Shear, M., Barlow, D. H., Gorman, J. M., Woods, S. W., Money, R., Etschel, E., Engel, R. R., & Leucht, S. (2009). Evidence-based guidelines for interpretation of the Panic Disorder Severity Scale. *Depression and Anxiety, 26*(10), 922-929.

Gratz, K. L., Tull, M. T., & Wagner, A. W. (2005). *Acceptance and mindfulness-based approaches to anxiety.* Springer.

Grohol, J. (2018). *What is exposure therapy?* Psych Central. https://psychcentral.com/lib/what-is-exposure-therapy/

Haigh, E., Craner, J., Sigmon, S., Yoon, K., Thorpe, G. (2018). Symptom attributions across the menstrual cycle in women with panic disorder. *Journal of Rational-Emotive & Cognitive-Behavior Therapy, 36,* 320-332. https://doi.org/ 10.1007/s10942-018-0288-4

Heimberg, R. G. (2002). Cognitive-behavioral therapy for social anxiety disorder: Current status and future directions. *Biological Psychiatry, 51*(1), 101-108.

Heimberg, R. G., Horner, K. J., Juster, H. R., Safren, S. A., Brown, E. J., Schneier, F. R., & Liebowitz, M. R. (1999). Psychometric properties of the Liebowitz social anxiety scale. *Psychological Medicine, 29*(1), 199-212.

Herbert, J. D., Rheingold, A. A., & Goldstein, S. G. (2002). Brief cognitive behavioral group therapy for social anxiety disorder. *Cognitive and Behavioral Practice, 9*(1), 1-8.

Hofmann, S. G., & Gómez, A. F. (2017). Mindfulness-based interventions for anxiety and depression. *Psychiatric Clinics, 40*(4), 739-749.

Hofmann, S. G., & Smits, J. A. J. (2008). Cognitive-behavioral therapy for adult anxiety disorders: A meta-analysis of randomized placebo-controlled trials. *The Journal of Clinical Psychiatry, 69,* 621–632.

Hofmann, S. G., Asnaani, A., Vonk, I. J., Sawyer, A. T., & Fang, A. (2012). The efficacy of cognitive behavioral therapy: *A Review of Meta-analyses. Cognitive Therapy and Research, 36*(5), 427–440. https://doi.org/10.1007/s10608-012-9476-1

Hollon, S. D., & Beck, A. T. (2013). *Cognitive and cognitive-behavioral therapies. Bergin and Garfield's handbook of psychotherapy and behavior change, 393-442.* Wiley.

Hope, D. A., Burns, J. A., Hayes, S. A., Herbert, J. D., & Warner, M. D. (2010). Automatic thoughts and cognitive restructuring in cognitive behavioral group therapy for social anxiety disorder. *Cognitive Therapy and Research, 34*(1), 1-12.

Horst, F., Den Oudsten, B., Zijlstra, W., de Jongh, A., Lobbestael, J., & De Vries, J. (2017). Cognitive behavioral therapy vs. eye movement desensitization and reprocessing for treating panic disorder: A randomized controlled trial. *Frontiers in Psychology, 8,* 1409.

Howell, H., Brawman-Mintzer, O., Monnier, J., & Yonkers, K. (2001). Generalized anxiety disorder in women. *Psychiatric Clinics of North America, 24*(1), 165-178. https://psycnet.apa.org/doi/10.1016/S0193-953X(05)70212-4

Jones, K. D. (2010). The unstructured clinical interview. *Journal of Counseling & Development, 88,* 220-226.

Kabat-Zinn, J. (1990). *Full catastrophe living: The program of the stress reduction Clinic at the University of Massachusetts Medical Center.* Dell Publishing.

Kaczkurkin, A. N., & Foa, E. B. (2015). Cognitive-behavioral therapy for anxiety disorders: An update on the empirical evidence. *Dialogues in Clinical Neuroscience, 17*(3), 337.

Kanji, N., & Ernest, E. (2000). Autogenic training for stress and anxiety: A systematic review. *Complementary Therapy and Medicine, 8,* 106-110.

Kennison, M. M., & Misselwitz, S. (2002). Evaluating reflective writing for appropriateness, fairness, and consistency. *Nursing Education Perspectives, 23*(5), 238-242.

Kessler, R., Berglund, O., Demler, R., Jin, K., Merikangas, R., & Walters, E. (2005). Lifetime prevalence and age-of-onset distributions of DSM-IV disorders in the National Comorbidity Survey Replication. *Arch. Gen. Psychiatry 62,* 593-602.

Kessler, R., Stang, P., Wittchen, H., Ustun, T., Roy-Burne, P., & Walters, E. (1998). Lifetime panic-depression comorbidity in the National Comorbidity Survey. *Arch Gen Psychiatry. 55*(9), 801–808. https://doi.org/10.1001/archpsyc.55.9.801

King James Bible. (2017). King James Bible Online. https://www.kingjamesbibleonline.org/ (Original work published 1769).

Kopala, M., & Keitel, M. (2017). *Handbook of counseling women* (2nd ed.). Sage Publications.

Lang, A. J. (2004). Treating generalized anxiety disorder with cognitive-behavioral therapy. The *Journal of Clinical Psychiatry, 65,* 14-19.

LeBeau, R., Glenn, D., Liao, B., Wittchen, H., Beesdo-Baum, K., Ollendick, T., & Craske, M. (2010). Specific phobia: A review of DSM-IV specific phobia and preliminary recommendations for DSM-V. *Depression and Anxiety 27,* 148-167. https://doi.org/10.1002/da.20655

Levin, J. S. (1991). The factor structure of the Pregnancy Anxiety Scale. *Journal of Health Society Behavior, 32,* 368- 381.

Linehan, M. M. (1993). *Cognitive-behavioral treatment of borderline personality disorder.* Guilford Press

Locke, A. B., Kirst, N., & Shultz, C. G. (2015). Diagnosis and management of generalized anxiety disorder and panic disorder in adults. *American Family Physician, 91*(9), 617-624.

Lothes, J., & Mochrie, K. (2017). The "what" and "hows" of mindfulness: Using DBT's mindfulness skills to reduce test anxiety. *Building Health Academic Communities, 1*(2), 10–20.

Manzoni, G. M., Pagnini, F., Castelnuovo, G., & Molinari, E. (2008). Relaxation training for anxiety: A ten-years systematic review with meta-analysis. *BMC Psychiatry, 8*(1), 41.

Masand, P. S., & Gupta, S. (2003). The safety of SSRIs in generalised anxiety disorder: Any reason to be anxious? *Expert Opinion on Drug Safety, 2*(5), 485-493.

Matsumoto, K., Sato, K., Hamatani, S., Shirayama, Y., & Shimizu, E. (2019). Cognitive behavioral therapy for postpartum panic disorder: A case series. *BMC Psychology, 7,* 53 https://doi.org/ 10.1186/s40359-019-0330-z

McLean, C., Asnaani, A., Litz, B., & Hofmann, S. (2011). Gender differences in anxiety disorders: Prevalence, course of illness, comorbidity and burden of illness. *Journal of Psychiatric Research, 8*(45), 1027-1035.

McRay, B., Yarhouse, M., & Butman, R. (2016). *Modern psychopathologies: A comprehensive Christian appraisal* (2nd ed.). InterVarsity Press.

National Institute of Mental Health. (2018). *Anxiety disorders*. https://www.nimh.nih.gov/health/topics/anxiety-disorders/index.shtml

Nolen-Hoeksema, S. (2000). The role of rumination in depressive disorders and mixed anxiety/depressive symptoms. *Journal of Abnormal Psychology, 109*, 504-511.

Norton, G. R., Harrison, B., Hauch, J., & Rhodes, L. (1985). Characteristics of people with infrequent panic attacks. *Journal of Abnormal Psychology, 94*(2), 216.

Ollendick, T., Allen, B., Benoit, K., & Cowart, M. (2011). The tripartite model of fear in children with specific phobias: Assessing concordance and discordance using the behavioral approach test. *Behaviour Research and Therapy, 49*(8), 459-465.

Öst, L. G. (1990). The Agoraphobia Scale: An evaluation of its reliability and validity. *Behaviour Research and Therapy, 28*(4), 323-329.

Our World in Data. (n.d.). *Mental health*. http://www.ourworldindata.org/mental-health#anxiety-disorders.

Parsons, T. D., & Rizzo, A. A. (2008). Affective outcomes of virtual reality exposure therapy for anxiety and specific phobias: A meta-analysis. *Journal of Behavior Therapy and Experimental Psychiatry, 39*(3), 250-261.

Phipps, M. G., Son, S., Zahn, C., O'Reilly, N., Cantor, A., Frost, J., Gregory, K. D., Jones, M., Kendig, S. M., Nelson, H. D., Pappas, M., Qaseem, A., Ramos, D., Salganicoff, A., Taylor, G., & Conry, J. (2019). Women's preventive services Initiative's well-woman chart: A summary of preventive health recommendations for women. *Obstetrics & Gynecology, 134*(3), 465-469.

Pittman, C., & Karle, E., (2015). *Rewire your anxious brain*. Harbinger Publications.

Rowa, K., & Anthony, M. M. (2005). Psychological treatments for social phobia. *The Canadian Journal of Psychiatry, 50*(6), 308-316.

Schwartz, J., & Begley, S. (2003). *The mind and the brain: Neuroplasticity and the power of the mental force*. Harper Collins.

Scully, J., Bechtold, D., Bell, J., Dubovsky, S., Neligh, G., & Peterson, J. (1990). *Psychiatry* (2nd ed.). Harwal.

Shapiro, F. (2001). *Eye movement desensitization and reprocessing (EMDR): Basic principles, protocols, and procedures*. Guilford Press.

Shapiro, F., & Maxfield, L. (2002). Eye Movement Desensitization and Reprocessing (EMDR): Information processing in the treatment of trauma. *Journal of Clinical Psychology, 58*(8), 933–946.

Shear, K., Belnap, B. H., Mazumdar, S., Houck, P., & Rollman, B. L. (2006). Generalized anxiety disorder severity scale (GADSS): A preliminary validation study. *Depression and Anxiety, 23*(2), 77-82.

Shear, M. K., Brown, T. A., Barlow, D. H., Money, R., Sholomskas, D. E., Woods, S. W., Gorman, J. M., & Papp, L. A. (1997). Multicenter collaborative panic disorder severity scale. *American Journal of Psychiatry, 154*(11), 1571-1575.

Smith, S., Anderson-Hanley, C., Langrock, A., & Compas, B. (2005). The effects of journaling for women with newly diagnosed breast cancer. Psycho-Oncology. *Journal of the Psychological, Social and Behavioral Dimensions of Cancer, 14*(12), 1075-1082.

Smyth, J. M., Johnson, J. A., Auer, B. J., Lehman, E., Talamo, G., & Sciamanna, C. N. (2018). Online positive affect journaling in the improvement of mental ditress and well-being in general medical patients with elevated anxiety symptoms: A preliminary randomized controlled trial. *JMIR Mental Health, 5*(4), e11290.

Snaith, R. P. (2003). The hospital anxiety and depression scale. *Health and Quality of Life Outcomes, 1*(1), 29.

Somerville, S., Dedman, K., Hagan, R., Oxnam, E., Wettinger, M., Byrne, S., Coo, S., Doherty, D., & Page, A. C. (2014). The perinatal anxiety screening scale: Development and preliminary validation. *Archives of Women's Mental Health, 17*(5), 443-454.

Spielberger, C. D. (1983). *State-Trait Anxiety Inventory for Adults (STAI-AD) [Database record]*. APA PsycTests. https://doi.org/10.1037/t06496-000

Spitzer, R. L., Kroenke, K., Williams, J. B., & Lowe, B. (2006). A brief measure for assessing generalized anxiety disorder. *Archives of Internal Medicine, 166*(10), 1092-1097. https://doi.org/10.1001/archinte.166.10.1092

Stanley, C. (2012). *A touch of his freedom*. Zondervan.

Sternberg, E., & Gold, P. (2002). The mind-body interaction in disease. *Sci Am (Special Edition), 12*(1), 82-89.

Stinson, F., Dawson, D., Chou, S., Smith, S., Goldstein, R., Ruan, W., & Grant, B. (2007). The epidemiology of DSM-IV specific phobia in the USA: Results from the national epidemiologic survey on alcohol and related conditions. *Psychological Medicine, 27*, 1047-1059. https://doi.org/10.1017/S0033291707000086S0033291707000086

Substance Abuse and Mental Health Services Administration. (2016). *Impact of the DSM-IV to DSM-5 changes on the national survey on drug use and health [Internet]*. https://www.ncbi.nlm.nih.gov/books/NBK519704/table/ch3.t10/

Taylor, S. E., Klein, L. C., Lewis, B. P., Gruenewald, T. L., Gurung, R. A. R., & Updegraff, J. A. (2000). Biobehavioral responses to stress in females: Tend-and-befriend, not fight-or-flight. *Psychological Review, 107*(3), 411–429. https://doi.org/10.1037/0033-295X.107.3.411

Tibi, L., van Oppen, P., Aderka, I., van Balkom., Al, Batelaan, N., Spinhoven, P., Pennix, B., & Anholt, G. (2015). An admisture analysis of age of onset in agoraphobia. *Journal of Affective Disorders, 180*(15), 112-115.

The Passion Bible. (2017). The Passion Translation Online. https://www.thepassiontranslation.com/

Tomas-Aragones, L., Voicu, C., & Marron, S. E. (2017). The clinical interview and assessment: General considerations. *Romanian Journal of Clinical and Experimental Dermatology, 4*(1), 6-13.

Valiente-Gómez, A., Moreno-Alcázar, A., Treen, D., Cedrón, C., Colom, F., Perez, V., & Amann, B. L. (2017). EMDR beyond PTSD: A systematic literature review. *Frontiers in Psychology, 8,* 1668.

Vollestad, J., Siversten, B., & Nielsen, G. (2011). Mindfulness-based stress reduction for patients with anxiety disorders: Evaluation in a randomized controlled trial. *Behavior Research and Therapy, 49,* 281-288.

Wardenaar, K., Lim, C., Al-Hamzawi, A., Alonso, J, Andrade, L., Benjet, C., Bunting, B., de Girolamo, G., Demyttenarere, K., Florescu, S, Gureje, O., Hisateru, T., Hu, C., Huang, Y., Karam, E., Kiejna, A., Lepine, J., Navarro-Mateu, F., Oakley Browne, M., …de Jonge, P. (2017). The cross-national epidemiology of specific phobia in the world mental health surveys. *Psychological Medicine, 47*(10), 1744-1760.

Watkins, P. C., Woodward, K., Stone, T., & Kolts, R. L. (2003). Gratitude and happiness: Development of a measure of gratitude, and relationships with subjective well-being. *Social Behavior and Personality, 3,* 431-452.

Wiederhold, B. K., Jang, D. P., Gevirtz, R. G., Kim, S. I., Kim, I. Y., & Wiederhold, M. D. (2002). The treatment of fear of flying: A controlled study of imaginal and virtual reality graded exposure therapy. *IEEE Transactions on Information Technology in Biomedicine, 6*(3), 218-223.

Wijma, K., Alehagen, S., & Wijma, B. (2002). Development of the delivery fear scale. *Journal of Psychosomatic Obstetrics & Gynecology, 23*(2), 97-107.

Wilson, J. B., Onorati, K., Mishkind, M., Reger, M. A., & Gahm, G. A. (2008). Soldier attitudes about technology-based approaches to mental health care. *Cyberpsychology & Behavior, 11*(6), 767-769. https://doi.org/10.1089/cpb.2008.0071

Wolpe, J. (1958). *Psychotherapy by reciprocal inhibition.* Stanford University Press.

Xu, Y., Schneier, F., Heimberg, R. G., Princisvalle, K., Liebowitz, M. R., Wang, S., & Blanco, C. (2012). Gender differences in social anxiety disorder: Results from the national epidemiologic sample on alcohol and related conditions. *Journal of Anxiety Disorders, 26,* 12-19. https://doi.org/10.1016/j.janxdis.2011.08.006

Zohar, J., & Westenberg, H. G. M. (2000). Anxiety disorders: A review of tricyclic antidepressants and selective serotonin reuptake inhibitors. *Acta Psychiatrica Scandinavica, 101,* 39-49.

Zoogman, S., Goldberg, S. B., Hoyt, W. T., & Miller, L. (2015). Mindfulness interventions with youth: *A meta-analysis. Mindfulness, 6*(2), 290-302.

CHAPTER 14
Counseling Women with Depression

DAVID R. BROWN, PH.D., MARANDA GRIFFIN, PH.D., & APRIL R. CRABLE, PH.D.

"For me, depression is not sadness. It's not having a bad day and needing a hug. It gave me a complete and utter sense of isolation and loneliness." ~Kristen Bell

"For I know the plans I have for you," declares the Lord, "plans to prosper you and not to harm you, plans to give you hope and a future." (Jeremiah 29:11, NIV)

Wisdom from Above: Standing in His Grace

Most of us can recall a dark and challenging time in our lives. In life's darkest moments, somewhere on your journey, you might feel as if your light is dimmed. Like the sons of Korah (Psalm 88:1-5), you may feel as if you have no strength and no way out. Depression can be experienced

subtly. But often, at its worst, depression is explicit, debilitating, and can affect anyone of any age for a number of reasons. That is why it is imperative that we "comfort those in any trouble with the comfort we ourselves receive" (*New International Bible*, 1973/2011, 2 Corinthians 1:4b). God desires something better for you. He wants to revive you. He wants to comfort and restore you. His presence enables us to walk with those who are hurting.

CHAPTER LEARNING OBJECTIVES

Upon completing this chapter, you should be able to:

- Identify the prevalence rates of women suffering from a depressive disorder
- Assess the various depressive disorders and issues related to symptoms of depression as identified in *DSM-5*
- Apply evidence-based treatment options while including a Biblical perspective
- Apply assessment and screening tools used to diagnose and identify a treatment plan
- Discover the need to consider gender-differences when diagnosing and treating depressive disorders

CHAPTER OVERVIEW

Depression is a mood disorder characterized by the presence of sadness, emptiness, or irritable mood. Depression is the leading cause of disability worldwide. Over 17 million, or approximately 7.1%, of all adults in the United States, have at least one depressive episode (National Institute of Mental Health [NIMH], 2017). Depression is most prevalent in women. Beginning in early adolescence, women experience depression at 1.5 to 3-fold higher rates (10.4%) compared to men (5.5%; National Center for Health Statistics, 2018). Based on the fifth edition of the *Diagnostic and Statistical Manual of Mental Disorders* (*DSM-5*), depression can appear at any age, but prevalence is in 18 to 29-year old individuals (American Psychiatric Association, 2013). Across diverse racial and ethnic groups, depression is more prevalent in white non-Hispanic (34.7%) clients (American Psychiatric Association, 2017). Minority clients are less likely to disclose symptoms and seek treatment. Further, statistics show that LGBTQ individuals experience depression 2.5 times more often compared to heterosexual individuals (American Psychiatric Association, 2017). Clients with depression may report a loss of interest in activities, weight loss, fatigue, worthlessness, and guilt. Sleep interruption, disturbance, or hypersomnia is common. Suicidal ideation is among the symptoms of depression that contribute to distress. Depression is an underlying cause of suicide attempts (Halverson, 2019). Depression also frequently occurs with other physical and mental health disorders. In this chapter, you will find an overview of the depressive disorders identified by the American Psychiatric Association (2017) and the prevalence of women for each disorder. Additionally, there are examples of screening tools and interventions offered to help build a "toolbox" for effective treatment of women diagnosed with a depressive disorder.

TYPES OF DEPRESSIVE DISORDERS

A chapter about mental health and depression is not complete without a discussion of the depressive disorders, as defined by the *Diagnostic and Statistical Manual and Mental Disorders* (5th ed.; *DSM-5*; American Psychiatric Association [APA], 2013). *Depression* is defined within the *DSM-5* as "the presence of sad, empty, or irritable mood, accompanied by somatic and cognitive changes that significantly affect the individual's capacity to function" (APA, 2013, p. 155). As we consider mental health diagnoses and clients, it is important to distinguish between normal feelings of sadness and clinically significant symptoms of depression. Almost everyone experiences loss, sadness, and grief at some point in life, but not all of these feelings are severe enough or persist long enough to meet the diagnostic threshold of a depressive disorder.

© Africa Studio/Shutterstock.com

For example, feelings of loss, helplessness, and despondence are common when grieving the death a loved one, losing one's job, or experiencing the end of a close relationship, and we should not automatically assume that people experiencing such symptoms are clinically depressed and/or require medication. While some of these symptoms are characteristic of general depression (APA, 2017), diagnosing a depressive disorder requires a client's symptoms to meet specific requirements. In some situations, feelings of grief, loss, and sadness can sometimes deepen into mental health concerns, such as a depressive disorder, and the *DSM-5* provides clinicians with guidance to discern whether the symptoms are sufficiently severe to warrant a diagnosis, as well as which diagnosis is appropriate (APA, 2013). As noted by the National Institute on Mental Health ([NIMH] 2019), depression is a treatable mental health disorder, but it can create impairments that have the potential to significantly interfere with a person's daily life and activities.

Over 7% of the United States population (or approximately 17.3 million people) reportedly struggle with depression, and women are roughly twice as likely to report symptoms of depression (Brody et al., 2018; NIMH, 2019).

Depression is commonly described as a *mood disorder*, a condition that involves "profound disturbances in emotion" (Kring & Johnson, 2018, p. 120). We can separate mood dis-

Bipolar disorder affects approximately 2.8% of adults each year in the United States. It is common for a person diagnosed with bipolar to have a history of depression (NIMH, 2017a). In the *DSM IV-TR*, bipolar disorder was categorized as a mood disorder, in the *DSM-5*, it is its own category (Bipolar and related disorders, APA, 2013).

orders into two broad categories: unipolar disorders and bipolar disorders. *Unipolar disorders* only contain depressive symptoms, which is what we will discuss here. *Bipolar disorders* contain both depressive symptoms and manic symptoms, which are periods of elation and irritability (APA, 2013).

Additionally, within the unipolar depressive disorders, we can identify two clusters: chronic depression and episodic depression (APA, 2013). *Chronic depression* encompasses disorders where depressive symptoms persist for two or more years and may fluctuate in intensity for lengthy periods. *Episodic depression* involves disorders where depressive symptoms may feel more severe at times (Psychology Today, 2019), but whose duration typically lasts from 3-6 months at a time (APA, 2013).

FIGURE 14.1

Sex Differences in Depression

According to the *DSM-5*, gender differences in diagnosis and experience tend to appear during early adolescence (APA, 2013); this is in agreement

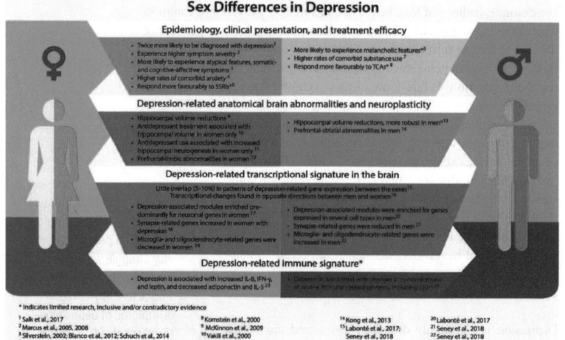

Infographic reprinted by permission of Vicky Earle, Medical/Scientific Illustrator.

with much research (Avenevoli et al., 2015). In addition, Riecher-Rössler (2018) discussed the importance of noting gender differences (e.g., etiologies, epigenetics, hormones, etc.), as a way to assist practitioners to better match treatments in order to improve outcomes. Hilt and Nolen-Hoeksema (2014) noted that while research indicates that factors related to gender contribute to a disproportionate number of women being diagnosed with a depressive disorder than men, once the diagnosis is given, factors unrelated to gender tend to determine how long a depressive episode persists. They discussed gender differences in depression as falling within three separate domains: a) biological explanations, b) psychological explanations, and c) social explanations.

Biological factors relate to the hormonal changes occurring in puberty, the menstrual cycle, postpartum, and menopause (Noble, 2005), when "levels of their gonadal hormones are undergoing substantial change" (Hilt & Nolen-Hoeksema, 2014, p. 357). Still, Steiner et al. (2003) suggested that changes in hormones are just one of various factors that lead to the development of a mood disorder. Psychological factors relate to various cognitive and interpersonal factors, as well as two personal characteristics that differ between genders: rumination and interpersonal orientation. Finally, social factors relate to stress exposure and sensitivity, especially from the context of responses to maltreatment, abuse, neglect, power differentials, and relationship concerns. As Hilt and Nolen-Hoeksema (2014) noted, many of these factors appear to have reciprocal relationships with depression: an increase in depression can bring about an increase in these factors and vice versa.

TYPES OF DEPRESSIVE DISORDERS

Within the depressive disorders category, disorders characterized as episodic unipolar depression are all types of major depressive disorder (MDD), premenstrual dysphoric disorder (PDD), and substance/medication-induced depressive disorder. This chapter will also discuss persistent depressive disorder (dysthymia), characterized as chronic unipolar depression. The *DSM-5* (APA, 2013) also includes a depressive disorder only diagnosed in children and adolescents (disruptive mood dysregulation disorder [PMDD]); but because this text focuses on counseling women, PMDD will not be discussed. Two additional depressive disorders noted in the *DSM-5* are diagnosable when observing depressive symptoms, but only at a sub-threshold level, or when a therapist concludes that more information is needed (other specified/unspecified depressive disorders). While these disorders will not be discussed in this chapter, it is important to understand that even sub-threshold depression can negatively affect an individual's daily functioning. Finally, the *DSM-5* depressive category contains one disorder for symptoms that occur from exposure to a medication or the intoxication or withdrawal from a substance, such as alcohol, marijuana (cannabis), or barbiturates: Substance/Medication-Induced Depressive Disorder. Because this disorder is diagnosed more frequently among males (APA, 2013), it will not be discussed.

Major Depressive Disorder

Catatonia is a diagnosable condition and is characterized by a decreased motor activity, interpersonal engagement, or "excessive and peculiar" motor activity (APA, 2013 p. 119). The presence of catatonia can range from unresponsiveness to a pronounced agitation that may appear similar to a manic episode.

One of the most widely documented and diagnosed of unipolar depressive disorders, **major depressive disorder** (MDD), requires the presence of several mood symptoms, among other criteria, prior to diagnosis. A primary requirement for MDD is the manifestation of either a "depressed mood most of the day" or a "markedly diminished interest or pleasure in all, or mostly all activities" (APA, 2013, p. 160) over at least a two-week period. A number of additional symptoms must be present in order to fulfill diagnostic requirements, including significant changes in weight (gain or loss), trouble falling asleep or staying asleep, psychomotor agitation, fatigue or loss of energy, feelings of worthlessness, inability to think or concentrate, and recurrent thoughts of death or dying. These symptoms, combined with the requirement of significant distress or impairment in daily functioning, as well as the symptoms not being attributable to substance use or another medical condition, represent a major depressive episode (APA, 2013). As Eid et al. (2019) noted, depression is a global mental health problem, a concern echoed by the World Health Organization ([WHO] 2018) and NAMI (2019). Depression can develop from a number of factors (e.g., social, environmental, genetic, psychological, temperamental) in a complex manner; the very nature of the depression means a person's symptoms are the cause of much of the impairment they experience on a daily basis (APA, 2013). This means that depressive symptoms not only affect how a person feels, they also affect that person's ability to go to work, spend time with family, enjoy hobbies, etc. Further, symptoms can vary in degree of severity, from very mild symptoms to complete incapacitation (catatonia). WHO (2018) also noted an interrelationship between symptoms of depression and physical illness. Treatment options are available and can be effective (Eid et al., 2019; Langan & Goodbred, 2016).

Prevalence among Women

It is noted in the *DSM-5*, that women are roughly twice as likely to be diagnosed with a depressive disorder (APA, 2013); this figure is noted consistently in professional literature (Brody et al., 2018; NIMH, 2019). Further, Kessler (2003) and Salk et al. (2017) reported that this ratio is a worldwide phenomenon, even among countries with equitable gender roles. Despite research and knowledge of this gender gap since the 1980's and 1990's (Salk et al., 2017), Kuehner (2017) wrote that explanations for it remain inconclusive. Still, gender differences among symptom manifestations are known; Eid et al. (2019) and Kuehner (2017) noted that women tend to report more atypical symptoms, primarily with an increased appetite (or weight gain), excessive fatigue, and hypersomnia, as well as other somatic symptoms, than do men. Further, Kuehner (2017) reported, "comorbidity with other internalizing disorders is higher among women than among men" (p. 147); these are disorders such as depressive disorders, anxiety disorders, obsessive-compulsive disorders, and trauma and stressor-related disorders.

Some research seems to indicate that the gender gap may be closing. Eid et al. (2019) suggested that current diagnostic criteria for MDD may not fully capture the way men experience depression, leading to lower rates of occurrence. Notably, Gili et al. (2014) reported that daily functioning among men and women diagnosed with a depressive disorder is equally impaired, meaning that men appear to experience the same level of impaired functioning as women when depressed. Parker et al. (2014)

discussed a similar finding in their research on different subtypes of depressive disorders; they conclude that gender gaps are not observed in some situations. In another study, Picco et al. (2017) reported that the gender gap appears to be narrowing in some countries; they speculate this may be due to changes in gender roles and how these changes may reduce stressors. In another example, Salk et al. (2016) reported that the emergence of depressive symptoms occurs with different trajectories: the rate of girls' diagnoses increased from ages 11-14, and the rate of boys' diagnoses increased from ages 15-18. This is a significant finding because Salk et al. (2016) informed us that gender differences in depression at age 18 in both boys and girls are not significantly different.

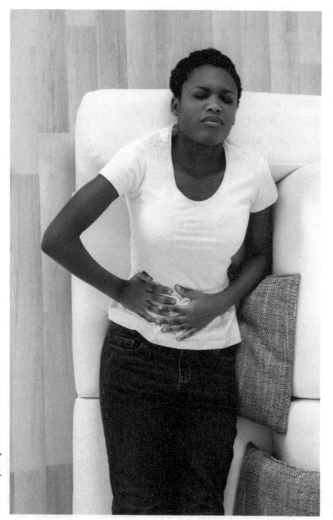

Premenstrual Dysphoric Disorder

Not to be confused with **premenstrual syndrome** (PMS), **premenstrual dysphoric disorder** (PMDD) is an episodic unipolar mood disorder where women experience both significant physiological and affective symptoms in the week prior to the onset of menses (APA, 2013; Hantsoo & Epperson, 2015). Ducasse et al. (2016) reported premenstrual symptoms to fall into one of three categories: 1) minor symptoms that do not cause significant impairment, 2) moderate to severe symptoms (e.g., PMS) that cause some distress, and 3) severe symptoms (e.g., PMDD) that significantly impair daily functioning. PMDD was designated a mental health disorder in the *DSM-5* (APA, 2013); prior to this, it was listed in the *DSM* as a condition for further research (Lanza di Scalea & Pearlstein, 2019).

A diagnosis of PMDD requires at least five of the following symptoms, with at least one symptom from two separate categories (APA, 2013; Hantsoo & Epperson, 2015). The first category (cognitive-affective symptoms) includes pronounced changes in mood, marked irritability, depressed mood, and noticeable anxiety. The second category (physiological symptoms) includes a decreased interest in typical activities, difficulty concentrating, easily fatigued, marked changes in appetite, changes in sleeping, feelings of being overwhelmed, and the presence of physical symptoms, such as breast tenderness or swelling, joint pain, muscle pain, bloating sensation, and weight gain (APA, 2013).

Lanza di Scalea and Pearlstein (2019) reported that comorbidity rates with other psychiatric disorders are high, especially with depressive and anxiety disorders. Etiology and treatment of PMDD is not settled, as a variety of competing theories exist; these include concerns such as abnormal responses to normal hormonal fluctuations, decreased or paradoxical sensitivity of certain receptors within the central nervous system, altered immune functions, altered circadian rhythms, genetic factors, and abnormal emotion processing, among others (Lanza di Scalea & Pearlstein, 2019). Additionally, a distinguishing feature of PMDD, to differentiate it from **dysmenorrhea** (a syndrome of painful menses) is that symptoms should begin prior to the onset of menses (APA, 2013). As noted in the *DSM-5*, PMDD symptoms may worsen when approaching menopause, but symptoms will cease post-menopause (APA, 2013).

Hantsoo and Epperson (2015) noted that any "unpleasant or undesirable physical, emotional, or behavior symptoms" (p. 87) occurring before or during menses are commonly referred to as PMS, which includes less severe or fewer symptoms than what is required for a diagnosis of PMDD (APA, 2013); a diagnosis of PMDD requires the presence of specific criteria. Further, symptoms must cause significant impairment to warrant a diagnosis of PMDD, not just discomfort and irritability experienced before and during menses.

Prevalence among Women

Lanza di Scalea and Pearlstein (2019) noted that estimates reveal approximately 85% of women will experience at least one mild premenstrual symptom (i.e., PMS), but only around 5% will report sufficient criteria for a PMDD diagnosis. Ducasse et al. (2016) also notes that approximately 20% of women with premenstrual symptoms will experience notable impairment in their daily functioning. The *DSM-5* notes that PMDD can develop any time after menarche (APA, 2013). In addition, Hantsoo and Epperson (2015) indicated that PMDD is clinically different from other depressive disorders by having "more irritability and anxiety-like features"

(p. 87). As a disorder within the *DSM-5*, both Hantsoo and Epperson (2015) and Lanza di Scalea and Pearlstein (2019) called for further research into PMDD; etiology and development remain somewhat uncertain.

Persistent Depressive Disorder (Dysthymia)

Viewed as a low-grade, persistent unipolar depression, the symptoms of **persistent depressive disorder** (PDD), or **dysthymia**, are considered less severe than MDD (Psychology Today, 2019). However, PDD is a chronic condition that can continue for years: whereas recovery from a major depressive episode may occur within three months of onset (APA, 2013), individuals with PDD may experience symptoms that endure longer than two years (Kring & Johnson, 2018). Symptoms of PDD are similar to those of MDD and may be just as severe; the primary differentiator is the chronicity or duration of symptoms. In fact, Köhler et al. (2018) reported that "approximately 30% of depressed patients have a chronic course of the disorder" (p. 18). PDD is a new depressive disorder within the *DSM-5*, representing a "consolidation" of two disorders from the *DSM-IV*: chronic major depressive disorder and dysthymic disorder (APA, 2013; Parker & Malhi, 2019), noting the overlapping similarity of the two disorders. Salk et al. (2016) discussed the idea of *chronicity* at length. Chronicity can be explained as the extent of the individual's suffering or the cost to society – the idea being that the longer an individual suffers, the greater the burden he/she carries. With this in mind, chronicity is a differentiator between PDD and MDD: although the symptoms may not be as numerous or as severe, individuals diagnosed with PDD may suffer more or have a greater burden to bear due to the longevity of the symptoms (Salk et al.,

2016). Walker and Druss (2015) noted that "persistent depression is influenced by a number of clinical, health-related, and psychosocial factors" (p. 702), indicating the complexity of diagnosis and treatment.

Prevalence among Women

Much like MDD, women are approximately twice as likely to be diagnosed with PDD as men (Kring & Johnson,

2018), although, conversely, Parker et al. (2014) reported that gender differences in depression are only distinct in symptoms and severity among bipolar disorders. Salk et al.'s (2016) longitudinal study confirms a gender disparity emerging around 13 years of age, noting that this finding is similar to research conducted throughout the 1980's and 1990's. As previously discussed, Salk et al. (2016) reported that despite different trajectories in the emergence of depressive symptoms, gender differences are not significant between boys and girls at age 18 and beyond; this finding suggests that chronicity is similar among men and women. Salk et al. (2016) speculate that different risk factors may explain the different emergent trajectories, although they also note that more research is necessary to confirm these findings. In their nationally representative study of persistent depression in adults, Walker and Druss (2015) reported intriguing results: women are almost two and a half times more likely to remain depressed over a 10-year period than men. Further, people who have never married were 2.42 times more likely to be depressed over the same 10-year period as those who are married. Walker and Druss (2015) noted that of all demographic variables they collected, gender and marital status are the most significantly associated with persistent MDD. As noted in our discussions with other depressive disorders, there is still much speculation regarding why women are roughly twice as likely to experience depression as men, and each study provides suggestions for future research that may lead to a resolution to this question.

OTHER CONCERNS AND DISORDERS

Postpartum Depression

Commonly known as **postpartum depression** (PPD), the symptoms of depression that develop during or after pregnancy are currently classified in the *DSM-5* as the "peripartum onset" specifier with both major depressive disorder (MDD) and persistent depressive disorder (PDD). The *DSM-5* notes that this specifier is used when a major depressive episode (or the most recent episode) occurs during pregnancy or within four weeks following delivery (APA, 2013). While we may be more familiar with the term *postpartum depression*, APA (2013) notes that "Fifty percent of 'postpartum' major depressive episodes actually begin prior to delivery" (p. 186), which necessitates using collectively applicable terminology.

© Tolikoff Photography/Shutterstock.com

Langan and Goodbred (2016) reported that "**Peripartum depression** (a major depressive episode occurring during pregnancy or within 4 weeks following delivery) affects up to one in seven women and is associated with significant maternal and neonatal morbidity if untreated" (p. 852).

Conversely, Kuehner (2017) noted that peripartum onset could be further subdivided due to situational factors (e.g., peripartal episodes vs. postpartal episodes), noting the differences in risk factors and prognosis. Regardless, PPD remains a significant concern for women.

We must also distinguish between the "baby blues" or "postpartum blues" and diagnosable depressive disorders. Noble (2005) reported that approximately 50-80% of women report a number of general depressive symptoms that tend to disappear within two weeks. Typical concerns are a depressed mood, mood swings, tearfulness, irritability, changes in sleep, and a decreased appetite. Since symptoms are so common, there should be no immediate concern that a depressive disorder is present. Still, Noble (2005) noted that approximately 25% of those reporting these symptoms will go on to experience PPD. It is, therefore, important to note the duration of symptoms, as they could be indicators that lead to a diagnosable condition.

Postpartum Depression

Sarah Savage

In August 2019, Sarah Savage posted a blog (https://auburn.citymomsblog.com/mom/postpartum-depression-almost-destroyed-me/) in a community parenting website, detailing her experiences with postpartum depression (PPD). It was not an easy task, writing and publicly sharing about something that she describes as a "very dark, lonely, and hopeless place." However, Sarah chooses to share her story, hoping that it helps other moms.

Sarah explains her pregnancy was relatively easy until the last week when her doctor wanted to induce labor. There was no indication of the darkness she would feel following delivery. Within the first couple of weeks after her daughter's birth, Sarah noticed that something just did not feel right. She initially believed she was still recovering and just worn down from a lack of sleep, but the sense of emptiness continued. She also thought she could handle it on her own, thinking that motherhood was just especially hard for some reason. She writes that "when the intense baby blues of the first couple weeks seemed to fade, they were replaced with deeper, more persistent feelings of despair." Sarah eventually sought help after her husband insisted, they do so. She agreed to meet with a therapist instead of a physician because she did not want to take medication.

Sarah reports finding therapy to be helpful. Foremost, she appreciates that her therapist was honest and willing to challenge her, especially when noting the importance of bonding with her daughter and the possible repercussions if bonding did not occur. Sarah did not like hearing this, but it helped her agree to visit the OB/GYN and accept a prescription for an antidepressant. Sarah also recalls feeling a deep shame because mothers are supposed to love their children from the moment they are conceived, and be obsessed with how cute their baby is, and want to cuddle, love, and nurture them – things she did not feel. Further, while expecting to be exhausted, drained, and needing to recover, Sarah did not expect to feel isolated, alone, and overwhelmed. As

© Jonathan Savage

Sarah reports that her greatest fear of admitting what she was feeling was that someone would take her daughter away from her.

a stay-at-home mom, Sarah recalls feeling an immense self-imposed pressure to resume life as normal as soon as she was discharged from the hospital: laundry, cooking, and grocery shopping… everything. Even when around other people, Sarah recalls feeling disconnected, isolated, and angry that others could walk around and be normal, as though nothing were wrong. She was surrounded by people, including her husband, and she recalls never feeling more alone in her life.

Looking back, Sarah indicates several things she would do differently, which are also her plans for future babies. First, she would hire a doula to help her through the birthing process, who could also be an advocate for her at the hospital. Second, she would focus on just the baby and herself for a while after birth – letting go of household chores and other things that may cause her to feel overwhelmed. Third, she would proactively contact her physician if she experienced any postpartum complications, noting that she had experienced several complications after the birth of her daughter. Fourth, she would be honest with her physician about how she was feeling and be willing to take medication. Fifth, she would begin exercising much sooner. And sixth, she would be much more willing to accept offers of help from friends, family, people at church, etc.

Sarah has a number of recommendations for moms, hoping they will not suffer needlessly when help is readily available. First, she wants other moms to know they are not alone; many women struggle with PPD, even if they do not talk about it. Sarah notes that PPD is very real, and it is not the mom's fault; they are not "crazy or defective," nor is it a reflection of their ability as a mother. Sarah also reminds moms that PPD will not last forever: their bodies will return to normal, they will eventually feel like themselves, and they will feel love for their babies. Sarah is adamant that moms should seek help as soon as possible: some post-delivery depression is normal, but if a mom is still struggling after a few weeks, she should tell someone she trusts, such as a physician, a therapist, or her spouse. She also encourages moms to take medication if needed – be willing to do whatever is necessary for your baby, yourself, and your family. Sarah recommends fathers take on as many burdens as possible, giving a new mom time to herself, time to rest, allowing her to cry and holding her. If help is needed, Sarah suggests fathers should gently push moms towards help and make it happen. As much as possible, fathers should take the initiative to schedule appointments and make any arrangements.

Freeman et al. (2018) highlighted a significant concern among women already diagnosed with a depressive disorder and taking antidepressant medication: whether to discontinue their medication during pregnancy. From their study of depression and unplanned pregnancy, Ekrami et al. (2019) reported that women who received counseling also indicate a reduced level of depression anxiety. It is important to note that Ekrami et al. 's (2019) study recruited women with no history of psychiatric disorders, meaning that their depressive symptoms developed during pregnancy. Interventions consisted of both individual and group counseling sessions, as well as routine pregnancy care. Noble (2005) also noted that the typical symptoms of depression often mirror the physiological changes in pregnancy, so therapists must carefully ascertain whether a woman's symptoms truly meet diagnostic criteria for a clinical disorder.

The onset of depression during pregnancy appears to somewhat common: Truijens et al. (2017) reported that up to 26% of women will experience depressive symptoms at some point during pregnancy, with approximately 4% of those women reporting persistent symptoms.

CONCEPT TO CONTEMPLATE

© ImageFlow/Shutterstock.com

It is not uncommon for counselors to have a strong response or experience intense feelings after hearing a client's story. These feelings can be evoked due to the counselor's own personal experiences or unsolved issues. After reading Sarah's story, what were your first reactions about Sarah and her experiences? Did you have a negative response or an empathetic one? Were you surprised by your feelings or thoughts about Sara's story?

Seasonal Affective Disorder

Sometimes called the *winter blues*, **seasonal affective disorder** (SAD) is listed as a specifier (or subtype) of major depressive disorder (MDD), which indicates recurring depressive symptoms that fit into a seasonal pattern (Melrose, 2015). SAD is a subtype of recurrent MDD and only occurs at a specific time of year, typically fall and winter; at other times during the year, depressive symptoms are in full remission (APA, 2013). According to Kring and Johnson (2018), SAD most often occurs during the winter months, and is more common in northern latitudes than in the south. Sandman et al. (2016) reported that SAD occurs more frequently among women than men, and is more common in North America than in Europe. Much like MDD and persistent depressive disorder (PDD), SAD is diagnosed approximately twice as often in women than in men, and symptoms tend to decrease with age (Chotai et al., 2004). Conversely, Melrose (2015) claimed that SAD occurs four times more often in women than in men.

"Light therapy involves daily exposure to artificial bright light for a set period of time, typically in the morning. The light is often delivered through a light box that is equipped with fluorescent tubes, a reflector, and a diffusing screen; or using fluorescent ceiling units" (Perera et al., 2016, p. 116).

There is speculation that SAD occurs in people who are sensitive to changes in daylight, specifically in the over-production of melatonin, which is a hormone produced within the pineal gland "that responds to darkness by causing sleepiness" (Melrose, 2015, p. 1). Although noting the effects of melatonin, Melrose (2015) claimed that it alone is not responsible for SAD. She also discusses the role of serotonin, which is a neurotransmitter that is believed to regulate mood. According to Melrose (2015), a "combination of decreased serotonin and increased melatonin impacts circadian rhythms" (p. 1), which is the body's internal "clock" that is influenced by the amount of daylight in each season. Thus, people who live farther from the equator have a greater chance of developing SAD due to more dramatic changes in the amount of daylight during winter. Kring and Johnson (2018) noted that SAD is a treatable condition, responding to antidepressant medication like other depressive disorders, however, they also reported that bright light treatments have been shown to be equally effective.

ASSESSMENT

Screening and assessments are tools that are available to support identification of depression (Hinz et al., 2016). Screening tools and assessments measure the presence and intensity of symptoms a client is experiencing. Screening results often inform if an individual requires further assessment. Diagnosing depression can be difficult as symptoms may overlap with a wide range of physical and mental health issues. Assessments often help support diagnostic criteria. A diagnosis should not be made solely based on the results of screeners and assessments. Evidence based screening and assessment tools have been developed and validated to aid identification and diagnosis of depression (Beck et al., 1961; Beusenberg et al., 1994; Cox et al., 1987; Hergueta & Weiller, 2013; Spitzer et al., 1999).

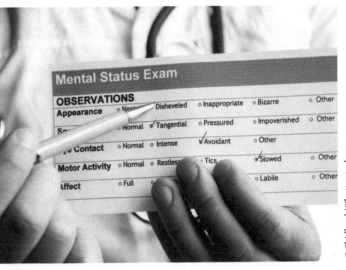

© Shidlovski/Shutterstock.com

Screening and Assessment Tools for Depression
- Beck Depression Inventory (BDI) is a 21-item widely used tool that measures symptoms of the severity of depression symptoms. BDI is a self-report rating tool (Beck et al., 1961).
- Edinburg Depression Scale (EDS) is a 10-item self- report scale to assess women for symptom of depression while pregnant and postnatal (Cox et al., 1987).
- Geriatric Depression Scale (GDS-15) is a 15-item self- report scale used to measure depression in older adults (Sheikh & Yesavage, 1986).
- Mini International Neuropsychiatric Interview (MINI) is a brief structured diagnostic interview to assess 17 prevalent disorders found in the *DSM-5* including depression (Hergueta & Weiller, 2013).
- Patient Health Questionnaire (PHQ-9) is a self-report tool used to assess, diagnose, and measure the severity of depression (Spitzer et al., 1999).
- Self-Reporting Questionnaire (SRQ) is a screening tool for mental health disorders including depression. Created by the World Health Organization, the SRQ has been translated into 20 languages (Beusenberg et al., 1994).

EVIDENCE-BASED TREATMENT OPTIONS

Many treatment options are available to treat depression. When looking at what options to use with your client, you want to utilize evidence-based treatment (EBT), evidence-based therapy or evidence-based practices. These options describe any treatment, therapy or practice that have been subject to scientific research and a body of evidence exists to support use of the treatment to address the issue. The main goal behind using EBTs is increased quality of care, accountability, and cost-effectiveness. In this section, we provide tools, interventions, and homework options for use with women with depression.

Psychotherapy Interventions

A number of interventions have empirical support for working with clients with depression. This section includes examples of interventions.

Cognitive Behavioral Therapy (CBT)

FIGURE 14.2

Cognitive Behavioral Model

CBT is a type of therapy that posits how you think influences how you feel and how you behave. Figure 14.2 below shows an illustration of this process, commonly known as the *cognitive behavioral model*.

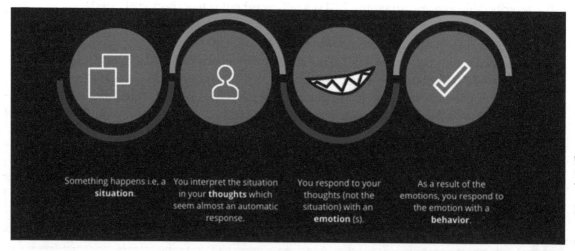

Something happens i.e. a **situation**.

You interpret the situation in your **thoughts** which seem almost an automatic response.

You respond to your thoughts (not the situation) with an **emotion** (s).

As a result of the emotions, you respond to the emotion with a **behavior**.

Source: Maranda Griffin

CBT focuses on modification of thoughts. Psychotherapists Aaron Beck and Albert Ellis are most widely known for pioneering this theory. Cognitive therapists help the client recognize exaggerated ways of thinking. In addition, these therapists engage clients in "rational thinking by asking them to examine the presuppositions that lead to depressive or anxious states" (Leahy, 2003, p. 1). Cognitive therapists rely on several techniques, some of which are highlighted in the *Homework* section, to reduce the symptoms associated with depression. CBT and interpersonal psychotherapy are among the most researched therapies for depression (Huibers et al., 2015).

Interpersonal Psychotherapy (IPT)

Researchers consider IPT as second to CBT for empirical efficacy in the treatment of depression (Markowitz & Weissman, 2004). IPT is a time-limited, 12-16-week therapy option for depression. The empirically validated treatment focuses on the client's outside environment and quality of relationships the client has with people. Improvement of relationships and social functioning are central to reduction of symptoms associated with depression. In counseling, the counselor focuses on four key areas with the client (see Figure 14.3).

Role disputes	**Role transitions**
Unresolved grief	**Interpersonal deficits**

FIGURE 14.3

Key Areas of Relational and Social Functioning

Source: Maranda Griffin

The therapeutic alliance is a key principle with this treatment approach. Counselors are present-focused with clients and approach the work in phases, beginning, middle, and end. The initial phase (beginning) focuses on diagnosis and identification of the interpersonal context in which symptoms present. In the middle phase of treatment, the counselor works with the client on the key area (Figure 14.3) to deal with the presenting issue. In the end phase, the counselor prepares the client for termination by focusing on the change in the relationship role in counseling, highlighting therapeutic gains, and independence. IPT is grounded in the work of Harry Stack Sullivan, Adolf Meyer, and John Bowlby (Overview of IPT, n.d.).

Gerald Klerman and Myrna Weissman are known for the development of IPT. Homework is not routinely used in IPT. IPT can be used in conjunction with psychopharmacology.

Pharmacotherapy and Psychotherapy

Research has found **Intravenous Ketamine** to be an effective treatment for people suffering from treatment resistant depression and for people at imminent risk of suicide (Price et al., 2009; Sinyor et al., 2018).

Women who suffer from a depressive disorder may choose a combination approach (i.e., prescription medication and psychotherapy therapy). For most depression disorders, psychotherapy and pharmacotherapy are effective independently; however, combined treatment has shown to be more efficacious in treating MDD (Cuijpers et al., 2013). In fact, Cuijpers et al. (2014) reported that combined treatment was far superior in the treatment of major depression compared to pharmacotherapy and psychotherapy individually. It is also important to consider that clients may not respond well to pharmacotherapy alone. Referred to as *treatment resistant depression*, some clients respond better overall when CBT is used as an adjunct to pharmacotherapy (Wiles et al., 2013).

A psychiatrist or a physician can work with the client to help the client find what works for them. Oftentimes, the medication prescriber will work with the client to ensure the dosage is balanced to address the client needs and minimize the side effects the client may experience. Counselors monitor client progress in therapy to ensure treatment gains. At times, despite the use of EBTs, the counselor may recommend the client to consult with a psychiatrist or a physician for medication consideration. A best practice when working with these clients is to educate the client on the benefit of communication with the psychiatrist or physician. The client can decide if they will authorize a release of information for the counselor to communicate with the prescribing doctor to aid successful treatment outcómes. It is anticipated that not all clients will be amenable to medication, even if it may be the best treatment option.

Group Counseling

Group counseling is considered to be an effective intervention for depression, as the efficacy of treating women suffering from depression has been well documented (Dastbaz et al., 2014; Hansson et al., 2008). Group counseling also provides a cost-effective treatment modality for people to participate in counseling. Additionally, it creates opportunities for access to services when the availability of counselors in the area is limited (Araya et al., 2006). For example, clients in rural towns may have to wait months before they are able to make an appointment for services, often leaving them vulnerable and increasing their risk of engaging in self-destructive behaviors. Group therapy is often used as a holding place until individual therapy becomes available. Community counseling agencies implement the groups as a *holding place*, allowing the agency to provide services at a lower cost, monitor and assess the client, and teach coping skills to help them manage their symptoms. Additionally, the group is often provided by a counselor in training (intern) or a counselor that is being supervised for licensure.

Psychoeducational, psychotherapy, and support groups are the most common groups to treat clients with depression. Counselors may integrate a variation of these options into one group curriculum. This decision should be based on the needs of the clients within the group. If your clients need basic understanding of depression or want to increase their knowledge on symptoms and skills, a psychoeducational group would be the ideal group for these clients. Psychoeducational groups serve the purpose of education, often teaching life skills. It is not considered a clinical processing group. In a psychoeducational group, the leader often takes a teacher

© Atstock Productions/Shutterstock.com

role. Unlike the counselor's role in a psychoeducational group, where a counselor serves as the facilitator of a psychotherapy group. Psychotherapy groups are grounded in a theory or a therapy model. A counselor may choose to implement a cognitive behavioral group or narrative group therapy to treat clients with depression. Both CBT and narrative group therapy have been found to be effective in alleviating symptoms of depression in women (Beatty & Koczwara, 2010; Dastbaaz, 2014; McDermut et al., 2001; Thimm & Antonsen, 2014).

Support groups are established to help clients find comfort and cope with their depression by being in a safe face to face or virtual environment with others who are also experiencing depression. Clients have found success in virtual support groups. Houston et al. (2002) reported that the participants of their one-year cohort study reported that engaging in a virtual support group helped their symptoms. Additionally, over one third of the 103 participants reported that they preferred virtual support groups to the traditional face-to-face model (Houston et al., 2002). Support groups help clients understand that they are not alone.

The members of support groups often encourage and empower each other during and after meetings. It is important for counselors to have a familiarity of support groups in their area so that they can make an informed recommendation to a client. If considering referring your client to a virtual support group, it is essential to assess your client for the appropriateness of this option. Support groups may be integrated in the client's treatment plan or as part of a step-down service after discharge.

Homework

One of the key attributes counselors use with clients is homework. Homework is a means for counselors to "help clients use the time between sessions as productively as possible" (Egan, 2010, p. 113). Counselors use homework as a way to support treatment, engage clients to action, and to help clients move to goal achievement. This section includes examples of homework that might be useful when confronting women with depression.

1. **The Cognitive Behavioral Model (CBM).** Provide your client a copy of the CBM (Figure 14.2). Using the CBM as a reference, the client is asked to think back about events (situations) where they may have had intrusive,

negative, or overwhelming thoughts. Instruct the client to write down (Figure 14.4) the event, the thought(s), and the emotion they associate with this. Lastly, have the client write down the behavior(s) that resulted.

FIGURE 14.4

Automatic Thought Record

Event/Situation	Thought	Emotion	Behavior

2. **Cognitive Distortions.** The client can be given the homework of identifying negative core beliefs that they have held about themselves and/or to monitor negative thoughts between appointments. The beliefs or thoughts are ones held within their subconscious. Instruct the client to make a list of these thoughts – for example, "I'll always be alone." Then ask the client to include evidence against the validity of the thought. Have the client reflect and meditate on Proverbs 23:7 (*King James Bible*, 1769/2017), "For as he thinketh in his heart, so is he: Eat and drink, saith he to thee; but his heart is not with thee". Using Philippians 4:6-8 (*King James Bible*, 1769/2017):

> Be careful for nothing; but in everything by prayer and supplication with thanksgiving let your requests be made known to God. And the peace of God, which passeth all understanding, shall keep your hearts and minds through Christ Jesus. Finally brethren, whatsoever things are true, whatsoever things are honest, whatsoever things are just, whatsoever things are pure, whatsoever things are lovely, whatsoever things are of good report; if there be any virtue, and if there be any praise, think on these things.

Have clients develop a new thought that is rational and aligns with the truth espoused in Philippians.

Thought	Evidence	New Rational Thought

Effective Treatment for Chronic Depression:
Cognitive Behavioral Analysis System of Psychotherapy (CBASP)
Written by Anita Kuhnley

What Is CBASP?

The national institute of health reports that the prevalence of Persistent Depressive Disorder (PDD) among women is higher than it is among men (NIMH, 2017b). Given the higher prevalence of this disorder among women it is important to discuss effective forms of treatment, CBASP is featured here because of its efficacy. For example, in previous research when CBASP is combined with medication it has treatment response rates up to 85%.

CBASP (McCullough, 2000) is not for all types of depression, but is specifically oriented toward the persistent unrelenting form of depression. In the *DSM-5*, what was previously called dysthymia and Major Depressive Disorder (MDD) were merged together under the diagnosis of Persistent Depressive Disorder (PDD), some researchers emphasize that the duration of depression symptoms is important whether the duration is more than one year or two (Blalock et al., 2013). However, some features of CBASP such as the situation analysis may be helpful for a range of situations, due to the emphasis on helping clients move toward desired outcomes. This is an important function in a variety of other therapeutic tools such as setting SMART goals, scaling, and the one-page miracle (Hawkins et al., 2019).

CBASP, a treatment for PDD, targets interpersonal processes of relationships. It is the only form of therapy designed specifically for clients with chronic depression (Klien, n.d.). It differs from many supportive therapies in that it is highly structured and has a focus on interpersonal experiences (Blalock et al., 2013). Despite the words "cognitive behavioral" in the name of the treatment, CBASP differs in distinct ways from traditional CBT and other supportive treatments. For example, therapist neutrality is not promoted in this approach, instead a technique called "disciplined interpersonal involvement" is used.

One of the goals of CBASP is to enhance "perceived functionality" (Jehele & McCullough, 2002), this means the client begins gaining self-awareness about the consequences of actions. "Situation analysis" (SA) provides a clear step by step process for navigating social problems while psychoeducational social skills are also included. In a situation analysis a CBASP therapist asks a client to identify some key components, starting with identifying a situation with beginning, middle, and end and also including: the actual outcome or end of the situation, several interpretations that contributed to the actual outcome, the desired outcome whether or not they accomplished their desired outcome, why they did or did not accomplish their desired outcome. Jehle and McCullough, Jr (2002, p. 267) indicate, "The essential purpose of SA is to teach patients that they are responsible for the outcomes they report (perceived functionality) and that their interpretations and behaviors contribute specifically to those consequences."

LOOKING THROUGH THE LENS OF CHRISTIANITY: BIBLICAL INTEGRATION

Clients present with complex cultural identities that include religion, spirituality, and faith. A growing body of literature supports the importance of religion, spirituality, and faith related to wellbeing (Ehsan et al., 2017; Loewenthal, 2019; Mengesha & Ward, 2012). In 2019, approximately 85% of the world's population identified with a religion (Loewenthal, 2019). A number of racial/ethnic groups, including Caucasian, African American, Asian, Latino/Hispanic, and Native American, emphasize spirituality (Sue

© Jacob_09/Shutterstock.com

& Sue, 2016). If religion or spirituality is important to the client, counselors should be aware of the potential need for Biblical integration when treating depression. EBTs can be adapted to clients with different religious beliefs. Adaptation of treatment approaches is consistent with the Association for Spiritual, Ethical and Religious Values in Counseling (ASERVIC) competencies for addressing spiritual and religious issues in counseling. "The professional counselor is able to modify therapeutic techniques to include a client's spiritual and/or religious perspectives" (ASERVIC, 2009, p. 2).

References to infertility are common in the Bible, often describing women as *barren*. Old Testament examples include Sarah, Rebekkah, Rachel, and Hannah. The value of family, including sustaining the bloodline, was central to the culture. The inability to conceive came with a heavy cultural weight, which is best illustrated in the story of Hannah in the book of 1 Samuel. Hannah was one of two wives to Elkanah. Elkanah's other wife, Peninnah, had children. Peninnah is described as an adversary in relationship to Hannah, "and her adversary also provoked her sore, for to make her fret, because the Lord had shut up her womb" (*King James Bible*, 1769/2017, 1 Samuel 1:6). In response to the provocation, Hannah is described as grieved, weeping, bitter, and not eating (*King James Bible*, 1769/2017, 1 Samuel 1:7-9). As portrayed, Hannah's symptoms are consistent with depression (Stein, 2010). In an effort to address her infertility, Hannah devised a plan and prayed, and God granted her petition. The use of prayer in Hannah's situation is seen as a contributing factor to her symptoms changing, "… and her countenance was no more sad" (*King James Bible,* 1769/2017, 1 Samuel 1:18b).

Biblical integration can be used as an adjunct to counseling and adapted by the counselor to compliment the client's worldview. When defining the integration of religion and spirituality in counseling interventions, three common views are noted (Mengesha & Ward, 2012). Mengesha and Ward (2012) found prayer to be consistent with the third view: the "use of actions or behaviors derived from religious practices" (p. 30). As seen in the case of Hannah, prayer was a strategy and seemingly a factor in her wellness. In addition to the use of prayer, Scripture reading, partnering with the faith community (i.e., clergy), and Christian cognitive therapy are all considerations for integration.

Prior to consideration of integrating religion, spirituality, or faith into counseling, self-awareness is important. Counselors must be mindful of their own beliefs, values, and bias specific to the intersection of religion, spirituality, and counseling. Self-awareness and being reflective as a counselor help minimize the risk of imposing your own values onto your clients. The American Counseling Association (ACA) *Code of Ethics* (2014) standard A.4.b., reinforces this need: "Counselors are aware of—and avoid imposing—their own values" (p. 5). Equally, self-awareness helps to acknowledge and recognize your limitations. Ultimately, it is important to understand that openness to integrate religion or spirituality into counseling can strengthen the therapeutic alliance (Mengesha & Ward, 2012).

CASE STUDY

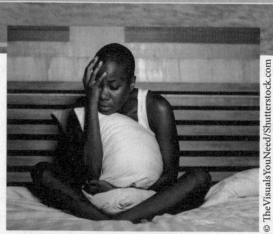

Andrea is a 28-year-old, single, Black woman who is seeking counseling at a local community agency at the prompting of her best friend Renée. Andrea stated that she initially visited the pastor at her church for guidance, noting that he has offered sound advice in the past. However, while he listened and appeared to understand her concerns, he did not offer any suggestions – just to pray and trust God. Upon intake, Andrea reports that she currently works full-time as an assistant manager at a large

© TheVisualsYouNeed/Shutterstock.com

chain retail store. She is also working on an MBA, taking classes in the evenings and weekends. Due to her busy schedule, Andrea reports being unable to spend as much time with friends and family as she would like; she reports that her schedule prevents her from dating anyone. Over the past couple months, Andrea says that she has felt "really down" almost every day and does not enjoy going out with her friends anyone. Andrea also notes that she finds it hard to get up in the morning to go to work, and she is having a hard time concentrating on her coursework – it seems to take twice as long to do everything. All she wants to do is sleep. Her appetite has decreased, and while she has lost some weight, Andrea claims it is still within a healthy range. Andrea reports that she only feels this way during the winter months, but this year is especially bad, which is why Renée is pushing her to seek counseling. Andrea also reveals that she is worried that her lack of interest in doing anything socially with her friends will prevent her from finding a date to Renée's New Year's party – something she has been anticipating for several months. However, Andrea also notes that despite her interest in attending the party, she just is not sure she has the energy to go and be around other people.

It appears Andrea meets the criteria for Seasonal Affective Disorder based on experiencing episodes of depression only during the winter months. Andrea reported a loss of energy, trouble concentrating, sleeping too much, and "feeling down" She also reported that she does not experience these symptoms for the rest of year. Creating a safe environment and building rapport with Andrea is the first step to ensure that she will feel comfortable to open up and engage in sessions.

If SAD is an unfamiliar diagnosis, it is imperative to learn more about the diagnosis through research, consultation, and supervision from other counselors in the area. As an aspect of providing a welcoming setting for Andrea, the counselor should carefully listen to her concerns and not make any assumptions about what she is experiencing or how her symptoms are affecting her lifestyle and daily functioning. Knowing that Andrea is involved enough within her church to seek advice from her pastor, the counselor should inquire more about Andrea's spiritual/religious beliefs; her beliefs can be integrated into therapy.

It is important to assess for SAD by conducting a diagnostic interview to gather the needed information regarding her symptoms and behaviors. Screening tools such as the Seasonal Pattern Assessment Questionnaire (SPAQ) (Rosenthal et al., 1986) and the Beck Depression Inventory-II (BDI-II) to monitor the severity of the depression symptoms (Beck et al., 1961). Additionally, completing a full clinical interview provides an opportunity to determine if there are any other diagnoses or concerns. The interview questions may be relevant to Andrea's psychiatric, mental health, and health history, current support system, and how well she is doing in school. Gathering additional information helps with identifying not only a diagnosis but also a treatment plan. The counselor should also inquire about Andrea's previous experiences with her symptoms, including asking questions regarding frequency, duration, and severity. Also knowing Andrea's previously sought advice from her pastor, you should ascertain Andrea's spiritual/religious preferences and if/how she would like these addressed in therapy. You may also want to propose an invitation to consult with Andrea's pastor to assist in integrating her faith in sessions.

As a counselor, you can incorporate Cognitive Behavioral Therapy (CBT), Group Therapy, and support groups. Psychoeducation is useful to help Andrea to understand the diagnosis and symptoms of SAD so that she can understand how the diagnosis is affecting her daily level of functioning during the winter months. Spiritual and religious practices (e.g., prayer, meditation, worship, etc.) can be woven into therapy to integrate Andrea's beliefs into treatment. Andrea may also be a good candidate for light therapy. It is best practice to review these treatment options with Andrea so that she can make an informed decision regarding the next steps. Because the treatment phase is a collaborative effort between Andrea and you as her counselor, investigating how she has previously dealt with

these symptoms will not only involve Andrea in the therapeutic process, but you can also incorporate the techniques and tools in sessions.

It is also important to refer Andrea to her primary care physician to rule out other possibilities for depressed mood. While working with Andrea, it is a good approach to assess her openness to a referral to a psychiatrist for a medication evaluation to determine the need for medication.

CONCEPT TO CONTEMPLATE

© pathdoc/Shutterstock.com

When we counsel women with diagnoses associated with depression it is important to remember that our communication of empathy and presence with them (regardless of intervention used) is a healing tool that may have spiritual implications. As they have a sense that we are present with them, and they are not alone in their depression, there may be a sense God is close to them, too. It is important to remember that clinical empathy also involves identifying agreed upon goals, and agreed upon treatment modalities (Hawkins et al., 2019).

How do you plan to remain present with your clients? What is your approach to show clinical empathy?

CHAPTER SUMMARY

Women suffering from depression may experience a diminished quality of life and limited psychosocial functioning. Because depression is common among women and the most seen disorder in treatment, it is important to understand the etiology and the gender specific treatment needs of women. In this chapter, the authors presented depressive disorders identified by the American Psychiatric Association, the prevalence rates of women, and the most widely used efficacious treatment modalities and screening tools used in clinical practice. Additionally, the authors provided tools to apply in clinical practice to accurately diagnose and effectively treat women suffering from depression.

KEY TERMS

Chronicity - the extent of the individual's suffering or the cost to society—the idea being that the longer an individual suffers, the greater the burden he/she carries

Chronic Depression - disorders where depressive symptoms persist for two or more years and may fluctuate in intensity for lengthy periods

Dysmenorrhea - a syndrome of painful menses

Episodic Depression - disorders where depressive symptoms may feel more severe at times but whose duration typically lasts from 3-6 months at a time

Peripartum Depression - a major depressive episode occurring during pregnancy or within 4 weeks following delivery

SUGGESTED RESOURCES

Websites

Anxiety and Depression Association of America: https://adaa.org/find-help-for/women/depression

Beck Institute: https://beckinstitute.org

Center for Addiction and Mental Health: https://www.camh.ca/en/health-info/mental-illness-and-addiction-index/depression

National Alliance of Mental Illness (NAMI): www.nami.org
National Institute of Mental Health (NIMH): www.nimh.nih.gov
U.S. Department of Health and Human Services – SAMHSA: www.
samhsa.gov
World Health Organization: www.who.int

REFERENCES

American Counseling Association. (2014). *2014 ACA code of ethics.* https://www.counseling.org/knolwedge-center

American Psychiatric Association. (2013). *Diagnostic and statistical manual of mental disorders* (5th ed.). https://doi.org/10.1176/appi.book.9780890425596

American Psychiatric Association. (2017). *What is depression?* https://www.psychiatry.org/patients-families/depression/what-is-depression

Araya, R., Flynn, T., Rojas, G., Fritsch, R., & Simon, G. (2006). Cost-effectiveness of a primary care treatment program for depression in low-income women in Santiago, Chile. *American Journal of Psychiatry, 163*(8), 1379-1387.

Association for Spiritual, Ethical, and Religious Values in Counseling. (2009). *Competencies for addressing spiritual and religious issues in counseling.* https://www.counseling.org/docs/default-source/competencies/competencies-for-addressing-spiritual-and-religious-issues-in-counseling.pdf?sfvrsn=aad7c2c_8

Avenevoli, S., Swendsen, J., He, J-P., Burstein, M., & Merikangas, K. R. (2015). Major depression in the national comorbidity survey-adolescent supplement: Prevalence, correlates, and treatment. *Journal of American Academy of Child & Adolescent Psychiatry, 54,* 37-44.e2.

Beatty, L., & Koczwara, B. (2010). An effectiveness study of a CBT group program for women with breast cancer. *Clinical Psychologist, 14*(2), 45-53. https://doi.org/10.1080/13284207.2010.500307

Beck, A. T., Ward, C. H., Mendelson, M., Mock, J., & Erbaugh, J. (1961). An inventory for measuring depression. *Archives of General Psychiatry, 4,* 561-571.

Bell, K. (2016). *Kristen Bell: I'm over staying silent about depression.* https://time.com/4352130/kristen-bell-frozen-depression-anxiety/

Beusenberg, M., Orley, J. H., & World Health Organization. (1994). *A user's guide to the self- reporting questionnaire* (SRQ No. WHO/MNH/PSF/94.8. Unpublished). Health Organization.

Blalock, J. A., Minnix, J. A., Mathew, A. R., Wetter, D. W., McCullough, J. P., & Cinciripini, P. M. (2013). Relationship of childhood trauma to depression and smoking outcomes in pregnant smokers. *Journal of Consulting and Clinical Psychology, 81*(5), 821–830. https://doi.org/10.1037/a0033381

Brody, D. J., Pratt, L. A., & Hughes, J. P. (2018, February). *Prevalence of depression among adults aged 20 and over: United States, 2013-2016 [NCHS Data Brief No. 303].* https://www.cdc.gov/nchs/data/databriefs/db303.pdf

Chotai, J., Smedh, K., Johansson, C., Nilsson, L. G., & Adolfsson, R. (2004). An epidemiological study on gender differences in self-reported seasonal changes in mood and behaviour in a general population of northern Sweden. *Nordic Journal of Psychiatry, 58*(6), 429-437. https://doi.org/10.1080/08039480410006052

Cox, J. L., Holden, J. M., & Sagovsky, R. (1987). Detection of postnatal depression: Development of the 10-item Edinburgh Postnatal Depression Scale. *The British Journal of Psychiatry, 150*(6), 782-786.

Cuijpers, P., Sijbrandij, M., Koole, S. L., Andersson, G., Beekman, A. T., & Reynolds III, C. F. (2013). The efficacy of psychotherapy and pharmacotherapy in treating depressive and anxiety disorders: A meta-analysis of direct comparisons. *World Psychiatry, 12*(2), 137-148.

Cuijpers, P., Sijbrandij, M., Koole, S. L., Andersson, G., Beekman, A. T., & Reynolds III, C. F. (2014). Adding psychotherapy to antidepressant medication in depression and anxiety disorders: a meta-analysis. *World Psychiatry, 13*(1), 56–67. https://doi.org/10.1002/wps.20089

Dastbaaz, A., Yeganehfarzand, S., Azkhosh, M., & Shoaee, F. (2014). The effect of group counseling "narrative therapy" to reduce depression and loneliness among older women. *Iranian Rehabilitation Journal, 12*(20), 11–15.

Dastbaz, A., Yeganehfarzand, S. H., Azkhosh, M., Shoaee, F., & Salehi, M. (2014). The effect of group counseling. *Iranian Rehabilitation Journal, 12*(2), 11-15.

Ducasse, D., Jaussent, I., Olié, E., Guillaume, S., Lopez-Castroman, J., & Courtet, P. (2016). Personality traits of suicidality are associated with premenstrual syndrome and premenstrual dysphoric disorder in a suicidal women sample. *PLoS ONE, 11*(2), e0148653. https://doi.org/10.1371/journal.pone.0148653

Egan, G. (2010). *The skilled helper: A problem-management approach to helping.* Brooks/Cole Publishing.

Ehsan, N., Johar, N., & Zafar, F. (2017). The moderating role of religiosity among people suffering from depression. *Pakistan Armed Forces Medical Journal, 67*(5), 853-59. https://pafmj.org/index.php/PAFMJ/article/view/991

Eid, R. S., Gobinath, A. R., & Galea, L. A. M. (2019). Sex differences in depression: Insights from clinical and preclinical studies. *Progress in Neurobiology, 176*, 86-102. https://doi.org/10.1016/j.pneurobio.2019.01.006

Ekrami, F., Charandabi, S. M-A., Kheiroddin, J. B., & Mirghafourvand, M. (2019). The effect of counselling on depression and anxiety of women with unplanned pregnancy: A randomized controlled trial. *Community Mental Health Journal, 55*, 1047-1056. https://doi.org/10.1007/s10597-019-00428-2

Freeman, M. P., Claypoole, L. D., Burt, V. K., Sosinsky, A. Z., Moustafa, D., Noe, O. B., Cheng, L. J., & Cohen, L. S. (2018). Course of major depressive disorder after pregnancy and the postpartum period. *Depression & Anxiety, 35*, 1130-1136. https://doi.org/10.1002/da.22836

Gili, M., Castro, A., Navarro, C., Molina, R., Magallón, R., García-Toro, M., & Roca, M. (2014). Gender differences on functioning in depressive patients. *Journal of Affective Disorders, 166*, 292-296. https://doi.org/10.1016/j.jad.2014.05.030

Halverson, J. L. (2019). *What is the suicide rate among persons with depressive disorder.* https://www.medscape.com/answers/286759-14675/what-is-the-suicide-rate-among-persons-with-depressive-disorder-clinical-depression

Hansson, M., Bodlund, O., & Chotai, J. (2007). Patient education and group counselling to improve the treatment of depression in primary care: A randomized controlled trial. *Journal of Affective Disorders, 105*(1), 235-240. https://10.1016/j.jad.2007.04.007

Hantsoo, L., & Epperson, C. N. (2015). Premenstrual dysphoric disorder: Epidemiology and treatment. *Current Psychiatry Reports, 17*(11), 87. https://doi.org/10.1007/s11920-015-0628-3

Hawkins, R., Knight, A., Silvey, R., Sibcy, G., & Warren, S. (2019). *Research-based counseling skills: The art and science of therapeutic empathy.* Kendall Hunt Publishing.

Hergueta, T., & Weiller, E. (2013). Evaluating depressive symptoms in hypomanic and manic episodes using a structured diagnostic tool: Validation of a new Mini International Neuropsychiatric Interview (MINI) module for the DSM-5 'With Mixed Features' specifier. *International Journal of Bipolar Disorders, 1*(1), 21.

Hilt, L. M., & Nolen-Hoeksema, S. (2014). Gender differences in depression. In I. H. Gotlib & C. L. Hammen (Eds.), *Handbook of depression* (3rd ed., pp. 355-373). The Guilford Press.

Hinz, A., Mehnert, A., Kocalevent, R. D., Brähler, E., Forkmann, T., Singer, S., & Schulte, T. (2016). Assessment of depression severity with the PHQ-9 in cancer patients and in the general population. *BMC Psychiatry, 16*(1), 22.

Houston, T. K., Cooper, L. A., & Ford, D. E. (2002). Internet support groups for depression: A 1-year prospective cohort study. *American Journal of Psychiatry, 159*(12), 2062-2068. https://doi.org/10.1176/appi.ajp.159.12.2062

Huibers, M., Cohen, Z., Lemmens, L., Arntz, A., Peeters , F., Cuijpers, P., & DeRubeis, R. (2016). Correction: Predicting optimal outcomes in cognitive therapy or interpersonal psychotherapy for depressed individuals using the personalized advantage index approach. *PLoS ONE, 11*(2), e0148835. https://doi.org/10.1371/journal.pone.0148835

Jehle, P. J., & McCullough, J. P. (2002). Treatment of chronic major depression using the cognitive behavioral analysis system of psychotherapy (CBASP). *Journal of Contemporary Psychotherapy, 32*, 263–271. https://doi.org/10.1023/A:1020520810062

Kessler, R. C. (2003). Epidemiology of women and depression. *Journal of Affective Disorders, 74,* 5-13. http://dx.doi.org/10.1016/S0165-0327(02)00426-3

King James Bible. (2017). King James Bible Online. https://www.kingjamesbibleonline.org/ (Original work published 1769)

Klein, D. N., Santiago, N. J., Vivian, D., Blalock, J. A., Kocsis, J. H., Markowitz, J. C., McCullough, J. P., Jr., Rush, A. J., Trivedi, M. H., Arnow, B. A., Dunner, D. L., Manber, R., Rothbaum, B., Thase, M. E., Keitner, G. I., Miller, I. W., & Keller, M. B. (2004). Cognitive-Behavioral analysis system of psychotherapy as a maintenance treatment for chronic depression. *Journal of Consulting and Clinical Psychology, 72*(4), 681–688. https://doi-org.ezproxy.liberty.edu/10.1037/0022-006X.72.4.681

Kohler, S., Chrysanthou, S., Guhn, A., & Sterzer, P. (2018). Differences between chronic and nonchronic depression: Systematic review and implications for treatment. *Depression & Anxiety, 36,* 18-30. https://doi.org/10.1002/da.22835

Kring, A. M., & Johnson, S. J. (2018). *Abnormal psychology: The science and treatment of psychological disorders* (14th ed.). John Wiley & Sons.

Kuehner, C. (2017). Why is depression more common among women than among men? *The Lancet Psychiatry, 4*(2), 146-158. https://doi.org/10.1016/S2215-0366(16)30263-2

Langan, R. C., & Goodbred, A. J. (2016). Identification and management of peripartum depression. *American Family Physician, 93*(10), 852-858.

Lanza di Scalea, T., & Pearlstein, T. (2019). Premenstrual dysphoric disorder. *Medical Clinics of North America, 103*(4), 613-628. https://doi.org/10.1016/j.mcna.2019.02.007

Leahy, R. L. (2003). *Cognitive therapy techniques: A practitioner's guide.* Guilford Press.

Loewenthal, K. M. (2019). Intersections among religion, culture, gender, and mental health. In J. A. Mena & K. Quina (Eds.), *Integrating multiculturalism and intersectionality into the psychology curriculum: Strategies for instructors* (pp. 143–156). American Psychological Association. https://doi.org/10.1037/0000137

Markowitz, J., & Weissman, M. (2004). Interpersonal psychotherapy: Principles and applications. *World Psychiatry, 3*(3), 136-9.

McCullough, J. P., Jr. (2000). *Treatment for chronic depression: Cognitive Behavioral Analysis System of Psychotherapy (CBASP).* Guilford Press.

McDermut, W., Miller, I. W., & Brown, R. A. (2001). The efficacy of group psychotherapy for depression: A Meta-analysis and review of the empirical research. *Clinical Psychology: Science and Practice, 8*(1), 98-116. https://doi.org/10.1093/clipsy.8.1.98

Melrose, S. (2015). Seasonal affective disorder: An overview of assessment and treatment approaches. *Depression Treatment and Research, 2015,* 1-6. http://dx.doi.org/10.1155/2015/178564

Mengesha, M., & Ward, E. C. (2012). Psychotherapy with African American women with depression: Is it okay to talk about their religious/spiritual beliefs? *Religions, 3*, 19-36.

National Alliance on Mental Health. (2019, September). *Mental health by the numbers.* https://www.nami.org/mhstats

National Center for Health Statistics. (2018). *National health and nutrition examination survey: Questionnaires, datasets, and related documentation.* https://wwwn.cdc.gov/nchs/nhanes/Default.aspx

National Institute of Mental Health. (2016). *Bipolar disorder.* https://www.nimh.nih.gov/health/topics/bipolar-disorder/index.shtml

National Institute of Mental Health. (2017a, November). *Prevalence of bipolar disorder among adults.* https://www.nimh.nih.gov/health/statistics/bipolar-disorder.shtml

National Institute of Mental Health. (2017b, November). *Prevalence of persistent depressive disorder among adults.* https://www.nimh.nih.gov/health/statistics/persistent-depressive-disorder-dysthymic-disorder.shtml

National Institute of Mental Health. (2019, February). *Major depression.* https://www.nimh.nih.gov/health/statistics/major-depression.shtml

New International Bible. (2011). New International Bible Online. https://www.thenivbible.com/ (Original work published 1973)

Noble, R. E. (2005). Depression in women [Supplement]. *Metabolism – Clinical and Experimental, 54*(5), 49-52. https://doi.org/10.1016/j.metabol.2005.01.014

Overview of IPT. (n.d.). *In international society for interpersonal psychotherapy.* https://interpersonalpsychotherapy.org/ipt-basics/overview-of-ipt/

Parker, G., & Malhi, G. S. (2019). Persistent depression: Should such a DSM-5 diagnostic category exist? *The Canadian Journal of Psychiatry, 64*(3), 177-179. https://doi.org/10.1177/0706743718814429

Parker, G., Fletcher, K., Paterson, A., Anderson, J., & Hong, M. (2014). Gender differences in depression severity and symptoms across depressive subtypes. *Journal of Affective Disorders, 167*, 351-357. https://doi.org/10.1016/j.jad.2014.06.018

Perera, S., Eisen, R., Bhatt, M., Bhatnagar, N., de Souza, R., Thabane, L., & Samaan, Z. (2016). Light therapy for non-seasonal depression: Systematic review and meta-analysis. *British Journal of Psychiatry Open, 2*(2), 116-126.

Picco, L., Subramaniam, M., Abdin, E., Vaingankar, J. A., & Chong, S. A. (2017). Gender differences in Major Depressive Disorder: Findings from the Singapore mental health study. *Singapore Medical Journal, 58*(11), 649-655. https://doi.org/10.11622/smedj.2016144

Price, R. B., Nock, M. K., Charney, D. S., & Mathew, S. J. (2009). Effects of intravenous ketamine on explicit and implicit measures of suicidality in treatment-resistant depression. *Biological Psychiatry, 66*(5), 522-526.

Psychology Today. (2019, February 7). *Persistent depressive disorder (Dysthymia).* https://www.psychologytoday.com/us/conditions/persistent-depressive-disorder-dysthymia

Riecher-Rössler, A. (2018, November 30). Introduction: Gender-specific issues relative to mental illness. *Psychiatric Times, 35*(11). https://www.psychiatrictimes.com/special-reports/introduction-gender-specific-issues-relative-mental-illness

Rosenthal, N. E., Sack, D. A., Jacobsen, F. M., James, S. P., Parry, B. L., Arendt, J., Tamarkin, L., & Wehr, T. A. (1986). Melatonin in seasonal affective disorder and phototherapy. *Journal of Neural Transmission Supplementum, 21*, 257-267.

Salk, R. H., Hyde, J. S., & Abramson, L. Y. (2017). Gender differences in depression in representative national samples: Meta-analyses of diagnosis and symptoms. *Psychological Bulletin, 143*(8), 783-822. http://dx.doi.org/10.1037/bul0000102

Salk, R. H., Petersen, J. L., Abramson, L. Y., & Hyde, J. S. (2016). The contemporary face of gender differences and similarities in depression throughout adolescence: Development and chronicity. *Journal of Affective Disorders, 205,* 28-35.

Sandman, N., Merikanto, I., Määttänen, Valli, K., Kronholm, E., Laatikainen, Partonen, T., & Paunio, T. (2016). Winter is coming: Nightmares and sleep problems during season affective disorder. *Journal of Sleep Research, 25,* 612-619. https://doi.org/10.1111/jsr.12416

Sheikh, J. I., & Yesavage, J. A. (1986). Geriatric depression scale (GDS): Recent evidence and development of a shorter version. *Clinical Gerontologist, 5,* 165-173.

Sinyor, M., Williams, M., Belo, S., Orser, B., Vincent, M., Mah, L., Zarate, C., Jr., Castel, S., Levitt, A. J., & Schaffer, A (2018). Ketamine augmentation for major depressive disorder and suicidal ideation: Preliminary experience in an inpatient psychiatry setting. *Journal of Affective Disorders, 241,* 103-109.

Spitzer, R. L., Kroenke, K., Williams, J. B., & Patient Health Questionnaire Primary Care Study Group. (1999). Validation and utility of a self-report version of PRIME-MD: The PHQ primary care study. *JAMA, 282*(18), 1737-1744.

Steiner, M., Dunn, E., & Born, L. (2003). Hormones and mood: From menarche to menopause and beyond. *Journal of Affective Disorders, 74,* 67-83. https://doi.org/10.1016 /S0165-0327(02)00432-9

Sue, D. W., & Sue, D. (2016). *Counseling the culturally diverse: Theory and practice.* Wiley.

Thimm, J. C., & Antonsen, L. (2014). Effectiveness of cognitive behavioral group therapy for depression in routine practice. *BMC Psychiatry, 14*(1), 292.

Truijens, S. E. M., Spek, V., van Son, M. J. M., Oei, S. G., & Pop, V. J. M. (2017). Different patterns of depressive symptoms during pregnancy. *Archives of Women's Mental Health, 20*(4), 539-546. https://doi.org/10.1007/s00737-017-0738-5

Walker, E. R., & Druss, B. G. (2015). Rate and predictors of persistent major depressive disorder in a nationally representative sample. *Community Mental Health Journal, 51*, 701-707. https://doi.org/10.1007/s10597-014-9793-9

Wiles, N., Thomas, L., Abel, A., Ridgway, N., Turner, N., Campbell, J., Garland, A., Hollinghurst, S., Jerrom, B., Kessler, D., Kuyken, W., Morrison, J., Turner, K., Williams, C., Peters, T., & Lewis, G. (2013). Cognitive behavioural therapy as an adjunct to pharmacotherapy for primary care based patients with treatment resistant depression: Results of the CoBalT randomised controlled trial. *The Lancet, 381*(9864), 375-384.

World Health Organization. (2018, March 22). *Depression.* https://www.who.int/en/news-room/fact-sheets/detail/depression

CHAPTER 15
Counseling Women with Eating Disorders

ANDREA BARBIAN, PH.D.

"In any given moment, we have two options: to step forward into growth or to step backward into safety" ~Abraham Maslow

"For you created my inmost being; you knit me together in my mother's womb. 1 praise you because 1 am fearfully and wonderfully made; your works are wonderful, 1 know that full well. My frame was not hidden from you when 1 was made in the secret place. When 1 was woven together in the depths of the earth, your eyes saw my unformed body." (Psalm 139: 13-16a, NIV)

Wisdom from Above: Standing in His Grace

As Christians, we have the assurance that our earthly bodies were intentionally created by God. We are masterpieces! The intricacies that compose the human body are not mistakes, but rather detailed systems that have been uniquely and delicately woven together by a Creator. As sin was introduced into God's perfect creation, so was shame. We see in Genesis 3:7 ("Then the eyes of both of them were opened, and they realized they were naked; so they sewed fig leaves together and made coverings for themselves" [*New International Bible*, 1973/2011]) that as Adam and Eve's eyes were opened to their nakedness, they felt shame and made coverings for themselves. Our fearfully and wonderfully made bodies are often looked at through a lens of shame or treated shamefully as a result of deep emotional wounds. Women struggle with healthy body image and eating disorders on a daily basis. We believe

the lies that we are not beautiful enough, thin enough, perfect enough, toned enough, or some other iteration of "not enough" to be acceptable. Acceptable to whom? Our creator sees our frame, sees HIS creation made in HIS image, and sees that it is good! As counselors, let us hunger and thirst for knowledge to help others reframe their thoughts and views surrounding their physical bodies.

CHAPTER OVERVIEW

When we consider individuals from a bio-psycho-social-spiritual model, the interconnection between social, psychological, and biological factors is apparent. Eating disorders have a widespread impact on an individual's physical, mental, emotional, social, and spiritual wellbeing, thus making them very complex in nature. Therefore, as we consider counseling women with eating disorders there are numerous factors that need to be considered. It is important that we have a general awareness of the impact of disordered eating and the comorbidities that are often associated with eating disorders. While all mental health counselors are not expected to be experts in treatment of eating disorders, it is important to have a basic knowledge of the signs and symptoms associated with the various feeding and eating disorders defined in the *DSM-5*. This chapter will specifically examine the diagnostic criteria related to anorexia nervosa, bulimia nervosa, and binge-eating disorder. Possible etiologies for disordered eating and evidence-based approaches to treatment will be discussed. As we acknowledge that individuals are also spiritual beings, we will also consider how Biblical principles can be integrated into counseling women with eating disorders.

CHAPTER LEARNING OBJECTIVES

Upon completing this chapter, you should be able to:

- Examine different types of eating disorders and their diagnostic criteria
- Identify the etiology of eating disorders
- Evaluate levels of care for eating disorder treatment
- Explore various evidence-based practices for treating eating disorders and their comorbidities
- Consider appropriate methods for integrating Biblical principles into eating disorder treatment

EATING DISORDERS DEFINED: DIAGNOSIS AND SYMPTOMOLOGY

Eating disorders have the highest rate of mortality of any mental illness, with one of five anorexia deaths occurring by suicide (National Association of Anorexia Nervosa and Associated Disorders, 2017). In terms of prevalence, in their lifetime 1% of American women will struggle with anorexia, 1.5% will struggle with bulimia, and 2.8% will struggle with binge eating disorder (National Association of Anorexia Nervosa and Associated Disorders, 2017). Statistics regarding the prevalence of eating disorders are ever changing and, in many ways, not an accurate reflection of the extent to which eating disorders are impacting lives daily. Due to their secretive nature, eating disorders are often underreported by individuals who are displaying signs and symptoms, as they are often in denial of the extent to which their physical, mental, and emotional health is being impacted or simply are not honest in their report. Additionally, in a culture that is fixated on body shape, weight, diet, and exercise, disordered eating is said to impact about 50% of the population. However, these sub-clinical eating disorders often go unrecognized and undiagnosed due to not fully meeting the diagnostic criteria. Figure 15.1 shows the eating disorders continuum.

FIGURE 15.1

Eating Disorders Continuum

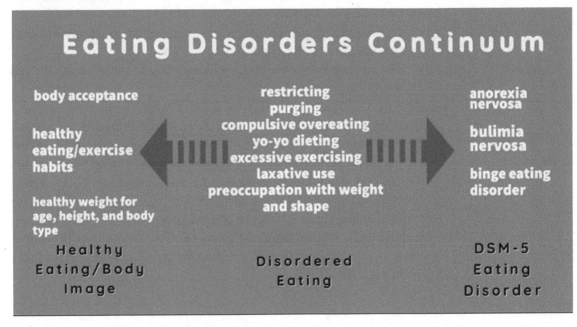

Source: Andrea Barbian

The *Diagnostic and Statistical Manual of Mental Disorders*, (5th ed.; *DSM-5*) characterizes feeding and eating disorders as those in which there is, "a persistent disturbance of eating or eating-related behavior that results in the altered consumption or absorption of food and that significantly impairs physical health or psychological functioning" (American Psychiatric Association [APA], 2013, p. 329). While the *DSM-5* includes disorders such as pica, rumination disorder, avoidant/restrictive food intake disorder, and other specified feeding or eating disorders in the feeding and eating disorder classification, for the purposes of this chapter we will focus on the three most prevalent disorders, anorexia nervosa, bulimia nervosa, and binge-eating disorder.

Anorexia Nervosa (AN)

Diagnosis

Criterion for the diagnosis of feeding and eating disorders underwent multiple changes with the revisions reflected in the *DSM-5*. According to the *DSM-5*, anorexia nervosa is characterized by the following diagnostic criteria:

- Persistent restriction of energy intake leading to significantly low body weight
- Intense fear of gaining weight or becoming fat, persistent behavior that interferes with weight gain
- Disturbance in the way body is experienced related to weight and shape

Depending on the presentation of symptoms over a three-month period, there are two subtypes of anorexia nervosa: restricting type and binge-eating/purging type. Restricting type is characterized by weight loss through dieting, fasting, and/or excessive exercise and an absence of binge eating and/or purging; whereas binge-eating/purging type is characterized by the presence of binge-eating or use of compensatory behaviors (i.e.- laxatives, purging, etc.). When diagnosing anorexia nervosa, the level of severity (mild, moderate, severe) is determined by the client's body mass index (BMI; APA, 2013).

Symptomology and Comorbidities

Clients struggling with anorexia nervosa are often hyper focused on physical size and appearance. Anorexia nervosa by nature is an obsessive and ritualistic eating disorder associated with behaviors such as, skipping meals, calorie counting, body checking, excessive exercise and food rituals. Medically speaking, signs and symptoms of anorexia nervosa include slow heart rate, orthostatic hypotension (when blood pressure decreases when moving from sitting to standing position), muscle loss and weakness, dry skin, hair loss, dizziness and fainting, constipation, and menstrual irregularities. Eating disorder behaviors are often complicated by the symptoms of their comorbidities. Common comorbidities for anorexia nervosa include anxiety disorders, depressive disorders, and cluster A and C personality disorders (i.e. – obsessive-compulsive disorder).

Bulimia Nervosa (BN)

Diagnosis

According to the *DSM-5*, bulimia nervosa is characterized by the following diagnostic criteria:

- Recurrent episodes of binge eating
  - Eating a large amount of food in a discrete period of time
  - Feeling a lack of control over-eating
- Recurrent compensatory behaviors (purging, laxative abuse, excessive exercise)
- Episodes occur at least once per week for 3 months
- Disturbance in the way body is experienced related to weight and shape

When diagnosing bulimia nervosa, the level of severity is based on the number of episodes of compensatory behavior use in a week's time period (APA, 2013).

Key Eating Disorder Assessment Points to Remember
- Absence of menstruation is no longer a diagnostic marker for anorexia nervosa
- Regardless of subtype, a diagnosis of anorexia nervosa requires significantly low body weight to be present
- Unlike anorexia nervosa and bulimia nervosa, binge eating disorder clients do not report a disturbance in the way they experience their body in relation to weight and shape
- Binge episodes reported by clients are subjective in nature
- Eating disorders are very secretive and deceptive in nature; therefore, self-report may not always be accurate
- Anorexia nervosa is the only eating disorder in which weight is a diagnostic marker

Symptomology and Comorbidities

Bulimia nervosa is often characterized by secretive and compulsive behaviors. Clients will often binge and purge in secret due to shame and guilt associated with their eating disorder. It is important to note that excessive exercise can also be a symptom of bulimia nervosa, as it is considered a compensatory behavior. Physically, it is not uncommon for individuals to experience electrolyte imbalances, inflammation of the esophagus, and tooth decay related to purging. Gastrointestinal issues are also common as the binge purge cycle of bulimia nervosa strains the gut. Approximately 10% of patients with a diagnosis of bulimia nervosa have a co-occurring substance abuse disorder (National Association of Anorexia Nervosa and Associated Disorders, 2019). In addition to anxiety and depressive disorders, which are also comorbidities of anorexia nervosa, comorbidities associated with bulimia nervosa include bipolar disorders and cluster B personality disorders (i.e. borderline personality disorder).

Binge Eating Disorder (BED)

Diagnosis

Despite being the newest addition to feeding and eating disorders in the *DSM-5*, binge eating disorder is the most common eating disorder. According to the *DSM-5*, binge eating disorder is characterized by the following diagnostic criteria:

- Recurrent episodes of binge eating (eating a larger than normal amount of food in a discrete period of time and a feeling of lack of control over-eating)
- Three or more:
    - Eating more rapidly than normal
    - Eating until feeling uncomfortably full
    - Eating large amounts of food when not physically hungry
    - Eating alone due to shame or embarrassment
    - Feeling disgusted with self, guilty or depressed afterwards
- Marked distress regarding binge eating
- Not associated with recurrent compensatory behaviors

When diagnosing binge eating disorder, the level of severity is based on the number of binge eating episodes in a week's time period (APA, 2013).

Symptomology and Comorbidities

Unlike with anorexia nervosa and bulimia nervosa, individuals with binge eating disorder see their body accurately in that they do not express an over evaluation of body shape or size. Life often centers around making time for their binges, which can have a devastating impact on social and personal lives. Health risks associated with binge eating disorder are primarily related to complications of obesity (i.e. - cardiac problems, high blood pressure, kidney problems, diabetes, sleep apnea, cancers, etc.). Similar to anorexia nervosa and bulimia nervosa, common comorbidities for binge eating disorder include anxiety, depression, substance use, and bipolar disorders.

EATING DISORDER ETIOLOGY

There are a variety of factors that lead to the development of an eating disorder. Biologically speaking, genetics play a significant role in setting the stage for eating disorder development. Approximately 80% of individuals with an eating disorder have a family history of disordered eating (Lob, 2016). Individuals may possess a predisposition to the inability to regulate appetite, mood, sleep, and/or stress, which can lead to disordered eating behaviors. Research continues to uncover more about the role of neurobiology in mental health, including its influence on eating disorders. However, research does indicate a relationship between cortisol levels and eating disorders such as binge eating disorder and bulimia nervosa (Vaz-Leal et al., 2018). Additionally, dysfunctions in serotonin circuitry have also been seen in individuals with anorexia nervosa and bulimia nervosa (National Eating Disorder Association, 2018). As research continues to uncover more about the relationship between neurobiology and eating disorders, it will be important for mental health counselors to explore opportunities to increase their understanding.

In addition to biological factors, psychological and psychosocial factors play a substantial role in eating disorder development. Individuals displaying disordered eating often exhibit difficulty regulating emotions.

Eating disorder behaviors such as restricting, bingeing, purging, etc. are often maladaptive ways of coping with or avoiding unpleasant emotions. In fact, a large aspect of eating disorder treatment is focused on learning to identify, tolerate, and cope with emotions. Additionally, high levels of impulsivity are typically seen in bulimia nervosa and binge eating, which is consistent with their comorbidities; while high levels of perfectionism are typically seen in anorexia nervosa, also consistent with its comorbidities (Lob, 2016). Finally, psychosocial factors commonly impact eating disorder development. Low self-esteem is commonly reported in women with eating disorders and can be impacted by a number of factors including peer pressure, societal expectations, social relationships, family environment, etc. Finally, research indicates that a history of trauma and/or abuse (e.g. sexual, physical, verbal, and/or emotional) can lead to a negative prognosis in terms of eating disorder development (APA, 2013).

TREATMENT OF EATING DISORDERS

Treating eating disorders and their comorbidities can be complex and challenging, especially for mental health counselors who do not have specialized training. From assessment to treatment planning to selecting interventions, there are several factors that must be taken into consideration. First, it is important that mental health counselors are well informed regarding treatment goals and select levels of care wisely based on the client's need and willingness to engage. Second, mental health counselors must be evidence-informed in their selection of treatment modalities and interventions. A variety of evidence-based treatment approaches are effective in treating eating disorders and their comorbidities. Additionally, mental health counselors should focus on building a healthy therapeutic relationship and maximizing the client's personal engagement. Fourth, effective eating disorder treatment involves improving interpersonal relationships and building a strong support network. Lastly, it is important to recognize and educate clients on the incremental nature of eating disorder recovery. Recovery from an eating disorder is arguably an indefinite process that requires incremental treatment goals in order to elicit confidence and feelings of empowerment for the client.

5 Practice Points for Mental Health Counselors Treating Eating Disorders
- Be evidence-informed
- Select levels of care wisely
- Maximize personal engagement
- Engage family and friends
- Accommodate incremental response

(Steiger, 2017)

Treatment Goals and Levels of Care

Treatment goals vary depending on symptomology, level of severity, and nature of comorbidities present. General treatment goals include: normalize eating and the client's relationship with food, decrease/eliminate eating disorder behaviors, weight restoration, medical stabilization, manage the impact of comorbidities, strengthen support networks, and improve peer relationships. Due to the complexity of treating eating disorders, a multidisciplinary treatment approach is necessary. Essential members of a multidisciplinary team include mental health counselors representing psychiatry, mental health counseling, nutrition, and medicine. It is important that members of the multidisciplinary team respect one another's scope of practice, openly collaborate with one another, and practice on-going communication (Dejesse & Zelman, 2013). As mental health counselors, it is essential that we understand the client's full treatment protocol. The interconnectedness of the client's biological, psychological, spiritual and social needs makes it important to have unified treatment goals that address the clients from a holistic perspective.

In terms of treatment, the level of care ranges from inpatient to outpatient and depends largely on the level of severity of the eating disorder. Inpatient care is focused heavily on medical and psychological stability. Often in this level of care, clients require 24/7 attention due to lack of medical stability, lack of nutritional stability, and possible suicidality. As clients become more medically and psychologically stable, they can step down to a residential level of care where the focus becomes weight restoration. Partial hospitalization or intensive outpatient care is focused on decreasing eating disorder behaviors and symptom use, medication compliance, normalizing eating, building support and improving interpersonal relationships, and decreasing symptoms of comorbidities such as anxiety, depression, etc. (Olmstead et al., 2013). The marker for step down to this level of care is typically when the client has reached 85-92% of their ideal body weight. Although an outpatient level of care is ideally focused on maintenance and relapse prevention, a large number of eating disorder clients

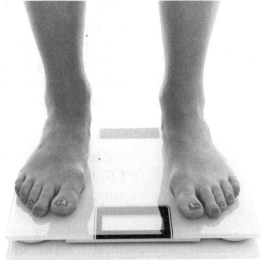

never seek a higher level of care due to financial and/or time restrictions and are treated in an outpatient setting.

Evidence Based Treatment Modalities

Given that eating disorders are complex and delicate, they should be treated with extra care. It is important that mental health counselors treating eating disorders utilize evidence-based treatments that have been shown to be effective and safe. The most widely used evidence-based treatments for eating disorders include cognitive behavioral therapy (CBT), dialectical behavior therapy (DBT), yoga/movement therapy, and expressive arts therapy.

Cognitive Behavioral Therapy

Cognitive behavioral therapy is one of the foremost widely used evidence-based practices for the treatment of eating disorders and their comorbidities. CBT successfully addresses the harmful behaviors and maladaptive beliefs associated with anorexia nervosa, bulimia nervosa, and binge-eating disorder. Additionally, it encourages a collaborative approach to the therapeutic relationship in which the counselor can challenge maladaptive coping skills and cognitive distortions which are often associated with comorbid anxiety and depression (Lob, 2016). Treatment is focused on mood intolerance, perfectionism, low self-esteem, and interpersonal difficulties.

Enhanced cognitive behavior therapy (CBT-E) is an enhanced form of CBT developed by Christopher Fairburn, specifically for the treatment of eating disorders. This trans-diagnostic approach to eating disorder treatment, consists of 20 individual therapy sessions which are focused and structured to be completed in a fixed time frame (Murphy & Fairburn, 2010). Sessions include regular eating and weekly weighing as a form of exposure therapy. The goal is for the counselor to work with the client to engage them in developing a case formulation of the processes that are used to maintain eating disorder behaviors. Essentially, they are seeking to answer the question, 'What purpose does the eating disorder serve?' while offering hope for recovery (Murphy & Fairburn, 2010).

Dialectical Behavior Therapy

Dialectical behavior therapy (DBT) is an effective therapeutic modality which integrates mindfulness and acceptance strategies to address affect dysregulation associated with eating disorders (Lenz et al., 2015). Maladaptive behaviors such as eating disorder symptom use (i.e. - bingeing, purging, restriction, excessive exercise, etc.) and self-harm (i.e. - cutting) are also addressed using DBT. Key strategies associated with DBT include validation, radical acceptance, paced breathing and self-soothing using the five senses. These strategies make DBT beneficial in addressing co-morbid personality disorders such as borderline personality disorder and exploring issues related to compliance and resistance. Figure 15.2 shows an example of an intervention utilized in DBT called a Behavior Chain Analysis (Linehan, 2015; Lob, 2016). The Behavior Chain Analysis is used in the counseling session to help explore vulnerabilities, prompting events, thoughts, feelings, behaviors, and consequences of eating disorder behavior use or self-harm.

FIGURE 15.2

Behavior Chain Analysis

Source: Andrea Barbian

For example, if a client came into session and reported purging a few days prior, the counselor and client would work through the Behavior Chain Analysis together to determine: 1) what circumstances may have made them vulnerable in the moment, 2) what event prompted their desire to use their behaviors (i.e. – a fight with a friend or family member, a negative comment made about them, etc.), 3) what behavior did they use (assess for duration, amount, frequency, etc. depending on behavior used), and 4) what were the consequences of using that particular behavior. After the counselor and client have worked through the scenario, they are able to identify links between thoughts, feelings, and behaviors, while working to increase the client's awareness of their vulnerabilities in order to prevent future behavior use.

Other Therapeutic Modalities

In addition to CBT and DBT, there are a variety of other therapeutic modalities that have been shown to be effective in treating eating disorders such as equine therapy, Yoga and movement therapy, and expressive arts and movement therapy. Equine therapy is an experiential modality and relational approach to therapy used to assist clients in building honest, authentic relationships and aid in self-discovery (Lac et al., 2013). Similarly, studies indicate that the use of therapy dogs (Animal Assisted Therapy) enhances therapeutic alliance in the group setting and decreases anxiety among clients in treatment settings (Wesley et al., 2009). Given that there is a mind-body disconnect associated with eating disorders, Yoga and Movement Therapy helps clients to increase awareness and connection with their bodies in a mindful and connected state (Douglass, 2011). Expressive Arts and Music Therapy can empower clients and increase awareness of their strengths while creating a mind/body connection (Lejonclou & Trondalen, 2009). In addition to these specific modalities, more general therapeutic interventions such as motivational interviewing, confronting, challenging, and distress tolerance are helpful in increasing awareness and addressing resistance.

Therapeutic Process

One of the first steps in the therapeutic process of treating eating disorders is building a strong therapeutic relationship. As mental health counselors, it is essential that we possess characteristics such as empathy, active listening, genuineness, acceptance, and optimism in order to build a strong therapeutic relationship with our clients (Hawkins et al., 2019; Rogers, 1975). It is important to define the role of the patient and the therapist as a framework for the therapeutic relationship. Allowing the patient to conceptualize their problem, while providing accepting understanding helps cultivate engagement in the treatment process. Throughout the therapeutic process, the counselor and client develop an interpersonal relationship that reflects cohesion and alliance in goals and motivation. Research indicates that the strength and quality of the therapeutic relationship positively impacts treatment outcomes in eating disorders (Antoniou & Cooper, 2014). Creating a safe environment that encourages self-exploration and self-disclosure is important in preventing early treatment termination, especially for clients with attachment anxiety or trauma history.

Unfortunately, resistance to treatment has detrimental and sometimes deadly impacts on treatment success and is a key factor in dropout. Resistance on the part of the client can either be conscious, where there is an awareness on the part of the individual, or subconscious, where the resistance is automatic and unmotivated (Fassino & Abbate-Daga, 2013). There are a number of strategies and interventions that can be used in the treatment process to help clients overcome resistance. One strategy is helping clients understand the root of their eating disorder and increasing their awareness of eating disorder behaviors. As clients become aware of their symptomology, we can help them identify alternatives to eating disorder behaviors. Additionally, encouraging clients to develop cognitive flexibility and a strong sense of self are instrumental in the therapeutic process. Using the Stages of Change model to assess for a client's willingness and readiness to engage in the therapeutic process can be beneficial in addressing resistance and treatment success (Hasler et al., 2004; Hoetzel et al., 2013; Robertson, n.d.).

FIGURE 15.3

Stages of Change Model for Eating Disorders

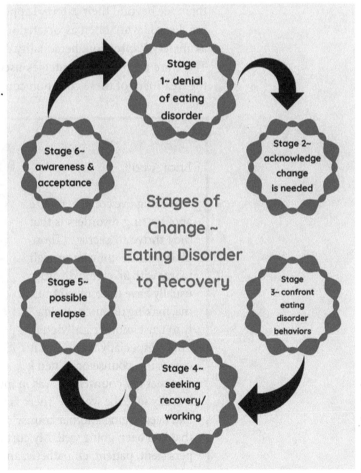

Biblical Integration in Treatment

The Word of God is living and active! For Christian counselors and clients, integrating Biblical principles into treatment is a powerful and effective tool. While the Bible does not specifically address eating disorders, God's Word does address His creation of our bodies. Genesis 1 speaks of the creation of man in God's image. Psalm 139 talks about being "fearfully and wonderfully made." It is advantageous to help women see that God has intricately created our bodies to not only carry out beautiful tasks of daily living, but also to bear children. For many women, giving purpose to their bodies that is not associated with visual or sexual pleasure, is important. As women, especially those struggling with disordered eating or poor body image, taking an opportunity to appreciate the uniqueness and the beauty of being created by a loving Father can be powerful in helping them see beyond their external appearance. As previously mentioned, eating disorders are often associated with other mental health concerns such as anxiety, depression, personality disorders, and substance use disorders. There are a variety of strategies used to integrate Biblical principles into the treatment of these common comorbidities as well.

Client Testimonial
Erica Averill

One thing I've come to realize about eating disorders is that they thrive in secrecy. Those of us who are unlucky enough to live with an eating disorder usually have unresolved trauma, making us much less likely to trust another individual. This is especially true when it comes to a counselor. When I first met my counselor, I was in intense denial about being sick. I had literally said the words, "There is nothing wrong with me." After all, I had been seeing another counselor for three years before and thought that had been going well. My current counselor was different, she was persistent, patient, empathetic, and compassionate.

© Erica Averill

I believe I went through every stage of grief before admitting that I had a problem with eating and every one of these values were essential to my mental health at the time. I needed her to be persistent with me, yet patient enough to know that I didn't understand and couldn't comprehend what was happening yet. She had faith in me that I didn't have during those sessions. She became the person that helped slowly build my self-confidence while showing me that I can also be the one to do it myself. She showed me empathy in the moments when I became beaten down and compassion by sharing some of her own stories. It's so easy to feel alone and embarrassed but having the person you tell everything to relate to you feels good sometimes. We've celebrated the good moments, like stepping down from intensive treatment but knowing treatment was just starting. She also knew it was important to keep in touch with me due to abandonment issues. This is what great counselors do. It's about treating the root of the problem, not just the symptom (i.e. eating).

I'm amazed at the amount of insight and forgiveness that she has taught me to show my body. The journey has been incredibly long, and I have goals. In the end, all I want is to be cared for and listened to. Many patients with eating disorders have been through life or death situations. As patients, we just need your help to see that there is another way to cope, another way to live. There absolutely is another way!

SPECIAL CONSIDERATIONS

Perfectionism and Eating Disorders

The overwhelming influence of societal pressures for attaining the "perfect" body are no secret to most women. However, the relationship between perfectionism and eating disorders is far more complex. The distinction has been made between socially prescribed perfectionism and self-oriented perfectionism, with a combination of the two being the most maladaptive (Esposito et al., 2019; Wade et al., 2016). Perfectionistic tendencies (self-oriented perfectionism) have long been associated with eating disorders, specifically anorexia nervosa. The labeling of foods as "good" or "bad" or patterns of restricting and bingeing are examples of the all-or-nothing/black-and-white thinking attributed to perfectionism. Many clients with self-oriented perfectionistic tendencies strive to be high achieving. While the standards that they set for themselves often lead to success, their failure to perfectly achieve can lead to feelings of shame and guilt. Historically, the school of thought has been that perfectionism is a negative quality and in order to help our clients we must focus on ridding them of their perfectionistic tendencies. But what if perfectionism wasn't all together a bad thing?

Philip Gnilka suggests that perfectionism is a multidimensional construct which consists of perfectionistic concerns, or one's inner critic, and perfectionistic strivings (Phillips, 2019). He further argues that one's self-critical perfectionism is what often leads to negative mental health concerns; therefore, the focus of interventions should be on the client's inner critic. When we consider the "eating disorder voice," it is often a manifestation of the client's inner critic. Clients often report that their eating disorder criticizes their lack of will-power, self-esteem, physical appearance, and overall value as a person. The eating disorder voice is harsh and often described as an abuser. Treatment interventions aimed at ridding clients of their perfectionistic tendencies without addressing their inner critic isn't effective. The complexity then becomes helping the client develop an adaptive or healthy form of perfectionism that focuses on high standards but low self-criticism. In other words, the goal becomes harnessing the individual's desire for high achievement while quieting their critical inner voice.

Effective treatment interventions include creating realistic reframes, softening the inner critic's voice, focusing on progress not outcomes, exploring the grey area, and practicing self-compassion (Phillips, 2019). Negative self-talk and irrational thoughts are very common in women with eating disorders, especially those exhibiting perfectionistic tendencies. Encouraging clients to reframe their negative, irrational thoughts provides an opportunity for them to acknowledge their uncomfortable emotions and explore a more positive outlook. Furthermore, when perfectionistic clients are focused on a high standard they have set for themselves, they often become very self-critical and beat themselves up if they do not perfectly achieve their goal. Focusing on progress rather than outcomes allows for greater flexibility, builds self-confidence, and provides opportunities for affirmation and validation. Finally, encouraging clients to practice self-compassion is monumental in softening their critical inner voice. It can be very beneficial and powerful for clients to step outside of themselves, imagine how they would talk to a friend who was in the same situation, and respond to themselves in the same manner. Often clients respond in a less harsh and more compassionate way.

Trauma and Eating Disorders

Various studies indicate that there is a link between traumatic experiences and eating disorder development (Backholm et al., 2013; Muehlenkamp et al., 2010; Reyes- Rodriguez et al., 2011; Tagay et al., 2013). In terms of risk and prognostic factors for bulimia nervosa specifically, the *DSM-5* indicates that childhood sexual or physical abuse puts individuals at a higher risk for developing bulimia nervosa (APA, 2013). Trauma is a broad term that encompasses a range of perceived negative experiences; thus, making characterizing and quantifying the frequency and nature of trauma challenging for mental health counselors. Assessing for trauma is an essential component of any eating disorder assessment, which also serves to acknowledge and validate the client's experience.

Responses to trauma can be physical, behavioral, cognitive, emotional, and spiritual in nature, varying among individuals. Studies indicate that women who have an eating disorder diagnosis and have reported exposure to trauma subsequently report increased severity of eating disorder symptoms, negative self-image, increased feelings of shame, psychosocial impairment, psychiatric comorbidities, and **alexithymia** (a difficulty in identifying, differentiating, and articulating emotions and feelings) (Backholm et al., 2013; Franzo et al., 2013; Reyes-Rodriguez et al., 2011).

> **Alexithymia:** a difficulty in identifying, differentiating, and articulating emotions and feelings.

Approximately three quarters of clients with anorexia nervosa and half of clients with bulimia nervosa report having difficulty describing their feelings and are often confused by their emotions, a phenomenon known as alexithymia (Franzo et al., 2013; Van Der Kolk, 2014). In his book, *The Body Keeps the Score* (2014), Dr. Bessel Van der Kolk discusses how traumatized individuals suffering with alexithymia have trouble discerning what is going on in their body. This often leads to them being out of touch with their needs and inhibits their ability to take care of themselves, specifically in terms of getting the appropriate amount of food and sleep.

Additionally, studies indicate that psychological and somatoform dissociative symptoms (physical symptoms that are not traceable to a physical cause) are more prevalent in eating disorder patients with reported childhood trauma, specifically in those exhibiting bingeing and purging behaviors (Palmisano et al., 2017; Seubert & Virdi, 2019). Trauma is also associated with feelings of loss or lack of control. It is not uncommon for abuse or trauma victims to turn to controlling their food intake and/or body size as a way to feel a sense of control.

Treating an eating disorder in and of itself can be complex. Therefore, as mental health counselors we must take care when treating individuals with a trauma history and co-occurring eating disorder. First and foremost, the goal must be to restore adequate nutrition. This allows for normalized brain function, which increases clarity of thought and the ability to process mentally and emotionally. Next, we must aid our clients in developing the capacity to identify and regulate their emotions. One of the primary treatment goals when treating individuals with co-occurring eating disorder and alexithymia or dissociative symptoms becomes re-creating a healthy mind body connection. From this point, we can help clients identify abuse and end the cycle of repeated victimization. As clients stabilize, we are then able to address feelings of shame and aid our clients in developing self-compassion that is lacking as a result (Kearney-Cook & Striegel-Moore, 1994).

Pregnancy and Eating Disorders

Although amenorrhea (irregular or loss of menstruation) is no longer a diagnostic marker for anorexia nervosa, it remains a complication of eating disorders which commonly leads to fertility issues. While the past or present diagnosis of an eating disorder can make becoming pregnant more challenging, it does not necessarily mean a woman will not become pregnant. It is recommended that women postpone their efforts to become pregnant until they are in recovery (National Association of Anorexia Nervosa and Associated Disorders, 2019). However, if a woman becomes pregnant, it is important to be aware of increased risks and complications to both the woman and the baby when disordered eating is present during pregnancy (Table 15.1).

TABLE 15.1

Risks to Mother and Baby during Pregnancy When Disordered Eating Is Present

Risks to Mother	Risks to Baby
• Poor nutrition and dehydration • Cardiac irregularities • Gestational diabetes • Preeclampsia • Miscarriage/stillbirth • Premature labor • Labor complications • Increased risk of cesarean section • Trouble nursing • Depression (during pregnancy and postpartum)	• Premature birth • Low birth weight • Delayed fetal growth • Respiratory distress • Feeding difficulties • Other perinatal complications

Source: American Pregnancy Association, 2019; Eckern, 2019; National Association of Anorexia Nervosa and Associated Disorders, 2019; National Eating Disorder Association, 2018

Many of the physical experiences surrounding being pregnant (i.e.- frequent weighing and measuring of a woman's body, increased nutritional focus, body changes, morning sickness, etc.) can be triggering for women who have or are currently struggling with an eating disorder. Not to mention the emotional and hormonal shifts that are occurring during pregnancy and postpartum. Without targeted support and a multidisciplinary treatment team, this can be a dangerous time for a woman with disordered eating. As counselors, it is important that we encourage our clients to:

• Be honest regarding their past or present struggles with an eating disorder when speaking with their prenatal healthcare provider.
• Schedule more frequent appointments to closely monitor their health during pregnancy.
• Work with a nutritionist to develop a plan for healthy eating and weight gain/loss during pregnancy and postpartum.
• Maintain individual counseling.
• Consider support groups or other classes related to pregnancy, childbirth, and parenting.

It is also important that we help our clients focus on body positivity and appreciation during this period. Helping women to focus on the amazing work that their body is doing and the human life that they are carrying

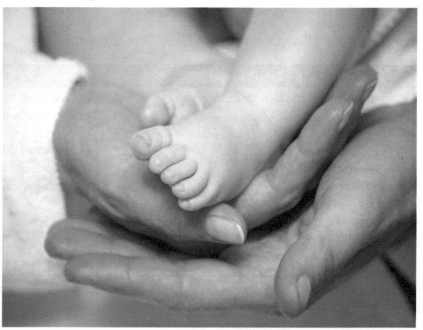

is often helpful in fostering appreciation for their body rather than hate. Finding solace in the fact that God chose them to carry this precious life can be invaluable. Women also respond positively to being reminded that the physical triggers and uncomfortable changes that they are experiencing are temporary. When they can rationally see that pregnancy lasts nine months and are reminded that they will not be in their pregnant body forever, it helps them emotionally cope with the triggers rather than respond with eating disorder behavior use.

Female Athletes and Eating Disorders

Being an elite athlete puts a great deal of focus on one's physical image; whether it be related to physical performance or physical appearance. A study performed on female athletes aged 17-30 found that in addition to high levels of body dissatisfaction and disordered eating symptomology, 60% reported pressure from coaches concerning their body shape and size (Kong & Harris, 2015). In addition to stigma that exists in a sports culture that is not well informed about mental illness, diagnosis and treatment of female athletes with eating disorders is often complicated as participation in competitive sports often requires a higher focus on diet and exercise compared to that of the typical population. Therefore, athlete specific screening tools, such as the *Athletic Milieu Direct Questionnaire* and the *Physiologic Screening Test to Detect Eating Disorders Among Female Athletes*, have been used and shown to be more effective in early detection of disordered eating (Wagner et al., 2016). While athletic performance often suffers in conjunction with an eating disorder, female athletes who display disordered eating are often also at higher risk for musculoskeletal injury due to low bone mineral density. Female athletes are at risk for a condition known as the female athlete triad, which refers to the interrelationship between decreased bone mineral density, menstrual dysfunction, and low energy availability in female athletes with disordered eating (Conviser et al., 2018; Joy et al., 2016; Nazem & Ackerman, 2012). An additional screening tool published by the Female and Male Athlete Triad Coalition (2019) aims to more effectively identify disordered eating in female athletes with the following questions:

- Have you ever had a menstrual period?
- When was your most recent menstrual period?
- How old were you when you had your first menstrual period?
- How many periods have you had in the past 12 months?
- Are you presently raking any female hormones (estrogen, progesterone, birth control pills)?
- Do you worry about your weight?
- Are you trying or has anyone recommended that you gain or lose weight?
- Are you on a special diet or do you avoid certain types of foods or food groups?
- Have you ever had an eating disorder?
- Have you ever had a stress fracture?
- Have you ever been told you have low bone density (osteopenia or osteoporosis)?

With proper assessment, diagnosis, and treatment from a multidisciplinary team the Female Athlete Triad is not only treatable, but preventable. Thus, enabling female athletes to successfully compete and perform without risking their overall health and wellbeing.

FIGURE 15.4

Female Athlete Triad

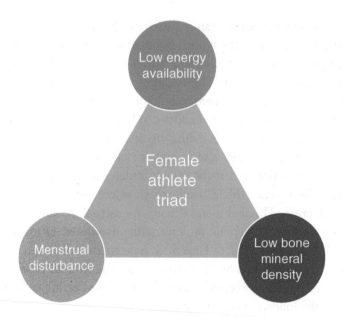

Source: Andrea Barbian

Celebrity Spotlight: Christy Henrich (1972-1994)

Christy Henrich was a famous USA gymnast who passed away from multiple organ failure, a complication of her eating disorder, at the young age of 22. Throughout her struggle with her eating disorder, Henrich abused laxatives, restricted her caloric intake, and engaged in excessive movement in order to achieve and maintain a low body weight. Henrich was 4'10" and 95 pounds at the peak of her career. When she passed away, she weighed 47 pounds. Despite the aggressive care she was receiving, her body simply could not function with a lack of fuel.

Henrich stated in an interview, "My life is a horrifying nightmare. It feels like there's a beast inside me, like a monster. It feels evil" (Noden, 1994). Although Henrich received intensive care, she was unable to win the battle against her eating disorder. Her story has impacted female athletes since.

Henrich's full story can be found in the article "Dying to Win" located in the *Suggested Resources* section of this chapter.

© ImageFlow/Shutterstock.com

To Refer or Not to Refer … That Is the Question!

As mental health counselors, we are legally and ethically bound to principles such as *nonmaleficence* (avoiding actions that harm our clients). Consider the importance of nonmaleficence regarding the treatment of eating disorders. Spend some time considering what actions you would take if a client presented to your office with an eating disorder. Given your knowledge and comfort level regarding diagnosing and treating eating disorders:

- What steps would you take to determine whether you should treat the client or refer them to a specialized mental health counselor?
- If you choose to treat the client, what steps would you take in ensuring that you practice nonmaleficence?
- If you choose to refer the client, how would you approach that conversation with the client?

CASE STUDY: THE CASE OF JAMIE, AND THE TWINS!

Jamie is a 28-year old female being seen for outpatient eating disorder treatment. Jamie has a previous diagnosis of anorexia nervosa, in conjunction with anxiety. Jamie successfully completed inpatient and partial hospitalization treatment for her eating disorder in her early twenties. Jamie has done well maintaining her recovery with the help of her dietician, physician, and mental health counseling. Her Christian faith has been a big part of her recovery as well. Jamie has struggled with infertility and recently found out that she is pregnant with twins. While Jamie and her husband are very excited about their new additions, they are fearful that her pregnancy will trigger eating disorder thoughts, feelings, and behaviors. How would you approach treatment with Jamie?

First, it is important that a multidisciplinary team is in place. Ideally, Jamie's dietician would help her create and monitor meal plans for different stages of her pregnancy to make sure that she is getting the proper nutrition to maintain her pregnancy and allow for healthy growth and development for the babies. Jamie's OB/GYN would be responsible for establishing healthy weight gain benchmarks and monitoring Jamie's vital signs and other health concerns. Since Jamie is currently effectively managing her anxiety without medication, medication management from a physician or psychiatrist is not needed. Given that Jamie and I already have a strong therapeutic relationship, it would be important to maintain the relationship and address any resistance or concerns regarding motivation. Additionally, Jamie is a Christian and values integrating Biblical principles into our work, we will continue this throughout her pregnancy.

As Jamie expresses anxiety and concern about the expected weight gain associated with pregnancy, we will focus our work on adjusting her outlook and motivation for remaining in recovery. In addition to reviewing risks to both Jamie and the babies, we will discuss possible triggers to eating disorder behavior that may present during pregnancy. Jamie has indicated that one of her greatest concerns is weight gain and how her changing body will look. She is afraid to have pictures taken throughout her pregnancy, even though she knows that this is a normal thing that women do to document their pregnancy. In addition to other interventions focused on reframing her thoughts and feelings around weight gain from negative to positive. Jamie will practice appreciation for her body and the ability to carry her babies through two specific exercises.

First, Jamie has previously enjoyed the process of journaling throughout her recovery as it helps her to process her thoughts and emotions. Jamie will continue journaling throughout her pregnancy with a gratitude and prayer focus. Jamie will be given a list of prompts targeted toward body appreciation, Bible verses, and other inspiration quotes to help her focus her journal entries and encourage reframing her thoughts around weight gain from negative to positive. Finally, Jamie, her husband, and I will work together on a special gift for the twins to document their journey in the womb. Each month Jamie's husband will take a picture of her standing by her favorite tree in their yard. Each month, after the picture is taken, Jamie and her husband will write a short letter to each of the twins expressing her excitement and anticipation of their arrival, documenting special events (i.e.- today we assembled your crib, this weekend we will be having a baby shower, this week we saw you via ultrasound, etc.), etc. Jamie will bring her picture and letter into session that month and we will process the experience together. The goal is for Jamie to focus on the miracle of her pregnancy with the twins and appreciate her body for the hard work that it is doing. Looking at the photos and processing the letters together will help her when she is struggling to reframe her negative thoughts about her weight gain and changing body. This will also serve as a special gift for her babies to document their life in the womb.

CHAPTER SUMMARY

Eating disorders are a very serious mental health concern with detrimental outcomes if not appropriately treated. As counselors, it is important that we are aware of the signs and symptoms commonly present with not only clinical eating disorders as defined by the *DSM-5*, but also with disordered eating. Collaborating with a multidisciplinary team and using evidence-based treatment modalities are essential in treating these delicate disorders. Various additional factors such as anxiety, depression, substance use, personality disorders, trauma, perfectionism, and pregnancy can complicate treatment and require specialized care. It is essential that mental health counselors have a basic understanding of eating disorders and seek further education if they desire to specialize in eating disorder treatment.

KEY TERMS

Alexithymia - a difficulty in identifying, differentiating, and articulating emotions and feelings

Amenorrhea - irregular or loss of menstruation

Nonmaleficence - avoiding actions that harm our clients

Orthostatic Hypotension - when blood pressure decreases when moving from sitting to standing position

Somatoform Dissociative Symptoms - physical symptoms that are not traceable to a physical cause

SUGGESTED RESOURCES

Articles

Celebrity Spotlight: "Dying to Win," *Sports Illustrated* by M. Noden
https://vault.si.com/vault/1994/08/08/dying-to-win-for-many-women-athletes-the-toughest-foe-is-anorexia-gymnist-christy-henrich-lost-her-battle

Books

Binge Eating
Overcoming Binge Eating by Christopher Fairburn
The Binge Eating and Compulsive Overeating Workbook by Carolyn Coker Ross, MD, MPH

Eating Disorder Recovery
8 Keys to Recovery from an Eating Disorder: Effective Strategies from Therapeutic Practice and Personal Experience by Carolyn Costin and Gwen Schubert Grabb
Goodbye Ed, Hello Me by Jenni Schaefer
Healing Your Hungry Heart by Joanna Poppink, MFT
Intuitive Eating: A Revolutionary Program that Works by Elyse Resch and Evelyn Tribole
Life Inside the Thin Cage by Constance Rhodes
Life Without Ed by Jenni Schaefer

Eating Disorder Treatment
Cognitive Behavior Therapy for Eating Disorders by Christopher Fairburn
Dialectical Behavior Therapy for Binge Eating and Bulimia by Safer, Telch, and Chen
The Eating Disorder Sourcebook by Carolyn Costin, MA, MED, MFCC

Pregnancy
ANAD's Eating Disorders and Pregnancy: A Comprehensive Book for Women and Healthcare Professionals by Patricia Santucci, MD, FAPA, FAED

Trauma
The Body Keeps the Score by Bessel Van Der Kolk, MD
Trauma-informed Approaches to Eating Disorders by Andrew Seubert and Pam Virdi

Organizations
Academy for Eating Disorders (AED): https://www.aedweb.org/resources/fast-facts
Association for Size Diversity and Health (ASDAH)/ Health at Every Size (HAES): https://www.sizediversityandhealth.org/content.asp?id=76
Eating Disorder Hope: https://www.eatingdisorderhope.com
National Association of Anorexia Nervosa and Associated Disorders (ANAD): https://anad.org

National Eating Disorders Association (NEDA): https://www.
nationaleatingdisorders.org
The Female and Male Athlete Triad Coalition: https://www.
femaleandmaleathletetriad.org

REFERENCES

American Pregnancy Association. (2019). *Eating disorders and pregnancy*.
https://americanpregnancy.org/pregnancy-health/pregnancy-and-eating-
disorders/

American Psychiatric Association. (2013). *Diagnostic and statistical manual
of mental health disorders* (5th ed.). https://doi.org/10.1176/appi.
books.9780890425596

Antoniou, P., & Cooper, M. (2014). Psychological treatments for eating
disorders: What is the importance of the quality of therapeutic alliance for
outcomes? *Counselling Psychology Review, 28*(4), 34-46.

Backholm, K., Isomaa, R., & Birgegard, A. (2013). The prevalence and
impact of trauma history in eating disorder patients. *European Journal of
Psychotraumatology, 4*(1), 22482.

Conviser, J. H., Tierney, A. S., & Nickols, R. (2018). Assessment of athletes
with eating disorders: Essential for best practice. *Journal of Clinical Sport
Psychology, 12*(4), 480-494.

Dejesse, L. D., & Zelmann, D. C. (2013). Promoting optimal collaboration
between mental health providers and nutritionists in the treatment of eating
disorders. *Eating Disorders 21*, 185-205.

Douglass, L. (2011). Thinking through the body: The conceptualization of yoga as
a therapy for individuals with eating disorders. *Eating Disorders, 19*, 83-96.

Eckern, J. (2019). *Eating disorders and pregnancy.* https://www.eatingdisorderhope.
com/treatment-for-eating-disorders/special-issues/pregnancy

Esposito, R. M., Stoeber, J., Damian, L. E., Alessandri, G., & Lombardo, C.
(2019). Eating disorder symptoms and the 2 x 2 model of perfectionism:
Mixed perfectionism is the most maladaptive combination. *Eating and
Weight Disorders- Studies on Anorexia, Bulimia, and Obesity, 24*(4), 749-755.

Fassino, S., & Abbate-Daga, G. (2013). Resistance to treatment in eating
disorders: A critical challenge. *BMC Psychiatry, 13*(282), 1-4.

Franzo, E., Gualandi, S., Caretti, V., Schimmenti, A., Di Pietro, E., Pellegrini,
G., Crapar, G., Franchi, A., Verrotti, A., & Pellicciari, A. (2013). The
relationship between alexithymia, shame, trauma, and body image
disorders: Investigation over a large clinical sample. *Neuropsychiatric
Disease and Treatment, 9*, 185-193.

Hasler, G., Delsignore, A., Milos, G., Buddeberg, C., & Schnyder, U. (2004). Application of Prochaska's transtheoretical model of change to patients with eating disorders. *Journal of Psychosomatic Research, 57*(1), 67-72.

Hawkins, R., Knight, A., Sibcy, G., Silvey, R., & Warren, S. (2019). *Research-based Counseling Skills: The Art and Science of Therapeutic Empathy*. Kendall Hunt.

Hoetzel, K., von Brachel, R., Schlossmacher, L., & Vocks, S. (2013). Assessing motivation to change in eating disorders: A systematic review. *Journal of Eating Disorders, 1*(38), 1-9.

Joy, E., Kussman, A., & Nattiv, A. (2016). 2016 update on eating disorders in athletes: A comprehensive narrative review with a focus on clinical assessment and management. *British Journal of Sports Medicine, 50*(3), 154-162.

Kearney-Cook, A., & Striegel-Moore, R. (1994). Treatment of childhood sexual abuse in anorexia nervosa and bulimia nervosa: A feminist psychodynamic approach. *International Journal of Eating Disorders, 15*(4), 305-319.

Kong, P., & Harris, L. M. (2015). The sporting body: Body image and eating disorder symptomatology among female athletes from leanness focused and nonleanness focused sports. *The Journal of Psychology, 149*(2), 141-160.

Lac, V., Marble, E., & Boie, I. (2013). Equine-assisted psychotherapy as a creative relational approach to treating clients with eating disorders. *Journal of Creativity in Mental Health, 8*, 484-498.

Lejonclou, A., & Trondalen, G. (2009). "I've started to move in my own body": Music therapy with women suffering from eating disorders. *Nordic Journal of Music Therapy, 18*(1), 79-92.

Lenz, A. S., Taylor, R., Fleming, M., & Serman, N. (2014). Effectiveness of dialectical behavior therapy for treating eating disorders. *Journal of Counseling and Development, 92*(1), 26-35.

Linehan, M. (2015). *DBT skills training manual* (2nd ed.). Guilford Press.

Lob, M. (2016). *In the trenches: Effective therapy modalities for eating disorders.* [PowerPoint slides]. www.iaedp2016.pathble.com

Muehlenkamp, J. J., Claes, L., Smits, D., Peat, C. M., & Vandereycken, W. (2010). Non-suicidal self-injury in eating disordered patients: A test of a conceptual model. *Psychiatry Research, 188*(1), 102-108.

Murphy, R., & Fairburn, C. (2010). British team promotes 'enhanced' CBT. *Eating Disorders Review, 21*(1), 3.

National Association of Anorexia Nervosa and Associated Disorders. (2017). *Eating disorder statistics.* https://anad.org/education-and-awareness/about-eating-disorders/eating-disorders-statistics/

National Association of Anorexia Nervosa and Associated Disorders. (2019). *Pregnancy.* https://anad.org/product-category/anad-products/

National Eating Disorder Association. (2018). *Pregnancy and eating disorders.* https://www.nationaleatingdisorders.org/pregnancy-and-eating-disorders

Nazem, T. G., & Ackerman, K. E. (2012). The female athlete triad. *Sports Health, 4*(4), 302-311.

New International Bible. (2011). New International Bible Online. https://www.thenivbible.com/ (Original work published 1973).

Noden, M. (1994, August 8). *Dying to win.* Sports Illustrated. https://vault.si.com/vault/1994/08/08/dying-to-win-for-many-women-athletes-the-toughest-foe-is-anorexia-gymnist-christy-henrich-lost-her-battle

Olmstead, M. P., McFarlane, T., Trottier, K., & Rockert, W. (2013). Efficacy and intensity of day hospital treatment for eating disorders. *Psychotherapy Research, 23*(3), 277-286.

Palmisano, G., Innamorati, M., Susca, G., Traetta, D., Sarracino, D., & Vanderlinden, J. (2017). Dissociative phenomena in eating disorders: Level and association with the severity of binge eating symptoms. *Journal of Trauma & Dissociation, 19*(1), 88-107.

Phillips, L. (2019). The messy reality of perfectionism. *Counseling Today, 61*(8), 32-37.

Reyes- Rodriguez, M. L., Von Holle, A., Ulman, T. F., Thornton, L.M., Klump, K. L., Brandt, H., Crawford, S., Fichter, M. M., Halmi, K. A., Huber, T., Johnson, C., Jones, I., Kaplan, A. S., Mitchell, J. E., Strober, M., Treasure, J., Woodside, D. B., Berrettini, W. H., Kaye, W. H., & Bulik, C. M. (2011). Posttraumatic stress disorder in anorexia nervosa. *Psychosom Med, 73*(6), 491-497.

Robertson, S. [Sarah]. (n.d.). *Discover ideas about bulimia recovery* [Pinterest Post]. Retrieved March 4, 2020, from https://www.pinterest.it/pin/229120699765349732/.

Rogers, C. R. (1975). Empathic: An unappreciated way of being. *The Counseling Psychologist, 5*(2), 2-10.

Seubert, A., & Virdi, P. (2019). *Trauma-informed approaches to eating disorders.* Springer Publishing Company.

Steiger, H. (2017). Evidence-informed practices in the real world treatment of people with eating disorders. *Eating Disorders, 25*(2), 173-181.

Tagay, S., Schlottbohm, E., Reyes-Rodriguez, M. L., Repic, N., & Senf, W. (2013). Eating disorders, trauma, PTSD, and psychological resources. *Eating Disorders: The Journal of Treatment & Prevention, 22*(1), 33-49.

The Female and Male Athlete Triad Coalition. (2019). *What is the female athlete triad?* https://www.femaleandmaleathletetriad.org

Van der Kolk, B. (2014). *The body keeps the score: Brain, mind, and body in the healing of trauma.* Penguin Books.

Vaz-Leal, F. J., Ramos-Fuentes, M. I., Rodriguez-Santos, L., Chimpen-lopez, C., Fernandez-Sanchez, N., Zamora-Rodriguez, F. J., Beato-Fernandez, L., Rojo-Moreno, L., & Guisado-Macias, J. A. (2018). Blunted cortisol response to stress in patients with eating disorders: Its association to bulimic features. *European Eating Disorders Review, 26*(3), 207-216.

Wade, T. D., O'Shea, A., & Shafran, R. (2016). Perfectionism and eating Disorders. In F. Sirois, & D. Molnar (Eds.), *Perfectionism, health, and well-being* (pp. 205-222). Springer.

Wagner, A. J., Erickson, C. D., Tierney, D. K., Houston, M. N., & Welch-Bacon, C. E. (2016). The diagnostic accuracy of screening tools to detect eating disorders in female athletes. *Journal of Sport Rehabilitation, 25*(4), 395-398.

Wesley, M. C., Minatrea, N. B., & Watson, J. C. (2009). Animal-assisted therapy in the treatment of substance dependence. *Anthrozoos, 22*(2), 137-148.

Wisniewski, L. & Ben-Porath, D. D. (2015). Dialectical behavior therapy and eating disorders: The use of contingency management procedures to manage dialectical dilemmas. *American Journal of Psychotherapy, 69*(2), 129-140.

CHAPTER 16
Women and Substance Abuse

JONNA BYARS, PH.D.

"What is addiction, really? It is a sign, a signal, a symptom of distress. It is a language that tells us about a plight that must be understood."
~Alice Miller, Breaking Down the Wall of Silence

"No temptation has overtaken you except what is common to mankind. And God is faithful; he will not let you be tempted beyond what you can bear. But when you are tempted, he will also provide a way out so that you can endure it."
(1 Corinthians 10:13, NIV)

Wisdom from Above: Standing in His Grace

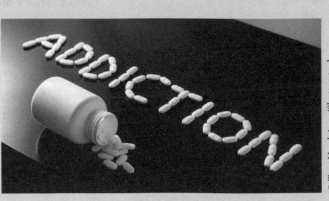

© Tero Vesalainen/Shutterstock.com

Counselors inevitably encounter addiction in their professional life. They, like the rest of society, encounter addiction in private life too through significant others, family members, friends, acquaintances, clients, clients' families, etc. Denial is a common quality that those struggling with addiction are likely to show. An acronym that describes the frustration of denial is **D**on't **E**ven k**N**ow **I** **A**m **L**ying. Often, addicts do not believe there is a problem, and trying to confront the denial directly rarely works. One strategy that may bear more fruit is to work *with* the client – to meet them where they are. For Christians, this could be considered a WWJD (What Would Jesus Do?) perspective. How did Jesus work with people who were in denial? How did he work with those who were lost or did not understand? How did he meet them where they were? One theme that is repeated in the gospels is a willingness

to share the humble circumstances of those who were deemed outcasts and sinners. Jesus met the woman at the well and dined with tax collectors. He exhorted only those who were without sin to stone the adulterous woman. He was modeling and teaching *humility*. Those suffering from addiction are highly resistant to change. Consider the enormous physiological changes wrought by drug addiction, and the nature of their task – they must alter their chemistry in an extremely painful process of recovery. No matter how resistant a client is, a WWJD perspective calls us to respond with the fruits of the spirit – love, peace, patience, gentleness, and self-control. To respond as a partner and fellow-sufferer, not as a righteous and angry defender. We are told in the Bible, "Let he who is without sin throw the first stone" (*New International Bible*, 1973/2011, John 8:7). That perspective connects us to the *grace* that is free to all who follow after Christ.

CHAPTER LEARNING OBJECTIVES

Upon completing this chapter, you should be able to:

- Evaluate the scope of the addiction problem and the place of women in the world of addiction
- Assess the signs and symptoms of addiction
- Explain the diagnostic criteria as defined in the *DSM*
- Know treatment options and strategies for counseling women with addictive disorders

CHAPTER OVERVIEW

Addiction (an inability to stop using a chemical, drug, activity, or substance, despite harm or injury that the use is causing) often follows a predictable path in the public mind. A user becomes dependent, hits bottom, goes to rehab, resumes regular life, and all too often repeats the cycle. Those who suffer from, and treat, addictive disorders understand that the story is much more complex. This one size fits all template becomes even more problematic when we attempt to apply it to women's addiction experiences. There are both biological and cultural differences between men and women in the area of substance abuse. The social and economic consequences to women are significantly different than those experienced by men. Many of these consequences are the result of social structures in which women bear a greater share of child care responsibilities. Economically they must find a way to support themselves and their children. Emotionally, they often must overcome the guilt that may come with struggling with addiction while raising children. Many women must take into account the negative consequences they may face if their addiction becomes public knowledge – further exacerbating the problems of stigma and shame. In the last several years, women and substance abuse disorders have been the subject of an increasing amount of research and study. We know more about the effects of alcohol and drugs on women's physiology and on pregnancy, how to treat women, the impact of trauma, **dual diagnosis** (the presence of a mental illness and substance abuse) and the importance of accounting for gender in scientific work, research, and in counseling. This chapter will explore these issues in addition to covering diagnosis of substance related disorders.

WHAT IS ADDICTION?

Addiction is an inability to stop using a chemical, drug, activity, or substance, despite harm or injury that the use is causing. It is both psychological and physiological in nature. The addict experiences strong cravings which may be uncontrollable even when there is a desire to quit, and the substance use comes to dominate their life (American Psychiatric Association, 2013).

Compulsive use despite clear harmful consequences is by its nature a complex situation. It has ceased to be a rational ordering of one's priorities and values. Some of the stigma may stem from the perceived incongruence of a person acting against their interests, or worse, those of their children (National Institute on Drug Abuse [NIDA], 2019a; Peters et al, 2013; Substance Abuse and Mental Health Services Administration [SAMHSA], 2019). But addiction is not a failure of will. It is a physiological condition that alters the function of the brain (Erickson et al., 2008; Van Vliet-Ruissen et al., 2014).

Addiction changes how the brain functions. Imaging studies show that the parts of the brain that control decision-making, learning, memory, and judgment all are affected by addiction as a simple matter of neurophysiology. Simply put, addiction changes the "wiring" of the brain. Behavior and thinking are distorted (Stankovic & Trikos, 2008; Van Vliet-Ruissen et al., 2014).

Substances most frequently associated with addiction are tobacco, opioids, alcohol, marijuana, hallucinogens such as PCP and LSD, inhalants including glue and solvents, sedatives, and stimulants like methamphetamine and cocaine (SAMHSA, 2019).

Myth: Substances alter people's behavior only while they are intoxicated. Intoxication, the intense high or calm, or pleasure caused by the drug, is the most visible period of substance affect (World Health Organization [WHO], 2018). However, the changes to the brain are not at all confined to the immediately perceived effects of the drug; they last much longer.

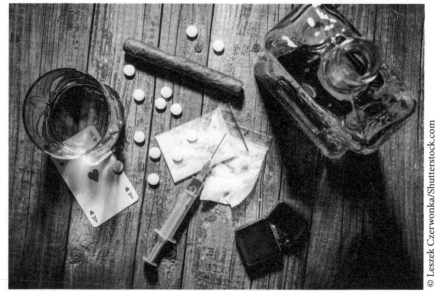

© Leszek Czerwonka/Shutterstock.com

Statistics

According to the National Center for Drug Abuse Statistics (2019) around 10 percent of the population is addicted to drugs or alcohol. For a sense of the scope of the problem, reflect that this makes it more common than many diseases, such as diabetes. According to SAMHSA (2018) 45 percent of women use alcohol every year, and six percent report illicit drug use. In 2017, 5.2% of women age 12 and older had a substance use disorder. These numbers cover all females ages 12 and up (SAMHSA, 2018). Twenty million adult women (18 and older) have used illicit drugs in the past year. The rate of overdose deaths has increased dramatically in recent years, principally due to synthetic opioid use. Opioid use and misuse has reached epidemic proportions in the United States. The Centers for Disease Control (2017) says that the rate of overdose deaths in 2016 was three times the rate in 1999. The financial, social, emotional, and medical consequences to women and their families are enormous.

Biological Issues Affecting Women

Women face a different experience than men with addictive substances. They typically have a shorter time frame between initial substance use to problematic use and health problems (SAMHSA, 2019). Women reach **intoxication** (a result of the intake of psychoactive substances that results in impairment of consciousness, thoughts, emotions, responses and behaviors) more quickly than men when drinking alcohol, partly as a factor of less water in the body and a greater proportion of body fat. Fatty tissue retains alcohol, and water dilutes it. A woman's tissues and organs are therefore more affected. Women also have lower levels of the enzymes that break down alcohol in the body. This means women absorb more alcohol before the breakdown happens (SAMHSA, 2019).

Alcohol consumption increases the risk of breast cancer (and other cancers). Women develop heart and nerve damage, as well as cirrhosis of the liver, in a shorter period of heavy drinking than men. Women also have greater risk of liver disease, kidney disease, and bacterial infections (Capuzzi & Stauffer, 2016; NIDA, 2018).

Women who smoke are twice as likely to have a heart attack as men and are more likely to get lung cancer (Capuzzi & Stauffer, 2016). Additionally, it has been found that women become addicted to stimulants faster than men, and that estrogen is a likely cause of this phenomenon. They may take larger doses than men because of this basic difference in the reward received from stimulants like meth and cocaine (Ait-Daoud et al., 2017).

The accelerated progression from initial use to dependence and seeking treatment is called **telescoping** (enhanced movement from initial use to dependence in women). This phenomenon is especially noticeable for women who use alcohol, opioids, and marijuana (Greenfield et al., 2011).

Substance use affects menstrual cycles and can play a role in infertility. The possibility of pregnancy is among the most serious concerns. Many women use without knowing they are pregnant. Some ignore pregnancy symptoms, assuming they are associated with their substance use. Pregnancy complicates detoxification and the medications that may be used for treatment (SAMHSA, 2019).

Women and Addiction in Society

It is important to consider the question of whether women face greater *social stigma* than men who abuse substances. Some cultures may view excess in substance use as a masculine trait, leading to greater stigma for

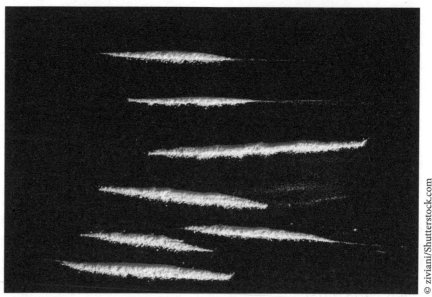

© ziviani/Shutterstock.com

women (Kulis et al., 2010). Women may, and indeed do, delay or avoid seeking treatment or help from friends and family. Such circumstances may be even worse for women of color or for members of other socially marginalized groups. These groups may also have higher risk factors. Black Women are more likely to be victims of domestic violence and sexual assault (National Organization for Women [NOW], 2018). This increases the risk for substance use, along with a host of other health problems. Screening for interpersonal violence is highly recommended by the United States Preventive Services Task Force (USPSTF; Watson et al., 2013).

Men and women approach stimulants in particular with different agendas. Men often treat stimulants as a tool for entertainment – using methamphetamine or cocaine, for example, to continue having a good time. Women report using stimulants to gain energy for work and family responsibilities or for weight loss. Men are also more likely to substitute a different drug if they cannot get their preferred stimulant (Ait-Daoud et al., 2017). Additionally, women are more likely than men to seek treatment for mental health issues in general, and this includes treatment for addiction. Women are more likely to stay in treatment if they have intensive individual care, and are far more likely than men to

Society may use different language to avoid stigma. Alcoholism. Alcohol addiction. Alcohol dependence. Whatever the words used, the issue being described is addiction.

value relationship building as a core component of the treatment process (SAMHSA, 2019).

WHAT CAUSES ADDICTION?

There is general agreement among professionals that addiction does not have a single cause but is a complex disease including many causal factors. These may include biological and genetic factors, as well as psychological, social, familial, cultural, and other environmental factors.

Most women who do have an addiction have one or more of the following root causes associated with their use:

- Trauma, often in the form of physical and emotional abuse by persons who are known and trusted. Research shows about 60% of women addicted to a substance have a history of trauma. Early trauma can affect cognitive development and the integration of thinking and feeling (Delker & Freyd, 2014; Winnington, 2010).
- Poor coping skills for dealing with stress (NIDA, 2019a).
- Family history of addiction. Genetic factors are extremely important in predicting addiction. The NIDA reports that genes account for 50% of an individual's risk of becoming addicted (NIDA, 2019b).
- Negative thinking, such as an all-or-nothing approach to life (Hart & Ksir, 2015).
- Underlying anxiety or depression (Ait-Daoud et al., 2017).
- Having a pain condition and taking opioid drugs (NIDA, 2019a).

> Women cite a particular set of reasons for drug use:
> Weight Control
> Coping with Pain
> Dealing with Exhaustion
> Self-Treatment for Mental Health

Gender Differences in Substance Abuse

The differences between men and women play a role in treatment possibilities. According to the Harvard Medical School (2010), the basic differences are in susceptibility, recovery, and risk of relapse:

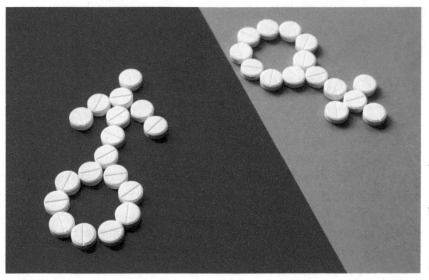

Susceptibility

- Men become addicts more frequently than women
- Men more frequently cite social factors as contributing to their substance abuse
- Women move from use to abuse to dependence at a faster pace than men
- Women are more likely to use substances to self-medicate

Recovery

- Men tend to maintain a stable level of substance abuse more frequently than women
- Withdrawal (emotional and/or physical reaction when a substance is discontinued) is usually worse for men
- Women are more likely to experience the side effects of substance abuse than men
- Women are more likely to overdose than men

Risk of Relapse

- Men relapse less frequently, with longer periods of recovery
- Women experience social consequences to a greater degree than men
- Women experience cravings with greater intensity, and relapse more often
- It is harder for women to quit

Men and Women Quit Smoking Differently?

It is more difficult for women to quit smoking. This is usually attributed to the fact that women metabolize nicotine faster than men. This means that nicotine gum or "the patch" do not work as well for women as for men (NIDA, 2019a). Men are simply more sensitive to the properties of nicotine that are connected to addiction (Miller & Carroll, 2019; NIDA, 2019a). Women, however, may be more susceptible than men to the elements of smoking addiction that are not related to nicotine. These factors may include sensitivity to sensory triggers like sights and smells, and self-image factors like concern about weight gain if they quit smoking (NIDA, 2019a).

Hole in Heart Phenomenon

Substance abuse is itself a symptom of a deeper problem. As with many other human foibles and struggles, such behavior indicates that there is something missing, and the addiction is part of a scramble to fill up the empty places in one's heart. This "hole in the heart" principle helps explain why so many people can stop using but maintain the same patterns, compulsions, and even neurobiology that lead them back to using again.

That hole has to be filled. Counselors do clients a disservice when we focus only on cessation of use. We need to focus on filling that *hole* as part of a plan to make the person *whole*. Not a band-aid, but a comprehensive healing that addresses the pain that so many addicts have at the heart of their problem. Getting at the root of the psychological, physical, or emotional pain prepares a client to fill the void in the heart.

Christian counselors understand that grace can fill those voids. That the Spirit serves to fill us with God's love. The Bible instructs us that it is unwise yet all-too-common for people to give their lives over to things that are *not* God – the idolatry of giving something else the prime place reserved for *Him*. Romans 12:2, *New International Bible* (1973/2011) encourages us to also renew our minds; consider the Scripture, "Do not conform to the pattern of this world, but be transformed by the renewing of your mind. Then you will be able to test and approve what God's will is—his good, pleasing and perfect will." The good news is that He *will* fill us if we open our hearts and help our clients to learn that the substances cannot fill this hole or void but the Spirit *can* and *will*.

SYMPTOMS AND DIAGNOSIS

The National Institute on Drug Abuse (2019) uses the term *addiction* to describe compulsive drug seeking despite negative consequences. However, *addiction* is not a *specific* diagnosis in the *Diagnostic and Statistical Manual of Mental Disorders (DSM-5)*—a diagnostic manual for clinicians that contains descriptions and symptoms of all mental disorders classified by the American Psychiatric Association (APA, 2013). The *DSM-5* recognizes substance disorders that stem from ten different kinds of drugs: alcohol; caffeine; cannabis; hallucinogens (phencyclidine or similarly acting arylcyclohexylamines, and other hallucinogens, such as LSD); inhalants; opioids; sedatives, hypnotics, or anxiolytics; stimulants (including amphetamine-type substances, cocaine, and other stimulants); tobacco; and other or unknown substances. The last category can form the basis of a diagnosis that does not belong to one of the named substances.

The brain's process of giving "rewards" is a major part of the issues arising from drug use. The feeling a person gets from taking a drug can be so rewarding to the brain that drug-taking becomes the most important activity in a person's life. The way this system works can be different depending on the drug, but the issue is the *high* – the sensations of pleasure that a person gets from their substance.

Not all people are equally vulnerable to addiction. Some have greater physiological susceptibility, and some have less self-control, which can put them at risk for developing disordered use. Reasons for using vary also. Some people use to avoid pain and some do it more to seek pleasure. There are of course other reasons, but alternate reasons for using generally fall under either the pain-avoidance mentality or pleasure-seeking mentality.

There are two groups of substance-related disorders: substance-use disorders and substance-induced disorders.
- **Substance-use disorders** are patterns of symptoms resulting from the use of a substance that you continue to take, despite experiencing problems as a result.
- **Substance-induced disorders**, including intoxication, withdrawal, and other substance/medication-induced mental disorders, are classed as a separate issue from substance use disorders. (APA, 2013)

The *DSM-5* (APA, 2013) lists 11 diagnostic criteria, and the severity of the problem can be determined by how many elements of the criteria are present within a 12-month period. Two or three elements of the criteria constitute a "mild" disorder, four or five is "moderate", and six or more indicate a "severe" condition:

DSM-5 Criteria (APA, 2013)
1. Taking the substance in larger amounts or for longer than you are meant to
2. Wanting to cut down or stop using the substance but not managing to
3. Spending a lot of time getting, using, or recovering from use of the substance
4. Cravings and urges to use the substance
5. Not managing to do what you should at work, home, or school because of substance use
6. Continuing to use, even when it causes problems in relationships
7. Giving up important social, occupational, or recreational activities because of substance use
8. Using substances again and again, even when it puts you in danger
9. Continuing to use, even when you know you have a physical or psychological problem that could have been caused or made worse by the substance
10. Needing more of the substance to get the effect you want (**tolerance**) (diminishing effect from substance abuse use that happens over time with the need to increase the consumption of the substance to acquire desired effect)
11. Development of withdrawal symptoms, which can be relieved by taking more of the substance (APA, 2013).

Addiction Terminology

It is important to be clear when talking about addiction, and correctly using the vocabulary of the field is helpful. **Intoxication** is a condition that follows the administration of a psychoactive substance, such as drugs or alcohol, and results in disturbances in the level of consciousness, cognition, perception, judgement, affect, or behavior, or other psychophysiological functions and responses (World Health Organization, 2018).

© travelcamera/Shutterstock.com

Physical dependence is a physical condition caused by chronic use of a tolerance-forming drug, in which abrupt or gradual drug withdrawal causes unpleasant physical symptoms (Hart & Ksir, 2015). Physical dependence may develop with daily use of a substance, even if it is legal and taken as prescribed by a doctor. The human body gets used to frequent exposure, and symptoms occur because the body reacts to the drug being taken away (Ruiz & Strain, 2014). **Tolerance** is the need to take more of a drug to get the effects of the drug a person is used to (Miller & Carroll, 2019), or the diminishing effect of a drug when taken over time (Clements, 2011). Tolerance and dependence frequently happen together and sometimes it is difficult to tell them apart (Capuzzi & Stauffer, 2016). **Withdrawal** is the reaction of the body when the substance is taken away. Withdrawal symptoms can be severe and painful, both physically and emotionally (Answer Addiction, 2017; Miller & Carroll, 2019).

Dual Diagnosis

A co-occurring disorder, or **dual diagnosis** (the presence of a mental illness and substance abuse), is when someone has a mental illness and a substance use problem at the same time. Either condition can happen first. People who have a mental health disorder may take substances to self-medicate. However, research shows that alcohol and other drugs worsen the symptoms of mental illnesses, and in fact the interaction of the two may make both conditions worse (Bersani & Prevete, 2017). Both disorders should be treated at the same time to improve the likelihood of success.

Approximately half of women with an addiction have a secondary diagnosis (NIDA, 2015; SAMHSA, 2019; Winnington, 2010). This is such a significant number that dual diagnosis needs to be considered with all female clients who show signs of addiction. Women with co-occurring mental and substance use disorders are likely to experience serious physical health problems (NIDA, 2019a; SAMHSA, 2019). Women who have mental disorders can have more difficulty adhering to health-related treatment recommendations, such as treatment attendance, diet restrictions, or medication compliance (Miller & Carroll, 2019; NIDAa, 2019).

Women who have substance use disorders are more likely to meet diagnostic criteria for mood disorders specific to depressive symptoms, ago-

Did You Know?

The United States government defines different categories of drugs depending on the acceptable medical use and the potential for misuse and dependency. Knowing these categories may help a counselor understand and assess the risk of a client developing a psychological or physiological addiction, or both (United States Department of Justice Drug Enforcement Administration [USDDEA], 2019).

Schedule I
Schedule I drugs, substances, or chemicals are defined as drugs with no currently accepted medical use and a high potential for abuse. Some examples of Schedule I drugs are: heroin, lysergic acid diethylamide (LSD), marijuana (cannabis), 3,4-methylenedioxymethamphetamine (ecstasy), methaqualone, and peyote

Schedule II
Schedule II drugs, substances, or chemicals are defined as drugs with a high potential for abuse, with use potentially leading to severe psychological or physical dependence. These drugs are also considered dangerous. Some examples of Schedule II drugs are: Combination products with less than 15 milligrams of hydrocodone per dosage unit (Vicodin), cocaine, methamphetamine, methadone, hydromorphone (Dilaudid), meperidine (Demerol), oxycodone (OxyContin), fentanyl, Dexedrine, Adderall, and Ritalin

Schedule III
Schedule III drugs, substances, or chemicals are defined as drugs with a moderate to low potential for physical and psychological dependence. Schedule III drugs abuse potential is less than Schedule I and Schedule II drugs but more than Schedule IV. Some examples of Schedule III drugs are: Products containing less than 90 milligrams of codeine per dosage unit (Tylenol with codeine), ketamine, anabolic steroids, testosterone

Schedule IV
Schedule IV drugs, substances, or chemicals are defined as drugs with a low potential for abuse and low risk of dependence. Some examples of Schedule IV drugs are: Xanax, Soma, Darvon, Darvocet, Valium, Ativan, Talwin, Ambien, Tramadol

Schedule V
Schedule V drugs, substances, or chemicals are defined as drugs with lower potential for abuse than Schedule IV and consist of preparations containing limited quantities of certain narcotics. Schedule V drugs are generally used for antidiarrheal, antitussive, and analgesic purposes. Some examples of Schedule V drugs are: cough preparations with less than 200 milligrams of codeine or per 100 milliliters (Robitussin AC), Lomotil, Motofen, Lyrica, Parepectolin

(United States Department of Justice Drug Enforcement Administration, 2019)

raphobia with or without panic attacks, posttraumatic stress, and eating disorders. For women, literature suggests that the onset of psychiatric disorders is likely to precede substance use disorders (Greenfield et al., 2011). Women with depression, for example, are more likely to develop a problem with alcohol after their first depressive episode.

When women seek treatment, it is typically for mental illness symptoms, and it is most often to a general practice physician or to mental health professionals. Men, in contrast, are more likely to go straight to addiction specialists/treatment, with symptoms clearly indicating that addiction is the presenting issue (Hawkings & Gilburt, 2004). This means that women's addiction and substance problems often are not addressed until later in the process, are misdiagnosed, or may even be missed entirely. Women who have a childhood history of abuse (whether sexual, physical, or emotional) are far more likely to have substance misuse problems, and because they may also show clear symptoms of PTSD, treatment may focus on that disorder instead of the addiction (Galvani & Humphries, 2007). Treatment for dual diagnoses must take into account the specific mental illness a client has and the substance they use. The many possible combinations that may exist make it necessary for a counselor to have a good understanding of a variety of issues.

Pertinent examples include:

Cannabis. There is ample evidence to show that cannabis is associated with negative mental health outcomes, such as psychosis, and long-term effects can persist even in a person who used cannabis only once (*Flor-Henry & Edmonton,* 2018). There remains, however, a serious debate about whether this connection proves that cannabis causes these disorders. The so-called causality theory on the basis that the rate of psychosis has not increased along with increases in cannabis use in recent history.

ADHD. About 25% of those who have a substance use disorder also have attention-deficit hyperactivity disorder (Nelson & Galon, 2012). People with ADHD use drugs at a younger age, and are harder to treat. Drug cravings are more intense, and success rates of treatment are lower (Nelson & Galon, 2012; SAMSHA, 2013).

Autism Spectrum Disorder. In contrast to ADHD, people with autism are far less likely to abuse substances. Being an introvert with a high level of inhibition naturally leads to that outcome, and people with autism are much less likely to engage in behavior that seeks a "high" (van Wijngaarden-Cremers, 2016). Alcohol is a type of substance abuse that does sometimes occur, and it does tend to worsen symptoms of autism spectrum disorder (SAMSHA, 2013; van Wijngaarden-Cremers, 2016).

Opioids and Pain. One of the most destructive trends in substance abuse is the misuse of opioid pain killers. The number of people using prescription opioids has increased, as has the percentage who become addicted (United States Department of Health and Human Services [USDHHS], 2016). Most national health organizations agree that the epidemic of misuse and addiction has reached crisis levels, with serious consequences for public health (NIDA, 2017). Women are prescribed opioid pain killers at much greater rates than men, and women aged 40-59 are the most likely demographic group to die from opioid overdose (Quintiles IMS Institute, 2017).

Treatment in Dual Diagnosis

© Dmytro Zinkevych/Shutterstock.com

Most people with co-occurring disorders do not receive treatment for both. According to the National Survey on Drug Use and Health (SAMHSA, 2018) an estimated 2.7 million adults aged 18 or older reported a co-occurring major depressive episode and alcohol use disorder during the previous year. Among these adults, 40.7 percent did not receive treatment for either disorder.

Several different methods may be used to treat co-occurring disorders. *Partial treatment* treats the condition that is considered most severe. *Sequential treatment* treats the most serious disorder first, then moves on to the other. *Parallel treatment* treats both conditions simultaneously, usually from two different sources. *Integrated treatment* treats both conditions and is coordinated among all providers who develop a single, coherent treatment plan incorporating all relevant

> "Addiction is about our hungers and thirsts, about our ultimate concern, about the clinging and longing of our hearts, and about giving ourselves over to these things. When it is in full cry, addiction is finally about idolatry."
> ~Cornelius Plantinga (Roberts & Talbot, 1997)

factors. Integrated treatment is considered the most reliable and effective course of action (Kelly & Daley, 2013).

EVIDENCE BASED TREATMENTS FOR SUBSTANCE ABUSE

Many critics and scholars have noted that most traditional behavioral science scholarship was undertaken by male researchers and used male subjects (Galvavani & Humphreys, 2007; Hillhouse & Fiorentine, 2001; Kulis et al., 2010; Lamberson, 2018). When treatment is considered it may be useful to remember that much research remains to be done, and there is a degree of uncertainty about how women will respond. It is wise to keep an open mind about sex and gender differences when one designs a treatment plan.

Cognitive Behavioral Therapy (CBT)

CBT is often used for clients with substance abuse and alcoholism problems. This evidence-based therapy is an effective way to help people abstain from use. This therapy considers how a person thinks, and how that connects to their behavior. The techniques used in this kind of therapy are

© BlurryMe/Shutterstock.com

an extremely important part of a client's plan for avoiding relapse (Epstein & McCrady, 2009).

At its heart, CBT therapy is a way for an individual to understand and modify how they think about themselves, the world, and other people. It also helps them understand that how they act affects their thoughts and feelings – a *cognitive* aspect and a *behavioral* aspect (Cayoun, 2011). In contrast to other forms of talk therapy, CBT focuses on immediate problems and difficulties. Rather than digging deep into past issues to explore the root causes of their problems, this approach looks for ways to improve the current state of mind (Rhodes, 2014).

- CBT is often used when addiction is combined with co-occurring issues such as anxiety, depression, social phobia, eating disorders, Obsessive Compulsive Disorder (OCD), Post-traumatic Stress Disorder (PTSD), and schizophrenia (Alladin, 2016). CBT for addiction focuses on helping clients *recognize* the situations in which they are most likely to use drugs and alcohol, *avoid* those situations when appropriate, and *cope* more effectively with a range of problems and problematic behaviors that are associated with substance abuse (Cayoun, 2011; Epstein & McCrady, 2009).
- CBT helps people break problems down into smaller parts that may be easier to handle. Techniques can include situational awareness to avoid the temptation to use, and coping mechanisms for problems and behaviors related to their substance use (Cayoun, 2011; Rhodes, 2014).

Dialectical Behavioral Therapy (DBT)

DBT is a type of cognitive behavioral therapy. The term "dialectical" comes from the idea that bringing together two opposites in therapy (*acceptance* and *change*) brings better results than either one alone (Roes, 2008). One important feature of DBT is its focus on acceptance of a patient's experience as a way for counselors to reassure them, and balance the work needed to change negative behaviors. DBT often focuses on high-risk, tough-to-treat patients. Three of the most common DBT techniques can easily be implemented into addiction treatment. These skills are mindfulness, reality acceptance, and a nonjudgement stance (Tartakovsky, 2018).

© G-Stock Studio/Shutterstock.com

The Matrix Model

The Matrix Model is a geared toward treating stimulants like methamphetamine and cocaine, and has been very successful. The Matrix Model uses many different styles of therapy, and is practiced as an intensive outpatient program (IOP). This means full days geared toward treatment, multiple days each week. The model is integrative, meaning that it combines multiple forms of therapy (CBT, Motivational Interviewing, family therapy, 12-step, etc.).

This model is highly structured, designed with planned topics and activities for each session and phase of treatment, and time-limited, designed to last for 16 weeks with an option for extension if necessary.

The ability to integrate treatment methods from the most effective styles helps make the Matrix Model a very good option for newly recovering people, or those who have not had success in previous efforts. Multiple studies have shown the benefit of this model, and many organizations including the National Institute on Drug Abuse (2019a) support its use.

Contingency Management (CM)

CM is a system of positive reinforcement in which rewards are earned by positive behavior – abstaining from use (Petry et al., 2017). One form is

Voucher-Based Reinforcement (VBR) which has been used successfully in community settings, often for people with heroin and cocaine addictions (particularly as they go through methadone detoxification). Clients get a voucher for clean drug tests, and can buy food, movie passes, etc. *Prize Incentives CM* uses cash prizes instead of vouchers. Clients earn the chance to win small cash prizes in a random drawing from a bowl, for example. Participants may also win chances to draw for attending counseling sessions and completing weekly goal-related activities (Petry et al., 2017).

Motivational Interviewing and Motivational Enhancement Therapy

Both Motivational Interviewing (MI) and Motivational Enhancement Therapy (MET) are brief, evidence-based treatments. They are used to help a person find the motivation to change. These treatments offer acceptance and compassion for clients as they begin and implement these changes (Miller & Rollnick, 2013).

Clients who engage in self-destructive behaviors may often be ambivalent or have little motivation to change their behavior, even if they understand the negative consequences of their behavior on health, family, and social functioning (Huang et al., 2011). MI is designed to empower clients to change through increased awareness of their behaviors, and by identifying appropriate goals to focus upon. MET is a more specific type of MI, based on the principles of motivational psychology (DiClemente et al., 2017).

© Kheng Guan Toh/Shutterstock.com

MET is based on five motivational principles (Miller & Rollnick, 1991; SAMSHA, 2013):

- **Express empathy:** Therapists create a supportive environment in order to help an individual feel accepted and respected, and they engage in reflective listening rather than direct confrontation. The therapist will listen to what an individual is saying and then reflect it back, with slight but deliberate modifications. The modifications both let the individual know that the therapist has heard and understood and encourage the individual to elaborate.
- **Develop discrepancy:** In MET, the therapist directs attention toward the discrepancy between an individual's desired state of being and that individual's actual state of being. This discrepancy may help aid in recognizing the ways that current behaviors hinder one from achieving goals, and it can also provide a strong incentive for behavior change.
- **Avoid argumentation:** A therapist will avoid attacking an individual or an individual's behavior, as this is thought to result in defensiveness and resistance. Other, gentler methods are used to raise awareness of any problems, and any statements regarding a need for change should come from the individual, not the therapist.
- **Roll with resistance:** Instead of directly confronting any resistance on the part of the individual, the therapist tries to defuse it, often through reflective listening or by simply going along with what an individual is saying. This approach may seem counterintuitive, but it decreases the odds of further defensiveness and may make it more likely that an individual will remain in therapy and benefit from other aspects of the intervention.
- **Support self-efficacy:** One's motivation to change typically depends not only on the reasons for modifying behavior but also on the belief that one is able to perform the tasks required for change. One aspect of a therapist's role is to help individuals become aware of their ability to successfully undertake the actions needed for change.

FIGURE 16.1

Principles of MET

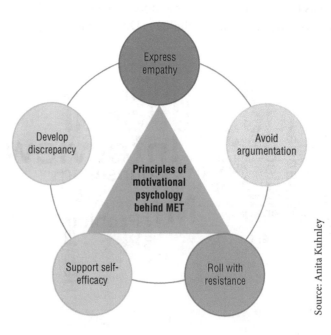

Source: Anita Kuhnley

© Asier Romero/Shutterstock.com

"Thou shalt have no other gods before me" (*New International Bible*, 1973/2011, Exodus 20:3). This is a central tenet of the Christian faith, and one that believers surely take to heart. Do not give anything else the place that belongs to God. But idolatry is often much more covert than making a conscious and visible decision to worship the golden calf instead of God. What rules your life? What has your time, attention, and resources? A person suffering from addiction almost by definition finds herself in a place where the substance is at the center of her life, occupying that prime position.

Is it possible to make that connection without introducing shame in the way we respond to addiction? It is a disorder – no one would think of accusing the sufferer of simply making the choice to put alcohol in God's place. But could it not be a component of recovery to think of framing the issue in spiritual terms, allowing ourselves to reclaim that space for God and his infinite mercy and grace?

Perhaps this is a way for counselors to relate to clients. Surely we can all understand the experience of struggling to keep the concerns of this world from pulling our attention from where it belongs; and we understand that the necessary response is not condemnation – *lift your gaze*, not *hang your head*.

What do you think? Is the concept of idols and false gods one that can be used productively when understanding and treating addiction?

Family Behavior Therapy (FBT)

FBT addresses multiple issues in addition to addiction, such as conflict in families, behavior issues, and other issues one would expect to encounter in a family therapy setting. The therapy involves the patient along with at least one significant other, such as a cohabiting partner or a parent (in the case of adolescents). The counselor includes family members in using the techniques discussed during meetings, with the goal of improving the home environment with new skills. During each session, behavioral goals are reviewed, and rewards may be provided by significant others when goals are accomplished (Lambert et al., 2018).

Twelve-Step Facilitation Therapy

Modified from © iQoncept/Shutterstock.com

Twelve-step facilitation therapy is the most well-known recovery system for substance abuse. Twelve step programs allow those in recovery gain support from others who are also struggling. Many who successfully practice abstinence from their substance of choice remain in twelve-step groups for life. The most widely known of these groups are Alcoholics Anonymous (AA) and Narcotics Anonymous (NA).

Twelve-step programs are so widely available, and their methods are so well-known, many treatment centers use their methods alongside many other of the techniques presented here. Since the steps of the program are based in spiritual principles, many patients develop or strengthen their spiritual beliefs. The most famous statement of belief associated with twelve-step programs is the serenity prayer, originally understood to have been originally composed by theologian Reinhold Niebuhr (Shapiro, 2014). The version most commonly used is:

God grant me the Serenity to accept the things I cannot change,
Courage to change the things I can,
and Wisdom to know the difference.

For Christians, a powerful component of recovery is expressed in the willingness to surrender one's will to God, an idea that is actively encouraged by twelve-step program methods. Overall, three key ideas animate twelve-step methodology:

- **Acceptance**: the belief that addiction is a disease that a person cannot control, that continuing the use of substances has caused life to become unmanageable, and that willpower alone is insufficient to enable abstinence.
- **Surrender:** giving oneself over to a higher power and accepting the necessity of being supported by other recovering addicts in the program.
- **Active involvement** in 12-step meetings.

While the efficacy of 12-step programs (and 12-step facilitation) in treating alcohol dependence has been established, the research on its usefulness for other forms of substance abuse is still ongoing with mixed results, but the treatment appears promising for helping drug abusers sustain recovery (Giannelli et al., 2019). Research also has shown that twelve-step programs work at least as well for women as for men. Some studies have indicated that women are more likely than men to join twelve-step programs, and several have concluded that women get *more* benefits from programs than men (Hillhouse & Fiorentine, 2001; Rush, 2002).

The many treatment strategies available for different kinds of clients show that a counselor must be comfortable with many different approaches to treating addiction. While this creates a challenge for those who are learning the field, it enables counselors to exercise creativity and gives them the flexibility to tailor each client's treatment to their unique situation.

CASE STUDY: SUSIE

© Couperfield/Shutterstock.com

Susie's substance use began at the age of 19, when she was a student at a prestigious ivy league college. To help pay her expenses, she took a job at a nightclub, where she drank for free with co-workers after hours – and in short order the drinking was happening every night. Susie was smart and academically gifted enough to maintain her GPA and graduate, but she had become a full-fledged alcoholic. She drank while working, after hours, and before work during the day. She moved on from her home state to California to attend graduate school in one of the most highly ranked programs in her field. There, her lifestyle brought her into a relationship with Hank, who introduced her to heroin. They dated for a year before getting married. Six months after the wedding, Hank was killed in a car accident while under the influence.

Susie was left broken, addicted, and suicidal. She entered counseling, and finally confronted some of the factors that left her susceptible to the life she had been living. Her mother was an alcoholic. Her parents constantly pushed her to excel, even while her mother inflicted emotional abuse and her father neglected her emotionally.

Recovery first focused on getting Susie sober. She went to inpatient detox for four weeks, and was treated with methadone for heroin and alcohol withdrawal. Her counselor came for sessions in the treatment facility twice a week, and she attended three to four group sessions each day.

After inpatient treatment came an intensive outpatient program. The program featured daily group sessions, and she still saw her counselor twice a week. The counselor's strategy included Motivational Interviewing and Cognitive Behavioral Therapy, with a focus on family of origin issues. This strategy helped Susie break the cognitions that had held her self-esteem at rock-bottom since childhood. Susie also found a supportive AA group and religious community to support and not judge her as she worked through her recovery. One of Susie's most important reflections about this process is about her fear that she would be judged or condemned if she joined a church community. Instead of condemnation, she felt the 'gentleness' of restoration described in the letter to the Galatians, and that her church community had a genuine desire to "bear each other's burdens in love" (Galatians 6:1). Seven years later, Susie is still sober. She reports that alcohol is still a temptation, but heroin is not. Her own summary of the most important things she has confronted is how she never formed healthy attachments to her parents, and how their abuse and poor role modeling contributed to her addiction. Finding a spiritual center, supportive AA group, and consistent counselor to follow alongside her have been critical to recovery.

CHAPTER SUMMARY

Substance abuse is an ever-present problem, leaving 10 percent of the population addicted to drugs or alcohol. There are important differences in how these problems affect women compared to men. Women reach intoxication more quickly and have a shorter time frame from initial use to health problems and misuse. Women also face different social consequences and are motivated to use substances by different factors than men. Women relapse at greater rates than men when recovering, and are more likely to overdose when using. Women's psychological, physiological, and social experiences need to be understood by the counseling profession.

When counselors work with women who have substance use disorders, it is important to consider the possibility of co-occurring disorders and dual diagnoses. Counselors should be especially vigilant for the signs and symptoms of depression, anxiety, bipolar disorder, and PTSD. Treatment may take many forms, and counselors should be conversant in many different techniques depending on the needs of each client.

With addiction, counselors often encounter denial and resistance. Christians may find great benefit in Jesus's example (see Philippians 2) as we humble ourselves to do His work with those who may feel like "the least of these".

KEY TERMS

Addiction - an inability to stop using a chemical, drug, activity, or substance, despite harm or injury that the use is causing

Dual Diagnosis - the presence of a mental illness and substance abuse

Intoxication - a result of the intake of psychoactive substances that results in impairment of consciousness, thoughts, emotions, responses and behaviors

Physical Dependence - physical condition that develops as a result of chronic use to the point of unpleasant symptoms developing during steady or rapid withdrawal

Telescoping - enhanced movement from initial use to dependence in women

Tolerance - diminishing effect from substance abuse use that happens over time with the need to increase the consumption of the substance to acquire desired effect

Withdrawal - emotional and/or physical reaction (may be severe) when a substance is discontinued

SUGGESTED RESOURCES

Organizations

SAMHSA Peer Recovery Support Services: https://store.samhsa.gov/product/What-Are-Peer-Recovery-Support-Services-/SMA09-4454

SAMHSA Focus on Prevention: https://store.samhsa.gov/product/Focus-on-Prevention/sma10-4120

HHS Office on Women's Health: https://women.smokefree.gov/ https://www.womenshealth.gov/

NIH Office of Research on Women's Health (ORWH)

Research: https://orwh.od.nih.gov/research

Treatment: https://www.drugabuse.gov/related-topics/treatment

U.S. Food and Drug Administration: www.fda.gov/womens

Toolkit

Opioid Epidemic Practical Toolkit: https://www.hhs.gov/sites/default/files/hhs-partnership-ctr-opioid-practical-toolkit-unremediated.pdf

Treatment Centers

To find a publicly funded treatment center in your state, call 1-800-662-HELP or visit: https://findtreatment.samhsa.gov/

REFERENCES

Ait-Daoud, N., Blevins, D., Khanna, S., & Sharma, S. (2017). Women and addiction. *Journal of Psychiatric clinics of North America, 40*(2), 285-297.

Alladin, A. (2016). *Integrative CBT for anxiety disorders: An evidence-based approach to enhancing cognitive behavioural therapy with mindfulness and hypnotherapy.* Wiley.

American Psychiatric Association. (2013). *Diagnostic and statistical manual of mental disorders* (5th ed.). https://doi.org/10.1176/appi.books.9780890425596

Answer Addiction. (2017). *Addiction terms, phrases, and definitions*. https://www. answeraddiction.com/alcohol-and-drug-abuse-resources/addiction-glossary/

Bersani, G., & Prevete, E. (2017). Novel psychoactive substances (NPS) use in severe mental illness (SMI) patients: Potential changes in the phenomenology of psychiatric diseases. *Human Psychopharmacology, 32*(3), 1-5.

Capuzzi, D., & Stauffer, M. (2016). *Foundations of addictions counseling* (3rd ed.). Pearson Education.

Cayoun, B. (2011). *Mindfulness-integrated CBT: Principles and practice*. Wiley-Blackwell.

Center for Behavioral Health Statistics and Quality. (2017). *Results from the 2016 national survey on drug use and health: Detailed tables*. Substance Abuse and Mental Health Services Administration. https://www.samhsa.gov/data/sites/default/files/NSDUH-DetTabs-2016/NSDUH-DetTabs-2016.pdf.

Centers for Disease Control and Prevention. (2017). *Annual surveillance report of drug-related risks and outcomes: United States, 2017*. https://www.cdc.gov/drugoverdose/pdf/pubs/2017-cdc-drug-surveillance-report.pdf

Clements, T. (2011). Substance abuse and behavioral addictions. In T. Clinton, & R. Hawkins (Eds.), *The popular encyclopedia of Christian counseling: An indispensable tool for helping people with their problems* (pp. 375-388). Harvest House Publishers.

Delker, B. C., & Freyd, J. J. (2014). From betrayal to the bottle: Investigating possible pathways from trauma to problematic substance use. *Journal of Traumatic Stress, 27*, 576-584.

DiClemente, C., Corno, C., Graydon, M., Wiprovnick, A., & Knoblach, D. (2017). Motivational interviewing, enhancement, and brief interventions over the last decade: A Review of reviews of efficacy and effectiveness. *Psychology of Addictive Behaviors, 31*(8), 862-887.

Epstein, E. E., & McCrady, B. S. (2009). *A cognitive-behavioral treatment program for overcoming alcohol problems: Therapist guide*. Oxford University Press.

Erickson, E., Blednov, Y., Harris, R., & Mayfield, D. (2008). Glial gene networks associated with alcohol dependence. *Scientific Reports*, (9), 1-13.

Flor-Henry, P., & Edmonton, A. (2018). Brain changes during cannabis-induced psychosis: Clarifying the marijuana medicine/harm dichotomy. *Journal of Psychiatry and Brain Science, 23*(3), 239-252.

Galvani, S., & Humphreys, C. (2007). *The impact of violence and abuse on engagement and retention rates for women in substance use treatment*. National Treatment Agency.

Giannelli, E., Gold, C., Bieleninik, L., Ghetti, C., & Gelo, O. (2019). Dialectical behaviour therapy and 12-step programmes for substance use disorder: A systematic review and meta-analysis. *Counselling and Psychotherapy Research, 19*(3), 274-285.

Greenfield, S., Back, S., Lawson, K., & Brady, K. (2011). Substance abuse in women. *Psychiatric Clinics of North American, 33*(2), 339-355.

Hart, C., & Ksir, C. (2015). *Drugs, society, and human behavior* (16th ed.). McGraw-Hill.

Harvard Medical School. (2010, January). *Addiction in women.* Harvard Mental Health Newsletter. https://www.health.harvard.edu/newsletter_article/addiction-in-women.

Hawkings, C., & Gilburt, H. (2004). *Dual diagnosis toolkit.* Rethink and Turning Point Services. https://amhp.org.uk/app/uploads/2017/08/dualdiagnosistoolkit.pdf.

Hillhouse, M., & Fiorentine, R. (2001). 12-step program participation and effectiveness: Do gender and ethnic differences exist? *Journal of Drug Issues, 31*(3), 767-780.

Huang, Y., Tang, T., Lin, C., & Yen, C. (2011). Effects of motivational enhancement therapy on readiness to change MDMA and methamphetamine use behaviors in Taiwanese adolescents. *Substance Use & Misuse, 46,* 411–416.

Kelly, T., & Daley, D. (2013). *Integrated treatment of substance use and psychiatric disorders.* Social Work in Public Health, *28*(0), 388-406.

Kulis, S., Marsiglia, F., & Nagoshi, J. (2010). Gender roles, externalizing behaviors, and substance use among Mexican-American adolescents. *Journal of Social Work Practice in the Addictions, 10*(3), 283-307.

Lamberson, K. (2018). Sociological theory. In P. Lassiter, & J. Culbreth (Eds.), *Theory and practice of addiction counseling* (pp. 161-176). Sage.

Lambert, S. F., Utnterberg, H., & Riggo, M. (2018). Family systems theory. In P. Lassiter, & J. Culbreth (Eds.), *Theory and practice of addiction counseling* (pp. 177-197). Sage.

Miller, W. R., & Carroll, K. M. (2019). *Rethinking substance abuse: What the science shows, and what we should do about it.* Guilford Publications.

Miller, W. R., & Rollnick, S. (1991). *Motivational interviewing: Preparing people to change addictive behavior.* Guilford.

Miller, W., & Rollnick, S. (2013). *Motivational interviewing: Helping people change* (3rd ed.). Guilford.

National Center for Drug Abuse Statistics. (2019). *Drug abuse statistics.* https://drugabusestatistics.org/

National Institute of Drug Abuse. (2017). *Opioid crisis.* https://www.drugabuse.gov/drugs-abuse/opioids/opioid-crisis.

National Institute on Drug Abuse. (2019a). *Substance use in women.* https://www.drugabuse.gov/publications/drugfacts/substance-use-in-women

National Institute on Drug Abuse. (2019b). *Women and drugs.* https://www.drugabuse.gov/related-topics/women-drugs

National Organization for Women. (2018). *Black women and sexual violence.* https://now.org/wp-content/uploads/2018/02/Black-Women-and-Sexual-Violence-6.pdf

Nelson, A., & Galon, P. (2012). Exploring the relationship among ADHD, stimulants and substance abuse. *Journal of Child and Adolescent Psychiatric Nursing, 25*(3), 113-118.

New International Bible. (2011). New International Bible Online. https://www.thenivbible.com/ (Original work published 1973).

Peters, T. J., Millward, L., & Foster J. (2013). Quality of life in alcohol misuse: Comparison of men and women. *Archives of Women's Mental Health, 6*(4), 239–243.

Petry, N., Alessi, S., Olmstead, T., Rash, C., & Zajac, K. (2017). Contingency management treatment for substance use disorders: How far has it come, and where does it need to go? *Psychology of Addictive Behaviors, 31*(8), 897-906.

QuintilesIMS Institute. (2017). *An analysis of the impact of opioid overprescribing in America.* https://www.planagainstpain.com/wpcontent/uploads/2017/09/PlanAgainstPain_USND.pdf

Rhodes, J. (2014). *Narrative CBT: distinctive features.* Routledge.

Roberts, R., & Talbot, M. (Eds.). (1997). *Limning the psyche: Explorations in Christian psychology.* Eerdman's.

Roes, N. (2008). DBT fits well in addiction treatment. *Addiction Professional, 6*(6), 35-36.

Ruiz, P., & Strain, E. (2014). *Substance abuse handbook.* Wolters Kluwer Health Publishers.

Rush, M. (2002). Perceived social support: Dimensions of social interaction among sober female participants in Alcoholics Anonymous. *Journal of the American Psychiatric Nurses Association, 8*(4), 114-119.

Shapiro, F. R. (2014, April 28). *Who wrote the serenity prayer?* The Chronicle Review. https://www.chronicle.com/article/Who-Wrote-the-Serenity-Prayer-/146159/

Stankovic, M., & Trikos, L. (2008). Cognitive impairment and severity of alcohol consumption *European Psychiatry, 23*(2), 321-322.

Substance Abuse and Mental Health Services Administration. (2013). Substance abuse treatment for persons with co-occurring disorders. *Treatment Improvement Protocol (TIP) Series, 42.* https://store.samhsa.gov/system/files/sma13-3992.pdf

Substance Abuse and Mental Health Services Administration. (2018). *Results from the 2017 national survey on drug use and health: Detailed table.* https://www.samhsa.gov/data/sites/default/files/cbhsq-reports/NSDUHDetailedTabs2017/NSDUH DetailedTabs2017.pdf.

Substance Abuse and Mental Health Services Administration. (2019). Substance abuse treatment: Addressing the specific needs of women. *Treatment Improvement Protocol (TIP) Series, 51.* https://store.samhsa.gov/system/files/sma13-4788.pdf.

Tartakovsky, M. (2018). *3 DBT skills everyone can benefit from.* https://psychcentral.com/blog/3-dbt-skills-everyone-can-benefit-from/

U.S. Department of Health and Human Services. (2016). *Opioid epidemic practical toolkit: Helping faith and community leaders bring hope and healing to our communities.* https://www.hhs.gov/about/agencies/iea/partnerships/opioid-toolkit/index.html

U.S. Department of Health and Human Services. (2017, April 19). *Secretary Price announces HHS strategy for fighting opioid crisis.* https://www.hhs.gov/about/leadership/secretary/speeches/2017-speeches/secretary-price-announces-hhs-strategy-for-fighting-opioid-crisis/index.html

United States Department of Justice Drug Enforcement Administration. (2019). *Lists of scheduling actions, controlled substances, regulated chemicals.* Drug and Chemical Evaluation Section (DRE), Diversion Control Division. https://www.deadiversion.usdoj.gov/schedules/orangebook/orangebook.pdf#search=drug%20scheduling

Van Vliet-Ruissen, C., McKinlay, A., & Taylor, A. (2014). Adult functioning of mothers with traumatic brain injury at high risk of child abuse: A pilot study. *NeuroRehabilitation, 34*(2), 373-380.

van Wijngaarden-Cremers, P. (2016). Autism and substance use comorbidity: Screening identification and treatment. *European Psychiatry, 33*, 21-22.

Watson, J., Fayter, D., Mdege N., Stirk, L., Sowden, A. J., & Godfrey, C. (2013). Interventions for alcohol and drug problems in outpatients' settings: A systematic review. *Drug and Alcohol Review, 32*(4), 356-367.

Winnington, J. (2010). Women and dual diagnosis. In P. Philips, O. McKewn, & T. Sandord (Eds.), *Dual diagnosis: Practice in context* (pp. 130-138). Wiley-Blackwell Publishing Ltd.

World Health Organization. (2018). *Management of substance abuse: Acute intoxication.* https://www.who.int/substance_abuse/terminology/acute_intox/en/

CHAPTER 17

Counseling Women with Sexual and Pornography Addiction

REBECCA WALDENSTROM, PH.D.

"Never trade temporary pleasure for permanent regret." (Davewillis.org)

"Guard your heart above all else, for it determines the course of your life."
(Proverbs 4:23, NLT)

Wisdom from Above: Standing in His Grace

© Daniilantiq/Shutterstock.com

Shhhhhh….The words *pornography addiction* are not ones that we like to talk about in social circles, and especially in church circles. It is certainly not a topic that women think is appropriate dinner conversation. Hence, a reason sexual addiction and pornography go untreated. We are uncomfortable talking about it; therefore, women feel ashamed.

From the beginning of time, sin has permeated our hearts, minds, and souls. When you read about Eve in Genesis 3:1 ("The serpent was the shrewdest of all the wild animals the Lord God had made. One day he asked the woman, 'Did God really say you must not eat the fruit from any of the trees in the garden?'" [*New Living Bible*, 1996]), she was tempted by the enemy to take something the Lord said was forbidden. God's restriction was not a punishment, but rather a protection. Yet, the enemy convinced her she was missing out. We know her disobedience was devastating to herself, to Adam, and to ultimately mankind. Christ came to this earth and died for our sins. Sin essentially started with impulse control, which led to disobedience. Just as Eve was forbidden to eat from the tree of knowledge of good and evil, God has also placed limits on what we should and should not do when it comes to sexual behavior. It is not that he wants to withhold from us, but rather he wants to protect us from what he knows will bring devastation to our personal thoughts, desires, and relationships.

CHAPTER LEARNING OBJECTIVES

Upon completing this chapter, you should be able to:

- Recognize causes, symptoms, and definitions of addiction
- Assess the signs and symptoms of addiction
- Assess the correlation between addiction and other mental health disorders
- Identify best treatment options for sexual addiction in women
- Know what Scripture says about sexual dysfunction, addiction, and intimacy

© Carlos E. Santa Maria/Shutterstock.com

CHAPTER OVERVIEW

Sexual addiction is an increasing problem in our culture, and not just for men, but also for women. This is a human issue, and an emerging global problem. (Carlisle et al., 2016). We as Christian counselors can try to bury our head in the sand and pretend this is not an issue for women, but that simply is not true. Our job as counselors is to acknowledge this issue, educate others about it, and advocate for women to get help if they suffer from it.

None of us are immune to being drawn into an inappropriate relationship and/or behavior. It happens more than we think, and because it is considered taboo, it is often kept secret. Unfortunately, women may suffer in silence for a significant length of time due to the secrecy of the problem. Addiction, specifically pornography addiction, starts off slowly and subtly. Anyone with an addiction will tell you it started with an "it can't happen to me" or an "I will be different" statement. Unfortunately, once a woman starts down the slippery slope of pornography, it is difficult to stop. Before she knows it, she requires more and more stimuli to satisfy her desires.

People, and women specifically, may look to pornography or to the Internet because it provides an outlet for their fantasies that cannot be provided by their primary partner (Atwood & Schwartz, 2002). However, sexual addiction is dangerous to all domains of development including, the mind, body, and soul (Phillips et al., 2015). It impacts every aspect of a woman's life, but pornography, unlike other poisons, is not labeled as life threatening. In this chapter, you will learn about gender differences in addiction, the definition of sexual addiction, and treatment options.

GENDER DIFFERENCES

How are women different than men relative to sexual addiction? What are the signs a woman is headed down a bad road? These are questions to think about when counseling women with reported compulsive sexual behaviors.

Women often participate in sexual activities due to dysfunction in relationships, role expectations, and cultural influences (Clayton & Kornstein, 2002; Kopala & Keitel, 2017). Women are often looking for connectedness and affection, and therefore begin looking to outside sources for a definition of love and passion, especially if they feel their needs are not being met with their partner. Women want to be validated, and your client may report she started engaging in compulsive sexual behavior because she felt invisible or unappreciated. She may not feel anyone sees her, or she may believe past experiences have made her unlovable. Her behavior may be related to self-worth, identity, or even past abuse and trauma (Harvey & Vigorito, 2015).

A woman may only come to counseling after realizing the devastating effects of pornography. She may recognize she is suffering from impulse control and other maladaptive behaviors that are impacting her interpersonal relationships, goals, and activities (Reid, 2015). It will be important for the counselor to assess the reasons for behavior prior to creating a treatment plan. If your client is engaging in sexual behavior due to abuse and/or trauma, it is imperative you have training in these issues, and understand treatment outcomes for disorders such as post-traumatic stress disorder (PTSD).

DEFINITION OF THE PROBLEM

A diagnosis is given to classify behavior and provides some tentative causes and explanation of symptoms. In addition, a diagnosis is provided so an individual gains an understanding of their behavioral patterns. It can also be used to assist the client in seeking appropriate treatment options. It is important to remember that a diagnosis is not static, but rather is a dynamic process and provides an explanation regarding the client's progress or setback in functioning. It is an important part of the treatment process (Sanders, 2013).

Issues to be considered when deciding on a diagnosis are related to behaviors that interfere with daily functioning and course of treatment. There must be evidence of disruption of cognitive and/or emotional functioning for a mental disorder to be diagnosed. A clinician will determine a diagnosis based on *DSM-5* criteria. While clients may not experience any given diagnosis the same way as other individuals, a diagnosis must meet diagnostic requirements. The *DSM* provides specific diagnostic guidelines about age, time frames, and patterns of behavior. The *DSM* also provides information about differential and provisional diagnoses. Therefore, a clinician should consult with the *DSM* if there is a question on how to present more than one diagnosis.

So, what is sexual addiction? Does watching pornography mean you have a mental health disorder? Is pornography harmful? These are questions you may be asked as a professional counselor. They do not present with easy answers, and even those in the counseling field cannot agree on how to define sexual addiction (Kaplan & Krueger, 2010; Kraus et al., 2016; Rosenberg et al., 2014).

The *DSM-5* does not have a definitive diagnosis for sexual addiction; therefore, counselors and clinicians continue to debate, and are often confused, as to how to proceed with diagnostics. One problem with sexual addiction is the lack of agreement on diagnosis due to limited scientific classification of this issue (Hughes, 2012). The problem with defining this issue, is while most clinicians treat it as an addiction, there is no solid consensus among professionals as to whether or not it could also be an impulse control problem, an obsessive-compulsive disorder, or brain disease (Barrilleaux, 2016). While the *DSM-5* has criteria on both obsessive-compulsive disorder and addiction, it does not categorize pornography or sexual addiction specifically under either category. Due to the lack of consensus clinicians, will often treat it as an addiction, There is no definitive criteria in diagnosing sexual addiction; however, factors to consider are excessiveness, frequency and duration of behavior, level of impairment in interpersonal relationships, consequences of behavior, level of risk taking, and cravings and urges (Reid, 2015; Tubino-Scanavino et al., 2013).

The American Society of Addiction Medicine (ASAM) defines addiction this way: "Addiction is a treatable, chronic medical disease involving complex interactions among brain circuits, genetics, the environment, and an individual's life experiences. People with addiction use substances or engage in behaviors that become compulsive and often continue despite harmful consequences" (ASAM, 2019, para. 1). Clients are often classified as "hypersexual", and the counselor may have difficulty determining if sexual addiction is the primary condition, or rather a symptom of another presenting mental health disorder. Some counselors diagnose a woman with obsessive-compulsive disorder, rather than with an addiction, because she is unable to stop her behavior and it impairs functioning. Those who adhere to the impulse control and obsessive disorder criteria describe the behavior as "impulsive and obsessive, and often includes the feeling of craving. There is often interference with life (work, relationships, hobbies, etc.), repeated attempts to control or quit the behavior, development of tolerance, and withdrawal symptoms (Phillips et al., 2015, p. 168).

Regardless of diagnosis whether it be compulsion, hypersexual activity, or addiction, treatment should focus on the symptoms. Due to the difficulty in determining a diagnosis, and lack of consensus among professionals, treating the symptoms will ensure the client is getting the best guidance from the counselor. Typically, treatment consists of individual therapy (most often cognitive behavioral therapy), group therapy, and/or peer support groups (Rosenberg et al., 2014). It is important for the counselor and the client to work together to identify triggers, learn strategies to

manage symptoms, work on conflict resolution, and focus on other mental health issues that may be the result of the said addiction or compulsion (Rosenberg et al., 2014). Clinicians, who want to specialize in treating sexual dysfunction and pornography related disorders, should be trained in how to recognize substance use, compulsion, and addiction (Hartman et al., 2012).

It is also important to note that those who work in neuroscience believe sexual addiction is a brain disorder due to the impairment in behavior and the continued craving for new experiences (Gola et al., 2017; Goleman, 2011). How does one undo what they have seen, and how do you replace behaviors that have brought pleasure? Sexual addiction, specifically an addiction to pornography, is difficult to overcome due to the visual process associated with brain activity. We know from research that the brain is literally re-wired when you engage in pornography (Gola et al., 2017). Continued exposure prohibits one to interact in relationships in a healthy manner. Healthy relationships are built on trust and impulse control, as well as the ability to express feelings and relate to another person (Goleman, 2011). Continued exposure to pornography inhibits the ability to interact in a healthy manner, and this is related to executive functioning impairment.

One of the reasons a woman will engage in sexual behavioral is because it brings temporary pleasure. Often it is done in private, and therefore a woman thinks nobody will know. However, the temporary pleasure can bring about long-term consequences and even permanent relationship damage. Therefore, treating sexual addiction is complex because every domain of development is impacted. A woman who is addicted to pornography is impacted physically, socially, psychologically, and spiritually (Phillips et al., 2015). It impacts the brain, creates an emotional attachment to images that cannot be obtained, causes rifts within interpersonal relationships, and separates us from a close relationship with God. The brain is made up of complex functional structures that are interwoven and overlapping. One division of the brain does not act alone. This is important to remember when working with someone with maladaptive behavior. Pornography use provides a short-term reward to the brain and body, making it difficult to treat and replace behavior.

DISCRIMINATION AGAINST WOMEN WITH SEXUAL ADDICTION

Studies indicate that gender bias is evidenced in personality assessment techniques and self-report inventories (Hersen & Turner, 2003; Reddick & Heiden-Rootes, 2016; Widiger & Samuel, 2005). Clinicians who rely on these evaluations to assist in clinical diagnostics may be using biased tools to assess dysfunction and addiction. Therefore, practitioners who do not conduct a comprehensive evaluation may inadvertently misdiagnose women, or not recognize symptoms effectively. Why is this important? Because research shows women who report maladaptive sexual activity are often discriminated against, even by counselors and those in the helping professions. Studies show the counselor often views behaviors associated with sexual addiction by females more negatively than with their male counterparts. Female clients who are in non-monogamous relationships and maladaptive sexual behaviors are treated differently, and are often reported as more difficult, annoying and resistive (Reddick & Heiden-Rootes, 2016, p. 547). There is a stigma associated with pornography use, especially in the female population. It is not typically thought of as a woman's issue. Therefore, some women will not initially report all their symptoms, or may try to pass their issue off as another disorder, such as depression, anxiety, or even relationship issues.

Gender bias is especially important to identify due to treatment interventions. If a diagnosis has been made based on gender stereotypes or bias, then ultimately the treatment plan will be altered (Hersen & Turner, 2003). This is unhelpful for the client and could compound the problem of personal dysfunction. Therefore, it is important for clinicians to be aware of bias and diagnose sexual addiction after a comprehensive interview and evaluation of the client.

CONCEPT TO CONTEMPLATE

Due to gender bias related to sexual addiction, your job as a counselor is to educate and advocate for this issue. Although it is an uncomfortable topic, you must be willing to dialogue, even in churches and Christian circles, about the dangers of pornography, and the increasing numbers of women engaging in maladaptive sexual behavior. Please think about how you, as a future counselor, will combat bias. How can you present this information to an audience that is reluctant to hear it?

STATISTICS

A recent study found that pornography use is reported by approximately six percent of the general population (Gola & Potenza, 2018). You may have heard women say, "this is a man's issue, so we don't need to talk about it"; however, in a study by the secular magazine *Marie Claire,* 1/3 of women confessed to watching pornography at least once a week, with 35% of Internet downloads being pornographic in nature (Willis, 2019). Pornography is available anytime, anywhere, due to the accessibility of the Internet on laptops, tablets, and phones. Pornography is also widely available, as research shows that "30% of all Internet data is related to pornography. Porn sites receive more visitors than Amazon, Netflix, and Twitter combined. The leading pornography site, Xvideos, receives an estimated 4.4 million viewers per month" (Negash et al., 2016, p. 690).

These statistics give us a glimpse into the problem; however, it is important to note they may not be entirely accurate. We know pornography and maladaptive sexual behavior are difficult topics to talk about; therefore, women who are addicted to pornography or other destructive sexual behaviors may not have reported the issue due to embarrassment, guilt, and/or shame.

SEXUAL ADDICTION AND MENTAL HEALTH

Sexual addiction and compulsive sexual behaviors (CSB) are often treated when a client reports continued use of pornography, excessive masturbation, and/or multiple casual partners (Tubino-Scanavino et al., 2013). These are the symptoms a clinician wants to assess, and any one of the above will direct the treatment planning.

For a therapist to be effective in counseling a woman with sexual and/or pornography addiction, rapport must be established quickly. It is essential your client trust that you will not approach the subject with judgment (McMinn, 2011). Listening without judgment does not mean we condone the behavior. We may need to use a soft confrontation within the course of treatment, realizing that a woman will not talk about her addiction if she feels she is going to be judged or condemned. Yet, this is often what happens when they approach a pastor or spiritual counselor. Due to moral standards, it is not always acceptable for a woman to talk about her sexual issues in the open, especially in Christian counseling settings. So, she keeps it a secret, and therefore does not receive the help she needs.

© Antonio Guillem/Shutterstock.com

THERAPEUTIC ALLIANCE AND ASSESSMENT

Due to the secret nature of pornography and sexual addiction, there is often guilt and shame, which can lead to mental health disorders such as depression, anxiety, compulsion, and substance use. This is why a counselor must assess for other disorders. It is also important to note a woman may come to counseling for depression or anxiety only to reveal that her symptoms are related to compulsive sexual behaviors.

Working with someone who appears to have engaged in immoral behavior is something a counselor will face (Sanders, 2013). Helpers who have difficulty in treating someone who presents with behaviors that are often considered immoral should consult with their supervisor and/or a colleague. You will not be able to effectively help a woman who presents with a sexual addiction if you have an attitude of judgment. It is important a counselor work through their own issues and bias prior to treating women who present with compulsive sexual behaviors.

In the exploration and intake stage, it is best to use "why" questions minimally, or not use them at all (Petersen, 2015). Asking open ended questions can provide a great deal of information and prevent the client from simply responding "yes" or "no" during the initial interviewing sessions. Asking "why" questions can make the client feel defensive, and can make the helper appear critical (Petersen, 2015). Open-ended questions that are reflective or probing are more effective in engaging a client in conversation and exploring feelings about varying topics. The exploration stage is to build trust. It is best if the client does not feel defensive in the first stage of helping, but rather perceive warmth and interest from the counselor. Asking "why" questions should only be used as the helping process develops and the client begins to gain insight about their feelings and circumstances. Once entering that aspect of the therapeutic process, the client has built a trusting relationship with her helper and will not perceive criticism as easily as when the relationship is new and in the first processes of exploration.

Look beyond the behavior and see the need.

So why do women seek help? The counselor must be aware that many women will come to the session with another presenting problem, such as depression and or anxiety. She may not reveal in the opening session that addiction is what is driving the need for help. However, she is not functioning in her daily routine and relationships. She may even come to the office for marital problems, only to disclose that her own addiction is contributing to marital dysfunction.

There is a bumper sticker that says, "It's only kinky the first time". When you read this, what are your thoughts? Does this make you feel uncomfortable? What is your response if a client makes this type of statement? How will you combat bias in the counseling session?

Comfort levels with discussing feelings openly and honestly in a counseling session may be influenced by one's culture and family background (Clayton & Kornstein, 2002). A woman who comes from a culture that does not openly discuss feelings may not be as open to discussing her sexual activity. You may also find women who come from conservative, Christian backgrounds may be embarrassed about their behavior. Feelings and emotions, however, are crucial to an individual's perceptions, and ultimately her everyday experiences (Hill, 2004, p. 145). The ability to convey feelings and emotions is important in making progress in the helping process and gain insight for effective change. Therefore, rapport must be established quickly. Without trust, goals will not be established, and treatment will be ineffective.

© panitanphoto/Shutterstock.com

Depression and Anxiety

It is imperative counselors assess for depression and anxiety at intake and in every subsequent counseling session. Clinical depression and anxiety, although separate disorders, are similar in that they present with distinct symptoms that impair functioning (Clinton & Langberg, 2011). If the client is presenting with depression, it will be important to assess for the severity of impairment and whether the client can work on higher-level goals. A referral to a psychiatrist may be needed for temporary medication management, if the client is not able to function in her daily routine and relationships. A client will not be able to address addiction if her depression is the primary condition. It is important for the counselor to assess whether the depression is chronic or is an underlying issue related to guilt, shame, and impulse control. Please refer to the chapters on depression and anxiety for further information on how to assess and treat this specific disorder.

Compulsions

As stated earlier in the chapter, sexual addictions are often considered compulsions and/or impulses that are classified under obsessive-compulsive disorder (OCD). Please refer to the *DSM-5* for specific criteria on diagnosing OCD. Addiction may present with fears of acting out in such fantasies or impulses (Barrilleaux, 2016). Therefore, sexual addiction is difficult to diagnose, because there is no consensus of what it is and how to treat it. Counselors do not know whether to treat the compulsions or address cognitive processing of pleasure associated with visual processing.

Substance Use

It is not uncommon for a woman who is addicted to pornography to also find herself addicted to alcohol and or other drugs/substances. Often clients will resort to using chemical substances to cope with the guilt and shame of their sexual issues, which then in turn may lead to substance dependence (Hartman et al., 2012). It is important to recognize the signs and symptoms of substance use. Most states require a counselor to have extensive training in substance use before engaging in treatment for this issue. If you suspect your client is abusing or addicted to substances, please consult with a supervisor or colleague on best treatment options for co-occurring disorders (having both a mental health issue AND a substance abuse issue).

Physical Health

Assessing physical health is especially important for women. Every client should have a full medical work up to rule out any conditions such as thyroid, hormone, diabetes or heart condition that can alter mood and contribute to maladaptive behavior.

Mental Health

Client mental health, particularly the presence of suicidal or homicidal ideations, is important to assess in every session. It is often required to be documented in case notes in a formal tracking system. It is also important to note that stress can be a trigger for hypersexual activity, impulse control issues, and pornography (Brewer & Tidy, 2017).

Any of the above can hinder treatment and should be assessed within the first session. This is especially true because as noted in this chapter, sexual addiction impacts all domains of development and can coincide with other physical and mental health disorders.

TREATMENT OPTIONS

Cognitive Behavioral Therapy

According to research out of the University of California, pornography uses two powerful parts of the body that are not sexual in nature—the eyes and the mind (Arthur, 2005, p. 201). Once images are seen, they get locked in the brain, (Arthur, 2005). These images then continue to replay over in the memory screen, which then leads to arousal for the viewer. This explains why pornography is so addictive and why changing thought processes is so important. It should be noted that due to the visual processes and brain impact of this behavior, treatment can be extensive, and it is not uncommon for the client to have setbacks.

Cognitive behavioral therapy is a treatment modality that can help a woman change her thought processes about sex and impulsive behavior. Cognitive behavioral therapy can be an effective treatment modality because the focus is to change thinking and acting rather than only expressing causes of feelings (Murdock, 2013). Rational emotive behavior therapy (also referred to as REBT) is a form of cognitive behavioral therapy in which the client is taught to change behavior by adjusting their thought processes and belief systems about life events. Regardless of using traditional CBT or

© Monkey Business Images/Shutterstock.com

REBT, the client must be motivated for change for treatment to be effective (Harvey & Vigorito, 2015). Someone with sexual compulsive behaviors must be willing to look internally at causes, triggers, emotions, and even trauma that may facilitate the addictive behavior.

Do I Confront a Client about Her Behavior?

When using CBT or its derivative, REBT, as a treatment modality, it may be necessary to confront a client about her thought processes and/or behavior. It is important for the counselor to remember that soft confrontation should be used instead of severe and harsh criticism, especially if a woman is embarrassed about her behavior and is motivated to change. Challenges that are presented in a question format often get a better response than declarative statements by the counselor. It is also vital that the helper be aware of any cultural implications for challenges. What is acceptable in Western societies may not bode well with clients of other races, ethnicities, and cultures (Hill, 2004).

Counselors should not initiate a challenge (soft confrontation) with women who have sexual addiction until there is a trusting relationship established (Hill, 2004). There must be enough exploration by the counselor to have a basic understanding of circumstances and feelings. The client is not usually ready to hear a challenge at the start of the helping process (Hill, 2004). The motive to challenge by the counselor should be only to assist the client in gaining further insight, point out discrepancies, or gain awareness of destructive behaviors. The counselor should never challenge to meet their need of superiority or impose their beliefs (McMinn, 2011). Using a challenge can be effective if it moves the client forward in gaining insight and using healthier coping skills; however, as with other techniques, this should be used minimally and only when viewed as necessary to give the client a new perspective on their motivations and behaviors.

> It is important to remember confidentiality is key to building a trusting relationship. Privileged communication is how confidentiality is protected. Laws or statutes are put into place to ensure that the therapeutic relationship is protected, and confidentiality is adhered to. Communications are privileged, unless the client presents information that identifies harm to self or others.

Finally, counselors should display empathy and support throughout the entire process. If a client is reluctant to change, the counselor should allow the client further exploration and insight about possible interventions (Neukrug, 2014). If one intervention does not work for the client, the counselor should explore additional options and ideas about what might work best for the client. As counselors, we should not rely on only one intervention simply because it has worked for previous clients.

Group Therapy

For sexual addictions, it may be helpful for the client to attend group therapy, in addition to individual therapy. Twelve step programs are often effective because the client comes to realize she is not alone in her problem and recovery (Rosenberg et al., 2014). Due to the secrecy of the issue, the counselor may find it difficult to get a client to attend a group session (Harvey & Vigorito, 2015); however, the counselor should encourage the client to attend because it has been found to be the most effective and potent way to treat sexual addiction. While individual therapy provides clinical management of symptoms, group therapy provides accountability, while also allowing the client to feel they are supported in their experiences.

Residential Treatment

As noted above, sexual addiction can be likened with a number of psychological disorders, specifically symptoms of mood (depression), anxiety,

and substance-related disorders (Niño De Guzmán et al., 2016). There-fore, residential treatment may be recommended if the client is suffering from another disorder and is unable to function in daily relationships and routines. Due to the cost of this type of treatment, this may not be an option for most of your clients. Treatment facilities are sparse, and it is not reasonable to think every client who presents with sexual addiction is a candidate for residential treatment. However, there are some clients who will benefit from intensive inpatient treatment, and it can be effective in addressing sexual addiction for extreme cases or if sexual addiction is related to another psychological disorder.

Medication

Psychopharmacology is the study of chemical substances (specifically medications) and their effects on the brain and psychological functioning. Psychotropic medications are used to alter brain activity and create bal-ance in the receptors (Freeth, 2005). There has long been a debate between the field of psychology and the discipline of psychiatry as to whether mental disturbances are biologically or emotionally triggered. Clinicians, however, now have a better understanding that some disorders (such as chronic depression or bipolar disorder) are the interaction of genetics and environmental stressors. Therefore, therapy alone is not always enough to assist individuals with certain disorders (Schatzberg et al., 2005). Though there is debate about selective serotonin reuptake inhibitors (SSRIs) and other pharmacological treatments, researchers and clinicians believe these to be a safe and effective way to treat depression and other psycholog-ical disturbances. Combinations of medications or dosage changes may be necessary to adequately treat symptoms. It is important to remember that psychotropic medications are offered to alleviate or modify symp-toms. They are not provided as a definitive cure for any specific illness, especially addiction.

While pharmacological intervention may be helpful, it can be overused when treating mental disturbances. There are some medications that pres-ent with side effects (Malhi & Berk, 2002). Individuals with mental distur-bances such as bipolar disorder, chronic depression, and anxiety are better able to cope in daily activities and personal interactions with continued pharmacological treatments; however, this may not be the best treatment of choice for sexual addiction or pornography.

Spiritual Guidance

Due to the secretive nature of this issue, a woman may not seek counseling within the church setting. If she feels there is condemnation, she may seek counseling with a professional that will listen without judgment (McMinn, 2011). However, spiritual preferences should be addressed at intake, and will be an important part of treatment planning. If a woman comes from a Christian background, she may feel more guilt and shame related to sexual addiction than a woman who does not profess any religious preferences. If the counselor is not familiar with Scripture related to sexual morality, then it will be imperative to direct a woman to a spiritual mentor and accountability partner.

If you are working as a spiritual counselor, then prayer, Scripture, and Christian resources should be incorporated into the session (McMinn, 2011).

Self-Help Books

Self-help books and materials are available, but women may be embarrassed to buy such materials. It may seem like an admission of the problem, and many women may be afraid of their family members finding materials in their home, especially if their spouse is unaware that they are secretly watching pornography or having an affair. However, as a counselor, you should be aware of self-help resources and books if you are going to counsel women with sexual addictions (See the *Suggested Resources* section at the end of the chapter). If a woman comes into your office and is motivated to change behavior, you may want to assign homework of books, websites, and journaling. This will help a woman identify her triggers for destructive behavior. She needs to know why she engages in addictive tendencies. Additionally, a starting point in treatment is for a woman to be educated about her issue and understand why her behaviors are considered maladaptive. It will also be important for her to learn how to verbalize her reasons (causes) for addiction. Using self-help materials will help the client after treatment has ended. She will continue to have the resources available to her if she ceases to attend formal counseling and/or group therapy.

LOOKING THROUGH THE LENS OF CHRISTIANITY: BIBLICAL INSIGHT

What does the Bible say about this topic? The Scriptures are clear that sexual immorality is a sin. We can assume that culture has drifted from Biblical standards of sexual morality. What is often referred to as a traditional view is now considered old-fashioned, stifling, or even hateful (Heimbach, 2004).

© pixelheadphoto digitalskillet/Shutterstock.com

God gave the gift of sex. It truly is a gift when it is shared between a husband and a wife. However, the Bible is clear that sexual activity outside of marriage is prohibited (Arthur, 2005). Jesus says that if you look at another person with lust in your heart, then you have committed adultery ("You have heard that it was said, 'You shall not commit adultery. But I tell you that anyone who looks at a woman lustfully has already committed adultery with her in his heart'" [*New International Bible*, 1973/2011, Matthew 5:27-28]). This is why pornography and sexual addiction are so dangerous. It grieves the heart of God, and it is destructive to interpersonal relationships. Reading graphic novels and watching sexual material leads to desire, which then in turn leads to adultery in the heart. What happens in the mind has such power and leads to escalation. More viewing is required to satisfy the body's desires (Arthur, 2005). Over time, there is an increasing need for more stimulant to get the same effect.

Scripture that can be used in the counseling session is found in Romans 13:12-14 ("The night is almost gone, and the day is near. Therefore, let us lay aside the deeds of darkness and put on the armor of light. Let us behave properly as in the day, not in carousing and drunkenness not is sexual promiscuity and sensuality,

> When we listen with empathy, it is not that we condone sin—we do not! But we should be available to support and guide. There is a difference between accountability and shaming. We do not shame—even when we are holding another person accountable for their behavior. This is an important concept to remember as a counselor.

not in strife and jealousy. But put on the Lord Jesus Christ and make no provision for the flesh in regard to lust" [*New Living Bible*, 1996, Romans 13:12-14]). It is important to remind your client that God loves her, and restoration is always his goal (McMinn, 2011). God wants relationships with his children, and there is nothing so shameful that God will not forgive, restore, heal, and make new. Psalm 119:11 (*New Living Bible*, 1996) says "*I have hidden your word in my heart that I might not sin against you*". It is impossible to stay away from sin without consistent intake of God's Word.

CASE STUDY

Jessica is a 30-year-old woman coming to you with reported symptoms of depression and anxiety. After the initial interview and first session Jessica provides a possible explanation of her symptoms and why she is seeking help. She believes it is related to her sexuality, which is impacting family relationships. Gaining an understanding of her cultural background will be an important first step in exploration, especially if she comes from a family that does not openly talk about problems or is condemning of those who admit addiction. Questions such as "Tell me about your family life?" or "What is a day like at home?" will not only provide some cultural background but will also allow Jessica to explore her feelings about her family and their apparent misgivings about her sexual behavior. It will give Jessica an opportunity to discuss her own values and discuss how they differ from her family's belief systems. This will provide the counselor some information about Jessica's personal perspectives and beliefs.

It will also be important to obtain a sexual history. This is not usually a standard exploration topic while taking a case history; however, Jessica presented it as a reason for seeking help, and therefore her sexuality and past relationships must be explored

© Photographee.eu/Shutterstock.com

through open-ended questions. Asking about what age she began watching pornography and her sexual activity will allow her to explore those feelings openly without judgment.

It is imperative to reflect on Jessica's feelings and restate what she has revealed during the first couple of sessions, which is that she is having difficulty discussing her feelings openly with her family. Therefore, initially, Jessica needs to feel she is being heard and understood more than anything else. She should be allowed to dictate which issue she wants to deal with first, whether it is her family interactions, or the actual addictive behaviors. Jessica could be a client that may or may not move to action. She may only need an outlet to be heard and explore the possibility of group treatment. It is not appropriate to discuss action too quickly with her. She needs time to gain insight about her family conflict, sexual behaviors, and consequences for choices. Treatment modality will be determined based on these goals. Getting her into a support group may be imperative for effective helping so that she does not feel alone in her experiences and has some accountability for her continued behavior.

Using cognitive behavioral therapy, it is important to start evaluating her negative thought processes. She will need to identify her triggers (i.e. having an argument with her family). Her focus will then be on self-management and self-regulation of behavior. For example, she may say "due to my high sexual desire and need to be loved, I view pornography". She may even think, "it is not harming anyone, it only impacts me". It's not harmful to watch pornography because I am not being physical with someone." She will have to work on changing these thoughts to "I can find other ways to deal with my conflict". She will also have to work on self-esteem and identify the qualities she possesses that are valuable and lovable.

If Jessica professes to be a Christian and is feeling shame and guilt because of her value system, it will be important to remind her that "There is therefore now no condemnation to them which are in Christ Jesus, who walk not after the flesh, but after the Spirit" (*King James Bible,* 1769/2017, Romans 8:1). She can receive forgiveness. The Holy Spirit can do more than we can do or even imagine (Ephesians 3:20) and can help Jessica in overcoming her destructive behaviors. She can work on finding her identity in Christ, even if she does not receive validation from her family.

CONCEPT TO CONTEMPLATE

© Digital Storm/Shutterstock.com

Unfortunately, this issue is not just impacting men. If it were, then examples of "soft" pornography (description of sex typically without detail or violence) would not have the success they have seen in the last few years. In the last decade the term "mommy porn" (pornography that is geared toward women and also viewed by women) has become popular and even joked about in public media. Young women are viewing violence in relationships more acceptable,

> We as counselors who follow Christ should be willing to dialogue about this topic. It is not that you should fill your head with images that are ungodly or topics that are not godly…but you should to be vigilant in this spiritual fight that is occurring—it is hurting young women.

and intimacy is being redefined by the media (Leistner & Mark, 2016; Upstone, 2016).

Why do you think the book and movie series *50 Shades of Gray* has become so popular with women? This book and movie series is proving to be destructive; but because it is presented in a novel format, I have heard women say, "it's just a story". This is not a love story—this is simply a way for women to become addicted to pornography. The message that is being sent to women is that they cannot have a pleasurable sexual experience without it being violent. Unfortunately, this version of pornography has created a cause and effect in long-term relationships. We, in the counseling community, are seeing an increase in an association of intimacy and violence (Leistner & Mark, 2016; Upstone, 2016). Please think about that.… Violence should never be associated with intimacy and love. That is not what God intended relationships to be. God is very clear about what love is and what it looks like in our everyday interactions and long-term relationships.

God's description of love can be found in I Corinthians 13: 4-8 (*New Living Bible*, 1996). Consider these descriptions:

> Love is patient, love is kind, love is not jealous, or boastful or proud or rude. It does not demand its own way. It is not irritable, and it keeps no record of being wronged. It does not rejoice about injustice but rejoices whenever the truth wins out. Love never gives up, never loses faith, is always hopeful and endures through every circumstance.

Does compulsive sexual behavior meet any of the above criteria found in this well-known passage of Scripture? Pornography is a distorted view of love and intimacy. It is not what God created, but rather what the enemy would like a woman to believe. Just as the enemy deceived Eve, he seeks to deceive women into believing there is no harm in their watching pornography or having other compulsive sexual behaviors. We as counselors must be willing to talk openly and honestly about this destructive behavior. We should recognize the signs of pornography and encourage women to get help due to the destruction it brings to her physically, mentally, emotionally, and spiritually.

KEY TERMS

Soft Porn-Pornography - describes sex without violence and in a non-detailed way

Mommy Porn Pornography – geared toward women and viewed by women, especially middle-aged women

SUGGESTED RESOURCES

If you search the Internet, there are ample sources for help regarding immoral sexual behavior, and specifically pornography addiction. These can be helpful tools in the counseling sessions and can be used as accountability resources for your client. A few suggestions are listed below.

Websites
Fight the New Drug: www.fightthenewdrug.org
Covenant Eyes: www.covenanteyes.com
Marriage Today – Dave & Ashley Willis: www.davewillis.org

Books
Facing the Shadow (3rd ed) by Patrick Sanders
Sex Addiction 101: A Basic Guide to Healing from Sex, Porn, and Love Addiction by Robert Weiss

REFERENCES

American Society of Addiction Medicine. (2019). *Definition of addiction.* https://www.asam.org/resources/definition-of-addiction

Arthur, K. (2005). *The truth about sex.* Waterbrook Press.

Atwood, J., & Schwartz, L. (2002). Cyber-Sex: The new affair treatment considerations. *Journal of Couple & Relationships Therapy, 13,* 37-56.

Barrilleaux, J. C. (2016). Sexual addiction: Definitions and interventions. *Journal of Social Work Practice in the Addictions, 16,* 421-438. https://doi.org/10.1080/1533256X.2016.1235425

Brewer, G., & Tidy, P. (2017). Sex addiction: Therapist perspectives. *Relationship Therapy,* 40-53. https://doi.org/10.1080/146819942017.1347618

Carlisle, K., Carlisle R., Polychronopoulose, G., Good-Man-Scott, E., Kirk-Jenkins, A. (2016). Exploring internet addiction as a process addiction. *Journal of Mental Health Counseling, 38*(2), 170-182.

Clayton, A., & Kornstein, S. (2002). *Women's mental health.* The Guilford Press.

Clinton, T. & Langberg, D. (2011). *The quick reference guide to counseling women.* Baker Publishing.

Freeth, R. (2005). Information sheet P8: Psychopharmacology and counseling and psychotherapy. *Counseling & Psychotherapy Journal, 16*, 25-28.

Gola, M., & Potenza, M. (2018). The proof of the pudding is in the tasting: Data are needed to test models and hypotheses related to compulsive sexual behaviors. *Arch Sex Behavior, 47*, 1323-1325. https://doi.org/10/1007/s10508-018-1167-x

Gola, M., Wordecha, M., Sescousse, G., Lew-Startowicz, M., Kossowksi, B., Wypych, M., Makeig, S., Potenza, M., & Marchewka, A. (2017). Can pornography be Addictive? An MRI study of men seeking treatment for problematic pornography use. *Neuropsychopharmocology, 42*, 2021-2031. https://doi.org/10.1038/npp.2017.78

Goleman, D. (2011). *The brain and emotional intelligence: New insights.* More Than Sound LLC.

Hartman, L., Ho V., Arbor, S., Hambley, J., & Lawson, P. (2012). Sexual addiction and substance addiction: Comparing sexual addiction treatment outcomes among clients with and without comorbid substance use disorder. *Sexual addiction and Compulsivity, 19*, 284-309. https://doi.org/10.1080/10720162.2012.7335515

Harvey, D., & Vigorito, M. (2015). *Treating out of control sexual behavior: Rethinking sex addiction.* Springer Publishing.

Heimbach, D. (2004). *True sexual morality: Recovering Biblical standards for a culture in crisis.* Crossway Books.

Hersen, M., & Turner, S. (2003). *Adult psychopathology and diagnosis.* (4th ed.). John Wiley & Sons.

Hill, C. (2004). *Helping Skills: Facilitating exploration, insight, and action* (2nd ed.). American Psychological Association.

Hughes, B. (2012). Sexual addiction: Diagnosis and treatment in clinical practice. *BMC Proceedings, 6*, 33. https://doi.org/10.1186/1753-6561-6-S4-P33

Kaplan, M., & Krueger, R. (2010). Diagnosis, assessment, and treatment of hypersexuality. *The Journal of Sex Research, 47*, 181-198.

King James Bible. (2017). King James Bible Online. https://www.kingjamesbibleonline.org/ (Original work published 1769)

Kraus, S., Voon, V., & Potenza, M. (2016.) Should compulsive sexual behavior be considered an addiction? *Addiction, 11*, 2097-2106. https://doi.org/ 10.1111/add13297

Kopala, M., & Keitel, M. (2017). *Handbook of counseling women* (2nd ed.). Sage Publications.

Leistner, C., & Mark, K. (2016). Fifty shades of sexual health an DBSM identity messaging: A thematic analysis of the fifty shades series. *Sexuality & Culture,20*, 464-485.

McMinn, M. (2011). *Psychology, theology, and spirituality in Christian counseling.* Tyndale House Publishers.

Malhi, G., & Berk, M. (2002). Pharmacotherapy of bipolar disorder: The role of atypical antipsychotics and experimental strategies. *Human Psychopharmacology, 17,* 407-412.

Murdock, N. (2013*). Theories of counseling and psychotherapy: A case approach* (3rd ed.). Pearson.

Negash, S., Van Ness Sheppard, N., Lambert, N., & Fincham, F. (2016). Trading later rewards for current pleasure: Pornography consumption and delay discounting. *Journal of Sex Research, 53,* 689-700. https://doi.org/10.1080/0 0224499.2015.1025123

Neukrug, E. (2014). *A brief orientation to counseling: Professional identity, history, and standards.* Brooks/Cole Publishing.

New International Bible. (2011). New International Bible Online. https://www. thenivbible.com/ (Original work published 1973)

Niño De Guzmán, I., Arnau, R., Green, B., Carnes, S., Carnes P., & Jore, J. (2016). Empirical identification of psychological symptom subgroups of sex addicts: An application of latent profile analysis. *Sexual Addiction & Compulsivity, 23,* 34-55. https://doi.org/10.1080/10720162.2015.1095139

New Living Bible (1996). New Living Bible. https://www.biblegateway.com/ versions/New-Living-Translation-NLT-Bible/

Petersen, J. C. (2015). *Why don't we listen better? Communicating and connecting in relationships* (2nd ed.). Petersen Publications.

Phillips B., Hajela, R., & Hilton, D. (2015). Sex addiction as a disease: Evidence for assessment, diagnosis, and response to critics. *Sexual Addiction & Compulsivity, 22*(2), 167-192. https://doi.org/10.1080/10720162.2015.1036184

Reddick, G., & Heiden-Rootes. (2016). Therapists assessments in treating sex addiction and their relationship to clients' gender, relationship status, and exclusivity status. *Journal of Marital and Family Therapy, 43,* 537-553.

Reid, R. (2015). How should severity be determined for the DSV 5 proposed classification of hypersexual disorder? *Journal of Behavioral Addiction, 4,* 221-225.

Rosenberg, K., Carnes, P., & O'Connor, S. (2014). Evaluation and treatment of sex addiction. *Journal of Sex & Marital Therapy, 40,* 77-91. https://doi.org/1 0.1080/0092623X.2012.701268

Sanders, R. (2013). *Christian counseling ethics: A handbook for psychologists, Therapists, and Pastors* (2nd ed.). IVP Academic.

Schatzberg, A., Cole, J., & DeBattista, C. (2005). *Manual of clinical psychopharmacology* (5th ed.). American Psychiatric Publishing, Inc.

Tubino-Scanavino, M., Ventuneac, A., Abdo, C., Tavares, H., SantAna do Amaral, M., Messina, B., dos Reis, S., Martins, J., & Parsons J. (2013). Compulsive sexual behavior and psychopathology among treatment seeking men in Brazil. *Psychiatry Research, 209,* 518-524. https://doi.org/10.1016/j.psychres.201301.021

Upstone, S. (2016). Beyond the bedroom: Motherhood in E. L. James's fifty shades of grey triology. *Frontiers: A Journal of Women Studies, 37,* 138-164.

Widiger, T., & Samuel, D. (2005). Evidence–based assessment of personality disorders. *Psychological Assessment, 17,* 278-287.

Willis, D. (2019). *Survey finds one and three women watch pornography.* https://fightthenewdrug.org/survey-finds-one-in-three-women-watch-porn-at-least-once-a-week

CHAPTER 18

Understanding and Responding to Client Trauma: Neurobiology, Conceptualization, and Treatment

ROBYN TRIPPANY-SIMMONS, ED.D. & KRISTY FORD, PH.D.

"We must eventually choose whether we will love again, care again, reach for another human being again. Trauma took away choice. Surviving and then telling our story returns that to us." ~Diane Langberg in Suffering and the Heart of God

"'For the mountains may depart and the hills be removed, but my steadfast love shall not depart from you, and my covenant of peace shall not be removed,' says the Lord, who has compassion on you." (Isaiah 54:10, ESV)

Wisdom from Above: Standing in His Grace

© Pictrider/Shutterstock.com

The words of Isaiah 54:10 (*New International Bible*, 1973/2011), "For the mountains may depart and the hills be removed, but my steadfast love shall not depart from you, and my covenant of peace shall not be removed,' says the Lord, who has compassion on you" carry the promise that when our earth feels shattered, God does not leave us. In the face of tragedy, God will still provide His peace. This is not easily understood in the aftermath of any traumatic experience, be it sexual abuse, violent crime, natural disaster, sudden loss, or any other earth-shaking event. How can peace ever be recaptured? How is it that a good, loving Father could allow the event in the first place? In Wang's (2014) discussion of the Christian paradox of how evil and suffering can exist if God is both good and omnipotent, he wrote that "Biblical lament language is the language of the soul, of lived human experience, of uncensored feelings spoken freely and audaciously before the presence of God" (p. 285). Because humans live in a broken world, broken things happen. However, the turning to God in the face of those broken things allows for a deeper level, a soul level, healing to occur. Consider the words in Psalm 107: 13-16 (*English Standard Bible*, 2001):

CHAPTER LEARNING OBJECTIVES

Upon completing this chapter, you should be able to:

- Compare various definitions of trauma
- Evaluate the impact of critical events on emotional and mental functioning
- Explain the process of adaptive functioning and its impact on development
- Describe trauma's impact on the brain from a neurobiological framework
- Summarize various evidence-based practices for treating trauma
- Consider appropriate methods for integrating Biblical principles into trauma treatment

Then they cried to the Lord in their trouble, and he delivered them from their distress. He brought them out of darkness and the shadow of death, and burst their bonds apart. Let them thank the Lord for his steadfast love, for his wondrous works to the children of man! For he shatters the doors of bronze and cuts in two the bars of iron.

God made a way to dismantle the chains of trauma. He created our hearts to seek Him in distress, He designed our brains to be able to rewire our understanding of experiences so that the trauma no longer feels as traumatic, and He placed a calling on some to walk with others along this journey of healing. He is faithful to His promise of love, peace, and freedom.

CHAPTER OVERVIEW

It is estimated that 51% of women experience some form of trauma in their lifetime (SAMHSA-HRSA, n.d.). Further, it is estimated that 90% of clients who seek counseling have a trauma history, whether or not that trauma is the presenting issue (Floen & Elklit, 2007; SAMHSA-HRSA, n.d.). In particular, Floen and Elklit (2007) noted that the most commonly occurring critical incidents include physical injury, neglect as a child, witnessing harm to others, and events which evoked terror. The least commonly occurring included natural disasters, fire, and combat. Thus, in your role as counselor, you can expect that trauma will be revealed in a significant number of clients with whom you will work. As such, it is necessary to understand the neuroscience implications of trauma as well as how to conceptualize and deliver treatment to clients.

RELEVANT DEFINITIONS OF TRAUMA

When you think of trauma, you may envision mass destruction, a devastating event, or a profound violation. These descriptors do indeed encompass trauma. However, these are not necessarily the only manner in which trauma is experienced. And to be more precise, trauma is the impact the event has on a person's emotional and mental functioning in the wake of the event. The Substance Abuse and Mental Health Services Administration (SAMHSA) and Health Resources and Services Administration (HRSA) defined trauma as resulting "from an event, series of events, or set of circumstances... as physically or emotionally harmful or life-threatening with lasting adverse effects on the individual's functioning and mental, physical, social, emotional, or spiritual well-being" (SAMHSA-HRSA, n.d., para. 1).

Traumatic events are actually critical incidents, which will be defined here as activating events. The critical incident may be a significant, or *Big T* (Big Trauma), event or a less potent, or *little t* (little trauma), event. Barbash (2017) indicated that Big T events (e.g., a devastating natural disaster, a mass murder, prolonged sexual abuse, a violent criminal attack, a high-conflict divorce, significant medical diagnosis, etc...) can result in a sense of powerlessness and lack of control, while little t events (e.g., death of a pet, minor vehicle accident, betrayal of a friend, etc...), though not as serious, may still impact ability to cope and impact emotions. A powerful, negative emotional response to the event, whether Big T or little T, is what is considered a crisis. It is important to note that not all critical events will lead to emotional crisis or traumatic response.

The impact of the critical incident is idiosyncratic to the individual experiencing it. Consider this example: a young child who observes a larger dog attack a smaller dog (critical incident) and becomes afraid and tearful in the face of this attack (crisis) later develops a significant fear of dogs, which causes disruptions in functioning (traumatization). If the witness of this event was instead a veterinarian, the impact (crisis/traumatization) would likely be significantly different. It is possible that a different child could witness the same event, but not necessarily be traumatized.

While not a comprehensive list of critical incidents, it is important to name some common experiences that could result in crisis or traumatization. As

© Yupa Watchanakit/Shutterstock.com

indicated in the introduction, some physical experiences of abuse, be it physical violence or sexual abuse, has been identified as a primary source of long-term negative impact on the mental health of an individual (Floen & Elklit, 2007). A sexual assault or violence in a romantic relationship can also lead to traumatization. Natural (e.g., hurricanes, tornado, flooding) and man-made (e.g., mass violence such as 9-11, school shootings, and public building bombings) have the potential to create a trauma response. While not as obviously potential precipitators for traumatization, marital infidelity, divorce, loss of a loved one, witnessing harm to someone else, watching news coverage of critical incidents that are not personally experienced, among others can also result in a traumatic injury.

ADAPTIVE FUNCTIONING: CSDT AND TRAUMAGENIC DYNAMICS

It is theorized that there is an emotional/mental adaptation process for individuals who experience prolonged trauma. van der Kolk (2014) indicated that, specifically for sexual trauma, an individual cannot return to the previously held view of self and world as all post-trauma events are reconstructed through the lens of that experience. Recall from your readings in human growth and development that Jean Piaget (1957) proposed that learning follows an adaptive process, relying on the functions of assimilation and accommodation for which individuals work to make sense of new information through working to make it fit or assimilate with existing information (e.g., if it walks on all fours and does not speak like a human being, then it is an animal) or adjusting to accommodate when it does not fit within the existing schema (e.g., it is similar to a dog but does not say "woof" rather it says "baa" so it is a sheep).

When a woman experiences a critical incident, she must assimilate and/or accommodate that information into her existing schema. Freud (1920) indicated that the inability to assimilate the critical incident resulted in survivors repressing the trauma response but experiencing the emotionality as a reaction to present stimuli (e.g., hyperarousal, exaggerated feelings of betrayal or abandonment, etc...). Thus, cognitive distortions for understanding contemporary events occurs. The framework of Constructivist Self-Development Theory suggested that the accommodation process challenges the once-held beliefs, or existing schemas of sense of self and understanding of the world (CSDT; McCann & Pearlman, 1990; Pearlman & Saakvitne, 1995; Saakvitne et al., 2000). In this way, the adaptation becomes a form of self-protection (Neswald-Potter & Trippany Simmons, 2016). These changes, while perhaps irrational, are a method of coping to counter the impact of emotional trauma. Owens and Chard (2001) reported that the cognitive distortions that occur as a result of this accommodation are in contradiction to the needs of safety, trust, power, esteem, and intimacy, resulting in anxiety, avoidant behaviors, sense of betrayal, feelings of powerlessness, anger, and passivity.

McCann and Pearlman (1990), in the development of CSDT, suggested that accommodation and assimilation occurs as a function of traumatic experiences. Pearlman and Saakvitne (1995) noted that within this framework, the adaptation to trauma is individually grounded in "personality and personality history and the traumatic event and its context, within the social and cultural contests for the event and its aftermath" (p. 57). Thus, not all survivors experience and respond to critical incidents in the same manner. Thus, the constructivist element of traumatization is subjective and you, as a counselor, will need to hear each client's story to understand how each client is processing their experience. Further, the construction of meaning is not a 'one and done.' Rather, as new information and new experiences are encountered, meaning will shift in response (Pearlman & Saakvitne, 1995).

Pearlman and Saakvitne (1995) described CSDT as an integration of constructivism, social learning theory, and cognitive development theory which focuses individual adaptive functioning in response to trauma. The adaptive responses or symptoms (i.e., dissociation, self-injury, relational instability, etc…) are, in essence, adaptations to the trauma and serve a protective function for the survivor (Pearlman & Saakvitne, 1995). In this theory, trauma impacts the individual's frame of reference (i.e., world view, identity, and spirituality), self-capacities (i.e., ability to maintain a sense of self and sense of connection with others), ego resources (i.e., ability to meet psychological needs and relate to others), psychological needs (i.e., safety, trust, esteem, intimacy, and control), and memory and perception (i.e., verbal memory, imagery, bodily memory, and interpersonal memory). Frame of reference is foundational understanding and perceiving self and the world (McCann & Pearlman, 1990). As the frame of reference interprets causality and attribution, disruptions can result in misunderstanding and disorientation. As an example, a survivor of a horrific car accident second guesses her decision to not stay home or to take a different route. Self-capacities reflect an individual's ability to regulate their emotions, to maintain a positive sense of self, and to appropriately function in relationships. When these are compromised, individuals may experience emotional responses that are in excess of what is a normal response, or may not be able to convey relational needs to friends and family or know how to navigate to meet their own needs. Ego resources allow for self-protection and may include intelligence, insight, awareness, capacity for self-growth, setting boundaries, understand consequences, among other self-protective abilities (Pearlman & Saakvitne, 1995). The psychological needs of safety, trust, esteem, intimacy, and control are intrapersonal and interpersonal needs. Saakvitne and Pearlman (1996) proposed that those areas which are associated with interpersonal relational functioning are the most vulnerable to symptomatic adaptation. As noted, CSDT conceptualizes that memory and perception, which are foundational to perception of life (Trippany et al., 2006). Memories may represent fragments of events and, as a result, can interfere with awareness and perception if not integrated.

The theory behind Traumagenic Dynamics also indicates a shift in development as a result of trauma experienced in childhood (Finkelhor & Browne, 1985). In particular, it is theorized that childhood sexual trauma survivors experience an assimilation and accommodation of the abuse. Finkelhor and Browne's (1985) seminal work on Traumagenic Dynamics explained the process for which children accommodate abuse. This model postulates that the experience of childhood abuse results in a sense of betrayal (i.e., not feeling protected or safely cared for), stigmatization (i.e., shame and guilt), powerlessness (i.e., afraid of perpetrator; feeling trapped in abuse), and traumatic sexualization (i.e., normal trajectory of sexual development is altered). These dynamics then impact cognitive schema regarding self, worldview, and emotional regulation.

THE NEUROBIOLOGY OF TRAUMA

In addition to impacting individuals along the domains of cognition, emotion, and a sense of self, trauma has an impact at the biological, and in particular, neurological level. Intense and prolonged trauma experiences have the potential to interfere with neurobiological development and/or current brain functioning (Cook et al., 2005). The body's natural fight or flight response, which is necessary for self-preservation during a life-threatening event, may become chronically activated, resulting in sustained arousal, re-experiencing, panic, and aggression (Viamontes & Bietman, 2009). More persistent and intense trauma, particularly when combined with decreased social support, results in more ingrained neurobiological alterations, leading to maladaptive behaviors and compromised functions across multiple domains, such as disruptions in relational attachments (Zilberstein, 2014) and impairments in memory systems (Siegel, 2003). A brief review of the basics of neurobiology can help with understanding the critical impact of trauma on the brain and support the application of effective treatments in therapy.

The Triune Brain

The Triune Brain, as termed by Maclean (1985), is made up of the brainstem, the limbic system, and the cerebral cortex. This three-part structure, when framed simplistically, is described as a primitive brain, housed within a more advanced brain, housed within an increasingly complex brain.

Brain evolution

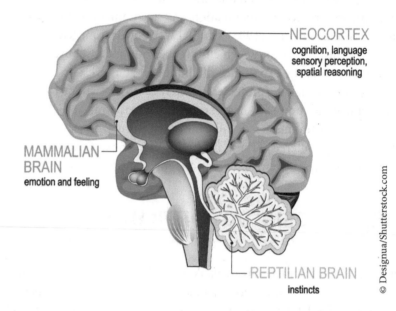

Brainstem

First, the **brainstem**, which Maclean (1985) termed the reptilian brain, is the most primitive part of the brain and is shared with all animals that have a backbone. As the brain's inner core, the brainstem oversees the body's regulating temperature, heart rate, and basic reflexes such as blood flow and respiration, and is further responsible for activation, arousal, homeostasis, and reproductive drives. The brainstem is located in the lowest region of the brain and its main function is guaranteeing survival; therefore, it is responsible for producing the adrenaline surge associated with the fight, flight, or freeze effect in response to fear (Cozolino, 2017). During the activation of the brain stem, access to the more advanced area of the brain responsible for executive function (EF) is circumvented, inhibiting the ability to process information clearly (Viamontes & Beitman, 2009).

Limbic System

Secondly, the **limbic system** is responsible for the processes involved in learning, motivation, memory, and experience of emotion, reacting to external stimuli with both instinctive and learned responses (Cozolino,

2017). This area of the brain surrounds the brainstem and includes the amygdala and the hippocampus. Located within the central region of the brain, the limbic system is involved in processes related to survival instincts, including feelings of pleasure, such as those experienced from eating or sex, as well as negative emotions such as fear or anger (Schore & Schore, 2008). This system is responsible for the storage of emotional memories, which are created and stored during strong emotional experiences, and which are easily triggered by external events that activate the core beliefs associated with the memories. When the limbic system has been triggered by an intense emotional memory, the brainstem's fight or flight system may also be activated, creating a similar biological response as though the original memory is recreated in the present moment and producing an overabundance of unnecessary and counterproductive adrenaline that surges through the brain and body (Schore, 2002a).

Cerebral Cortex

Finally, the cerebral cortex empowers the brain's ability for conscious thought, problem solving, and self-awareness as the outermost and most complex region of the brain (Cozolino, 2017). Involved in executive functioning (EF), the cerebral cortex organizes experiences and interactions with the world (Viamontes & Beitman, 2009). This advanced area includes differentiated areas of specialization and two hemispheres, right and left, that communicate via the corpus callosum. As part of the cerebral cortex, the frontal lobe is responsible for critical functions of higher order thinking, including motor behavior, expressive language, executive function, abstract reasoning, directed attention, and the integration of cognitive and emotional processing. If the frontal lobe is not working properly, the resulting state of psychological dysfunction could include various disruptions in the maintenance of adaptive thoughts, feelings, or behaviors by affecting important processes such as reasoning, judgment, learning, and impulse control. Additionally, the prefrontal cortex is involved in personality expression, planning, strategy, and working memory, as well as constructing ideas about the beliefs, intentions, and perspectives of others.

Normal Brain Development

Normal brain development occurs over time in response to interactions between the self and the environment, particularly interpersonal exchanges. At birth, the brainstem is fully functional while the limbic system is primed and ready to be organized by early experiences; but the cerebral cortex develops slowly throughout the lifespan (Cozolino, 2006). The field of neurobiology emphasizes the emotional and interpersonal learning that occurs during the earliest years while the most primitive brain is still in control (Siegel, 1999). This learning precedes explicit memory, problem solving, or perspective, which all require the higher functioning capacities of the cerebral cortex (Schore, 2002b). Additionally, bonding occurs between the infant and caretaker through a biologically based communication system in which spontaneous emotional communication is shared between limbic systems, contributing to the early organization of personality and the complex formation of attachment schemas (Zilberstein, 2014).

Neural Integration

As the infant brain develops, it depends on experiences in the environment in order for neurons to begin the process of differentiation and formation of specialized neural networks for specific functions. Neural networks refer to the connection of neurons, which link together into organized associations. Neural networks encode and organize all behaviors from reflexes to comprehension. Additionally, neural networks interconnect with other networks, allowing for interaction and integration among the systems. Learning is reflected in neural changes including changes in connectivity, expansion of existing neurons, and growth of new neurons. Neurons grow in reaction to new experiences and learning through the expansion and branching of the dendrites, increasing interconnectivity (Cozolino, 2017). Evidence of brain neuroplasticity, or the ability of the brain to be altered through the development of new neurocircuitry, is displayed in early development as the nervous system changes physically in response to ongoing experience (Schwartz & Begley, 2002). The goal is for these specialized networks to become integrated, so that various networks that focus on responsibilities such as thinking, feeling, relating, or problem solving might collaborate toward a singular, goal-directed purpose. Siegel (2010b) explained that integration refers to a process in which separate areas of the brain are allowed to specialize in their function and then to become linked together in a network. Neural integration involves maximizing the flow and flexibility of energy through neural networks, while psychopathology is caused by difficulties, not just in a specific region of the brain, but also in the interactions among participating systems.

Pathways of Integration

Ideally, an integrated neural system is regulated from the top down, meaning that the cerebral cortex in full control and is regulating the reflexes, impulses, and emotions generated by the brainstem and limbic system (Siegel, 2010b). Top-down networks strengthen the capacity for executive function control which is vital for affect regulation. Similarly, neural network integration is ideally executed from the left to the right hemisphere (Siegel, 2010b). Left-right integration is the ability to utilize input from both the left and right cerebral cortex and lateralized limbic regions for balanced and optimal functioning (Cozolino, 2017). While both hemispheres exercise dominance over specific functions, the blending of strengths allows for maximum integration of cognitive and emotional functioning. The right hemisphere processes information holistically and often unconsciously, appraising safety and danger, interpreting the emotional aspects of language, organizing a sense of self, and focusing on negative stimuli, avoidance behavior, and threat-related vigilance (Viamontes & Beitman, 2009). Conversely, the left hemisphere processes information consciously, involving intentional coping and problem solving while interpreting spoken and body language. The left hemisphere, then, is biased toward positive emotion and social approach behaviors, maintaining responsibility for both anger and aggression toward others as well as successful, optimistic navigation of the social world. Ultimately, the left hemisphere synthesizes all available information from the experience of

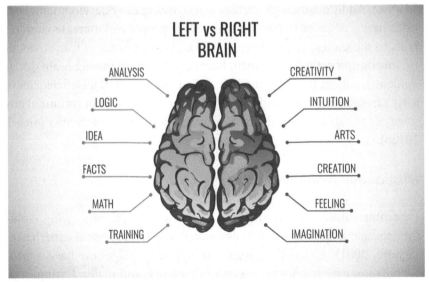

the environment and generates a coherent narrative for the conscious social self (Schore, 2002b). While emotional stability is best accomplished through left to right processing, participation of both hemispheres is required for balance and integration (Cozolino, 2017).

Neural Dis-integration in Trauma

Neural dis-integration refers to specialized areas of the brain that are not integrated, meaning they are not cooperating systemically with other specialized areas of the brain (Siegel, 2010b). The brain reacts to trauma by dis-integrating neural networks. Traumatic experiences leave their traces in the amygdala, imprinted as implicit, emotional memories and eliciting fearful and anxious responses, without requiring cognitive awareness of the cause of the reaction (Bettman & Jasperson, 2010). Whether the stress is chronic or acute from immediate threat, trauma changes the baseline production, availability, and regulation of critical neurochemicals (Cozolino, 2017), and relational trauma is particularly linked with negative impacts on right brain development (Schore, 2001).

Cortisol, often called the stress hormone, is a neuromodulator that enhances memory, mobilizes energy, and helps restore homeostasis after stress (Cozolino, 2017). As the key activator in the fight or flight response, cortisol is useful for brief periods of stress, but prolonged cortisol release due to sustained stress is correlated with memory deficits and dysregulated affect. Additionally, high cortisol levels during early developmental periods have a negative impact on brain development and increase vulnerability to subsequent stress (Schore, 2001). The experience of fear, stress, or trauma during early development has the potential to impact brain development, resulting in neural dis-integration (Schore, 2001). Deficiencies in early caretaking, genetic and biological vulnerability, and/or trauma at any stage of life can result in the lack of integration among networks (Siegel, 2010b).

Dissociation from Experience

First, unresolved trauma disrupts integrated neural processing, splitting conscious awareness from emotional and physiological experiences (Schore, 2001). Elevated endogenous opioids (analgesics) have a profoundly negative impact on cognition, memory, and reality testing, sup-

© Lightspring/Shutterstock.com

porting emotional blunting, dissociation, and depersonalization, which are all associated with a sense of distance from the traumatized body (Cozolino, 2017). Additionally, high levels of glucocorticoids decrease hippocampal volume and are related to memory deficits (Viamontes & Beitman, 2009). Dissociation seems to allow the traumatized individual to escape the trauma via several biological and psychological processes. Trauma can impair interactions across memory domains, and is capable of dissociating the normally integrated tracks of sensation, emotion, behavior, and conscious awareness.

Dis-Integration in Left-Right Balance

Secondly, neurochemical changes impede integration of right and left hemisphere functions, impeding interpersonal bonding and fear arousal regulation (Siegel, 2010b). For example, increased norepinephrine released from the amygdala prepares the body for fight or flight, boosting a primitive stimulus-response pairing that results in increased arousal, anxiety, irritability, and an easily triggered startle response. Simultaneously, increased dopamine correlates with hypervigilance, paranoia, and perceptual distortions as well as social withdrawal and avoidance of new or unfamiliar situation, while lowered serotonin levels are correlated with irritability, depression, and hyper-arousal (Cozolino, 2017).

Dysregulation in Affect

Lastly, trauma results in difficulties with emotional regulation. Schore (2002a) emphasized the dysregulatory role of trauma, particularly trauma experienced in early attachment relationships. The brain naturally organizes defensive coping strategies to reduce anxiety, embedding these in unconscious memory to assist with the selection of what is approached or avoided through assumptions used to organize experience (Cozolino, 2017). However, as alternating episodes of hyperarousal and dissociation mark early relational interactions between caregiver and child, the developing right hemisphere and its corresponding limbic system and autonomic nervous system becomes imprinted with implicit memories of dysregulated trauma response (Schore, 2002a). Consequently, due to the structural nature of these changes, coping mechanisms that are normally focused on limbic system regulation and autonomic nervous system responses are rendered insufficient (Schore, 2002a).

Neural Reintegration

The first task of treatment for PTSD and trauma symptoms is the integration of fragmented neural networks (Siegel, 2010b). Top-down and right-left integration is an experience-dependent process requiring assistance with affect regulation through accessible and secure relationships. Therapy provides an opportunity for building rapport through the therapeutic relationship, and then focuses on top-down integration through the activation of memory and the conscious processing of associated stimuli and on emotional and cognitive integration, resulting in right-left balance through participation of both hemispheres (Siegel, 2010b; Siegel, 2007). Avoidance of the negative emotions stirred by the attempt at creating narratives may result in stories that are incoherent due to unresolved trauma. Narratives that encourage the struggle toward integration by putting frightening experiences into words may initiate emotional healing by simultaneously creating cortical activation and increasing top-down control over subcortically triggered emotions. In this way, therapy emphasizes adaptation to stress and trauma, activating dissociated neural networks in an attempt toward reintegration of brain processes. In the struggle to create an integrated narrative, forgotten memories stored in the amygdala can intrude into adult consciousness, particularly when associated with early childhood trauma (Cozolino, 2006).

Attachment schemas are related to implicit memory and may be reenacted in therapy between client and therapist as traumatic childhood memories are activated as implicit memory systems retain fears from early childhood experiences. Therapy attempts to inhibit the amygdala response by convincing implicit memory systems that the danger is no longer present, thereby assimilating the traumatic experience through the process of re-integration (Cozolino, 2017). Therapy, then, serves as a psychosocial relationship whereby new relational and healing processes can be learned and implemented (Samardzic & Nikolic, 2013), scaffolding hope for healing from the impact of trauma.

CLINICAL CONCEPTUALIZATION OF TRAUMA

The nature of critical incidents varies and the extent of the crisis or traumatization because of the event are dependent on the individual experiencing it, her ego resources, support network, resilience, among other mitigating factors. A diagnostic conceptualization will be necessary in helping you identify the extent to which the critical incident has impacted the client and thus provide you with an understanding of the necessary treatment approach. However, it is important to note that not all those who experience trauma will meet criteria for a diagnosis.

In the fifth edition of the *Diagnostic and Statistical Manual of Mental Disorders* (*DSM-5*; American Psychiatric Association [APA], 2013), diagnoses which previously were encapsulated under other categories (i.e., Disorder Usually First Diagnosed in Infancy, Childhood, and Adolescence; Anxiety Disorders, and Adjustment Disorders) in the *Diagnostic and Statistical Manual of Mental Disorders, Fourth Edition, Text Revision* (*DSM IV-TR*; APA, 2000) now are conceptualized under the category of Trauma- and Stress-Related Disorders. Other disorders that may be associated with traumatization (i.e., Dissociative Identity Disorder, Borderline Personality Disorder, etc...) still fall under their previous categorizations. These changes speak to the ever-increasing understanding of why it is critical for mental health professionals to understand the impact traumatization has on mental health functioning.

In particular, it will be important for you to be familiar with the following diagnoses: Post-Traumatic Stress Disorder (PTSD), Acute Stress Disorder,

Adjustment Disorder, and Dissociative Identity Disorder (DID). Further, there are some clinical conceptualizations in the professional literature which are not included in the *DSM-5* but would be beneficial for you to consider, including Trauma Reenactment Syndrome (Miller, 2005; Trippany et al., 2006) and Complex PTSD (C-PTSD; Cloitre et al., 2009; Cook et al., 2005; Little et al., 2009).

PTSD, Acute Stress Disorder, and Adjustment Disorder

PTSD is a constellation of symptoms that result after an individual is exposed to threat of or experienced serious injury or sexual violence or threat of violent or accidental death (APA, 2013), whether it is through individual experience, witnessing someone else's experience (whether in person or in media), or as a function of a job (e.g., firefighter, police officer). As a result of the experience, the individual may experience intrusive imagery (e.g., memories, nightmares, flashbacks, etc...) which result in a visceral response (i.e., physiological reactions).

Attempts to avoid the traumatic material (i.e., memories, feelings, people, places, situations, etc...) are present. Further, individuals with PTSD will experience negative shifts in cognitive schemas, mood, relationships, expectations, etc... and marked changes in arousal (i.e., hypervigilance, increased startle response, etc...) and reactivity (i.e., angry outbursts, self-destructive behavior, etc...; APA, 2013). While individuals with PTSD may use and abuse substances, the symptoms must not be attributed to that use and abuse. Rather, the symptoms must be associated with the trauma. For the diagnosis of PTSD to be given, these symptoms must occur for longer than a month after the event and must result in distress or functional impairment. If these symptoms are experienced between 3 days and 1 month of the same criteria for the critical incident, you would diagnose it as Acute Stress Disorder (APA, 2013). Less intense in presentation than PTSD or Acute Stress Disorder, Adjustment Disorders result from a stressful experience or event and result in disproportionate distress which creates a marked change in mood, anxiety, and/or conduct (APA, 2013). For an individual to be diagnosed with an adjustment disorder, the symptoms must not persist beyond 6 months after the stressor/consequences of the stressor have ceased.

> If you would like to view a well-developed representation of PTSD in film, consider watching the movie *Welcome to Marwen*.

Dissociative Identity Disorder (DID)

Perhaps the most compelling diagnosis, DID is a trauma-based disorder in which an individual can experience two or more alters, or fragments, of personality. These alters are distinct from the individual, or host, and the host is often unaware of their existence until therapeutic integration efforts are involved. For the client suffering from DID, there is a recurring dissociative amnesia (i.e., loss of memory, time, information beyond normal forgetting) and there is a "discontinuity in sense of self and sense of agency" (APA, 2013, p. 292). DID is developed as a result of extreme childhood experiences of trauma, abuse, or significantly overwhelming experience, although symptoms may not be expressed until adulthood. In particular, there is a 90% prevalence of childhood abuse and neglect for those diagnosed with DID (APA, 2013). The International Society for the Study of Trauma and Dissociation (ISSTD; 2011) stated:

> Severe and prolonged traumatic experiences can lead to the development of discrete, personified behavioral states (i.e., rudimentary alternate identities) in the child, which has the effect of encapsulating intolerable traumatic memories, affects, sensations, beliefs, or behaviors and mitigating their effects on the child's overall development. Secondary structuring of these

discrete behavioral states occurs over time through a variety of developmental and symbolic mechanisms, resulting in the characteristics of the specific alternate identities. The identities may develop in number, complexity, and sense of separateness as the child proceeds through latency, adolescence, and adulthood. (p. 122)

You may wish to view movies such as *Sybil, The Lives of Truddi Chase,* and *The Many Faces of Eve* which are based on real clinical cases of women diagnosed with DID.

It is not likely that an experience of trauma in adulthood will develop into DID as the etiology of DID is associated with the interference of critical developmental periods in childhood for which intense and overwhelming experiences occurred and caregiver-attachment was compromised (ISSTD, 2011).

Borderline Personality Disorder, Trauma Reenactment Syndrome, and Complex PTSD

Battle et al. (2004) indicated that childhood trauma is associated with the development of Borderline Personality Disorder (BPD; APA, 2013) at the rate of 30-90% in the clinical population. Further, Widom et al. (2009), in a longitudinal study of children who had adverse childhood experiences, were significantly more likely to meet the criteria for BPD as adults.

A personality disorder is characterized by consistent patterns of intrapersonal and interpersonal functioning. According to the *DSM-5* (APA, 2013), these patterns are divergent from what is typical of the cultural norms and expectations in functioning. To meet the criteria of a personality disorder, in general, the patterns are manifested in at least two of these areas: 1) cognitions about self, others, and events; 2) emotional response; 3) relational functioning; and 4) impulse control. In particular, someone who meets the criteria of BPD will have unstable interpersonal relationships, sense of self, emotional dysregulation, and impulsiveness. Further, individuals would need to meet five or more of the following patterns:

1. frantic efforts to avoid real or imagined abandonment. Note: Do not include suicidal or self-mutilating behavior covered in Criterion 5.
2. a pattern of unstable and intense interpersonal relationships characterized by alternating between extremes of idealization and devaluation

3. identity disturbance: markedly and persistently unstable self-image or sense of self

4. impulsivity in at least two areas that are potentially self-damaging (e.g., spending, sex, substance abuse, reckless driving, binge eating). Note: Do not include suicidal or self-mutilating behavior covered in Criterion 5.

5. recurrent suicidal behavior, gestures, or threats, or self-mutilating behavior

6. affective instability due to a marked reactivity of mood (e.g., intense episodic dysphoria, irritability, or anxiety usually lasting a few hours and only rarely more than a few days)

7. chronic feelings of emptiness

8. inappropriate, intense anger or difficulty controlling anger (e.g., frequent displays of temper, constant anger, recurrent physical fights)

9. transient, stress-related paranoid ideation or severe dissociative symptoms. (APA, 2013, p. 663)

However, Trippany et al. (2006) suggested "while it is possible, and often likely, that the sexual trauma survivor's symptoms are similar to the diagnostic criteria of BPD, it is imperative that clinicians consider the underlying motivations for such symptoms before offering a BPD diagnosis" (p. 101). As previously discussed, symptoms serve the adaptive function of helping to make sense of the abuse. Thus, the symptoms are symbolic of, or reenactments of the trauma. Trauma Reenactment Syndrome (Miller, 2005) theorized that trauma survivors experience thoughts, feelings, and behaviors that are symbolic of the rage, shame, and fear which resulted from their trauma. Miller (2005) indicated that self-harming actions (e.g., relational instability, eating disorders, suicidal gestures, self-injury, etc…) further serve a protective functioning through creating distance in relationships.

Attaching a label of BPD can further traumatize the client because of the stigma associated with that diagnosis. Additionally, Trippany et al. (2006) suggested that counselors often focus on the characterological nature of BPD in therapy rather than the source of the symptom constellation. Miller (2005) stressed that the focus of counseling should be on helping trauma survivors understand their patterns of behavior through a trauma-sensitive lens rather than pathologizing the maladaptive behaviors.

Little et al. (2009) reported that women who experienced sexual traumatization in childhood are four times more likely to receive a personality disorder diagnosis in adulthood than the general population. This statistic

© fizkes/Shutterstock.com

seems to indicate that an experience that is out of the control of the "experiencer" results in a pathology of personality. However, based on what you have read about the psychological adaptations in cognition and the impact of trauma on brain functioning, it seems that the impact of the trauma is not necessarily on personality, but rather on the ability to adjust to the traumatization.

Similar to Trauma Reenactment Syndrome, C-PTSD is not included as a diagnostic category in the *DSM-5*. C-PTSD, however, provides a conceptualization for individuals who experience more than one traumatization. Cloitre et al. (2009) indicated "exposure to sustained, repeated or multiple traumas, particularly in the childhood years, has been proposed to result in a complex symptom presentation that includes not only posttraumatic stress symptoms, but also other symptoms reflecting disturbances predominantly in affective and interpersonal self-regulatory capacities such as difficulties with anxious arousal, anger management, dissociative symptoms, and aggressive or socially avoidant behaviors" (pp. 399-400). What distinguishes C-PTSD from PTSD is that in addition to the physiological and neurological symptoms of flashbacks, nightmares, hypervigilance, avoidant behaviors, and other criteria for PTSD, an individual experiencing C-PTSD will also have interpersonal challenges, negative self-concept, and emotional dysregulation (Cloitre et al., 2014). While these additions seem consistent with BPD, C-PTSD is theorized as being distinct from BPD in that there is absence of impulsiveness, recklessness, relational instability, self-harm, erratic mood, and lack of paranoid thinking. Thus, Cloitre et al. (2014) proposed a spectrum diagnosis, for which C-PTSD bridges a gap in between PTSD and BPD. Such a conceptualization provides a more respectful, and potentially ethical, approach to working with those who suffered because of something out of their control.

Recognizing that not all movies represent a Biblical worldview and care in viewing is appropriate, it is a challenge to suggest a film for educational purposes to view which illustrates BPD due to the stigma associated with this disorder. However, it is more important to offer you a glimpse into the symptom constellation whether you will conceptualize this a personality disorder or reenactment of trauma. Girl, Interrupted is perhaps the most appropriate film to illustrate this, although Fatal Attraction has been identified as another film for which this symptom constellation is present.

TREATMENT APPROACHES IN TRAUMA

Empirically Supported Treatment of PTSD

Empirically supported treatments for PTSD include approaches that begin with a solid theoretical rationale for their effectiveness, followed by the development of a manualized protocol for administration of the treatment and training of administrators (Monson et al., 2014). Furthermore, empirically supported treatments have been submitted to research that includes randomized controlled trial (RCT) designs and comparisons to other established therapies as to their efficacy in reducing symptoms of PTSD, demonstrating clinically and statistically significant differences between groups. While numerous PTSD treatment approaches show promise in the alleviation of problematic symptoms, only two treatments currently meet the qualifications to be considered empirically supported for adults:

© Feng Yu/Shutterstock.com

cognitive processing therapy (CPT) and prolonged exposure therapy (PE), which will both be reviewed below. In addition, trauma-focused cognitive behavioral therapy (TF-CBT) is an empirically supported treatment for children and adolescents with trauma symptoms.

Cognitive Processing Therapy

Based on a social cognitive theory of PTSD, cognitive processing therapy (CPT) focuses on the meaning that the patient has assigned to the trauma event as a method of regaining a sense of control over life (Monson et al., 2006). This assigned meaning is presumed to create secondary responses in addition to the initial response of anger or fear. CPT also addresses the primary emotions that may emerge from the fight or flight response to perceived danger, but goes a step further to address the secondary emotions such as self-blame or shame that may emerge based on how the event is individually interpreted (Monson et al., 2006). In other words, these secondary emotions are considered the result of cognitions about the event, rather than related to the event itself.

CPT follows a manualized protocol that was initially developed to treat PTSD symptoms in survivors of sexual assault (Resick & Schnicke, 1993; Resick et al., 2008) but has been updated and applied to other populations including combat veterans (Barlow, 2014). CPT can be delivered in either individual or group formats, and is a 12-session, structured program. Clients are first introduced to PTSD symptoms and basics of CPT, then are asked to write an *Impact Statement*, which describes the effect of their most distressing traumatic event. In the statement, clients are asked to focus on any self-blame experienced in regard to the trauma as they consider the effects of the event on their beliefs about the self and others. The *Impact Statement* is then used to assist with understanding how the client may have cognitive distortions and overgeneralizations about the cause of the event or its meaning, and how this distortion has affected their daily functioning. (Resick et al., 2008). The next phase of therapy focuses on a written account of the trauma event, which is read aloud in session. The therapist then challenges distorted cognitions, particularly those associated with self-blame, guilt, or shame. The final phase of therapy focuses on cognitive therapy skills such as tracking automatic thoughts, and then on beliefs or themes (i.e. regarding safety, trust, power, control, or intimacy) that may have been affected by the traumatic event, connecting them to the "stuck points" that the patient has identified throughout the treatment process (Resick et al., 2008).

Empirical support for CPT includes a study by Monson et al. (2006) that demonstrated significant improvements in PTSD symptoms for military veterans treated with CPT. Additionally, research by Chard (2005) examined the impact of CPT on sexual abuse survivors, with participants from the CPT treatment group reporting significant differences in the reduction of PTSD symptoms compared to waitlist control. No significant differences in treatment gains were found at a 1-year follow-up, indicating the stability of treatment outcomes (Chard, 2005).

Prolonged Exposure

Prolonged exposure (PE) is an empirically supported treatment for symptoms of PTSD, originally developed by Foa et al. (1991) for victims of rape. The purpose of extended exposure as a treatment approach, whether in vivo or imaginal, is to directly address the avoidance behavior associated with PTSD (Foa et al., 2007). The avoidance strategy has a reinforcing effect on PTSD symptoms, serving as a reward mechanism and maintaining the behavioral pattern by creating feelings of temporary safety. On the other hand, approaching the fear causes the autonomic nervous system to become flooded with anxiety, resulting in temporarily increased physiological responses. However, the physiological consequences diminish as the anxiety is tolerated, allowing the brain's fight or flight reaction to follow a natural course of dissipation. PE encourages the approach of internal and external reminder cues, so that the feared stimuli can purposefully induce a response of emotional and physiological anxiety.

The PE treatment approach begins with an information gathering, treatment planning, and explanation of treatment phase (Foa et al., 2007). Next, the therapist and patient collaborate to create a hierarchical list of fearful stimuli. In therapy, the patient uses imaginal exposure to relive the trauma by retelling the event in detail, beginning with a memory that produces moderate anxiety and then moving progressively through the list. By recording the sessions, patients may then listen to the recording at home as homework, moving eventually toward in vivo exposure by approaching previously feared stimuli in real life scenarios (Monson et al., 2014). The requirements to become a certified PE therapist include a four-day intensive workshop and two PE cases under a PE certified consultant, making the relative simplicity of training a strength of the PE approach for master's level clinicians.

Empirical support for PE includes a study by Foa et al. (2005) that demonstrated PE as superior to wait-list control in the reduction of PTSD symptoms in a sample of 171 female assault survivors. Although much of the research has focused on female rape victims, studies have demonstrated the effectiveness of exposure techniques with combat veterans (Keane et al., 1989), establishing the applicability of the PE approach to diverse populations that present with varying types of trauma.

Trauma-Focused Cognitive Behavioral Therapy (TF-CBT)

TF-CBT addresses the unique needs of children and adolescents struggling with PTSD symptoms, depression, behavioral issues, or other difficulties related to adverse childhood experiences (ACEs). TF-CBT is appropriate for children between the ages of 3 and 18 who have been sexually abused or exposed to other forms of trauma, as well as for parents or caregivers who did not participate in the abuse. TF-CBT is a cognitive behavioral approach that incorporates principles related to attachment theory, family systems theory, developmental psychology, and neurobiology that focuses on a strengths-based approach to personal empowerment (Cohen et al., 2017).

TF-CBT is a short-term treatment manualized to be delivered in as few as 12 sessions, but which may be provided for longer periods of time depending on client needs. Individual child/adolescent sessions, as well as joint parent/caregiver and child sessions include specific components of TF-CBT summarized by the acronym PRACTICE. First, *Psychoeducation* is provided to children and their caregivers about the impact of trauma and common childhood reactions. Parenting skills are provided to optimize children's emotional and behavioral adjustment. *Relaxation* and stress management skills are individualized for each child and parent. *Affective* expression and modulation are taught to help children and parents identify and cope with a range of emotions. *Cognitive* coping and processing are enhanced by illustrating the relationships among thoughts, feelings, and behaviors. This helps children and parents modify inaccurate or unhelpful thoughts about the trauma. An important component to treatment is the *trauma* narration, in which children describe their personal traumatic experiences. *In vivo* mastery of trauma reminders is used to help children overcome their avoidance of situations that are no longer dangerous, but which remind them of the original trauma. *Conjoint* child-parent sessions help the child and parent talk to each other about the child's trauma. The final phase of the treatment, *Enhancing* future safety and development, addresses safety, helps the child to regain developmental momentum, and covers any other skills the child needs to end treatment (Cohen et al., 2017).

TF-CBT is the most researched treatment for childhood trauma, with 21 completed randomized controlled trials comparing TF-CBT to other treatment conditions (Cohen et al., 2004). Results indicate that TF-CBT is consistently superior to active comparison conditions for reducing PTSD symptoms in adolescents (Cohen et al., 2004), as well as minimizing affective symptoms (depression, anxiety, fear [Cohen et al., 2005]), behavioral problems (internalized, externalized, total behavior, and sexual behavior [Cohen & Mannarino, 1997]), dissociative symptoms [Cohen et al., 2005], and relational and adaptive functioning issues (Friedman et al., 2014).

TF-CBT has been implemented in urban, suburban, and rural environments and in clinics, schools, homes, residential treatment facilities, foster care, refugee camps, juvenile justice settings, and inpatient settings. It has demonstrated effectiveness with children and families of different cultural backgrounds including Caucasian, Black, and Hispanic children from all socioeconomic backgrounds (Weiner et al., 2009), and has been adapted for Latino, Native American, and hearing-impaired populations. It is a highly collaborative approach in which the therapist, parent/caregiver, and child work together to identify and attain common goals for therapy (Pollio & Deblinger, 2018).

Other Evidence-Based Treatments for Trauma

Evidence-based practice in the treatment of trauma includes approaches that indicate moderate or early research support with positive outcomes in the treatment of PTSD and trauma symptoms, but allow for a wider inclusion of protocols that do not necessarily adhere to the strict requirements of empirically supported treatments (Knight et al., 2019). Stress inoculation training and eye-movement desensitization and reprocessing therapy are discussed below as evidence-based practice approaches.

Stress Inoculation Training (SIT)

SIT, developed by Meichenbaum (1985) as a method for mastering fear, is a treatment approach for PTSD that demonstrates modest research support. This approach focuses on the development of coping skills to deal with feelings such as stress and anxiety related to exposure to trauma (Monson et al., 2014). The first phase of treatment is psycho-education, helping the patient to increase their understanding of how the physical, behavioral, and cognitive reactions to trauma can impact current emotional states. The second phase of treatment revolves around training in coping skills that are related to these reactions. For example, deep muscle relaxation and breathing exercises target the physical reactions to trauma, visualization and role play exercises target the behavioral reactions to trauma, and thought stopping exercises along with guided self-dialogue target the cognitive reactions to trauma. SIT focuses on the acquisition of skills that support the survival of a trauma event by managing stress and anxiety, fostering resiliency, and developing a sense of mastery over fear. Because avoidance of the physical and emotional reminders of trauma is considered a maintenance mechanism of PTSD symptoms, a strength of this treatment is that it supports an attitude of approach, rather than encouraging the tendency to avoid fearful stimuli. Additionally, the flexible, psycho-educational nature of this approach makes it easy to tailor to diverse populations (Monson et al., 2014).

Research by Foa et al. (1999) demonstrated the superiority of SIT over waitlist control to reduce PTSD symptom severity in female victims of assault. Following treatment, 58% of the SIT treatment group participants no longer met the criteria for a diagnosis of PTSD (Foa et al., 1999). However, in spite of being one of the earliest approaches to PTSD treatment, SIT requires additional research support in order to be considered empirically supported, and is often utilized in conjunction with other approaches as a component of treatment (Monson et al., 2014).

Eye Movement Desensitization and Reprocessing (EMDR)

Although sometimes thought of as controversial, eye movement desensitization and reprocessing (EMDR) is considered an effective treatment for PTSD symptoms, with strong but conflicting research support (Davidson & Parker, 2001). Developed by Shapiro (2001), the core process of EMDR originated from a personal experience in which her anxious, upsetting thoughts were alleviated as her eyes followed the back and forth motion of leaves swaying in the wind. As a clinician and researcher, Shapiro discovered positive outcomes while trying the technique on others, instructing clients to process disturbing memories while coaching them to make specific movements with their eyes, moving them from side to side at a particular speed. The EMDR manualized protocol (Shapiro, 2001) outlines 8 phases of treatment that include history taking, client preparation, target assessment, desensitization, installation, body scan, closure, and reevaluation of treatment effects. In overview, the core components focus on the identification of a traumatic event, the identification of negative cognitions related to the event, and the creation of rating scales for the distress related to various cognitions about the event. The client is instructed to visualize the traumatic memory, mentally rehearsing the negative cognitions, and paying attention to the physical location of anxiety in the body. Meanwhile, the client is further instructed to move their eyes back and forth, usually tracking with the movement of the therapist's finger, although other bilateral stimulation may also be used. Following this EMDR process, the client is asked to once again rate the levels of distress related to their previously identified negative cognitions.

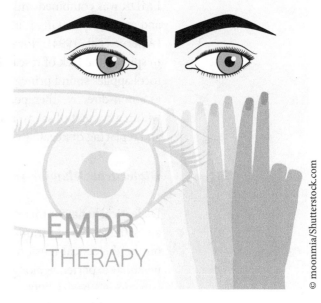

Although the mechanism of change in EMDR is often ridiculed, the proponents of the treatment insist that the theoretical basis is sound, asserting that unresolved trauma is the result of poorly integrated cognitive, emotional, or sensory aspects of the memory and that EMDR supports adequate neurological processing. A randomized controlled trial by Rothbaum et al. (2005) demonstrated that EMDR was superior to a waitlist control group in the reduction of PTSD symptoms; however, other research studies such as Devilly and Spence (1999) have demonstrated that EMDR is inferior to cognitive behavioral therapy. A meta-analysis by Davidson and Parker (2001) reviewed 34 studies that focused on EMDR outcomes with various populations, concluding that EMDR appears to be no more effective than other exposure-based techniques. Furthermore, this study asserts that the eye movements are an unnecessary component of treatment, finding no significant differences in outcomes when comparing the same procedures with and without eye movements (Davidson & Parker, 2001).

Often criticized as a "mystical" or a "quick-fix" approach, many researchers and clinicians accuse EMDR proponents of being unscientific in their methods to researching and reporting therapy outcomes due to a theoretical rationale that has not been clearly explicated and a mechanism of change that is impossible to measure (Acierno et al., 1994). Additionally, in virtually all of the published case studies that report positive outcomes, treatment with EMDR was combined with other interventions such as relaxation training and exposure, making it impossible to assign the improvements to EMDR (Acierno et al., 1994). However, Hyer and Brandsma (1997) pointed out that in spite of the lack of research support for eye-movement, the EMDR protocol applies sound principles for the alleviation of trauma symptoms such as a non-directive therapeutic stance, the processing of trauma memories within a context of safety, a strong therapeutic alliance, and the processing and replacing of negative cognitions.

Dialectical Behavior Therapy (DBT)

Dialectical behavior theory (DBT), developed by Linehan (1993), provides an evidence-based   framework for various clinical interventions focused on the dialectical tension involved in both radical acceptance of painful personal experience alongside the need to make meaningful changes in behavior (Wheelis, 2009). DBT is an empirically supported treatment for Borderline Personality Disorder (Linehan et al., 2006; Neacsiu et al., 2010; Stoffers et al., 2012), a diagnosis often associated with trauma reenactment syndrome and complex PTSD. Furthermore, multiple research studies indicate the success of DBT techniques in the treatment of symptoms often comorbid with trauma such as self-harm (Feigenbaum, 2010; Pistorello et al., 2012; Tormoen et al., 2014), distress tolerance and emotion regulation (Neacsiu et al., 2014; Welch & Kim, 2012; Lynch et al., 2006), substance abuse (Linehan et al., 2002), and the intrusive and dissociative symptoms associated with complex PTSD (Bohus et al., 2019). In practice, dialectical behavior therapy employs mindfulness techniques that focus on increasing self-awareness and being emotionally present in the present-moment as a process of the acceptance of pain, as well as reflective techniques, such as meditative exercises, prayer, and the purposeful assignment

of meaning to suffering (Linehan, 1993). The fundamental treatment components of DBT include: (1) an analysis of the problem and support for implementation of alternative solutions, (2) the validation of personal experience to convey acceptance of thoughts, feelings, and behaviors, and (3) an emphasis on dialectical thinking that understands the vacillation between extreme emotion and dysfunctional behavior, with the goal of holding both in a point of tension; thus, seeking to validate prior and current functioning while emphasizing the need for change and problem solving in order to move forward with increasing health (Wheelis, 2009).

INTEGRATING BIBLICAL PRINCIPLES IN TRAUMA TREATMENT

Conversations around forgiveness are common in Christian circles, as God's offer of forgiveness to all through the sacrifice of Christ on the cross is foundational to our faith. However, when discussed in the context of trauma, particularly relational trauma, forgiveness becomes a much more challenging topic. Consider Colossians 3:13 (*Holman Christian Standard Bible*, 2003) which states, "The Lord has forgiven you, so you also must forgive" and Ephesians 4:32 (*New Living Translation*, 1996) which states, "Be kind to each other, tenderhearted, forgiving one another, just as God through Christ has forgiven you." These words may sound sweet and the concepts may be basic to our Christian faith; however, their true weight is realized when faced with the daunting work of offering forgiveness to an abuser.

Forgiveness in Relational Trauma

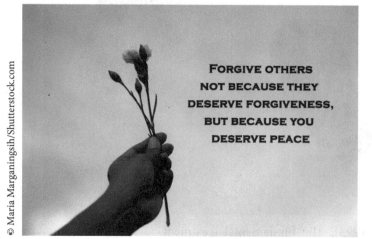

FORGIVE OTHERS NOT BECAUSE THEY DESERVE FORGIVENESS, BUT BECAUSE YOU DESERVE PEACE

While trauma may originate from any experience of threat, relational trauma, generally originating from someone who should have cared for us but instead caused harm, can often have the most devastating impact for women. Particularly, childhood sexual abuse has the potential to leave a lifetime scar on its victims. Relational trauma initiates challenges related to ongoing interpersonal hypervigilance, highlighting the need for interventions that consider the application of interpersonal forgiveness in treatment while remaining sensitive to the deep wounds left by the abuse. Forgiveness is understandably difficult, and the topic is often met with a defensiveness that needs extreme validation and patience on the part of the clinician. Being ready to offer forgiveness to someone who has inflicted severe abuse may require an ongoing process, and it is important to emphasize that forgiveness is not the same as reinstating trust for the abuser. When working with relational trauma survivors, counselors should understand that healing will not come easily for our clients. Encouraging forgiveness is sometimes counterintuitive, particularly when the abuse was severe, and when we emotionally identify with the client's anger and outrage. However, research in the area of post traumatic growth indicated that the process of forgiveness has implications for success in treatment (Neul et al., 2019; Schultz et al., 2010).

One Client's Perspective on Forgiveness

One client, a female survivor of long-term childhood sexual abuse described her journey with forgiveness as part of her treatment in this way: *Forgiveness is really hard to do. It is like a power struggle with your own self. Working to forgive someone of the trauma they caused you is like working out with a resistance band. When you finally let go, you realize you are stronger from the struggle. The struggle to forgive grows your emotional muscles.*

If I did not have the resistance band...if I had never had the trauma...I would never have had to work out those muscles. When I have to choose to forgive again and again, each time I grow a little more because I work those muscles out again and I get even stronger. Every day I wake up, I know I could absolutely STOP choosing it too. If I stop choosing to forgive, I know I will stop making progress. I could go right back to that weak place. No one would blame me. But I keep struggling and getting stronger in the struggle. I keep choosing to forgive.

As you consider these heartfelt words that represent years of personal and therapeutic hard work, we encourage you to consider the importance of approaching the topic of forgiveness in your counseling work, particularly when working with Christian clients. Forgiveness is never easy, but the journey is worthwhile.

CONCEPT TO CONTEMPLATE

© ImageFlow/Shutterstock.com

Consider critical incidents you have experienced in your life. Do you feel like you have experienced a traumatic response to any of these? How might you apply these concepts to your experience? What was it like for you to consider forgiveness toward those who have harmed you? If you have not already, consider seeking counseling to assist you in this before you begin counseling others.

When Jamie, now 26, was in the 2nd grade, her house burned down the day after her birthday. Her family lost everything they owned, including the gift of a sapphire birthstone ring that she was so thrilled to receive for her birthday. The fire happened in the middle of the night because of faulty wiring in their rented home. She remembers her mother and father screaming for she and her younger sister to climb out the window. She remembers the smell of the fire. She remembers being very confused as to why she could not go out the front door. She remembers being told she could not go back in the house for her ring. She remembers it was cold outside and she was barefooted. She remembers her mother's sobs. She also remembers how long it took for them to find a new place to live, staying in a crowded one-bedroom apartment with her grandparents.

While she had not thought of the fire in several years, lately she had been remembering it like it was just happening. Eight years ago, as a freshman in college, she was walking home from the library late one evening. On her way home, she was jumped by two men who stole her backpack which contained a brand new laptop and her wallet, which contained her parents' credit card, $50 in cash, and her ID with her address. These men did not sexually assault her, but they did physically assault her when she struggled to keep her backpack. The police were never able to find these men and Jamie lived in fear that they would come to her apartment and hurt her again as they had access to her address. She did receive a few counseling sessions at the university counseling center but did not like feeling vulnerable to her emotions, so she stopped attending. However, she never stopped feeling afraid that these men would track her down. Jamie presented for counseling after a friend was killed in a car accident a month ago. She indicated since this accident, she had been having anxiety attacks, nightmares, and flashbacks of the fire and the mugging.

Based on Jamie's clinical presentation, it appears she may meet the criteria for Posttraumatic Disorder (PTSD). However, during the initial sessions, it is essential to gather information from Jamie to assess her symptoms and to ensure she does meet criteria for PTSD. After the information gathering and a PTSD diagnosis have been determined, you will need to establish which treatment model would be most effective for Jamie. Because Jamie has an extensive trauma history and has a diagnosis of PTSD, she is appropriate for Cognitive Processing Therapy. Before implementing CPT with Jamie, it is your ethical responsibility to receive the proper training. You also want to make sure that you introduce the intervention by explaining the expectations and to get Jamie's written consent to participate in the treatment. While using CPT, it is highly recommended that you follow the sessions in order outlined in the manual.

As Jamie's counselor, it is important for you to address her previous counseling experience in which she terminated counseling because she did not like feeling "vulnerable to her emotions". You will also need to continue to have frequent check-ins with Jamie to discuss her level of comfort throughout treatment and affirm for her that this is a safe environment to speak freely about her concerns. If Jamie expresses, she is a Christian and is open to Spiritual integration, you should assess her relationship with God because she has experienced several traumas. Some clients lose faith or often feel abandoned by God after experiencing trauma. Integrating Scripture in your sessions with Jamie may help reduce her fear and anxiety. Remind Jamie that in Joshua 1:19, God reminds us not to be frightened but to remain strong and courageous because he is always with us and of Psalm 55:22, that we should place our burdens onto God and he will take care of our needs.

CHAPTER SUMMARY

The focus of this chapter was to help you gain an understanding of how trauma develops, from the experience of a critical incident to what may or may not result in traumatization. The intention of the chapter is to provide you with the knowledge of the impact trauma has on the individual, from adaptations and shifts in cognitive perspectives to the effect of trauma neurologically and neurochemically. Further, knowledge and awareness of traumatization's impact on the mental health of survivors can assist with your diagnostic and case conceptualization of clients.

KEY TERMS

Brainstem - termed the reptilian brain, is the most primitive part of the brain and is shared with all animals that have a backbone

Cerebral Cortex - empowers the brain's ability for conscious thought, problem solving, and self-awareness as the outermost and most complex region of the brain

Limbic System - responsible for the processes involved in learning, motivation, memory, and experience of emotion, reacting to external stimuli with both instinctive and learned responses

Neural Dis-integration - specialized areas of the brain that are not integrated, meaning they are not cooperating systemically with other specialized areas of the brain

Trauma – results from an event, series of events, or set of circumstances that are physically or emotionally harmful or life-threatening with lasting adverse effects on the individual's functioning and mental, physical, social, emotional, or spiritual well-being

Traumatic Events - critical incidents, defined here as activating events

SUGGESTED RESOURCES

Books

Suffering and the Heart of God: How Trauma Destroys and Christ Restores by Diane Langberg

Women who Hurt Themselves: A Book of Hope and Understanding by Dusty Miller

The Body Keeps the Score: Brain, Mind, & Body in the Healing of Trauma by Bessel van der Kolk

Videos

Perry, B. D. (The ChildTrauma Academy). (2013, September 6). *Seven slide series: The human brain* [Video]. YouTube. https://www.youtube.com/watch?v=uOsgDkeH52o

Perry, B.D. (The ChildTrauma Academy). (2013). *Seven slide series: Threat response patterns* [Video]. YouTube. https://www.youtube.com/watch?v=sr-OXkk3i8E&feature=youtu.be

Perry, B. D. (The ChildTrauma Academy). (2013). *Seven slide series: Sensitization and tolerance* [Video]. YouTube. https://www.youtube.com/watch?v=qv8dRfgZXV4

Certifications and Trainings

Information on certification as a CPT therapist: https://cptforptsd.com/achieving-provider-status/

Information on DBT certification: https://dbt-lbc.org/

Information on training and certification in EMDR: https://www.emdria.org/emdr-training-education/emdr-certification/

Information on becoming a certified TF-CBT therapist: https://tfcbt.org/certification-process/

Prolonged Exposure Therapy Training: https://www.med.upenn.edu/ctsa/certification_requirements.html

REFERENCES

American Psychiatric Association. (2000). *Diagnostic and statistical manual of mental disorders* (4th ed., text revision). Author.

American Psychiatric Association. (2013). *Diagnostic and statistical manual of mental disorders* (5th ed.). https://doi.org/10.1176/appi.books.9780890425596

Acierno, R., Hersen, M., Van Hasselt, V. B., Tremont, G., & Meuser, K. T. (1994). Review of the validation and dissemination of eye-movement desensitization and reprocessing: A scientific and ethical dilemma. *Clinical Psychology Review, 14*(4), 287-299.

Bettmann, J. E., & Jasperson, R. A. (2010). Anxiety in adolescence: The integration of attachment and neurobiological research into clinical practice. *Clinical Social Work Journal, 38*, 98-106.

Barbash, E. (2017, March 13). *Different types of trauma: Small 't' versus large 'T.'* Psychology Today. https://www.psychologytoday.com/us/blog/trauma-and-hope/201703/different-types-trauma-small-t-versus-large-t.

Barlow, D. H. (Ed.). (2014). *Clinical handbook of psychological disorders: A step-by-step treatment manual.* Guilford publications.

Battle, C. L., Shea, M. T., Johnson, D. M., Yen, S., Zlotnick, C., Zanarini, M. C., Sanislow, C. A., Skodol, A. E., Gunderson, J. G., Grilo, C. M., McGlashan, T. H., & Morey, L. C. (2004). Childhood maltreatment associated with adult personality disorders: Findings from the collaborative longitudinal personality disorders study. *Journal of Personality Disorders, 18*, 193–211.

Bohus, M., Schmahl, C., Fydrich, T., Steil, R., Muller-Engelmann, M., Herzon, J., Ludascher, P., Kleindienst, N., & Priebe, K. (2019). A research programme to evaluate DBT-PTSD, a modular treatment approach for complex PTSD after childhood abuse. *Borderline Personality Disorder and Emotion Dysregulation, 6*(7). https://doi.org/10.1186/s40479-019-0099-y

Chard, K. M. (2005). An evaluation of cognitive processing therapy for the treatment of posttraumatic stress disorder related to childhood sexual abuse. *Journal of Consulting and Clinical Psychology, 73*, 965-971.

Cloitre, M., Garvert, D. W., Weiss, B., Carlson, E. B., & Bryant, R. A. (2014) Distinguishing PTSD, complex PTSD, and borderline personality disorder: A latent class analysis. *European Journal of Psychotraumatology, 5*, 1-10.

Cloitre, M., Stolbach, B. C., Herman, J. L., van der Kolk, B., Pynoos, R., Wang, J., & Petkova, E. (2009). A developmental approach to complex PTSD: Childhood and adult cumulative trauma as predictors of symptom complexity. *Journal of Traumatic Stress, 22*, 399–408

Cohen, J. A., & Mannarino, A. P. (1997). A treatment study for sexually abused preschool children: Outcome during a one-year follow-up. *Journal of the American Academy of Child and Adolescent Psychiatry, 36*(9), 1228-1235.

Cohen, J. A., Deblinger, E., Mannarino, A. P., & Steer, R. A. (2004). A multi-site randomized controlled trial for children with sexual abuse-related PTSD symptoms. *Journal of the American Academy of Child and Adolescent Psychiatry, 43*(4), 393-402.

Cohen, J. A., Mannarino, A. P., & Deblinger, E. (2017). *Treating trauma and traumatic grief in children and adolescents* (2nd ed.). The Guilford Press.

Cohen, J. A., Mannarino, A. P., & Knudsen, K. (2005). Treating sexually abused children: One year follow-up of a randomized controlled trial. *Child Abuse and Neglect, 29*(2), 135-145.

Cook, A., Spinazzola, J., Ford, J., Lanktree, C., Blaustein, M., Cloitre, M., DeRosa, R., Hubbard, R., Kagan, R., Liautaud, J., Mallah, K., Olafson, E.,

& van der Kolk, B. (2005). Complex trauma in children and adolescents. *Psychiatric Annals, 35,* 390-398.

Cozolino, L. (2006). *The neuroscience of human relationships. Attachment and the developing social brain.* Norton & Company.

Cozolino, L. (2017). *The neuroscience of psychotherapy: Healing the social brain* (3rd ed.). W. W. Norton.

Davidson, P. R., & Parker, K. C. (2001). Eye movement desensitization and reprocessing (EMDR): A meta-analysis. *Journal of Consulting and Clinical Psychology, 69,* 305-316.

Devilly, G. J., & Spence, S. H. (1999). The relative efficacy and treatment distress of EMDR and a cognitive behavioral trauma treatment protocol in the amelioration of post traumatic stress disorder. *Journal of Anxiety Disorders, 13,* 131-157.

Feigenbaum, J. (2010). Self-harm – the solution not the problem. The dialectical behaviour therapy model. *Psychoanalytic Psychotherapy, 24*(2), 115-34.

Finkelhor, D., & Browne, A. (1985). The traumatic impact of child sexual abuse: A conceptualization. *American Journal of Orthopsychiatry, 55,* 530–541.

Floen, S. K., & Elklit, A. (2007). Psychiatric diagnoses, trauma, and suicidality. *Annals of general psychiatry, 6,* 12. https://doi.org/10.1186/1744-859X-6-12.

Foa, E. B., Dancu, C. V., Hembree, E. A., Jaycox, L. H., Meadows, E. A., & Street, G. P. (1999). A comparison of exposure therapy, stress inoculation training, and their combination for reducing posttraumatic stress disorder in female assault victims. *Journal of Consulting and Clinical Psychology, 67,* 194-200.

Foa, E. B., Hembree, E. A., Cahill, S. P., Rauch, S. A. M., Riggs, D. S., Feeny, N. C., & Yadin, E. (2005). Randomized trial of prolonged exposure for posttraumatic stress disorder with and without cognitive restructuring: Outcome at academic and community clinics. *Journal of Consulting and Clinical Psychology, 73,* 953-964.

Foa, E. B., Rothbaum, B. O., Riggs, D., & Murdock, T. (1991). Treatment of post-traumatic stress disorder in rape victims: A comparison between cognitive-behavioral procedures and counseling. *Journal of Consulting and Clinical Psychology, 59,* 715-723.

Foa, E., Hembree, E., & Rothbaum, B. (2007). *Prolonged exposure therapy for PTSD: Emotional processing of traumatic experiences therapist guide.* Oxford University Press.

Freud, S. (1920). Beyond the pleasure principle. In J. Starchey (Ed.), *Complete psychological works* (3rd edition). Hogarth Press.

Friedman, M. J., Kean, T. M., & Resick, P. A. (2014). *Handbook of PTSD: Science and practice.* A Division of Guilford Publication Inc.

Holman Christian Standard Bible (2003). https://www.bhpublishinggroup.com/tag/holman-christian-standard-bible/

Hyer, L., & Brandsma, J. M. (1997). EMDR minus eye movements equals good psychotherapy. *Journal of Traumatic Stress, 10*(3), 515-522.

International Society for the Study of Trauma and Dissociation. (2011). Guidelines for treating dissociative identity disorder in adults, third revision. *Journal of Trauma & Dissociation, 12,* 115–187.

Keane, T. M., Fairbank, J. A., Caddell, J. M., & Zimering, R. T. (1989). Implosive (flooding) therapy reduces symptoms of PTSD in Vietnam combat veterans. *Behavior Therapy, 20,* 245-260.

Knight, A., Ford, K., & Sibcy, G. A. (2019). Research, program evaluation, and the counselor. In R. Simmons, S. Lilley, & A. Knight (Eds.), *Introduction to counseling: Integration of faith, professional identity, and clinical practice.* Kendall Hunt Publishing Company.

Langberg, D. (2015). *Suffering and the heart of God: How trauma destroys and Christ restores.* New Growth Press.

Linehan, M. M. (1993). *Cognitive behavioral treatment of borderline personality disorder.* The Guilford Press.

Linehan, M. M., Comtois, K. A., Murray, A. M., Brown, M. Z., Gallop, R. J., Heard, H. L., Korslund, K. E., Tutek, D. A., Reynolds, S. K., & Lindenboim, N. (2006). Two-year randomized controlled trial and follow-up of dialectical behavior therapy vs therapy by experts for suicidal behaviors and borderline personality disorder. *Archives of General Psychiatry, 63*(7), 757-766.

Little, A. S., Trippany, R. L., & Rush-Wilson, T. (2009). Complex posttraumatic stress disorder: Diagnostic reconceptualization for childhood sexual abuse survivors. *Journal of Counseling: Research and Practice, 1,* 5-13.

Lynch, T. R., Chapman, A. L., Rosenthal, M. Z., Kuo, J. R., & Linehan, M. M. (2006). Mechanisms of change in dialectical behavior therapy: Theoretical and empirical observations. *Journal of Clinical Psychology, 62,* 459-480.

Maclean, P. (1985). Evolutionary psychiatry and the triune brain. *Psychological Medicine, 15*(2), 219-221. https://doi.org/10.1017/S0033291700023485

McCann, I. L., & Pearlman, L. A. (1990). *Psychological trauma and the adult survivor: Theory, therapy, and transformation.* Brunner/Mazel.

Meichenbaum, D. H. (1985). *Stress inoculation training.* Pergamon.

Miller, D. (2005). *Women who hurt themselves: A book of hope and understanding.* Basic Books.

Monson, C. M., Resick, P. A., & Rizvi, S. L. (2014). Posttraumatic stress disorder. In D. H. Barlow (Ed.), *Handbook of psychological disorders: A step-by-step treatment manual* (5th ed.). The Guilford Press.

Monson, C. M., Schnurr, P. P., Resick, P. A., Friedman, M. J., Young-Xu, Y., & Stevens, S. P. (2006). Cognitive processing therapy for veterans With military-related posttraumatic stress disorder. *Journal of Consulting and Clinical Psychology, 74,* 898-907.

Neacsiu, A. D., Lungu, A., Harned, M. S., Rizvi, S. L., & Linehan, M. M. (2014). Impact of dialectical behavior therapy versus community treatment by experts on emotional experience, expression, and acceptance in borderline personality disorder. *Behaviour Research and Therapy, 53,* 47-4.

Neacsiu, A. D., Rizvi, S. L., & Linehan, M. M. (2010). Dialectical behavior therapy skills use as a mediator and outcome of treatment for borderline personality disorder. *Behaviour Research and Therapy, 9,* 832-839.

Neswald-Potter, R., & Trippany Simmons, R. (2016). Regenerative supervision: A restorative approach for counselors impacted by vicarious trauma. *Canadian Journal of Counselling and Psychotherapy, 50,* 75-90.

New International Bible. (2011). New International Bible Online. https://www.thenivbible.com/ (Original work published 1973)

New Living Bible (1996). New Living Bible. https://www.biblegateway.com/versions/New-Living-Translation-NLT-Bible/

Neul, H., Sung-Man, B., & Myoung-Ho, H. (2019). The effect of forgiveness writing therapy on post-traumatic growth in survivors of sexual abuse. *Sexual and Relationship Therapy, 34*(1), 10-22. https://doi.org/10.1080/14681994.2017.1327712

Owens, G., & Chard, K. (2001). Cognitive distortions among women reporting childhood sexual abuse. *Journal of Interpersonal Violence, 16,* 178-191.

Pearlman, L. A., & Saakvitne, K. W. (1995). *Trauma and the therapist: Countertransference and vicarious traumatization in psychotherapy with incest survivors.* W.W. Norton.

Piaget, J. (1957). *Construction of reality in the child.* Routledge & Kegan Paul.

Pistorello, J., Fruzzetti, A. E., MacLane, C., Gallop, R., & Iverson, K. M. (2012). Dialectical behavior therapy (DBT) applied to college students: A randomized clinical trial. *Journal of Counseling and Clinical Psychology, 80*(6), 982-994.

Pollio, E., & Deblinger, E. (2018). Trauma-focused cognitive behavioural therapy for young children: Clinical considerations. *European Journal of Psychotraumatology, 8*(7), 1433929. https://doi.org/10.1080/20008198.2018.1433929

Resick, P. A., & Schnicke, M. K. (1993). *Cognitive processing therapy for rape victims: A treatment manual.* Sage.

Resick, P. A., Monson, C. M., & Chard, K. M. (2008). *Cognitive processing therapy veteran/military version: Therapist's manual.* Department of Veterans' Affairs.

Rothbaum, B. O., Astin, M. C., & Marsteller, F. (2005). Prolonged exposure versus eye movement desensitization and reprocessing (EMDR) for PTSD rape victims. *Journal of Traumatic Stress, 18,* 607-616.

Saakvitne, K. W., & Pearlman, L. A. (1996). *Transforming the pain: A workbook on vicarious traumatization.* W.W. Norton.

Saakvitne, K. W., Gamble, S., Pearlman, L. A., & Tabor Lev, B. (2000). *Risking connection: A training curriculum for working with survivors of childhood abuse.* Sidran Press.

Samardzic, L., & Nikolic, G. (2013). Neurobiology of psychotherapeutic relationship: New perspectives. *Scientific Journal of the Faculty of Medicine in Nis, 30*(2), 55-61.

Schore, A. N. (2001). The effects of early relational trauma on right brain development, affect regulation, and infant mental health. *Infant Mental Health Journal, 22*(1-2), 201-269.

Schore, A. N. (2002a). Dysregulation of the right brain: A fundamental mechanism of traumatic attachment and the psychopathogenesis of posttraumatic stress disorder. *Australian and New Zealand Journal of Psychiatry, 36*(1), 9-30.

Schore, A. N. (2002b). The neurobiology of attachment and early personality organization. *Journal of Prenatal and Perinatal Psychology and Health, 16*(3), 249-263.

Schore, J. R., & Schore, A. N. (2008). Modern attachment theory: The central role of affect regulation in development and treatment. *Clinical Social Work Journal, 36*, 9-20.

Schultz, J. M., Tallman, B. A., & Altmaier, E. M. (2010). Pathways to posttraumatic growth: The contributions of forgiveness and importance of religion and spirituality. *Psychology of Religion and Spirituality, 2*(2), 104-114. https://doi.org/10.1037/a0018454

Schwartz, J. M., & Begley, S. (2002). *The mind and the brain: Neuroplasticity and the power of mental force.* HarperCollins Publishers.

Shapiro, F. (2001). *Eye movement desensitization and reprocessing: Basic principles, protocols and procedures* (2nd ed.). Guilford Press.

Siegel, D. J. (1999). *The developing mind: How relationships and the brain interact to shape who we are.* Guilford Press.

Siegel, D. J. (2003). An interpersonal neurobiology of psychotherapy: The developing mind and the resolution of trauma. In M. E. Solomon & D. J. Siegel (Eds.), *Healing trauma: Attachment, mind, body, and brain* (pp. 1-56). Norton.

Siegel, D. J. (2010b). *The mindful therapist: A clinician's guide to mindsight and neural integration.* W. W. Norton & Company.

Stoffers, J. M., Vollm, B. A., Rucker, G., Timmer, A., Huband, N., & Lieb, K. (2012). Psychological therapies for people with borderline personality disorder. *Cochrane Database Systematic Review, 8*(8), CD005652. https://doi.org/10.1002/14651858.CD005652.pub2.

Substance Abuse and Mental Health Services Administration-Health Resources and Services Administration. (n.d.). *Trauma.* https://www.integration.samhsa.gov/clinical-practice/trauma

Tormoen, A. J., Groholt, B., Haga, E., Brager-Larsen, A., Miller, A., Walby, F., Stanley, B., & Mehlum, L. (2014). Feasibility of dialectical behavior therapy with suicidal and self-harming adolescents with multi-problems: Training, adherence, and retention. *Archives of Suicide Research, 18*(4), 432-444. https://doi.org/10.1080/13811118.2013.826156.

Trippany, R. L., Helm, H. M., & Simpson, L. (2006). Trauma reenactment: Rethinking borderline personality disorder when diagnosing sexual abuse survivors. *Journal of Mental Health Counseling, 28*, 95-110.

Trippany, R. L., White, V. E., & Wilcoxon, S. A. (2004). Vicarious trauma: What counselors should know about working with trauma survivors. *Journal of Counseling and Development, 82,* 31-37.

van der Kolk, B. (2014). *The body keeps the score: Brain, mind, and body in the healing of trauma.* Penguin Books.

Viamontes, G. I., & Beitman, B. B. (2009). Brain processes informing psychotherapy. In G. O. Gabbard (Ed.), *Textbook of psychotherapeutic treatments.* American Psychiatric Publishing.

Wang, D. C. (2014). Secondary and vicarious trauma: Implications for faith and clinical practice. *Journal of Psychology and Christianity, 33,* 281-286.

Weiner, D. A., Schneider, A., & Lyons, J. S. (2009). Evidence-based treatments for trauma among culturally diverse foster care youth: Treatment retention and outcomes. *Children and Youth Services Review, 31*(11), 1199-1205.

Welch, S. S., & Kim, J. (2012). DBT-enhanced cognitive behavioral therapy for adolescent trichotillomania: An adolescent case study. *Cognitive and Behavioral Practice, 19*(3), 483-493.

Wheelis, J. (2009). Theory and practice of dialectical behavioral therapy. In G. O. Gabbard (Ed.), *Textbook of psychotherapeutic treatments.* American Psychiatric Publishing.

Widom, C. S., Czaja, S. J., & Paris, J. (2009) A prospective investigation of borderline personality disorder in abused and neglected children followed up into adulthood. *Journal of Personality Disorders, 23,* 433–446.

Zilberstein, K. (2014). Neurocognitive considerations in the treatment of attachment and complex trauma in children. *Clinical Child Psychology and Psychiatry 19*(3) 336–354.

CHAPTER 19
Counseling Women Who Have Been Sexually Abused

JAMA DAVIS, PH.D. & REBECCA TAYLOR, PH.D.

"You see them and who they are, but you must also always see who they were."
~Dr. Diane Langberg

"Be strong and courageous. Do not be afraid or terrified because of them, for the LORD your God goes with you; he will never leave you or forsake you"
(Deuteronomy 31:6, NIV)

Wisdom from Above: Standing in His Grace

Sexual abuse and injustice grieve the heart of God. In 2 Samuel 13, Tamar was raped by her half-brother, and experienced both rape and incest at the hands of Amnon, an heir to the throne of King David. God's law in Leviticus 18:11 was violated when Amnon was intentional in his disobedience. Tamar's life was forever changed, and she lived her life as a "desolate woman" (*New International Bible,*1973/2011, 2 Samuel 13:20). King David also failed Tamar by not holding Amnon accountable for this atrocity. Pain runs deep for survivors of sexual abuse. God hates sexual abuse and grieves with those who experience it. He is also a God of healing and offers hope, a hope that Tamar was unable to grasp. God promised in Isaiah 60 that those who have felt alone and uncared for will be made beautiful. As counselors, we have the privilege of hearing and holding stories of those who have been abused. We have the opportunity to be

CHAPTER LEARNING OBJECTIVES

Upon completing this chapter, you should be able to:

- Articulate the definition of sexual abuse
- Identify the characteristics and consequences of sexual abuse
- Understand evidence-based treatment phases while also incorporating Biblical insights
- Recognize the process of transitioning clients from victim to survivor and into healthy functioning

conduits of hope and help restore dignity through our presence and willingness to listen, hear, and guide their healing process. May we not take this privilege lightly, and instead, we should enter each encounter with a sexual abuse survivor by offering respect, dignity, and hope.

CHAPTER OVERVIEW

Shame, unanswered questions, uncertainty, loss of hope, body memories, and emotional triggers are some of what lives in the minds of sexual abuse survivors. The woman's innocence, her joy, her smile, her hope, and all other areas that were impacted are altered when the abuse occurred, whether it was one time or repeated. Abuse changes a person. It changes their view of life. What once felt safe might be riddled with fear. Where laughter once occurred may bring memories of pain. Innocence may have turned to shame (Trickett et al., 2011). Recognizing the statistics that represent women who have been abused, it is likely that many women reading these words have been sexually abused at some point in their lives. We know the statistics for reported abuse. What we do not have are the numbers of unreported cases. Most likely, many women never became part of the known statistics (Murray et al., 2015). We want to be mindful of the many women around us who may have been abused and perhaps even our personal history with abuse.

Before going further, it is important to be clear regarding the need for anyone who is working with sexual abuse survivors to ensure they have addressed their woundedness. If you have a history of sexual abuse in your past, do not work with other survivors until you have addressed your own healing through your own personal counseling. Please do not read this as a suggestion. Rather see this as a requirement, professionally and ethically. We cannot sit with others and hear their stories of trauma without those stories impacting us. If we have not done our personal work for sexual abuse or other trauma that may be part of our history, we may be triggered during sessions and issues of countertransference may occur. Counseling is always about the client, not about having our own emotional needs met. Countertransference occurs when counselors are triggered by their own history and respond out of their unmet needs or lack of healing. This then shifts the focus from the client to the counselor's unresolved history. In this chapter, you will learn how to define sexual abuse along with the characteristics and consequences. A treatment approach consisting of three phases will be presented as will a discussion of transitioning clients to healthy functioning. This single chapter is in no way comprehensive. Rather we hope it will provide the groundwork and guide your work with sexual abuse survivors.

SEXUAL ABUSE

"Me, too.", the two words that have taken on a powerful and distinct meaning since 2018. These words link friends and strangers alike in the shared experience of childhood sexual abuse. Child sexual abuse can happen anywhere and to any family. No demographic is safe from childhood sexual abuse. Children are the least able to protect themselves, and perpetrators offend against those who are most vulnerable. The consequenc-

© oleschwander/Shutterstock.com

es, if left untreated, may become a lifetime influence over relationships, a woman's sense of self, and the inability to cope through other adverse life events. There may be long term impact on emotional, physical, and social well-being for the individual.

In the United States, estimates are that 1 in 3 girls and 1 in 5 boys have been sexually abused (The Advocacy Center, n.d.), often by those who are closest to them, either in proximity or in familial relationships. Some estimates place the number of children who have been sexually abused much higher at nearly 40% for all children in the United States. (American College of Obstetricians and Gynecologists [ACOG], 2011). The Rape Abuse and Incest National Network (2019) reported that every 9 minutes, a claim of child sexual abuse is substantiated by investigators. It is estimated that there are more than 42 million survivors of childhood sexual abuse (CSA) in the United States (National Association of Adult Survivors of Child Abuse, n.d.). For too many years, sexual abuse was a topic avoided and became secrets kept, often across generations.

Secrets kept often become secrets that harm. Sharing the secret of sexual abuse is complex. Secrets tend to negatively influence the emotional health of victims, as well as relationships across generations. There is a cost to secret keeping. McElvaney and colleagues (2012) found that the cost was most often emotional. The secret had a tendency to leak out and negatively impact relationships. When the pressure to keep the secret becomes too great, the feelings of anger, shame, guilt, and sadness will impact the individual's ability to cope with day to day life (McElvaney et al., 2012). Clients often come to counseling due to an overwhelming sense of shame and guilt as a direct result of secrets kept. A child may not understand what is happening to them from a developmental perspective, but they do feel shame and guilt, because they have been told not to tell or that

© chrisdorney/Shutterstock.com

what is happening is their fault. Depending on the developmental stage of the child when the abuse occurred, the impact of sexual abuse negatively influences the development of identity, trust, purpose in life, and how to make and maintain proper boundaries with others.

Shame and guilt may be complicated by possible sexual and emotional responses to the abuse. Children are not emotionally or cognitively equipped to manage the physiological responses associated with sexual abuse (American Academy of Child and Adolescent Psychiatry, 2014). Balter and colleagues (2016) noted that as children develop, curiosity about their body increases, but this curiosity develops within the context of the environment. If CSA is present, natural curiosity is complicated by emotional and physical responses to the abuse. If guilt and shame are part of this emotional and physical response, the long-term consequences of abuse become embedded in the emerging self.

In the 1980s, emerging CSA literature provided a conceptual framework for trauma, integrating concepts of psychological adjustment, pubertal development, and physiological stress (Trickett et al., 2011). Psychobiological factors such as pubertal development and physiological stress related to childhood sexual abuse may impact biopsychosocial development and psychological adjustment (Putnam & Trickett, 1987; Putnam & Trickett, 1993; Trickett et al., 2011). Irish et al. (2009) linked childhood sexual abuse at an early age with psychobiological and behavioral factors across the lifespan. Factors influencing positive development outcomes included the duration of the sexual abuse, frequency of the sexual abuse, how the child was related to the abuser, whether physical violence was present, and the age of onset all influenced the long term psychological outcomes for childhood sexual abuse. These early studies not only demonstrated that childhood sexual abuse created long term consequences, but defined the parameters of these consequences. Recent research conducted by Easton (2019) found that the level of public awareness, societal attitudes, as well as resources for recovery, have become exponentially available over the past few decades. The more open, current discussion of sexual abuse has created public awareness and understanding that the abuse harms children. Greater access to resources for recovery increases the possibility that CSA will become part of the individual narrative, but not the entire story.

Child Sexual Abuse Defined

Sexual abuse defined by the *DSM-5* (APA, 2013) as any sexual act involving a child for the sexual gratification of a parent, caregiver, or another individual or individuals who are responsible for the safety and well-being of a child includes "fondling of genitals, penetration, incest, rape, sodomy or indecent exposure" (American Psychiatric Association [APA], 2013, p. 718) and is defined by the *DSM-5* (APA, 2013) as any sexual act involving a child for the sexual gratification of a parent, caregiver, or another individual or individuals who are responsible for the safety and well-being of a child. Sexual abuse also involves the kissing of genitals or forcing the child to view pornography, according to Tong and Gillespie (2011). Non-contact exploitation by a parent or caregiver includes "force, tricking, enticing or threatening" (APA, 2013, p. 718). Any sexual contact between an adult and a child who has not reached the age of consent is considered sexual abuse (Murray et al., 2015).

Incest Defined

Incest is defined as a sexual relationship between close biological relatives, including between father and child, mother and child, grandparents or other relatives, and the child. Incest is also sexual abuse. Gomes et al. (2014) noted that paternal incest is one of the "most serious forms of intrafamilial sexual abuse with clinical, social, and legal relevance" (p. 255). Sibling sexual abuse is potentially as harmful as incestuous sexual abuse by a parent (Yates, 2016). A broader definition by Gomes et al. (2014) included step-parent or step-sibling sexual relationships. One characteristic of incest is the hidden nature of the abuse. An open or closed family system not only has an impact on the possibility of abuse but the ability to hide what is happening. Open family systems allow individuals to receive and share information, as well as free access to others. A closed family system does not allow outside information in and establishes secrecy. The emotional ties between the abuser and the child contribute to secret-keeping.

One-third of all cases of incest are intrafamilial and have been noted as a "silent health emergency" by the World Health Organization (WHO; 2017). Father-daughter incest is considered one of the most severe forms of intrafamilial sexual abuse with legal consequences, clinical implications for the child, and intrafamilial relationships (Gomes et al., 2014). Father-daughter incest (FDI) is responsible for 13% of all sexual crimes (Gomes et al., 2014). Although limited in scope, a study by Stroebel et al. (2013) provided insight into the nature of FDI and potential risk factors. In families where parents participated in verbal or physical fighting, the risk of FDI increased by five times. For those families where father-daughter nudity or where maternal affection was lacking, risk also increased. The most significant finding was that living in homes of single-parent mothers or a non-biologically related male increased the risk by more than ten times (Goodyear-Brown et al., 2012), with some estimates of increased risk as high as 20 times.

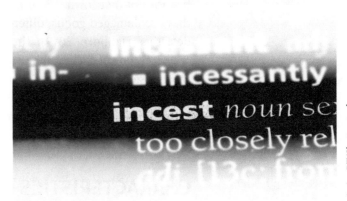

© Casimiro PT/Shutterstock.com

The most prevalent form of sexual abuse in families is sibling sexual abuse (Carlson et al. 2006; Kreinert & Walsh, 2011; Thompson, 2009). Historically, sibling sexual abuse has not raised the same red flags as FDI or abuse at the hands of other abusers. Yates (2016) noted that sibling sexual abuse is possibly just as harmful as sexual abuse by a parent, despite the lower reported incidents. Other research found that sibling sexual abuse occurs twice as often as other forms of abuse within families and may be five times more common than FDI (Carlson et al., 2006; Monahan, 2010). As with any abuse, there is a stigma attached, and families may fear that, if reported to a service provider, protective services will become involved. Secrets are kept, abusers are protected, and the child may come to believe that they are not worthy of protection.

Mother-child incest represents a very significant disruption in the relationship between a child and the caregiver, charged with their safety and security (Haliburn, 2017). Attachment theory posits that the primary nurturer and protector of an infant is the mother (Bowlby, 1988). For many years, a lack of acknowledgment that mother-child incest was even possible created a gap in the literature for this particular form of sexual abuse. According to Haliburn (2017), mother-child incest is a double betrayal, violating trust and exploiting the needs and dependent nature of the relationship. Strickland (2008) found that female sex offenders, when compared to other perpetrators of child sexual abuse, have complex trauma histories of their own. Victims of mother-daughter incest often feel that they are damaged goods, different from others, and believe that they are defective (Haliburn, 2017). The consequences of mother-daughter incest are based on the lack of the mother to provide safety and security in the most basic sense. Mother-son incest is an underreported form of incest, but the emotional consequences for males are guilt, along with desire, confusion, anger, and a love/hate relationship with his mother (Haliburn, 2017).

CHARACTERISTICS OF VULNERABILITY

Some environmental characteristics may increase the risk of sexual abuse for the child. These risk factors may be comprised of family dynamics, single-parent households, a boyfriend, or stepfather living in the home, and a lack of paternal affection (Goodyear-Brown et al., 2012). The WHO (2004) included being female, social isolation, parents with substance abuse issues, foster children, and children who are physically or mentally handicapped as factors that contributed to increased risk for victimization. Murray et al. (2015) noted that sexual abuse often co-occurs with other forms of abuse and neglect, including low caregiver warmth, high-stress family systems, and lack of support for parents. The risk of a single-parent household is a lack of supervision, and a misplaced trust reflected in the 27% increased risk related to a non-biologically related male in the home (Goodyear-Brown et al., 2012).

Disclosure

Many factors contribute to a child or adolescent disclosure of sexual abuse. Disclosure is defined as the child or adolescent sharing information about the sexual abuse to others. An earlier discussion noted that the level of attachment and connectedness to primary caregivers, particularly the mother, influence whether a child discloses sexual abuse (Wamser-Nanney & Sager, 2018). Age of the child, characteristics of the sexual abuse, and child reported abuse stressors are essential predictors of maternal support following disclosure (Wamser-Nanney & Sager, 2018). Factors for disclosure are related to intrapersonal barriers, relationship barriers, and societal barriers, including stigma (Collin-Vezina et al., 2015).

© Yeexin Richelle/Shutterstock.com

Barriers to disclosure may include a lack of information regarding knowledge about one's body and how to set or maintain personal boundaries (Brattfjiell & Flam, 2018). The emotional responses to sexual abuse include shame and guilt, which also become dual barriers to disclosure. Internal factors discussed by Collin-Vezina et al. (2015) included self-blame, stage of development, or an emotional protective factor. Disclosure means that the child must relive the abuse, reexperiencing the feelings associated with the abuse. Shame and guilt are the result of the secretive nature of the abuse, as well as developmental and cognitive unfolding. The child may love the abuser and feel a need to protect him or her. The child may also choose to not disclose due to threats of harm to the child or the family. These could include threats of parental divorce or harm to cherished pets if the child discloses.

Sorensen and Snow (1991) suggested that the process of disclosure often involves denial, reluctance, disclosure, recantation, and affirmation. Other factors, such as powerlessness, betrayal, stigmatization, and traumatic sexualization, distort the individual's ability to view the world as a safe place (Finkelhor & Browne, 1985). In the family, if there is a close attachment relationship, and strong family connectedness is present, the child is more likely to disclose, secure with the knowledge that their sharing will be believed. Depending on the reactions of the person to whom the disclosure is made, healing may begin or might be deferred, sometimes over the lifespan. It is important to remember that secrets held are secrets that may harm. The goal of counseling is to come alongside the individual, walking with them as they share their story and move from victim to survivor.

FIGURE 19.1

The Process of Disclosure

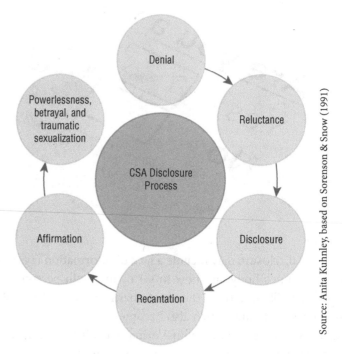

Source: Anita Kuhnley, based on Sorenson & Snow (1991)

Theories of healing after CSA note that disclosure and being believed are the critical first steps towards long term positive outcomes, socially and emotionally (Easton, 2019). When a child discloses, the first reaction by caregivers may be anger, perhaps towards the child, or towards the individual who has caused the harm. It is important to remember that children when they do not understand what is happening, may attribute blame to themselves. When a parent or other individual is trusted enough for the child to disclose, it is critical that anger not be displayed. Zawastak (2018) provided a plan of action for parents or others when a child discloses sexual abuse. The first is not to overreact. Strong emotions are often present for the adult, but it is so crucial for the child to not see themselves as having done something wrong. Easton (2019) found that secondary prevention programs encourage children to report the abuse, never keep secrets, and continue telling adults until someone takes action.

Stigma

Stigma (means that others attribute blame to the one being sexually abused, not the perpetrator, for what happened to him or her. Stigma feels like a mark of disgrace for the one who has been abused) related to sexual abuse contributes to the shame and guilt carried by the individual. As the individual develops a sense of self, stigma becomes the burden for actions committed by another against the child or adolescent. Stigma also means that others attribute blame to the one being sexually abused, not the perpetrator, for what happened to him or her. A child is never, ever responsible for sexual abuse, and it is the responsibility of those who care for children to ensure that a child feels safe and secure in this knowledge.

Research has also found that the stigma of CSA contributes to the development of disruptions in the formation of intimate relationships, emotionally and sexually. As the adolescent attempts to move through developmental stages of identity formation, fear, and hopelessness because of the sexual abuse become incorporated into their identity. The task following identity formation involves intimacy and isolation. Feiring et al. (2009) noted that intimacy for those who have been sexually abused, but who have not received treatment, is associated with fear and shame, rather than the caring and optimistic sharing with another, socially, emotionally, and sexually.

© Vitezslav Vylicil/Shutterstock.com

Adolescents, as they move towards adulthood, seek to make, and maintain long term relationships with others at the most intimate level. With stigma, there is often a sense that the child or adolescent is alone and that no one else has ever had this happen to them. It is only through sharing the experiences that a personal narrative of shame can be changed to reflect hope and healing for what has happened that was beyond the control of a child. It is possible to move from victim to survivor, and the next section of this chapter will focus on specific interventions designed to create a new narrative of healing.

PERPETRATOR CHARACTERISTICS

There is no definitive system of profiling that will predict who will perpetrate sexual abuse against a child. Any individual in the home, school, religious institution, or any other setting where children are present has the potential to perpetrate against children. Several factors are related to the characteristics of those who are sexually abused, as well as perpetrator characteristics. Teaching our children about "Stranger Danger" does not address the real scope of the problem and may leave them vulnerable to sexual abuse by those they know and trust. For this chapter, it is important to note that danger for most children exists in the home and among friends (Smallbone & Wortley, 2001). Parents must be aware of any changes in behaviors or emotional responses, as well as grooming behaviors used by perpetrators (Smallbone & Wortley, 2001).

Recent studies have sought to identify perpetrator characteristics. Prediction is difficult due to numerous other interrelated intrapersonal and interpersonal characteristics (Hassan et al., 2014). Parents and other caregivers must be aware and sensitive to anything that does not feel "right" between their children and others with whom they come in contact. Juvenile and adult males commit the majority of sex offenses against children, but female perpetrators do exist (Hassan et al., 2014). Juvenile perpetrators represent a category separate from other perpetrator demographics, with differing predispositions, including a history of previous physical or sexual abuse, as well as witnessing family violence (Ryan & Ontichar, 2007). Research investigating juvenile perpetrators found that one-half of all sex offenses by juveniles were committed against a sibling (Malin et al., 2014).

Mediating factors for perpetrator characteristics include age at first offense, issues of mental illness, sexual orientation, preferences for males or female children, personality traits, and whether or not the individual him or herself was also sexually abused as a child. Ryan and Hall (2007) proposed that individuals who perpetrate against children may experience feelings of inferiority or lack age-appropriate relationships due to lack of emotional maturity. The authors also noted that reduced assertiveness, use of passive-aggressive behaviors, and cognitive distortions about appropriate decision making are present (Ryan & Hall, 2007). Those who perpetrate against children may report disturbance of affect, emotional dysphoria, anxiety, and personality disorders, primarily **Cluster B and C personality disorders** (Cluster B personality disorders are characterized as unpredictable and acting with overly dramatic and emotional behavior. Cluster C personality disorders are characterized by a high level of anxiety) (Ryan & Hall, 2007).

Characteristics of juvenile perpetrators who are younger than 16 are more complicated, primarily due to age differential from the child being sexually abused, stage of psychosocial development, and environmental risk factors. According to Hassan et al. (2014), the inability to form relationships with peers, the experience of rejection, and lack of family cohesion are factors that generate significant risk. These risk factors can be seen in a lack of connectedness through peer and family bonding, a lack of family cohesion, and environments that do not model positive coping behaviors across interpersonal and social stressors.

Many juvenile perpetrators are male and have often been sexually abused (Ryan & Ontichar, 2007). Ryan and Ontichar (2007) found that, in comparison, juvenile perpetrators were more likely to have been physically or sexually abused or had been exposed to sexual violence within the family. All of these risk factors create a situation where the individual may perpetrate against younger children to bolster a sense of power and control, or a sense of connectedness to others through inappropriate sexual contact.

Grooming

Grooming in the most general terms, involves gaining access to the child, gaining trust, and then progressing to sexual abuse. Grooming refers to a process where the child is engaged in behaviors that encourage trust, allows the perpetrator to have access to the child successfully, and keeps the child and others free of suspicion regarding the perpetrator's intentions towards the child (Wolf & Pruitt, 2019). Bennet and O'Donohue (2014) proposed that grooming includes inappropriate behavior on the part of the adult and that this behavior serves to increase the likelihood of future abuse. Grooming can also include subtle everyday actions that may consist of interest by an adult that goes beyond casual contact. For example, the perpetrator has a focused interest in one child of a family, seeks opportunities to spend time with a child, and buys gifts for one child in a family (American Bar Association [ABA], 2015). The ABA goes on to note that the grooming process includes activities with a child that arouse sexual feelings in individuals who have a sexual interest in children, such as bathing the child. The National Center for Victims of Crime (NCVC; 2019) added other elements to the grooming process. The grooming process may include identification of the intended victim, such as a preference for a specific age group or gender (Ryan & Hall, 2007). When the ecology of the child is at risk, either through insecure attachment, parental characteristics, or other risk factors, vulnerability for sexual abuse increases. Other grooming behaviors included playing a significant role in the life of the child or using emotional manipulation to coerce the child into a secret and sexually abusive relationship. Controlling the relationship, initiation of sexual contact, and isolating the child from family or friends all contribute to the secretive nature of abuse. Some perpetrators have been able to successfully abuse the child, even while in the presence of others (NCVC, 2019).

From a forensic and legal perspective, a more concrete definition would be helpful, as well as a way to identify and measure grooming behaviors. This would, in turn, allow counselors to more accurately determine if grooming is occurring before the actual abuse occurs (Bennett & O'Donohue, 2014). Unfortunately, as with perpetrators, there is no one definitive pattern for grooming. Those who sexually abuse children very often manipulate children and families into trusting them (ABA, 2015), which makes grooming behaviors challenging to identify.

FIGURE 19.2

Grooming Behaviors

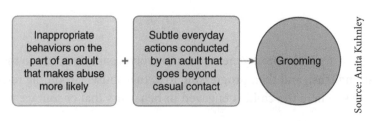

Source: Anita Kuhnley

POST SEXUAL ABUSE CONSEQUENCES

The existing literature has noted long term consequences of CSA. In 2011, the American College of Obstetricians and Gynecologists (ACOG) stated that the long-term consequences vary with the individual, are interrelated with interpersonal and environmental factors, and can be emotionally devastating to the individual. These consequences may be psychosocial, psychosexual, and/or behavioral. Adverse outcomes also include emotional and physical sequelae. CSA was related to gastroenterological, gynecological, and cardiopulmonary concerns in adulthood

(Irish et al., 2009). A recent study by Klumparendt and colleagues (2019) found that those who experienced childhood maltreatment were at increased risk for major depressive disorders in adulthood. Klumparendt et al. (2019) further noted that maltreatment may include sexual, physical, and/or emotional abuse.

Fergusson et al. (2013) extended previous research, finding that childhood sexual abuse influenced a broad spectrum of adult developmental outcomes. These include **post-traumatic stress disorder (PTSD)** symptoms, risky sexual behaviors, and increased risk for mental health concerns (Fergusson et al., 2013). CSA elevates the risk for risky sexual behaviors, including promiscuity, according to Abajobir et al. (2017).

As noted earlier, there are transgenerational consequences for CSA. Cush (2018) provided insight into the emerging field of neurological effects for CSA. In addition to altered interpersonal relationships, the body chemistry of the individual is altered in response to stress hormones. These elevated stress hormones may alter genetic coding, thus impacting succeeding generations. Traumatic disruption in the environment can either turn a gene on or off and is classified as epigenetic change (Cush, 2018). Research is ongoing in the area of genetics, but there is evidence that two epigenetically mediated effects influence the genetic transmission of trauma. The first epigenetic mediated effect consists of maternal stress both during pregnancy and after the child is born. The second epigenetic impact is through preconception trauma of parents, thus influencing the biological inheritance for stress related influences (Yehuda & Lehrner, 2018). Thus, the long-term consequences of stress may be passed down to subsequent generations through genetic alterations.

Mental health consequences of CSA include anxiety, depression, and possible recurring symptoms of dissociation (Hall & Hall, 2011). ACOG (2011) noted that fear, shame, humiliation, guilt, and self-blame contributed to anxiety and depression. Individuals who have experienced sexual abuse are at increased risk for depression, anxiety, and suicidal behaviors, especially during adolescence (Brown et al., 1999). Other consequences of CSA include greater levels of reported trauma related symptoms and lower levels of secure attachment relationships in adulthood. Since the primary task of adolescence is identity formation, when this is disrupted through experiences of CSA, a coherent sense of self may be compromised. For some children who have been sexually abused, PTSD is a severe emotional outcome. The *DSM-5* (APA, 2013) uses specific criteria for a diagnosis of **PTSD** (a mental health disorder characterized by difficulty recovering from experiencing or being witness to an event where actual or threatened death, serious injury or sexual violence occurred, according to the *DSM-5*). These criteria include, but are not limited to, exposure to actual or threatened death of the child or loved one, presence of intrusion symptoms, persistent avoidance of stimuli associated with the traumatic event(s), and negative changes in how one thinks about the abuse or mood changes. The *DSM-5* (APA, 2013) goes on to note that PTSD is associated with physical, emotional, and occupational disability. Functional impairment has an impact on every relationship for the individual, across all domains of his or her ecological system. The National Institute of Mental Health (NIMH; 2019) does not distinguish between trauma that results in PTSD symptoms; however, the report does indicate that children can have extreme responses to trauma. These symptoms may not be the same as those of adults and may include reexperiencing, avoidance, reactivity and behavioral symptoms (NIMH, 2019).

Featured Practitioner
Diane Langberg, Ph.D.

I began seeing clients in 1972 after finishing my master's degree and while working on my doctorate. I worked at the university counseling center and also with a Christian private practice group. There were very few females in the field (I was the only one in my doctoral program). Women requested to meet with me, not because I knew anything (I was 23) but because I was female. I heard things like, "My father did weird things to me" or "My husband gets angry sometimes". I had no idea of the stories behind such words. I asked questions and little by little began to learn of the sexual abuse, rape, violence and humiliating behaviors many girls and women endured alone. I was also working with Vietnam vets and it eventually dawned on me that the soldiers and the women had the same symptoms. My conclusion was that there was more than one kind of war zone. Keep in mind that Posttraumatic Stress Disorder was not a diagnostic category until 1980.

There was nothing in my graduate work about trauma, abuse, violence against women or combat. The feminist movement was just beginning to talk about rape. I told my clients there were no resources and that I did not know what would help them. I told them that if they were willing to help me understand what it was like to be them, I would do my best to find ways to help them look at hard and ugly things and then search together for ways to alleviate their pain and help them to be safe and learn how to flourish. So began a journey that would determine the focus of my work and change me in many ways. It has been one of the greatest privileges of my life to learn from victims and walk with them in their courageous journey toward truth, health and freedom.

Best practices for working with survivors are not techniques or models – all of which can be very helpful. They are adjunct. Your character is preeminent. Have you studied trauma and abuse and what it does to precious people made in the image of God? Are you a safe person? Do you have tested and tried integrity? Are you aware of your own impact on the one in front of you? Are you humble, knowing that no matter how many stories you hear you still do not know what it was like for the next person. Even if you, yourself, have suffered abuse, each person, story and the impact are unique. Never assume you know. Can you wait – for words, feelings and questions? Can you be steady in the storm of doubts and fears without having to find a "quick fix" in part to ease your own pain or discomfort?

You are the tool. That also means you must learn how to take good care of yourself. Trauma and abuse are ugly, chaotic, evil, overwhelming and painful. Seek antidotes to these things. Seek beauty. Deliberately and consistently find ways to inject beauty, order, quiet and respite into your life. I find very human things like music, nature and safe friends, who know how to laugh, to be necessary if I am to continue. Ultimately, all of those things are found in Jesus Christ. Nurture your life in him. Study his word, his character and his response to suffering. Pursue him. He will use this work to pursue you as he is always working both sides. The work is a front row seat to his redemptive work. But this work will also expose you to yourself. Seek Christ as Teacher, as Refuge and as the Potter. He who will one day redeem all things will use the suffering and darkness brought to you by others as a place of redemption – for them and for you. Ultimately the work is a call to incarnate the character of Jesus Christ in the flesh. Whatever the outcome of a particular case, we delight the heart of the Father when we bear the aroma of his Son in our lives.

Contributed by Diane Langberg. © Kendall Hunt Publishing Company.

TREATMENT

Chapter 18 introduced evidence-based therapies for working with clients who experienced trauma. In this chapter, we will focus on some interventions specific to sexual abuse. Sexual abuse survivors develop personal narratives that unfold with the abuse. Included in the narratives of those who have been sexually abused are questions related to identity, responsibility, guilt, shame, and victimization.

© tsuponk/Shutterstock.com

Assessment

A thorough **psychosocial assessment** (the process of gathering information related to the current issue, past history of treatment, current level of functioning and then making treatment decisions to guide work in the counseling relationship) is essential to develop an understanding and an appropriate approach to treatment. Included in this assessment is an exploration of the religious or spiritual history of the client. Pressley and Spinazzola (2015) recognized this spiritual assessment as leading to an understanding of spiritual distress, and examining how spiritual and religious beliefs impact a person's view of their trauma history along with their view of God. Spiritual assessments can be instrumental in bringing this information to the surface in ways that might otherwise be difficult for the client to express. Christian counselors will enter the counseling relationship with the understanding that people are image-bearers of God's likeness. Clinicians working with Christian clients can assist trauma survivors toward healing that includes "adopting new beliefs about the self as a person of worth" (Pressley & Spinazzola, 2015, p. 10).

Additionally, when trauma occurs, a person's system of meaning is altered. This personal meaning-making can include a loss of faith, hopelessness, and despair. For Christian clients who have lost a sense of hope and faith or recognize this has been an intense wounding, there is the opportunity for Christian counselors to connect "deeply and sensitively" in restoring this hope and faith (Pressley & Spinazzola, 2015, p. 11).

Counseling Implications

Abuse shatters a sense of stability in all areas of life. As we work with clients, understanding the depth of the impact is extremely important. Dr. Diane Langberg (2015b) stated that "trauma can shape and also shatter meaning", discussing how trauma assaults an individual and turns a person's beliefs about themselves, others, and God literally "upside-down" (Langberg, 2015b). With **trauma** (any physical or emotional experience that has long term emotional, physical, or social consequences for the individual), and in this case specifically CSA, a person's world changes. What may have seemed safe becomes insecure. The abused child becomes frozen at the time of the abuse and begins to view life through the framework of abuse. Questions that were not previously present now fill the survivor's mind. CSA impacts families and generations. Developing trust in relationships and intimate marriages can bring a level of difficulty that others without this experience are unable to comprehend (Godbout et al., 2009; Jeong & Cha, 2019).

Who am I? What is wrong with me? Will I always see myself as a victim? How did this happen to me? Why wasn't I protected? Will my life ever be the same? Will I ever be loved for who I am? What does this mean? Will I ever be able to trust? Where was/is God? Will I ever feel safe?

FIGURE 19.3

Survivor Questions

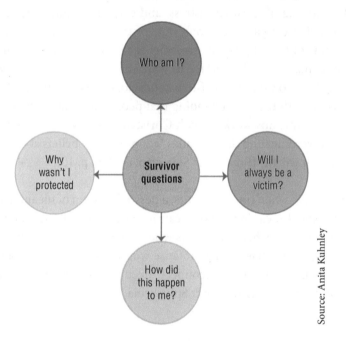

Source: Anita Kuhnley

Recognizing they are no longer able to cope with their history of sexual trauma, seeking help can leave a survivor feeling uncertain and weak. It is important for the counselor to help the client reframe their decision to seek help as being one of courage (Herman, 1992). When a client recognizes the reality of their situation and decides to step towards change, this empowers the survivor. Some survivors may see the decision to seek help as one of weakness and giving a "win" to the abuse when, in reality, it is quite the opposite. It takes strength to step toward support and work to end the silence and isolation. Counselors need to be intentional in their efforts to help clients realize they are not responsible for what happened to them and understand the abuse history informs their present life but does not have to dictate their life. Sexual abuse was a part of their life but is not the lens that determines their future.

TREATMENT PROCESS

Though it is understood that CSA is a prevalent problem, the healing process for those impacted is not clearly identified and understood in the research. Jeong and Cha (2019), realizing a specific theoretical model of treatment for childhood sexual abuse survivors had not been tested, sought to describe the healing experience portrayed by CSA survivors in the literature from 2007-2017. Drauker et al. (2011) proposed a four-stage model of healing that includes: struggling with the meaning of CSA, identifying the meaning of CSA, addressing the effects of CSA, and recovering a sense of control over one's life. Jeong and Cha (2019) also reviewed studies that were focused on coping and found these limited as they did not move individuals towards healing. Jeong and Cha (2019) indicated a lack of evidence surrounding the healing experience of CSA survivors, which led to their study on the experience of healing. It is vital in working with CSA survivors to facilitate growth, moving from coping to healing and recovery.

Judith Herman (1992) offered a phased treatment model. Over time, this model has become the foundation for treating complex trauma, including sexual abuse, and is referred to extensively by Gingrich (2017) and Langberg (1997).

FIGURE 19.4

Herman's (1992)
Model Includes
Three Phases of
Treatment

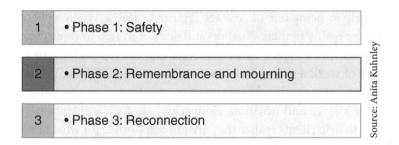

1	• Phase 1: Safety
2	• Phase 2: Remembrance and mourning
3	• Phase 3: Reconnection

Source: Anita Kuhnley

Establishing Rapport

Building a strong therapeutic relationship (the process by which the counselor and the client are able to trust one another and work towards treatment goals for the client) is essential before beginning any counseling, regardless of approach, and even more critical when working with sexual abuse survivors. Survivors need time to develop trust, and the time necessary for this can vary. Counselors need to be patient in this process and intentionally aware of times when they sense trust is increasing. Reaffirming themselves as trustworthy and safe is essential throughout the process. This sense of safety includes things that may seem unrelated though essential, including, for example, being on time for appointments, alerting the client if there are any unexpected changes to upcoming schedules or appointments, or alerting the client if the office will be changed in any way. These connect in with the client's sense of safety and security that was shattered by the abuse. Proactive communication and predictability increase a sense of safety, facilitating the development of trust.

Sexual abuse, as with any trauma, is much more than what occurred in the past. At the point of trauma, emotional and physical sensations were present and imprinted in the mind and body. In the present, these are experienced not just as memories but as unsettling physical reactions (Van Der Kolk, 2014). Counselors need to work with sexual abuse survivors to find ways to calm themselves and be present in the current time and space, followed by maintaining a sense of calm when responding to images and sensations connected with the past abuse. There becomes this sought balance for clients of being fully engaged and aware of others around them - both fully present and engaged. Helping clients understand the importance of not keeping secrets is important (Van Der Kolk, 2014). Secrecy breeds isolation and loneliness, furthering the sense of shame. Putting a voice to secrets allows truth to surface and recognition of the ways the woman worked to survive both during the abuse and in the time since the abuse.

Building an approach based on Herman's (1992) model, we will explore three phases:

> Phase 1: Developing Safety and Stability
> Phase 2: Remembering, Mourning and Processing the Trauma
> Phase 3: Reconnecting and Strength Development

Herman (1992) described recovery as occurring in three stages, with central tasks in each stage. The first stage involves establishing safety with the second stage focusing on remembrance and grief. The third stage involves the survivor reconnecting with her ordinary life. Herman (1992) recognized the stages attempt to bring order and ease to a process that is better described as unsettled and complicated. Though there are stages identified, it is important to recognize these are not straightforward and linear. Often progress is made, and then earlier issues surface in memory and are later revisited with an increased level of integration of learning from the recovery process. This is like a prism. When the client continues through counseling, the light shifts. New reflections are seen, and new insights are gained.

Phase 1: Developing Safety and Stability

Treating sexual trauma is complex and, therefore, needs to be comprehensive. Appropriate treatment is essential at each stage, with shifts from one approach to another as the client progresses through treatment. What was helpful at one stage may not be at another. A willingness of the counselor to be attuned to these shifts is important. Clients develop a sense of empowerment when there is a validation of their trauma and what occurred (Herman, 1992). For the woman who experienced sexual abuse, this validation and naming of what happened gives her language for her experi-

ences and begins to break the silence that may have been years in the making. So often, the counselor is the first person who has been trusted enough for the client to share what happened to them. The process of developing a safe and trusting environment can seem arduous for both the survivor and counselor, and at times there can be a desire from both the survivor and counselor to move quickly. When this happens, the movement into the therapeutic work comes prematurely, and the survivor's level of safety is compromised. This prematurity can result in an end to the therapeutic relationship with the survivor feeling compromised in some way. It is imperative to build a strong therapeutic relationship that provides a foundation for the healing work ahead.

Social Support – Safety

Support systems are critical for survivors. Arias and Johnson (2013) identified the importance of supportive relationships in the healing process. Supportive relationships bring the opportunity to lessen the impact of the abuse with a negative response compounding the deep hurt (Herman, 1992). The survivor needs to know their support system, even if only one person, will not abandon her. Abandonment would replicate the feelings of aloneness that were present at the time of the abuse. It is vital in this stage of stabilization to inquire about the client's social support. Is her social support safe, available, and reliable? Does she understand how to utilize her support system appropriately? Gingrich (2017) recognized that some survivors do not experience healthy relationships; therefore, the counselor needs to actively engage this process of discernment of whether relationships are safe and healthy. If not, the client may need assistance in the development and/or movement to an environment that is safe from those who create hurt. Also critical is a thorough assessment of the client's safety from self. Suicidality needs to be evaluated and monitored throughout treatment with clear safety plans in place. The client will be unable to move forward in healing without an overall safe environment.

Phase 2: Remembering, Mourning, and Processing the Trauma

This processing begins only after safety has been established, the client has identified social support, and is engaging with the support system. Moving too quickly into this phase jeopardizes the healing process, as the client will not be prepared without safety and social support systems in place. The processing of horrific sexual abuse memories can be difficult for clients and counselors. The reinforcement of social support is essential to support clients through this process (Gingrich, 2017). In this processing, the counselor needs to be especially aware of the need to balance the reality of what happened with the abuse and the client's need for safety (Langberg, 1997).

In this time of processing, clients may experience an intense time of grieving over what has occurred. Some may attempt to hold back tears, for fear that once they begin to cry, they will be unable to stop. Grieving may not be something considered in the healing process. Clients will need to mourn the loss of their childhood and innocence that comes with that part of the healing process. A lost sense of safety, competence, and moral integrity are all part of the intense grief that is present (Langberg, 1997). There may also be grieving over stillborn children due to not having prenatal care, forced abortions, and babies taken from them at birth of whom they do not know the whereabouts (Langberg, 1997). So, we see that grief is both deep and wide for these women and is not to be moved through quickly or minimized in any way. The time it takes to grieve the losses is different for each woman. Though the deep pain of grief does not feel "normal", the process of moving through this season of deep grief does need to be normalized. In this time of grief, the Christian counselor has the opportunity to be the representative of God (Langberg, 1997) found in Isaiah 61:1-7, maintaining mindful professionalism in this role.

Memories

Gingrich (2017) described a method for accessing and processing memories and the intense emotions that accompany them. It is beyond the scope of this chapter to discuss this in detail yet very important to gain an understanding of how to appropriately address the memories and manage the sessions in a way that allows for a sense of safety for the client. It is imper-

© sebastianosecondi/Shutterstock.com

ative to avoid suggesting memories of any type. Framing questions with intentionality and absent suggestion is fundamental. Consider a woman who states, "I see a person coming toward me." Rather than asking a leading question such as, "Is that the perpetrator?" or "Is that your cousin?" use a **reflective statement** (used by the counselor to reflect back to the client what has been said or observed. This encourages the client to expand on what he or she has chosen to share in counseling) that is not suggestive. Examples of this would be: "Tell me more about what you are seeing" or "Describe the figure coming toward you." A reflective statement holds to the client telling their story without any suggestion from the counselor.

In this phase, clients may be confronted with their **dissociation** (the inability to recall all or part of a traumatic event) which is a defense mechanism. Dissociation is the client's "effort to retain a positive sense of self while simultaneously suppressing parts of the trauma from consciousness" (Underwood et al., 2007, p. 406). For some, this dissociation previously blunted their emotions and, in essence, may have helped them survive their past abuse. For these clients, any emotional expression may be accompanied by a sense of fear. For Christian clients, they may sense they are dishonoring God if negative emotions surface. It is important to remind clients that God is aware of their pain and emotions and how these have impacted them and desires for them to be free of this negative impact. For others, there may have been outbursts and difficulty regulating emotional expressions (Gingrich, 2017). In this stage, the survivors need to be reminded of the safety in the counseling room and how allowing intense emotions to surface makes space for healing to occur. Giving voice to feelings moves survivors out of the darkness and hiding and into the light where healing and restoration can occur. It is also important to teach the client how to use grounding techniques in order to remain emotionally present during this time of processing memories and times when they may feel triggered (see *Suggested Resources*—Grounding Techniques).

Langberg (1997) also identified confrontation and forgiveness as part of this phase. Confrontation, if appropriate, needs to be purposeful and guided with care, maturity, and truth. Not every survivor will confront their perpetrator and should not be forced to do this. For confrontation to occur, the client needs to be fully ready to speak the truth in love. Without this position, there is an increased potential for more pain to occur. Confrontation should also not be seen as the "answer" for recovery and healing. For some, this is part of the process. For others, this is not necessary or even recommended. The overall safety of the client must be factored into this decision. For someone who plans to confront, it is important to help the client set appropriate goals, have a realistic outlook, and carefully plan what will be said, including the specifics such as when and where this will occur, who will be present, how will the seating be arranged, and a planned time for the client to remain with the therapist to process further provided this confrontation occurs in the counselor's office (Langberg, 1997). In preparation for confrontation, role-playing exercises can be very powerful for the client, helping her to gain strength in using her voice.

Phase 3: Reconnecting and Strength Development

Remembering the process of treatment can be circular rather than linear is essential. In this phase, emotions from previous phases may resurface as clients begin to gain a sense of their identity as a survivor and one moving into healing rather than a focus on a victim identity. In this phase, the clients are unable to dissociate from their experiences and must be fully present (Gingrich, 2017). A strong therapeutic relationship has been built, and the client is more hopeful in what the future brings. Langberg (1997) identified four significant areas to address in the third phase of treatment: continued work in developing healthy relationships, the survivor reclaiming her body, the survivor creating the life she desires, and termination of therapy. We also want to acknowledge that clients may return to therapy when circumstances in their lives change. For example, the birth of a child or when the child is the same age as when the mother's abuse occurred may trigger new emotional responses.

Changing Relationships

Relational changes and challenges can occur. Patterns developed in a marriage that underscored the client as a victim will be challenged as the client moves further into a place of healing. A client who has been in a dependent role in the marriage and becomes more independent will desire to be more of an equal, using their voice and expressing their needs. The spouse would have developed a relationship with the former, more dependent person, and may "consciously or unconsciously sabotage continued growth" (Gingrich, 2017, p. 248). The survivors may also realize changes in their parenting styles and their adult friendships. It is important to remember that relationships were formed when the client was operating from the victim's stance, and with growth and healing, they will change. This change will impact all relationships. For the client, understanding this is crucial as they navigate these relationships. Decisions may need to be made to intentionally discontinue relationships with those who are unable to connect with the client as she continues to heal. The balance of the relationship will change. Helping the client to continue to see the positives in her personal growth is vital, while allowing space to grieve the loss of relationships that may occur.

In cases of incest, when disclosure occurs, family members may choose sides, and the client needs to be prepared for this to happen. Helping the client navigate the changing relationships and the forthcoming emotions are essential. Clients may not understand the decisions of family members and may feel either deeply hurt or supported. Providing support for the client to process their emotions surrounding this experience is very important.

Marriage

Throughout treatment, it is essential to give some attention to the client's marriage, as it is inevitably impacted by a woman's history of sexual abuse. The spouse may not understand the woundedness that occurs with sexual abuse, the therapeutic process, and the impact on the marriage.

Nurturing empathy and increased understanding from the spouse promote hope and healing for the wounded spouse and the marriage. During times of sexual connection and intimacy, flashbacks may occur that may surprise both husband and wife. Providing psychoeducation on grounding techniques to be present is essential. Langberg (1997) suggested these questions to help the client be fully present in the moment. With eyes open, the client will process (silently or verbally): Where is she? Who is she currently involved with sexually? Where is she (location)? What is different now than when the abuse occurred? Some survivors can process these questions internally, while others may need to stop and process verbally with their husbands (Langberg, 1997). Helping to normalize what does not seem normal and knowing how to work through those times with support, love, and care brings healing to the survivor and the marriage. Without some level of knowledge and understanding, more profound hurt may occur. Spouses must be taught how to respond and not expected to know what to do or say.

Forgiveness

Clients need to understand this is a process occurring over time, and that forgiveness (a decision to release feelings of revenge against a person who has harmed one) does not require reconciliation (the process by which an individual claims the harm that he or she has done to another and the survivor is able to continue a relationship with the perpetrator). Reconciliation requires the perpetrator to acknowledge the wrongdoing. If the perpetrator minimizes or denies the abuse occurred and/or if there is a continued risk of the abuse occurring again, reconciliation is not advised (Gingrich,

2017). Christian counselors can easily make the mistake of encouraging forgiveness too early and then mandating reconciliation as a requirement for healing. Doing this minimizes the healing process and will leave the client with unresolved trauma. Counselors must carefully consider their personal background with forgiveness and reconciliation and how this impacts their approach. If a counselor has unresolved background issues, it is important personally and ethically to seek appropriate personal counseling to resolve these issues. The goal is to avoid transference and countertransference, as well as ensure they are practicing ethically and in the best interest of the client. The Bible is clear in the importance of forgiveness, prompting a discussion with clients that God sees them, is aware of their heart, and understands this process. Being in the process of forgiveness, though it may take some time, places them in the mindset of forgiveness. Clients who move through these phases of treatment often arrive at this point themselves. With forgiveness comes a release of any hold the perpetrator has held on the survivor. This release brings freedom for survivors that they are prepared to grasp when they have a full understanding of how the abuse has impacted their lives. Forgiveness is a gift the survivor gives herself, even if the perpetrator never knows what she has done.

CONCEPT TO CONTEMPLATE

© Asier Romero/Shutterstock.com

What might be some implications, therapeutically and ethically, of encouraging forgiveness too quickly? How might forgiveness impact the client's healing process, personally and spiritually?

Transitioning to Termination

Termination of treatment often brings apprehension for survivors as they have grown to see counseling as a place of safety, perhaps feeling safe for the first time in their lives. Counseling should not be stopped abruptly, but instead, spacing out appointments and engaging in the process of termination is important. It may be advisable to schedule appointments every other week and then three weeks to monthly and beyond. Often by the time the client is coming only monthly, they are aware of their personal empowerment and ability to cope in various situations. They see the fruits of their healing process being lived out in their daily lives. It is at this time termination can be discussed, with the caveat that the client can return to counseling if they sense a need. Returning to counseling does not indicate failure or a lack of progress, but rather, it shows strength to know when additional support can be beneficial. In my (Jama Davis) 30+ years of experience, I have found this leads to a minimal number of sessions, sometimes only one, before the client is able to gain their strength again and lean into living life out of a place of healing, gaining the confidence they can do this.

LOOKING THROUGH THE LENS OF CHRISTIANITY: BIBLICAL INTEGRATION

Singh et al. (2013) and Arias and Johnson (2013) reinforced the importance of including religion and spirituality in the healing process for CSA survivors. Leaning into this importance, understanding the worldview of the client is essential as we work with all clients. With this understanding and informed consent, counselors can appropriately tailor treatment plans. Christian counselors are encouraged to pray for clients outside of the session and silently during sessions. A counselor does not separate who they are from the process, yet must be ethical and honoring to all clients. Explicit prayer during the session cannot be used without clear, informed consent being given by the client, and this must be properly documented in case notes (McMinn 2011; Tan, 2011). When Informed Consent is given for in-session prayer, it is important to ensure that prayer is used appropriately and not in a manner that creates an unhealthy dependence upon the counselor. Empowering the client and honoring client choice is imperative.

Counselors need to use care and recognize how Scripture may have been misused as a false means to portray support for the abuse that occurred, and

© sundora14/Shutterstock.com

how this results in damage for the client. Sexual abuse may have involved a perpetrator who was affiliated with the church or portrayed themselves as a Christian. Merely providing a verse of Scripture and expecting the client to take it in may be quite unrealistic, leading to a misuse of Scripture that could be viewed as another form of abuse. Counselors must be mindful of their spiritual development to ensure accuracy with Scripture as well as ethical guidelines for spiritual interventions (McMinn 2011; Tan, 2011).

Healing narratives take time to build. The process through the three identified phases takes time and is individual to each abuse victim. It is not to be rushed, and instead should always be entered with deep respect and honor for the woman who suffered the abuse. Without safety and stability, clients will not be able to process the depth of grief that is present for them. Remembering and processing trauma is part of the healing process that ultimately leads to reconnection and the development of strength to move forward in ways the woman may have never imagined.

Featured Practitioner
Jama Davis, PhD, LMHC, LPC, NCC

© Randall Davis

In over 30 years of working with survivors, I have witnessed how sexual abuse changes a woman. Many women have held onto their story of abuse, living for years in silence and pain. Stepping into a counselor's office may bring mixed emotions of apprehension and uncertainty, along with some level of hope that life can be different. Their sexual abuse history has defined them. With care and healing, the women realize their history informs their present life but no longer defines who they are or dictates their future. They are empowered and able to grasp hope for themselves and generations to follow. Women who do the hard work of healing can live a life of peace and hope.

Opportunity awaits counselors who are willing to sit with women who are wounded, modeling a level of respect and care the survivor often feels is undeserving. Healing is possible and hope can be restored. Working with trauma survivors will change you. Counselors, prepare yourself well, do what is right, be merciful and walk humbly with God into this work (Micah 6:8).

652

Patricia was referred to counseling by her primary care physician after reporting she had been sexually abused as a child and believed she needed to speak with someone. The initial counseling session focuses on gathering Patricia's history. This information-gathering typically asks that the client share her story. Patricia discloses that a close family friend, who resided with her family, sexually abused her when she was 14. Patricia shares that she has been feeling afraid and reported she has been engaging in unhealthy behaviors.

Clients need to feel safe and secure in the counseling room. Trust and relationship building (Herman, 1992) are the foundations for all the hard work that follows, which can be very difficult with clients who have experienced abuse. It is also critical to empower Patricia to share her story, be in charge of the content, and when sharing is done. It is an act of bravery to enter into counseling. It is important affirm Patricia's decision to take that step. It is challenging for many survivors to move past the shame and guilt associated with sexual abuse because they may feel responsible or have been told it was their fault.

Although Patricia wants counseling, she is very resistant to any discussion related to her sexual abuse. She notes that her sister was also sexually abused as a child, and this abuse has not impacted her sister. Patricia reports that she and her sister had decided to keep their abuse a secret. Deep shame and guilt are present with Patricia. She believes the lie that she is responsible for her abuse.

Allender (2008) identified three typical responses to childhood sexual abuse. These include being the "tough" girl, who hardens herself from ever again becoming vulnerable. A second response is to seek sexual attention from others and engage in risk-taking behaviors by becoming a "party" girl (Allender, 2008). The third response, according to Allender (2008) is to be the "good" girl, who tries to gain the approval of others by becoming a "pleaser". From her history, Patricia appears to have deep wounds in her ability to understand boundaries, her self-worth, and a sense of what may be risky behaviors. Patricia seems to present as a tough girl as she denies the trauma of her own sexual abuse.

The initial goal of counseling is to establish a sense of safety and stability in the counseling process. Patricia's boundaries have been violated in a way that not only stole her childhood but interfered with her ability to understand that it is appropriate and necessary to set boundaries with others. The counseling room needs to be a safe place for Patricia to share her thoughts and feelings. Her childhood sexual abuse interferes with her ability to make and maintain relationships with men from a healthy position. Patricia must learn how to identify the characteristics of a healthy relationship.

Processing the trauma allows Patricia to express feelings, long suppressed, and denied fully. When working with Patricia, the focus needs to be on her need to think differently about those experiences, by reconnecting with herself emotionally and to build on her strengths. Additionally, the goal is to empower Patricia to see herself as a strong woman, not through the lens of a powerless child.

Patricia reports that she has lost her faith in God and does not want Spiritual integration as a part of her sessions. As a counselor, you must respect Patricia's wishes and work with her in the manner she feels most comfortable. You can pray for Patricia, both during and between sessions. You can rely on faith to guide your words, actions, and interventions. The hope and prayer for Patricia is that she experiences something different in the counseling relationship that may open the possibility of a rebirth in Jesus Christ.

CHAPTER SUMMARY

Awareness of childhood sexual abuse has increased over the past thirty years, but most recently, the "Me, Too" movement has underscored the need for counselors to be aware of the magnitude of the harm done to children. The statistics speak for themselves, and counselors should assume that they will treat those who have been sexually abused. The "Me, Too" movement has also given a voice to those who have been sexually abused, as they come forward and courageously share their stories with counselors. Our focus here has been counseling with female survivors of childhood sexual abuse so that they may no longer feel the shame, fear, and loss associated with childhood sexual abuse. Identification of what constitutes abuse, along with understanding the risk factors for those who may be abused and how perpetrators groom their victims, is essential as we begin our counseling work with survivors. We must also understand the traumatic nature of childhood sexual abuse and how this trauma can have lifelong consequences. Through the ministry of compassionate and knowledgeable counselors, the trauma can be remediated and those who have been abused can become survivors. Survivors are better able to embrace life with joy and wholeness. The most important message for those who have been sexually abused is that healing is possible, and their sexual abuse history does not define them as individuals or in any way dictate their future.

KEY TERMS

Countertransference - when a counselor is triggered by their own history and responds out of their unmet needs or lack of healing. This then shifts the focus from the client to the counselor's unresolved personal concerns

Disclosure - the child, adolescent, or adult sharing information about the sexual abuse to others

Dissociation - the inability to recall all or part of a traumatic event

Forgiveness - a decision to release feelings of revenge against a person who has harmed one

Grooming - a process where the child is engaged in behaviors that encourage trust, allow the perpetrator to have access to the child successfully and keeps the child and others free of suspicion regarding the perpetrator's intentions towards the child

Incest - a sexual relationship between close biological relatives, including between father and child, mother and child, grandparents or other relatives, and the child

Psychosocial Assessment - the process of gathering information related to the current issue, past history of treatment, current level of functioning and then making treatment decisions to guide work in the counseling relationship

Post-traumatic Stress Disorder (PTSD) - a mental health disorder characterized by difficulty recovering from experiencing or being witness to an event where actual or threatened death, serious injury or sexual violence occurred

Recovery - the process through which individuals are able to reclaim their lives and reach their fullest potential

Reconciliation - the process by which an individual claims the harm that he or she has done to another and the survivor is able to continue a relationship with the perpetrator

Reflective Statement - used by the counselor to reflect back to the client what has been said or observed. This encourages the client to expand on what he or she has chosen to share in counseling

Sexual Abuse - as any sexual act involving a child for the sexual gratification of a parent, caregiver, or another individual or individuals who are responsible for the safety and well-being of a child

Stigma - others attribute blame to the one being sexually abused, not the perpetrator, for what happened to him or her. Stigma is a mark of disgrace for the one who has been abused

Therapeutic Relationship - the process by which the counselor and the client are able to trust one another and work towards treatment goals for the client

Trauma - any physical or emotional experience that has long term emotional, physical, or social consequences for the individual

SUGGESTED RESOURCES

Books
Healing the Wounded Heart by Dan Allender
Counseling Survivors of Sexual Abuse by Diane Langberg

On the Threshold of Hope by Diane Langberg

The Body Keeps Score: Brain, Mind, and Body in the Healing of Trauma by
Bessel Van Der Kolk

Videos

Langberg, D. (2017). Lessons from a Life of Counseling. Retrieved from
https://www.youtube.com/watch?v=8neKS93z7Qg

Langberg, D. (2015) What mistakes do Christians frequently make in
trying to help someone scarred by abuse? [video file]. Retrieved
from https://foclonline.org/answer/what-mistakes-do-christians-
frequently-make-trying-help-someone-scarred-abuse

Langberg, D. (2016). The spiritual impact of sexual abuse and other
trauma. [video file]. Retrieved from https://www.youtube.com/
watch?v=ABXxJdQavhQ

Organizations

Child Welfare Information Gateway: www.childwelfare.gov

RAINN (Rape, Abuse & Incest National Network): www.rainn.org

The Advocacy Center: www.theadvocacycenter.org

National Association of Adult Survivors of Child Abuse: www.naasca.org

Child Sex Abuse Prevention and Protection Center:
www.charitychoices.com

National Center for Missing and Exploited Children: www.missingkids.org

Website Resources

Grounding Techniques Worksheet: https://www.therapistaid.com/
worksheets/grounding-techniques.pdf

Child sexual abuse education and prevention: www.
childmolestationprevention.org

National Sex Offenders Registry: https://www.nsopw.gov/

Stop It Now! Prevents the sexual abuse of children by mobilizing adults,
families, and communities to take actions that protect children
before they are harmed: www.stopitnow.org

The National Children's Alliance (NCA) is the national associate and
accrediting body for Children's Advocacy Centers (CACS):
www.nationalchildrensalliance.org

Resources dedicated to prevention of child sexual abuse:
www.preventchildabuse.org

Resources dedicated to prevention of child sexual abuse:
www.publichealth.org

American Academy of Pediatrics tips for parents for prevention and identification of Child Sexual Abuse: www.aap.org/en-us/about-the-aap/aap-press-room/news-features-and-safety-tips/Pages/Parent-Tips-for-Preventing-and-Identifying-Child-Sexual-Abuse.aspx

American Psychological Association Information related to understanding and prevention of child abuse: www.apa.org/pi/families/resources/understanding-child-abuse

REFERENCES

Abajobir, A. A., Kisely, S., Maravilla, J. G., Williams, G. & Najman, J. M. (2017). Gender differences in the association between childhood sexual abuse and risky sexual behaviours: A systematic review and meta-analysis. *Child Abuse and Neglect, 63*, 249-260. https://doi.org/10.1016/j.chiabu.2016.11.023

Allender, D. (2008). *The wounded heart: Hope for adult victims of childhood sexual abuse.* Tyndale.

American Academy of Child and Adolescent Psychiatry. (2014). *Sexual abuse. \facts for families.* Retrieved October 22, 2019, from https://www.aacap.org/AACAP/Families_and_Youth/Facts_for_Families/FFF-Guide/Child-Sexual-Abuse-009.aspx.

American Bar Association. (2015). *Understanding sexual grooming in child abuse cases.* Retrieved October 22, 2019, from https://www.americanbar.org/groups/public

American College of Obstetricians and Gynecologists. (2011). *Adult manifestations of childhood sexual abuse, 498.* Retrieved October 22, 2019, from https://www.acog/Clinical-Guidance-Publications/Committee-Opinions/Committee-on-Health-Care-for-Underserved Women.

American Psychiatric Association. (2013). *Diagnostic and statistical manual of mental disorders* (5th ed.). American Psychiatric Association.

Arias, B. J., & Johnson, C. V. (2013). Voices of healing and recovery from childhood sexual abuse. *Journal of Child Sexual Abuse, 22*, 822-841. https://doi.org/10.1080/10538712.2013.830669

Balter, A., van Rhijn, T. M., & Davies, A. W. J. (2016). The development of sexuality in childhood in early learning settings: An exploration of early childhood educators' perceptions. *Canadian Journal of Human Sexuality, 25*(1), 30-40. https://doi.org/10.3138/cjhs.251-A3

Bennet, N., & O'Donohue, W. (2014). The construct of grooming in child sexual abuse: Conceptual and measurement issues. *Journal of Child Sexual Abuse, 23*(8), 957-976. https://doi.org/10.1080/10538712.201.960632

Bowlby, J. (1988). *A secure base: Parent-child attachment and healthy human development*. Basic Books.

Brattfjiell, M. L., & Flam, A. M. (2018). "They were the ones that saw me and listened." From child sexual abuse to disclosure: Adults' recall of the process towards final disclosure. *Child Abuse and Neglect, 89,* 225-236. https://doi.org/10.1016/j.chiabu.2018.11.022

Brown, J., Cohen, P., Johnson, J., & Smailes, E. M. (1999). Childhood abuse and neglect: Specificity of effects on adolescent and young adult depression and suicidality. *Journal American Academy of Child and Adolescent Psychiatry, 38*(12), 1490-1496.

Carlson, B. E., Maciol, K., & Schneider, J. (2006). Sibling incest: Reports from forty-one survivors. *Journal of Sexual Abuse, 15*(4), 19-34. https://doi.org/10.1300/j070v15n04_02

Collin-Vezina, D., De La Sablonniere-Griffin, M. Palmer, A. M., & Milne, L. (2015). A preliminary mapping of individual, relational, and social factors that impede disclosure of childhood sexual abuse. *Child Abuse & Neglect, 43,* 123-134. https://doi.org 10.1016/j.chiabu.2015.03.010

Cush, E. (2018). *Impacts of intergenerational trauma: How #MeToo affects us all.* Good Therapy. Retrieved October, 22, 2019, from https://goodtherapy.org.

Drauker, C. B., Martsolf, D. S., Boller, C., Knapik, G., Ross, R., & Stidham, A. W. (2011). Healing from childhood sexual abuse: A theoretical model. *Journal of Child Sexual Abuse, 20,* 435-466. https://doi.org/10.1080/10538712.2011.588188

Easton, S. D. (2019). Childhood disclosure of sexual abuse and mental health outcomes in adulthood: Assessing merits of early disclosure and discussion. *Child Abuse & Neglect, 93,* 208-214. https://doi.org/10.1016/j.chiabu.2019.04.005

Feiring, C., Simon, V. A., & Cleland, C. M. (2009). Childhood sexual abuse, stigmatization, internalizing symptoms, and the development of sexual difficulties and dating aggression. *Journal of Counseling and Clinical Psychology, 77*(1), 127-137. https://doi.org/10.1037/a0013475

Fergusson, D. M., McLeod, G. F. H., & Horwood, L. J. (2013). Childhood sexual abuse and adult developmental outcomes: Findings from a 30-year longitudinal study in New Zealand. *Child Abuse and Neglect, 37,* 664-674. https://doi.org/10.1016/j.chiabu.2013.03.013

Finkelhor, D., & Browne, A. (1985). The traumatic impact of child sexual abuse: A conceptualization. *American Journal of Orthopsychiatry, 55*(4), 530-541. https://doi.org/10.1111/j.1939-0025.1985.tb02703.x

Gingrich, H. D. (2017). Sexual abuse and dissociative disorders. In H. D. Gingrich & F. Gingrich (Eds.), *Treating trauma in Christian counseling* (pp. 232-256). InterVarsity Press.

Godbout, N., Sabourin, S., & Lussier, Y. (2009). Child sexual abuse and adult romantic adjustment: Comparison of single- and multiple-indicator

measures. *Journal of Interpersonal Violence, 24,* 693–705. https://doi.
org/10.1177/0886260508317179

Gomes, V., Jardim, P., Taveira, F., Dinis-Oliveira, R., & Magalhaes, R. (2014).
Alleged biological father incest: A forensic approach. *Journal of Forensic
Sciences, 59*(1), 255-259. https://doi.org/10.1111/1556-4029.12310

Goodyear-Brown, P., Fath, A. & Myers, L. (Eds.). (2012). *Child sexual abuse: The
scope of the problem. Handbook of child sexual abuse.* John Wiley and Sons.

Haliburn, J. (2017). Mother-child incest, psychosis, and the dynamics of
relatedness. *Journal of Trauma and Dissociation, 18*(3), 409-426. https://doi.
org10.1080/15299732.2017.1295424

Hall, M., & Hall, J. (2011). *The long term effects of childhood sexual abuse:
Counseling implications.* American Counseling Association. Retrieved
October 22, 2019, from http://counselingoutfitters.com/vistas/vistas11/
Article_19.pdf

Hassan, M. A., Gary, F., Killion, C., Lewin, L., & Totten, V. (2014). Patterns
of sexual abuse among children: Victims and perpetrator characteristics.
Journal of Aggression, Maltreatment & Trauma, 24, 400-418. https://doi.org/
10.1080/10926771.2015.1022289

Herman, J. (1992). *Trauma and recovery: The aftermath of violence—from
domestic abuse to political terror.* Basic Books.

Irish, L., Kobayashi, I., & Delahanty, D. L. (2009). Long-term physical health
consequences of childhood sexual abuse: A meta-analytic review. *Journal of
Pediatric Psychology, 35*(5), 450-461. https://doi.org/10.1093/jpepsy/jsp118

Jeong, S., & Cha, C. (2019). Healing from childhood sexual abuse: A meta-
synthesis of qualitative studies. *Journal of Child Sexual Abuse, 28*(4), 383-
399. https://doi.org/0.1080/10538712.2019.1574945

Klumparendt, A., Nelson, J., Barenbrugge, J., & Ehring, T. (2019). Associations
between childhood maltreatment and adult depression: A mediation analysis.
BMC Psychiatry, 19(36), 1-11. https://doi.org/10.1186/s12888-019-2016-8

Kreinert, J. L., & Walsh, J. A. (2011). Sibling sexual abuse: An empirical analysis
of offender, victim, and event characteristics in national incident-based
reporting system (NIBRS) data, 200-2007. *Journal of Child Sexual Abuse, 20,*
353-372. https://doi.org/10.1080/10538712.2011.588190

Langberg, D. M. (1997). *Counseling survivors of sexual abuse.* Tyndale.

Langberg, D. (2015a). *Suffering and the heart of God: How trauma destroys and
Christ restores.* New Growth Press.

Langberg, D. (2015b). What mistakes do Christians frequently make in trying
to help someone scarred by abuse? [Video File]. Retrieved from https://
foclonline.org/answer/what-mistakes-do-christians-frequently-make-
trying-help-someone-scarred-abuse

Malin, H. M., Saleh, F. M., & Grudzinskas (2014). Recent research related to
juvenile sex offending: Findings and directions for further research. *Current
Psychiatry Reports, 16,* 440. https://doi.org/10.1007/s11920-014-0440-5

McElvaney, R., Greene, S. & Hogan, D. (2012). Containing the secret of child sexual abuse. *Journal of Interpersonal Violence, 27*(6), 1155-1175. https://doi.org/10.1177/0886260511424503

McMinn, M. R. (2011). *Psychology, theology and spirituality in Christian counseling* (Rev. ed.). Tyndale.

Monahan, K. (2010). Themes of adult sibling sexual abuse survivors in later life: An initial exploration. *Clinical Social Work Journal, 38,* 361-369. https://doi.org/10.1007/s10615-010-0286-1

Murray, L. K., Nguyen, A., & Cohen, J. A. (2015). Child sexual abuse. *Journal of Child and Adolescent Psychiatry, 23*(2), 321-337. https://doi.org/10.1016/j.chc.2014.01.003

National Association of Adult Survivors of Child Abuse. (n.d.). *Statistics of child abuse.* http://www.naasca.org/2012-Resources/010812-StaisticsOfChildAbuse.htm

National Center for Victims of Crime. (2019). *Child abuse statistics.* Retrieved October 22, 2019, from https://www.victimsofcrime.org

National Institute of Mental Health. (2019). *Post-traumatic stress disorder.* Retrieved February 19, 2020 from, https://www.nimh.nih.gov/health/topics/post-traumatic-stress-disorder-ptsd/index.shtml#part13.

Pressley, J., & Spinazzola, J. (2015). Beyond survival: Application of a complex trauma treatment model in the Christian context. *Journal of Psychology & Theology, 43*(1), 8-22. https://doi.org/0091-6471/410-730

Putnam, F. W., & Trickett, P. K. (1987). *Psychological effects of sexual abuse: A longitudinal study.* WT Grant Foundation.

Putnam, F. W., & Trickett, P. K. (1993). Child sexual abuse: A model of chronic trauma. *Psychiatry, 56,* 82-95.

Rape, Abuse and Incest National Network. (2019). *Children and teens: Statistics.* https://www.rainn.org/statistics/children-and-teens

Ryan, C. W., & Hall, R. (2007). A profile of pedophilia definition, characteristics of offenders, recidivism, treatment outcomes, and forensic issues. *Mayo Clinic Proceedings, 82*(4), 457-471.

Ryan, E. P., & Otonichar, J. M. (2016). Juvenile sex offenders. *Current Psychiatry Reports, 18*(67), 1-10. https://doi.org/10.1007/s11920-016-0706-1

Singh, A. A., Garnett, A., & Williams, D. (2013). Resilience strategies of African American women survivors of child sexual abuse: A qualitative inquiry. *Counseling Psychologist, 41,* 1093–1124. https://doi.org/10.1177/0011000012469413

Smallbone, S. W., & Wortley, R. K. (2001). Child sexual abuse: Offender characteristics and operandi. *Australian Institute of Criminology, 194,* 1-6.

Sorensen, T., & Snow, B. (1991). How children tell: The process of disclosure in child sexual abuse. *Child Welfare League of America,* 3-15.

Strickland, S. M. (2008). Female sex offenders: Exploring issues of personality, trauma, and cognitive distortions. *Journal of Interpersonal Violence, 23*(4), 474-489. https://doi.org/10.1177/0886260507312944

Stroebel, S. S., Kuo, S., O'Keefe, S. L., Beard, K. W., Swindell, S., & Kommer, M. J. (2013). Risk factors for father-daughter incest: Data from an anonymous computerized survey. *Sexual Abuse: A Journal of Research and Treatment, 25*(6), 583-605. https://doiorg/10.1177/1079063212470706

Tan, S.-Y. (2011). *Counseling and psychotherapy: A Christian perspective.* Baker Academic.

The Advocacy Center (n.d.). *The facts about youth sexual abuse.* http://www.theadvocacycenter.org/adv_abuse.html

Therapist Aid (2019). GroundingTechniques. https://www.therapistaid.com/worksheets/grounding-techniques.pdf

Thompson, K. M. (2009). Sibling incest: A model for group practice with adult female victims of brother-sister incest. *Journal of Family Violence, 24*(7), 531-537. https://doi.org/10.1007/s10096-009-9251-6.

Tong, E., & Gillespie, M. (2011). Childhood sexual abuse: Help to make it 'safe to say'. *British Journal of Nursing, 20*(9), 555-558.

Trickett, P. K., Noll, J. G., & Putnam, F. W. (2011) The impact of sexual abuse on female development: Lessons from a multigenerational, longitudinal research study, *Development & Psychopathology, 23,* 453-476. https://doi.org/10.1017/S095457941000174

Underwood, L., Stewart, S. E., & Castellanos, A. M. (2007). Effective practices for sexually traumatized girls: Implications for counseling and education. *International Journal of Behavioral Consultation and Therapy, 3*(3), 403-419. http://dx.doi.org/10.1037/h0100815

Van Der Kolk, B. (2014). *The body keeps score: Brain, mind and body in the healing of trauma.* Penguin Books.

Wamser-Nanney, R., & Sager, J. C. (2018). Predictors of maternal support following children's sexual abuse disclosures. *Child Abuse & Neglect, 81,* 39-47. https://doi.org/10.1016/j.chiabu.2018.04.016

World Health Organization (n.d.). *Child sexual abuse.* Retrieved October 22, 2019, from https:www.who.int>resources>publications>guidelines_Chap7.

World Health Organization (2017). *Violence against women.* Retrieved October 22, 2019, from http://www.who.int/news-room/fact-sheets/detail/violence-against-women.

Wolf, M. R., & Pruitt, D. K. (2019). Grooming hurts too: The effects of types of perpetrator grooming on trauma symptoms in adult survivors of child sexual abuse. *Journal of Child Sexual Abuse, 28*(3), 345-359. https://doi.org/10.1080/10538712.2019.1579292

Yates, P. (2016) Sibling abuse: Why don't we talk about it? *Journal of Clinical Nursing, 26,* 2482-2494. https://doi.org/10.1111/jocn.13531

Yehuda, R., & Lehrner, A. (2018). Intergenerational transmission of trauma effects: Putative role of epigenetic mechanisms. *World Psychiatry, 17*(3), 243-257. https://doi.org/10.1002/wps.20568

Zawastak, H. (2018). *What to do (and not do) when your child discloses sexual abuse.* GoodTherapy. Retrieved October 22, 2019, from https://goodtherapy.org.

CHAPTER 20

Counseling Women Facing Emotional and Physical Abuse

Jama Davis, Ph.D., Cynthia Doney, Ph.D., & Daria White, Ph.D.

"Change is hard, and sometimes we're only motivated to change when the pain of staying the same becomes greater than the fear or pain of making the change."
~Leslie Vernick

"The LORD is close to the brokenhearted and saves those who are crushed in spirit."
(Psalm 34:18, NIV)

Wisdom from Above: Standing in His Grace

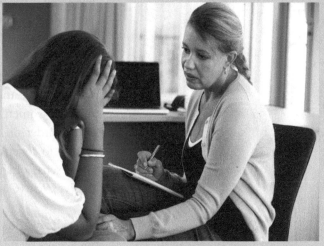

© Monkey Business Images/Shutterstock.com

Finding hope amid abusive situations can be difficult, yet we are assured of God's care and attentiveness to those who are suffering. In the life of Jesus (Mark 15), we see where He was victimized and ridiculed unjustly. Jesus stood before Pilate and listened to the people cry out to crucify Him though He had done no wrong. He was profusely beaten, and a crown of thorns was placed on His head. Imagine the physical pain Jesus endured as He was forced to walk to Golgotha, the place of His crucifixion, carrying his crucifixion cross along part of the path. Along the route, He endured verbal mocking and insults. In this journey, He was physically beaten and emotionally ridiculed. Jesus understands the plight of those who are experiencing all types of abuse. Yet during this physically painful, emotionally challenging, and horrific experience, Jesus showed compassion. His rejection did not make Him unworthy.

CHAPTER LEARNING OBJECTIVES

Upon completing this chapter, you should be able to:

- Evaluate patterns of domestic abuse and intimate partner violence (IPV)
- Identify interventions and evidence-based treatments
- Discover resources available to assist women in restoring healthy functioning

He understood what it meant to be brokenhearted as those who were close to Him betrayed Him. As you enter this journey to work with women who have been abused, we hope that you will work with your clients with the compassion and care that Jesus showed throughout His life and during His time of death and resurrection.

CHAPTER OVERVIEW

Domestic abuse and intimate partner violence (interchangeable terms describing a current or past relationship that involved physical, sexual or psychological abuse) are not topics of typical dinner table conversation. Most often, they are hidden, and women are silent in their pain, rationalizing what is occurring, and not identifying the personal destruction as abuse. In emotionally abusive relationships, there are no visible scars, yet the internal damage is intense and lasting. Friends and family may not be aware of what is happening as the batterer blames the woman for his outburst, and the woman often blames herself (Enander, 2010; Ganley, 1995). She often believes that if she would only be a better person or spouse and try harder, the abuse would stop. This thought process is part of the pattern of lies that result from the abusive relationship where her abuser convinces her the abuse is her fault. Angry gestures are used to manipulate and control. In contrast, with physical abuse, there are overt signs of the violent episodes. Yet often the women, using the same internal dialogue of needing to try harder or be a better person, find themselves making excuses to cover up what is happening. Often, this is a result of the sense of shame that has developed while living in the abusive cycle (Graham-Bermann et al., 2017).

Not to be overlooked is the fact that perpetrators of abuse are not always men. Women have also been found to be abusive in all of the same ways. For this chapter however, we will focus only on women who are victims of physical, emotional, verbal, economic, and spiritual abuse. But keep in mind, much of the information is transferrable between the genders.

So then, as we examine abuse and intimate partner violence, we are looking for patterns. A single abusive event, though impactful, does not mean a person is evil and a pattern is present. It does, however, warrant close attention and intervention. In Romans 12:21 (*New International Bible*, 1973/2011), we are instructed by Paul to "not be overcome by evil but overcome evil with good." We are not to be passive in addressing abusive relationships. Instead, it is vital to support and empower abuse victims to help them move into safety and the healing process. In this chapter you will learn definitions of abuse and how to identify abusive patterns. Evidence-based treatment and interventions will be presented to bring understanding in assisting women who are victims of abuse in their movement toward restoration and healthy functioning.

DESCRIPTION OF DOMESTIC ABUSE AND INTIMATE PARTNER VIOLENCE

Domestic abuse and intimate partner violence (IPV) are recognized cultural issues. The National Coalition Against Domestic Violence (NCADV) Statistics (2019) show that 25% of women will experience a severe domestic violence incident in their lifetime, that there will be 536 gun-related domestic violence fatalities during the year, and most shocking of all, that

© dizain/Shutterstock.com

domestic violence incidents account for 15% of all violent crime in the United States. Additionally, both the NCADV and the Juvenile Justice Bulletin agree on the problematic statistic that 1 in 15 children are exposed to IPV each year (Finkelhor et al., 2011).

The *Diagnostic and Statistical Manual of Mental Disorders* (5th ed.; *DSM-5*; American Psychiatry Association [APA], 2013) does not explicitly distinguish domestic violence as its own diagnostic category. Instead, it is included as a subcategory under any number of primary disorders. When diagnosing, domestic violence is most easily included under the identifier of Adult Maltreatment and Neglect Problems. Within this category, physical violence (confirmed T74.11 or suspected T76.11), sexual violence (confirmed T74.21 or suspected T76.21), spouse/partner neglect (confirmed T74.01 or suspected T76.01), and psychological abuse (confirmed T74.31 or suspected T76.31) are all referenced as subcategories. Violence against others may also be included as a subtype of Schizophrenia Spectrum and Other Psychotic Disorders, Trauma and Stressor-Related disorders, [most often Post-Traumatic Stress Disorder (F43.10)], Sleep-Wake disorders, Sexual Dysfunctions, Disruptive Impulse Control and Conduct Disorders, and Substance-Related and Addictive disorders. As a result of the variety of violence types often being coupled as a secondary, co-occurring disorder in relation to a primary disorder (APA, 2013), diagnoses and treatment interventions are more commonly related to the disorders within the primary categories.

The Battered Women's Movement (Timeline of the Battered Women's Movement, 2008), began to gain a serious foothold in the United States, in the early 1970s. However, broader societal awareness and advocacy only started to emerge in the late 20th century. Progressing into the 21st century, understanding of issues leading to the development of community programs, has made the terminology and concepts, much more common in mainstream society. The existence and issues of domestic violence are on the minds of many: social justice warriors, medical professionals, psychologists, school and clinical mental health counselors, community advocates and helpers. But most commonly, domestic violence is on the minds of those who live with it, or have lived with it, as a reality of their existence. When domestic violence is an aspect of one's daily life, it becomes the primary belief that this is the normal function of family life (Goldsmith, 2018). To alter the mindset that promotes the cycle of violence in families, counselors need to develop a greater understanding of how society has come to understand it through the years.

THEORIES OF DOMESTIC ABUSE AND INTIMATE PARTNER VIOLENCE

So then, is it possible to identify behavioral characteristics and living environments that may seem to lead to situations of domestic violence and other incidents of abuse? There are many theoretical perspectives that attempt to explain the how and why of abusive behaviors. However, after decades of dismissing the problem by saying that abused women were the primary cause of violent events, such as victim blaming or claiming she brought it upon herself (Campbell & Raja, 1999; Kippert, 2017; Zorza, 1998), the validity of those ideas were eventually dismissed and replaced with more plausible theories. The following progression of theories on domestic violence and abuse have developed as research and advocacy have advanced.

Learned Behavior Theory

Learned Behavior Theory establishes that children (most often boys) learn behaviors of violence by witnessing it in the home throughout childhood. In turn, that child/boy is much more likely to become an abuser himself (Lemkey, 2001).

Loss of Control Theory

The Learned Behavior Theory evolved into the concept of the abuser losing control, only in isolated situations. The prevailing mentality of the abuser is that he could dismiss his actions as a momentary loss of control, minimizing the behaviors as "losing it" or "this is not really me; blame it on the alcohol." The abuser is then able to excuse his conduct as a momentary lapse in judgment (Klein et al., 1997).

Batterer's Choice Theory

Batterer's Choice Theory is another theory of domestic violence that is predicated on the batterer losing control. However, the premise of this theory is that he only loses control in specific and targeted situations. As an example, a batterer may become infuriated at his work colleague, but is unlikely to assault that person. Instead, he makes the specific choice to control himself. He might then go home and take his frustrations out on the targets there; his wife and family (Klein et al., 1997). Exhibiting that ability to constrain himself until he is in a private setting, where his behaviors will likely go undetected, actually illustrates that he has genuinely NOT lost control. Instead, he has decided to choose his environment, his victim, and often his method, to release his violent feelings, without detection or repercussion (Schechter & Ganley, 1995).

Learned Helplessness Theory

The Learned Helplessness Theory perspective is rooted in Seligman's classic theories (2016) and includes a learned loss of will. The belief is that the victim has adopted ideas and behaviors that, no matter what they try to do to avoid victimization, they can do nothing to change it; so, they become resigned to it. They have learned to be helpless, which in turn, empowers the perpetrator and makes the victim more vulnerable (Maier & Seligman, 2016). And while this is quite possibly a valid perspective, it does lean toward placing the responsibility for the violence (or at least, the shared responsibility) onto the victim.

Power and Control Theory

The Power and Control Theory, as depicted in the *Power and Control Wheel,* is now the most broadly accepted explanation for the cause of domestic abuse. The concept of the *Power and Control Wheel* was initially formulated by Ellen Pence and focused on advocacy (Dasgupta, 2010) in partnership with the Domestic Abuse Intervention Programs in Duluth, MN. These initiatives were the outgrowth of a 1981 experimental program by the community, which established what is now known as the Duluth Model. Its purpose was to determine better methods for assisting battered women (Pence & Paymar, 1993). Observation of victims led to the concept that abusers can maintain control over their victims because of the perceived power differential that exists between the two partners (illustrated in the graphic below). This may be an actual power differential or merely a perceived differential. But the result is the same. If the victim is unable to see a way to escape their abuser, they will remain trapped in a violent relationship. Additionally, the feelings of helplessness can be so overwhelming to the victim, that even when liberated from her abuser, the victim may return to him. This decision could be a reflection of *learned helplessness* in action.

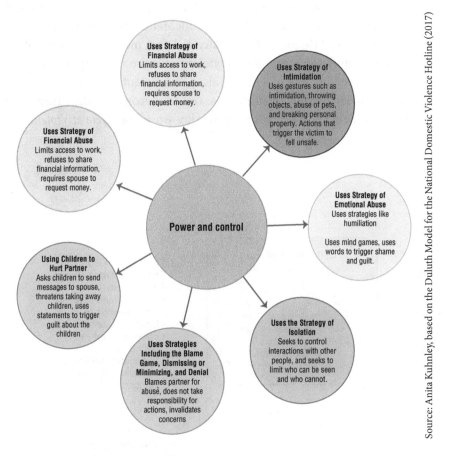

Source: Anita Kuhnley, based on the Duluth Model for the National Domestic Violence Hotline (2017)

FIGURE 20.1

The Power and Control Wheel

Cycle of Violence Theory

Does anything on the *Power and Control Wheel* surprise you? Perhaps you find yourself saying, "I never realized that was a form of abuse." You may be wondering why a woman would allow herself to be drawn to an abuser when she experienced the horrors of it throughout childhood. Well it could simply be the fact that since the woman has lived a lifelong existence in an abusive environment, that lifestyle is her norm. She is drawn to the type of man similar to the man who perpetrated the abuse during her developmental years (Goldsmith, 2018; Widom et al., 2008; Vargas et al., 2005). Once this concept of "violence as the norm" is grasped, it is easier to draw connections to the *why*: to why victims of abuse hide their mistreatment, while protecting or defending the abuser, and to why so many victims refuse to leave an abuser, even when assistance is available. The most comprehensive theoretical explanation of why victims will accept "violence as the norm" is encapsulated in the graphic (below) commonly referred to as the *Cycle of Violence*, a theoretical perspective created by Lenore Walker (1995). Walker contended that most victims of violence lived in a similar environment of violence for the majority of their lives. Studies show that 30% of women raised in a violent environment will enter into abusive adult relationships, or will become abusers themselves (Rakovec-Felser, 2014). This pattern is known as the *Cycle of Violence*.

FIGURE 20.2

The Cycle of
Violence

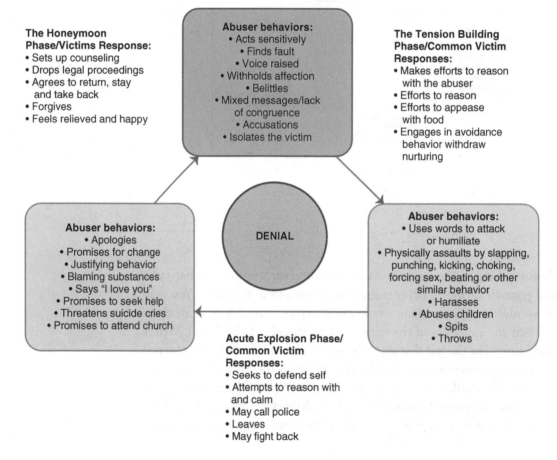

The Honeymoon Phase/Victims Response:
• Sets up counseling
• Drops legal proceedings
• Agrees to return, stay and take back
• Forgives
• Feels relieved and happy

Abuser behaviors:
• Acts sensitively
• Finds fault
• Voice raised
• Withholds affection
• Belittles
• Mixed messages/lack of congruence
• Accusations
• Isolates the victim

The Tension Building Phase/Common Victim Responses:
• Makes efforts to reason with the abuser
• Efforts to reason
• Efforts to appease with food
• Engages in avoidance behavior withdraw nurturing

DENIAL

Abuser behaviors:
• Apologies
• Promises for change
• Justifying behavior
• Blaming substances
• Says "I love you"
• Promises to seek help
• Threatens suicide cries
• Promises to attend church

Abuser behaviors:
• Uses words to attack or humiliate
• Physically assaults by slapping, punching, kicking, choking, forcing sex, beating or other similar behavior
• Harasses
• Abuses children
• Spits
• Throws

Acute Explosion Phase/ Common Victim Responses:
• Seeks to defend self
• Attempts to reason with and calm
• May call police
• Leaves
• May fight back

Source: Anita Kuhnley, based on Walker (1994/2000)

COUNSELING WOMEN

TYPES OF DOMESTIC ABUSE AND INTIMATE PARTNER VIOLENCE

Domestic abuse and IPV descriptors typically fall into three broad categories, and then a fourth that is often overlooked or dismissed. The most recognized types of abuse are physical, emotional and verbal, and economic abuse (Domestic Violence Roundtable, 2019). The existence of spiritual abuse is often dismissed as being invalid or is dismissed by religious communities as not actually being abuse. Each category has specific identifiers. Additionally, there are characteristics of each that overlap with the others. Following are some of the defining identifiers:

Physical Abuse

This is the most easily understood type of domestic violence because it is exactly what its name says. According to the New York State Office of

Children and Family Services, **physical abuse** (holding physical power over someone, hitting, and physically harming another; the use of physical force to intentionally inflict pain, bodily harm, or impairment on another person) is the use of physical force to intentionally inflict pain, harm, or impairment on another person (Tracy, 2012). In discussions on the general topic, most people's minds go to the physical aspect. According to the National Domestic Violence Hotline (2019), incidents of physical domestic violence will not look the same in any two environments.

Some of the most common types of physical violence include:

- Pulling hair, punching, slapping, kicking, biting or choking
- Forbidding victim from eating or sleeping
- Hurting her with weapons
- Preventing the woman from calling the police or seeking medical attention
- Physically harming the children (Domestic Violence Roundtable, 2019)

Emotional Abuse

This type of abuse takes advantage of the emotions and the psyche of the victim. **Emotional abuse** (criticism, name-calling, humiliation, looks and gestures that create fear, isolation, constant monitoring of another; plays on the present fears and emotional weaknesses of a woman) plays on the present fears and emotional weaknesses of a woman, or to weaken her to the point that she develops new debilitating fears. Again, the National Domestic Violence Hotline (2019) submits a partial list of examples:

- Abandoning her in unfamiliar places
- Driving recklessly or dangerously placing her at risk
- Calling her names, insulting, or continually criticizing
- Refusing to trust her and acting jealous or possessive
- Isolating her from family or friends; monitoring where she goes, or who she calls
- Trapping her in her home or preventing her from leaving
- Punishing by withholding affection
- Threatening to hurt her, the children, her family, or pets
- Humiliating or belittling her in both public or private settings
- Blaming her for the abuse
- Gaslighting – using manipulation to confuse the victim's thinking, i.e. projecting their issues as the victim's, telling the victim she's crazy, constant denial and lying, etc. This topic is discussed in more detail in Chapter 21.

Verbal Abuse

Contrary to common belief, simply throwing verbal insults at someone's partner, is not typically considered abuse. It becomes **verbal abuse** (most often occurs with other types of abuse as a means to coerce and control) when it is used regularly to coerce and control a woman. Additionally, verbal abuse is often coupled with other types of abuse, especially physical harm, and when the two are connected, the perpetrator's power over his victim is amplified (Ganley, 1995; Outlaw, 2009).

© fizkes/Shutterstock.com

Economic Abuse

This is a lesser-known or understood type of abuse. However, it carries a great deal of power because economic abuse (withholding financial resources and information regarding finances, preventing from employment, preventing access to basic life necessities) prevents a woman from having access to the basic necessities of life and survival. With this type of mistreatment, the abuser typically limits the income of a woman and monitors what she does have, very closely. He may also control and refuse access to all bank accounts. Another tactic may be that the abuser does not allow the victim to work at all. She must ask for food, clothing, and all other items needed for self-care and preservation. It is a debilitating form of abuse (Adams et al., 2008; Postmus et al., 2012; Postmus et al., 2020).

Spiritual Abuse

This is one of the most challenging categories of abuse to address because there are such widespread beliefs about what the defined roles are within marriages based on faith practices. In fact, in some circles of faith, the violent experiences previously discussed, would not be considered abusive (Zakar et al., 2013). However, the discussion here is not about the actual roles of men and women, as defined by religion. Rather, the conversation here defines spiritual abuse (use of religion to exert a sense of power and in an entitled manner) as the pervasive practices of men who use religion as an excuse to exert power and to do it in an entitled way. The abuser construes elements of their faith beliefs to claim his status as not only *head of the household* but also as *a high priest* (Domestic Violence Roundtable, 2019). This narcissistic mentality leads to the perpetrator's assertion that because he holds this position, he is also the most important person in the home. His word is law. He is to be served and obeyed. These attitudes leave the victim and her children vulnerable as they are considered subjects to his ultimate authority (Aaron, 2016; Stetzer, 2014). In recent years, there has been an onslaught of revelation involving every type of abuse within religious institutions; clergy and staff members at all levels, lay leaders, and families within the churches, synagogues, and mosques. Many are practicing or experiencing domestic abuse under the umbrella of faith practice (Earls, 2019).

Unfortunately, despite the growing societal awareness of the signs and symptoms of domestic abuse and intimate partner violence, the prevalence continues within communities and families of all races, financial status, and religious creeds (Ganley, 1995). This may be partially due to a lack of understanding within the professional community, on methods for detection and confirmation of abuse, weak educational systems that teach acknowledgment and management procedures, and gaps in professional development that offer improved evidence-based interventions to those who are in need. Whatever the reasons for the continued presence of violent behaviors in family settings, it is hopeful that with increased cognizance of the issues, abusive incidents will decrease over time. Advocacy for potential victims who are at highest risk should advance these goals, and the primary avenue of advocacy should come through the training of clinicians. This can be accomplished through increased responsiveness to potential victims, along with education and application of broadly accepted intervention techniques.

Featured Practitioner
Leslie Vernick

© Melissa Anthony

1. What led you into the work of counseling women experiencing verbal and emotional abuse or domestic violence?

I've always been an advocate for those who are abused. I am the oldest child of a broken home when broken homes were rare. I was physically and emotionally abused by my mother who struggled with alcoholism and mental illness. However, even as an adult, even after becoming a Christian and a licensed clinical social worker, I could not figure out how to honor my mother without dishonoring myself. Forty-five years ago, there was little said about familial abuse, especially from a Biblical or Christian perspective.

After graduate school, I began working in a mid-size hospital educating the emergency room doctors and nurses to recognize and report child abuse as reporting became mandatory. I also started advocating with church leaders to screen nursery and childcare workers. At the time, church leaders found it hard to grasp that someone who claimed to be a Christian and belonged to a church would harm child. These days no church would consider not having these protocols for the safety of children.

When I was writing my third book, *Defeating Depression* I began to notice that women who were clinically depressed were often in emotionally, verbally and sometimes physically and sexually abusive marriages.

I began to ask myself and the Holy Spirit some questions. Does God care more about the sanctity of marriage than he does for the safety and sanity of the woman in it? Is it godly or healthy for an abused wife to suffer silently, numbing out or taking antidepressants for her entire lifetime just to endure living with her oppressor? And what about the kids? Neuroscience was an emerging field and we were learning how early childhood trauma impacts a child's brain and capacity to learn and grow. Does their development matter to God?

Does God mandate a wife and her children to sacrifice their health and well-being in order to stay in the same household with their oppressor? To silently endure mistreatment, pretending at church and with outsiders that everything is fine at home? Who does that approach serve or help? It doesn't help the oppressed woman or her children nor does it help the oppressor wake up and repent. Does that approach glorify God?

Or does God call her to something more risky and redemptive? What about verses that call her to speak the truth in love, expose the unfruitful deeds of darkness, and stand up against injustice and abuse of power?

I began to dig deeper into Scripture and discovered that God has a lot to say about the oppressor and the oppressed. About the abuse of power, whether it be in a nation, a church or a home. Both the Old and New Testament are very clear about the power of our words and their toxic effects on others. I continue to be perplexed when current Christian counselors or leaders minimize or invalidate emotional or verbal abuse when the Scriptures are quite clear that it's real and its impact harmful to the soul, spirit and body of the recipient.

2. What do you see as being the best practices for working with women experiencing verbal and emotional abuse/domestic violence?

Working with an abused woman is multifaceted. First, as the counselor you must understand that she is traumatized by her interpersonal relationship. Research indicates that CTSD (Complex Traumatic Stress Disorder) is common among victims of abuse, especially chronic abuse like domestic abuse. When she finally comes for help, she may not report being abused, but she may be depressed, numbed out, a shell of a person, even suicidal.

As therapists we must be cognizant that a victim's story may not always sound logical or sequential. Her facts may be fuzzy. She may not remember things at first and be easily triggered. She may be unable to make a decision for herself or be emotionally labile or volatile. These symptoms are not necessarily indicative of a personality disorder but rather the effects of repeated trauma and fear of disclosure. Be careful not to label her prematurely with a diagnosis that she will later have to fight about in court if she is in a custody evaluation for her children.

Safety is the first treatment goal. As the counselor, be careful not to take ownership of her safety at home. That is something she must be empowered to do with your help. However, you must make sure that you create a safe environment for her to disclose what's going on. One of the ways you do that is to let her disclose at her pace, respect her "no" and validate her voice, and don't pressure her to do anything, especially reconcile, or drop a Protection Order, or even separate from her spouse. She has been treated as child or slave or worse in her marriage and therefore she must begin to get a sense that you see her as an adult who is capable of making decisions for herself that are respected. She must begin to sense her own power to think for herself, to be heard, be known, to make choices, and be believed.

Marriage counseling is contraindicated. Abuse is never a marriage problem, it causes marriage problems for sure, but abuse is an individual character issue stemming from various factors. When marriage counseling is the first treatment plan, the responsibility for repairing the marriage often falls on the victim's shoulders. "You just need to trust him again, he said he won't act that way anymore." Or "Why are you pushing his buttons, you know this makes him mad." Or "If only you were willing to have more sex, he wouldn't act like this." Or, "You're just overreacting because of your own childhood issues."

The abuser needs his own treatment plan and if willing, work on why he acts the way he does when he's frustrated, disappointed, hurt, or anxious. His wife is not responsible to make his life 100% stress free, or to control his tongue and temper. That is impossible. He needs to learn to manage his emotions and his tongue so that he does not continue to cause harm. If he is unwilling to engage in his own individual treatment plan, the marriage cannot be repaired, and nothing will change. Unchallenged, abusive behaviors tend to increase in frequency and intensity over time, increasing her level of danger.

Work with her to help her develop her CORE strength, be honest, take responsibility for herself and her own choices, overcome evil with good yet not enabling destructive behavior to continue to harm her or her children. Don't focus on saving the marriage, focus on strengthening the victim.

3. How do you see Biblical headship being used as a cover for emotional and verbal abuse?

The misuse of headship is rampant among abusers. Abusive men misuse their God given power (physical power, economic power, spiritual power), to control their spouse and get their own way, relegating her to the status of a child, or a slave. She has no voice and no choice. He is to be obeyed as if he was god.

This is not a Biblical picture of marriage, nor headship. God created woman as an equal partner in marriage. That does not negate the need for authority or leadership however, when Jesus taught his disciples about what leadership or headship looked like, he demonstrated it by washing their dirty feet. Biblical headship is never described as demanding your own way, forcing others to submit, or verbal battering when one does not obey or submit. Those behaviors have other Biblical words: selfishness, sin, abusive speech and oppressor.

Jesus made the definition of Biblical headship very clear. After washing the disciple's feet, they argued over who would get to sit at Christ's right hand in heaven. They still didn't understand headship. He clarified it to them. He said, "You know that those who are regarded as rules of the Gentiles lord it over them, and their high officials exercise authority over them. Not so with you. Instead, whoever wants to become great among you must be your servant, and whoever wants to be first must be slave of all. For even the Son of Man did not come to be served, but to serve, and to give his life as a ransom for many" (*New International Bible*, 1973/2011, Mark 10:42).

Jesus specifically instructs us as Christians against the misuse of authority and "lording" it over someone. If anyone does have authority, as certainly Jesus did, he or she is to serve and give not to demand and strut one's authority as a license for getting one's own way.

Be careful of this mistake especially if you're seeing a couple together because you aren't fully aware of all the abuse at home. Sometimes a woman will resist submitting to a legitimate request her spouse asks of her. There is no perfect wife and at times you will find yourself liking the husband more than the wife. When a woman has been filled with resentment or is depressed or depleted, she does not respond in an ideal "Biblical" way. And her spouse will use that as a reason or justification for why he abused. "If she only would submit, stop arguing, do what I say, follow my leadership, this wouldn't happen." Be alert. As the therapist it's tempting to try to solve his "anger or abuse problem" by turning to her and trying to help her to stop aggravating him or challenging him, or pushing his buttons, or not cooperating with him. Don't do it. Instead, stay with him. Validate his legitimate pain or anger or frustration with his wife's refusal to follow his leadership and instead challenge him with how he handled himself when she refused.

He is 100% responsible for how he handles his own emotional upsets and it's not his wife's responsibility to become the perfect wife, so she never upsets him. Notice whether or not he takes responsibility to manage and control his own emotions and words. If he continues to blame-shift or skirt around the issue, recognize that marriage counseling is contraindicated. It's not that the wife doesn't need help to stop escalating a situation, but don't do that work in front of her abuser. That feeds his entitlement thinking and validates his perspective that she is the problem in their marriage.

4. What advice/message would you offer to the Christian counselors desiring to work in this field?

Get good training and supervision from experts in the field. Never stop learning and growing yourself. Listen to your clients. They will teach you more than you will teach them. If you find yourself defensive or argumentative with feedback your client gives you, get supervision, don't assume they are wrong. Don't be fake. If you're not doing your own work to grow closer to God, getting healthier emotionally and relationally, and walking the walk, you will do more harm than good. Have integrity.

Recognize your limits. Don't over-function. You are not their hero or savior. When we try, it strokes our ego, but it's harmful to our clients. Help your clients connect with the true Savior and teach them how to become the hero of their own story. Be creative. Remember you are not just helping them to think differently, but to live differently.

Last, but not least, take good care of you, your mind, body and spirit. Compassion fatigue and burnout are common among people helpers. Sitting all day is not good for your body or spirit. Give yourself breaks in the day to stand up, go outside, and move around. Have clear and firm boundaries. Take time off. Don't neglect your real relationships and invite people who are truth tellers and not afraid to tell you what they see. Challenge yourself with fresh goals and dreams that are not professional. Be a whole person, not just a therapist.

Copyright © Leslie Vernick. Reprinted by permission.

TREATMENT CONSIDERATIONS FOR DOMESTIC VIOLENCE AND ABUSE

Given the secrecy surrounding intimate partner violence (IPV) and the way a woman may become habituated to its normalcy, seeking services might take time. By the time a woman reaches out for help, solutions could be extreme, perhaps requiring relocating and starting from ground zero in order to find safety. As we discuss evidence-based treatments and techniques, remember that the task of the counselor with domestic vio-

© Nikki Zalewski/Shutterstock.com

lence victims is greater than providing mental support. Many women will need a real lifeline as they exit highly dangerous situations and become independent again.

Studies exhibit a correlation between women who formally seek help for experiences with IPV, and higher education, PTSD symptoms, or severity of emotional and psychological trauma (Nnawulezi & Murphy, 2019). Black women seek the services of the police and their religious leaders more often, while being white is a significant predictor for seeking mental health services (Nnawulezi & Murphy, 2019). Women of a minority status initiate connection but do not keep up the appointments, which may relate to a less positive therapeutic experience and/or different expectations for therapy outcomes compared to the therapist (Klopper et al., 2014). It is essential when you work with women of minority status to check in early with them about their expectations and comfort level with the counseling process, making every effort to establish a relationship characterized by therapeutic rapport and trust.

Another consideration for treatment for all survivors of IPV relates to intimate partner violence experiences. Researchers have found that some factors complicate treatment for women who have experienced abuse. Kubany and Watson (2002; see also Kubany et al., 2004) describe four factors that complicate the treatment of abused women:

- The severity and duration of IPV differs from single-episode trauma.
- Intimate attachment of IPV leads to ambivalence not shared by other trauma survivors.

- Often IPV victims have had multiple abusive relationships and are in danger of being re-victimized.
- Feelings of guilt and shame often are part of the IPV experience.

FIGURE 20.3

Factors That Complicate the Treatment of Abused Women

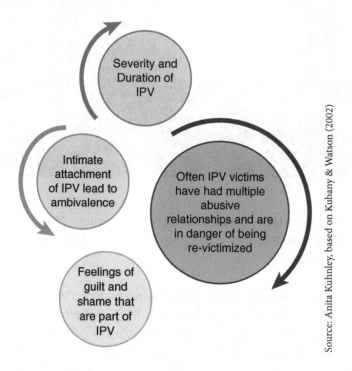

Source: Anita Kuhnley, based on Kubany & Watson (2002)

Other barriers to treatment-seeking are mental health barriers, health barriers, practical barriers, partner-related barriers, cultural barriers, and perceived systemic barriers (Hasselle et al., 2019). Given all the difficulties to be surmounted when entering treatment, a woman who comes for help needs all the encouragement and support you and your organization can offer to set her up for success.

Safety First

What are the basics for treating women who are/were victims of IPV? No matter what type of therapy is used with treating a woman after IPV, the most important rule for each case is: safety, safety, safety. When a woman makes this first phone call to a crisis hotline or a domestic violence shelter, an advocate will go over a script with her. Creating a safety plan is a

© smahok/Shutterstock.com

priority. Safety could be separated in some loose categories: safety during an explosive incident; safety when the woman prepares to leave; safety in her home; safety if she already has a protective order; safety in public and when at work; and safety and emotional health (see Deaton & Hertica, 2001). Deaton and Hertica's *Growing Free: A Manual for Survivors of Domestic Violence* is a small book that could be shared with women considering leaving or in the process of leaving an abusive partner. A specific chapter of the book addresses the creation of safety plans. Safety during an explosive incident would include going into a room that has an exit, having a bag ready with the most important things, informing a neighbor, using a code word with others when they need to call the police, having a safe place to go after she leaves the house, and following a gut instinct.

There are many websites to help guide a woman through the process of leaving and finding resources. Assisting women in navigating this information is essential. For those currently in abusive situations, they may be apprehensive about looking for information or having a number on their cell phone out of fear the abuser may be monitoring this information. The National Domestic Violence Hotline provides information, live-chat options, and 1-800 call numbers where help is available to navigate safety planning, leaving a relationship, legal advice, definitions of abuse, etc. Visit their website here: https://www.thehotline.org

CONCEPT TO CONTEMPLATE

© Asier Romero/Shutterstock.com

In the field of social workers and mental health providers, we rarely speak of the unintended consequences of leaving an abusive environment. Unexpected losses are crucial to consider: loss of emotional and physical safety for themselves and their loved ones; loss of social support; loss of finances; loss of their home and roots; loss of control over parenting; and loss of freedom due to the fear of being found (Thomas et al., 2015).

For example, a client had to change her name and leave a highly abusive environment that involved severe physical and sexual abuse. Due to safety reasons, her real name was changed and never disclosed. By running away and changing her identity, she experienced an unintended consequence of losing her family, her home, and the connection to her community. Unintended consequences can matter a great deal to someone's well-being and core identity.

As you ponder this information, consider: Do you know the resources in your local area? If so, do you have the contact information readily available? If not, take some time to explore nearby resources and organize their contact information so it is easily accessible. Once you have contact information available, consider visiting a local women's shelter or support center to learn all that is offered.

Resilience

In treatment, one key factor to explore is the current level of the woman's resilience, along with ways to increase resilience. There are many definitions of resilience. In simple words, resilience is the ability to bounce back after adversarial environmental situations. Successful coping strategies can lead women to be more resilient. It is important to explore the individual factors that could make women more resilient such as physical activity, altruism, control over their lives, introspection, optimism, rediscovering, creativity, spirituality, new projects and goals, focus on the present, and a sense of humor. These factors of support increased resilience for Spanish women who had experienced IPV (Lopez-Fuentes & Calvete, 2015). You could choose to focus on one or two of these or create a list to go over together with some stronger and weaker areas to develop, perhaps incorporating the process into weekly homework assignments. External factors for resiliency are the provision of housing, informal support, and formal social support (Lopez-Fuentes & Calvete, 2015). Often domestic violence agencies work on case management, helping women sign up for Section 8 housing (government assistance in paying for rental housing for low-income households in the United States) through formal supportive agencies such as community centers (U.S. Department of Housing and Urban Development, 2020).

Resiliency also connects to the communities and culture with which the individual identifies. A study conducted in 11 countries with adolescents discovered that identity, material resources, social justice, power, belonging, relationships, and the way these factors interconnected with each other led to higher levels of resilience (Ungar et al., 2007). What are the places and who are the people the woman trusts and is committed to? Are there traditions, religious events, or cultural markers that could help her overcome the present hurdles and focus on a new future? How can she increase her chances for meaningful and useful connections in a new place, especially when she has entered a shelter or has moved away because of the abuse? Can she find meaningful work (Rothman et al., 2007)? One thing to explore with women is the number of violent relationships they have been in and their duration, which could lead to lowered resiliency. In contrast, spirituality may bring comfort and enhance resilience, especially in Black women (Howell et al., 2018).

TREATMENT

A range of treatments are available to use with women who have experienced IPV. Some of them are specific to this phenomenon, while others treat PTSD and trauma or could have specific applications to IPV. The American Psychiatric Association ([APA] 2013) lists evidence-based practices that have been successful in treating IPV. These include Cognitive Behavioral Therapy (CBT), Skills Training in Affective and Interpersonal Regulation (STAIR), Dialectical Behavior Therapy (DBT), Interpersonal Psychotherapy (IPT), Cognitive Processing Therapy (CPT), Eye Movement Desensitization and Reprocessing (EMDR), Helping to Overcome PTSD through Empowerment (HOPE), Relapse Prevention and Relationship Safety (RPRS), Grady Nia Project, Cognitive Trauma Therapy for Battered Women (CTT-BW), and psychopharmacological treatments. No matter the treatment chosen, it is important to create a setting that will be trauma-informed and inviting for domestic violence survivors. This section will begin with describing trauma-informed practice and then focus on a few of the specific treatments listed above.

Trauma-Informed Practice

One of the essential parts of treating women who have experienced IPV is creating the right atmosphere: treatment begins at the door. Some recent research has suggested that the programs created to help are shown to retraumatize, further stigmatize, and disempower women contrary to the goal of empowerment (Glenn & Goodman, 2015). Wilson et al. (2015) studied publications that explored the environment and approach of trauma-informed practice (TIP), noting six clusters of TIP:

1. **Promote emotional safety.** In your organization, is the environment designed to minimize triggers? Is the staff trained to have a nonjudgmental approach sharing the policies clearly and safely?
2. **Restore choice and control.** Is the approach of your organization and therapy-work top-down or collaborative? Due to the crisis mode of the work, it is easy to take control and tell survivors what to do. Make sure you are not constantly operating in that crisis mode. Your pre-session prep could involve finding a quiet place alone to pause,

pray, and focus so that you could enter a highly stressful situation with a clear head and diminished anxiety.

3. **Facilitate connection.** Build relationships, connect genuinely with survivors and let them have opportunities to associate if there is communal living involved. Many come with apprehension and use unhelpful parenting skills. It is important to support them in their relationship with their children and build respect. Help them establish healthy relationships and learn how to use those skills in a new community.

4. **Support coping.** Help survivors develop strategies for coping and support coping related to domestic violence. Target a holistic culture of healing as you look at the big picture of their life and future. Everything might feel like a crisis in the moment but coping with daily life and learning a calm existence will be key!

5. **Respond to identity and context.** Even though there are many commonalities about those who have experienced trauma, especially IPV trauma, there will be women from many walks of life and identities. Is the physical space inclusive for them? Does the organization represent the diversity of clients?

6. **Build strengths.** Refer back to the earlier paragraph on resilience. Make sure to recognize the personal strengths of each woman and help them develop leadership skills.

STAIR: Skills Training in Affective and Interpersonal Regulation

STAIR is the most widely researched and published cognitive behavioral approach to trauma (National Center for PTSD, 2019). Its main premise is that trauma and PTSD impact individuals mostly in two areas: the ability to self-regulate and relationship dynamics. The STAIR approach consists of eight basic skills described in its modules. Clients come for eight sessions that cover key aspects, techniques, and tools as they learn how to regulate through breathing; connect through emotional awareness; learn of emotional regulation and emotionally engaged living; practice changing relationship patterns; and become more aware of agency and flexibility in relationships.

Self-regulation is the ability to name and sort through different feelings, communicate them, engage in emotional regulation skills, and learn distress tolerance. To help clients who are not aware of their emotions, who feel numb and are mostly down, the counselor could offer a simple list of different feelings (National Center for PTSD, 2019). For example, ask the client to identify a time in the last week when she experienced a lot of emotion as a way for her to begin exploring and naming the different feelings present throughout her days. Another helpful tool in naming feelings is the *Feeling Wheel* (see Figure 20.4 below), which helps the client become more specific in her words used. Show her how to use a self-monitoring form throughout the week to discover the connection between thoughts, feelings, and behaviors (National Center for PTSD, 2019).

FIGURE 20.4

Feeling Wheel

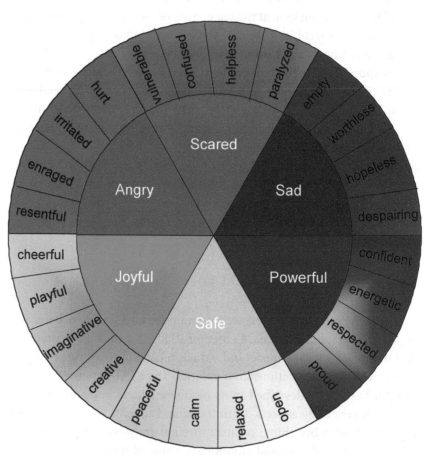

Source: National Center for PTSD (2019)

Once the client has been able to name emotions, the STAIR approach identifies the comfort zone of strategies has she used so far, explores whether or not these have been helpful, and asks what other strategies could she employ. Women are asked to find their comfort zone in thoughts, body, and action. **Distress tolerance** is the woman's ability to endure certain pain and discomfort to achieve the desired goal. Does she want to go back to school? Is there a class she would like to take? Does she want to engage with the community she is in? Let these guide her decisions and determination to work through the painful process of getting there.

CONCEPT TO CONTEMPLATE

Are you able to identify your emotions? Do you ever find yourself using "thinking" words instead of "feeling" words? Do you notice yourself saying "I think I feel…" rather than "I feel…"? Over the next few days, be intentional in identifying how you are feeling. Work on saying "I feel…."

© Digital Storm/Shutterstock.com

Following the exploration of emotions and distress tolerance, STAIR moves to explore relationship patterns. Women who have been in abusive relationships have had mostly negative experiences that have produced rigid interpersonal schemas and ways they could interact with others. The *Interpersonal Schemas Worksheet* below helps them identify how old beliefs might have been damaging in their interactions with others. Role-playing with clients could help them find better ways to express frustration and gain their voice, learning how to avoid passive and aggressive behaviors and become assertive instead. "I-messages" are central to learning how to do this. Finally, there are power dynamics in each relationship, from equal to unequal - parent-child, boss-worker, husband-wife. Explore with women how to say no in each of these types of relationships. Help them create new Interpersonal Schemas (National Center for PTSD, 2019).

FIGURE 20.5

Interpersonal
Schemas Worksheet
Examples

INTERPERSONAL SCHEMAS WORKSHEET I

Interpersonal Situation	What did I feel and think about myself?		What were my expectations about the other person?		My Resulting Behavior
What happened?	My Feelings	My Thoughts	Their Feelings	Their Thoughts	What did I do?

Interpersonal Schema: WHEN_____ THEN_____

https://www.ptsd.va.gov/apps/STAIR/Session5/010501----.htm#

INTERPERSONAL SCHEMAS WORKSHEET II

Interpersonal Situation	What did I feel and think about myself?		What were my expectations about the other person's thoughts and feelings?		My Resulting Behavior
What happened?	My Feelings	My Thoughts	Their Feelings	Their Thoughts	What did I do?

Interpersonal Schema: WHEN_____ THEN_____

Interpersonal Goals for Situation	What did I feel and think about myself?		What alternative expectations can I have about the other person's thoughts and feelings?		My Resulting Behavior
What are my goals in this situation?	My Feelings	My Thoughts	Their Feelings	Their Thoughts	What else could I do?

Alternative Schema: WHEN_____ THEN_____

https://www.ptsd.va.gov/apps/STAIR/Session6/010501----.htm#

Source: U.S. Department of Veterans Affairs and the National Center for PTSD

By following the links below the pictures of Figure 20.5, you can then access session materials at the bottom left corner of the webpage. You will find handouts for the basic steps of a role-playing exercise and the *Interpersonal Schemas Worksheets*. The U.S. Department of Veterans Affairs offers eight hours of certified CE training on the STAIR model that covers core treatment components. After registering on their website, the training is free for practitioners and people engaged in emergency services.

Helping Overcome PTSD through Empowerment (HOPE)

HOPE addresses five areas of dysfunction: safety, trust, esteem, intimacy, and control, and teaches women how to cope with PTSD symptoms (Johnson & Zlotnik, 2009). It is a program designed to be developed in shelters together with case management and advocacy services. There are three stages through which therapy progresses: establishing safety and empowerment, managing PTSD symptoms, and improving relationships.

Cognitive Trauma Therapy for Battered Women (CTT-BW)

CTT-BW brings down the depression and anxiety, and increases self-esteem and quality of life and leads to a reduction of guilt and shame (Beck et al., 2016). CTT-BW includes: (1) exploration and exposure to the previous trauma; (2) PTSD psychoeducation; (3) homework through the imagined and in vivo; (4) psychoeducation on maladaptive self-talk; (5) relaxation training and stress management stress; (6) cognitive therapy addressing the guilt (7) psychoeducation on assertiveness and responses to verbal aggression; (8) managing unwanted contacts with former partners; (9) learning to identify potential perpetrators and avoid revictimization; and (10) psychoeducation on positive coping strategies that focus on self-advocacy and self-empowerment (e.g., placing oneself first, decision-making that promotes self-interest) (Beck et al., 2016). Homework incorporates listening to audiotapes of the sessions, in-vivo and imaginal exposure to abuse-related reminders, playing a relaxation tape, and self-monitoring of negative self-talk.

Dialectical Behavior Therapy (DBT)

Difficulty in managing emotions results from feeling vulnerable along with consistent invalidation through criticism, contempt, disregard, and crazy-making behaviors. A small study proved that there was statistical significance pre and post-intervention in depression, hopelessness, social adjustment (Iverson et al., 2009). Researchers used DEARMAN = the needed skills to achieve the objectives (Describe, Express, Assert, Reinforce, stay Mindful, Appear confident, Negotiate) for a 12-week program. Utilizing Marsha Linehan's (2015) *DBT® Skills Training: Handouts and Worksheets* manual can be beneficial for planning exercises and homework to target specific behaviors as they relate to Domestic violence and interpersonal abuse. Counselors are encouraged to seek additional training in Dialectical Behavior Therapy (Linehan, 2015) to learn to use all DBT skills appropriately.

Understanding treatment approaches and being intentional in their application is very important. Counselors need to be focused on their approach. Victims of emotional and physical abuse are vulnerable, and we want to model safety and trust in the way we care for them. Often the counselor may hold the hope for the client. Staying hopeful for her and patient in the process, while trying different approaches and ideas, will continue to energize your time together and help her engage in the steps of change.

LOOKING THROUGH THE LENS OF CHRISTIANITY: BIBLICAL INTEGRATION

God desires for people to be loved and cherished. Man's brokenness, selfishness and greed open unintended doors to abuse, and it breaks God's heart for women to be victimized in this way. Scripture, in 2 Timothy 3:1-7 (*New International Bible*, 1973/2011) describes this brokenness:

> But mark this: There will be terrible times in the last days. People will be lovers of themselves, lovers of money, boastful, proud, abusive, disobedient to their parents, ungrateful, unholy, without love, unforgiving, slanderous, without self-control, brutal, not lovers of the good, treacherous, rash, conceited, lov-

ers of pleasure rather than lovers of God— having a form of godliness but denying its power. Have nothing to do with such people. They are the kind who worm their way into homes and gain control over gullible women, who are loaded down with sins and are swayed by all kinds of evil desires, always learning but never able to come to a knowledge of the truth.

We opened the chapter acknowledging God's care for those who are hurting and brokenhearted (Psalm 34:18). As we work with clients, we want to ensure our foundation of hope in God's care is present. The most important thing we can do in preparation for this work is to pray. Our mental preparation is indeed important. Having discernment from the Holy Spirit is essential. Seeking discernment in our encounters with clients, our approach to client treatment, and our personal spiritual growth is imperative. Counselors need to be cognizant of the importance of spiritual armor (Ephesians 6) for what lies ahead in working with abuse victims. We need to be messengers of true peace. This means we are peacemakers, not peacekeepers. We walk in Truth and work to bring truth to difficult situations. We trust in the process of truth and the importance of bringing into light what has been hidden in a way that is respectful and honoring of our clients. Mark 4:22 (*New International Bible*, 1973/2011) speaks to this saying, "For whatever is hidden is meant to be disclosed and whatever is concealed is meant to be brought out into the open."

© Rachata Sinthopachakul/Shutterstock.com

Counselors need to be prepared with accurate Biblical understanding to bring clarity to clients who may have misinterpreted Scripture or received misinformation. Holding firm to abuse not being part of God's desire and being proactive regarding the safety and well-being of our clients is essential. Identifying situations where Scripture has been misused as inappropriate justification for abuse is the counselor's responsibility. Jesus modeled the importance of safety when he intentionally avoided places (Judea) and people that had intent to harm him (John 7:1). In I Samuel 18-31 we read where David was fearful for his own life and fled. God did not ask David to stay and submit to King Saul's anger while trusting God to care for him. Instead, David was respectful of the king's position and set a boundary by fleeing to protect and care for himself. God is aware when abuse is occurring and offers a promise that "there is nothing concealed that will not be disclosed, or hidden that will not be made known" (*New International Bible*, 1973/2011, Luke 12:2).

CASE STUDY

Have you ever known anyone who was living life with domestic violence? While you would hope that none of your friends or family would experience domestic violence, at least one woman in your world may be living this terrible reality. You may not even be aware who that person is, but it is possible that you do know someone who is suffering in a violent and abusive relationship.

Joye seemed to be an exceptionally happy woman. She attended church and was engaged in the community, an upper-middle-class congregation with the majority of members being well-educated. Joye's husband presented as a mild-mannered, easy-going, and affable guy. By all appearances, Joye and her husband were well-connected and happy in their marriage.

Joye played on community sports teams with many women in the church. Over some time, the women from the church noticed that Joye often had a new injury. Every month, she had another broken, sprained, or bruised appendage. She would sometimes have bruises on her face or neck, as well. Yet, she was always able to give reasonable explanations for her injuries. Sometimes she would say that she had tripped and fallen. Other times she would claim that she had dropped something heavy on a foot or hand. And then there were times that she stated she had run into something, such as a door frame or a wall. Several women on the team frequently discussed how the injuries appeared to be odd, but no one ever asked or knew for sure if Joye was being abused. Over time, many of the other women began to suspect some type of abuse was occurring. One of the women approached Joye privately and encouraged her to seek professional support from a counselor. Joye was hesitant, fearing her husband would find out and retaliate.

So, in working with this client, keep in mind the previously presented concept treatment begins at the door. As soon as Joye comes to you as her counselor, best practices would lead you to begin to immediately implement evidence-based treatments in assisting her. Solution-focused therapy (SFT) is the most advisable therapeutic intervention as a starting point, when beginning to work with a victim. This means that you are helping Joye to establish solutions for her immediate and concrete problems. First and most importantly, you must ensure Joye's safety. This involves creating a safety plan with her. Recall our earlier chapter discussion on these actions. Your conversation with her must consider how she would be able to maintain her safety at home, at work, and in the community. In all of these locations, she must have a clear plan for how to escape her abuser when a volatile crisis arises. As she establishes a safety plan with your guidance, she must be cognizant of her need to access money for transportation, food, shelter, and clothing. Finally, it is important for Joye to figure out, ahead of a violent incident, a destination to escape to, for safety and protection.

Once Joye is stabilized and has a clear safety plan in place, you are ready to move forward from SFT into an expanded treatment plan. This would include facilitating Joye in the process of acknowledging and exploring the personal history and family cycles that drew her into an abusive relationship to begin with. While a variety of interventions could be used with Joye, the most basic starting point is to implement empathic listening techniques in a non-judgmental way, allowing her to tell her story, and being believed. This will quickly build rapport as you establish the therapeutic relationship.

From that point, you as the counselor, must choose a therapeutic intervention path that seems best for each specific client, bringing that client into the process of establishing her therapy goals. Keep in mind Joye's specific situation and her emotional strengths and weaknesses, and then decide if you want to approach treatment from a perspective of PTSD. This is the most common approach to treating victims of domestic violence, but it may not always be the best. From this perspective, interventions would require treatment tactics or a curriculum, proven to be effective for PTSD. Cognitive Behavioral Therapy (CBT), HOPE (Helping to Overcome PTSD through Empowerment), or STAIRS (Skills Training in Affective and Interpersonal Regulation) are all proven approaches in assisting a victim like Joye.

Your other treatment options might be to address the behavioral and cognitive processes that influenced Joye in becoming involved with an abuser in the first place. Some of the most effective interventions for this approach to treatment are Interpersonal Psychotherapy (IPT), Cognitive Processing Therapy (CPT), Eye Movement Desensitization Reprocessing (EMDR), or Cognitive Trauma Therapy for Battered Women (CTT-BW). This is not an all-inclusive list of evidence-based treatment approaches, but are some of the most used, evidence-based interventions in the field. Of course, some of these and other very effective interventions are specialized and require specific training.

Finally, as a clinician of faith, if your client has given consent, you may want to include principles of faith in your intervention approach. As Christians, there are many Scripture passages and Biblical concepts that teach the value and worth of all people, including women (Psalm 139:13-16, Ephesians 2:10, 1 Corinthians 6:20). There are distinctive scriptural passages that offer examples of the strong qualities a woman should strive to possess (Proverbs 31), and the power she has because of her Divine connection (Galatians 2:20). As you create a comprehensive treatment plan for Joye, keep all of these factors in mind.

CHAPTER SUMMARY

The prevalence and impact of physical and emotional abuse is more widespread than many realize or are willing to accept. With intentionality, counselors can help women regain their voices that are lost in abusive relationships and learn to live outside of the shame they have internalized. Women are not called to be martyrs in abusive relationships. They are offered opportunity to walk in the grace of God's light and truth. Living in relationship with someone who "prefers deceit and darkness and who twists and manipulates the truth" (Vernick, 2013, p. 70) is stressful and not how God designed relationships to be. Counseling women seeking true peace in their lives can be challenging yet also rewarding. In this chapter, we discussed definitions and patterns of emotional and physical abuse, provided information on various interventions and evidence-based treatments, and offered additional helpful resources to encourage women in their journey to restoration of healthy functioning. This information can be a catalyst to expand your understanding of the broad spectrum of physical and emotional abuse and how as a counselor, you may engage with clients on their path to healing.

KEY TERMS

Domestic Abuse and Intimate Partner Violence (IPV) - interchangeable terms describing a current or past relationship that involved physical, sexual or psychological abuse

Economic Abuse - withholding financial resources and information regarding finances, preventing from employment, preventing access to basic life necessities

Emotional Abuse - criticism, name-calling, humiliation, looks and gestures that create fear, isolation, constant monitoring of another; plays on the present fears and emotional weaknesses of a woman

Physical Abuse - holding physical power over someone, hitting, physical harming another; any non-accidental use of force that results in bodily injury, pain, or impairment

Section 8 Housing - government assistance in paying for rental housing for low-income households in the United States

Spiritual Abuse - use of religion to exert a sense of power and in an entitled manner

Verbal Abuse - most often occurs with other types of abuse as a means to coerce and control

SUGGESTED RESOURCES

Books

Healing Trauma: A Pioneering Program for Restoring the Wisdom of your Body by Peter Levine

DBT® Skills Training: Handouts and Worksheets (2nd ed.) by Marsha Linehan

The Emotionally Destructive Marriage: How to Find your Voice and Reclaim Hope by Leslie Vernick

The Emotionally Destructive Relationship: Seeing it, Stopping it, Surviving it by Leslie Vernick

Training

National Center for PTSD provides training for practitioners: https://www.ptsd.va.gov/professional/continuing_ed/index.asp

Training for church leaders and counselors to recognize and respond to abusive behaviors: https://leslievernick.com/counselors/

Assessments

The American College of Obstetricians and Gynecologists (ACOG) provides screening questions for practitioners: https://www.acog.org/Clinical-Guidance-and-Publications/Committee-Opinions/Committee-on-Health-Care-for-Underserved-Women/Intimate-Partner-Violence?IsMobileSet=false

The Substance Abuse and Mental Health Services Organization SAMHAS provides resources for clinicians, organizations, patients, and policymakers on intimate partner violence with IPV screening and assessment tools; information on at-risk populations: https://www.integration.samhsa.gov/clinical-practice/intimate-partner-violence#Providers

Facts and Statistics

The World Health Organization (WHO) provides basic facts and statistics on IPV: https://apps.who.int/iris/bitstream/handle/10665/77432/WHO_RHR_12.36_eng.pdf;jsessionid=BE293677284EAD0404B3A291BB942D34?sequence=1

REFERENCES

Aaron, C. (2016, February 5). *Domestic abuse in the church, a 'silent epidemic.'* CBN. https://www1.cbn.com/cbnnews/us/2016/January/Combating-Domestic-Abuse-in-the-Church

Adams, A. E., Sullivan, C. M., Bybee, D., & Greeson, M. R. (2008). Development of the scale of economic abuse. *Violence Against Women, 14*(5), 563-588. https://doi:10.1177/1077801208315529

American Psychiatric Association. (2013). *Diagnostic and statistical manual of mental disorders* (5th ed.). https://doi.org/10.1176/appi.books.9780890425596

Beck, J. G., Tran, H. N., Dodson, T. S., Henschel, A. V., Woodward, M. J., & Eddinger, J. (2016). Cognitive trauma therapy for battered women: Replication and extension. *Psychology of Violence, 6*(3), 368-377. http://dx.doi.org.ezproxy.liberty.edu/10.1037/vio0000024

Campbell, R., & Raja, S. (1999). Secondary victimization of rape victims: Insights from mental health professionals who treat survivors of violence. *Violence and Victims, 14*(3), 261–275. https://doi:10.1891/08866708.14.3.261

Dasgupta, S. D. (2010). My friend, advocate Ellen Pence. *Violence Against Women, 16*(9), 985-991. https://doi.org/10.1177/1077801210379254

Deaton, W. S., & Hertica, M. (2001). *Growing free: A manual for survivors of domestic violence.* Haworth Maltreatment and Trauma Press; The Haworth Press.

Domestic Violence Roundtable. (2019). *What Is domestic violence.* https://www.domesticviolenceroundtable.org/whatisdv

Earls, A. (2019, May 21). Churchgoers split on existence of more sexual abuse by pastors: More sexual abuse revelations to come? https://lifewayresearch.com/2019/05/21/churchgoers-split-on-existence-of-more-sexual-abuse-by-pastors/

Enander, V. (2010). "A fool to keep staying": Battered women labeling themselves stupid as an expression of gendered shame. *Violence Against Women, 16*(1), 5-31. https://doi.org/10.1177/1077801209353577

Finkelhor, D., Turner, H., Ormrod, R., & Hamby, S. (2011). Children's exposure to intimate partner violence and other family violence. https://www.ncjrs.gov/pdffiles1/ojjdp/232272.pdf

Ganley, A. L. (1995). *Understanding domestic violence. Improving the health care response to domestic violence: A resource manual for health care providers.* https://andvsa.org/

Glenn, C., & Goodman, L. (2015). Living with and within the rules of domestic violence shelters: A qualitative exploration of residents' experiences. *Violence Against Women, 21*(12), 1481-1506. http://dx.doi.org.ezproxy.liberty.edu/10.1177/1077801215596242

Goldsmith, T. (2018). What causes domestic violence? *Psych Central.* Retrieved November 8, 2019, from https://psychcentral.com/lib/what-causes-domestic-violence/

Graham-Bermann, S. A., Cater, Å. K., Miller-Graff, L. E., & Howell, K. H. (2017). Adults' explanations for intimate partner violence during childhood and associated effects. *Journal of Clinical Psychology, 73*(6), 652–668. https://doi.org/10.1002/jclp.22345

Hasselle, A. J., Howell, K. H., Bottomley, J., Sheddan, H. C., Capers, J. M., & Miller-Graff, L. E. (2019). Barriers to intervention engagement among women experiencing intimate partner violence proximal to pregnancy. *Psychology of Violence.* Advance online publication. http://dx.doi.org/10.1037/vio0000253

Howell, K. H., Thurston, I. B., Schwartz, L. E., Jamison, L. E., & Hasselle, A. J. (2018). Protective factors associated with resilience in women exposed to intimate partner violence. *Psychology of Violence, 8*(4), 438-447. http://dx.doi.org/10.1037/vio0000147

Iverson, K. M., Shenk, C., & Fruzzetti, A. E. (2009). Dialectical behavior therapy for women victims of domestic abuse: A pilot study. *Professional Psychology: Research and Practice, 40*(3), 242-248.

Johnson, D. M., & Zlotnick, C. (2009). HOPE for battered women with PTSD in domestic violence shelters. *Professional Psychology: Research and Practice, 40*(3), 234-241.

Kippert, A. (2017, August 23). Why we blame victims for domestic violence. https://www.domesticshelters.org/articles/identifying-abuse/why-so-many-are-quick-to-blame-victims-of-domestic-violence

Klein, E., Campbell, J., Soler, E., & Ghez, M. (1997). *Ending domestic violence: Changing public perceptions/halting the epidemic.* Sage Publishing.

Klopper, J. J., Schweinle, W., Ractliffe, K. C., & Elhai, J. D. (2014). Predictors of mental healthcare use among domestic violence survivors in shelters. *Psychological Services, 11*(2), 134-140.

Kubany, E. S., Hill, E. E., Owens, J. A., Iannce-Spencer, C., McCaig, M. A., Tremayne, K. J., & Williams, P. L. (2004). Cognitive trauma therapy for battered women with PTSD (CTT-BW). *Journal of Consulting and Clinical Psychology, 72*(1), 3-18.

Kubany, E. S., & Watson, S. (2002). Cognitive trauma therapy for formerly battered women with PTSD; Conceptual bases and treatment outlines. Cognitive *and Behavioral Practice, 9*(2), 111-127.

Lemkey, E. (2001). *Domestic violence: Theories of causation.* Domestic Violence Group ActionProject. Retrieved November 9, 2019, from http://wost201h_domviol.tripod.com/groupactionproject/id4.html

Linehan, M. M. (2015). *DBT® skills training: Handouts and worksheets* (2nd ed.). Guilford.

López-Fuentes, I., & Calvete, E. (2015). Building resilience: A qualitative study of Spanish women who have suffered intimate partner violence. *American Journal of Orthopsychiatry, 85*(4), 339-351.

Maier, S. F., & Seligman, M. E. P. (2016). Learned helplessness at fifty: Insights from neuroscience. *Psychological Review, 123*(4), 349–367. https://doi.org/10.1037/rev0000033

National Center for PTSD (2019). *Skills training in affective and interpersonal regulation (STAIR).* Retrieved from https://www.ptsd.va.gov/professional/continuing_ed/STAIR_online_training.asp

National Coalition Against Domestic Violence [NCADV] (2019). *Statistics.* https://ncadv.org/statistics

New International Bible. (2011). New International Bible Online. https://www.thenivbible.com/ (Original work published 1973)

Nnawulezi, N., & Murphy, C. (2019). Understanding formal help-seeking among women whose partners are in abuser intervention programs. *Psychology of Violence*, Advanced online publication.

Outlaw, M. (2009). No one type of intimate partner abuse: Exploring physical and non-physical abuse among intimate partners. *Journal of Family Violence, 24*(4), 263-272.

Pence, E., & Paymar, M. (1993). *Education groups for men who batter: The Duluth Model* (p. xiii). Springer Publishing Company. https://www.theduluthmodel.org/wpcontent/uploads/2017/03/PowerandControl.pdf

Postmus, J. L., Hoge, G. L., Breckenridge, J., Sharp-Jeffs, N., & Chung, D. (2020). Economic abuse as an invisible form of domestic violence: A multicountry review. *Trauma, Violence, & Abuse, 21*(2), 261–283. https://doi.org/10.1177/1524838018764160

Postmus, J. L., Plummer, S. B., McMahon, S., Murshid, N. S., & Kim, M. S. (2012). Understanding economic abuse in the lives of survivors. *Journal of Interpersonal Violence, 27*(3), 411-430. https://doi.org/10.1177/0886260511421669

Rakovec-Felser, Z. (2014). Domestic violence and abuse in intimate relationship from public health perspective. *Health Psychology Research, 2*(3). https://doi.org/10.4081/hpr.2014.1821

Rothman, E. F., Hathaway, J., Stidsen, A., & de Vries, H. F. (2007). How employment helps female victims of intimate partner violence: A qualitative study. *Journal of Occupational Health Psychology, 12*(2), 136-143.

Sayers, S. L. (2014). *Coming back together: A guide to successful reintegration after your partner returns from military deployment.* New Harbinger Publications.

Schechter, S., & Ganley, Anne L. (1995). *Domestic violence: A national curriculum for family preservation practitioners.* Family Violence Prevention Fund.

Stetzer, E. (2014, June 20). *The church and its response to domestic and sexual violence pastors must address domestic and sexual violence.* https://www.christianitytoday.com/edstetzer/2014/june/church-and-its-response-to-domestic-and-sexual-violence.html#bmb=1

The National Domestic Violence Hotline (2017). *Is this abuse?: Abuse defined.* https://www.thehotline.org/is-this-abuse/abuse-defined/

Thomas, K. A., Goodman, L., & Putnins, S. (2015). "I have lost everything": Trade-offs of seeking safety from intimate partner violence. *American Journal of Orthopsychiatry, 85*(2), 170-180.

Timeline of the Battered Women's Movement. (2008). Department of Social Services. http://www.ncdsv.org/images/NYCHRADSS_TImelineBWM_2008.pdf

Tracy, N. (2012, July 26). *What is physical abuse?* HealthyPlace. Retrieved February 28, 2020, from https://www.healthyplace.com/abuse/adult-physical-abuse/what-is-physical-abuse

Ungar, M., Brown, M., Liebenberg, L., Othman, R., Kwong, W. M., Armstrong, M., & Gilgun, J. (2007). Unique pathways to resilience across cultures. *Adolescence, 42*(166), 287-310.

Vargas, L., Cataldo, J., & Dickson, S. (2005). Domestic violence and children. In G.R. Walz & R.K. Yep (Eds.), *VISTAS: Compelling perspectives on counseling* (pp. 67-69). American Counseling Association.

Vernick, L. (2013). *The emotionally destructive marriage: How to find your voice and reclaim hope.* Waterbrook.

Walker, L. E. A. (1984/2000). *The battered woman syndrome.* Springer.

Walker, L. E. A. (1995). Understanding battered woman syndrome. *American Association for Justice, 31*(2), 30+.

White Ribbon Australia (2019). *The cycle of violence*. Brisbane Domestic Violence Service: Micah Projects, Brisbane. https://www.whiteribbon.org.au/understand-domestic-violence/what-is-domestic-violence/cycle-of-violence/

Widom, C., Czaja, S., & Dutton, M. (2008). Childhood victimization and lifetime revictimization. *Child Abuse & Neglect, 32*, 785-796.

Wilson, J. M., Fauci, J. E., & Goodman, L. A. (2015). Bringing trauma-informed practice to domestic violence programs: A qualitative analysis of current approaches. *American Journal of Orthopsychiatry, 85*(6), 586-599.

Zakar, R., Zakar, M. Z., & Kraemer, A. (2013). Men's beliefs and attitudes toward intimate partner violence against women in Pakistan. *Violence Against Women, 19*(2), 246–268.

Zorza, J. (1998). Batterer manipulation and retaliation in the courts: A largely unrecognized phenomenon sometimes encouraged by court practices. *Domestic Violence Report, 3*(5), 67-70. https://www.civicresearchinstitute.com/online/article_abstract.php?pid=18&id=1025&aid=6721

CHAPTER 21

Counseling Women Dealing with Intimate Betrayal Trauma

BARBARA STEFFENS PH.D. & JANICE CAUDILL PH.D.

"When all of earth turns against you, all of heaven turns toward you."
~Max Lucado in *When the Angels Were Silent*

"The Lord is close to the brokenhearted and saves those who are crushed in spirit."
(Psalm 34:18, NIV)

Wisdom from Above: Standing in His Grace

Isaiah 61:3 (*New International Bible*, 1973/2011) says "...to provide for those who grieve in Zion—to bestow on them a crown of beauty instead of ashes, the oil of joy instead of mourning, and a garment of praise instead of a spirit of despair. They will be called oaks of righteousness, a planting of the LORD for the display of his splendor." God has let us know His heart for those who have been deeply wounded. Those who experience betrayal at the hands of trusted loved ones need to know that He hears, He knows, He heals, and He redeems! Consider how the LORD has restored you after a major disappointment or betrayal at the hands of someone you trusted. Thank Him for His redemptive power in your life!

© VladGavriloff/Shutterstock.com

CHAPTER LEARNING OBJECTIVES

Upon completing this chapter, you should be able to:

- Define the concept of intimate betrayal trauma (IBT)
- Evaluate the situations that can bring about IBT in women
- Know the associated experiences and symptoms of IBT
- Identify the areas of focus in counseling and support when there is IBT
- Apply the trauma informed framework for addressing relational/IBT

CHAPTER OVERVIEW

Some of the questions that will be answered in this chapter include: What is Intimate Betrayal? How is it traumatic? What does it look like? What causes it? How can the betrayed person find help and restoration after betrayal? What is the role of the counselor after Intimate Betrayal Trauma?

Intimate betrayal in committed relationships can bring about strong and often traumatic responses in the betrayed person. Imagine the following scenarios: What do you think they have in common?

- Susan goes to the family computer to look up something and sees a website URL in the browsing history she does not recognize. She clicks on the link and then is frozen in place as she sees a pornographic website with graphic images fill her screen. Her heart races, she feels frozen in place but continues looking at other URLs in the history and finds that there are several over several days. She paces the floor, has trouble catching her breath, and feels like time stands still. Only one other person in the home could have accessed these sites - her husband.

- Estell's cell phone rings with a number she does not recognize but decides to answer the call. The caller states she is woman who works at the same place as her accountant husband and proceeds to say that she and Estell's husband have been having an affair, and that she intends to convince Estell's husband to leave the marriage for her. Estell hears the woman say, "he loves me, not you!" before the woman hangs up. Estell is frozen in place, feels her heart beating so hard she thinks it might stop beating altogether, she cannot breathe, and her mind begins to race.

Now fast forward to about four weeks after these events. Each woman is now experiencing difficulty sleeping, lack of appetite, numbness at times or extreme emotional swings, intrusive thoughts, and has fears about what else might she not know about her husband's life or behavior. The women find they cannot get some thoughts from spinning or intruding in their mind, and they are easily startled by any loud noise or unexpected movement of those around her. Images or reminders, such as a phone or computer or even their loved one's face, can "trigger" strong emotions and fear. They keep thinking thoughts like "How could I not have known?" "What is wrong with me? Am I not enough?" "What else don't I know?" "Who is this person I thought I knew?" "Am I safe? Have I been exposed to sexually transmitted illnesses?" Each woman is internally trying to make sense of something that has blindsided them and has put everything in their life and future into question. Their bodies and minds are reeling, and they are feeling extreme terror and anxiety. They are most likely experiencing Intimate Betrayal Trauma (IBT). **IBT** is defined as the experience of someone in an intimate romantic, sexual, and/or committed relationship with someone else who has deceived them and betrayed their trust. It occurs in relationships where there is an expectation of safety and honesty. It is the result of betrayal in a committed relationship leading to symptoms consistent with traumatic stress of posttraumatic stress.

This chapter will focus on the unique experiences and traumatic responses in women when there is sexual betrayal within committed, intimate relationships. The chapter will cover why and how this type of intimate betrayal is traumatic and will provide a framework or model for helping women who experience Intimate Betrayal Trauma.

INTIMATE BETRAYAL TRAUMA

The concept of intimate betrayal trauma is relatively new in the psychological and counseling literature. Intimate Betrayal Trauma (IBT) can be thought of or conceptualized in a variety of ways, all within the context of committed relationships, such as a marriage or other romantic relationship. Some in the trauma field find it difficult to identify betrayal as traumatic, but when the symptoms are explored and identified, a clear picture emerges of traumatic stress in many women who experience this level of betrayal. As with other traumatic life events, these are events that occur outside the control of the wounded individual. They are not responsible for the traumatic events. They have common emotional, physiological, cognitive, and spiritual responses to the events that happen to them.

Counselors need to respond in ways that do not pathologize the individual who experiences intimate betrayal (American Counseling Association [ACA], 2014; Herman, 1992). The traditional medicalized treatment model "implicitly locates the pathology of trauma within the individual instead of within the person(s) who perpetrated the harm" (Gómez et al., 2016, p. 165). It is important to remember that women who are betrayed are not responsible for their own betrayal. They are responsible for how they care for themselves.

Intimate betrayal can also be viewed as a breach of a covenant, or covenantal betrayal (Maxwell, 2017). Maxwell suggested a definition of *covenant* as "the permanent sealing of God's relationship with man, as well as the terms in which they relate" (p. 248). Cheselka, (1995 as cited in Maxwell, 2017) said that betrayal is "a violation not only of trust and of the other, but of the sanctity of intimate relationships...an implicit covenant has been broken or denied..." (p. 249).

Statistics

It is difficult to estimate how many women are impacted by IBT, since it is a relatively new way of understanding betrayal and trauma. However, there are statistics on related experiences of women. For example, many women who experience IBT are in relationship with someone who has compulsive or problematic sexual behavior that may be secret or unknown to them. They may experience infidelity or chronic infidelity. They may experience other forms of relational betrayal or violations of safety and trust.

It is estimated that around 3%-6% of adults struggle with sexual behaviors to the level of addiction (Karila et al., 2014). Sexually compulsive behavior or addiction is a primary context for IBT among women. There are no estimated numbers regarding those in relationship with sexual addicts, but the majority of addicts seeking treatment are in some type of committed relationship. In a study regarding betrayal trauma, Goldberg and Freyd (2006) found high levels of traumatic events by someone close to them, with 16.8% experiencing forced sexual contact, and 37.8% experiencing emotional and psychological abuse. So, you can see that a high percentage of women experience some level of betrayal, breach of safety, and trust in their lifetimes.

How Is Intimate Betrayal *Traumatic*?

The following sections will cover the various ways counselors and other helpers might "conceptualize" or understand intimate betrayal trauma. These are some of the ways IBT can be experienced as traumatic.

Event or Shock Trauma

This type of IBT occurs when there is the *discovery* of betrayal. This is that point in time where something happens that is unexpected and that leaves the person feeling unsafe or at risk of physical or relational harm. It comes without warning. It is much like any other traumatic event that is an unexpected or where the individual cannot escape. It can also be considered **shock trauma** As was discussed in Chapter 18, a traumatic event is one where the person is exposed to an event or stressor such as "actual or threatened death, serious injury, or sexual violence" (American Psychological Association [APA], 2013, p. 271). Betrayed women report experiencing the event of discovery of sexual and intimate betrayal as life threatening or sexually abusive, thus meeting the *DSM* requirements if only in the betrayed person's perceptions of the events (Steffens, 2005).

Professionals in the field of infidelity have long understood that finding out about betrayal in a relationship can be traumatic (Glass, 2002; Gordon et al., 2004; Lusterman, 2004; Scuka, 2015; Warach & Josephs, 2019). They understood that the sudden awareness of relational intimate betrayal could bring about traumatic stress related symptoms in the betrayed spouse.

© arloo/Shutterstock.com

Some studies focus specifically on the discovery of repeated infidelity, or sexual addiction. Steffens (2005) found that 70% of women in her study who experienced the sudden discovery of sexual betrayal by their spouse experienced all clinical symptoms of posttraumatic stress disorder (PTSD). In a more recent study, 299 betrayed women completed the *Posttraumatic Stress Checklist* (PCL-5) and 47.5% met the criteria for PTSD with symptoms measured in terms of severity within the last month (Woods, 2017). In the same study, Woods found that 74.2 % of the women had no idea about the hidden sexual behaviors until sometime into their relationship.

In one research study, 75% of discoveries occurred by the spouse uncovering or finding information related to the betrayal (Steffens, 2005; Steffens & Rennie, 2006). The remaining percentages of discoveries occurred by a third party disclosing, or by the betrayer confessing (Steffens, 2005; Steffens & Rennie, 2006). Discoveries can be via finding concrete evidence (for example, on the computer, receipts, texts, or emails, etc.) or by the betrayed partner confronting the betrayer and receiving affirmation of the behaviors. Discoveries can also be initiated by a third party or by consequences such as loss of a job, blackmail, legal consequences, or revelations from a child who has stumbled upon evidence. Woods (2017) found that 79.6 % of the partners discovered the secret sexual behaviors themselves. Of these women, 45.8 % believed there were still secrets hidden by their husbands. Woods also found that the peak time for experiencing PTSD and depression was between 6-12 months following discovery, with 87.5% of these women meeting all of the symptomatic criteria for PTSD.

CONCEPT TO CONTEMPLATE

© ImageFlow/Shutterstock.com

In Her Shoes

What is it about *experiencing intimate betrayal* that could be experienced as "life threatening" or traumatic? What areas of your life would be impacted if this happened to you? If this has happened to you, what did you experience? (There are resources at the end of this chapter to address this.)

Betrayal Trauma

Betrayal Trauma is a specific term or model that describes how betrayal in close relationships can be traumatic for the betrayed individual. Initially described and studied by Dr. Freyd and associates in relation to childhood abuse (Freyd, 1996), the concept of Betrayal Trauma has been expanded to describe the traumatic impact of betrayal in close or dependent relationships (Birrell & Freyd, 2006; Freyd, 1999, 2013). Freyd and her associates also use the concept to describe betrayal by a system or institution that should be there to assist or protect a victim of abuse, called Institutional Betrayal (Smith & Freyd, 2013). Freyd also stressed that a major component of Betrayal Trauma is the "not knowing" as part of a trauma response (Freyd, 1999; Freyd & Birrell, 2013). The concept "points to the importance of social relationships in understanding posttraumatic outcomes, including reduced recall" (Freyd et al., 2007, p. 295).

For someone in a committed relationship, such as a marriage or partnered relationship, there can be significant reasons why it is difficult for the betrayed person to fully recognize betrayal without specific concrete evidence. When someone is being betrayed, and before receiving concrete evidence, she may experience feeling as if something is not right; she may notice some changes in the relationship or strange behaviors and yet not recognize that she is being betrayed. In their book, *Blind to Betrayal*, Freyd and Birrell (2013) stated:

Betrayal has a significant impact on the life of the betrayed, even in how she views her world. It can change everything. "Moreover, the discovery of betrayal always seems to prompt a profoundly new awareness: the world is not the same" (Freyd & Birrell, 2013, pp. 8-9).

ongoing betrayal can occur only when there is some deception that is not fully detected. Sometimes this lack of knowledge is the result of insufficient information, but other times the obliviousness is in part the result of betrayal blindness—unawareness of information that is present but is somehow 'whooshed away'. (p. 8)

For the betrayed person, once direct evidence of deception appears that removes doubt, she can now fully know that betrayal has occurred or is occurring. This awareness then changes everything.

Sexual Trauma

Another way to view or conceptualize IBT is the concept of sexual trauma or sexual betrayal. When there is IBT in a committed romantic relationship, typically there is some form of sexual betrayal as part of the activities. Whether the sexual betrayal took the form of a single affair, or there was *virtual* infidelity such as the use of pornography or online sexual encounters, the betrayed partner may have sexual-related distress in response. Sexual betrayal in intimate relationships can bring about concern over the betrayed woman's sexual health, through possible exposure to sexually transmitted illnesses. Conley et al. (2012) found that those who were sexually unfaithful engaged in less protected sexual behaviors and had fewer episodes of being tested for sexually transmitted infections (STI's), leaving the faithful partner at higher risk of experiencing transmission of STI's.

Women who experience IBT may also have a limited sense of ability to give full consent to sexual behaviors within the primary relationship due to a lack of open information about their loved one's sexual history and behaviors .They may be unaware their loved one is engaging in sexual behaviors outside of the relationship, and so cannot consent to having safe sexual experiences with their partner. They may also experience uncomfortable or coercive sexual experiences with a partner who is being unfaithful or who exploits their romantic partner. Utley (2017) conducted a review of the literature regarding violence experienced in relationships where there was also infidelity or betrayal and found several types of intimate partner violence (IPV) experienced by women. Utley found the following types of IPV (as identified in the following table):

TABLE 21.1

Intimate Partner Violence

Social Aggression	Curtailing social contact
Economic Aggression	Controlling ability to acquire/use economic resources
Emotional Aggression	Undermining self-respect and sense of worth
Psychological Aggression	Undermining sense of safety and security
Sexual Violence	Nonconsensual sexual acts or transfer of STIs
Physical Violence	Intentional use of physical force

Another source of potential sexual trauma within IBT is focused on uncomfortable or coercive sexual behaviors introduced into the primary relationship or actual sexual abuse of the primary partner. Intimate partner sexual assault or sexual violence is another form of sexual betrayal a woman can experience. In a study of intimate partners who sought help at a sexual assault center, the researchers found that "sexual assaults by intimate partners should be viewed as serious as an assault by other assailants by law enforcement, the judiciary, and the public" (Seyller et al., 2016, p. 516).

Women can experience IBT in their primary relationships through experiences of sexual assault or marital rape. Women who experience sexual assault or rape in their primary relationships have a difficult time either recognizing the acts as assault (due to prior episodes of giving consent to being sexual) or may have a belief that rape is not possible in a marriage relationship (Jaffe et al., 2017). The authors found that women who experienced intimate partner rape (IPR) "were less likely than women who reported rape by another perpetrator to label their victimization experiences as rape" (p. 13).

Infidelity

Chapter 8 of this textbook covers some of the difficulties that women face such as divorce. The issue of **infidelity** ("sexual and/or emotional act engaged in by one person within a committed relationship, where such an act occurs outside of the primary relationship and constitutes a breach of trust and/or violations of agreed upon norms [overt and covert] by one or both indi-

As you read the Bible, it is clear that our Father God has strong feelings in response to people who are unfaithful. In Psalms 43:1 (*New International Bible*, 1973/2011) it states "Vindicate me, my God, and plead my cause against an unfaithful nation. Rescue me from those who are deceitful and wicked". Proverbs 11:3 (*New International Bible,* 1973/2011) reads "the integrity of the upright guides them, the unfaithful are destroyed by their duplicity" and in verse 6, says "the righteousness of the upright delivers them, the unfaithful are trapped by evil desires." Fidelity and faithfulness are high values in a Christian worldview, as well within other standards of appropriate and moral behaviors.

viduals in that relationship in relation to romantic/emotional or sexual exclusivity" [Blow, 2008, p. 13]) is a common precipitating event leading to divorce. As stated earlier in this chapter, researchers and clinicians have recognized and treated trauma reactions in women (and men) following disclosure of infidelity in committed relationships (Glass, 2002; Gordon, et al., 2004; Lusterman, 2004; Scuka, 2015; Warach & Josephs, 2019). Some studies suggest that "20% to 25% of married Americans have had extramarital sex at some point" (Atkings et al., 2001, as cited in Warach et al., 2018). It is estimated that for those who experience infidelity, more than half end up separated or divorced (Allen & Atkins, 2012).

Infidelity can take the form of in-person sexual contact, online engagement with others, emotional connection, and/or the use of pornography without the knowledge of the committed partner (Dean, 2011). The basic underlying theme defining infidelity is that it constitutes a *breach of trust*. Infidelity can also be considered abusive, especially by those who have been betrayed this way. Utley (2017) quoted an anonymous woman in her study of infidelity and betrayal who said, "I really understand infidelity as abuse. It's abuse. It's abusive. It's without consent. It's a serious violation. I think I would like it if we culturally started talking about the dynamic" (Forsythia, as cited in Utley, 2017). A person who has experienced infidelity can experience lack of consent, violation of trust, emotional pain, loss of a sense of safety, and threat to future economic security.

CONCEPT TO CONTEMPLATE

In Her Shoes
What are the economic, physical, emotional, relational, sexual, or social consequences following infidelity? How might a woman be particularly at-risk following infidelity betrayal?

© Digital Storm/Shutterstock.com

Chronic Infidelity: Sexual Addiction

At this point, it seems important to consider the impact of chronic infidelity or repeated sexual betrayal, and its relation to IBT. A frequently used term used to describe this pattern of repetitive or out-of-control sexual behavior is *sexual addiction*. A common definition of sexual addiction is sexual behavior that is "compulsive and yet continues despite adverse consequences" (Carnes & Adams, 2013, p. 5). Other terms used to describe this compulsive sexual behavior include hyper-sexuality, sexual compulsion, problematic sexual behavior, or compulsive sexual behavior disorder (CSBD). This newly adopted diagnosis by the World Health Organization will be part of the *International Classification of Diseases and Related Health Problems* (11th ed.; *ICD-11*) as a mental disorder. (The *ICD-11* definition of CSBD is "a persistent pattern of failure to control intense, repetitive sexual impulses or urges resulting in repetitive sexual behavior" (ICD-11, as cited in Heaney, 2018, para. 2).

For the intimate partner or spouse of someone with CSBD or sex addiction, the traumatic impact of finding out about a loved one's repeated sexual infidelities and deception is profound. Research has found high levels of PTSD symptoms in wives of self-identified "sex addicts" (Keffer, 2018; Skinner, 2017; Steffens, 2005; Steffens & Means, 2009; Steffens & Rennie, 2006). Betrayed women describe the experiences with statements such as "'It left me shell shocked", "I threw up, couldn't sleep, couldn't eat, cried constantly", "I had fear for my health and for our children", "It was devastating, traumatic", and "The initial disclosure was one of the darkest times of my life- it rocked me to the core of my soul" (Steffens, 2005, p. 99).

© Lane V. Erickson/Shutterstock.com

CONCEPT TO CONTEMPLATE

A trauma-informed conceptualization of a betrayed partner allows for accurate assessment of symptoms and respects the experiences of the client. How would you put this quotation into your own words to help explain it to your client? "The partner of a sex addict has responses that serve as reactions to a stressor that is traumatic in nature, in predictable emotional, behavioral, and physiological ways as her mind and body attempt to survive and adapt to a dangerous situation. *She seeks what she cannot find: safety in an unsafe situation*" (Steffens & Rennie, 2006, p. 262). Symptoms experienced by the betrayed woman are to be expected, due to the traumatic nature of her wounds.

A person with CSBD can participate in any number/types of sexual behaviors as part of the compulsion. Typical sexual behaviors discovered by the betrayed spouse can include chronic masturbation, pornography use (print media, online, etc.), virtual sexual activity online such as in online chat rooms, hiring sex workers, multiple affairs, same sex acting out, and any other sexual activity one can imagine. Schneider et al. (2012) reported, "Results show that even when sexual behaviors are limited to online, partners can lose trust in their loved ones, feel the need to seek assistance, and identify themselves as victims of trauma" (p. 123). Intimate partners or spouses can learn that their loved one has engaged in sexual activities that were believed to be outside of the values of the individual or relationship.

Part of the trauma for betrayed spouses certainly centers on the secretive nature of these behaviors. The betrayed partner can learn that the sexual acting out of their loved one existed for years prior to it being discovered, leaving the betrayed partner in shock, and questioning their own history in the relationship. Keffer's (2018) term **intimate deception**, describes the nature of betrayal associated with months and often years of hidden activity where the injured or betrayed spouse had no opportunity to give consent to being in this kind of relationship. They had no idea. They were blindsided. In Steffens' (2005) study, the average length of marriage at the time of initial discovery was 15 years. Woods (2017) reported "...partners whose husbands' addictive sexual behaviors were limited to pornography experienced the same degree of PTSD and depression severity as partners whose husbands had engaged in a range of sexual behaviors including sexual and emotional affairs with others" (p. 208).

Imagine what it would be like to find out about secrets held for over a decade that impact your view of your loved one, your relationship, your safety and security, and your own perception of your history.

The **discovery** (the act of suddenly or unexpectedly learning of or finding evidence of sexual secrets and sexual deception) of sexual deception and betrayal can be devastating across all areas of a woman's life. In a study conducted by Carnes and O'Conner (2016), the researchers found that the betrayed partner experienced significant negative consequences due to the discovered sexual behaviors of their loved one, including family conflict, health consequences, financial damage, loss of important relationships, and even loss of employment. The study also revealed that the addictive behaviors (95%) and the hidden nature of the behaviors (93%) were detrimental to the relationship.

Although some of the early literature on partners or spouses of sexual addicts regarded these partners as co-dependent or *co-addicted* (Carnes, 2001), more recent research clearly identifies and conceptualizes these survivors as distressed, experiencing trauma responses (Steffens, 2005), and "overall psychologically healthy" (Reid et al., 2010, p. 218). Women are not responsible for the secrets or behaviors of someone else, but have often experienced feelings of blame, or were told they were suffering because of who they choose, so in effect were told they were in some way culpable for what has happened. A trauma-informed model helps reduce the pain partners of the sexually addicted have experienced.

Featured Practitioner Interview

Dr. Steffens, who is an expert regarding intimate betrayal and trauma, was interviewed about intimate betrayal by Dr. Robert Weiss, a highly recognized expert in the area of sexual addiction and sex therapy (Steffens, 2018). Listen to this interview at: https://sexandrelationshiphealing.com/blog/betrayal-trauma-and-healing-with-dr-barbara-steffens/

© Dan Ledbetter

CONCEPT TO CONTEMPLATE

© ImageFlow/Shutterstock.com

In Her Shoes

Go back to Susan's case study at the beginning of this chapter. How do you understand her responses after reading this section? Write out a few sentences that describe her experience that reflect the shock and trauma at discovery.

Attachment Trauma

Close, trusting relationships provide a sense of belonging and safety. The term *attachment* describes the bonds in secure relationships where safety is expected. John 1:18 (*New International Bible,* 1973/2011) describes such a relationship or attachment: "No one has ever seen God, but the one and only Son, who is himself God and is in closest relationship with the Father, has made him known." Jesus also describes this type of safe relationship as He prayed to the Father before He was crucified. John 17:21-22 (*New Living Bible*, 1996) records Jesus saying, "I pray that they will all be one, just as you and I are one- I am in them and you are in me. May they experience such perfect unity that the world will know that you sent me and that you love them as much as you love me." The closeness of the Son and the Father and our relationship with them serves as a picture of what strong, secure attachments can provide. Strong attachments provide security; attachment ruptures bring fear and pain.

Researchers in the area of attachment recognize the significant negative impact of betrayal on the attachment between two committed individuals (Johnson, 2002; Schade & Sandberg, 2012; Warach & Josephs, 2019). Bowlby (1988), author of *A Secure Base*, described healthy attachment as involving any behaviors that "the person engages in from time to time to

© fizkes/Shutterstock.com

obtain and/or maintain a desired proximity" (p. 28). He also stated that "enduring attachment, or attachment bonds" are limited to only a small group of people (p. 28). The primary attached relationship for adults is the pair-bonded or committed relationship, such as in marriage. This attached relationship becomes a safe place or "safe haven" – the place the individuals return to bring calm and safety again (Johnson, 2002).

When there is a breach in this attachment, such as through betrayal or deceit, the attachment is ruptured or strained. The more significant or prolonged the rupture of safety, the more the distressful impact on the betrayed member of the relationship, causing a significant rupture. Returning to the original attached individual no longer brings a sense of safety or calm, but instead brings about insecurity, anxiety, and/or fear. Along with this insecurity and fear comes "angry protest, clinging, depression, and despair...culminating eventually in detachment" (Johnson, 2002, p. 39). Infidelity and intimate betrayal can bring about this response, called attachment trauma. Someone experiencing this attachment trauma might have high anxiety, anger, fear, a desire to be close, and a desire to stay away from the offending partner. A study participant put it this way: "I loved my husband and I wanted his comfort, yet he was the source of my searing pain" (Steffens, 2005, p. 110).

Emotional and Psychological Abuse Related Trauma

Most of the wounds related to IBT are invisible. They cannot be seen like a bruise or broken bone but are just as real as physical traumatic injuries. This is true for the emotional or psychological abuse-related traumas often experienced as part of IBT. How might betrayal be abusive? To put it another way, what about IBT is emotionally or psychologically abusive?

Recall that IBT typically occurs in secret, then is discovered. There is betrayal behavior occurring that the betrayed party typically has no knowledge of in terms of tangible evidence until after the betrayal is discovered or disclosed. The betrayer often utilizes emotional or psychological manipulation communication tactics to divert attention away from the secret. The types of diversion behaviors most often used are comprised of emotional and psychological manipulation and abuse. This section will include information on emotional abuse but will primarily focus on the psychological abuse tactic known as gaslighting (Dorpat, 1996; Stern, 2007). For more in-depth information on emotional abuse, see Chapter 20 of this text.

As a reminder, emotional abuse consists of behaviors such as "verbal assault, dominance, control, isolation, ridicule, or the use of intimate knowledge for degradation (Gondolf et al., 2002, as cited in Karakurt & Silver, 2012, p. 804). Karakurt and Silver (2012) found that women, especially young women, experience emotional abuse in the form of isolation most frequently. Isolation can include controlling interpersonal relationships outside of the primary relationship or physically confining the woman (not permitting her to leave the home without permission). For someone who is experiencing IBT, certainly, these types of emotional control and abuse can restrict their ability to obtain help and support. Emotional or psychological abuse tactics tend to be repetitive and distressing for the abused person.

Gaslighting

Another form of abuse or control tactic often experienced by those with IBT is gaslighting. First defined by Dorpat (1996), Stern (2007) raised the issue of this type of psychological manipulation and abuse in a self-help book about how to spot and recover from this type of abuse. Fuchsman (2019), in a review of Stern's book, describes gaslighting as a tactic saying, "a *gaslighter* seeks to manipulate another or others into thinking that their own perceptions of reality are mistaken, and for the *gaslightee* or *target* to believe what the manipulator claims instead" (p. 74). Stark (2019) stated, "the aim of gaslighting is to get another to see her own plausible perceptions, beliefs, or memories as groundless" (p. 221). The overall goal and effect of gaslighting as an abuse tactic is to manipulate and control the perceptions and beliefs of another person. Hightower (2017) found "there is a strong relationship between psychological abuse and gaslighting" (p. 92).

Within the experience of IBT, gaslighting is most often said to serve the purpose of taking the focus off of the betrayer and placing it onto the betrayed by highlighting the deficits or lack of understanding of the betrayed. Here is an example of what a gaslighting conversation might look like in this situation:

Betrayed: I think maybe you are not telling me the truth! I found information on the computer and it looks like you have been chatting with other women! What is going on?

Gaslighter: I don't know what you are talking about! What are you doing snooping on the computer anyway? Are you spying on me? You must be paranoid!

Betrayed: I wasn't spying...I just...I just was feeling like you were distant, so I looked at the computer and there it was...

Gaslighter: Spying! You're a spy! You are a jealous spy! You are a lot like your mom that way- never believing your father. Now you are doing it too!

Betrayed: I am not like my mother- at least not this time. But I can see where you are upset that I looked at stuff because I was afraid you were cheating. I am sorry I hurt you by looking.

Gaslighter: I hope you get help for this jealousy and paranoia.

Can you see here how the conversation shifted from the betrayed person's concern to a focus on her potential deficits? Gaslighting serves the purpose of deflecting the focus by labeling the confronter and highlighting some real or imagined deficit or weakness. The person on the receiving end of gaslighting will leave the conversation feeling confused, focused perhaps on their faults, and with no resolution to the original complaint about the online chats. In gaslighting, the betrayed is labeled, her reality distorted, and her needs are not responded to. The effect over time is a diminished sense of trust in their perceptions of reality.

Psychological abuse again serves the purpose of controlling the awareness of the betrayed by the betrayer's actions or seeking to minimize the perception of the impact of the betrayal. However, it can also be a method of reality manipulation, even after the betrayal has been discovered as a means of exerting control in the relationship. Another way of understanding or describing psychological manipulation and control is the concept of DARVO (Harsey et al., 2017). DARVO is the acronym for a three-phase process: Deny, Attack, Reverse Victim and Offender. Jennifer Freyd (1997) described this strategy or process whereby a betrayer or offender defends and seeks to silence the person they betrayed. Freyd believed this process serves to confuse the victim/betrayed person and reduces the likelihood of consequences of the offense.

In this strategy, the offender ends up sounding like the victim. See the chart below (Figure 21.1) that describes the DARVO process:

Deny	Offender denies accusation
Attack	Attacks person doing the confronting
Reverse victim offender	Confronter becomes the accused

Source: Janice Caudill

FIGURE 21.1

The DARVO Process

In the above scenario, DARVO would sound like this:

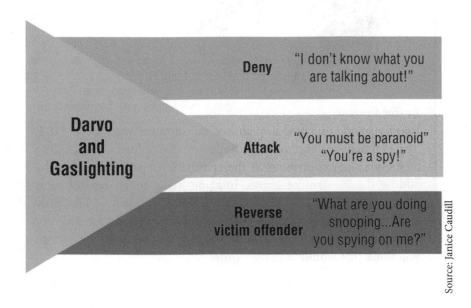

FIGURE 21.2

Sample Gaslighting Responses in the Context of DARVO

Source: Janice Caudill

In this process, the offender becomes the offended. The betrayer becomes the betrayed.

CONCEPT TO CONTEMPLATE

In Her Shoes

Emotional and psychological abuses are common when there is IBT. The cumulative effect of these types of psychological controlling techniques can contribute to the traumatic impact of betrayal by adding the element of abuse. Imagine living in an environment where you attempt to communicate about a concern or fear, only to leave the conversation confused and feeling blamed for the very thing you are trying to address in the other person. What impact do you think that would have over time?

TRAUMA SYMPTOMS FOLLOWING BETRAYAL

Using discovery of betrayal as the distressing event, Steffens (2005; Steffens & Rennie, 2006) identified PTSD in 70% of the research participants, with 48% reporting moderate to severe symptoms levels, and 72% demonstrating severe functional impairment in major life areas. This is consistent with Skinner (2017) who found that 75% of those experiencing sexual betrayal met criteria B, C, D, and E for PTSD. This study of 6000 identified a wide array of symptoms consistent with the profile described after betrayal in previously cited research. The chart below depicts frequently reported symptoms experienced by betrayed partners and shows examples of how IBT victims experience trauma. The quotations are from the Steffens' (2005) research study on women's responses following disclosure of hidden sexual behaviors of their spouse.

TABLE 21.2

Quotations from Betrayal Partners (Steffens, 2005)

Trauma Symptom Profile	Quotes from Betrayed Partners
Criterion B: Intrusive Symptoms Intrusive and obsessive thoughts Compulsive checking Repetitive questioning Dissociative experiences	"I had disturbing dreams frequently." (p. 72)
Criterion C: Avoidance Behaviors Increased isolation Emotional numbing Attempts to avoid thoughts or reminders of betrayal	"I was like an ostrich with my head in the sand, hoping my husband didn't have a problem, or would straighten it out on his own. . ."
Criterion D: Negative Thoughts and Mood Shifting emotions Depression Anxiety, fear, terror Abandonment Anger, jealousy, rage, revenge Loss of self-esteem	"I felt horror, anger, rage, terror, fury at God." (p. 72) "I loved my husband and I wanted his comfort, yet he was the source of my searing pain." (p. 110) "In one moment, your heart and breathing stops. . . you have been completely thrown into an alternate universe." (p. 98) "I had fear for the children and their safety. . . I didn't know what he had done or how far he had gone. . . fear for my health." (p. 99)
Criterion E: Altered Arousal/Reactivity Hypervigilance to signs of additional betrayal Shock Difficulty concentrating Sleep disturbance Physiological disturbances	"It left me shell-shocked." (p. 98) "The initial disclosure was devastating, traumatic—it was hell." (p. 99) "I was shocked. . . I threw up, I couldn't sleep, couldn't eat. . . I felt crazy." (p. 99) "In one moment, your heart and breathing stops. . . you have been completely thrown into an alternate universe." (p. 98) "I needed medical attention." (p. 99) "I lost my ability to concentrate." (p. 99)

Hopefully, you can clearly see that it is common for women who experience betrayal trauma to often experience significant and distressing symptoms consistent with posttraumatic stress and PTSD.

COMMON CRISES OR RELATED ISSUES FOLLOWING INTIMATE BETRAYAL

When a woman experiences betrayal in her intimate relationship, not only does she have to cope with the experiences related to the betrayal (such as breach of trust, fear, potential loss of the relationship, and the other traumatic consequences), she often has other related life events to which she must respond. Like a stone thrown into a pond, the act of betrayal can generate other events or crises. The ones covered in this section are financial realities, isolation, disclosing to others, and spiritual or existential effects of betrayal.

Financial Issues

As discussed earlier in this chapter, IBT can bring about significant life changes and crises, including divorce. Crouch and Dickes (2016) studied the impact of infidelity on economic realities for the family, including the divorced spouse. They found evidence that divorce due to infidelity "results in substantial economic and social externalities resulting from family fragmentation" (p. 62). What types of things impact the financial reality of a woman who experiences IBT? Certainly, divorce has a negative impact on women and their economic realities. In a recent study regarding the economic impact of divorce on women, Leopold (2018) found that women experience greater negative consequences in the areas of household income, and risks of poverty. Even if the relationship does not end in divorce, there can be economic realities such as costs for separation, any legal costs, loss of income due to inability to work, costs for counseling support, and costs for childcare needed during the time of extreme stress.

Isolation

Women who experience IBT can experience extreme social isolation. Betrayed women can be isolated due to some of the emotional and psychological manipulation and abuse discussed earlier in this chapter. Isolation may also be driven by shame. Thaggard and Montayre (2019) found themes related to shame among women who experienced interpersonal violence. The themes they discovered are very similar to what professionals hear from women who experience IBT. The themes include: "the shame of it all", "shame and isolation", and "shame and selfhood" (Thaggard & Montayre, 2019, pp. 221-222). In an informal survey of betrayed partners of sexual addicts, women described experiencing shame internally, as well as receiving highly negative or shaming responses from those from whom they sought help, even when seeking help from their faith communities (Caudill & Steffens, 2019). For example, one woman said she was told that "it was my fault for not being submissive enough and not giving my husband enough sex." Another woman shared she was told she had an anger problem for being upset about her spouse's use of pornography. When the betrayed person feels internal shame or receives perceived shame from those they try to tell about their experiences, they are less likely to seek and receive the support they need and deserve.

Disclosure to Others

Common questions people have once they are aware of intimate betrayal include questions like: Who else needs to know? What else do I not know? How do I find out what I do not know? How can I ever know that I know everything? What do I tell my family, friends, or children? Do I tell my children? A woman who has experienced IBT must carefully consider the consequences of any action to disclose to others. A trained, caring support person can help a betrayed woman work through these difficult decisions.

Researchers have explored why people hold or reveal secrets. One research team explored the process by which people decided to reveal secrets and found there is an internal process of assessing the risk of disclosing (Afifi & Steuber, 2009). They stated that "this risk assessment is what predicts people's readiness or willingness to reveal them" (p. 145). The secret holder assesses the potential positive and/or negative consequences of revealing the secret to the *target* (person to receive this information) .Afifi and Steuber also explored considerations in terms of the target, such as closeness of relationships, any pressure from the target, or the target's need to know the information. Another risk is the potential response when the secret or betrayal is shared with others. The experience of not being believed, feeling dismissed, or having the secret exposed unintentionally to others can bring additional stress into an already difficult situation. Additionally, disclosing during help-seeking attempts (going to a counselor, a clergy member, or other support person) can bring about less than helpful responses. Smith and Freyd (2013) coined the term **institutional betrayal** to describe the re-traumatizing experience of receiving no help or being harmed again while seeking help. Woods (2017) studied the correlation between positive or negative social supports and PTSD symptoms in betrayed women. She found a statistically significant correlation between negative social support exchanges and total PCL-5 scores (p.172). When betrayed women receive negative support responses, or no responses, this has the effect of increasing the trauma symptoms they experience.

For betrayed women, it is important that they consider the need to share versus the potential consequences. Once a secret is out, it cannot be returned! However, the holding of secrets can also carry difficult consequences. Trauma is best healed in community when the experience can be shared (Herman, 1992). Later in the chapter, we will focus on support and treatment needs of betrayed women.

Spiritual and/or Existential Consequences

Any time a person experiences traumatic life events including intimate betrayal trauma, the impact can set off a sense of disconnection from the rest of the world, from those around them, and from their higher power or God. In her book *Trauma and Recovery*, Judith Herman (1992, 1996) puts it this way. She stated that traumatic events "undermine the belief systems that give meaning to human experience. They violate the victim's faith in a natural or divine order and cast the victim into a state of existential crisis" (p. 51). She also described the impact on the traumatized person when cries for assistance or help go unanswered (by the betrayer, or by her community or church) saying, "traumatized people feel utterly abandoned, utterly alone, cast of the human and divine systems of care and protection that sustain life" (p. 52). Experiencing any type of trauma can bring about this response. Imagine the impact when the trauma comes from the person she trusts the most and with whom she has the most vulnerable of relationships. The next section of this chapter will cover spiritual implications in more depth.

BIBLICAL VIEWS OF BETRAYAL AND ADULTERY/INFIDELITY

What does the word *adultery* mean? A good dictionary response or definition is "voluntary sexual intercourse between a married person and a person who is not his or her spouse". Other words used to describe this include infidelity and cheating. Synonyms for infidelity include the words betrayal, duplicity, and faithlessness. The first-time Scripture addresses the issue of adultery (or intimate sexual betrayal) is in Exodus 20:14 as part of what is called the Ten Commandments. Exodus 20:14 (*New International Bible*, 1973/2011) clearly states "You shall not commit adultery." Jesus, during His time on earth, expanded the idea of what constitutes adultery when He said, "...but I tell you that anyone who looks at a woman lustfully

© fizkes/Shutterstock.com

has already committed adultery with her in his heart" (*New International Bible*, 1973/2011, Matthew 5:28). Is adultery an act or an attitude or heart condition? According to these Scriptures, it seems to be both! Jesus also said, "For out of your heart come evil thoughts- murder, adultery, sexual immorality, theft, false testimony, slander" (*New International Bible*, 1973/2011, Matthew 15:19). A reasonable conclusion from looking at these Scriptures is that committing adultery or infidelity is not within God's will for His people, and that God takes the behavior quite seriously.

CONCEPT TO CONTEMPLATE

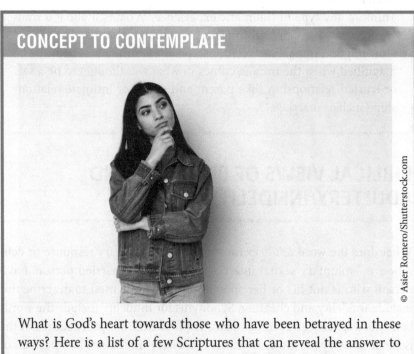
© Asier Romero/Shutterstock.com

What is God's heart towards those who have been betrayed in these ways? Here is a list of a few Scriptures that can reveal the answer to this question. Take a few minutes to read them on your own. Write a sentence or two to summarize what you find. How would you share this with a client? All of the following Scriptures are from the New International Version of the Bible (1973/2011).

- Malachi 2:14 "You ask, "Why?" It is because the LORD is the witness between you and the wife of your youth. You have been unfaithful to her, though she is your partner, the wife of your marriage covenant."
- Psalm 55:12-14 "If an enemy were insulting me, I could endure it; if a foe were rising against me I could hide. But it is you, a man like myself, my companion, my close friend, with whom I once enjoyed sweet fellowship at the house of God as we walked about among the worshipers."
- Lamentations 1:2 "Bitterly she weeps at night, tears are on her cheeks. Among all her lovers there is no one to comfort her. All her friends have betrayed her; they have become her enemies."
- Matthew 26:24 "The Son of Man will go just as it is written about him. But woe to that man who betrays the Son of Man! It would be better for him if he had not been born."
- Psalm 9: 9-10 "The LORD is a refuge for the oppressed, a stronghold in times of trouble. Those who know your name trust in you, for you, LORD, have never forsaken those who seek you."
- Isaiah 43:2-3a "When you pass through the waters, I will be with you and when you pass through the rivers, they will not sweep over you. When you walk through the fire, you will not be burned; the flames will not set you ablaze. For I am the LORD your God, the Holy One of Israel, your Savior."
- Isaiah 61:1-3 "The Spirit of the Sovereign LORD is on me, because the LORD has anointed me to proclaim good news to the poor. He has sent me to bind up the brokenhearted, to proclaim freedom for the captives and release from darkness for the prisoners,[a]2 to proclaim the year of the LORD's favor and the day of vengeance of our God to comfort all who mourn, 3 and provide for those who grieve in Zion—to bestow on them a crown of beauty instead of ashes, the oil of joy instead of mourning, and a garment of praise instead of a spirit of despair. They will be called oaks of righteousness, a planting of the LORD for the display of his splendor."

COUNSELING CONSIDERATION AND RECOMMENDATIONS

As discussed earlier, the discovery of betrayal can be very difficult and traumatic for women, especially due to the intimate nature of the betrayal. A betrayed woman may seek out support from a variety of sources, such as from a friend, faith leader or clergy, support group, online resources, or counselor. As the counselor, you will need to know how to identify this as a presenting problem, how to respond to the crisis, how to assess for possible trauma responses, and how to help the betrayed woman navigate through the crisis and subsequent issues that will arise. These can be quite complicated cases!

A Trauma-Informed Model for IBT

Dr. Steffens, Dr. Caudill, and their colleagues (Association of Partners of Sex Addicts Trauma Specialists [APSATS], 2012) developed a model used for treatment planning and intervention when there is IBT in the form of chronic sexual infidelity or sex addiction. The model is based on an adapted three-phase model first introduced by Judith Herman in her book *Trauma and Recovery* (1992). Herman's model was developed to meet the clinical needs of those traumatized within the context of dependent relationships, such as parent-child, captor-captive, abuser-abused in domestic/interpersonal violence, and where the threat is ongoing or repetitive. The victim of this type of traumatization has an inability to escape due to physical or economic reasons or any form of captivity. This adaptation of Herman's trauma resolution model fits well with this population of traumatized women. Herman's three-phase model has been used and adapted for a variety of traumatic recovery scenarios where the trauma occurred within the context of dependent/interdependent relationships. Researchers have noted the effectiveness of a three-phase model for recovery from infidelity (Gordon et al., 2004; Scuka, 2015), and for women dealing with addiction (Covington, 2008). This three-phase model allows for variety among clients in terms of what they need, while giving a framework for understanding the process toward healing. The specific model for helping after chronic infidelity or CPSB is called the *Multidimensional Partner Trauma Model* (APSATS, 2012; Steffens, 2019).

The three phases for this trauma resolution model are *Safety and Stabilization, Remembrance and Mourning,* and *Reconnection* (APSATS, 2012;

Herman, 1992). Think of these three phases as categories for the types of activities or interventions that occur within each category. Also think of the phases as a process. A traumatized person must achieve a sense of safety in Phase One, feeling stable enough in the here-and-now before moving on to the challenge of grief and trauma work that would occur in the Phase Two, *Remembrance and Mourning*. Phase Three, *Reconnection*, occurs when the person is coming out the other side of the trauma and is ready to re-engage in life and vision for their future. A variety of tasks and interventions exist within each of these phases. This model has been adopted and adapted by an organization that trains counselors on how to respond to the trauma of betrayal with partners of sexual addicts (APSATS, 2012; Steffens, 2019). All of this work supporting a betrayed woman *must* be done within the context of a safe, healing relationship.

Treatment Process

The following structure (Steffens, 2014) can be helpful as you plan your counseling treatment plan with women (see Figure 21.3). These phases and tasks can be addressed in individual, group, or when appropriate, in couples counseling sessions.

Phase One: Safety and Stabilization counseling interventions include items such as crisis intervention, safety assessment, symptom assessment and management, referral for medication evaluation, psychoeducation on trauma and intimate betrayal, disclosure of any additional information needed by the betrayed woman, management of trauma symptoms using tools such as mindfulness techniques and possible psychopharmacological interventions. Safety related boundary setting and awareness of potential emotional, psychological, or sexual abuse in the relationship with the betrayer is also necessary at this point. ***Goals: Safety and empowerment.***

Phase Two: Remembrance and Mourning counseling interventions can include narrative therapy interventions (telling of her story), grief work, and trauma resolution techniques (such as EMDR, CBT, etc.). During this phase, you would continue to assess for any safety needs. Provide help and support with decision making around the status of the relationship. Psychoeducation on healthy or protective boundaries can be very helpful, as is assertive communication. Techniques/strategies that help with trauma help with IBT. ***Goals: Complete grief work and trauma resolution.***

Phase Three: Reconnecting tasks focus on re-engaging or visioning for a future. This can include relationship focused interventions if the relationship remains intact and can move into helping others (giving back) by supporting others or engaging in other positive life activities. Resilience building, skill building, communication and relationship skills growth can be occurring throughout. ***Goals: Finding meaning, moving on.***

FIGURE 21.3

Trauma-Informed Model

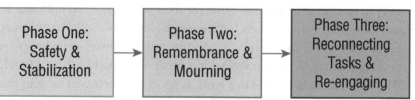

Source: Patti Hinkley

If at any time there is another betrayal in the intimate relationship, the client will likely return to Phase One needs, focused on safety and stabilization. It is difficult for any trauma survivor to begin a healing process if there is continued trauma (such as betrayal, IPV, emotional abuse, etc.).

CONCEPT TO CONTEMPLATE

© ImageFlow/Shutterstock.com

In Her Shoes
What are some other traumatic events or conditions that could complicate healing for someone who experiences IBT? How would you continue to assess for this with your client?

Individual counseling and group support have been found to be very helpful with trauma survivors and with those experiencing IBT. Gómez et al. (2016) suggested a relational cultural therapy (RCT) model of support for those who experience betrayal trauma. The authors state that the differences in this model are the focus on mutuality, along with empathy and connection, versus a sense of disconnection, which can occur following trauma and within traditional medical treatment models. This is consistent with the three phased model above, which also seeks to normalize or non-pathologize the responses to intimate betrayal trauma. A growing number of support groups are available for betrayed women, both counselor and peer lead, as well as groups facilitated by training professional life coaches.

CASE STUDY

Now, return to one of the initial cases at the beginning of this chapter and consider the story of Susan. Recall that Susan discovered pornographic material on her home computer and reacted with great shock and distress. Here is what happened next with Susan. Susan then confronted her husband and he confessed to looking at pornography secretly for about one month. Susan was not convinced that she had all of the truth and so asked more questions over the next month and scoured the computer for more evidence. Between the answers she received from her husband and what she was able to uncover online, she believed her husband was frequently and compulsively viewing explicit pornography on the home computer, on his work computer, and was stopping by adult bookstores on his way home from work. She believes this has been going on for approximately five years without her knowledge or consent. This behavior is totally outside of her beliefs as a Christian, and she is stunned that her husband, also a Christian, would engage in these behaviors. She cannot believe God allowed this to happen to her and wonders why God did not protect her.

Susan comes to you seeking counseling support due to her symptoms of intrusive thoughts, anxiety, difficulty with eating and sleep, anger, rage, difficulty concentrating, and being easily "triggered" (certain places or objects would take her right back to the moment she first found the porn). She has strong beliefs against pornography, and she tells you (her counselor) that her husband was fully aware that she was opposed to pornography in general and would not approve of her spouse viewing porn. She also tells you that she had been aware of her husband behaving differently; he had been withdrawn, irritable, distracted, and had periods of time that he could not account for after work. She felt something was not right, had asked him only to have him say things to her like "You are a nag" or "Things are fine, why do you always try to make trouble where there isn't any!" or "You are just paranoid! Nothing is wrong!". He refuses to go to a counselor himself, saying she is making "a mountain out of a molehill! Everyone uses porn!" She says his mood and behaviors have gotten worse over the past year or two. At the point she comes to see you, Susan says her husband has promised he will not use porn again, but she has no sense that he is telling her the truth about this. She is overwhelmed and terrified that the betrayal using pornography will not stop and she is terrified she still does not know everything. She says, "What if he had affairs or saw prostitutes? What else don't I know?" She has researched online about sexual addiction and believes that it may be what is going on. She continues to search for signs that he has stopped and is telling her the truth. Just yesterday, she found out her husband has a second email account she knew nothing about. She wonders what else he may be hiding and feels like she is in a horror movie. She has no idea what is going to happen next or how it will end. She just wants the pain and fear to stop. You are the first person she has told about what has happened.

During the first few sessions, it is important to work on establishing a rapport and trust with Susan by creating a safe place and affirming her decision to seek out counseling. It is important to have an awareness that this may be difficult due to the betrayal she has just experienced with her husband. Because of Susan's disclosure of experiencing intimate betrayal trauma, you can implement Steffens (2014) three-phase treatment model to help assist the client in safety and stabilization, remembrance, and mourning, and planning her future. As Susan's counselor, it is essential that you identify treatment interventions that are evidence-based and appropriate for Susan.

Additionally, the timing for introducing Susan to interventions is also important. While working with Susan, you must not bring your judgments and values into the counseling sessions. Your responsibility is not to provide Susan with advice but to walk alongside her while she is determining her future with or without her husband. Furthermore, the focus of the sessions must remain on Susan and not on Susan's marriage or her husband.

Although Susan is questioning God's decision right now, you want to assess whether she is open to integrating her faith into sessions. If she is open to it, you may suggest she focus on the words found in Psalm 62: 5-8 (*New International Bible*, 1973/2011) "Yes, my soul, find rest in God; my hope comes from him. Truly he is my rock and my salvation: He is my fortress; I will not be shaken. My salvation and my honor depend on God; He is my mighty rock, my refuge. Trust in Him at all times, you people; pour out your hearts to Him, for God is our refuge." You may also recommend that Susan speak to her spiritual leader about what is going on with her marriage. Susan has been forthcoming with sharing that she has not spoken to anyone else about the betrayal. Women who have experienced intimate partner betrayal often feel alone and embarrassed. It is essential to help normalize Susan's feelings by connecting her with support groups and resources in her community.

CHAPTER SUMMARY

Intimate Betrayal Trauma (IBT) in women occurs when there is a breach of trust and violation of agreed upon or understood boundaries within a committed relationship. This can occur in situations such as infidelity and chronic infidelity (such as found in sexual addiction, or CSBD). Relationships, where there is IBT, can also include abuses, such as sexual or emotional/psychological abuse, as part of the betrayal or protection of the sexual secrets and deceit. IBT may also be viewed as a significant betrayal of the covenant implicit in committed relationships such as marriage. The effects of IBT can include trauma or posttraumatic stress-related responses that can be debilitating. IBT can also bring about additional crises into the life of the betrayed woman. Counselors need to be aware of this reality in their clients and be adequately prepared to respond in informed, ethical, and respectful ways. There is a real need for further research in this area! If this is an area of interest for you, see the resources listed at the end of this chapter for more information.

KEY TERMS

Compulsive Sexual Behavior Disorder (CSBD) – a persistent pattern of failure to control intense, repetitive sexual impulses or urges resulting in repetitive sexual behavior

Discovery - the act of suddenly or unexpectedly learning of or finding evidence of sexual secrets and sexual deception

Gaslighting - an abuse tactic is to manipulate and control the perceptions and beliefs of another person

Infidelity - as a sexual and/or emotional act engaged in by one person within a committed relationship, where such an act occurs outside of the primary relationship and constitutes a breach of trust and/or violations of agreed upon norms (overt and covert) by one or both individuals in that relationship in relation to romantic/emotional or sexual exclusivity

Institutional Betrayal - the re-traumatizing experience of receiving no help or being harmed again while seeking help

Intimate Betrayal Trauma - the experience of someone in an intimate romantic, sexual, and/or committed relationship with someone else who has deceived them and betrayed their trust

Intimate Deception - describes the nature of betrayal associated with months and often years of hidden activity where the injured or betrayed spouse had no opportunity to give consent to being in this kind of relationship

Sexual Addiction - sexual behavior that is compulsive and yet continues despite adverse consequences

SUGGESTED RESOURCES

Books

Full Disclosure: How to Share the Truth after Sexual Betrayal by Dan Drake and Janice Caudill

Intimate Deception: Healing the Wounds of Sexual Betrayal by Sheri Keffer

Your Sexually Addicted Spouse: How Partners can Cope and Heal by Barbara Steffens and Marsha Means

Moving Beyond Betrayal: The 5-Step Boundary Solution for Partners of Sex Addicts by Vicki Tidwell-Palmer

Websites

The American Psychological Society (APA) has some great resources on trauma from a general perspective. Other resources on Intimate Betrayal Trauma can be found at APSATS.org or Betrayal Trauma Recovery.org.

Association of Partners of Sex Addicts Trauma Specialists. (APSATS). Organization that trains and certifies clinicians and life coaches to help following intimate betrayal from a trauma-informed model for the entire system: https://www.apsats.org

Covenant Eyes. Faith based organization that provides information and blocking software to provide screen accountability. Also has blogs and booklets for information for men, women, and faith leaders: https://covenanteyes.com

Disclosing Secrets after Betrayal: Full Disclosure: How to share the Truth after Sexual Betrayal What to Tell the Children? https://vickitidwellpalmer.com/what-to-tell-the-children/

Society for Advancement of Sexual Health. (SASH). SASH has a diverse international membership focused on sexual health research, education, and intervention: https://www.sash.net

REFERENCES

Afifi, T., & Steuber, K. (2009). The Revelation Risk Model (RRM): Factors that predict the revelation of secrets and the strategies used to reveal them. *Communications Monographs*, *76*(2), 144-176. https://doi.org/10.1080/03637750902828412.

Allen, E. S., & Atkins, D. C. (2012). The association of divorce and extramarital sex in a representative U.S. sample. *Journal of Family Issues, 33*(11), 1477-1493. https://doi.org/10.1177/0192513X12439692.

American Counseling Association. (2014). *2014 ACA Code of ethics*. https://www.counseling.org/knowledge-center

American Psychological Association. (2019). *Trauma*. Retrieved October 21, 2019, from https://www.apa.org/topics/trauma/

Association of Partners of Sex Addicts Trauma Specialists. (2012). *The multidimensional partner trauma model* [Unpublished curriculum]. https://www.apsats.org

Birrell, P., & Freyd, J. (2006). Betrayal trauma: Relational models of harm and healing. *Journal of Trauma Practice, 5*(1), 49-63.

Blow, A. J. (2008). Key considerations for clinicians working with couples and infidelity. *Family Therapy Magazine*, 7, 12-14.

Bowlby, J. (1988). *A secure base: Parent-child attachment and healthy human development*. Basic Books.

Carnes, P. J. (2001). *Out of the shadows: Understanding sexual addiction*. Hazelden Publishing.

Carnes, P., & Adams, K. (2013). *Clinical management of sex addiction*. Routledge.

Carnes, S., & O'Connor, S. (2016). Confirmatory analysis of the Partner Sexuality Survey. *Sexual Addiction & Compulsivity, 23*(1), 141-153. https://doi.org/10.1080/10720162.2015.1039151.

Caudill, J., & Steffens, B. (2019). *Survey data: Faith-based help seeking of partners of sex and pornography addicts* [Unpublished manuscript].

Conley, T. D., Moors, A. C., Ziegler, A., & Karathanasis, C. (2012). Unfaithful individuals are less likely to practice safer sex than openly non-monogamous individuals. *The Journal of Sexual Medicine, 9*(6), 1559-1565 .

Covington, S. S. (2008). Women and addiction: A trauma-informed approach. *Journal of Psychoactive Drugs, 377-85*.

Crouch, E., & Dickes, L. (2016). Economic repercussions of marital infidelity. *International Journal of Sociology and Social Policy, 36*(1/2), 53-65.

Dean, C. (2011). Psychoeducation: A first step to understanding infidelity-related systemic trauma and grieving. *The Family Journal: Counseling and Therapy for Couples and Families, 19*(1), 15-21. https://doi.org/1177/1066480710387487

Dorpat, T. L. (1996). *Gaslighting, the double whammy, interrogation, and other methods of covert control in psychotherapy & analysis*. Jason Aronson, Inc.

Drake, D., & Caudill, J. (2019). *Full disclosure: How to share the truth after sexual betrayal (A comprehensive guide for the disclosing individual)*. Publisher .

Freyd, J. (1997). Violations of power, adaptive blindness and Betrayal Trauma Theory. *Feminism & Psychology, 7*(1), 22-32.

Freyd, J. J. (1999). Blind to betrayal: New perspectives on memory for trauma. *The Harvard Mental Health Letter, 15*, 4-6.

Freyd, J., & Birrell, P. (2013). *Blind to betrayal: Why we fool ourselves we aren't being fooled*. Wiley.

Freyd, J. J., DePrince, A. P., & Gleaves, D. H. (2007). The state of betrayal trauma theory: Reply to McNally- Conceptual issues and future directions. *Memory, 15*(3), 295-311. https://doi.org/10.1090/0965821070125614.

Fuchsman, K. (2019). Gaslighting. *The Journal of Psychohistory, 47*(1). 74-78.

Glass, S. P. (2002). Couple therapy after the trauma of infidelity. In A. S. Gurman & N. S. Jacobson (Eds.), *Clinical handbook of couple therapy* (3rd ed., pp. 488-507). Guilford.

Goldberg, L. R., & Freyd, J. J. (2006). Self-reports of potentially traumatic experiences in an adult community sample: Gender differences and test-retest stabilities of the items in a brief betrayal-trauma survey. *Journal of Trauma & Dissociation, 7*(3), 39-62. https://doi.org/10.1300/J229v07n03_04.

Gómez, J. M., Lewis, J. K., Noll, L. K., Smidt, A. M., & Birrell, P. J. (2016). Shifting the focus: Nonpathologizing approaches to healing from betrayal trauma through an emphasis on relational care. *Journal of Trauma and Dissociation, 17*(2), 165-185. https://doi.org/10.1080/15299732.2016.1103104.

Gordon, K. C., Baucom, D. H., & Snyder, D. K. (2004). An integrative intervention for promoting recovery from extramarital affairs. *Journal of Marital and Family Therapy, 20*, 213-231.

Harsey, S. J., Zurbriggen, E. L., & Freyd, J. L. (2017). Perpetrator responses to victim confrontation: DARVO and victim self-blame. *Journal of Aggression, Maltreatment, & Trauma, 26*(6), 644-663. https://doi.org/10:1080/10926771.2017.1320777.

Heaney, K. (2018, July 11). *Compulsive sexual behavior is now classified as a mental-health disorder*. The Cut.

Herman, J. (1992, 1996). *Trauma and recovery: The aftermath of violence - from domestic abuse to political terror*. Perseus Books Group.

Hightower, E. (2017). *An exploratory study of personality factors related to psychological abuse and gaslighting* (Publication No. 10642512) [Doctoral dissertation, William James College]. ProQuest Dissertation & Theses Global.

Jaffe, A. E., Steel, A. L., DiLillo, D., Messman-Moore, T. L., & Gratz, K. L. (2017). Characterizing sexual violence in intimate relationships: An examination of blame attributions and rape acknowledgment. *Journal of Interpersonal Violence, 0*(00), 1-22. https://doi.org/10.1177/0886260517726972.

Johnson, S. (2002). *Emotionally focused couple therapy with trauma survivors: Strengthening attachment bonds*. Guildford Press.

Karakurt, G., & Silver, K. E. (2013). Emotional abuse in intimate relationships: The role of gender and age. *Violence and Victims, 28*(5), 804-821. https://doi.org/10.1891/0886-6708.

Karila, L., Wery, A., Weinstein, A., Cottencin, O., Petit, A., Reynaud, M., & Billieus, J. (2014). Sexual addiction or hypersexual disorder: Different terms for the same problem? A review of the literature. *Current Pharmaceutical Design, 20*(0), 1-9.

Keffer, S. (2018). *Intimate deception: Healing the wounds of sexual betrayal.* Revell.

Leopold, T. (2018). Gender differences in the consequences of divorce: A study of multiple outcomes. *Demography, 55*(3), 769-797. https://doi.org/10.1007/s13524-108-0667.6.

Lusterman, D. D. (2004). Infidelity: Theory and treatment. In M. Harway (Ed.), *Handbook of couple's therapy* (pp. 337-351). Wiley.

Maxwell, P. C. (2017). Betrayal trauma and covenant: Theologically understanding abuse trauma and traumatically reforming theological understanding. *Journal of Spirituality in Mental Health, 19*(4), 241-267. https://doi.org/10.1080/10349637.2016.1260514.

Merriam-Webster. (n.d.). Discovery. In *Merriam-Webster.com dictionary.* Retrieved February 18, 2020, from https://www.merriam-webster.com/

New International Bible. (2011). New International Bible Online. https://www.thenivbible.com/ (Original work published 1973)

New Living Bible (1996). New Living Bible. https://www.biblegateway.com/versions/New-Living-Translation-NLT-Bible/

Reid, R. C., Carpenter, E. D., Draper, E., & Manning, J. C. (2010). Exploring psychopathology, personality traits, and marital distress among women married to hypersexual men. *Journal of Couple & Relationship Therapy, 9*(3), 203-222.

Schade, L. C., & Sandberg, J. G. (2012). Healing the attachment injury of marital infidelity using Emotionally Focused Couples Therapy: A case illustration. *The American Journal of Family Therapy, 40*(5), 434-444. https://doi.org/10.1080/01926187.2011.631374.

Schneider, J. P., Weiss, R., & Samenow, C. (2012). Is it really cheating? Understanding the emotional reactions and clinical treatment of spouses and partners affected by cybersex infidelity. *Sexual Addiction & Compulsivity, 19*(1-2), 123-139.

Scuka, R. F. (2015). A clinician's guide to helping couples heal from the trauma of infidelity. *Journal of Couple & Relationship Therapy, 14*(2), 141-168. https://doi.org/10.1080/15332691.2014.953653.

Seyller, M., Denis, C., Dang, C., Boraud, C., Lepresle, A., Lefevre, T., & Chariot, P. (2016). Intimate partner sexual assault: Traumatic injuries, psychological symptoms, and perceived social reactions. *Obstetrics & Gynecology, 127*(3), 516-526. https://doi.org/10.1097/AOG.0000000000001288.

Skinner, K. (2017). *Treating trauma from sexual betrayal: The essential tools for healing.* Skinner Corp.

Smith, C. P., & Freyd, J. J. (2013). Dangerous safe havens: Institutional betrayal exacerbates sexual trauma. *Journal of Traumatic Stress, 26*, 119-124. https://doi.org/10.1002/jts.

Stark, C. (2019). Gaslighting, misogyny, and psychological oppression. *The Monist, 201*, 221-235. https://doi.org/10.1093/monist/onz007

Steffens, B. (2005). *The effects of disclosure on wives of sex addicts* [Unpublished doctoral dissertation]. Regent University.

Steffens, B. (2014). *MPTM Treatment planning* [Unpublished work].

Steffens, B. (2018, July). *Betrayal trauma and healing with Dr. Barbara Steffens* [Audio podcast]. https://www.sexandrelationshiphealing.com/blog/betrayal-trauma-and-healing-with-dr-barbara-steffens/

Steffens, B. (2019, October). *A framework for helping those impacted by CSBD/PSB: An introduction to the Multidimensional Partner Trauma Model* [Keynote presentation]. Society for Advancement of Sexual Health Conference, St. Louis, MO, United States.

Steffens, B., & Means, M. (2009). *Your sexually addicted spouse: How partners can cope and heal.* New Horizon Press.

Steffens, B., & Rennie, R. (2006) The traumatic nature of disclosure for wives of sexual addicts. *Sexual Addiction & Compulsivity, 13*(2-3), 247-267. https://doi.org/10.1080/10720160600870802.

Stern, R. (2007). *The gaslight effect: How to spot and survive the hidden manipulations other people use to control your life.* Morgan Road Books.

Thaggard, S., & Montayre, J. (2019). "There was no one I could turn to because I was ashamed": Shame in the narratives of women affected by IPV. *Women's Studies International Forum, 74*, 218-223.

Utley, E. (2017). Infidelity's coexistence with intimate partner violence: An interpretive description of women who survived a partner's sexual affair. *Western Journal of Communication, 81*(4), 426-445. https://doi.org/10.1080/10570314.2017.1279744.

Warach, B., & Josephs, L. (2019). The aftershocks of infidelity: A review of infidelity-based attachment trauma. *Sexual and Relationship Therapy*, 1-24. https://doi.org/10.1080/14681994.2019.1577961

Warach, B., Josephs, L., & Gorman, B. (2018). Pathways to infidelity: The roles of self-serving bias and betrayal trauma. *Journal of Sex and Marital Therapy, 44*(5), 497-512. https://doi.org/10.1080/0092623X.2017.1416434

Woods, J. (2017). *Examining the psychological impact of male sex addiction on female partners from a social-cognitive processing perspective: The relationship of social support, cognitive assumptions, and posttraumatic stress and depression* [Unpublished doctoral dissertation]. James Cook University, Singapore.

World Health Organization. (2019). *International statistical classification of diseases and related health problems* (11th ed.). https://icd.who.int/

CHAPTER 22
Considerations for Lay Counselors in Counseling Women in the Church

CHARITY WILLIAMS, PH.D.

"The malpractice for advice-giving is like five times as much as a craniotomy."
~Nicole Krauss, *Man Walks into a Room*

"If you remain in Me and My words remain in you, ask whatever you wish and it will be done for you." (John 15:7, NIV)

Wisdom from Above:
Standing in His Grace

© Halfpoint/Shutterstock.com

Prayer needs to be the first step taken when considering the beginning of any ministry. If you are a counselor or church leader and are wondering about the benefits of a lay counseling ministry at your church, a prayerful approach as you look at the details will benefit you greatly. We can often desire to do more in the name of Jesus, but *more* may not be what Jesus desires of us. It is important that we slow down and seek Him in genuine conversation so that we can understand what it is He has for us. This can mean that we need to step away from our areas of ministry, take some dedicated time, and really ask Him if He is moving us toward a new place of service for Him. Knowing whether or not He is leading us toward a new ministry is non-negotiable. If we simply forge ahead because it sounds like a good idea, or because it stirs up our emotions, then we may be moving forward based on our intentions rather than His. He reminds us in John 15:5 (*Holman Christian Standard Bible*, 2003/2009) "I am the vine; you are the branches. The one who remains in

CHAPTER LEARNING OBJECTIVES

Upon completing this chapter, you should be able to:

- Define lay counseling and lay helping
- Explore ways lay counseling can be utilized within the church
- Discover the Biblical basis for lay counseling
- Examine ethical and legal issues surrounding lay counseling
- Explore traits of an effective lay counselor
- Examine the importance of training and supervision of lay counselors
- Value the significance of lay counseling ministry for women

Me and I in him produces much fruit, because you can do nothing without Me".

A lay counseling ministry, even though it offers much in the way of helping hurting people and providing areas of service for believers, will be a futile effort if this is not the path God has for this body of believers. Praying and seeking God fervently about what His plans are should be the first step that is taken before any lay counseling ministry is established. If He has called you to pursue the path of creating a lay counseling ministry, it is my hope and prayer that this brief resource will get you started on the journey. But even if this is not part of your calling, I hope you will learn more about the ministry of lay counseling and see how this effort could support the discipleship journey in local congregations and offer much needed assistance to women.

CHAPTER OVERVIEW

Lay counseling, or lay helping, is assistance provided by those with little to no professional counseling training. The Christian church has utilized lay helpers for years, but the role has increased in demand recently due to changing health care standards. Lay helpers can provide needed assistance to those within the church who desire not only to be assisted with difficulties but who also desire to grow in their relationship to Christ. Lay counselors need training, supervision and direction to pursue their helping role. They need to be made aware of the responsibility of helping others and the ethical standards needed to practice with integrity. Women within church congregations are especially in need of female lay helpers, as often the ministerial team is comprised of men who may not be able to relate to the needs of women the way other women can. Discussion is provided regarding the establishment of a lay counseling ministry, the Biblical basis for such a ministry, the relationship between lay counseling and discipleship, and the skills and training necessary for lay counselors.

LAY COUNSELING FOR WOMEN

Lay Counseling Definitions and Differences

Lay counseling or lay helping is best understood to be assistance provided by individuals who have little to no professional counseling training. While lay counseling has been a part of the Christian church experience for years, there has been an increase in its role and significance over time. Much of that increase has to do with the current climate of health care, especially that of mental health services. With managed care setting standards for individuals, there are less options for mental health services, and few people can afford long term counseling provided by professionals. As a result, people are turning to other options such as lay counseling, which might be provided by local churches or parachurch organizations. These lay counselors often provide their services free of charge, which provides an affordable alternative for many who would otherwise not be able to receive any type of counseling (Tan, 2002).

> **Lay counseling/lay helping** is best understood to be assistance provided by individuals who have little to no professional counseling training.

Considering that the lay counselor has little to no training, it is important to distinguish how this form of counseling differs from other counseling roles. For instance, one may wonder how lay counseling differs from pastoral counseling or even Christian counseling. To better clarify, an examination of terms will be important. Considering the definitions provided by professional literature, for this text, counseling will be defined as a formal process whereby a counselor and client embark in a professional relationship to address certain cognitive, emotional, behavioral, and/or relational matters in order to help the client reach desired goals (Gladding, 2018; Mudge & Worrell, 2009). This definition offers insight into those in a professional counseling role but gives those in other counseling positions a general understanding of what counseling entails. When considering pastoral counseling, a definition surmised by a review of the literature is a form of counseling provided by those with roles in the church such as pastors or ministers who have been set apart by their church and/or denominational authority, and who often have received additional training in counseling skills (Gladding, 2018; American Association of Christian Counselors [AACC], 2014).

Based on various definitions of the term in the literature (Clinton et al., 2011; Clinton & Ohlschlager, 2005; Gladding, 2018; McMinn, 2011), for the purposes of this text Christian counseling is defined as follows: a professional-ministry relationship characterized by a helper dependent on the Holy Spirit who assists a care seeker to experience a healing encounter with Christ and to move toward spiritual maturity and psycho-social-emotional wellness. While there are many goals present in Christian counseling, the greatest concern is "helping clients become more like Christ and grow into a deeper intimacy with God and with one another" (Clinton et al., 2011, p. 11).

> "As licensed clinicians, we strongly advocate the need for highly trained, properly equipped, thoroughly competent and authentically Christian therapists. However, we are equally fervent about the important role of the local church and its responsibility to function as God's ambassadors of compassionate caregiving and reconciliation."
> (Tan & Scalise, 2016b, p. 47)

Yet another relevant term is spiritual direction. Spiritual direction may best be defined as the process of one believer in Jesus Christ offering another believer help in the journey toward understanding God's will and working in that individual's life and encouraging surrender to His direction and purpose. While this was often thought to be the role of pastors, ministers, or those specifically trained, there is a continued redefining of the idea which now promotes that this is a responsibility of all believers. Considering the definitions for spiritual direction as well as Christian counseling, there is not always a clear distinction between them. Collins (2007) notes, "Counseling tends to be more problem-centered, while spiritual direction is Spirit-centered. Counseling seeks to resolve problems, but spiritual direction focuses more on helping the person grow in his or her relationship with God" (p. 38). So, while lay counselors are not trained in the same way as those with professional licensed credentials, there are common elements in the desire to help those who are hurting or need direction.

Lay Counseling and the Church

Since lay counseling is most often utilized within the church or in parachurch organizations, understanding this dynamic is important. Lay counseling can support the work of the local church in many ways such as assisting the pastoral staff with counseling of church members, leading support groups, and following up with care seekers. Lay counselors can provide leadership in small group ministries, mentoring relationships, or with specific needs such as divorce recovery or grief sharing (Bland, 2003). Other concerns addressed by lay counselors include marital disputes, premarital work, vocational topics, anxiety, and parenting difficulties (Tan & Scalise, 2016a). Often within the regular meetings of the church's small groups, concerns are brought forth by the members, and lay counselors may be utilized to address those needs or to refer to professional counselors if the issue is beyond their expertise. These natural situations that arise during regular ministry of the church are both part of the reason for the need for lay counselors but also one of the cautions (Edwards, 2003).

© MIA Studio/Shutterstock.com

Lay counselors can also provide relevant information to pastoral staff regarding community concerns. The lay counselors could offer input regarding ideas for targeting community needs such as support groups for single moms or groups for addiction recovery. Once the need has been established, the lay leaders can be instrumental in providing relevant care for the concerns presented (Spriggs & Sloter, 2003). Lay counselors can further aid the busy pastoral staff by conducting ministry visits, serving as informal leadership, taking referral cases or long-term counseling visits, providing support groups and following up with care seekers (Tan & Scalise, 2016a). Considering that many pastoral teams are comprised mainly of male pastors, the relevance of having women referrals for female care seekers is one in need of examination.

While it is noted that more than half of most congregations are composed of women, there are still few females that serve in senior ministry roles (Barna, 2017). This uneven dynamic creates difficulty when women need counsel from someone who respects their faith journey. One option for women, then, is to have a female lay counselor who will assist them when they are facing challenges. This underscores the need for a lay counseling ministry which is specifically geared toward women and their issues. While men may have been trained in counseling skills and have the necessary tools, there is considerable need for women to have other women who can relate to their journey as only another woman can. In Titus 2: 3-4 (*New American Standard Bible*, 1960/1995) the apostle Paul writes,

© Asier Romero/Shutterstock.com

Women have a unique journey and role within family life, but also within the church. Women bear the responsibility of caring for the children with the biological changes and needs which are a part of that process. Women often are responsible for the tasks of a household, such as cooking and cleaning, and yet many are part of the workforce, too. Even as Barna (2017) noted, women make up most of our churches, and yet are not well represented within senior ministry staff.

Considering that people will most often seek a minister for assistance first, women who follow that trend are often met by a male minister who simply cannot relate to her journey in the same way another woman might. The male minister may also feel uncomfortable meeting with a woman alone, or for more than just a few times before seeking referral options. He might consider bringing his wife in, but if she is uncomfortable or unwilling to be in that role, then he is left with little choice. Women who are both called and trained to provide ministry and/or counseling are needed to aid other women on their journey. Adding women to a senior ministry role could support this work, but if that is a concern due to differing beliefs, then female lay counselors could be a way to bridge this gap. Female lay counselors could offer a way to minister to women who are juggling many responsibilities and who want to have a Biblical perspective to life's challenges. What are some of the ways lay counseling could benefit women specifically?

"...older women are to ...encourage the young women". Another woman may be able to assist a struggling female who may feel more comfortable sharing her journey with a woman rather than a man. Current research even indicates that professionally trained counselors often do not receive much training on gender related issues, so women helping other women would help lessen the gap from a male counselor to a female care seeker (Schwartz et al., 2011).

Lay Counseling Models

Garzon et al. (2009) noted four classifications of lay counseling models. Their classification included active listening approaches, cognitive and solution-focused approaches, inner healing approaches, and mixed approaches. In the active listening model, Rogerian principles such as empathy, positive regard and listening skills are emphasized. In the cognitive approaches, the emphasis is on the role of automatic thoughts, self-talk, and core beliefs and their role in the creation of difficulties. Prayer and Scripture are part of the process that will be utilized to bring thoughts toward a more Christ centered place. Considering that cognitive behavioral therapy is an empirically supported treatment modality, there are considerable resources which examine this model from a Christian perspective including *Cognitive Behavioral Therapy for Christians with Depression: A Practical Tool-Based Primer* (Pearce, 2016).

Solution-focused lay models point toward helping the care seeker envision life or the future without the problem in place. Care seeker strengths and resources are emphasized in efforts toward this future. Kollar's (2011) *Solution-Focused Pastoral Counseling: An Effective Short-Term Approach for Getting People Back on Track* utilizes a solution focused model. An inner healing approach seeks to take the care seeker on a journey toward the past to uncover any personal, family or other experiences that may be contributing to present concerns. This journey must be done with the Holy Spirit's leading and is centered on prayer along with encounters with Christ as the catalyst for change. An example may be found in the work of Anita Sorenson who explored the protracted grief of a woman over the loss of her twin sister (Sorenson et al., 2017).

Finally, in the mixed approach, there is a greater emphasis on using several different psychological theoretical perspectives, but there is also a willingness to explore the role of the flesh and even the demonic influence within emotional disturbances (Garzon et al., 2009). In a study by Pan et al. (2013) findings tended to indicate that if a person was seeking some type of pastoral counseling or care, there was a desire for explicit Christian interventions to be part of the process. While they acknowledged the sample size was small, they noted that this finding helps support the "clinical, ethical, and professional use of spiritual resources" (p. 146).

Biblical Basis for Lay Counseling

When we consider the earlier definitions of counseling, spiritual direction, and even Christian counseling, there is a common thread of helping those who are struggling to move them toward healing and growth. In the lay counselor role, specifically those who are seeking to aid others from a Christ centered perspective, consideration must be made as to whether this is a responsibility for all believers, and if so, how this looks within the church. Questions must also be asked regarding the goals for lay counseling within the church and the qualifications that will be required of the helper.

The goals of discipleship and the goals of counseling are not that different. Consider what Ed Stetzer notes as eight attributes of a maturing Christian or disciple (follower) of Christ: "Bible engagement, obeying God and denying self, serving God and others, sharing Christ, exercising faith, seeking God, building relationships and unashamed transparency" (Gallaty, 2015, p. 12.)

Robby Gallaty in his 2015 book *Rediscovering Discipleship: Making Jesus' Final Words our First Work*, discusses the differences in the Hebraic and Western mindsets. While the Western mindset often speaks of a personal relationship with God, the Hebraic view is more corporate in nature. We see this idea represented specifically in *The Lord's Prayer*. Jesus prays "Our Father" rather than "My Father". In Matthew 6:9a (*Christian Standard Bible,* 2017/2020) Jesus informs His disciples, "Therefore, you should pray like this: Our Father in heaven...". In Jewish culture, community was key. There was an expectation that life would be lived together, not separated. These ideas inform discipleship. Community life is an expectation among believers. Celebrations and sorrows are experienced together. When one member of the body is hurting, the whole body of believers is impacted. Considering that lay counseling addresses those who are hurting or in need, there is support for the ministry within these principles.

Gallaty (2015) goes on to clarify that "discipleship has an end goal: to be formed into the image of Christ-to talk the way he talked, walk the way he walked, and respond the way he responded" (p. 79). Noting again a portion of the definition of Christian counseling from Clinton and Hawkins (2011) the goal is "helping clients become more like Christ and grow into a deeper intimacy with God and with one another" (p. 11). If we as believers consider Christ as our example, then His responses to life's struggles and celebrations are to be how we model our own responses. Hackney (2010) acknowledges that sin, or responding outside of God's desires for our lives, destroys the image of God in humanity. His thoughts are that sanctification, or the process of spiritual maturity, involves the reversal of that corruption. Hackney believes that "the humanity of Christ provides a prototype of human flourishing" (p. 197). Should lay counselors then consider the principles of discipleship and Christ following as the foundations for goals regarding their work with care seekers? Garzon et al. (2009) even note in their review of the literature that Scripture is quoted more often in lay counseling than in professional counseling. They also pointed out that prayer and application of the Scripture was an important component within lay counseling models.

> "Christ Himself, in rebuking the Pharisees because religious form took precedence over their concern for others, said, 'I desired compassion and not a sacrifice' (New International Bible, 1973/2011, Matthew 12:7). In taking this admonishment to heart, the decision for many pastors and churches may then become, not 'If we should begin to provide ministry in these areas,' but 'How and where should we start?'"
> (Tan & Scalise, 2016b, p. 47)

Crabb (2003) indicates that the greatest and most lasting change occurs when there is authentic relationship. This relating might well happen within the confines of a counseling office or in a church small group. Collins (2007) posits a similar idea regarding the ideas of community and spiritual transformation. He states that "isolation generally leads to spiritual barrenness. Spiritual formation and transformation must be nurtured through community. We need companions for the spiritual journey" (p. 37). Collins also concedes that the lines are not always clear between the disciplines of counseling and spiritual direction.

Walters (2000) reflected to counseling students regarding the difference that Christianity makes in psychology stating that the changes within a client or care seeker "progresses toward goals suggested by Scripture: inward awareness, outward peace, corporate connectedness, and ultimate health of the client" (p. 272). These changes are consistent whether the counseling is professional or lay centered.

CONCEPT TO CONTEMPLATE

© ImageFlow/Shutterstock.com

For the Christian helper, considering how Jesus' teachings will influence the goals and foundations of counseling is key. Discipleship and the process of **sanctification** (the process of "being made holy" or "becoming more like Jesus"). Another way to discuss sanctification is to consider "Christian growth or maturation" (Mathis, 2013, p. 14) in the life of a believer as it helps to inform day to day beliefs and actions. If a care seeking believer desires to grow in their walk with Christ and live as He desires, then should not counseling and discipleship ideas closely align?

LEGAL ISSUES OVER THE WORD *COUNSELING*

State laws may prohibit the use of the word *counselor* by anyone who is not a licensed professional counselor. This issue could impact the naming of the lay counseling ministry. Other proposed ideas are lay helpers or even lay caregivers (Tan, 2013a). Tan and Scalise (2016a) mention a similar concern and note that to decrease the risk of being sued, ministries would benefit from not using the word *counselor* or *counseling*. Considering the previous discussion, a possible name could be *discipleship conversations.* While not all therapy models lean toward the idea that the counselor is the expert, there is enough of a perception that the simple word *counselor* brings up images of a person who will lead the care seeker toward health from a prescribed picture. The Christian lay counselor or helper, who is not trained in specific models, would best assist a care seeker if they had in mind the idea of discipleship, or following Christ, as the ultimate goal.

Even in working with beginning counseling students, many have offered that learning models that do not require them to be the expert has brought them great relief. Lay counselors may feel empowered to know that they are not expected to function beyond their expertise but are instead inviting care seekers toward a deeper relationship with Jesus Christ and are accomplishing that goal through intentional conversation and living life together.

This idea would support the work of the church that often struggles in the intentional task of discipleship. In a December 2015 study by Barna,

© Freedomz/Shutterstock.com

only 1% of church leaders said that "today's churches are doing very well at discipling new and young believers" (para. 9). A majority, 60%, felt that churches were not discipling their members well.

Peter Scazzero (2010), pastor of the multi-ethnic New Life Fellowship in Queens, New York, and author of multiple books on emotional health in the church had this to say: "The link between emotional health and spiritual maturity is a large, unexplored area of discipleship" (p. 18). He goes on to note: "Sadly, for too long have we delegated 'emotional' issues to the therapist's office and taken responsibility only for 'spiritual' problems in the church. The two are inseparably linked and critical to a fully Biblical discipleship" (p. 19).

Albritton (2016), in a study conducted of 51 pastors, sought to determine their understanding and approach toward counseling as part of the discipleship process within the local church setting and as part of their own growth. While the congregation size varied, the largest percentage of churches represented were over 1000 in attendance. Of the pastors surveyed, only 11 of the 51 pastors (or 22%) had counseling as part of their plan for discipleship. Of those Albritton surveyed, only 23 (46%) offered lay counseling. Albritton also included a question about the pastors' personal experiences with counseling, and the responses indicated that the percentage of those who had sought professional counseling in the past was only slightly higher than those who had never sought any type of counseling. Albritton (2016) provided this reflection: "If a pastor himself is unwilling to pursue any form of help, then it is highly unlikely that the church will decide on its own to do that. In order for the church to start the process, it must begin with the pastor himself" (p. 113).

Albritton's (2016) work seems to underscore the importance of how the pastor's beliefs about counseling can have a great impact on the willingness of the church to consider counseling as a needed part of the ministry it provides. As mentioned earlier, counseling efforts with a goal of discipleship or helping believers mature in their walk with Christ could help provide some much needed relief to pastors and ministry staff who have multiple levels of responsibility and could provide women a much needed source of help. Lay counseling efforts, or discipleship conversations, could serve to help bridge the gap expressed by Scazzero (2010) and noted by the Barna (2015) research and Albritton's (2016) work. Still, the literature denotes the terms lay counselor and lay counseling often, so they will be utilized in this discussion.

PERSONHOOD OF THE LAY COUNSELOR

Character Traits of the Lay Counselor

There is much written about the characteristics or traits of a person who makes a good counselor. While lay counselors are not required to be educated in the same manner as professional counselors, there are still some characteristics which would be of benefit for any helper to possess. Ohlschlager and Clinton (2002) outline ideas regarding several types of helpers and the traits which would assist any counselor in their work. One such notation includes the professional clinician's dedication to understanding

how all realms of living (biological, psychological, social, and spiritual) are interrelated. The pastoral or Biblical counselor holds true to their relationship with Christ, has a high view of Scripture, and pursues maturity in Christ as the highest goal. Lay counselors often possess a natural empathy, a strong desire to listen, and a helpful attitude. Charismatic counselors rely heavily on the presence of the Holy Spirit, the discernment gift, and their strong belief in divine healing. Other counselors emphasize cognitions and false beliefs and strive to assist clients in replacing faulty ideas with Biblical and rational truth. Family systems or relational counselors look to interpersonal relationships as a primary healing agent. These emphases fit well into an overall view of the idea of lay counseling and discipleship.

While these points are commendable, there must be more than just the outward actions of the counselor to be viewed considering the personhood aspect. As Jesus reminds the scribes and Pharisees in Matthew 23, simply considering outward behavior does not mean the person's motivations are pure and God-honoring. Scazzero (2010) describes his reflection this way:

> To truly love God with all our heart, soul, mind and strength requires that we know not only God but also our interior-the

nature of our own heart, soul and mind. Understanding that world of feelings, thoughts, desires, and hopes with all its richness and complexity is hard work. It also takes time - lots of it. (p. 57)

For the lay counselor, or disciple-maker, continuing her own journey toward spiritual maturity must be a non-negotiable as she works with others. Examining her motivations will be vital as she must be committed first to her relationship with Christ, and then as part of her growing connection to Him, her service will be an outward sign of her inner relationship with Jesus.

Langberg (2006) reminds us that as human beings we will be an image bearer, but the question remains, whose image will we reflect? Langberg, a therapist herself, offers counselors thoughts that center on how the care seekers or clients will impact the helpers. She says that counselors will be impacted or shaped by the therapy they provide, and to think otherwise is a deception. Considering the reverse, she also strongly emphasizes that care seekers will be shaped by their interactions with counselors, and that in some way they will bear the image of their counselor within their person. A heavy responsibility not to be taken lightly, counselors should then be willing to ask themselves whether they are reflecting the image of the Creator God. It is only in His reflection that we as helpers can serve as the "redemptive force in this world" (Langberg, 2006, p. 262).

Langberg (2006) calls herself a "disciple undergoing training" (p. 263), offering thoughts about disciplines she feels God uses in her life to create change. First, she noted the importance of worship. Acknowledging Almighty God and praising Him for His attributes reminds the counselor of their place. Reading Scripture, praying, and obeying God's will and work in her life is an important task for the counselor who desires to proceed with working in a way that honors God. A 2016 study by Sutton, Arnzen, and Kelly, indicated that personal spirituality practices of Christian clinicians predicts their use of Christian interventions within their work with clients.

Listening Skills

A skill noted as essential in the work of counseling is that of being a good listener. A practical book is James Petersen's work *Why Don't We Listen Better? Communicating and Connecting in Relationships* (2015). Petersen believes that "real listening gets us inside each other" (p. 7). He also acknowledges that while better communication skills can improve relationships, they are not the entire picture. He says, "The need-to-win and put ourselves above others in relationships causes even more problems than shoddy communication" (p. 7). Another text used for teaching counseling skills is *Research-based Counseling Skills: The Art and Science of Therapeutic Empathy* (Hawkins et al., 2019), which emphasizes the idea that empathy is an umbrella skill and that, if listening skills are used, they only tend to be effective if conducted under the umbrella of empathy.

Lay counselors might assume this resource would be beneficial only to those they help, but this idea of empathy and value of others is an essential idea for the helpers to understand as well. Even in the counseling relationship, there can be a tendency for the helper to shift focus from the one seeking help back to the counselor. This can be very problematic as the attention is to be on the one who is coming for assistance, not the one providing it. The lay counselor must be working on their own spiritual maturity and life in Christ in order to keep themselves from such behaviors. The counselor or helper must be in counseling or in an accountability relationship on their own so that any blind spots or areas of unhealthy actions can be identified and addressed so that their helping connections are not marred by sinful attitudes or beliefs.

CONCEPT TO CONTEMPLATE

The counselor or care giver cannot take a care seeker somewhere they themselves have never been. If the counselor is not working on her own journey toward Christlikeness and spiritual maturity, then she cannot expect to walk with a care seeker toward health in that area.

Screening of Lay Counselors

Careful screening of potential lay counselors or helpers is a task that should be undertaken prior to the beginning of any such ministry. Criteria could include such things as spiritual maturity, a genuine interest and love for people, appropriate spiritual giftedness, availability, teachability, and an ability to maintain confidentiality. An interview process could also include assessment of psychological and emotional stability, though formal psychological testing of potential lay counselors should be avoided or conducted only according to ethical guidelines (Tan, 2013a).

McMinn (2011) offered challenging thoughts and questions concerning the characteristics of those in the role of a Christian counselor that could also apply to those who would serve in a lay counseling role as a church ministry. McMinn noted that while understanding spirituality does not lend itself to any status or credential, the counselor would do well to spend time studying and practicing the ideas of Christian theology. A counselor would find that a care seeker will desire a helper who has values they respect. McMinn highlights the idea that a counselor who is involved in prayer, Scripture study, solitude, fasting, and corporate worship is an essential ingredient in the work in a session with a care seeker. The personhood of the counselor will only be transformed by the work of the Holy Spirit in the life of the care giver. The counselor who understands that they are a sinful human needing a Savior and who are willing to admit their own brokenness and limitations will offer their care seekers an authenticity that cannot be denied. The counselor who practices under ethical guidelines, seeking supervision and offering referrals when needed, is one who offers the best standards of care.

Jesus taught His disciples about the most important characteristics of following God in Mark 12: 29-31 (*New Living Bible*, 1996):

> "This is the most important," Jesus answered, "Listen, Israel! The Lord our God, the Lord is One. Love the Lord your God with all your heart, with all your soul, with all your mind and with all your strength. The second is: Love your neighbor as yourself. There is no other commandment greater than these".

Self-Care

Self-care is a discipline that is often misunderstood, even within the Christian community. Many espouse a theology that elevates others but dismisses the individual. When looking at Mark 12:31a, Jesus informs us that we are to love others "as yourself". Now He is not promoting a selfish or self-centered love, but rather an acknowledgement that while we are to love others, we are also not to practice self-condemnation and are to realize we are loved by the Father as well. We are not expected to be capable of always being there as God is for us, as we are finite humans. The practice of self-care gives us opportunity to rest, to rejuvenate and to re-center our focus. Along with the chance to rest, the practice of self-care allows us to practice good boundaries and understand our limits.

Those who may not have been exposed to the concepts of *burnout* or even *compassion fatigue*, such as the lay counselor applicant, might feel that self-care or boundary setting goes against Christian faith principles and, therefore, might need some instruction on the importance of taking care of themselves as they seek to minister to others. According to Peter Scazzero, a pastor and author of many books on emotional health, the inner emotional work one does is part of the process of self-care. When there is an understanding of why a person must keep serving rather than slow down, then a recognition of that tendency can be acknowledged and dealt with rather than face burnout or fatigue. Emotional health impacts the ability to serve others. Scazzero (2015) says this: "We cannot give what we do not possess.

We cannot help but give what we do possess" (p. 38). If a person is not emotionally healthy and on the journey toward spiritual maturity, then there is an inability to lead someone else on that path. But if there is movement toward growth, then one cannot help but share that with another. Therefore, the counselor's own path is crucial in her work with others.

It is important that the lay helper spend time in care of herself. She may need to become involved in a hobby. She will need to pay attention to her physical health as well. Helpers often seek to serve others but neglect their own health. Setting up a schedule of regular physical activity is vital. Personally, determining a process that allows for functioning within God-given rhythms is key. It is not that engagement at other times as needed won't happen but living in ways that allows for personal responsibilities to be completed and self-care to occur is also vital. Determining the best schedule and plan for helping others which also takes care of herself, her personal relationship with God, and her family responsibilities is an important task in the helper's life. As the lay helper is on the journey toward maturing in Christ herself, she might best consider herself less an expert and more a fellow pilgrim.

CONCEPT TO CONTEMPLATE

© Digital Storm/Shutterstock.com

Consider your own personality traits. Are you an introvert? An extravert? Do you find yourself energized by being alone or being around others? Do you have more focus in the mornings or in the evenings? Finding a schedule that works best for you is important. There may be certain responsibilities that must fit into your schedule regardless of your personal preferences, but are there ways to organize certain tasks so that it fits you best? For example, scheduling things in the early morning may not be ideal, so afternoon and early evenings may be when appointments are preferred. Do you know what works best for you?

EFFECTIVENESS AND NEED OF LAY COUNSELING

Effectiveness and Limitations

Garzon and Tilley (2009) reviewed the research conducted on lay Christian counseling approaches and noted its limitations. They were not able to conclude its effectiveness based on their study. In another study by Gilat et al. (2012) responses to suicidal messages by both trained volunteers and lay individuals were reviewed to see if the responses differed. While it was noted that offering emotional assistance was the most pervasive technique employed by the participants of the study, it was also clear that the trained volunteers provided this assistance more often than the lay individuals. The trained volunteers offered emotional support to almost all the messages while the lay individuals provided this type of support in about 70 percent of the interactions. The volunteers did not necessarily differ from the lay individuals in their ability to offer such support, but rather seemed to realize the necessity of using this technique in helping interactions, and therefore were more likely to employ it. This encourages the idea of training for volunteers and lay helpers because even though they may be naturally inclined to a helping response, training reinforces these tendencies.

Tan (2013b) states that lay counseling has received support from the literature concerning its effectiveness and pointed out that lay counselors have generally been found to be as effective therapeutically as their professional counterparts. Tan did point out that more research is needed in this area, especially with regards to Christian lay counselors within the local church context. Collins (2007) warns that even with good intentions, some non-professional caregivers may do more harm than good. Collins reminded that lay caregivers would vary in their levels of training, therapeutic skills, sensitivity, psychological knowledge and even ability to aid.

Options for Health is a methodology which uses motivational interviewing (MI) to intervene in efforts to reduce sexual risk. An evaluation of lay counselors' ability to successfully deliver the intervention after training noted a failure in proficiency so a study was conducted to evaluate the impact of a refresher training and ongoing supervision. The 2014 study by Dewing et al. noted a positive impact from the ongoing training and supervision experience. While counselors did not always attain proficiency in the required protocol, basic communication skills and therapeutic approach did see an improvement which allowed for better quality counseling (Dewing et al., 2014).

Tan and Scalise (2016a) in a review of the outcome studies conducted which compared professional therapy to lay counselors noted that the majority found lay counseling to be generally as effective when working with the most common issues. Again, the reminder is that more study needs to be conducted before definitive conclusions can be reached.

Toh and Tan (1997) conducted the only controlled outcome study regarding the effectiveness of lay Christian counseling within a church setting. In the 1997 study Toh and Tan found a significant improvement in clients who were randomly assigned to a lay Christian counseling treatment group versus those who were randomly assigned to the non-treatment control group. The gains created were maintained at a one month follow up.

PSYCHOLOGIST'S NEED FOR CHRISTIAN COUNSELORS

Gorusch (2002) noted that psychologists have often considered ministers only in the sense of being a possible referral source for clients. But Leung (1991) clarified that the two have different divisions of labor. Ministers, and possibly Christian lay counselors, are better suited for helping with direction in spiritual searching and understanding of Biblical truths while trained professionals such as psychologists would be capable of addressing personality disorders and major relational challenges. Leung (1991) pointed out that a psychologist might not have more training than an average lay person on spiritual matters and to hold a "position that a psychologist can do whatever a minister can encourages unethical practice" (p. 123).

While there is a need for trained professional counselors and other related professions, there is also a need for those who are dedicated to serving a hurting population struggling with issues related to faith and spirituality. Many who are facing challenges insist on contact with a counselor who shares their perspective on belief in God and a relationship with Him as a starting point for healing (Ohlschlager & Clinton, 2002).

© fizkes/Shutterstock.com

TRAINING, STRUCTURE, SUPERVISION AND FEES

Lay counselors are by definition those without professional training or credentials in the area of counseling. That does not mean that it would not be beneficial or even necessary to provide training and structure for a lay counseling ministry. A likely resource for training and supervision for a lay counseling ministry would be a trained professional in the mental health field. It would be important to note that like Tan and Scalise (2016a) mention, supervisors are often held responsible for any counselors they directly supervise. Making sure that the person, or persons, who will offer supervision is aware of this detail is important. Training will be a crucial part of protecting the care seekers, the lay helpers, and the supervisors, not to mention the church who will sponsor this ministry. If a desire is present to begin a lay counseling ministry, other resources would need to be consulted in order to be prepared. A great resource to start the journey is *Lay Counseling: Equipping Christians for a Helping Ministry* by Siang-Yang Tan and Eric Scalise (2016a).

While it may be preferable that the supervisor of the lay counseling ministry be a mental health professional, it is not essential and in some rural locations may not be possible. Even if the supervisor is not a professional, some basic knowledge and training in the field is appropriate and a licensed counselor should be used as a consultant. Ongoing, regular supervision is expected and would include weekly meetings for at least an hour. These supervisory times could be done on an individual basis or in pairs or small groups. Other options are possible if a weekly meeting is not feasible. Individual supervision should always be made available for whenever the need arises. Observation of the lay counselor's work should be part of the supervisory process and could include direct observation, co-counseling, or recorded sessions with care seeker consent (Tan & Scalise, 2016a).

Tan (2013b) suggested that while obtaining malpractice insurance for lay counselors might be a good practice, it is not always feasible for churches to provide this due to the expense. The licensed mental health professional who is providing direct supervision would need to obtain malpractice insurance due to the potential liability involved in working with lay helpers. The encouragement is still that lay counselors obtain malpractice insurance, as in some locations it is required for them to do so.

For the lay counselor to practice within their level of competence, training would include information regarding situations of high risk in which appropriate referral and/or consultation would be required. Some possible high risk scenarios would be: belief in simple spiritual solutions for complex situations, counseling psychotic or suicidal care seekers, advice against medical or psychological treatment, denial of the existence of psychological disorders, improper care of client information, sexual relationships with a care seeker or violations of confidentiality (Tan & Scalise, 2016a).

Tan (2013b) also warns against lay counseling with an employee or relative. He also encourages lay helpers to adequately represent themselves and use care when speaking in public. With regard to fees for lay counseling, Tan discourages the practice, noting it to be a high-risk situation. When attempting to reduce the risk of being sued for malpractice, not charging or even asking for donations keeps the lay counseling ministry within bounds of safer practice.

While the training of lay counselors is recommended, the type of training and model that the lay counselors would ultimately utilize would depend on several things. Consideration would need to be given to the focus or clientele that the counseling ministry would serve. The theological orientation of the church and the theoretical counseling preference of the training counselor would also play a role in the development of both the training system and the chosen model for the lay counseling ministry (Tan & Scalise, 2016a). The types of lay counseling models that might be chosen include the spontaneous and informal type which occurs in settings like homes or restaurants where meetings occur without prior planning. Little training or supervision occurs in this model, but if training is desired it could be easily implemented. The second model of lay helping still occurs in informal locations such as homes, hospitals or restaurants but the caregiver has been screened and carefully selected prior to receiving specialized training. This informal, organized model also creates supervision of the lay counselor by a trained person. The last model is the formal, organized model of lay helping. Again, the lay counselors are screened, trained and supervised but in this method the counseling takes place in a more formal location such as the lay counseling center of a local church. Appointments are made and meetings happen with an individual, couple or family at an arranged time and place (Tan, 2013a).

Several training models exist for a lay counseling ministry. Some of these include models created by Lawrence Crabb, Gary Sweeten, Horace Lukens, and Kenneth Haugk (Tan & Scalise, 2016a). Crabb's (2013) model includes three levels of counseling. He believes that all Christians can be involved in Level I counseling and others can be trained for Level II and Level III efforts. This model is discussed more fully in his work, *Effective Biblical Counseling: A Model for Helping Caring Christians Become Capable Counselors* (Crabb, 2013).

> Dr. Eric Scalise, co-author of the book *Lay Counseling: Equipping Christians for a Helping Ministry* (Tan & Scalise, 2016a) provided insights into the development of a lay counseling model by offering his training program. Within this program he outlines six clear steps for addressing a crisis within counseling. This model will be described in brief detail, but if the reader desires to understand his model more fully, the author gives more information within the book.
>
> 1. *Achieve* a connection with the care seeker. Understand the ministry of presence. Listen empathically. Encourage expression of feelings. Maintain a sense of calm and self-control. Don't minimize or underestimate what the care seeker is experiencing. Begin where

the care seeker is. Accept the person as they are, though this does not mean acceptance of choices or behaviors.

2. *Break down* the elements of the problem. Look for key themes or ideas. Determine the critical nature of the situation in terms of thoughts, behaviors, feelings or experiences. Realize that the care seeker may not be giving you the whole story. Ask yourself whether there is a need for immediate intervention. Are there threats to life? Determine whether any issues can be resolved immediately. Look at attempts that have been made previously. Make steps toward appropriate ownership of the problem.

3. *Commit* to action. What sources of support exist? Encourage the development of a plan of action, considering the strengths, resources, and limitations of the care seeker. Consider the structure of the plan and include smaller goals to meet prior to complete resolution. Time limits will help organize and create deadlines to meet. Supportive encouragement will be important. Resistance is likely. If needed, have referral resources ready.

4. *Document* important information. Relevant details should be written down including important points discussed and actions decided. If there were any ethical, legal, or liability concerns these should be documented, and all information kept confidential.

5. *Explain* action steps. The care seeker should understand what the goals are and what next steps are. The plan should be repeated back by the care seeker and clarifications made as necessary. If there are others who need to understand the plan of action, emphasizing who needs to be made aware should be another step. Follow up by the care giver is expected.

6. *Follow up* with the care seeker. Reach out to the care seeker on the agreed upon day and verify that the plan is in progress or completed. Ongoing support and accountability would also be expected. Encourage care seeker involvement in relevant support systems both inside and outside the church community (Tan and Scalise, 2016a, pp. 58-60).

> Lay counselors should experience regular training and ongoing supervision. Policies should be in place prior to beginning a lay helping ministry regarding the practices and procedures.

Concerning training, there are many elements that should be part of the process. Boundaries would be a key point to address. Scazzero (2010) has written about his own struggles embracing the limits God has placed on

© Freedom Studio/Shutterstock.com

him in his role as a pastor. Scazzero acknowledges Jesus as a model when it comes to limits, reminding us that He did not do any miracles as far as we know the first 30 years of His life. Jesus embraced the limits that He was given by God and lived within those limits. Christ did not heal every sick and demon-possessed person He encountered. Jesus did not meet the needs of every person around Him, and therefore, embraced limitations. Lay counselors would be remiss if they tried to live without limits or boundaries.

Tan (2018) mentioned several characteristics that distinguish therapists with more positive outcomes for clients. Training may not be able to create these characteristics within a person, however, as noted by the study by Gilat et al. (2012), training helps to remind a person to employ certain behaviors more often than if they had not received training. Tan (2018) included flexibility, appropriate response to clients' needs, awareness of the helper's own experiences, ability to connect with the care seeker's story, and a compassionate and caring nature as some of the noted factors. Others included an ability to deal with the any negative emotions felt in response to client situations, an ability to be honest with self about acknowledging mistakes, and an ability to process feedback.

Other key reminders which can be emphasized as part of training include a discussion concerning how many people a lay helper should see before taking a break (Haynes, 2011). While a lay counselor may be able to serve in one capacity for a season of life, when other factors enter in, the lay counselor may need to take a break from their role and plans need to be in place to give much needed respite from soul care. The supervisor should be able to assist in helping the lay leader transition as appropriate (Scazzero, 2010).

With regards to a specific model of training for a lay counseling ministry within the church, referring to the earlier discussion is important. Seeking God regarding the vision for the church and the lay counseling

> Tan (2018) offered these characteristics of therapists who noted more positive outcomes for clients: flexibility, appropriate response to clients' needs, awareness of the helper's own experiences, ability to connect with the care seeker's story, compassionate and caring nature, ability to deal with any negative emotions in response to client situation, an ability to be honest with self about acknowledging mistakes, and an ability to process feedback.

ministry should be first steps. The ministry team, specifically senior staff, should be supportive of the idea. The supervisory role should be considered and the person(s) who will be responsible should have input into the training model used. Legal considerations must be made. Other factors for consideration include "the size of the community, the focus of the ministry, the nature of the ministry, and the qualifications of the lay counselors" (Haynes, 2011, p. 43.)

If you are considering starting a lay counseling ministry, make sure to gather more information about current needs and resources. Review the *Suggested Resources* included at the end of this chapter to begin your search.

SUPPORT FOR CHURCH COLLABORATION

As noted, there are many elements in the consideration of a lay counseling ministry. If church populations are representative of the world at large, one in four of the persons sitting on the pew at church struggles with a diagnosable mental disorder. While lay counselors may not be trained to deal with more complex disorders, they can assist with lesser relational troubles which could free up the professional counselors to treat those in need

© Lamppost Collective/Shutterstock.com

of longer-term care (Clinton & Ohlschlager, 2005). It is estimated that nearly 25% of those suffering from mental illness will seek help from a religious source (Wong et al., 2018).

Bland (2003), a clinical psychologist, participated in training individuals for a lay counseling ministry at Olathe Bible church and discovered that there was a high level of cooperation between the church and the field of psychology. He noted that the ultimate goal for this cooperation was not simply a clinic, but instead a place where people could reach their potential in Christ. Counseling was not the only aspect that they utilized within this partnership. They looked at outreach ministries, and even traditional programs such as Sunday School, as preventative instruments. Their desire was to see the problems experienced by humanity not as situations to be solved but rather as expected concerns of living within a fallen world. This mindset created a culture of intentional compassion and effective responses while also acknowledging the need for appropriate referral and follow up care.

Scazzero (2015) echoes a similar sentiment. In his pursuit of creating a culture of emotional health at the church he pastors, he acknowledged the need to engage many levels of the environment intentionally, from the exercise of authority to the conducting of relationships and beyond. Conflict resolution, spiritual growth pursuit, and community behaviors were other considerations. Scazzero believes that emotional health is too often a missing element in discipleship efforts. When considering lay counseling, one of the topics discussed throughout this work has been how lay counseling and discipleship often coincide. Scazzero's emphases fit well into the work that a lay counseling ministry could support within the church.

ETHICAL ISSUES AND BEST PRACTICES

Lay counselors can be trained to decrease certain risks associated with this ministry. Considering lay counselors from a church ministry position, leaders should place a continued emphasis on training regarding spiritual beliefs about the problems care seekers face. Lay counselors must be aware of ethical standards surrounding the use of Biblical and spiritual counseling practices. In the *AACC Christian Counseling Code of Ethics* (2014), counselors are reminded not to presume that care seekers will be open to Judeo-Christian interventions such as prayer for and with clients, the inclusion of Scripture reading and references, or the use of religious imagery or music.

Supervision and regular access to the trained overseer of the ministry can again be a way to keep risks low. While lay counselors will not have the same expectations as licensed mental health professionals, they might find best practices to be similar with regard to informed consent, record keeping, confidentiality and mandatory reporting of abuse. The supervisor should consider that the lay counselor's practices will reflect their own work. The development of a formal counseling policy would highlight structured procedures for target needs, organizational channels and accountability, supervision and training protocols, and determining insurance standards (Tan & Scalise, 2016a). The *AACC Christian Counseling Code of Ethics* (2014) reminds lay counselors that they are to function only under the supervision of the church, a Christian counselor, or a Christian counseling organization.

Paperwork given to care seekers would need to emphasize the limitations of the lay counseling ministry, as well as procedures for referral, how care seeker information will be shared in supervision, details on mandatory reporting, and limits of confidentiality. Encouragement from professionals in the field is for lay counselors to follow the standards of licensed mental health providers with regards to these matters. Since lay counselors are functioning as a ministry of the church, there could be issues regarding information learned within sessions and a correlation with a church's policy on church discipline. Having clients sign informed consent stating that they agree to abide by the designated policies set forth by the church with regards to the matter of church discipline prior to beginning work with a lay counselor would help lower risk with concern to this issue (Tan & Scalise, 2016a).

Considering that a lay counselor will likely be a fellow church member alongside a care seeker coming for assistance, an acknowledgment of the issue of dual relationships is vital. Training regarding this issue needs to specific as this is a situation which can create tension quickly. A clear definition of the relationship is important. There should be an examination of the potential for risk to the care seeker as she (he) is likely the most vulnerable. If the consequences are examined prior to proceeding, ethical codes have been consulted, and there is still a desire to move forward, then ongoing consultation and supervision can be utilized to process through the resulting dynamics (Tan & Scalise, 2016a).

CASE STUDY

Examining how this may look in a church lay counseling center may offer the reader more insight. Let us suppose we have a lay counselor named Melody who has been trained by her supervisor, Mary, before she begins her work with Kristy, a new church member.

Melody was excited to begin her journey. She had been trained as a lay counselor for her church and was about to meet with her first care seeker, Kristy. Melody had arranged to meet Kristy at 2

© SpeedKingz/Shutterstock.com

pm in the lay counseling center. Kristy was new to the church and a new Christian. She had not been married long but her husband was not yet involved in church. Kristy wanted to talk about how to respect her husband's wishes about not wanting to come to church, but also how to grow in her faith and what her role was as a wife.

Melody had been meeting with her supervisor, Mary, for several weeks prior to meeting with her first care seeker. She had been going through the extensive training, Mary, a licensed professional counselor, had provided and met her church's requirements for lay counselors. Mary had chosen to use *The ABCs of Crisis Intervention* (Tan & Scalise, 2016a, pp. 58-60) to help the lay counselors assist others. Mary had also talked in the training about how counseling from a Christian perspective was related to discipleship. Melody had felt more confident as she had been concerned about having to be an "expert" but thinking about being on the journey with her care seeker and simply assisting her along the way was an easier idea to consider. She knew these "discipleship conversations" should be focused on what Kristy wanted to accomplish, but Melody also knew that if she felt like Kristy needed more help than she could give she could get Mary's help to provide a referral for Kristy. Melody had paid close attention in the training to Mary's emphases on confidentiality, listening skills, and goals. She knew that she could not tell Kristy what to do but could listen to her and help ask questions that would assist Kristy in determining what she felt her next step should be. Melody had also read through *The Quick Reference Guide to Counseling Women: 40 topics, Spiritual Insights and Easy to use Action Steps* (Clinton & Langberg, 2011), and

had reviewed relevant sections prior to her afternoon meeting. She found the Assessment Interview, Wise Counsel and Action Steps sections to be especially helpful and had made careful notes for herself. Mary had also recommended *Shepherding Women in Pain: Real Women, Real Issues and What you Need to know to Truly Heal* (Hislop, 2010) among others.

Melody arrived early to the center and went into her assigned room. She made sure that the seating was appropriate and that the lighting was acceptable. Melody took a few moments to check the paperwork to see that everything was included. She gathered her thoughts and looked again over her notes. She finally bowed her head and prayed for God's guidance and wisdom. She was excited for the journey and felt confident in her training and in the knowledge that her supervisor was available if she felt unsure.

During her meeting with Kristy, she thought about all the things she had learned. She assessed Kristy as she asked relevant questions. She used the ABCs method (Tan & Scalise, 2016a) as she had been taught. She made sure to use Scripture and Biblical truth as appropriate. She saw herself not as the expert but as a disciple of Jesus Christ on the journey herself, helping another follower of Jesus on her path.

When their meeting was over, Melody made sure to store the completed paperwork securely. She thanked Kristy and scheduled a follow up appointment. She left her conversation with Kristy feeling confident that she had been an obedient disciple of Jesus who had acted according to her beliefs and training.

CHAPTER SUMMARY

Lay counseling has been demonstrated to be an effective and needed ministry for churches to consider. While there are concerns and even potential risks, with proper training and supervision, as well as consideration for legal issues, a church can coordinate a lay counseling ministry that would not only serve to assist the often overwhelmed mental health system but could support their disciple making efforts as well.

Hurting people are everywhere. They often fill the pews at worship services. Believers in Jesus Christ can assist with providing lay counseling to those within their reach. The church can look to a lay counseling ministry to support their efforts to help ones who are struggling but the lay counseling ministry can also help believers live out their calling and giftedness. The trained mental health professional who is also a believer can use her (his) skills and support the lay counseling ministry in a supervisory role, with training efforts, and/or as a referral. Every believer has a responsibility to use their gifts in a God-honoring capacity. As mentioned in 1 Peter 4:10 (*Holman Christian Standard Bible*, 2003/2009) "Based on the gift each one has received, use it to serve others, as good managers of the varied grace of God".

KEY TERMS

Christian Counseling - a professional-ministry relationship characterized by a helper dependent on the Holy Spirit who assists a care seeker to experience a healing encounter with Christ and to move toward spiritual maturity and psycho-social-emotional wellness

Counseling - a formal process whereby a counselor and client embark in a professional relationship to address certain cognitive, emotional, behavioral, and/or relational matters in order to help the client reach desired goals

Lay Counseling or Lay Helping - assistance provided by individuals who have little to no professional counseling training

Pastoral Counseling - a form of counseling provided by those with roles in the church such as pastors or ministers who have been set apart by their church and/or denominational authority and who often have received additional training in counseling skills

Sanctification - the process of spiritual maturity in the life of a believer in Jesus Christ

Spiritual Direction - the process of one believer in Jesus Christ offering another believer help in the journey toward understanding God's will and working in that individual's life and encouraging surrender to His direction and purpose

SUGGESTED RESOURCES

Books

Lay Counseling: Equipping Christians for a Helping Ministry (2016) by Siang-Yang Tan and Eric Scalise

Christian Counseling Ethics: A Handbook for Psychologists, Therapists and Pastors (2013) edited by Randolph Sanders

The Emotionally Healthy Church: A Strategy for Discipleship that Actually Changes Lives (2010) by Peter Scazzero

The Emotionally Healthy Leader: How Transforming your Inner Life will Deeply Transform your Church, Team and the World (2015) by Peter Scazzero

Why Don't we Listen Better? Communicating and Connecting in Relationships (2015) by Jim Petersen

Shepherding Women in Pain: Real Women, Real Issues, and What you Need to Know to Truly Help (2010) by Beverly Hislop

Rediscovering Discipleship: Making Jesus' Final Words our First Work (2015) by Robby Gallaty

The Quick Reference Guide to Counseling Women: 40 Topics, Spiritual Insights and Easy-to-use Action Steps (2011) by Tim Clinton and Diane Langberg

The Quick Reference Guide to Biblical Counseling: 40 Topics, Spiritual Insights and Easy-to-use Action Steps (2009) by Tim Clinton and Ron Hawkins

Effective Biblical Counseling: A Model for Helping Caring Christians Become Capable Counselors by Larry Crabb

REFERENCES

American Association of Christian Counselors. (2014). *AACC Christian counseling code of ethics.* American Association of Christian Counselors.

Albritton, J. E. (2016). *Discipleship counseling: Developing healthy, growing, multiplying followers of Jesus* [Doctoral dissertation, Liberty University]. http://www.digitalcommons.liberty.edu/doctoral/1308/

Barna (2017, March 8). *What Americans think about women in power.* http://www.barna.com/research/americans-think-women-power/

Barna (2015, December 1). *New research on the state of discipleship.* http://www.barna.com/research/new-research-on-the-state-of-discipleship/

Bland, E. D. (2003). Psychology-church collaboration: Finding a new level of mutual participation. *Journal of Psychology and Christianity, 22*(4), 299-303.

Christian Standard Bible. (2020). https://csbible.com/ (Original work published 2017)

Clinton, T. & Langberg, D. (2011). *The quick reference guide to counseling women: 40 topics, spiritual insights and easy-to-use action steps.* Baker Books.

Clinton, T. & Hawkins, R. (2009). *The quick reference guide to Biblical counseling: 40 topics, spiritual insights and easy-to-use action steps.* Baker Books.

Clinton, T. E., Hawkins, R. E., & Ohlschlager, G. (2011). Christian counseling described and defined. In T. E. Clinton, & R. E. Hawkins (Eds.), *The popular encyclopedia of Christian counseling: An indispensable tool for helping people with their problems.* Harvest House.

Clinton, T. & Ohlschlager, G. (2005). Introduction to Christian counseling: The 21st-century state of the art. In T. Clinton, A. Hart, & G. Ohlschlager (Eds), *Caring for people God's way: Personal and emotional issues, addictions, grief and trauma* (pp. 3-26). Thomas Nelson.

Collins, G. (2007). *Christian counseling: A comprehensive guide* (3rd ed.). Thomas Nelson.

Crabb, L. J., Jr. (2003). Invited introduction: Collaboration might be just what God has in mind. *Journal of Psychology and Christianity, 22*(4), 293.

Crabb, L. J., Jr. (2013). *Effective Biblical counseling: A model for helping caring Christians become capable counselors.* Zondervan.

Dewing, S., Mathews, C., Cloete, A., Schaay, N., Simabyi, L., & Louw, J. (2014). Lay counselors' ability to deliver counseling for behavior change. *Journal of Consulting and Clinical Psychology, 82*(1), 19-29. https://doi.org/10.1037/a0034659

Edwards, L. C. (2003). Psychology and the church: Collaboration opportunities. *Journal of Psychology and Christianity, 22*(4), 309-313.

Gallaty, R. (2015). *Rediscovering discipleship: Making Jesus' final words our first work.* Zondervan.

Garzon, F., & Tilley, K. A. (2009). Do lay Christian counseling approaches work? What we currently know. *Journal of Psychology and Christianity, 28*(2), 130-146.

Garzon, F., Worthington, E. L., Jr., & Tan, S. Y. (2009). Lay Christian counseling and client expectations for integration in therapy. *Journal of Psychology and Christianity, 28*(2), 113-123.

Gilat, I., Tobin, Y., & Shahar, G. (2012). Responses to suicidal messages in an online support group: Comparison between trained volunteers and lay individuals. *Social Psychiatry and Psychiatric Epidemiology, 47,* 1929-1935.

Gladding, S. T. (2018). *The counseling dictionary* (4th ed.). American Counseling Association.

Gorusch, R. L. (2002). *Integrating psychology and spirituality?* Praeger Publishers.

Hackney, C. H. (2010). Sanctification as a source of theological guidance in the construction of a Christian positive psychology. *Journal of Psychology and Christianity, 29*(3), 195-207.

Hawkins, R., Kuhnley, A., Silvey, J, Sibcy, G., & Warren, S. (2019). *Research-based Counseling Skills: The art and science of therapeutic empathy.* Kendall Hunt Publishing.

Haynes, J. W. (2011). *Equipping selected members of First Baptist Church, Biloxi, Mississippi to provide a lay counseling ministry.* New Orleans Baptist Theological Seminary.

Hislop, B. (2010). *Shepherding women in pain: Real women, real issues, and what you need to know to truly help.* Moody Publishers.

Holman Christian Standard Bible. (2009). https://www.biblegateway.com/versions/Holman-Christian-Standard-Bible-HCSB/ (Original work published 2003)

Kollar, C. A. (2011). *Solution-focused pastoral counseling: An effective short-term approach for getting people back on track.* Zondervan.

Langberg, D. (2006). The spiritual life of the therapist: We become what we habitually reflect. *Journal of Psychology and Christianity, 25*(3), 258-266.

Leung, W. Y. (1991). *Intervention to facilitate use of psychological services by Chinese Americans* [Unpublished master's thesis]. Fuller Theological Seminary.

Mathis, D. (2013). The search for sanctification's holy grail. In J. Piper, D. Mathis, D, K. DeYoung, E. Welch, R. Moore, & J. J. Williams (Eds.), *Acting the miracle: God's work and ours in the mystery of sanctification.* Crossway.

McMinn, M. R. (2011). *Psychology, theology and spirituality in Christian counseling.* Tyndale House Publishers, Inc.

New American Standard Bible. (1995). New American Standard Bible Online. https://www.biblestudytools.com/nas/ (Original work published 1960)

New Living Bible (1996). New Living Bible. https://www.biblegateway.com/versions/New-Living-Translation-NLT-Bible/

Pan, P. J., Deng, L. F., Tsai, S. L., & Yuan, J. S. (2013). Issues of integration in psychological counseling practice from pastoral counseling perspectives. *Journal of Psychology and Christianity, 32*(2), 146-159.

Pearce, M. (2016). *Cognitive behavioral therapy for Christians with depression: A practical tool-based primer.* Templeton Press.

Petersen, J. C. (2015). *Why don't we listen better? Communicating and connecting in relationships.* Petersen Publications.

Ohlschlager, G., & Clinton, T. (2002). The new Christian counselors: Who we are and what we do to help others. In T. Clinton, & G. Ohlschlager (Eds.), *Competent Christian counseling: Vol. 1.* (pp. 69-92). Water Brook Press.

Scazzero, P. (2010). *The emotionally healthy church: A strategy for discipleship that actually changes lives.* Zondervan.

Scazzero, P. (2015). *The emotionally healthy leader: How transforming your inner life will deeply transform your church, team and the world.* Zondervan.

Schwartz, R. C., Lent, J., & Geihsler, J. (2011). Gender and diagnosis of mental disorders: Implications in mental health counseling. *Journal of Mental Health Counseling, 33*(4), 347+.

Spriggs, J. D., & Sloter, E. (2003). Counselor-Clergy collaboration in a church-based counseling ministry. *Journal of Psychology and Christianity, 22*(4), 323-326.

Sorenson, A. L., Tisdale, T. C., & Bland, E. D. (2017). Deep calls to deep: Healing and renewal at the crossroads of psychoanalysis and spiritual formation. *Journal of Psychology and Christianity, 36*(4), 276+.

Sutton, G. W., Arnzen, C., & Kelly, H. L. (2016). Christian counseling and psychotherapy: Components of clinician spirituality that predict type of Christian intervention. *Journal of Psychology and Christianity, 35*(3), 204-214.

Tan, S. Y. (2002) Lay helping: The whole church in soul-care ministry. In T. Clinton, & G. Ohlschlager (Eds.), *Competent Christian counseling: Foundations and practice of compassionate soul care: Vol. 1.* (pp. 424-436). Water Brook Press.

Tan, S. Y. (2013a). Lay Christian counseling for general psychological problems. In E. L. Worthington, E. L. Johnson, J. N. Hook, & J. D. Aten (Eds.), *Evidence-based practices for Christian counseling and psychotherapy* (pp. 40-58). IVP Academic.

Tan, S. Y. (2013b). Lay counselor training. In R. K. Sanders (Ed.), *Christian counseling ethics: A handbook for psychologists, therapists and pastors* (pp. 382-396). InterVarsity Press.

Tan, S. Y. (2018). How and why some therapists are better than others: Empirical evidence and clinical applications from a Christian perspective. *Journal of Psychology and Christianity, 37*(2), 183-188.

Tan, S. Y. & Scalise, E. T. (2016a). *Lay counseling: Equipping Christians for a helping ministry* (Rev. ed.). Zondervan.

Tan, S. Y. & Scalise, E. T. (2016b). On belay: The role of the church in lay helping ministry. *Christian Counseling Today, 21*(2), 46-50.

Toh, Y. M. & Tan, S. Y. (1997). The effectiveness of church-based lay counselors: A controlled outcome study. *Journal of Psychology and Christianity, 16*(3), 260-267.

Walters, S. T. (2000). What difference does Christianity make? A note to the bewildered psychology student. *Journal of Psychology and Christianity, 19*(3), 270-274.

Wong, E. C., Fulton, B. R., Derose, K. P. (2018). Prevalence and predictors of mental health programming among U.S. religious congregations. *Psychiatric services, 69*(2), 154-160.

CHAPTER 23
Counseling Women to Balance Life

STACEY LILLEY, PH.D. & ANGEL GOLSON, PH.D.

"Whatever course you decide upon, there is always someone to tell you that you are wrong. There are always difficulties arising which tempt you to believe that your critics are right. To map out a course of action and follow it to an end requires courage."
~Ralph Waldo Emerson

"Above all else, guard your heart, for everything you do flows from it."
(Proverbs 4:23, NIV)

Wisdom from Above: Standing in His Grace

© bleakstar/Shutterstock.com

The search for wellness is not a new practice. The Bible introduces this topic as Eve was called to be a "helper" (Genesis, Chapter 2). However, her wellness was challenged as sin entered into her life and spread. She had to deal with the reality of shame, guilt, embarrassment, and not having any answers to her problem. As Genesis continues, Eve's basic needs were met (food, clothing, shelter), but there were struggles in balancing family life, child-rearing, and work (Genesis, Chapters 3-4). We only know a little about Eve based on the Bible, but as women, we can relate to Eve on many levels. Women are faced with daily challenges of being helpers to many by wearing multiple hats such as daughter, sister, mother, volunteer, friend, employee, counselor, mentor, neighbor, acquaintance, and the list goes on. With these many roles also come responsibilities

and expectations. Some of these expectations are reasonable, and others are too large to fathom. If Eve were your client today, how would you help her? She may come in presenting as overworked and extremely stressed, having difficulty in balancing it all. She may present as anxious or depressed, lacking energy just to keep up with daily tasks. She may be struggling with intimacy in her marriage. Modern Eve would be struggling with wellness. One of the best ways to begin this journey of wellness is with grace. "Let us then approach God's throne of grace with confidence so that we may receive mercy and find grace to help us in our time of need," (*New International Bible,* 1973/2011, Hebrews 4:16). We need God and His unlimited grace to help us make the right choices, forgive when necessary, shed light on areas of change, and give us the strength to be proactive in our areas of wellness.

CHAPTER LEARNING OBJECTIVES

Upon completing this chapter, you should be able to:

- Differentiate the factors related to Biblical holistic wellness
- Explain the developmental factors of wellness and how these relate to women
- Compare the cultural differences of women's wellness and how these relate to counseling
- Formulate treatment recommendations for counselors working with women to obtain a greater balance in their life

CHAPTER OVERVIEW

The process of maintaining wellness takes time, energy, and self-evaluation. This chapter is focused on promoting a healthy lifestyle to improve a client's overall quality of life, in addition to encouraging counselors to model behaviors promoting wellness. As counselors, being a role model that practices a well-balanced, healthy lifestyle can be very beneficial to your client; in fact, your example may be more influential than using multiple therapeutic techniques. Most of the early contributors to the modern wellness movement were physicians, such as Halbert Dunn, John Travis, and Bill Hettler (Miller, 2005). Even though the traditional medical training of physicians in the 1960s did not incorporate working with or researching healthy people, Dunn, Travis, and Hettler became fascinated by the idea of preventing diseases from ever occurring. They studied healthy people and made several efforts to promote the modern wellness movement (Hettler, 1998).

WHAT IS WELLNESS?

The term wellness brings many ideas to each individual. Early wellness models were focused on physical wellness, had a medical model focus, and occurred after something was broken (Larson, 1999). However, the last decade has been focused more on holistic treatment and looking at all areas of wellness, which includes spirituality.

Bill Hettler, a physician in 1984, defined wellness as "an active process through which people become aware of, and make choices toward, a more successful existence" (Sweeney, 2009, p. 14). He identified wellness as an individualized, active journey, and as an active process of development rather than a static destination (Myers & Sweeney, 2005). After reviewing the wellness literature and conducting their own research, Myers et al. (2000) defined wellness as "a way of life oriented toward optimal health and well-being in which body, mind, and spirit are integrated by the individual to live life more fully within the human and natural community" (p. 252). For the purposes of this chapter, wellness is defined as intentionally making decisions and disposing time and energy in areas of the body, mind, and spirit in order to increase self-actualization.

In addition, many contextual factors influence a woman's wellness, such as local, institutional, global, and chronometrical variables (Myers & Sweeney, 2005). The basis for considering these variables comes from Alfred Adler's theory of the social interest influence, which elaborates on the ideas of how present community, society, and environment affect an individual (Ansbacher & Ansbacher, 1964).

© Polarpx/Shutterstock.com

CHALLENGES WOMEN FACE IN MAINTAINING WELLNESS

What are the challenges today's women face in today's society? Some of the challenges may be viewed as daily, situational, seasonal, or part of on-going development. With all of these moving parts, it can be difficult to find a balance in wellness and maintain it. Not to mention that at each developmental stage, additional factors complicate the situation such as hormones, relationships, finances, etc. In some instances, women will reflect and desire to make changes for the future. One thing is for certain - each developmental state presents challenges, and as counselors, we must be able to work with women as they navigate through life's trials.

According to a recent Harvard Medical article, while men are stronger, they are by far the weaker sex when it comes to health and wellness (Harvard Health Publishing, 2019). The American lifestyle has changed over the last 100 years; however, the life expectancy gap has not. Women are still outliving men and having a longer life expectancy. There are many guesses as to why this occurs but a few themes put women at an advantage. Men are more prone to illness, and estrogen has some protective factors, while testosterone may contribute to some diseases like prostate cancer. Women also tend to engage in more substantial and more consistent so-

© BOKEH STOCK/Shutterstock.com

cial networks that allow women to connect and share their feelings. In their review of literature, Harvard found the most significant reason for the gap is behavioral factors among men: risky choices, aggressive behavior, lack of diet and exercise, and lack of medical care and routine checkups. It seems as though men are in greater need of counseling due to their genetics and choices; ironically, women are also more likely to seek counseling than men (Liddon et al., 2018).

The World Health Organization (WHO) in the 1940s viewed holistic health as "a state of complete physical, mental and social well-being and not merely the absence of disease or infirmity" (WHO, 2006, para. 2). While this definition fulfills part of the definition, women today have other factors to consider in their overall wellness. **Wellness** (intentionally making decisions and disposing time and energy in areas of the body, mind, and spirit in order to increase self-actualization) is no longer defined by being disease-free or solely based on a woman's physical health. The roles assumed throughout a woman's life will change with age and developmental stages. Counselors today must take into consideration where their female client is and how they are navigating through their developmental milestones. While childhood is important in a client's development for the purpose of this chapter and wellness, the adolescent stage will be the first explored.

THE IMPACT OF DEVELOPMENT

Development is a biological and psychological progression, which incorporates ways of adapting to the individual's environment (Rathus, 2017). By using developmental psychology and considering the stages women go through, clinicians have a greater understanding of all aspects of a women's health. Erik Erikson's Theory of Development will be used in relation to the ages and characteristics of each of the life changes. In addition, motherhood will be highlighted as a transitional period of development that some women experience. Even though all stages of development are important, this chapter will focus on the transitional periods from adolescence to late adulthood.

Adolescent Era

This time period, also known as pubescent years, presents with the most physical and emotional changes in a woman's life. Erik Erikson stated in his Theory of Development that adolescence is from 12 to 18 years of age (McLeod, 2018); however, some critics would argue this stage can linger on towards about 20 years of age (Good Therapy, 2018). Female teenagers will see growth spurts that affect their height and weight as well as physical changes in body parts and the shape of their physique (Rathus, 2017).

These are the noticeable changes, but the less obvious ones should not be discounted: intellectual and social changes. Intellectual changes may include thinking abstractly, concern regarding political/social issues, looking toward future events, and comparing oneself to others with regards to her future. Relationships during this time may be a struggle as an adolescent teen wants independence from her parents, peer influence is significant, peer relationships are made a priority, and the desire for a romantic relationship may present itself. To further complicate this state with all the many changes happening within the female, she may seek the need for social approval, and since she is more prone to make irrational choices, this can be a turbulent time. These choices may have strong consequences and affect the teen for the rest of her life.

For each teenager, these changes are inevitable but unique, as the timing is uncertain. Some will go through puberty quickly, and others will be late to develop, moving at slower rates through this stage. Some groups like the American Psychological Association ([APA] n.d.-a) have made it a priority to not focus on the stress that can occur during this time but look at "a new understanding of adolescent girls that affirms their strength and resilience needs to be developed" (para. 1). A task force created in 1996 was designed to help teenagers look beyond their appearances and focus on their future (APA, n.d.-a). The hope was to help teenagers move beyond social media and the barriers that society puts on adolescents.

However, social media and curiosity have complicated and clouded the feelings of teenage girls as they decide upon their standings regarding current trends and social issues. These teenagers must also work through complicated situations like cyberbullying, imposter syndrome, stalking, and the inability to practice personal skills in working through friendship issues. Recent survey results found that popular social media like Snapchat, Twitter, and Instagram all led to increased feelings of poor body image, feeling lonely, anxiety, and depression (Twenge et al., 2018).

Young Adulthood

This stage of life is usually after the teenage years and is sometimes referred to as the "in-between" stage, because it is sandwiched between adolescent and adult years. According to Erikson, this is the time when self-identity is cultivated, and creating roots from settling down is prevalent (Rathus, 2017). Erikson would say this stage of development typically begins around age 19 or when the individual is independent of their parents, and then ends at 40 years of age (Good Therapy, 2018; McLeod, 2018). Arnett (2000) argued that late teens through twenties (18-25) was a stage of emerging adulthood (EA) because individuals lack commitment or responsibility as adults, yet have countless opportunities for achievement and exploration as adolescents.

Traditionally, young adulthood comes with many possible transitions: college, full-time employment, independent living, and parenthood. Due to cultural expectations, more individuals go to college and stay longer. The National Center of Education Statistics reported that almost 60% of students graduate in six years, which drives up the cost of education and accrues unwanted debt (Hess, 2019). The U.S. Department of Labor (2019) reported that women ages 18 to 24 change jobs 5.4 times, and 69.9% quit a job in less than one year. Education and employment appear to be unstable and inconsistent, along with relationships, which seem to be developmentally delayed for this age group.

Some women find themselves caught in the middle of being dependent on their parents financially and striving for the independence to make their own decisions. This can be a frustrating process and transition. Arnett (2014) described this age group as exploring their identity, irritable, self-focused, feeling in-between, and optimistic. Arnett (2014) concluded that "rather than a time of deepening commitments to adult roles, during these years, the entry into marriage, parenthood, and stable employment has been postponed for most young people, sometimes through their desire to try various possibilities before making commitments" (p. 575).

Our culture has endless possibilities for achievement and change. Some women are taking advantage of new opportunities and exploring avenues that were not possible for the previous generations (Hess, 2019). While no fault lies in being determined and reaching for goals, it is important to acknowledge that we are only allotted a certain amount of energy and time. If a client wants to take the time and energy to explore options, she also needs to be aware of its benefits and consequences; and counselors have the opportunity to assist in this process (Arnett, 2014). This may include informing the client on financial, biological, health, and educational logistics. For example, counselors can help clients understand the advantages and disadvantages of staying in school longer or selecting a career (Hess, 2019). They also can provide information on delaying marriage and parenthood so that clients are well informed of how the choices of their today will affect their tomorrow (United States Census Bureau, 2018).

Motherhood

During this developmental stage, the two main stressors for women are getting married and having children. Women tend to delay getting married

© fizkes/Shutterstock.com

COUNSELING WOMEN

and having children in comparison to their mothers and grandmothers. In 1960, the median age for a woman's first marriage was 20.3 years in contrast to 27.8 years in 2018 (United States Census Bureau, 2018). Some women are choosing not to get married at all or being part of the 15% increase in single-person households. While a healthy marriage may attribute to a woman's mental and physical wellness, married women also report having more stress than single women (APA, n.d.-b). This stress may manifest in symptoms such as irritability, anger, crying, holding back tears, headaches, and fatigue.

Having children is also a stressor to women of this age group. They have more responsibilities and less time for themselves. Depending on a woman's partner situation, single women with children could be more stressed than those who are married with children. The delays in getting married and having children have not been the only changes for women. In 1945, women over the age of 16 made up only 28.6% of the workforce in comparison to 46.8% in 2016 (U.S. Department of Labor, n.d.). There have been gradual shifts in the developmental milestones of women. These shifts are additional influences on a woman's wellness and how she will adapt to the responsibilities, roles, and cultural influences. Women working outside the home may have additional internal stressors placed upon themselves with the balancing act of family and work. In addition to working and having a family, economic issues also can affect your client's wellness at this time. Families may accumulate additional debt during this stage as large purchases like a home, car, and childcare expenses may occur. Counselors need to be prepared to listen to their clients and help brainstorm ways the client can deal with their stressors, especially in those clients who developmentally may not be within the normative range.

Middle Adulthood

For those women putting off having children, they may become part of the sandwich generation (those women in their thirties or forties who feel stuck between taking care of their children and their aging parents). The sandwich generation is typically a generation in their thirties or forties who may feel the responsibility of taking care of their children and their aging parents (Lexico, 2019). The sandwich generation is faced with some unique circumstances concerning time, money, and career choices. When middle adulthood is supposed to be associated with an established career and consumed with family activities, this also can be a time based on a stagnation stage of development. According to Erikson's developmental theory, middle adulthood is either a stage of movement or of feeling stuck and self-absorbed. The focus of this life stage is on family and work in relation to investing in the next generation. Middle adulthood usually occurs around the 40s. In addition to expending energy into work and family, many women in their mid-forties are adding the role of caregiver to an aging parent (O'Donnell, 2016). According to the Family Caregiver Alliance, 53 to 68 percent of women are the primary caregiver for a parent, sibling, or additional family member (APA, n.d.-b). The U.S. Department of Health and Human Services (2018a) reported that 30 percent of those caregivers are spending at least 20 hours per week on these responsibilities. The additional and typically unexpected responsibilities modify the natural focus of a woman's development and can even affect their future career goals. Women, who are caregivers, report decreasing their work hours, leaving their current positions, and putting their jobs at risk (Birnstengel, 2018). When this should be an energized professional advancement stage of life, some women are experiencing as much stress and adjustment as they did in their young adulthood.

Late Adulthood

Based on Erikson's theory, this stage of development begins at 65 years of age and is known as Integrity versus Despair (Good Therapy, 2018). Late adulthood is characterized mainly with physical issues being noticed

© Rawpixel.com/Shutterstock.com

and occurring, which changes the quality of life. Most women reach the stage of menopause between ages 45 and 55; however, they could experience menopause as occurring as early as the 30s and as late as the 60s. During this stage, women may experience hot flashes, night sweats, irritability, and sleep difficulties. Osteoporosis is another concern for the older female. Nearly 80 percent of the estimated 10 million Americans who have osteoporosis are female due to their body structure (Rush University Medical Center, n.d.). Women begin with thinner, smaller bones and less bone tissue than men. Through most of their lives, women's bones are protected by estrogen, which may block a substance that kills bone cells. However, when women begin to lose estrogen during menopause, it causes loss of bone mass (osteoporosis). This loss takes a toll: Nearly 50 percent of women over 50 will break a bone because of osteoporosis (Rush University Medical Center, n.d.).

In addition to understanding the developmental stage that a woman is going through, it is also essential to look at other factors that will affect wellness. Some factors include culture, sleep patterns, sexual activity, and various life roles. These areas, along with the developmental stages, will impact a woman's wellness.

WHAT IMPACTS WOMEN'S WELLNESS?

Cultural Factors

Mom guilt is defined as "the feeling of guilt, doubt, anxiousness or uncertainty experienced by mothers when they worry they're failing or falling short of expectations in some way," (Collier, n.d., para. 4). Women tend to feel guilty about a variety of things: career, health, relationships, children, parents, appearance, and overall wellness (Cohen, 2010; Collier, n.d.). A poll on Workingmother.com reported that 57% of respondents reported feeling guilty daily, and 31% reported feeling guilty weekly (Cohen, 2010). Some women lean towards the unrealistic expectations that women are supposed to work outside their home and discount their work with the children. However, not just moms struggle with the guilty feelings of not performing up to their personal expectations. The feeling of guilt is a focus on behavior rather than self (Brown, 2010). For example, guilt would be

"I did something bad," and shame (the feeling or belief that we are bad and do not deserve to be happy, accepted or loved) would be "I am bad."

Even though some experts argue that guilt can be a good thing, feelings of guilt also can be detrimental to overall wellness (Purcell, 2019). Depression, anxiety, negative thoughts, addictive behaviors, overscheduling, and perfectionism are all consequences when feelings of guilt turn into shame, driving a woman to believe she is a failure or a bad person (Mihalich-Levin, 2017).

The feelings of guilt or shame tend to be self-inflicted by a woman's perception of herself and her environment. When defining perception, it is one's awareness of something using the senses: sight, hearing, smell, taste, and touch. Even though a person is consistently sensing information from the world around them, it is the interpretation or how the information is perceived that affects a person's behavior and cognition (Myers, 2010). We tend to organize and interpret sensory information based on our knowledge, experiences, and thoughts; then, we use it to consciously experience our lives (Myers, 2010). This process bleeds over into how women perceive themselves in relationship to others. It is especially true in how women compare and perceive themselves on social media sites.

In 2018, Facebook dominated social networking sites with 2.17 billion users, with 44% of women users predominantly between 18 to 44 years of age (Kemp, 2018). In another research study conducted by Pew Research in 2019, they reported that more women in the United States than men said they use Facebook, Instagram, and Pinterest as their online social networking site or messaging app (Perrin & Anderson, 2019). Unfortunately, with the consistent increase of social networking use, women continuously battle negative perceptions and comparisons about themselves. In Dr. Bridget Dibb's (2019) research study of social comparison and social media, she found that the participants who perceived themselves worse off

© Constantin Stanciu/Shutterstock.com

than others on Facebook reported more awareness of physical ailments. In addition, Dibb's reported that women more than men reported a greater awareness of physical health in relation to spending time on social networking sites (Dibb, 2019).

Guilt and social comparison are not the only culprits affecting women's wellness. The **Fear of Missing Out (FoMO)** (this fear creates anxiety or worry that others are experiencing more fun, wealth, happiness, or a more rewarding experience than you are) also impacts a woman's perception of herself and overall health. FoMO is associated with anxiety or worry that others are experiencing more fun, wealth, happiness, or having a more rewarding experience (Wiesner, 2017). These negative feelings can occur during or after observing an online media post of a friend or family member on social media or surfing the internet on social networking sites (Rifkin et al., 2015). FoMO can trigger feelings of anxiety, depression, inadequacy, and insecurities (Abel et al., 2016). Counselors need to be prepared for the ever-changing cultural pressures to fit in, belong and feel accepted. Guilt, social comparison, and FoMO all affect how a woman perceives herself in relationship to the world around, which indirectly affects her overall wellness.

Sleep

Sleep is essential for function and well-being. The National Sleep Foundation worked with 18 experts and researchers in the field to make recommendations for rest (National Sleep Foundation, n.d.-a). Adults should be getting 7-9 hours of sleep; specifically, women should be getting 20 more minutes than men (National Sleep Foundation, n.d.-a, n.d.-b). Unfortunately, almost half (46%) of women report sleep difficulties every night or nearly every night and state they do not feel refreshed when they wake up (National Sleep Foundation, 2007). Sleep deprivation causes havoc on women's minds and bodies. Not getting enough sleep is associated with heart disease, Alzheimer's disease, diabetes, obesity, decision-making problems, and a number of other issues (Jones, 2017). Women tend to be less patient, productive, and creative when they have not gotten adequate sleep (National Sleep Foundation, n.d.-a). Even though women may feel the constant nagging of those in need, women need to learn to slow their pace of life and be intentional about their overall wellness. Counselors need to be comfortable in assessing and evaluating sleep patterns to increase emotional regulation and mental health processing.

Stress may be a leading culprit causing women not to get enough sleep (National Sleep Foundation, n.d.-a). Stress triggers the sympathetic nervous system, or the fight/flight part of the brain, which sets the mind and body into motion. There are positive and negative types of stress (Myers &

© Syda Productions/Shutterstock.com

DeWall, 2015). For example, planning a wedding, graduating from school, or having a baby can all be positive and exciting events in a woman's life; however, with each event comes a level of adjustment and stress. Ideally, the event will pass, and the woman will adapt to life or environmental changes. Her parasympathetic or recovery part of the nervous system will help her mind and body return to baseline (Myers & DeWall, 2015).

For some women, they will report chronic stress, which can be long-term, low to extreme levels of stress (U.S. Department of Health & Human Services, 2019). This type of stress can do more damage to the mind and body. Chronic stress increases the risk of many illnesses and diseases: insomnia, hypertension, heart diseases, diabetes, constipation, irritable bowel syndrome, upper respiratory infections, infertility, and even cancer (Low Dog, 2012). The U.S. Department of Health and Human Services has dedicated staff and research to the Office on Women's Health (2019). In one of their articles on *Stress and Your Health*, stress was associated with the above risk in addition to headaches, migraines, obesity, menstrual cycle problems, decreased sex drive, depression, and anxiety (U.S. Department of Health and Human Services, 2019). The overall consensus is that long-term stress, no matter if it is low-level or extreme, can put a woman's health at risk. There is a complicated relationship between sleep and stress. Some women report they cannot sleep because they are stressed, and others report they are stressed because they cannot sleep (Low Dog, 2012). Interestingly, there is another interrelated connection that involves the relationships between sleep, stress, and sex.

Sex

Even though in some circles, sex is not a common topic, Abraham Maslow would argue that sex is one of the most basic physiological needs in his Hierarchy of Needs (Myers & DeWall, 2015). The benefits of sex for women surpass the idea that sex is only for reproduction (National Sleep Foundation, n.d.-b, para. 1). In one study, women, who indicated high levels of stress, reported a decrease in their sex drive and feeling more distracted during sex (Hamilton & Meston, 2013; U.S. Department of Health and Human Services, 2019). The National Sleep Foundation reported that "more sex helps you sleep, and more sleep boosts your sex drive" (n.d.-b, para. 1). During pleasurable sex for women, dopamine is released, triggering feelings of happiness and relaxation; endorphins also are released, which is the body's natural pain killer; and estrogen levels increase improving the deepest stage (REM) sleep (Clark, 2019; National Sleep Foundation, n.d.-b). Women should be able to talk about sex with their counselors, and in turn, counselors need to be comfortable talking about sex with their clients. Sex can have major benefits and repercussions; it will be important for counselors to be prepared for an open discussion, ask purposeful questions, and learn more about the connection between sex and women's overall health. Keep in mind that counselors are not medical doctors. Some clients may need to be referred to a physician to rule out any medical concerns. Counselors also need to be aware of the ethical standards, national and state regulations for sexual abuse. They will need to know the protocol for how to handle a minor or an adult disclosing sexual abuse (American Counseling Association [ACA], 2014).

Various Roles of Women

In the words of William Shakespeare, "All the world's a stage, and all men and women merely players: they have their exits and entrances, and one man in his time plays many parts" (1623/1963, 2.7.136-166). This quote captures the essence of the many roles a woman will play over the course of her life: daughter, sister, mom, wife, friend, professional, to name a few. With each role, there are certain expectations and responsibilities, along with a person, article, or book to tell them how to do it. These expectations reflect the unwritten rules about how one should behave in a particular situation or role (McLeod, 2008). The majority of the population conforms to the social norms within the current culture; however, some outliers will step out to create their own way of doing things. When this occurs, many women feel the resistance of others, possibly even conflict. In some instances, women might even feel shame because of her behavior.

Brown (2012) defined shame as "the intensely painful feeling or experience of believing that we are flawed and therefore unworthy of love and belonging" (p. 69). Unfortunately, shame traps its victims in believing that they are powerless and isolated (Tucker, n.d.). When women feel shame, they tend to avoid and withdraw from connected social situations. Then the avoidance and withdrawal only reinforce the shame. It becomes a vicious cycle of negative self-talk that is difficult to break. In addition, women have become professionals in shaming other women, especially using social networking sites and the media.

FIGURE 23.1

The Shame Cycle

Source: Anita Kuhnley, based on Tucker (n.d.) and Brown (2012)

Women have easy access at their fingertips allowing them to share their reflections of what they think someone should or should not do (Perrotto, 2013). Behind the screens, women can dissociate or even post anonymously, which means they are more likely to say or do something online that they would never say or do face-to-face. The media is no help with reinforcing shame. When evaluating marketing and advertising messages, many organizations use shaming as a tactic to get consumers to buy their products. Based on Brown's (2012) research, women experience shame among twelve categories: appearance, money, motherhood, family, parenting, mental/physical health, addiction, sex, aging, religion, surviving the trauma, and being stereotyped or labeled. Each category requires its own expectations and its own rules of behavior in how one should fulfill her role. These expectations are a lot to live up to for women.

Counselors will need to be prepared to help their clients think upstream in creating their personal path. Thinking upstream was derived from the medical field in response to the healthcare crisis; however, its definition can be helpful in how women cultivate their responses to social and cultural norms. Upstream thinking is defined as "taking wise collective action to ensure better outcomes rather than simply responding to and being overwhelmed by, crises we could have foreseen" (Meili, n.d., para. 1). The first portion of the definition relates to wisdom: "Listen to advice and accept discipline, and at the end, you will be counted among the wise" (*New International Bible*, 1973/2011, Proverbs 19:20). To have wise actions, women need to seek wise counsel. "Plans fail for lack of counsel, but with many advisers, they succeed" (*New International Bible*, 1973/2011, Proverbs 15:22). Once again, the Bible is instructing us to seek information from those who have experience and knowledge to offer. If women have wise counsel in their life, they know more about how to respond and behave without feeling overwhelmed or insecure about their decisions to live their life more fully.

The second portion of the definition refers to the preparation of crises (Meili, n.d., para. 1). With the many roles and responsibilities of women, perfection is impossible. There is no way to maintain flawlessness in all aspects of life at the same time (Brown, 2012). Someone is going to forget homework, get sick, be late, or if you are a homeowner you may have an unexpected disaster like a roof leak or an air conditioner break down. These are just a few of the everyday crises that women face at one time or another. Counselors need to be willing to listen to small concerns with just as much compassion as they do significant issues. This will help

© pathdoc/Shutterstock.com

counselors acknowledge the source of their client's concerns. For overall wellness, counselors can train clients in preparation and planning strategies that will help increase security and safety no matter the circumstances (Myers & Sweeney, 2005).

Because women exert energy in a variety of roles, it is important to seek wise counsel. Through knowledge and learning from other women they can be proactive in preparing and learn to handle and ultimately withstand any storm. Women need to know how to build their houses through living on a firm foundation; so that it is possible to hold up and persevere when unexpected circumstances occur. Matthew 7:25 (*New International Bible*, 1973/2011) states "The rain came down, the streams rose, and the winds blew and beat against that house; yet it did not fall, because it had its foundation on the rock." It is important to have the knowledge and guidance to know how to be strong and courageous during those difficult times. However, we are not equally made, and some women are not naturally gifted in this area. This stresses the importance of seeking wise counsel, being proactive, putting a plan in place, and delegating some of the responsibilities that may help women withstand the storm.

COUNSELING CONSIDERATIONS

During intake, your client's wellness should be assessed and evaluated in a holistic realm to determine not only deficits and signs of impairment but also what wellness issues are important to the client. Because wellness is multi-dimensional, there are several areas a counselor will want to address when working with a client. When reviewing the following section on counseling recommendations, please consider your overall personal wellness as well as the clients. The counselor needs to practice and model the same recommendations they are suggesting to the client. Along with being a good model for wellness, the counselor will use good judgment about disclosing areas that are more difficult for them personally in comparison to others.

It would be great if a counselor could remove the circumstances causing the stress in the client's life. Unfortunately, some women do not have the luxury of changing their situation. For example, they may have a set of circumstances that require responsibilities such as caregiving for a sick child, assisting a spouse losing a job, or coping with the death of a best friend. In other incidences, it may not be the situation causing all of the stress but rather the individual's perspective. Due to trauma or mental health problems, some women have a distorted perspective of their circumstances. Something that does not appear to be stressful to one person may seem very disturbing to another depending on their backgrounds, culture, and previous experiences.

> "A healthy outside starts
> from the inside."
> ~Robert Urich

Counselors are not magicians, and therefore cannot change the circumstances or perspectives of their clients. Counselors can create a safe place for client disclosure and help facilitate change. They can be competent in cognitive therapy for working with clients that have a distorted perspective of themselves or the world around them. Counselors can help women learn how to deal with stress and increase self-care. Deep breathing, healthy eating habits, adequate exercise, and meditation are a good start to managing stress (Low Dog, 2012; U.S. Department of Health and Human Services, 2019). Going to counseling and seeking support can help a client feel empowered and more resilient against stress. In the next section there are several suggestions to combat stress: mindfulness meditation, acupuncture, practicing gratitude (Lin & Yeh, 2014), and increasing humor/laughter (Low Dog, 2012). Even getting adequate rest can help reset the mind and body to be more equipped in handling stressful situations.

Counseling Recommendations and Treatments

The American Psychological Association (2018) revised the psychological recommendations for practitioners to use when working with women and girls. Because of the dramatic changes in the roles women play in the family, work, and relationships, the APA incorporated a more strength-based approach to mental health treatment and promoting the resilience of women (APA, 2018).

One of the most foundational pieces in evaluating the strengths and challenges of women is to use empathy (APA, 2018). Empathy (having an understanding of what another person is saying, feeling, and experiencing) is having an understanding of what the other person is saying, feeling, and experiencing. It can diffuse strong emotions such as anger, shame, and overpowering grief. As a counselor, demonstrating empathy for our clients is one of the most important things we can do to build rapport and establish a relationship. Some textbooks on counseling skills emphasize empathy as an umbrella skill that should be used with all oth-

er counseling skills to increase effectiveness and rapport (Knight et al., 2019). When empathizing, counselors should be aware of what the client is saying and how the client is saying it. Even though individuals seem to relate more to those that are similar in age, race, and gender, people of different backgrounds can empathize with one another. Brown (2012) suggests that empathy begins with compassion.

Counselors need to have compassion for their clients, even when they do not understand all of the circumstances (Myers, 2010). Sometimes situational factors are not as important as the emotional content and sources of their difficulties. Counselors cannot get caught up in the client's storytelling and consistently ask purposeful questions. Active listening, empathetic understanding, and purposefully questioning are all great skills when evaluating your client's wellness and helping them achieve their goals (Myers, 2010).

Because wellness is multi-dimensional, there are several areas counselors need to evaluate, address, and provide treatment recommendations (Myers & Sweeney, 2005). Some of the most common or more traditional areas are physical exercise, diet, relationships, and maintaining

> "The ability to be in the present moment is a major component of mental wellness."
> ~Abraham Maslow

regular medical check-ups. There are some alternative treatments such as mindfulness, gratitude, and laughter that will be briefly discussed as well (Low Dog, 2012).

Traditional Treatment Recommendations

Physical Exercise

Year after year, "getting more exercise" is one of the top three New Year's resolutions with "eating healthier" ranked at number one (Dickinson, 2018). Even though most women have the best intentions of meeting their goals, many feel the goals are unattainable and give up only after a short period. Counselors need to educate, model, and help clients develop realistic physical exercise goals to fulfill this aspect of wellness. Because we were made for movement, physical exercise can help lower our risk for illness and diseases along with increasing our mood and well-being. In the second edition of the *Physical Activity Guidelines for Americans,* adults should maintain 150 to 300 minutes of moderate to intense exercise weekly (U.S. Department of Health and Human Services, 2018b). Even though there are countless articles, books, and blogs advertising exercise is good for you, the U.S. Surgeon General reported that "60 percent of U.S. women do not engage in the recommended amount of physical activity, and 25 percent of U.S. women are not active at all" (U.S. Department of Health and Human Services, n.d., Facts section). The major health-related organizations all report many benefits to exercise, such as a decrease in heart disease, cancer, diabetes osteoporosis, and obesity. In addition to avoiding some of the most severe health-related diseases and illnesses, exercise can improve sleep, mood, and menstrual cycles (Horowitz, n.d.). According to Horowitz (n.d.), "many of the health issues that women face can be improved substantially with consistent exercise," (para. 4). One of the biggest excuses for not exercising is not having enough time, with the second being not enjoying the activity. Because of busy schedules and endless responsibilities, exercise must be intentional and scheduled. After a routine is established, the schedule may become more flexible; however, the beginning stages of starting or developing a consistent exercise program must be scheduled into the client's life. Please maintain awareness that you are not a medical doctor and should not prescribe physical exercise. Clients need to have a full annual exam by their physician to clear them for physical activity and the type of training they can maintain.

Diet

In addition to regular exercise, diet is another essential factor in women's overall wellness. The *2015-2020 Dietary Guidelines for Americans* reported that

63% of adult females were overweight or obese, and obesity is more common in adults ages 40 or older (U.S. Department of Health and Human Services and U.S. Department of Agriculture, 2015-2020). The guidelines have changed over the years of what and how much food is suggested; however, there are several consistencies: fruits and vegetables are at the top of the list, whole grains, and limited dairy (U.S. Department of Health and Human Services and U.S. Department of Agriculture, 2015-2020). Another significant suggestion by many nutritionists and physicians is to eat as close to nature as possible, which means decreasing processed food. Due to the increasing amount of sugar in processed foods, women need to be aware of label contents with a goal of reducing added sugar. Even though the American Heart Association states that women should only be consuming 6 teaspoons (25 g) of sugar daily, the common practice for adults consumption is 17 teaspoons (71.14 g) of sugar every day (University of California San Francisco, n.d.). Excessive sugar consumption is linked to heart disease, obesity, inflammation, diabetes, skin problems, and liver, pancreas, and kidney difficulties (Hughes, n.d.).

Making Connections

"Two are better than one because they have a good return for their labor: If one falls down his friend can help him up. But pity the man who falls and has no one to help him up," (*New International Bible*, 1973/2011, Ecclesiastes 4:9-10). Because God intrinsically designed the human species for connection, it is no wonder that the lack of connection comes with

© Yuriy Maksymiv/Shutterstock.com

serious consequences: obesity, smoking, anxiety, depression, weaker immune systems, and high blood pressure (House et al., 1988; Sepala, 2012). In a study of close confidantes from 1985 to 2004, Americans reported a drop of confidants from three to one, with 25% of Americans stating they did not have a close friend (McPherson et al., 2006). It goes against our original design to be isolated and withdrawn from the connection. Having close relationships is just as important as exercising and eating well to women's overall health.

Maintaining Regular Medical Check-Ups

A woman's health can be a difficult thing to measure. Therefore, it is crucial to have a baseline and get an annual check-up with a healthcare provider. The Center for Disease Control (2017) recommends regular check-ups to screen for potential illnesses and diseases and encourage preventative measures to increase well-being (Roth, 2019). During an annual check-up, women can build rapport with a doctor in order to ask questions and feel secure about disclosing any personal health problems. A regular check-up includes a discussion of family history and mental health screening (Center for Disease Control, 2017), which is vital for the doctor to know in case there are health-related issues in the future. Before counselors suggest starting a diet and exercise program, clients need to check in with their regular physician for the following: make sure the program is appropriate, rule out any other health-related difficulties, and screen for health problems associated with mental illnesses.

Alternative Treatment Recommendations

Mindfulness

A new but ancient approach to wellness has been reported to improve well-being, physical health, and mental health (Harvard Health, n.d.). Even though mindfulness meditation has been around for thousands of years in Eastern religious practices, it was not until the late 1970s that it was introduced in the mental health field. Jon Kabat-Zinn, the founder of the Stress Reduction Clinic at the University of Massachusetts Medical School, brought mindfulness meditation to mainstream psychology by developing a stress reduction program (Inbreath, n.d.).

© Nabilah Khalil/Shutterstock.com

Mindfulness meditation has been incorporated into religious and secular practices and can be found in Hinduism, Buddhism, Jewish and Christian religions, yoga, Positive Psychology, and Philosophy (Selva, 2019). **Mindfulness** (maintaining a moment-by-moment awareness of our thoughts, feelings, bodily sensations, and surrounding environment, through a gentle, nurturing lens) is based on practices of staying in the here-and-now, belly breathing, and redirecting intrusive thoughts. Some research has indicated that mindfulness can decrease anxiety and feelings of isolation and loneliness, along with increased resilience and intrusive thoughts (Mrazek et al., 2013). There are dozens of apps, websites, books, and articles dedicated to the benefits of mindfulness, along with instructions on how to be mindful and meditate. Living in a culture that promotes busyness as successful and imposes impossible expectations, mindfulness meditation is an easy cost-efficient treatment recommendation for clients to slow down, increase acceptance, acknowledge the truth, and be aware of outside negativity (Aitken, 2013).

Ecclesiastes 3:7 states, "a time to tear, and a time to mend, a time to be silent, and a time to speak" (*New International Bible*, 1973/2011). The Bible gives instructions about creating a time and space for everything; it is a balance that many in our culture find difficulty in achieving. "A time for everything, a season for every activity under the heavens" (*New International Bible*, 1973/2011, Ecclesiastes 3:3). God knew the human inclination for continuous movement of the body and mind. Therefore, He gives us permission to *be still,* and let go of our burdens unto Him (Proverbs 46:10). When recommending mindfulness, counselors need to be knowledgeable and competent in mindfulness meditation practices. Counselors also need to be willing to adapt certain practices for their clients in how much time and effort their clients are willing to commit.

Practicing Gratitude

Thankful people are happier, less stressed, and much more fun to be around. 1 Chronicles 16:34 (*New International Bible*, 1973/2011) says, "Give thanks to the LORD, for he is good; his love endures forever." Unfortunately, some people are experiencing difficulties and do not feel like practicing gratitude for their circumstances. For example, it would be hard to be thankful while taking care of a sick loved one or appreciative for the loss of a job. Yet even still, 1 Thessalonians 5:18 (*New International Bible*, 1973/2011) says, "give thanks in all circumstances; for this is God's will for you in Christ Jesus." Being thankful is "God's will for you." As my friend died recently? Yes! As my father battles cancer? Yes! As ….. (you fill in the blank)…? Yes. My friend is with the Lord, and my father will be at some point. If you want or need a boost today, read Romans 8:37 (*New International Bible*, 1973/2011) which after describing various trials, declares that we are "more than conquerors through him who loved us." In *the Gifts of Imperfection*, gratitude is described as an action, something that you do rather than you say (Brown, 2010). Some individuals seem to be naturally selfish creatures so they must

COUNSELING WOMEN

train and practice to be grateful. There are others, especially women, that are living their lives in such fast motion they move from crisis to crisis rather than acknowledging the good in their lives. Negative thinking, whining, and complaining can all become nasty habits. Therefore, counselors will need to help women combat, redirect, and train their brains to think differently; this is the practice of gratitude.

Humor, Laughter and Optimism

Along with a grateful heart, laughter can be one of the best medicines for a women's overall wellness. Even the world-famous, Dr. Patch Adams, suggests that humor and fun can be one of the best ways to stay healthy and combat loneliness (Low Dog, 2012). There are physical and psychological benefits to having a good chuckle. Dr. Lee Berk, a laughter expert, found that laughter is associated with the release of endorphins and neurotransmitters such as serotonin and dopamine (Ringer, 2019). The release of endorphins mimics the same type of release as moderate exercise, which can act as a natural painkiller, while serotonin and dopamine work on mood, anxiety, pleasure, and reward. Some of the physical benefits of laughter are improving the immune system and decreasing heart disease and stroke. Even though the body and mind are examined separately, Dr. Berk stated, "when we start to look at the whole person, we can see how interconnected the human body really is" (Ringer, 2019, para. 8). The inspiration for his research was Proverbs 17:22, "A cheerful heart is good medicine, but a crushed spirit dries up the bones" (*New International Bible*, 1973/2011).

There are several ways to prescribe laughter to clients: watching a funny movie, listening to upbeat happy music, sharing some time with someone that has a good sense of humor, reading a funny non-fiction book, reading the comics, and spending at least ten minutes a day smiling (Low Dog, 2012). In counseling, there will always be serious issues and matters that need critical attention; however, it is important to maintain laughter and fun as a good wellness practice. Like many of the other treatment recommendations, counselors need to be willing to model these practices.

Featured Practitioners

Kay Glidden and Beth Reynolds

Kay Glidden and Beth Reynolds Lewis, Co-Owners of Compassion Resiliency, are trainers for professionals working in trauma-exposed work environments. Kay and Beth each have 30 plus years working in the Behavioral Health field.

© Kay Glidden

"I (Kay) was a therapist for university students and in graduate school, and while working in the field, I did not receive any training on how to detach from my clients in a healthy way. I would listen to students all day long and then go home and worry about them. I was not aware of compassion fatigue/secondary trauma and how to keep healthy." We live in a culture that glorifies being busy. "Resting and restoring is just as important as working" (L. Cheung, personal communication, April 5 2015). Compassion fatigue goes beyond our daily stress as it is the cost of caring for a living thing in emotional pain. Compassion fatigue is a normal part of your job as a therapist. Police officers have protective gear, but what do we have? We have to create our own approaches to protect ourselves before, during, and after hearing emotional trauma from our clients.

© Beth Reynolds-Lewis

"I (Beth) am a wife and mother of three, and prior to working in public behavioral health, I worked in child protective services and as a forensic interviewer at a Child Advocacy Center. It has taken me years to understand that not everyone views the world as I do. My kids never sat on Santa's lap at the mall. Why?... because Santa is a predator (everyone knows that)? Secondary trauma has changed my worldview; it won't go back to unicorns and rainbows. There is no magic eraser big enough to erase what I have heard or seen in my career, but I have improved my awareness of my own triggers and skills to better manage my secondary trauma."

Kay Glidden and Beth Reynolds Lewis, Co-Owners of Compassion Resiliency, share the following recommendations to increase your awareness of personal wellness and maintain health and resilience:

1. Know what compassion fatigue, secondary trauma, burnout, and moral distress is and understand that self-care is NOT selfish. Finding positive peer support is key to sustaining your resiliency.

2. Be aware of your own individual signs and symptoms, and when your compassion fatigue and/or secondary trauma increases, your self-care should also increase.

3. Try different and new approaches to keep yourself healthy and re-silient for home and at work such as:
   a. mindfulness: meditation, daily deep breathing, nature, mindful walking/eating, grounding techniques
   b. reduction in trauma exposure
   c. taking breaks during the day – go outside, wash your hands, walk, movement in your office
   d. positive peer support and de-briefing tools

4. Be aware and remember the meaning and rewards of your work and what keeps you sustained.

If you would like to know more, Kay and Beth recommend getting *Help for the Helper: Psychophysiology of Compassion Fatigue and Vicarious Trauma* by Babette Rothschild and *The Compassion Fatigue Workbook: Creating Tools for Transforming Compassion Fatigue and Vicarious Trauma* by Francoise Mathieu.

LOOKING THROUGH THE LENS OF CHRISTIANITY: BIBLICAL INTEGRATION

In Matthew 13, Jesus talks about the parable of the sower. The Scripture shares an analogy of the sower who goes out and casts seed and, depending on where it lands, determines the consequence of the seed. We counselors are also like the sower with seed. As Christians, we feel called to help those who are hurting (John 17:4). We cast our knowledge and skills, but we have no idea which clients will make changes in their life. Jesus called us to "love one another" (*New International Bible*, 1973/2011, John 13:34) and to "serve others" (*New International Bible*, 1973/2011, Mark 10:45). While we strive to follow His commands personally and professionally, we each have our issues to reflect upon and deal with daily. At times, serving can feel draining and exhausting, and we must protect ourselves by reducing and avoiding burnout and compassion fatigue. As we aspire to grow more like Christ, our wellness becomes a foundation to assist in grounding ourselves to help our body, mind, and spirit feel whole, so we are more equipped to help others. The Bible calls us to be well, and we draw strength from not only Jesus's teachings but from the life he modeled. Like Christ, the best testimony as professionals we can provide to our clients is through our own self-care. We will be better equipped to deal with our client's issues while maintaining balance in our own life. So choose not to be hypocritical and talk to your clients about being well; instead, choose to be well and model this as only a Christian can.

CONCEPT TO CONTEMPLATE

© Asier Romero/Shutterstock.com

When was the last time you looked at yourself? Really looked at yourself and your self entirely? Now is the time to have a close inspection and an honest conversation. How would you rate yourself inspecting all areas of wellness: social, emotional, intellectual, spiritual, and occupational? If someone close to you were also doing an inspection, what would they see? Take time to note what you are balanced at and feel good about your focus. Find an area that you wish you were spending more time developing and create a plan. The best way is to choose one attainable aspect to change, master it, and then build upon that goal. You want to be a success, and repetition over time will produce results. Remember, it is hypocritical to encourage our clients to take steps towards their wellness when we, too are lacking in this area. It's not about being perfect; it's about working towards being our best. Christ has called us not to grow weary and do our best (Galatians, 9:9), and we continually evaluate and change as we work towards wellness.

Prayer of St. Teresa of Avila (1515-1582), Mystic
"Christ has no body but yours, no hands, no feet on earth but yours,
Yours are the eyes with which he looks with compassion on this world,
Yours are the feet with which he walks to do good,
Christ has no body now on earth but yours.
Yours are the hands, with which he blesses all the world.
Yours are the hands, yours are the feet,
Yours are the eyes, you are his body.
Christ has no body now but yours, no hands, no feet on earth but
yours,
Yours are the eyes with which he looks with compassion on this world."
(Manneh, 2018)

CASE STUDY

Jessica is a 40-year-old African American woman with a fifteen-year-old son, twelve-year-old son, and newborn daughter. She has been married for sixteen years to Curtis, who is 45 years old. Jessica worked as a high school teacher before the birth of her daughter, and she now works from home as an English and Math tutor. She states feeling overwhelmed, isolated, and exhausted. Her mom is her primary support system and helps with children and housework as much as she can. Even though Jessica is overweight, she says she does not have time to exercise and eats to stay awake. She explains that she thinks her husband is going through a midlife crisis. He seems frustrated and angry all of the time and said the other day that he was miserable. Jessica does not know how to help him because she feels the same way. In addition, she has a diagnosis of a skin disorder, which causes the skin to change the pigment and peel at times. Jessica is very insecure about the way she feels, but she admits not investing any time into her appearance. Another layer to Jessica's story involves the volunteer work she did before getting pregnant. Jessica volunteered at church as a mentor and lay counselor for young girls. She was very dedicated and said she felt like she was part of something bigger than herself. During some interactions with one of the pastors, he said some very sexually inappropriate things to her. At the time, she did not want to expose him in fear of what it would do to the church. Because of the internal conflict, she eventually told her husband, and they left the church. Since then, they found a church but are not heavily invested. So far, they are not serving in any capacity, which saddens Jessica. She comes into counseling with goals of not feeling so anxious and intense all of the time and wanting to help her husband and children. She battles feeling like a failure and meeting expectations. She said that she wanted this year to focus on feeling better and being well.

There are several different areas of wellness to incorporate in Jessica's overall treatment. First, there is Jessica's overall physical health and psychological well-being. Jessica will need a comprehensive evaluation to address any psychological symptoms, such as depression and anxiety. Her physical evaluation should be completed by her primary physician to find diet and exercise options that will fit into her schedule and lifestyle. If a client feels physically bad, more than likely, she will feel emotionally unhealthy as well.

Other factors impacting Jessica's wellness are her lack of connection, relationship issues, and previous trauma with the church. From a cognitive behavioral therapy (CBT) perspective, the therapist and client can assess these concerns and incorporate possible interventions. For example, mindfulness and keeping a gratitude journal may help Jessica combat some the negative thinking or stinking thinking. The mindfulness practices can help decrease anxiety and provide some relaxation in her demanding schedule. Another way the mindfulness practices can help Jessica will be to bring more awareness to the triggers and emotional responses to her circumstances.

Forgiveness therapy would be an excellent way to incorporate the spiritual concept to Jessica's treatment. This is an opportunity for the counselor to include Scripture, psychoeducation, and address emotional content. Possible Scriptures that may be inspirational to Jessica are Romans 8:31 ("What shall we say about such wonderful things as these? If God is for us, who can ever be against us" [*New Living Bible*, 1996, Romans 8:31]), Romans 15:13 ("I pray that God, the source of hope, will fill you completely with joy and peace because you trust in him. Then you will overflow with confident hope through the power of the

Holy Spirit" [*New Living Bible*, 1996, Romans 15:13]), Deuteronomy 31:6 ("So be strong and courageous! Do not be afraid and do not panic before them. For the Lord your God will personally go ahead of you. He will neither fail you nor abandon you" [*New Living Bible*, 1996, Deuteronomy 31:6]), Psalm 31:24 ("So be strong and courageous, all you who put your hope in the Lord!" [*New Living Bible*, 1996, Psalm 31:24]), and Isaiah 40:31("But those who trust in the Lord will find new strength. They will soar high on wings like eagles. They will run and not grow weary. They will walk and not faint" [*New Living Bible*, 1996, Isaiah 40:31]). Even though forgiveness therapy can be used for those without a religious affiliation, it can be a great asset to minister to Jessica's spirituality.

While addressing Jessica's cognitive process, the therapist can evaluate how her cognitions are affecting her behaviors and emotional responses. In many cases, clients are using avoidance and withdrawal behaviors to respond to anxiety provoking situations. Unfortunately, these behaviors only reinforce anxiety and increase the risk for isolation. Jessica stated feeling isolated and alone. Therefore, it will be important for Jessica to be aware of reinforcing inappropriate behaviors and search for a healthier way in dealing with her fear.

The counselor can provide Jessica accountability, support, psychoeducation, and encouragement as she works towards personal wellness. During the counseling process, the therapist will have to adapt and alter some interventions to better fit Jessica's personal goals and schedule. The counselor will have to remember that wellness is not a one size fits all approach. Wellness strategies must be personal and flexible for unexpected circumstances and developmental changes.

CHAPTER SUMMARY

This chapter identified different factors as they related to holistic wellness by presenting clinical and Biblical information. The different developmental stages by Erikson were reviewed as they related to women specifically. Additional factors were explored that also attribute to areas that women need to assess when looking at their wellness. Finally, this chapter looked at counseling recommendations and treatments when working with women to assist in gaining a great balance in their life.

KEY TERMS

Empathy - having an understanding of what another person is saying, feeling, and experiencing

FoMO - the Fear of Missing Out, this fear creates anxiety or worry that others are experiencing more fun, wealth, happiness, or a more rewarding experience than you are

Mindfulness - maintaining a moment-by-moment awareness of our thoughts, feelings, bodily sensations, and surrounding environment, through a gentle, nurturing lens

Sandwich Generation - those women in their thirties or forties who feel stuck between taking care of their children and their aging parents

Shame - the feeling or belief that we are bad and do not deserve to be happy, accepted or loved

Wellness - intentionally making decisions and disposing time and energy in areas of the body, mind, and spirit in order to increase self-actualization

SUGGESTED RESOURCES

Books
Life is your Best Medicine by Tieraona Low Dog
Daring Greatly or *The Gifts of Imperfection* by Brene Brown
Reshaping It All by Candace Cameron Bure with Darlene Schacht
So Long Insecurity by Beth Moore

Help for the Helper: Psychophysiology of Compassion Fatigue and Vicarious Trauma by Babette Rothschild

The Compassion Fatigue Workbook: Creating Tools for Transforming Compassion Fatigue and Vicarious Trauma by Francoise Mathieu

Podcasts

Brene Brown: Listening to Shame: https://www.ted.com/talks/brene_brown_listening_to_shame?language=en

Priscilla Shirer: Going beyond Ministries: Authentically Me: https://podcasts.apple.com/us/podcast/going-beyond-ministries-with-priscilla-shirer/id840242536?i=1000291465985

REFERENCES

Abel, J. P., Buff, C. L., & Burr, S. A. (2016). Social media and the fear of missing out: Scale development and assessment. *Journal of Business & Economics Research (JBER), 14*(1), 33-44. https://doi.org/10.19030/jber.v14i1.9554

Aitken, L. (2013, March 25). *All in the mind? Psychology, mindfulness and Christianity.* https://www.publicchristianity.org/all-in-the-mind-psychology-mindfulness-and-christianity/

American Counseling Association. (2014). *2014 ACA code of ethics.* https://www.counseling.org/knowledge-center

Amercian Psychological Association. (n.d.-a). *A new look at adolescent girls.* https://www.apa.org/pi/families/resources/adolescent-girls

American Psychological Association. (n.d.-b). *Gender and stress.* https://www.apa.org/news/press/releases/stress/2010/gender-stress

American Psychological Association. (n.d.-b). *Who are family caregivers?* https://www.apa.org/pi/about/publications/caregivers/faq/statistics

American Psychological Association. (2018). *APA guidelines for psychological practice with girls and women.* http://www.apa.org/about/policy/psychological-practice-girls-women.pdf

Ansbacher, H. L., & Ansbacher, R. R. (Eds.). (1964). *Alfred Adler: Superiority and social interest.* Northwestern University Press.

Arnett, J. J. (2000). Emerging adulthood: A theory of development from the late teens through the twenties. *American Psychologist, 55*(5), 469-480. https://doi.org/10.1037//0003-066X.55.5.469

Arnett, J. J. (2014). The new life stage of emerging adulthood at ages 18–29 years: Implications for mental health. *Lancet Psychiatry, 1*(7), 569-776.

Birnstengel, G. (2018). *The reason women are working less.* https://www.nextavenue.org/reason-women-working-less/

Brown, B. (2012). *Daring greatly: How the courage to be vulnerable transforms the way we live, love, parent, and lead.* Gotham Books.

Brown, C. B. (2010). *The gifts of imperfection: Let go of who you think you're supposed to be and embrace who you are.* Hazelden.

Center for Disease Control. (2017). *Regular check-ups are important.* https://www.cdc.gov/family/checkup/index.htm#

Clark, M. (2019). *What's going on in men's and women's brains and bodies before, during and after sex?* https://atlasbiomed.com/blog/whats-going-on-with-hormones-and-neurotransmitters-during-sex/

Cohen, L. (2010). *The anatomy of working mom guilt.* https://www.workingmother.com/2010/5/home/anatomy-working-mother-guilt

Collier, T. (n.d.). *Mom guilt is real. Here's how to beat it.* https://www.activekids.com/parenting-and-family/articles/mom-guilt-is-real-here-s-how-to-beat-it

Dibb, B. (2019). Social media use and perceptions of physical health. *Heliyon, 5*(1). https://doi.org/10.1016/j.heliyon.2018.e00989

Dickinson, K. (2018). *9 most common New Year's resolutions – and how to make them happen.* https://bigthink.com/personal-growth/succeed-common-new-years-resolutions

Good Therapy. (2018). *Erikson's eight stages of development.* https://www.goodtherapy.org/blog/psychpedia/erikson-eight-stages-development

Hamilton, L. D., & Meston, C. M. (2013). Chronic stress and sexual function in women. *The Journal of Sexual Medicine, 10*, 2443-2454. http://dx.doi.org/10.1111/jsm.12249

Harvard Health. (n.d.). *Benefits of mindfulness.* https://www.helpguide.org/harvard/benefits-of-mindfulness.htm

Harvard Health Publishing. (2019). *Mars vs. venus: The gender gap in health.* https://www.health.harvard.edu/newsletter_article/mars-vs-venus-the-gender-gap-in-health

Hess, A. (2019, June 19). *Graduating in 4 years or less helps keep college costs down - but just 41% of students do.* CNBC. https://www.cnbc.com/2019/06/19/just-41percent-of-college-students-graduate-in-four-years.html

Hettler, B. (1998). *The past of wellness.* www.hettler.com/History/hettler.htm

Horowitz, J. J. (n.d.). *Health benefits of exercise for women.* https://www.sutterhealth.org/health/womens-health/health-benefits-of-exercise-for-women

House, J. S., Landis, K. R., & Umberson, D. (1988). Social relationships and health. *Science, 241*(4865), 540–5.

Hughes, L. (n.d.). *How does too much sugar affect your body?* https://www.webmd.com/diabetes/features/how-sugar-affects-your-body

Inbreath. (n.d.). *The history of mindfulness.* https://inbreathe.com.au/the-history-of-mindfulness/

Jones, T. (2017). *How many hours of sleep do you really need?* https://www.healthline.com/nutrition/how-much-sleep-you-need

Kemp, S. (2018). *Digital in 2018: World's internet users pass the 4 billion mark.* https://wearesocial.com/uk/blog/2018/01/global-digital-report-2018

Knight, A., Sibcy, G., & Gantt, A. (2019). *Research-based counseling skills: The art and science of therapeutic empathy.* (R. Hawkins, A. Knight, A., J. Silvey, G., Sibcy, & S. Warren, Eds.). Kendall Hunt Publishing.

Larson, D. D. (1999). The conceptualization of health. *Medical Care Research and Review, 56,* 123-136.

Lexico. (2019). Sandwich generation. In *Lexico Powered by Oxford.* https://www.lexico.com/en/definition/sandwich_generation

Liddon, L., Kingerly, R., & Barry, J. (2018). Gender differences in preferences for psychological treatment, coping strategies, and triggers to help-seeking. *British Journal of Clinical Psychology, 57,* 42–58.

Lin, C. & Yeh, Y. (2014). How gratitude influences well-being: A structural equation modeling approach. *Social Indicators Research, 118*(1). https://www.researchgate.net/publication/263669224_How_Gratitude_Influences_WellBeing_A_Structural_Equation_Modeling_Approach.

Low Dog, T. (2012). *Life is your best medicine.* National Geographic Society.

Manneh, E. (2018). *Lessons from St. Teresa: How to be the eyes, hands, and feed of Christ.* https://bustedhalo.com/ministry-resources/lessons-from-st-teresa-how-to-be-the-eyes-hands-and-feet-of-christ

McLeod, S. A. (2008). *Social roles.* https://www.simplypsychology.org/social-roles.html

McLeod, S. A. (2018). *Erik Erikson's stages of psychosocial development.* https://www.simplypsychology.org/Erik-Erikson.html#ego

McPherson, M., Smith-Lovin, L., & Brashears, M. E. (2006). Social isolation in America: Changes in core discussion networks over two decades. *American Sociological Review 71*(3), 353-375.

Meili, R. (n.d.). *Theory: Upstream thinking.* https://solutions.thischangeseverything.org/module/upstream-thinking

Mihalich-Levin, L. (2017). *What exactly is mom guilt anyway? A clinical psychotherapists explains.* https://www.mindfulreturn.com/mom-guilt/

Miller, J. W. (2005). Wellness: The history and development of a concept. *Spektrum Freizeit, 27*(1), 84-106.

Mrazek, M., Franklin, M. S., Phillips, D. T., Baird, B., & Schooler, J. W. (2013). Mindfulness training improves working memory capacity and GRE performance while reducing mind wandering. *Psychological Science, 24*(5), 776–781.

Myers, D. G. (2010). *Psychology* (6th ed.). Worth Publishing.

Myers, D. G., & DeWall, C. (2015). *Psychology* (11th ed.). Worth Publishers.

Myers, J. E., & Sweeney, T. J. (2005). *Counseling for wellness: Theory, research, and practice.* American Counseling Association.

Myers, J. E., Sweeney, T. J., & Witmer, J. M. (2000). The wheel of wellness counseling for wellness: A holistic model for treatment planning. *Journal of Counseling & Development, 78,* 251-266.

National Sleep Foundation. (n.d.-a). *How much sleep do we really need?* https://www.sleepfoundation.org/articles/how-much-sleep-do-we-really-need

National Sleep Foundation. (n.d.-b). *Is sex helping or hurting your sleep?* https://www.sleep.org/articles/does-sex-affect-sleep/

National Sleep Foundation. (2007). *Summary of findings.* https://www.sleepfoundation.org/sites/default/files/inline-files/Summary_Of_Findings%20-%20FINAL.pdf

New International Bible. (2011). New International Bible Online. https://www.thenivbible.com/ (Original work published 1973).

New Living Bible (1996). New Living Bible. https://www.biblegateway.com/versions/New-Living-Translation-NLT-Bible/

O'Donnell, L. (2016). *The crisis facing America's working daughters.* https://www.theatlantic.com/business/archive/2016/02/working-daughters-eldercare/459249/

Perrin, A., & Anderson, M. (2019). *Share of U.S. adults using social media, including Facebook, is mostly unchanged since 2018.* https://www.pewresearch.org/fact-tank/2019/04/10/share-of-u-s-adults-using-social-media-including-facebook-is-mostly-unchanged-since-2018/

Perrotto, A. M. (2013). *Why do women shame other women?* https://www.nsvrc.org/blogs/feminism/why-do-women-shame-other-women

Purcell, J. (2019). *The surprising emotion that can make you a better person.* https://www.chatelaine.com/health/wellness/guilt-complex-emotion-explained/

Rathus, S. A. (2017). *Childhood & adolescence voyages in development* (6th ed.). Cengage Learning.

Rifkin, J., Chan, C., & Kahn, B. (2015). Fomo: How the fear of missing out leads to missing out. *Advances in Consumer Research, 43,* 244-248.

Ringer, J. (2019). *Laughter: A fool-proof prescription.* https://news.llu.edu/research/laughter-fool-proof-prescription

Roth, B. (2019, September 9). *Should you get an annual physical?* Duke Health. https://www.dukehealth.org/blog/should-you-get-an-annual-physical

Rush University Medical Center. (n.d.). *How gender affects health.* https://www.rush.edu/health-wellness/discover-health/how-gender-affects-health

Selva, J. (2019, October 25). *History of mindfulness: From east to west and religion to science.* https://positivepsychology.com/history-of-mindfulness/

Sepala, E. (2012, August 26). *Connect to thrive.* Psychology Today. https://www.psychologytoday.com/us/blog/feeling-it/201208/connect-thrive

Shakespeare, W. (1963). *As you like it.* (P. Negri & S. L. Rattiner, Eds.). Dover Publications. (Original work published 1623)

Sweeney, T. (2009). *Adlerian counseling and psychotherapy* (5th ed.). Routledge.

Tucker, J. (n.d.). *Motherhood, shame and society.* http://www.mothersmovement.org/features/bbrown_int/bbrown_int_1.htm

Twenge, J., Joiner, T., Rogers, M., & Martin, G. (2018). Increases in depressive symptoms, suicide-related outcomes, and suicide rates among U.S. adolescents after 2010 and links to increased new media screen time. *Clinical Psychological Science, 6*(1), 3-17. https://doi.org/10.1177/2167702617723376

University of California San Francisco. (n.d.). *How much is too much?* Sugarscience. https://sugarscience.ucsf.edu/the-growing-concern-of-overconsumption.html#.XeLr80FG1PZ

United States Census Bureau. (2018). *U.S. census bureau release 2018 families and living arrangements tables.* https://www.census.gov/newsroom/press-releases/2018/families.htm

U.S. Department of Health and Human Services and U.S. Department of Agriculture. (2015 – 2020). *Dietary Guidelines for Americans* (8th ed.). https://health.gov/dietaryguidelines/2015/guidelines/.

U.S. Department of Health and Human Services. (n.d.). *A report from the U.S. surgeon general physical activity and health.* https://www.cdc.gov/nccdphp/sgr/pdf/women.pdf

U.S. Department of Health and Human Services. (2018a). *CDC caregiving data factsheet.* https://www.apa.org/pi/about/publications/caregivers/faq/cdc-factsheet.pdf

U.S. Department of Health and Human Services. (2018b). *Physical activity guidelines for americans* (2nd ed.). https://health.gov/paguidelines/second-edition/pdf/Physical_Activity_Guidelines_2nd_edition.pdf

U.S. Department of Health and Human Services. (2019). *Stress and your health.* https://www.womenshealth.gov/mental-health/good-mental-health/stress-and-your-health

U.S. Department of Labor. (n.d.). *Facts over time - Women in the labor force.* https://www.dol.gov/wb/stats/NEWSTATS/facts/women_lf.htm#CivilianLFSex

U.S. Department of Labor. (2019). *News release Bureau of Labor Statistics.* https://www.bls.gov/news.release/nlsoy.nr0.htm

Wiesner, L. (2017). *Fighting fomo* [Master's thesis, University of Twente]. https://essay.utwente.nl/73690/1/Wiesner_MA_BMS%20Behavioural%2C%20Management%20and%20Social%20Sciences.pdf

World Health Organization. (2006). *Constitution of the world health organization* (45th ed.). https://www.who.int/governance/eb/who_constitution_en.pdf